BOURGOGNE AUVERGNE ESCALADE

David Atchison-Jones

INTRODUCTION - LA LIBERTÉ D'ESCALADE

Si votre seule expérience de l'escalade est en salle et que vous pensez aller grimper à l'extérieur, alors lisez ce qui suit. Le seul mot qui résume l'escalade en plein air est liberté. À l'extérieur, vous laissez de côté toutes les contraintes de l'escalade en salle avec les prises de couleur définies, et vous êtes libres d'utiliser n'importe quelle prise et selon la configuration que vous souhaitez. Après 4 mètres au-dessus du sol vous êtes libres de continuer sans qu'un instructeur vous demande de redescendre immédiatement. A 5 mètres, vous aimeriez avoir cet instructeur réalisant que vous êtes maintenant en difficulté, cependant vous vous ressaisissez et contrôlez votre descente. C'est en effet l'essence même de l'escalade à l'extérieur : grimper comme vous le souhaitez. Il n'y a pas d'heure d'ouverture ou de fermeture, seule la pluie ou la neige dictent une vie de plaisir à l'extérieur. En hiver le soleil peut-être votre meilleur ami en réchauffant confortablement une paroi rocheuse même les jours les plus froids. Mais en été le soleil peut être votre pire ennemi. Vous découvrirez cependant rapidement que toutes les falaises passent une partie de la journée à l'ombre, donc il vous suffit juste de bien choisir la meilleure heure pour grimper. L'escalade à l'extérieur permet également de voyager en dehors de votre localité, et avec d'autres personnes et vous finirez par partir pour des week-ends entiers et profiterez du merveilleux réseau de campings municipaux bon marchés à travers toute la France. Vous êtes libres de grimper le matin aussi tôt que vous le souhaitez, et le soir jusqu'à ce que le soleil se couche. Après un certain temps, les degrés de difficulté n'auront même plus trop d'importance. Grimper à l'extérieur pour moi offre la possibilité d'explorations merveilleuses de paysages magnifiques, tout en utilisant la force et les mouvements du corps que vous appréciez en salle.

Vous êtes libres de faire de l'escalade à l'extérieur partout dans le monde. Vous devrez cependant respecter les lois de chaque pays et adhérer aux règles d'éthique suivies par les grimpeurs du monde entier. La roche est votre challenge mais vous ne devez pas la changer. Un rocher ou une falaise peuvent vous paraître vides mais pour d'autres les petites prises donneront le soutien nécessaire pour pouvoir grimper. Si aucune prise n'est visible ne touchez pas à la roche – il faut grimper pour s'amuser pas pour abîmer la nature. Il y a environ 200,000 falaises dans toute la France mais seulement environ 1% sont en fait bien adaptées pour faire de l'escalade et ont des voies équipées pour grimper. La plupart des falaises sont soit difficiles d'accès, soit elles n'ont pas de prises naturelles permettant de grimper ou soit elles sont trop instables. Attention cependant car même les falaises équipées restent très instables et des effondrements sont possibles de part l'érosion naturelle. La tradition mondiale de l'équipement des voies veut que lorsqu'une broche est installée sur une falaise, elle doit être suffisamment solide pour que la personne qui l'ait installé puisse l'utiliser le jour même pour grimper sans danger. Attention car les broches ne sont pas nécessairement placées pour permettre de tomber en sécurité – à vous de choisir la manière dont vous souhaitez les utiliser. Elles sont laissées en place et font partie de l'environnement naturel et subissent l'érosion. Heureusement la majorité des falaises sont supervisées par les clubs d'escalade locaux qui vérifient régulièrement l'érosion des broches mais n'oubliez jamais qu'en fin de compte c'est vous qui prenez un risque et que vous avez toujours le choix de ne pas grimper.

Vous êtes en effet libres de partir si vous ne vous sentez pas en sécurité Grimper à l'extérieur vous permettra de visiter des lieux magnifiques tout autour du monde. En France, il vous faudra une vie entière pour visiter les meilleures 1000 falaises. J'ai divisé cette série en 4 livres pour permettre à tout grimpeur d'avoir une solution pratique pour visiter de nombreux sites d'escalade plutôt que d'apporter une valise de 50kg avec les guides d'escalade de chacun des sites ! Cette série est vraiment un produit de ma vie et de mon expérience de grimpeur. Jusqu'à l'âge de 20 ans, mon temps libre était passé à apprendre à grimper en débutant par des vacances en famille à Chamonix dés l'âge de 5 ans. De 20 à 40 ans, ce furent mes années de haute performance (7a-8a). J'ai grimpé sur une large sélection de falaises dans toute l'Europe et j'ai ouvert plus de 200 nouvelles voies. De 40 à 60 ans j'ai pris le temps de visiter toutes les falaises intéressantes et impressionnantes que j'ai loupé lorsque j'étais obsédé par les voies avec des degrés de difficulté élevés. J'ai également utilisé ces années pour écrire 14 livres d'escalade et aider de nombreuses personnes à découvrir et apprécier de nouveaux sites. J'ai maintenant la chance d'avoir atteint 60 ans mais les muscles ne sont plus aussi forts qu'ils l'étaient. Heureusement en France il y a suffisamment de falaises et de voies dans des degrés de difficulté 4a-6a ce qui devrait me permettre de rester occupé pendant les 20 prochaines années. Après ça qui sait peut être que je reprendrai l'escalade en salle.

LA CRÉATION DE GUIDES

J'ai toujours aimé l'aventure, c'est pourquoi je me suis beaucoup impliqué dans l'escalade de nouvelles voies, que ce soit en bloc, en escalade sportive ou en terrain d'aventure (en utilisant des coinceurs et des cames pour la protection). Cela peut sembler glamour - grimper une nouvelle ligne et lui donner un nom pour la première fois, mais cela demande souvent des heures de nettoyage et de préparation avant que le rocher soit sûr et agréable à grimper. J'ai souvent nettoyé des blocs à Fontainebleau qui avaient plusieurs centimètres d'épaisseur de mousse, pour découvrir qu'il y avait déjà un numéro peint - il y a 50 ans ; encore une fois, c'est raté ! Quand une voie est vraiment difficile, on se dit qu'aucun grimpeur ne l'a jamais faite. Cependant, Charles Albert a récemment escaladé «pieds nus» de nombreux problèmes de Fontainebleau de niveau 8a-c, alors qui sait ce que les grimpeurs préhistoriques ont pu réaliser, ou quels noms ils ont pu donner aux voies. Sur les falaises marines géantes, j'ai souvent descendu en rappel dans un chaudron océanique bouillonnant, en espérant que les embruns ne mouillent pas trop le rocher - personne ne l'a fait avant - au secours, c'est peut-être impossible. De nombreux grimpeurs occasionnels qualifieraient cette situation de «presque suicidaire», mais les nouveaux grimpeurs expérimentés restent calmes et qualifient simplement cette situation d'»atmosphérique». Il faut certainement être, à la fois mentalement et physiquement fort pour ouvrir de nouvelles voies de style classique. C'était la même chose avec l'escalade sportive dans les années 70, on ne plaçait un boulon que lorsque c'était vraiment nécessaire. La plupart des grimpeurs de tête étaient très performants en 7b/c, donc jusqu'à ce que la voie atteigne ce niveau, on ne voyait pas beaucoup de boulons, voire aucun. J'ai ouvert beaucoup de voies de ce type, mais je suis maintenant très heureux que ces voies soient rééquipées. L'escalade peut être rendue beaucoup plus sûre, et se casser les chevilles en tombant sur de petites corniches n'est pas du tout justifié. Pour tous ceux qui veulent recréer une ascension historique, il suffit de prendre 3 dégaines !

Après avoir escaladé une nouvelle voie, vous créez un topo. C'est la chose la plus simple à faire, cela prend moins de 60 secondes, et cela ne coûte rien à faire. Vous trouvez un petit morceau de papier (paquet de cigarettes vide des années 1960-80), vous dessinez quelques lignes simples, puis vous ajoutez quelques noms et grades, et vous le laissez dans un bac en plastique au pied de la falaise pour que tout le monde puisse l'utiliser. Tout semble plus difficile quand on est un pionnier, alors on baisse toujours le niveau de difficulté d'un ou deux degrés. Si vous vous lancez dans une deuxième ascension, vous savez que le degré risque d'être rétrogradé. En fait, la plupart des voies sur les forums Internet obtiennent une fourchette de 5 notes à partir des commentaires postés, il est donc préférable pour le rédacteur d'un topo d'observer les grimpeurs qui réussissent ou échouent sur une voie, pour donner une note juste. Aujourd'hui, la plupart des grimpeurs prennent une photo de leur topo, puis la mettent en ligne pour que tout le monde puisse la voir, l'utiliser et la commenter. Certaines personnes excellent dans ce domaine, et je dois féliciter les grimpeurs de la région de Beaune et Macon, qui se sont donnés beaucoup de mal pour obtenir des photos par drone, qui illustrent très bien toutes les voies, et qui sont disponibles pour tout le monde gratuitement sur Internet. Dans la plupart des autres régions, vous pouvez également trouver des topos gratuits sur Internet, mais cela demande un peu de persévérance. Tous les problèmes de bloc et les nouvelles voies sont un cadeau de tous les grimpeurs les uns aux autres, et devraient donc être partagés librement. La grande question que les gens se posent cependant est de savoir qui doit contribuer au rétro-boulonnage. Ma réponse de base est la suivante : les grimpeurs car c'est eux qui vont ensuite escalader les voies et profiter de la sécurité du rétro-boulonnage (un guide ne permet que d'accéder aux voies). Les différentes régions ont différentes façons d'essayer de collecter les contributions des grimpeurs «utilisant les boulons». Il va sans dire que si vous restez dans une région pendant une période prolongée, faites un effort pour voir si vous pouvez contribuer, cela sera très apprécié. Si vous utilisez fréquemment une falaise, proposez d'y contribuer fréquemment.

J'aime faire des guides d'escalade, simplement parce que je trouve que beaucoup de grimpeurs veulent beaucoup plus qu'une poignée de topos simples et gratuits faits par les premiers ascensionnistes. L'inspiration pour l'escalade peut provenir de toutes sortes de sources : une photo sur Internet, un article dans un magazine, une voie mentionnée par un ami, etc. Tous les grimpeurs vont ensuite réaliser leur rêve - ou non, en fonction de leur forme physique du jour. Cependant, le véritable pouvoir de ce livre n'est pas tant de fournir une inspiration individuelle pour une voie, mais d'illustrer clairement «les sites à ne pas manquer et qui sont si proches». J'ai sélectionné environ 250 falaises parmi 500 dans le centre de la France que vous ne devez tout simplement pas manquer au cours de votre vie de grimpeur. Avec ce livre en main, vous ne devriez jamais dire, oh quel dommage, nous avons manqué ça. Je trouve qu'Internet est génial pour trouver les choses que vous souhaitez chercher et dont vous avez entendu parler. Ce livre, en revanche, vous fera découvrir tous les sites d'escalade fantastiques... que vous ne chercheriez pas. Il vous montrera aussi des falaises qu'il est inutile de visiter, car les voies sont pour vous soit trop faciles, soit trop désespérées. En conclusion, espérons que ce livre deviendra votre compagnon amical, pour tous vos voyages dans le Centre de la France.

INTRODUCTION - Escalade Exterieur

Après avoir divisé la France en 4 zones d'escalade en extérieur, le but de ce topo est de recenser autant de falaises et de voies de tout niveau que possible. Comme la première visite d'un site est toujours complexe, j'ai pensé que présenter toutes les informations nécessaires sur une double page était le meilleur format. Tourner les pages n'est pas un problème quand vous connaissez déjà un endroit, mais pour la première utilisation, avoir une vue complète d'un coup d'œil est de loin la meilleure présentation que j'ai pu trouvée. Les falaises de grandes largeurs rentrent parfaitement dans ce format, les plus petites s'adaptent sur un simple page; et donc associée à une autre falaise du même type dans les environs. Ce design utilise un simple graphique noir et blanc de la falaise, recouvert d'un graphique couleur avec tous les itinéraires 3a à 8c dans différentes couleurs. Cela permet à tout grimpeur d'évaluer la pertinence de la falaise d'un seul coup d'œil, mais présente d'autres informations si vous voulez plus de détails. J'utilise des photos-topos pour la plupart des falaises, mais avec parcimonie. Je pense que le plus important dans un topo photo, c'est de vous permettre de reconnaître les principales voies et leurs caractéristiques pour une première visite, et d'avoir confiance dans le topo. Certains topos colorient simplement les voies en fonction de la cotation falaise de la voie, mais je n'ai jamais vu un grimpeur apprécier le 6a et le 6c+ de la même façon, l'écart étant trop grand. La plupart des grimpeurs restent dans des niveaux compactes 6a-b (bleu) ou 6c-7a (rouge) ou 7b-7c (noir). Ainsi, en utilisant pour ces cotations les couleurs déjà utilisées à Fontainebleau, vous retrouvez des couleurs reconnaissables pour la majorité des grimpeurs, De plus, si une voie en 6a comporte un seul pas de bloc, je peux la colorier en rouge tout en conservant la cotation 6a.

Les voies des falaises sont toutes numérotées de gauche à droite, avec les hauteurs approximatives du relais. J'ai essayé d'indiquer si les relais étaient facilement accessibles par le haut, ce qui permet la mise en place de moulinettes ou de système d'auto-assurage. Je passe beaucoup de temps à dessiner les falaises et j'ai vu malheureusement beaucoup d'accidents. Dans 99% des cas il s'agit de grimpeurs un peu trop ambitieux se lançant en tête et, qui, en chutant (malheureusement pas sous un surplomb) ont heurté le rocher – n'hésitez pas à faire une voie en moulinette d'abord pour plus de sécurité! L'orientation pour chaque secteur est indiquée, ainsi qu'un indice H (humidité), lié au nombre de jours pendant lesquels le secteur reste humide après de fortes pluies. Cela peut varier en été, mais c'est une bonne info si vous n'êtes pas familier avec la falaise. J'ai inscrit les noms des voies verticalement à côté de la ligne directrice, mais certains noms sont vraiment très longs...et donc abrégés. J'ai donc conservé la première partie du nom, En bas de chaque voie se trouve une petite série de cases (comme l'assureur), qui fournissent des informations supplémentaires pouvant être utiles. . La case du bas peut contenir 2 lettres décrivant le type d'escalade de la voie - A = Arête, P = Pilier (si possible en français), un index complet se trouve au dos du livre. Je n'utilise pas de pictogrammes indiquant le niveau de force ou de résistance car chaque grimpeur est différent, Je préfère donner les informations de base concernant la voie que vous avez choisie de faire - vous ne pouvez pas confondre un mur avec une arête! Cette lettre est sur un fond blanc et indique que la voie est au soleil. S'il y a du vert dans la case, cela indique à quelle hauteur sont les arbres, ou encore la portée de l'ombre sur la paroi. De cette façon, vous savez précisément pour chaque voie ce qui est au soleil ou à l'ombre pour l'assurage comme pour l'escalade- très utile en été.

Au-dessus des cases se trouve un cercle pour illustrer la nature de l'équipement. Les mini-cercles qui se touchent signifie que vous pouvez aller d'un point à un autre; un espace entre les deux signifie que vous aurez besoin d'une rallonge pour clipper si vous ne pouvez pas faire les mouvements, et un seul point d'assurage signifie que c'est un pas engagé. Un seul point sur un fond plat indique que vous pourriez heurter un rebord ou le sol si vous tombiez. C'est un réel avertissement, car beaucoup de voies de niveau inférieur nécessiteraient 30 points d'assurage pour les rendre aussi sures qu'en salle, et que tomber dans certaines parties de ces voies n'est tout simplement pas une option! Chacune des 6 sections de ce topo offre une vue d'ensemble des falaises et les informations nécessaires sur la page opposée. Chaque grimpeur trouvera différentes manières d'utiliser ces pages. J'ai essayé de regrouper les falaises sur un week-end et d'indiquer des campings et des lieux de pique-nique à proximité. J'ai indiqué les coordonnées GPS du parking en décimal, car c'est plus simple à rentrer dans votre cellphone. Je n'indique pas toujours le parking le plus proche, mais le plus pratique afin aussi de ne pas gêner les agriculteurs, etc. Essayez de bien faire attention aux accès aux champs et aux barrières lors du stationnement. J'indique la pente approximative des sentiers en % avec un + ou un – pour indiquer si cela monte ou descend. Les temps de parcours sont à plus ou moins 10 secondes, et en marchant doucement. Très important si c'est votre première sortie en extérieur, grimpez sous le contrôle de grimpeurs expérimenté et dans le doute, faites appel à des moniteurs d'escalade.

INTRODUCTION - FREEDOM

If you have only ever experienced climbing on indoor walls, and are perhaps thinking of wanting to go climbing outside, then read on, this is generally what it's all about. The one word that sums up outdoor climbing is Freedom. Outside, you leave behind you all the constrictions of climbing a coloured set of holds, and are free to use any hold you want and in any configuration you desire. After 4 metres off the ground, you are free to keep on going upwards – no wall attendant demanding you immediately return to the floor. At 5 metres, you wish for that attendant – realising that you are now in distinct peril, however – you compose yourself and climb down in control, and feel that lovely sense of having made the decision yourself. This is very much indeed the essence of climbing outside. There are no opening or closing times, rain or snow simply dictates a life of fun outdoors. The sun will be your friend in winter, comfortably warming up a rockface on even the coldest of winter days. In summer, the sun can be your enemy, but you soon realise that all rockfaces get shade at some part of the day, so you calculate wisely. Climbing outside, usually means travelling to somewhere outside of your locality, so you do it with others, forming some great friendships along the way. Climbing outside suits good weather, so you soon end up spending weekends away, and enjoying the wonderful network of inexpensive municipal campsites across France. You are free to climb as early in the morning as you want to, or even as the sun sets on the far horizon. These are the memories that you will treasure for years to come, after a while, the grades won't simply matter anymore. Climbing outside for me offers the total combination of; Wonderful exploration and stunning scenery, long lasting great friendships, psychological attentiveness - all in addition to the Physicality of strength and body flow that you enjoy indoors.

You are free to climb all over the world, and as such, you adapt the culture of world outdoor climbing. Each individual country will have its own legislature for climbing etc., but there is the overall climbing ethos that climbers from all over the world adhere to. The rock is your challenge, so you do not change it. A piece of rock may appear blank to you, but to others, the tiny holds will give support and make it climbable. Even when rock is totally blank, it should be left alone, we climb to enjoy - not destroy. There are probably around 200,000 cliffs across France, but only around 1% are actually well suited for climbing, and are therefore equipped with climbing bolts. Most cliffs are actually either too remote to access, too blank to climb, or too loose and friable. This said, all cliffs do however remain unstable, and will have parts that can collapse with natural erosion, it's how they were naturally created - 'beware.' Equipping outside has a Worldwide tradition. When a bolt is inserted into a cliff, it simply must be strong for the equipper to hang and lower off "on that day." In addition, not all bolts are necssarily placed in positions for falling on, or for your safety - how you use them, is totally your decision. Thereafter, they are left in place, and become part of the natural environment that naturally erodes. You simply trust any bolts at your own risk, as you do any piece of rock. You are free to climb as you want, but most importantly - are also free to simply walk away. Thankfully, most cliffs are supervised by local climbing clubs to check on bolt erosion, but never forget - "it is ultimately your risk, and you are free to walk away."

Climbing outside, should take you to some magnificent locations all over the world, and you should have some amazing trips ahead of you. In France, you will find it easily takes a lifetime to visit it's finest 1000 cliffs. I have devised this series of 4 compact books, to precisely enable any climber to do this with a practical solution, rathern than transporting a 50kg suitcase of individual cliff guidebooks! This series is very much a product of my climbing lifetime. Up to the age of 20, my spare time was spent learning to climb, starting with family holidays in Chamonix from the age of 5. From 20 to 40, these were my high performance years (7a-8a), and I climbed on a huge selection of cliffs all over Europe, plus opening over 200 new routes. In my 3rd period (40-60), I have enjoyed visiting all of the impressive and interesting cliffs that I missed when I was "over obsessed" about grades or pure difficulty. I have also used this time to write 14 climbing books and help many others discover and enjoy other climbing destinations. I am now lucky to have reached 60, but the muscles are nowhere near as strong as they used to be. Fortunately, in France there are more than enough cliffs and climbs in the lower grades (4a-6a), so I will hopefully be very occupied for the next 20 years, after that – who knows, maybe I will try indoor climbing again.

CLIMBING GUIDEBOOKS

I've always loved adventure, so have been heavily involved in climbing new routes, both in bouldering, sport climbing and terrain adventure (using natural nuts and cams for protection). It may sound glamorous - climbing a new line and giving it a name for the first time, but it often requires hours of cleaning and preparation before the rock is safe and enjoyable to climb. Many times, I have cleaned boulders in Fontainebleau which are several centimetres thick in moss, only to find that there is already a painted number - from 50 years ago; thwarted yet again! When a climb is really difficult, you think - surely no climber has ever done it. However, Charles Albert has recently climbed "in bare feet," many of the Fontainebleau grade 8a-c problems, so who knows what prehistoric climbers may have achieved, or what names they could have given to climbs. On giant sea cliffs, I have often abseiled down into a crashing boiling ocean cauldron, you hope that the sea spray will not make the rock too wet - nobody's done this before - help, it may be impossible. Many casual climbers would call this "verging on suicidal," but experienced new route climbers stay calm, and simply refer to this situation as "atmospheric." You certainly need be, both mentally and physically strong to open classic style new routes. This was the same with sport climbing in the 1970's, you only placed a bolt when it really was necessary. Most leading climbers were very profficient at 7b/c, so until the route got to this level, you wouldn't see many - if any, bolts. I opened lots of routes like this, but am now very happy that these routes are being retro bolted. Climbing can be made a lot safer, and breaking ankles in short falls onto small ledges is completely unnesseccary. For anyone who wants to re-create a historic ascent - simply - only take 3 quickdraws!

After you've climbed a new route, you create a topo. This is the most simple thing to do, it takes under 60 seconds, and it costs nothing to make. You find a small piece of paper (empty cigarette packet 1960's-80's), draw a few simple lines, then add some names and grades, and leave it in a plastic tub at the bottom of the cliff for everyone to use. Everything seems more difficult when you are pioneering, so you always drop the grade one or two. If you are going for a second ascent, you know it's going to be tough for the grade. In fact, most climbs on internet forums will get a range of 5 grades from comments posted, so a guidebook writer is best off, simply observing climbers succeeding or failing on a route, to give a fair grade. Today, most climbers will take a photo of the simple topo, then post it online for all to see, use, and comment. Some people excel at this, and I must congratulate the climbers of the Beaune and Macon area, who have gone to great lengths in getting drone photos, which illustrate all the climbs very well, and are available to everyone for free on the internet. In most other areas you can also find free topos on the internet, but it does take some perseverence. All boulder problems and new routes, are a gift from all climbers to each other, so should be freely shared. The big question that people ask however, is who should contribute to the retro bolting. My basic answer is, the climbers who then go and actually climb the routes, and enjoy the safety of the retro bolting, (a guidebook only gets you to the routes). Different areas have different ways of trying to collect contributions from climbers "using the bolts." It is needless to say that if you are staying in an area for a prolonged period, then do make an effort to see if you can contribute, you will be liked for doing so. If you use a cliff frequently, offer to contribute frequently.

I love to make climbing guidebooks, simply because I find that many climbers want a lot more than a handful of free simple topos made by the first ascentionists. People will get an inspiration to climb from all different parts of life; a photo on the internet, an article in a magazine, or a route mentioned by a friend, etc. All climber's then go and realise this dream - or not; how 'fit do you feel today.' The real power of this book however, is not so much as to provide individual route inspiration, but to illustrate clearly "what you are missing out on - that is so closeby." I have selected around 250 cliffs from 500 in Central France that you simply should not miss during your climbing lifetime. With this book in your hand, you should never end up saying, oh what a pity, we missed that. I find the internet is brilliant for looking up things that you want to look for, and have heard about. This book however, will hopefully throw up all the great climbing venues... that you actually weren't looking for. It will also show you cliffs that are pointless for you to visit, since the routes are perhaps too easy, or too desperate for you. In conclusion, let's hope that this book will end up as your friendly companion, to all your travels in Central France.

INTRODUCTION - Climbing Outside with this guidebook

After separating France in to 4 natural climbing areas, the task of this guidebook is to include as many cliffs and routes of all grades as possible. Everyone finds navigating a new climbing area confusing, and I find that presenting all relevant information on a double page spread is ideal. Turning pages is fine when you know somewhere, but as a first time user, to see the whole cliff in a simple but complete format, is by far the best presentation I have found to date. Most large cliffs fit perfectly into this format, and other medium sized cliffs fit into a single page layout, so are usually paired with another similar cliff nearby.

This design uses a simple black and white graphic of the cliff, and is overlaid with a colour graphic that illustrates all of the routes 3a-8c in colour. This allows for any climber to assess the cliff for suitability at an instant glance, but does has more information if you decide to examine the finer detail. I use photo topos for most cliffs, but these are used sparingly. I find the most essential part of a photo topo, is that so you can mostly recognise the major routes and features on a first visit, and have confidence in the guidebook. Some guidebooks simply colour routes according to the numbers of sport grades, but I do not see the same climbers enjoying 6a and 6c+ remotely, the gap is too huge. Most climbers fit into 6a-b (blue), or 6c-7a (red), or 7b-7c (black), so by colouring in these ranges with the colours already in use at Fontainebleau, you actually end up with colours that are useful to the majority of climbers. Additionally, if there is a 6a with a single desperate boulder move, I can colour it red and still retain the 6a grade.

All cliffs are numbered from left to right, with approximate heights to the belay (relais). I try to show if the belay can be easily accessed from above to allow straightforward top roping or self belaying methods. I spend a huge amount of time drawing cliffs and sadly see many accidents unfortunately. 99% of these incidents result from over ambitious leaders falling off non-overhanging rock, and hitting the rock whilst falling down. I personally, am never dissuaded from top roping a route in safety first. The orientation for each sector is given in big letters (Se-means 'South' but slightly south-east), along with an H (humidity) value, which indicates how many days the sector stays wet for after "very heavy rain." This can be different in summer, but is a good rough guide if you are not familiar with the cliff. I place the route names vertically next to the routes, but some are extrodinarrrrily long.... so are abbreviated. At the base of the route is a little series of boxes (like a belayer), that gives extra information which may be useful. The bottom box has room for 2 letters which describe the physical nature of the route; A=Aréte, P=Pilier (from French words where practical), a complete index is at the back of the book. I don't use pictograms for strenuous or powerful, because different climbers find things different, I prefer to give the basic element of what you are intending to climb - you 'should not' mistake a wall for a corner. This letter is on a white background, which indicates that sun is on the climb. If there is any green in the box, it indicates how far up the route the trees grow, or grey for rock shade. This is very useful in the hot summer months.

On top of the boxes is a circle, which can be used to illustrate the nature of equipping. Mini bolt circles touching, means you can literally touch bolt to bolt (oh so nice); a space between means you will need a clip stick if you cannot do the moves (boring), and just a single bolt means engagée (terrifying). A single bolt with a X at the bottom indicates that you could 'hit a ledge' or the 'ground,' if you fall. This is a big warning, since many routes 3a-6c would need 30 bolts to make them safe like indoor walls. Falling off whilst climbing outdoors in many instances, is quite simply - not a safe option!

The book divides into 6 sections, each with a good overview map, and data opposite. I try to group cliffs together for a weekend trip, and show nearby campsites and picnic spots. The GPS for parking is decimal for easy input into your phone. I don't always give the closest parking, but do try to give the most practical in terms of not annoying farmers etc. Please consider all gates and access to fields when parking. I give footpaths (approximate) ascent %, and plus or minus to show ascending or descending. Timings are to the nearest 10 seconds, and I walk quite slowly on purpose. Importantly, if this is your first time climbing outside, only proceed under the strict supervision of highly experienced climbers, or if in doubt - use professional climbing instructors, specifically qualified for outdoor climbing.

ROCK ON

BULGING WITH CLIMBING GEAR

Many shops claim to be climbing specialists.
At Rock On we sell Climbing/Mountaineering equipment
& Books and absolutely nothing else. NOTHING ELSE.
Now that's specialist.

Mile End Climbing Wall
Haverfield Road, Bow,
London E3 5BE
Tel: 020-8981 5066

Redpoint Climbing Centre
77 Cecil Street,
Birmingham B19 3ST
Tel: 0121 359 8709

Craggy Island Climbing Wall
9 Cobbett Park, Moorfield Rd, Slyfield Industrial Estate,
Guildford, GU1 1RU - Tel: 01483 565 635

www.rockonclimbing.co.uk

Area 1 - FONTAINEBLEAU (30 premier sectors)

Page	Blocs - Secteur			Arbre	Am-Pm	Crash	Enfants		Circuits (problems)					Approche	Ambience
16	B3	P14	91.1	H0	2-4m	1 +	0	0	47	84	0	47	0	10	Techinque, cool
16	B3	P14	95.2	H0	3-4m	2 +	0	0	0	84	41	43	28	8	Techinque, cool
15	C4	P7	Apremont Dames	H1	2-3m	1 +	0	0	0	40	45	0	40	4	Petit & Fun
15	C4	P7	Apremont Gorges-Chaos	H1	4-6m	3 +	46	0	42	28	44	46	35	8	Tech & Serieux
15	C4	P7	Apremont Ouest	H1	3-5m	2 +	0	0	0	29	57	40	0	6	Tech & Cool
14	A4	P1	Beauvais - Hameau	H2	2-4m	2 +	0	40	33	73	33	40	38	8	Jolie, Chaos
14	A4	P2	Beauvais - Nainville Bois	H2	2-3m	1	50	0	60	56	0	0	28	1	Jolie, traversée
14	A4	P2	Beauvais - Nainville Côte	H1	2-4m	1 +	50	50	0	30	50	40	30	1	Jolie, traversée
14	A4	P1	Beauvais - Télégraphe	H1	2-3m	1 +	50	50	38	38	38	0	0	1	Jolie, vue
16	B3	P12	Bois Rond	H1	2-4m	1	0	0	0	37	33	0	40	4	Jolie, traversée
17	A1	P18	Buthiers Canard-Cocci	H2	3-8m	4 +	27	0	0	34	38	36	22	1	Cool & Serieux
17	A1	P19	Buthiers Piscine	H1	3-8m	3 +	49	0	20	69	42	35	39	1	Cool & Serieux
16	B2	P17	Cailleau - JA Martin	H0	3-6m	2 +	38	0	54	46	50	50	0	1	Variant, Chaud
16	B3	P13	Canche aux Merciers	H0	2-3m	1	69	35	38	41	44	34	0	4	Jolie, traversée
15	C4	P7	Canon, Rocher	H2	3-4m	1 +	40	0	48	43	80	46	24	4	Technique
16	B3	P15	Cul de Chien	H0	3-5m	2 +	0	0	0	47	46	38	0	16	Physique, variant
14	C3	P4	Cuvier - Bas	H1	3-5m	2	0	0	0	50	48	42	30	1	Physique, tech
14	C3	P4	Cuvier - Rempart	H0	4-7m	3 +	0	0	0	0	0	0	47	14	Techinque, haut
17	C1	P21	Dame Jouanne-Requin	H1	3-9m	7 +	0	0	68	76	76	99	31	3	Crazy, superbe
17	C1	P20	Eléphant	H0	3-9m	5 +	32	0	49	?	84	0	40	3	Giant, cool
15	C3	P10	Franchard - Cuisinière	H1	3-7m	2 +	0	0	35	51	0	53	48	7	Tech, cool
15	C3	P9	Franchard - Isatis	H1	2-6m	1 +	0	0	0	45	50	62	50	1	Tech, physique
16	B2	P16	Guichot, Rocher	H1	2-4m	1	0	0	0	30	20	21	0	1	Jolie, technique
17	C1	P21	Maunoury	H1	3-9m	6 +	0	0	0	54	71	36	0	12	Serieux, Physique
14	A4	P3	Padole	H3	2-6m	2 +	0	0	52	55	65	59	32	1	Petit & Serieux
17	C1	P22	Petit Bois	H3	2-5m	1 +	0	0	54	0	70	50	36	0	Jolie, variant
16	B2	P16	Potala, Rocher du	H0	3-4m	1	0	0	40	57	47	55	0	7	Jolie, tech
17	D2	P23	Restant du Long Rocher	H2	2-4m	2 +	0	0	0	66	0	34	0	3	Jolie, variant
16	B3	P15	Sabots, Roche aux	H1	2-4m	1 +	0	40	0	42	50	34	0	3	Physique & tech
14	D3	P6	Saint Germain Est	H1	2-3m	1	51	0	49	31	36	34	0	5	Jolie

L'Angle du 30: 4c, *Mr. Jingo, Rocher Canon*

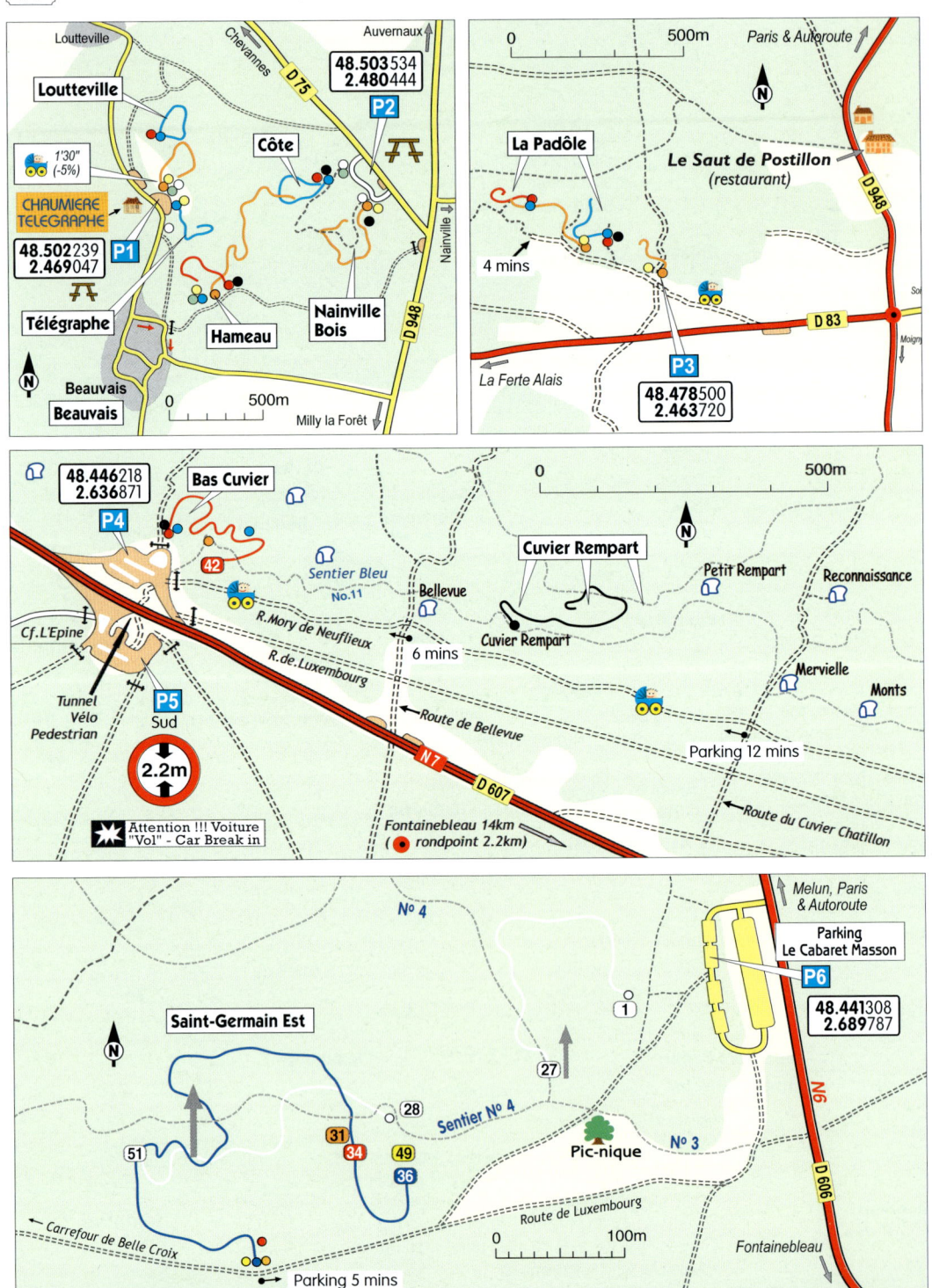

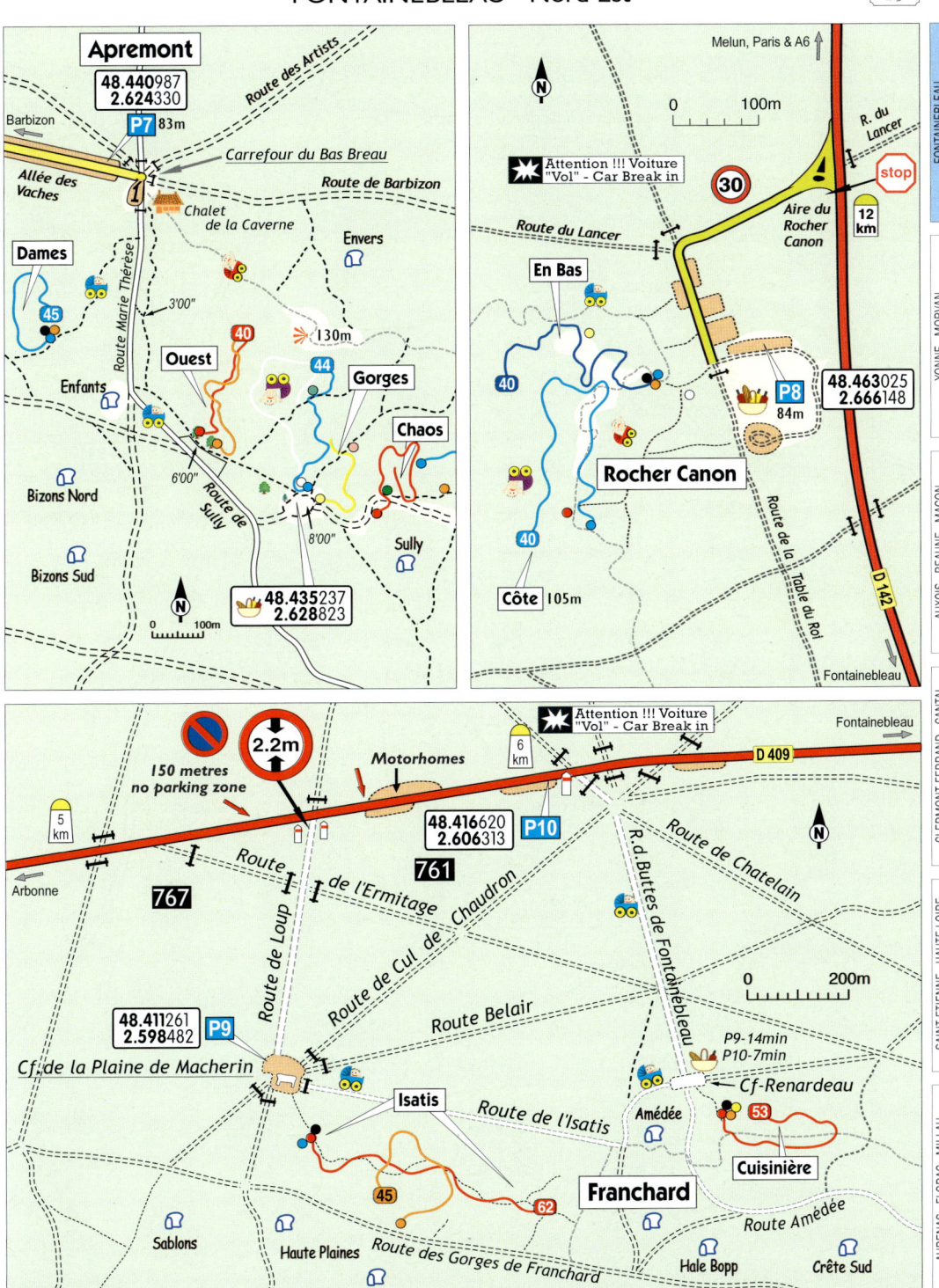

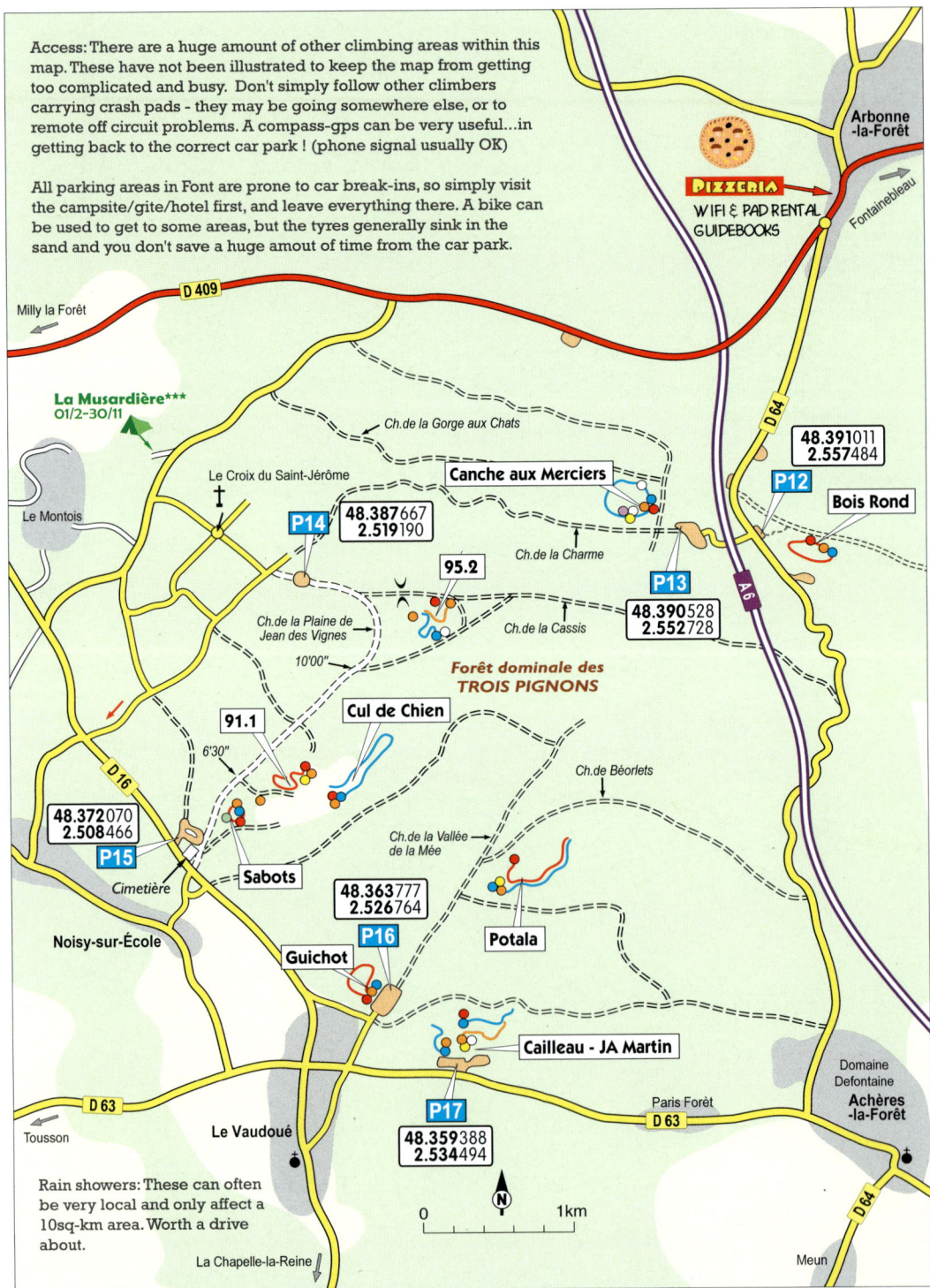

FONTAINEBLEAU - Sud

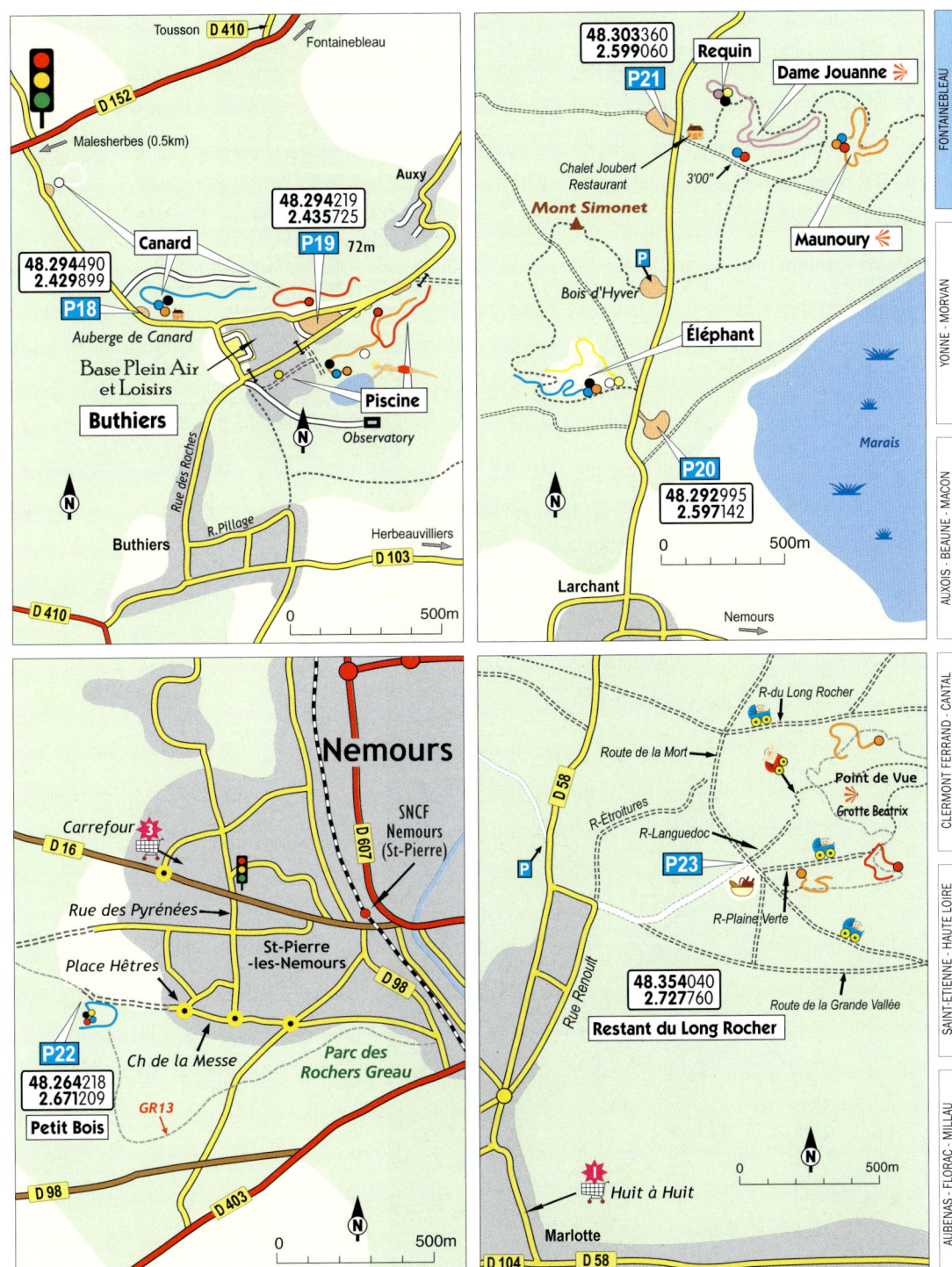

Area 2 - YONNE - MORVAN

Page	Falaise/Cliff	Alt	Arbre-Ori-Sèche	Am-Pm	Rocher	Longeur	\#1	\#2	\#3	\#4	\#5	\#6	Approche	Ambience
62	C2 Chien - Est	480m	E/H0-3		Granit	8-37m	2	13	12	1	2	1	0	Mur, Pilier
63	C2 Chien - Ouest	500m	W/H2-3		Granit	14-19m	4	4	3	0	0	0	3	Mur, Pilier
52	C3 Cousin - Avallon	197m	SW/H1-2		Granit	8-28m	9	6	8	0	0	0	1	dalle,Mur,Pilier
57	C3 Fées (Bloc)	500m	E&W/H1-2		Granit	2-8m	8	5	9	5	0	0	3	Mur, Surplomb
60	C2 Gués de Dun	380m	S/H1-4		Granit	6-35m	6	23	16	11	5	0	8	Mur, raide, Zzz
54	B2 Lormes-en bas	330m	SE/H2		Granit	11-13m	4	4	2	1	0	0	7	dalle, Mur, Zzz
54	B2 Lormes-en haut	370m	S/H1		Granit	7-10m	16	6	4	4	2	0	8	dalle,Mur,bloc
58	C2 Montal	430m	S&E/H1		Granit	10-13m	10	5	7	4	2	1	1	Mur, raide
53	C1 Moulins d'Yonne	405m	E/H1-3		Volcanic	8-11m	0	0	7	8	6	2	3	Mur, oomph
20	A4 Parc, Rochers	130m	SW/H0-1		Calcaire	12-28m	19	18	28	43	36	11	1	Mur, glissant
20	A4 Parc, Sud	130m	SW/H0-1		Calcaire	25-28m	3	3	11	19	5	0	2	Mur, glissant
26	A4 Saussois	140m	W&E/H0-1		Calcaire	17-35m	31	40	77	153	95	28	1	Mur, poches
26	A4 Saussois-Oise...	131m	W&E/H0-1		Calcaire	25-53m	3	7	13	22	2	1	1	Mur, glissant
40	A3 Surgy - Est	145m	E/H1-4		Calcaire	8-40m	11	30	83	91	44	24	6	Mur, poches
40	A3 Surgy - Sud	145m	S/H0-1		Calcaire	15-23m	16	12	15	5	1	0	2	Mur, glissant
64	D3 Vieux-Château	250m	S/H0-2		Granit	15-35m	33	31	25	14	4	3	5	dalle,mur,Pilier

MONO MANIA 7c+, *Laurent Pouillot, Saussois*

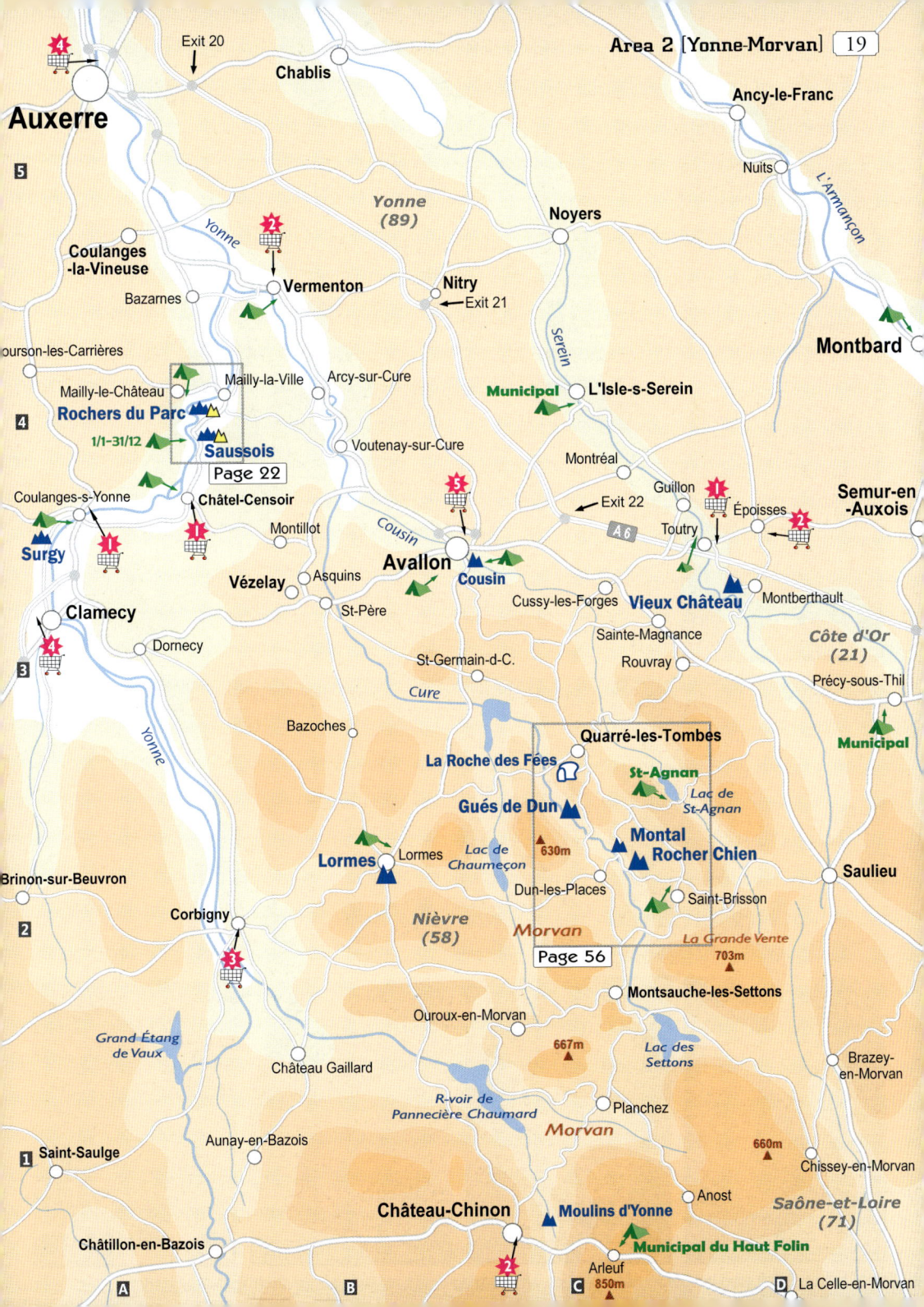

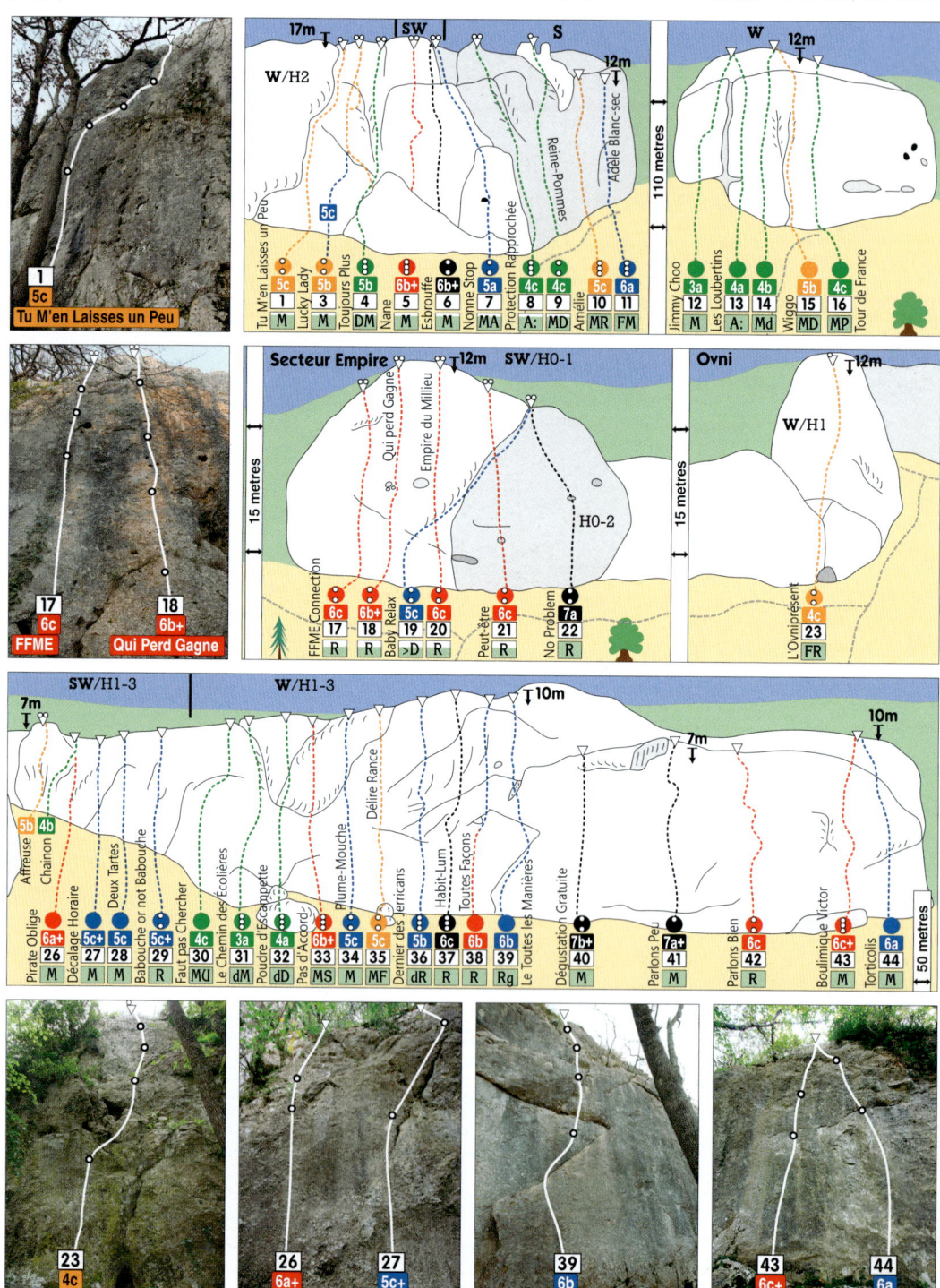

ROCHERS DU PARC

47.581070, 3.647917 — P2 — 21

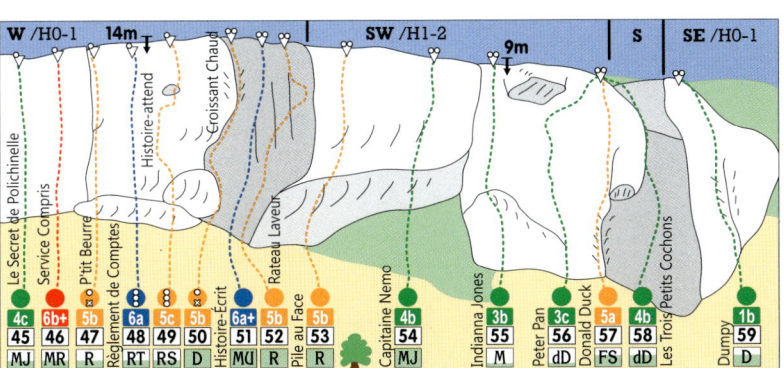

49 — 5c — L'Histoire n'Attend Pas

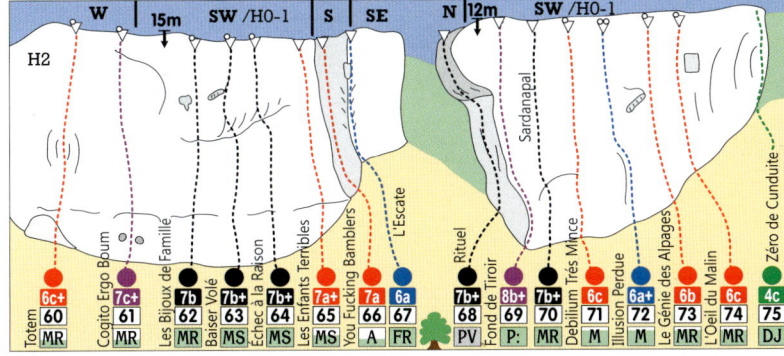

62 — 7b — Le Bijoux de Famille

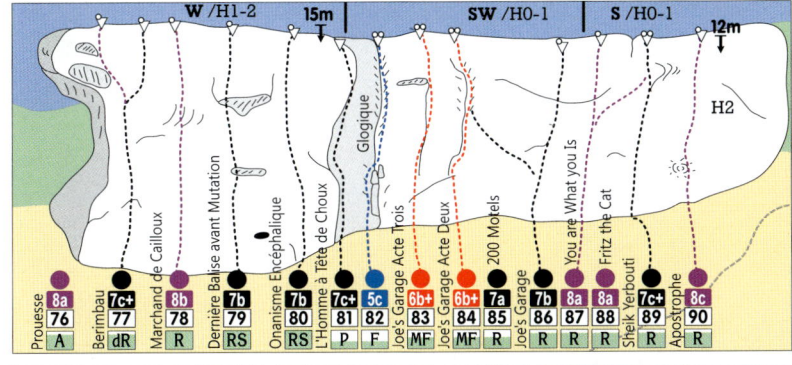

70 — 7b+ — Sardanapal

77 — 7c+ — Benimbau

82 — 5c — Glogique

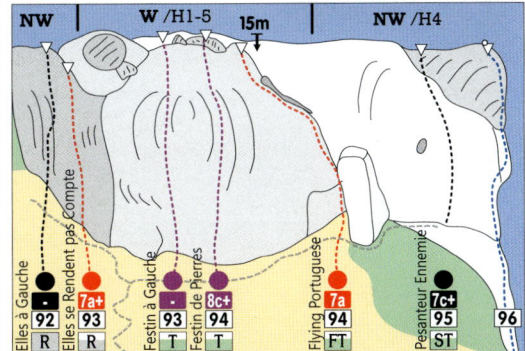

Some very impressive sections, small towers with minimal pockets - brutal for the fingers.

FONTAINEBLEAU — YONNE - MORVAN — AUXOIS - BEAUNE - MACON — CLERMONT FERRAND - CANTAL — SAINT-ETIENNE - HAUTE LOIRE — AUBENAS - FLORAC - MILLAU

ROCHERS DU PARC

P3 47.579749, 3.648920

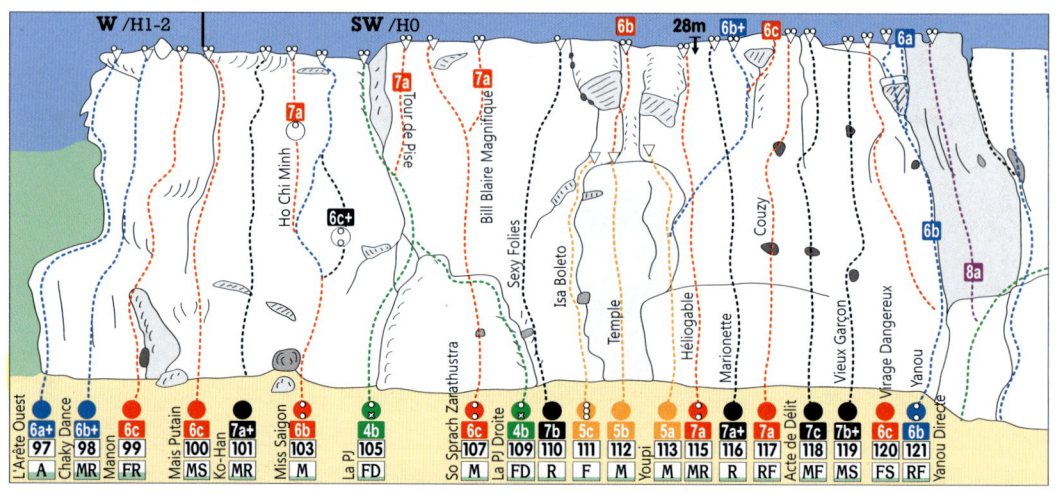

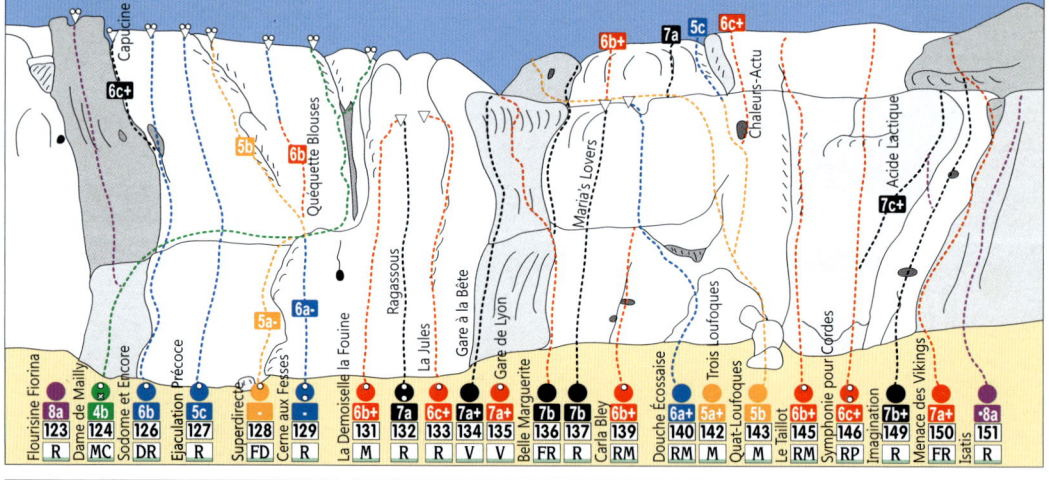

Most of the equipping is not generous (basically really unhelpful), you will find a clipstick very useful.

ROCHERS DU PARC

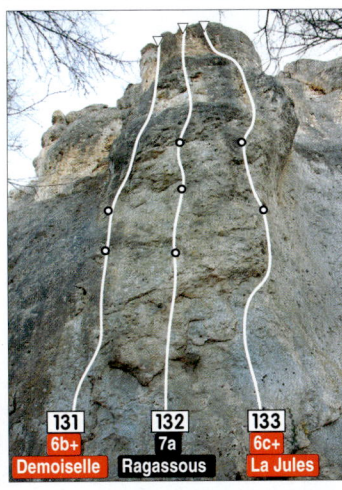

Some routes stay wet with drainage streaks, but most dry well in winter - so on a sunny day it can be glorious.

ROCHERS DU PARC

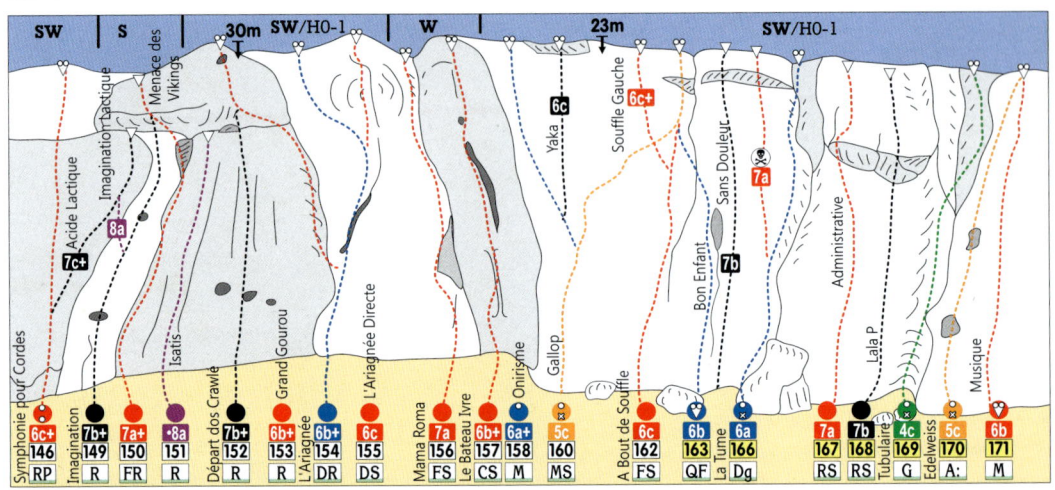
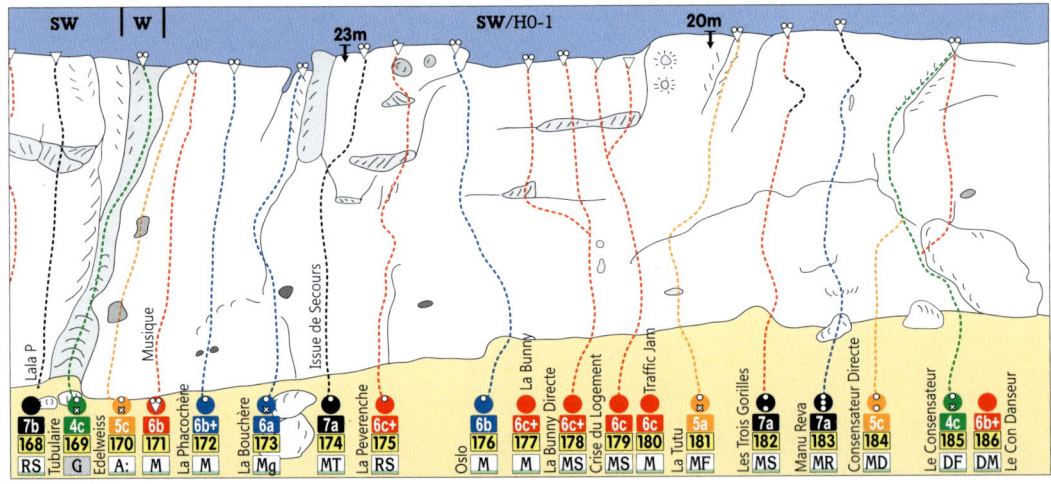
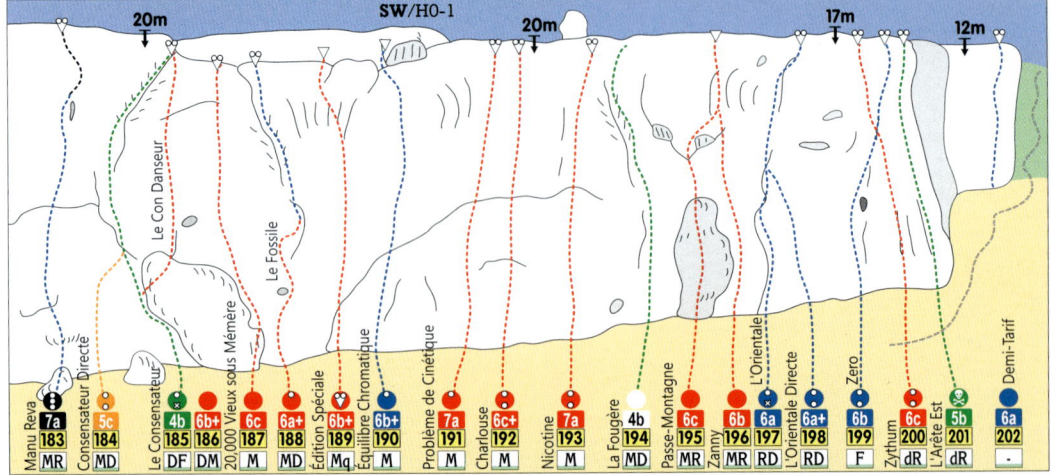

ROCHERS DU PARC (Sud) # 163-202 [15/2 - 03/06]   25

#	Grade	Name
156	7a	Mama Roma
157	6b+	Le Bateau Ivre
164	7b	Sans Douleur
165	7a	Le Miroir aux Alouettes
166	6a+	La Tume
169	4c	La Tubulaire
170	5c	L'Edelweiss
174	7a	Issue de Secours
175	6c+	La Pervenche
179	6c	Crise du Logement
181	5a	La Tutu
182	7a	Les Trois Gorilles
183	7a	Manu Reva
191	7a	Problème de Cinétique
192	6c+	Charlouse
197	6a	L'Orientale
198	6a+	L'Orientale Directe
199	6b	Zero
200	6c	Zythum
201	5b	L'Arête Est

FONTAINEBLEAU · YONNE - MORVAN · AUXOIS - BEAUNE - MACON · CLERMONT-FERRAND - CANTAL · SAINT-ETIENNE - HAUTE LOIRE · AUBENAS - FLORAC - MILLAU

Bird restriction will probably be variable. For top access at this time go straight up from P2.

LE SAUSSOIS (Bundao)

P4 47.565483, 3.648877

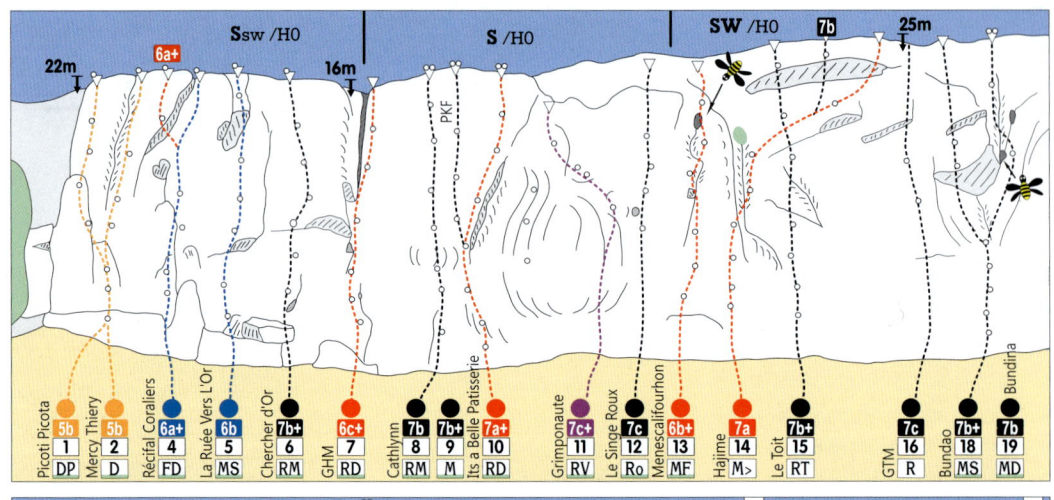

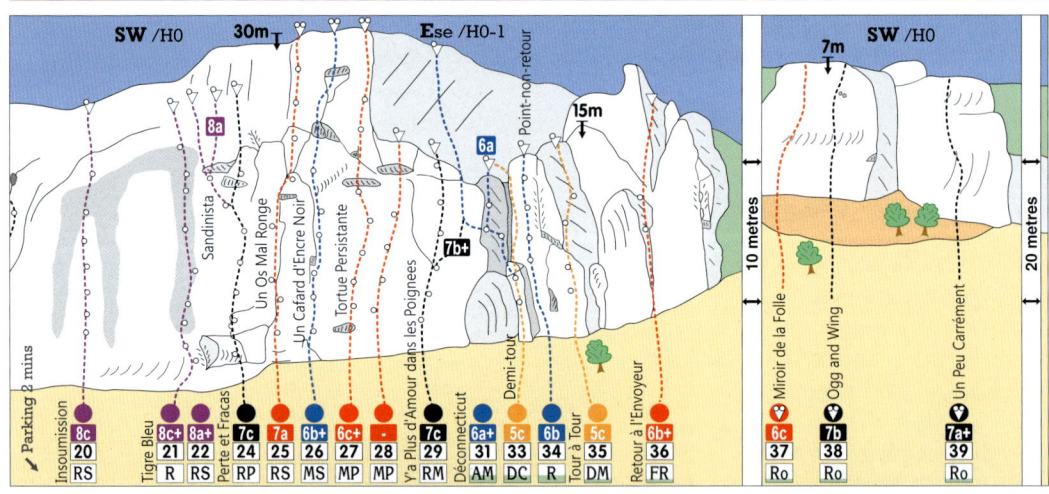

1	2
5b	5b
Picoti Picota	Merci Thierry

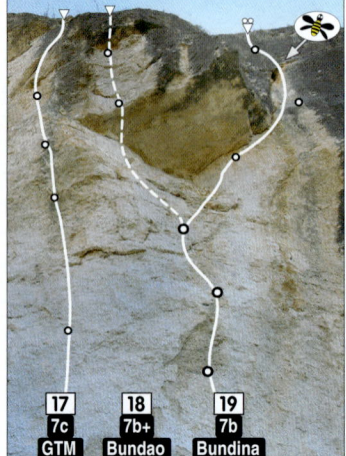

17	18	19
7c	7b+	7b
GTM	Bundao	Bundina

26	31
6b+	6a+
Un Cafard d'Encre Noir	Déconnecticut

Calcaire **** Some of the very best rock that you will find. Incredibly compact and strong, pockets of all different sizes.

LE SAUSSOIS (Locomotive)

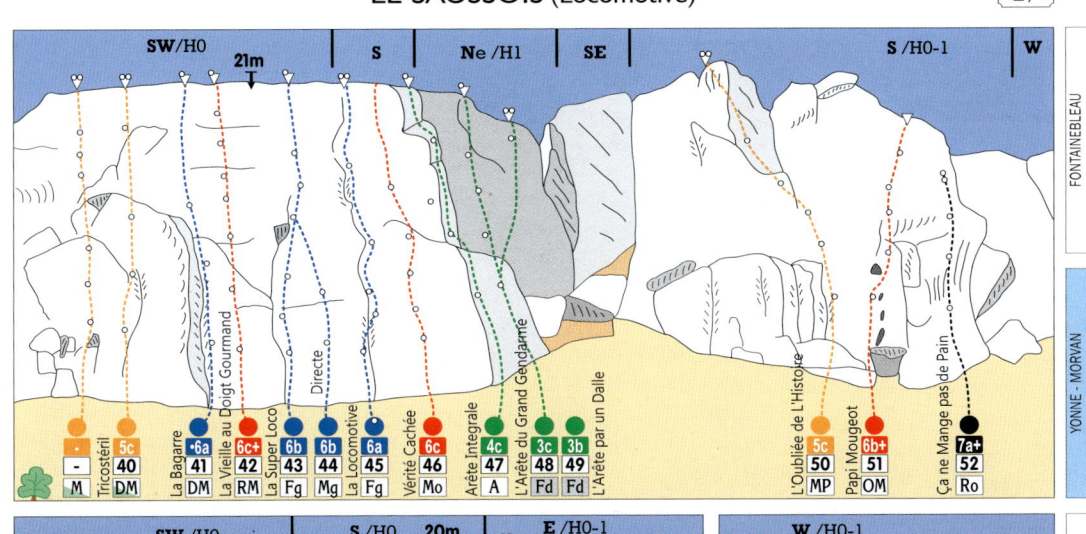

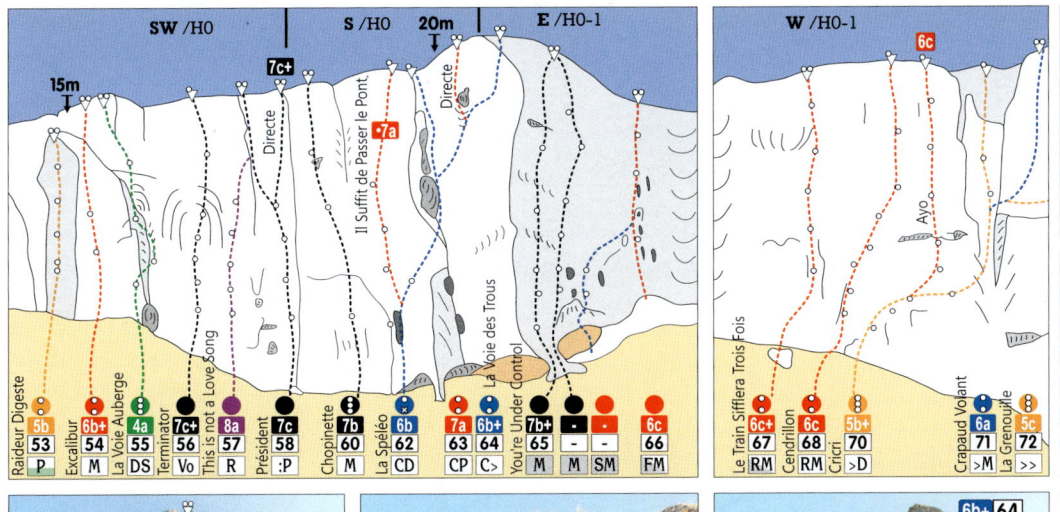

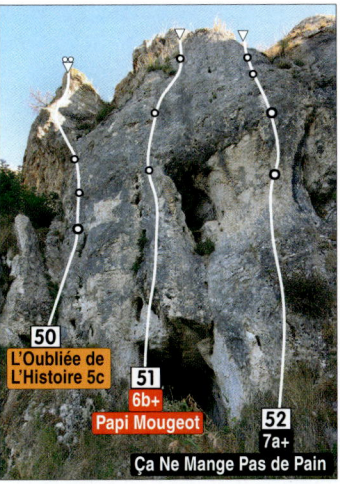

Two popular sectors with shorter routes, most are polished - but you need the pockets to be - to save your skin.

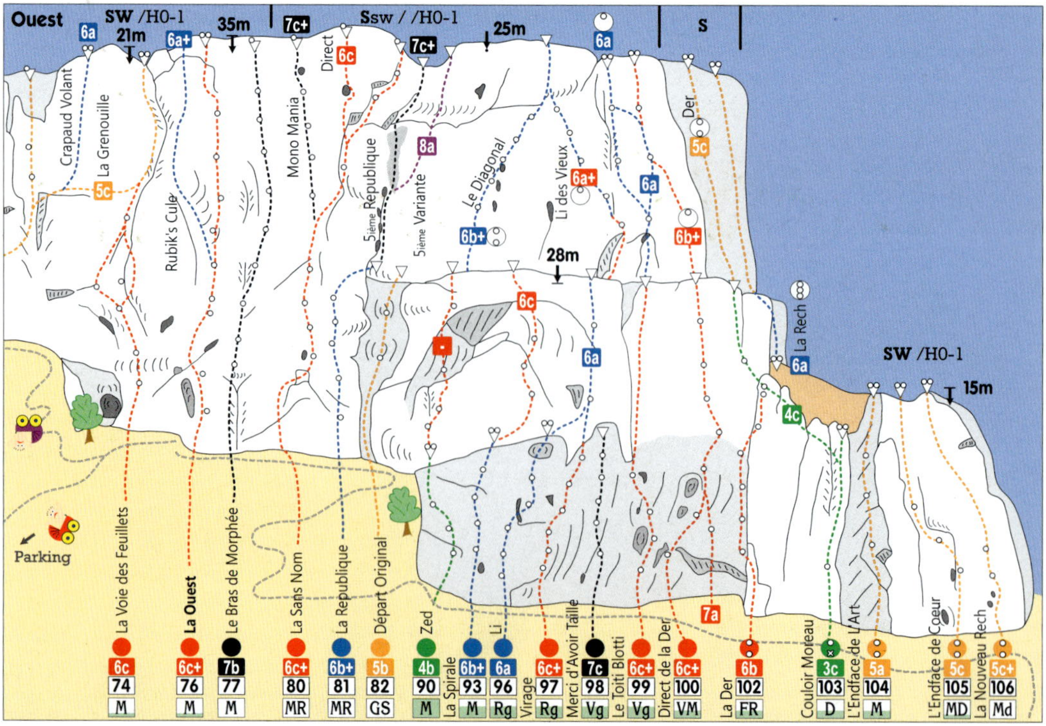

LE SAUSSOIS (Ouest)

P4 47.565483 , 3.648877

Page 28

Route labels on the cliff photo:
- Mono Mania **78** — 7c+
- La Sans Nom Direct **79** — 6c / 7c+
- Cinquième Variante **84** — 8a
- Éclectite — 6b / 6a / 6a / 5c / 6b+
- La Der — 6a
- La Sans Nom **80** — 6c+
- La Cinquième République **83**
- La Diagonale **85** — 6b+
- L'i des Vieux — 6a+
- Le Livre Ouvert — 6a
- Éclectite **102**
- **100**

Topo / schematic labels:
- Ouest — SW /H0-1
- 6a 21m — 6a+ 35m — 7c+
- Ssw //H0-1 — 7c+ Direct — 25m
- S
- 6a — Der — 5c
- Crapaud Volant — La Grenouille — 5c
- Rubik's Cube — Mono Mania
- 5ième République — 8a
- 5ième Variante — Le Diagonal — 6b+
- Li des Vieux — 6a+ — 6a — 6b+
- 28m
- 6c
- 6a
- La Rech
- 6a — SW /H0-1 — 15m
- 4c

	La Voie des Feuillets	La Ouest	Le Bras de Morphée	La Sans Nom	La Republique	Départ Original	Zed	La Spirale	Li	Virage	Merci d'Avoir Taillé	Le Toit Blotti	Direct de la Der	La Der	Couloir Moiteau	L'Endface de l'Art	L'Endface de Cœur	La Nouveau Rech
Grade	6c	6c+	7b	6c+	6b+	5b	4b	6b+	6a	6c+	7c	6c+	6a	6b	3c	5a	5c	5c+
#	74	76	77	80	81	82	90	93	96	97	98	99	100	102	103	104	105	106
	M	M	M	MR	MR	GS	M		Rg	Vg	Vg	Vg	VM	FR	D	M	MD	Md

Superb pocket pulling high up, overhanging gymnasium lower right. **VOIE DES TROUS 6b+**, *Jean-Claude André; Saussois (64)* ▷

LE SAUSSOIS

△ *Saussois-Est-Jardins & Renard* *Merry-sur-Yonne & Saussois* △△

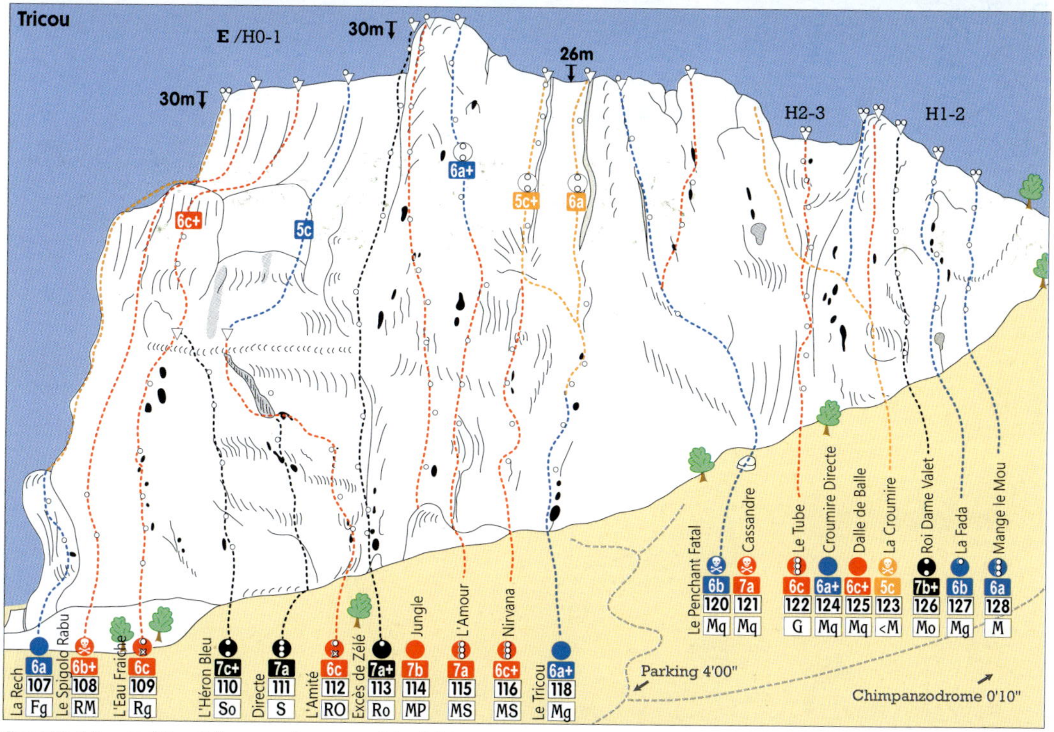

LE SAUSSOIS (Tricou)

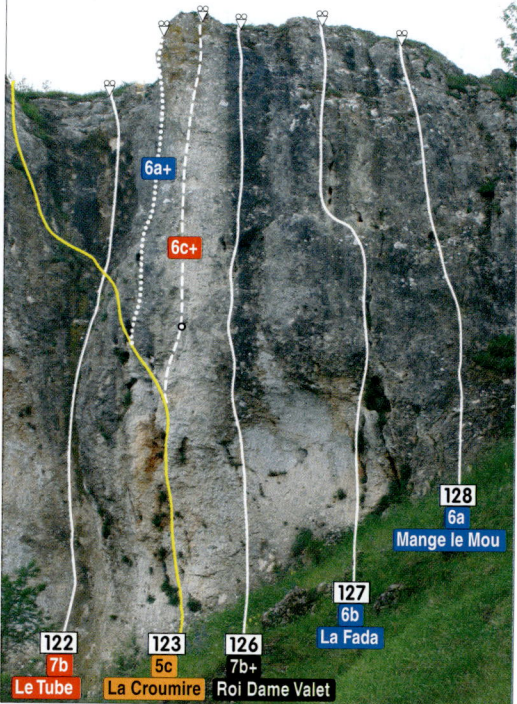

Some very impressive sections, small towers with minimal pockets - brutal for the fingers.

LE SAUSSOIS (Chimpanzodrome)

P4 47.565483 , 3.648877

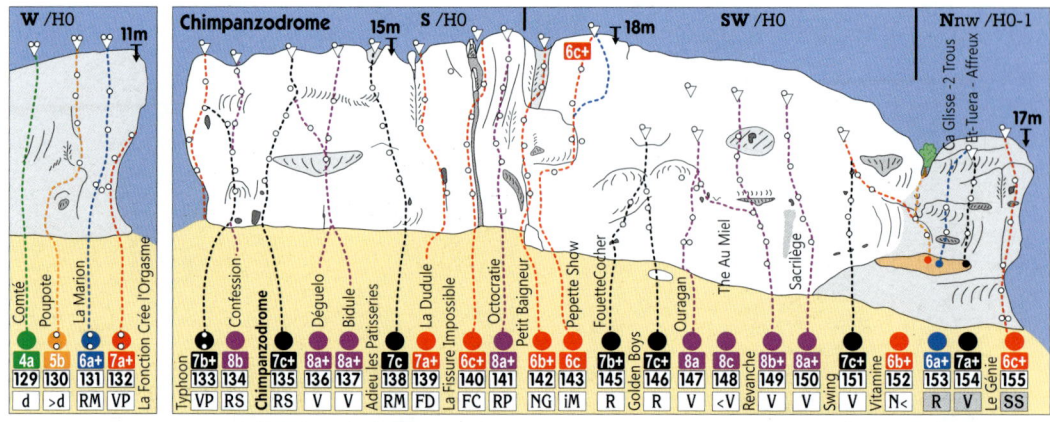

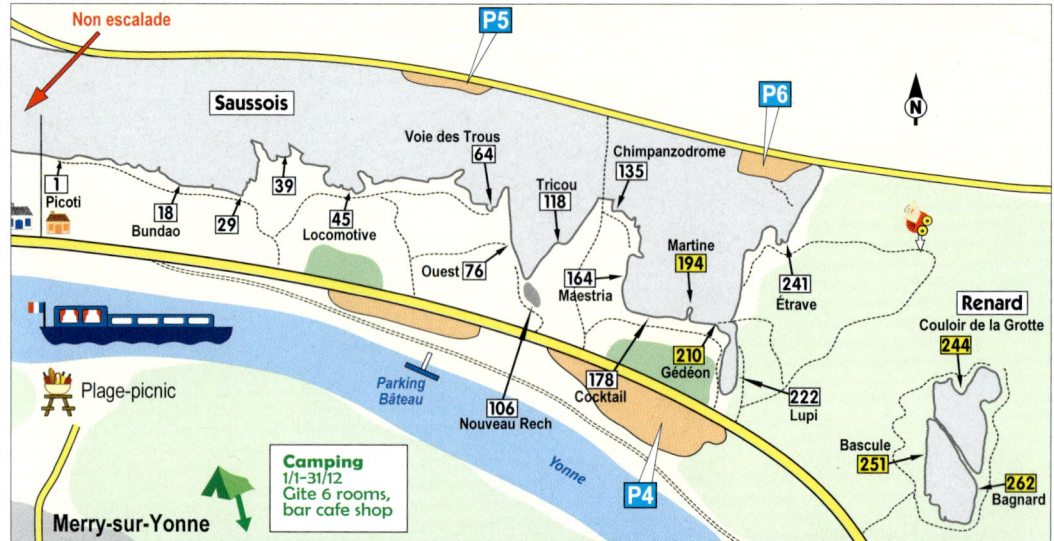

This sector can be approached easiest from the top parking, which also gives easy access to nice picnic spot with views.

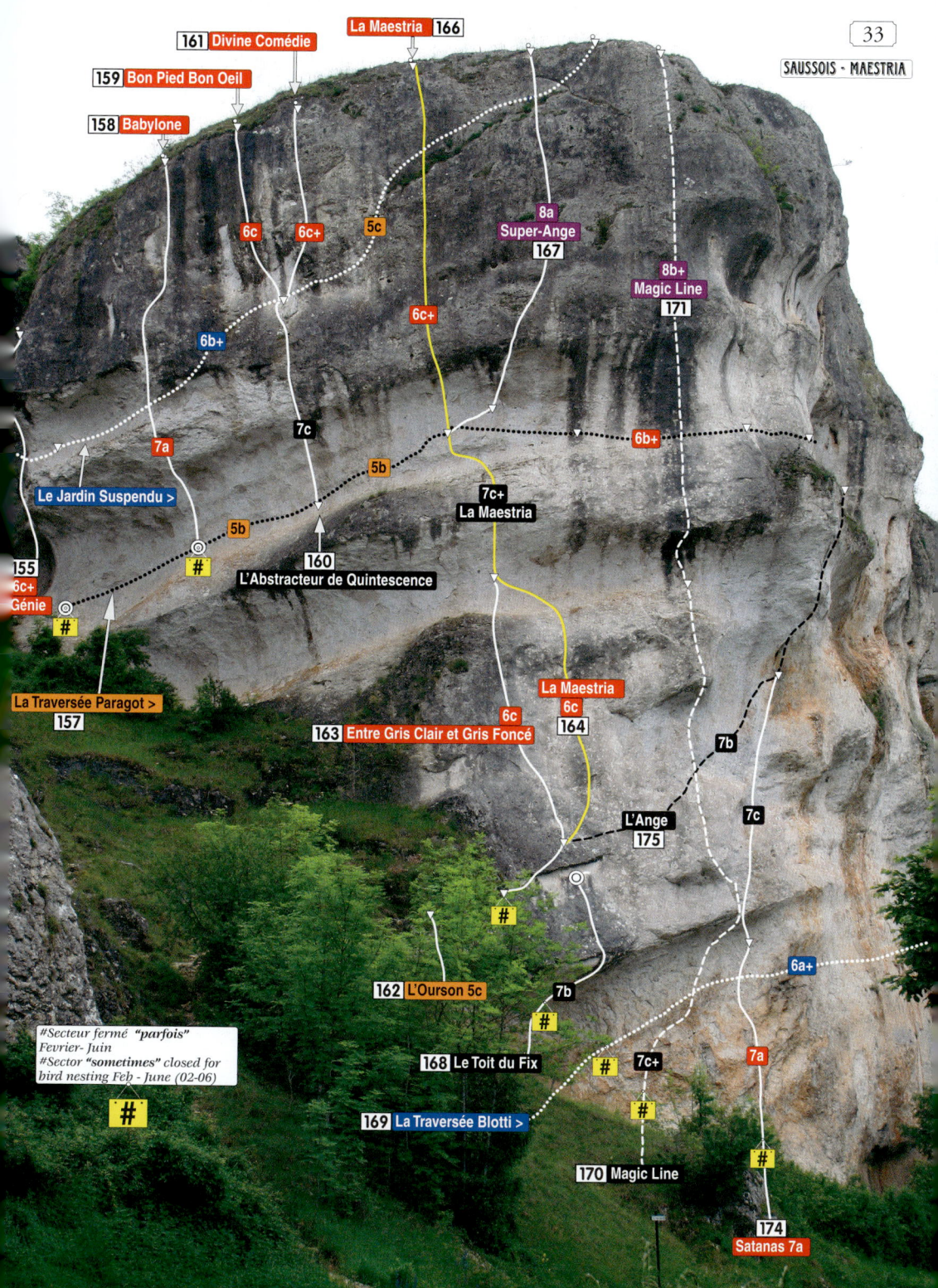

No holds are polished here "they are just incredibly smooth & slippery." Amazing climbing. Bird restriction - sometimes.

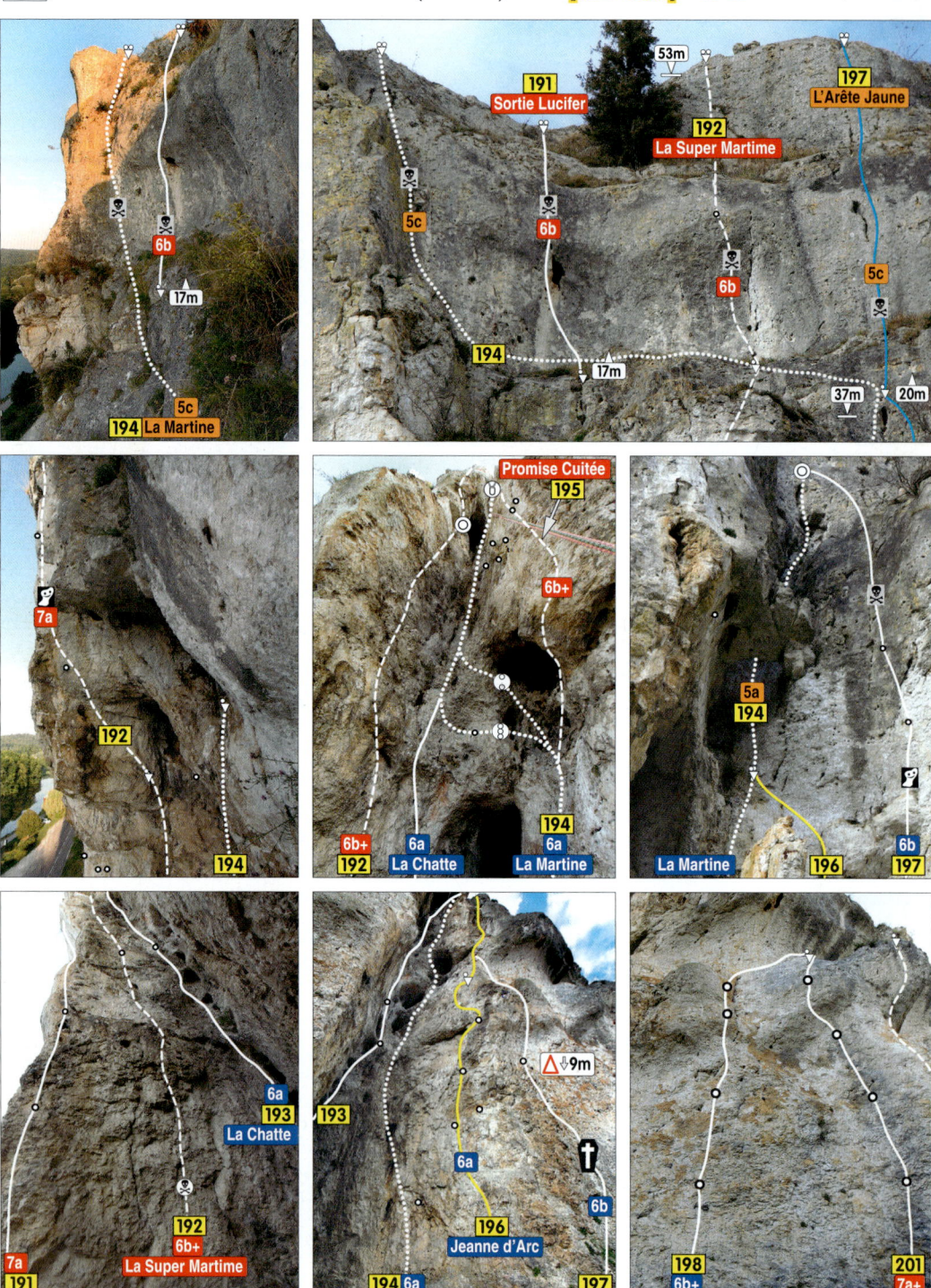

The - GLOOMY - "La Martine" sector has been polished by the birds to glass, it has some of the most bizzare bolting in France.

LE SAUSSOIS (Toufou-Étrave)

P4 47.565483 , 3.648877

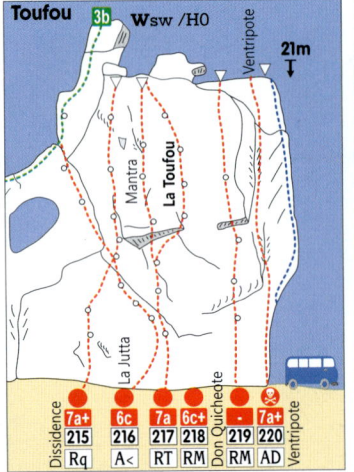
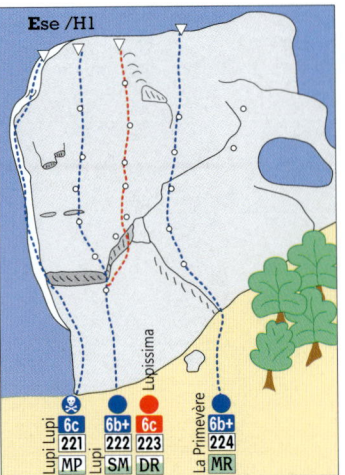
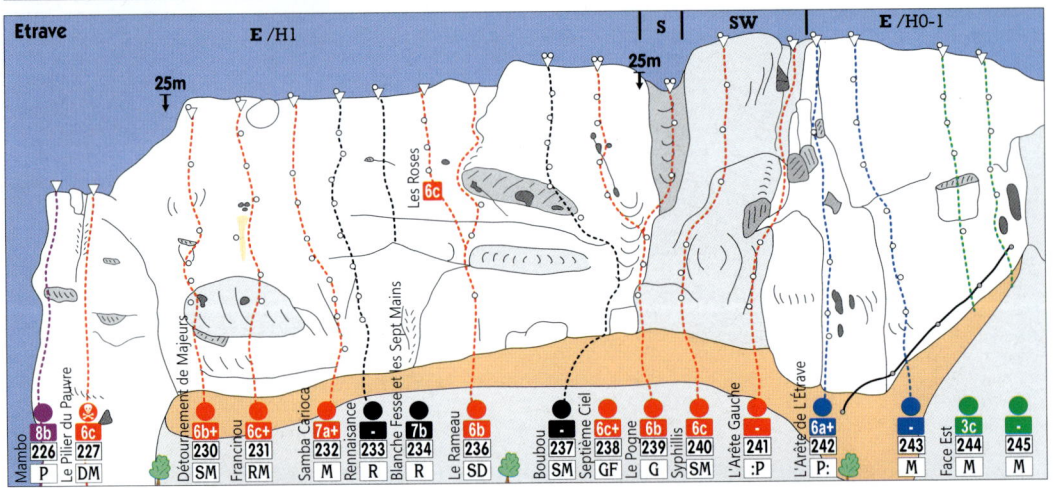

The Etrave sector is often quiet with cool afternoon shade. A nice place to retreat to on hot days.

LE ROCHER DU RENARD [15/2 - 03/06]

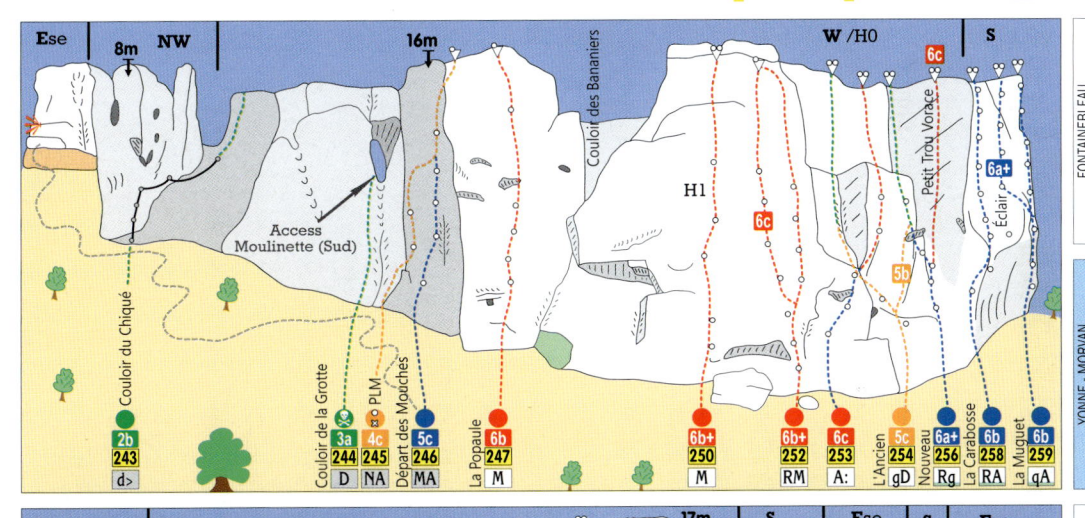

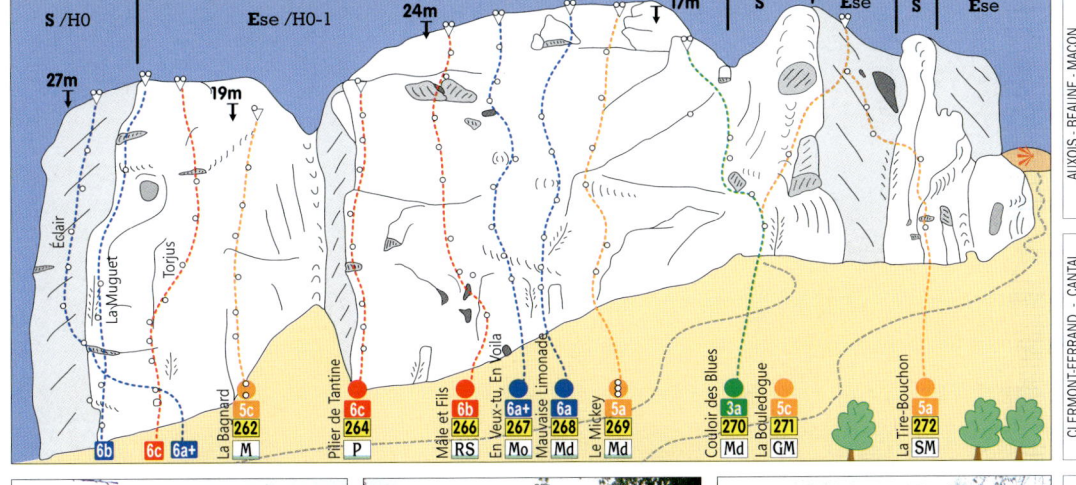

Renard: A lot of historic routes did not follow good lines & with crazy equipping. New lines being developed, in progress.

SURGY (Les Rochers de Basseville)

P7 47.493206, 3.507026

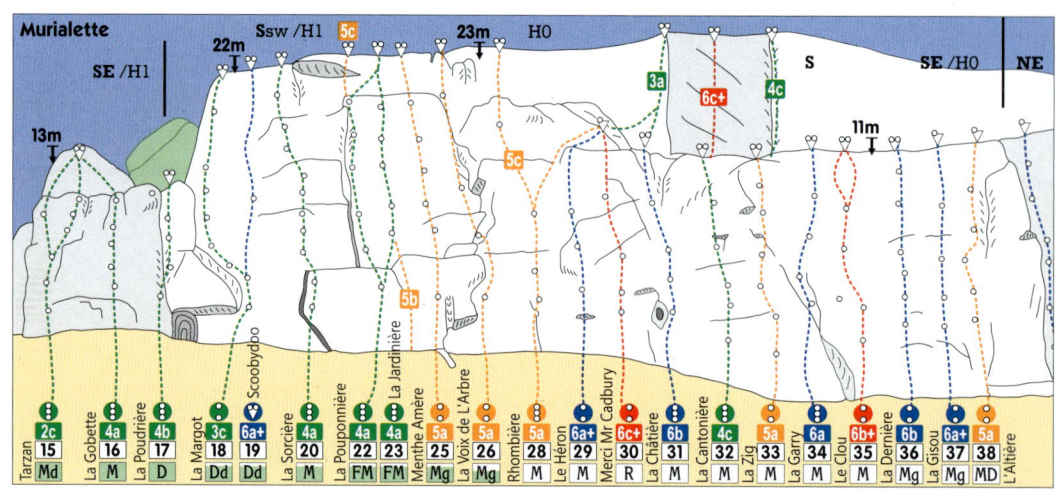

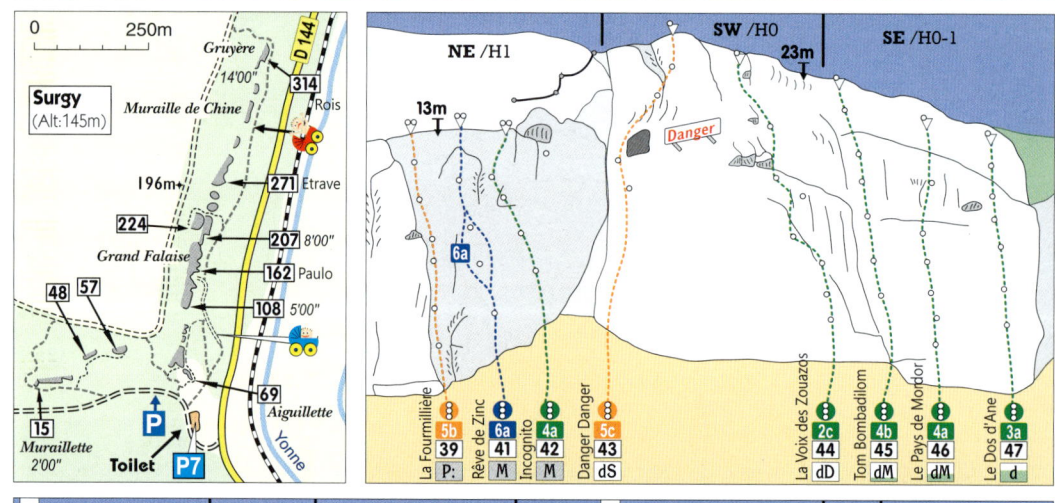

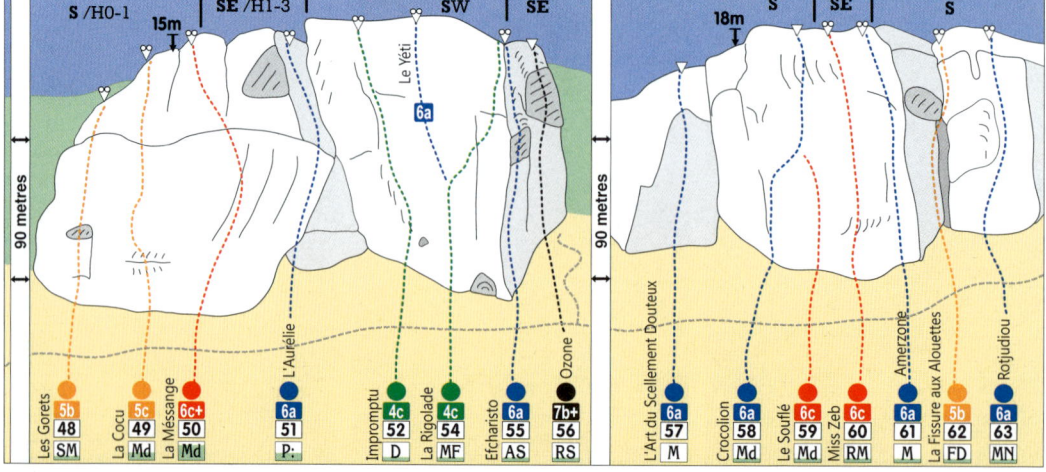

Routes 1-14 (not brilliant-not included). Calcaire**** Most of the rock here is excellent, sometimes a bit too blank.

SURGY (Secteur L'Aiguillette)

P7 47.493206, 3.507026

The Aiguillette will fall down one day !!! The other sectors are a lot more solid and give excellent climbing, enjoy.

A sector with lots of variety, certainly "not well equipped enough" for a lot of climbers - big caution.

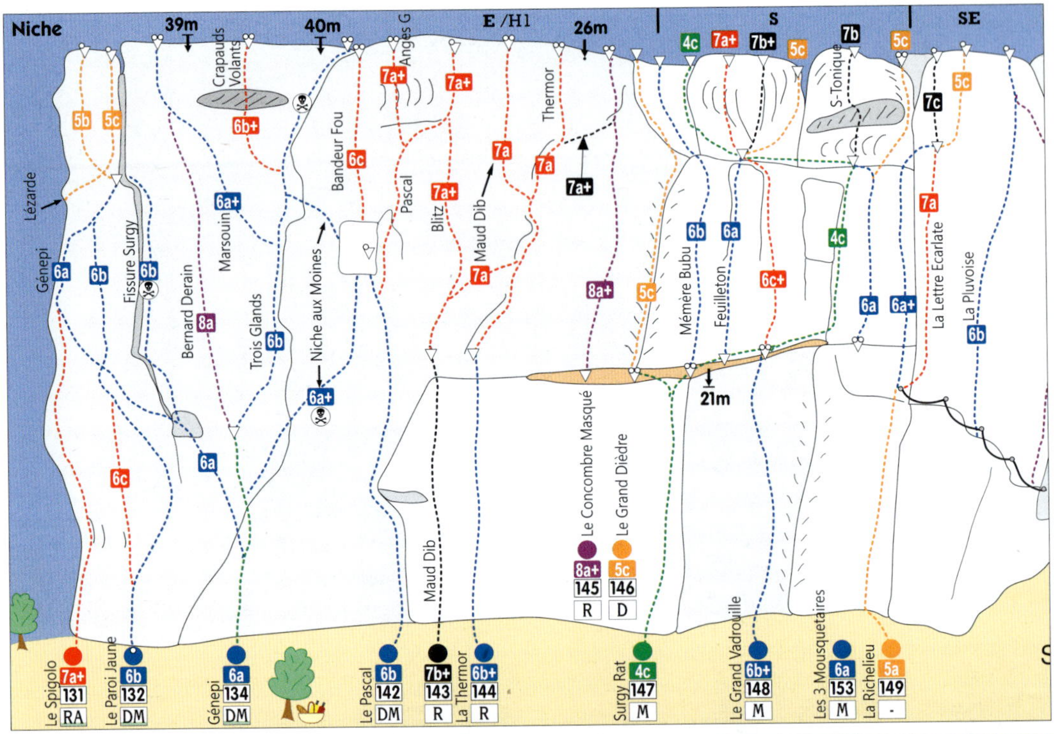

SURGY (Secteur Niche)

P7 47.493206, 3.507026

A very impressive bay with impressive and intimidating routes. Stays warm and muggy on hot days in the afternoon.

SURGY (Secteur Paulo)

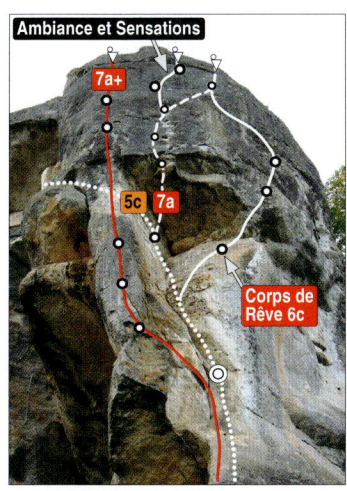

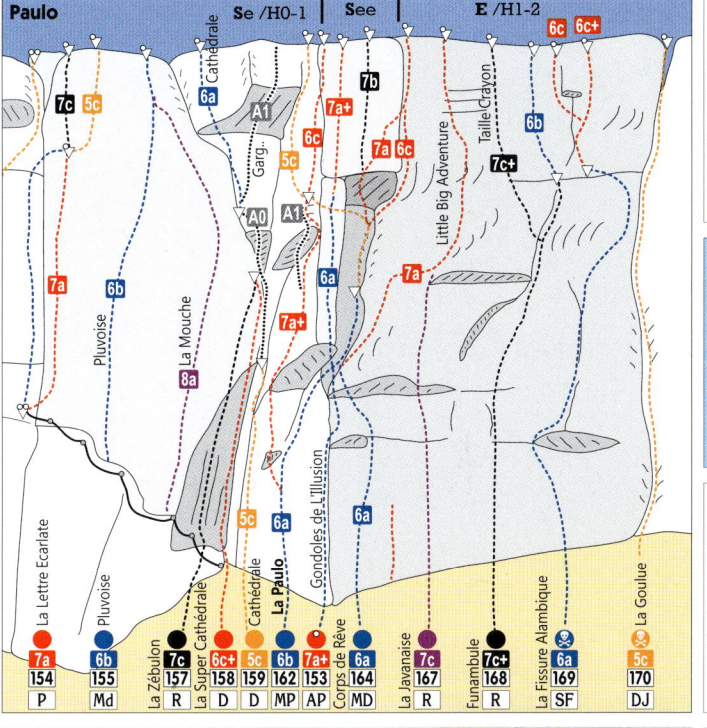

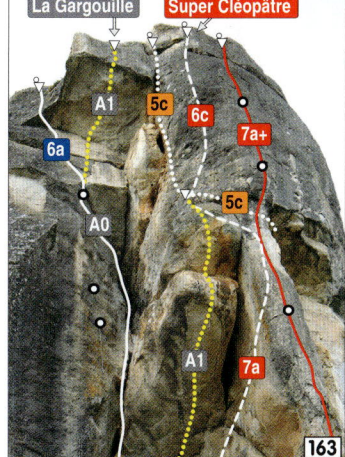

#	Name	Grade	Style
154	La Lettre Ecarlate	7a	P
155	Pluvoise	6b	Md
157	La Zébulon	7c	R
158	La Super Cathédrale	6c+	D
159	Cathédrale	5c	D
162	La Paulo	6b	MP
153		7a+	AP
164	Corps de Rêve	6a	MD
167	La Javanaise	7c	R
168	La Funambule	7c+	R
169	La Fissure Alambique	6a ☠	SF
170	La Goulue	5c ☠	DJ

This is a gigantic impressive prow. Ideal for the mid to high grade 7 Climber (6C/7a - it's a long way to haul up the clip stick).

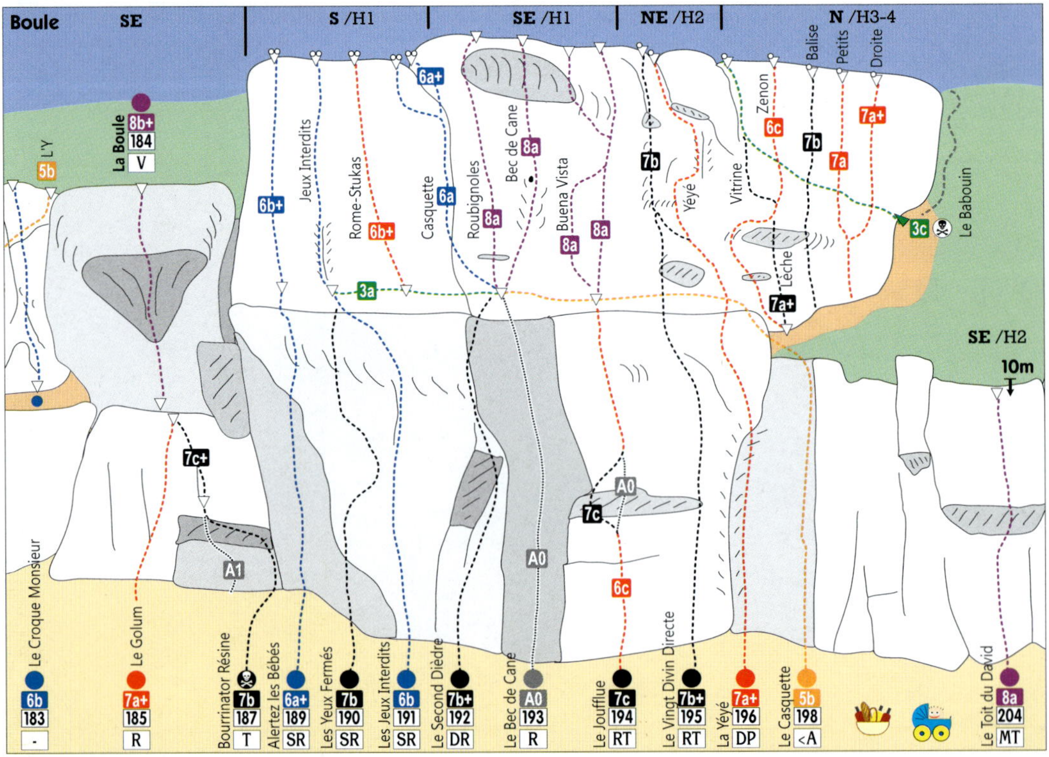

SURGY (Secteur Citadelle)

P7 47.493206, 3.507026

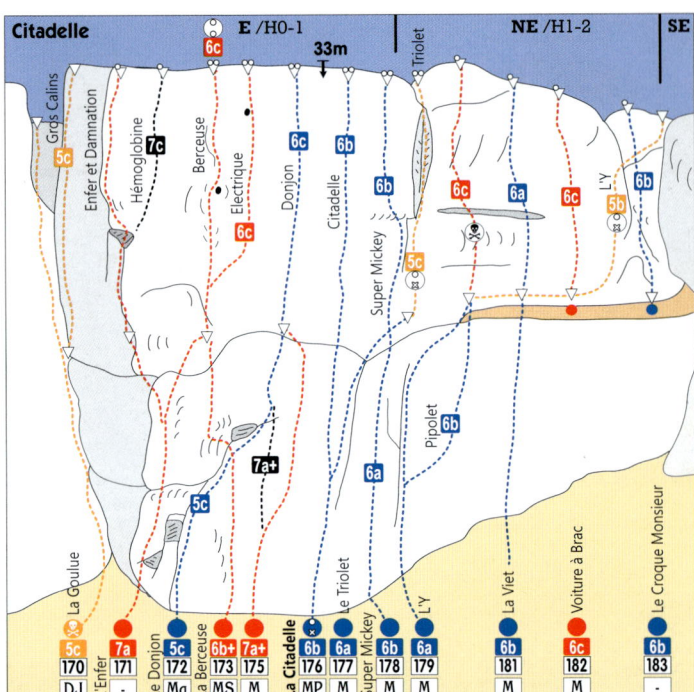

Some of the best and most stunning routes at Surgy. Does stay a bit damp, and a bit scary with slippery feet.

SURGY (Les Rochers de Basseville)

Big overhangs - big arms needed. Big flat walls high up with some monos, sometimes too many...sometimes not enough !

SURGY (Secteur Tourelle)

P7 47.493206, 3.507026

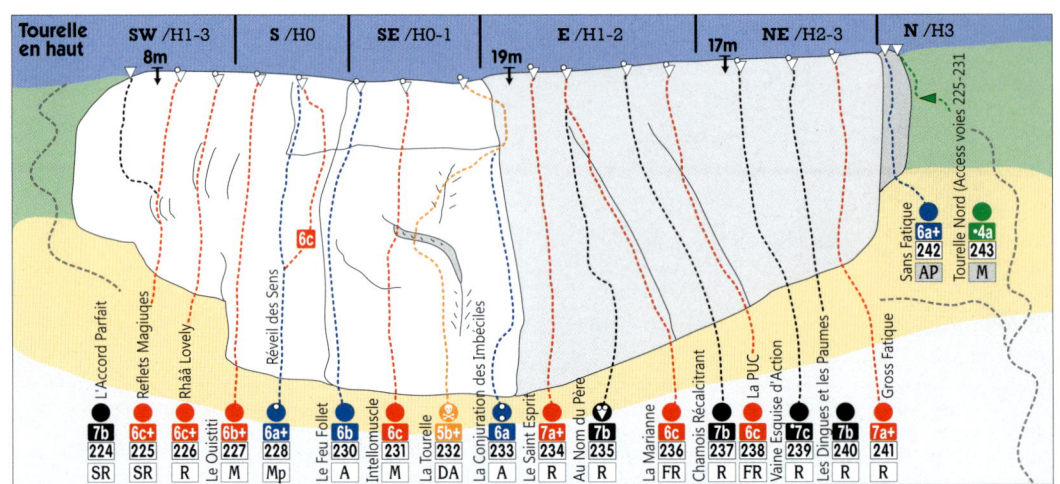

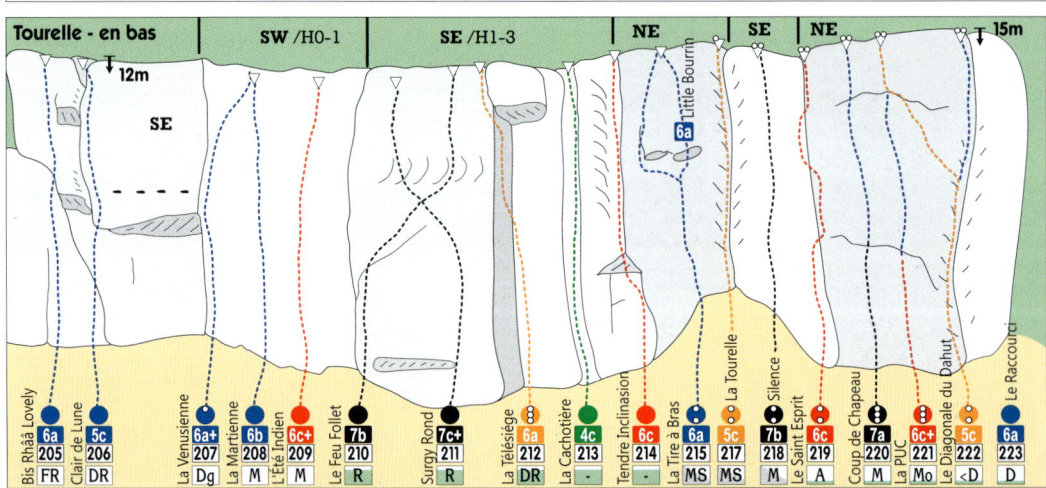

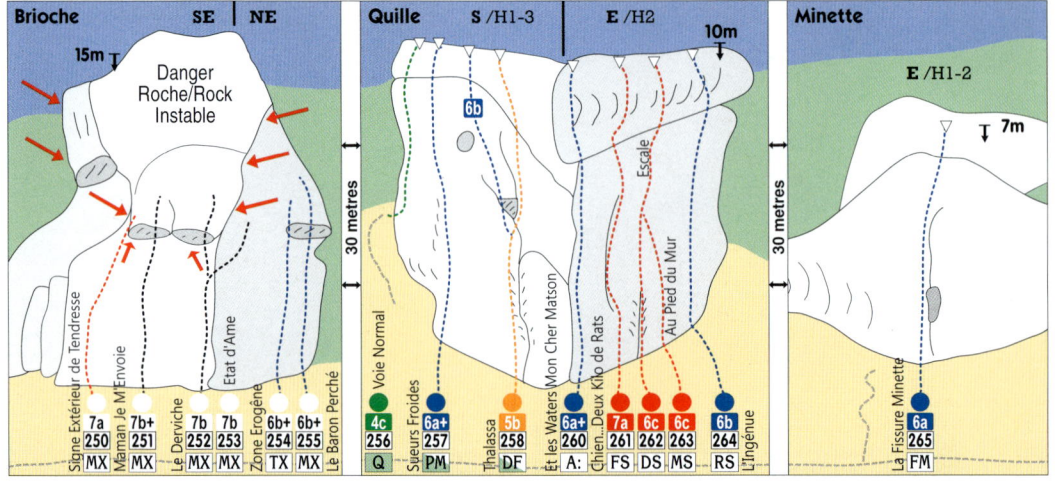

The Tourelle is the end of the main cliff, a nice selection of routes downstairs, and some great views from the top tier (en haut)

SURGY (Les Rochers de Basseville) 49

#	Grade	Name
227	6b+	Le Ouistiti
228	6a+	Réveil des Sens
230	6b	Feu Follet
231	6c	Intellomuscle
232	5b+	La Tourelle
236	6c	Marianne
237	7b	Chamois Récalcitrant
238	6c	P.U.C.
207	6a+	Venusienne
208	6b	Martienne
209	6c+	L'Été Indien
210	7b	Feu Follet
211	7c+	Surgy Rond
212	6a	Télésiège
213	4c	Cachotière
220	7a	Coup de Chapeau
221	6c	P.U.C.
222	5c	Diagonale du Dahut
256	4c	Voie Normale
257	6a+	Sueurs Froides
259	5b	Thalassa
260	6a+	—
261	7a	2 Kilos de Rats
262	6c	Escale à Deux
265	6a	La Fissure Minette

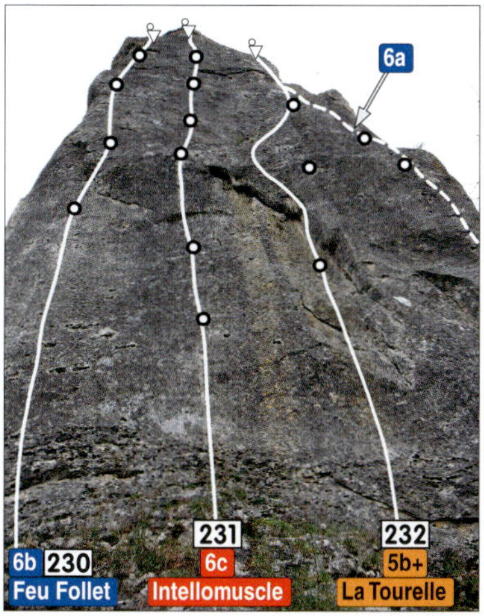

The cliff now becomes a sereis of small overhanging buttresses, very similar to Frankenjura - with difficulty to match.

SURGY (Muraille de Chine)

P7 47.493206, 3.507026

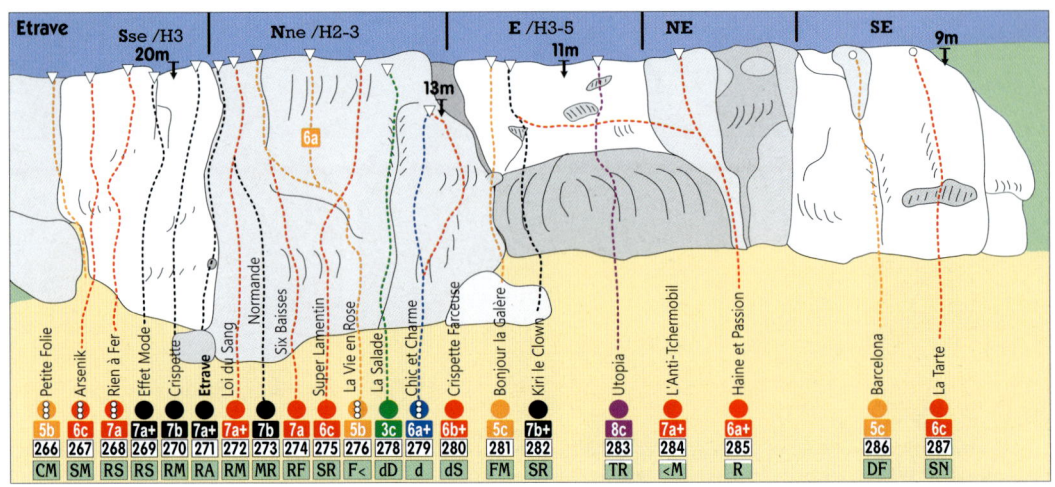

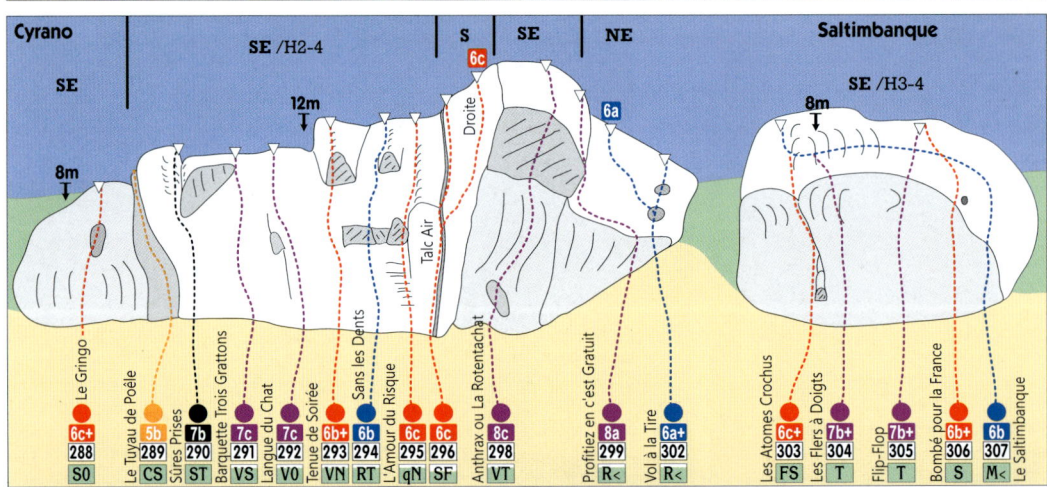

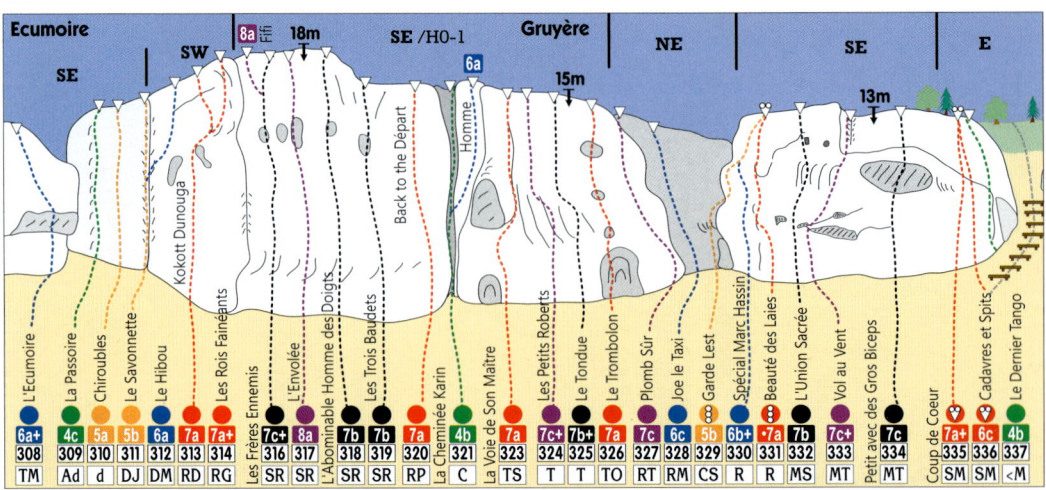

Secteur Etrave is very shady and a good place to climb in summer. Cyrano and Saltimbanque will appeal to boulderers.

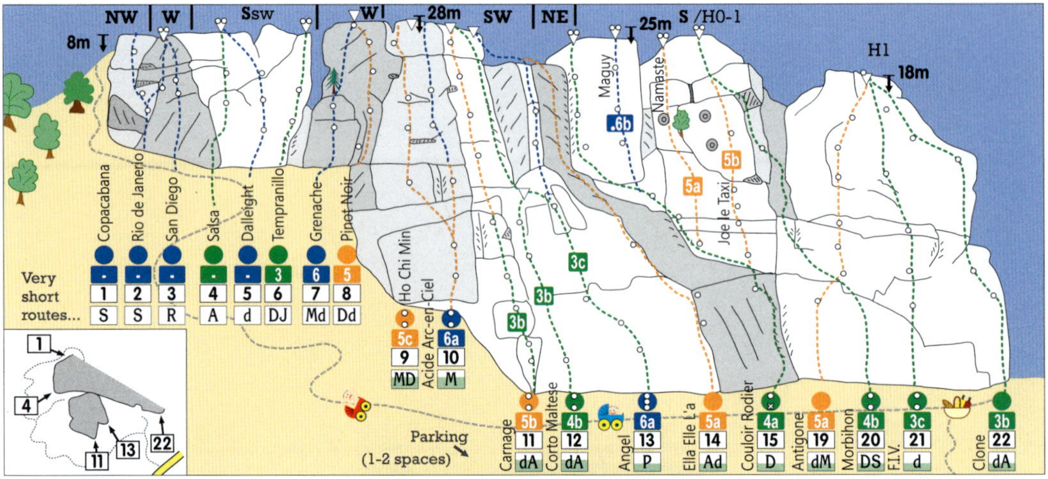

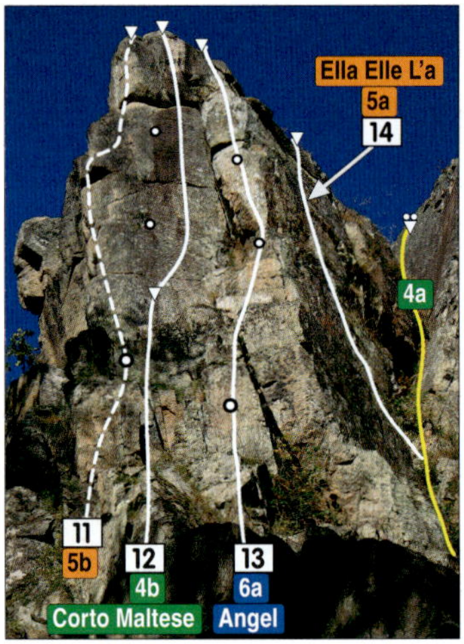

ROCHERS DU COUSIN

P1 47.480500, 3.912039

Granite*** Good quality. Only a few good routes, but worth visiting if staying at the camping overnight. Easy to top rope.

LES MOULINS D'YONNE

P2 47.066742, 3.952203 — 53

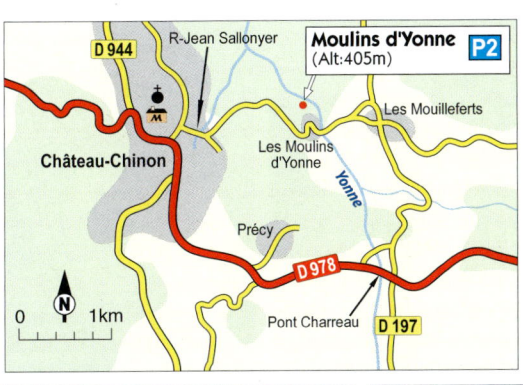
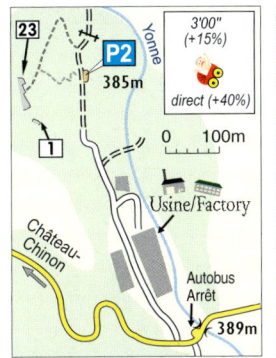
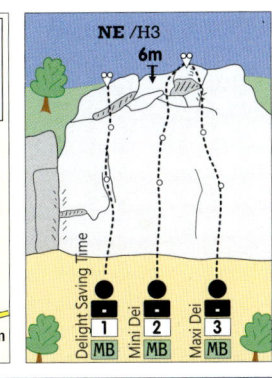

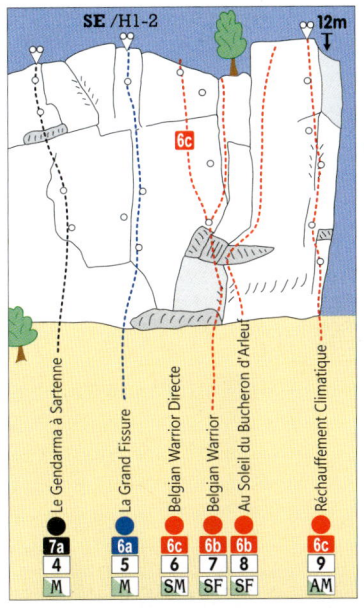
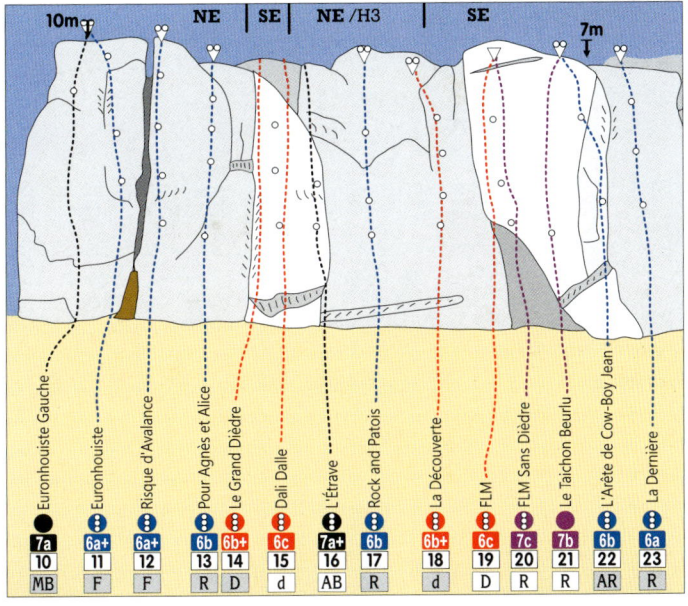

Volcanic*** Good small spot, boulder style - good landings, but most will enjoy a rope. Grades meaningless - font bloc colours.

LORMES

P1 47.284984, 3.812057

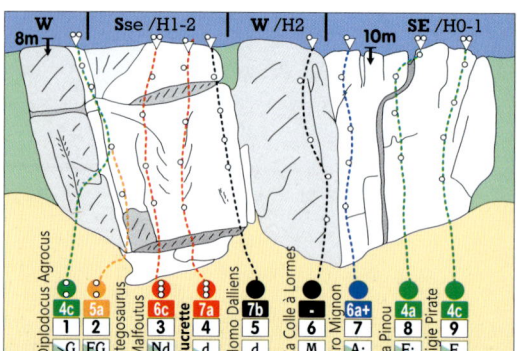
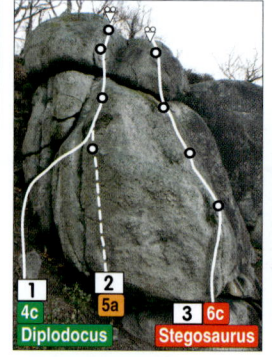
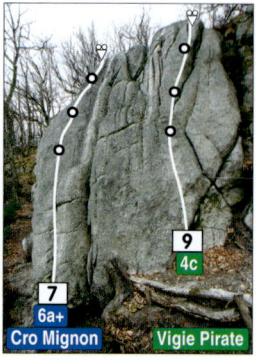
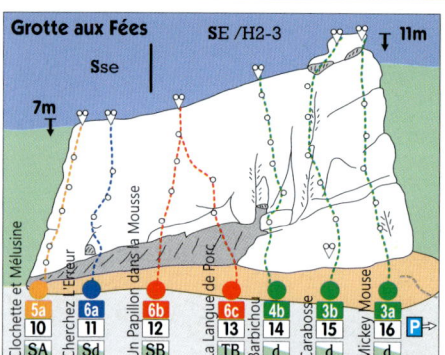
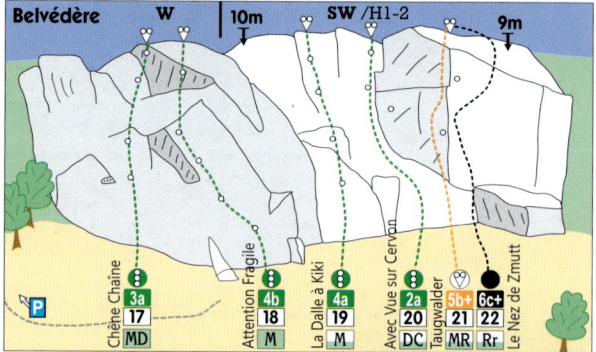
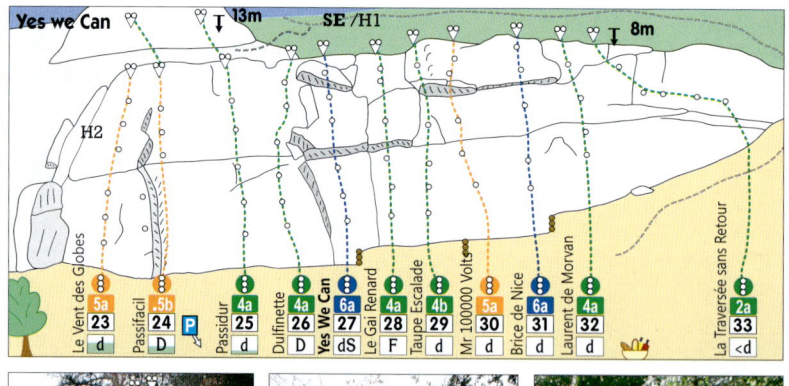
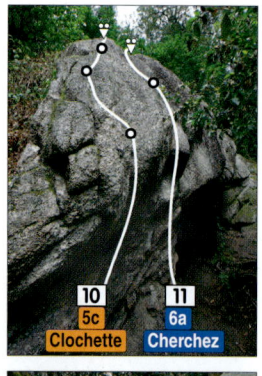
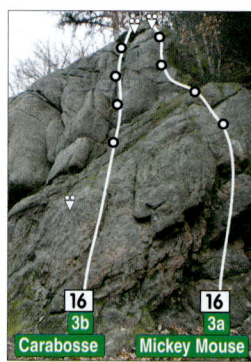

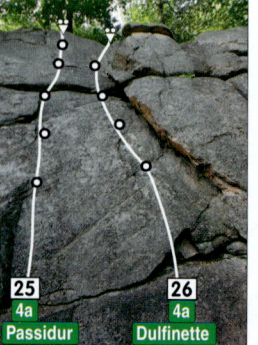
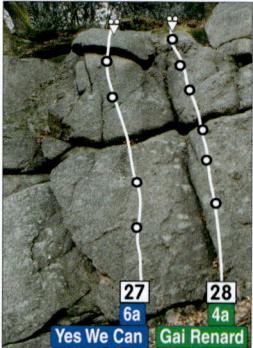

Granite **** Very rough, excellent friction, lots of bolts, great small venue and highly enjoyable. A good variety of short climbs.

LORMES

55

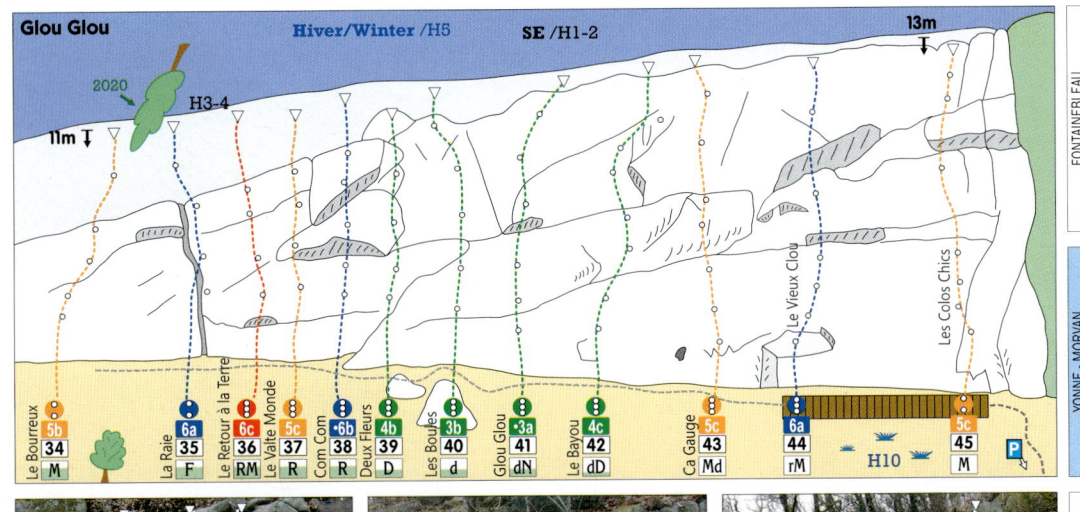

	Le Bourreux	La Raie	Le Retour à la Terre	Le Vaite Monde	Com Com	Deux Fleurs	Les Boules	Glou Glou	Le Bayou	Ça Gauge		Le Vieux Clou		Les Colos Chics
	5b	6a	6c	5c	•6b	4b	3b	•3a	4c	5c		6a		5c
	34	35	36	37	38	39	40	41	42	43		44	H10	45
	M	F	RM	R	R	D	d	dN	dD	Md		rM		M

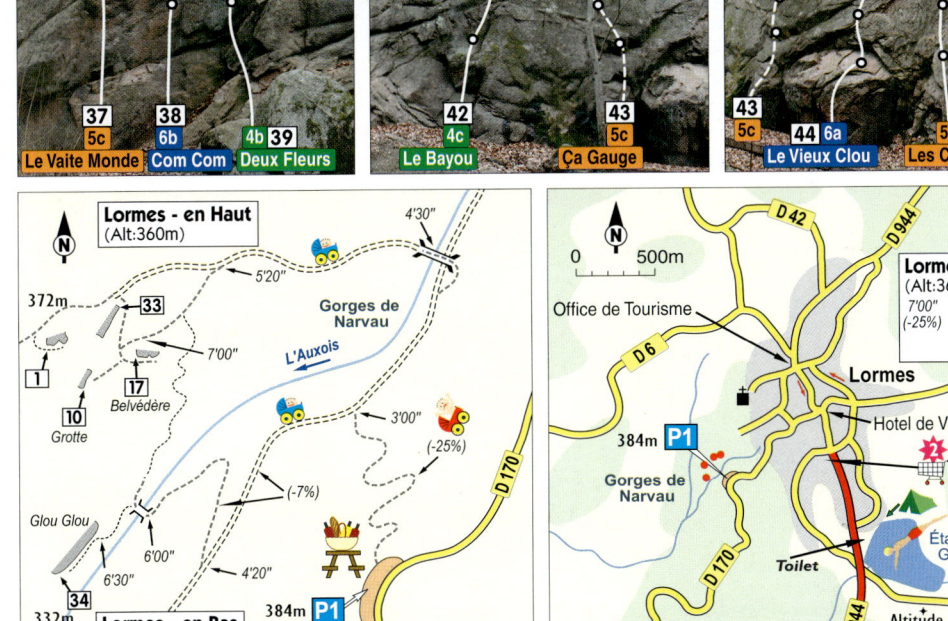

Glou Glou is set down in the gorge, a cool place - but still gets very hot in summer - no go in winter, top sectors all year possible.

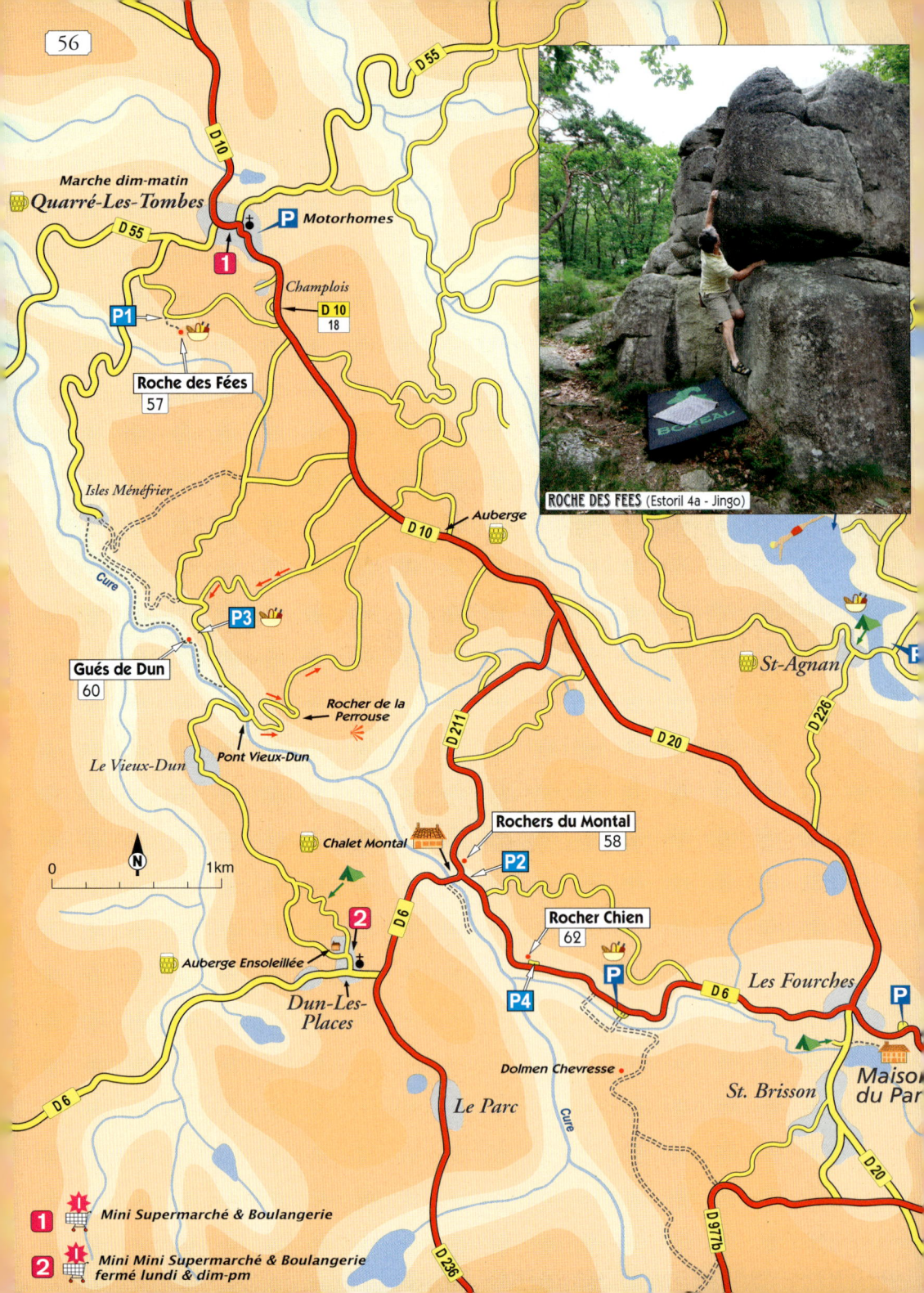

LA ROCHE DES FÉES

P1 47.356885, 3.987951

Fées (Alt:504m) E/H1-2 8m

+ cams (mid size)
Broches (ancien)
Cotation/Grades - Font

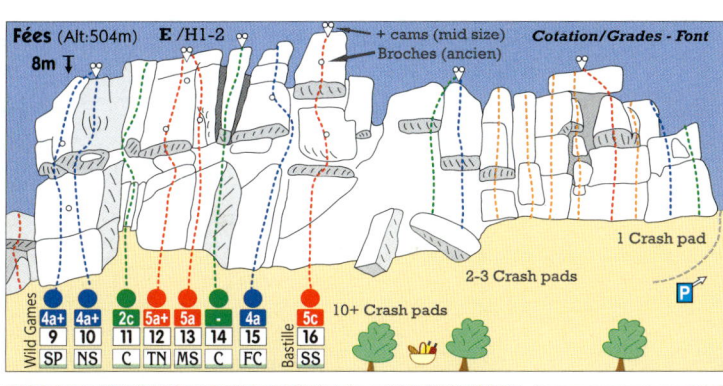
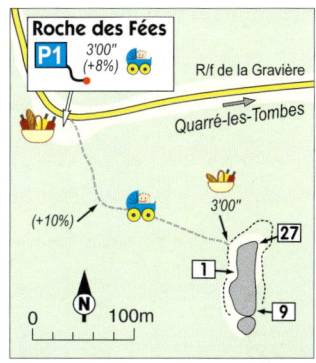

#	1	2	3	4	5	6	7	8	9	10	11	12	13	14	15	16
Name	Wild Games									Nuroloque						Bastille
Grade	4a+	4a+	2c	5a+	5a	-	4a	5c								
Notes	SP	NS	C	TN	MS	C	FC	SS								

1 Crash pad
2-3 Crash pads
10+ Crash pads

| 1 Asteroide 2a | 2 Virgin Mary 3a+ | 3 Dehli 2b | 4 Good Book 2a+ | 5 Barcelona 4a | 6 Estoril 4a | 7 Katalonya 4a | 8 |

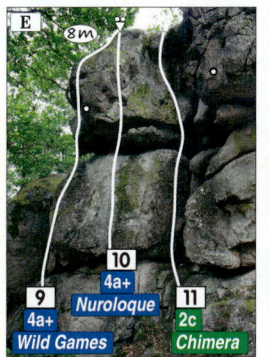

| 9 Wild Games 4a+ | 10 Nuroloque 4a+ | 11 Chimera 2c | 12 Tarzan 5a+ | 13 Beetlejuice 5a | 14 Jolie Jolie - | 15 Banjo Man 4a | 16 Bastille 5c |

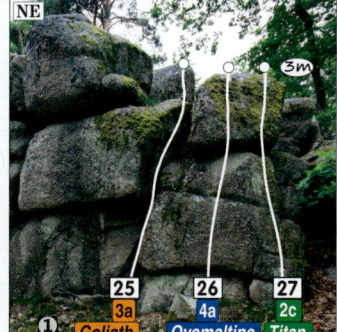

| 17 Plongée 2a | 18 Paranoide 4b | 19 Fizzure 3a | 20 Illusion 3a+ | 21 Hamlet 2b | 22 Pentacost 4a | 23 Le Guppy 3c | 24 Polaramine 5b | 25 Goliath 3a | 26 Ovomaltine 4a | 27 Titan 2c |

Granite**** Enough climbing for a fun afternoon, nice spot. Bring 2 pads, plus a rope with some cams to back up belay/relais.

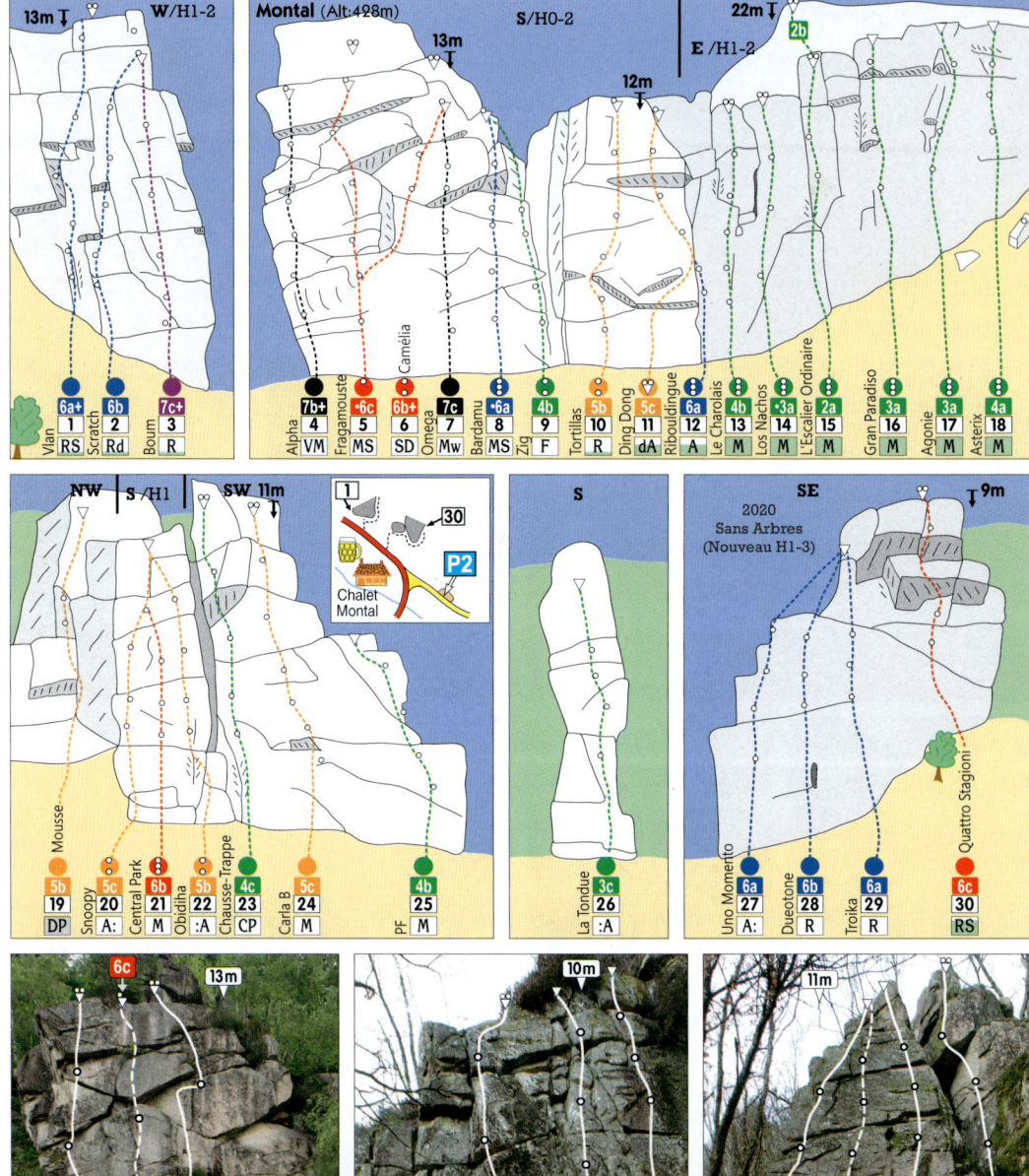

ROCHERS DU MONTAL

P2 47.294007, 4.033929

Granite** A nice couple of small cliffs only a few metres from the road. Can get roastingly hot. Tree shade recently cut down.

LE MORVAN

PERLE RARE 6b, *Carrie Atchison-Jones* ▽
GUES DE DUN

ROCHER CHIEN

TAMPONOIR 5b, *Hughes Biault* △

TRACES DE PNEUS 6c, *Chris Kestel* △
VIEUX CHATEAU

L'ARETE DANS LE CIEL 6a, *Katie Hopwood* △
VIEUX CHATEAU

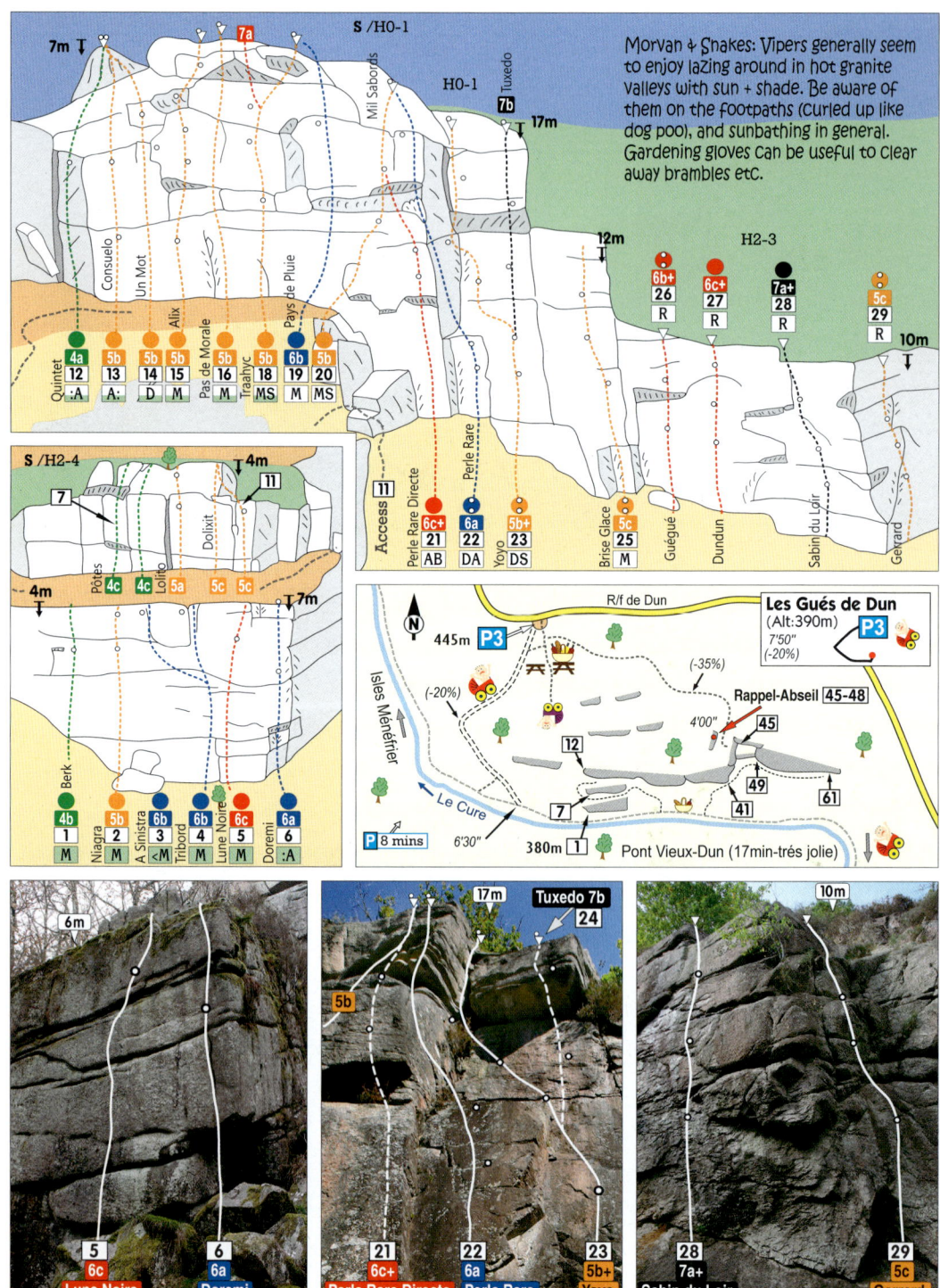

GUÉS DE DUN

P3 47.321841, 3.991803

Granite** Nice rock in a deep wooded valley. Most of the base is clear of trees, but undergrowth is prolific in summer.

GUÉS DE DUN

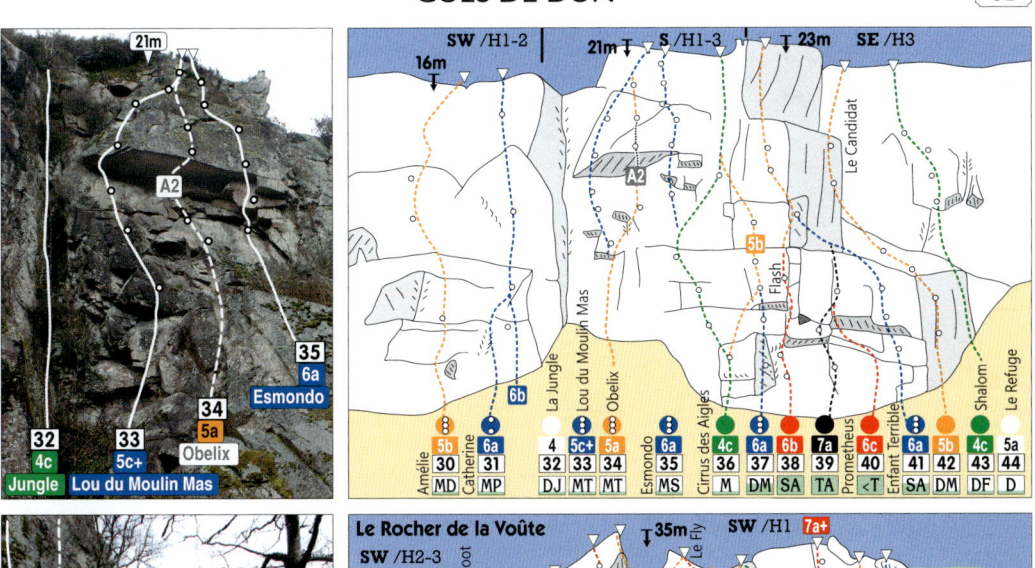

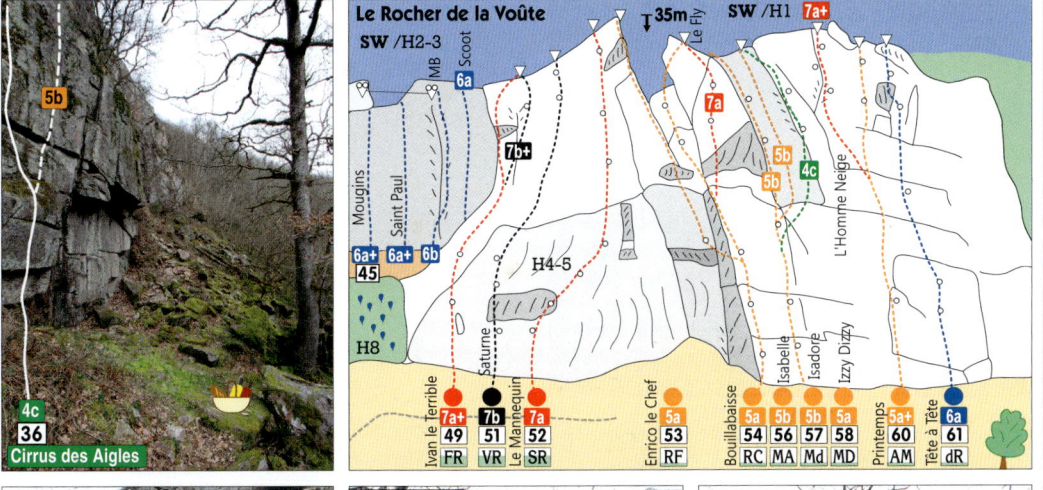

Not the super quality of Vieux Château, so it's much quieter. Can be very calm and mystical. Benifits from a dry spell.

ROCHES du CHIEN

P4 47.284373, 4.043682

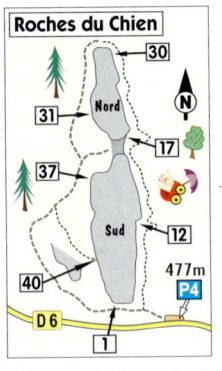
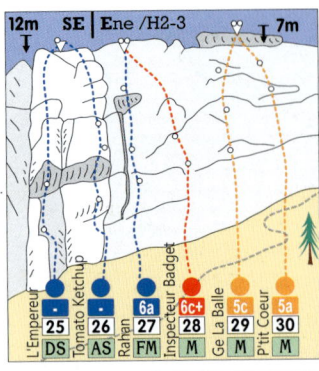
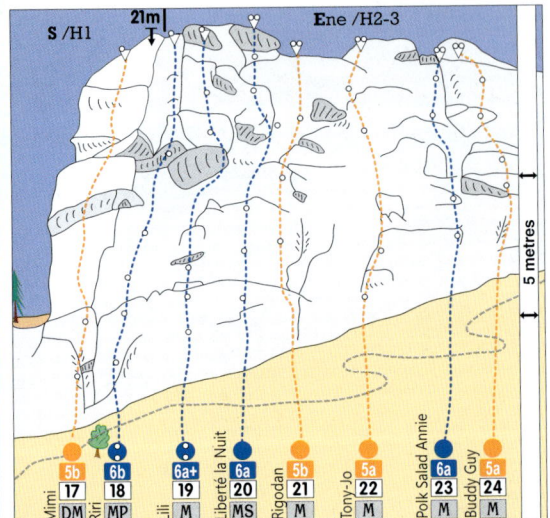
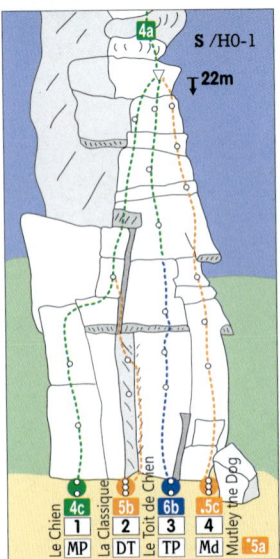
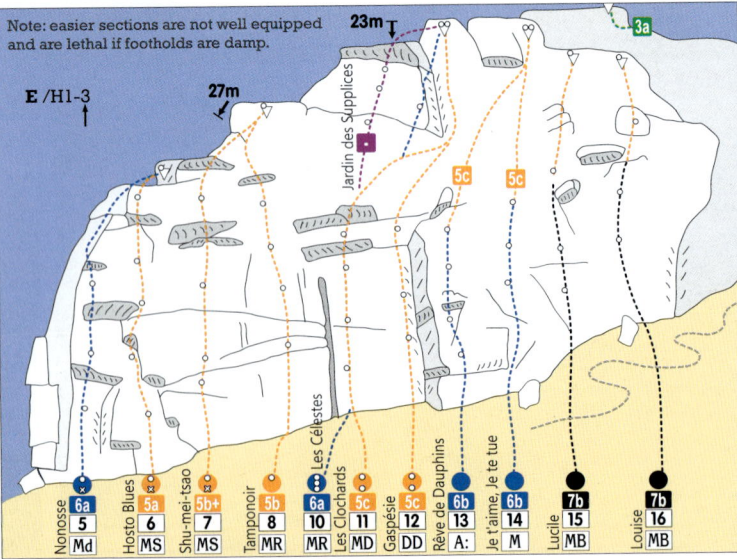

Granite*** A superb set of towers going up the hill. Almost a drive in cliff, and a great place on hot afternoons.

ROCHES du CHIEN

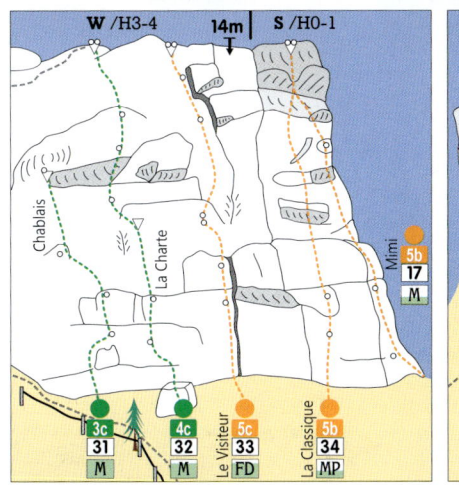
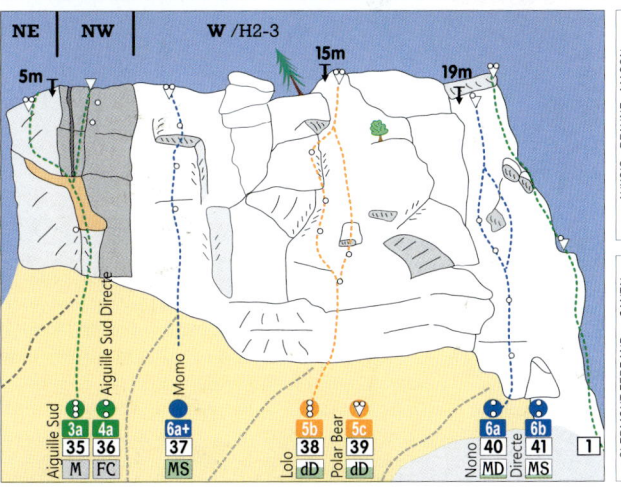

The routes on the west side are less impressive and not so well equipped, but are still definitely worth doing (moulinette).

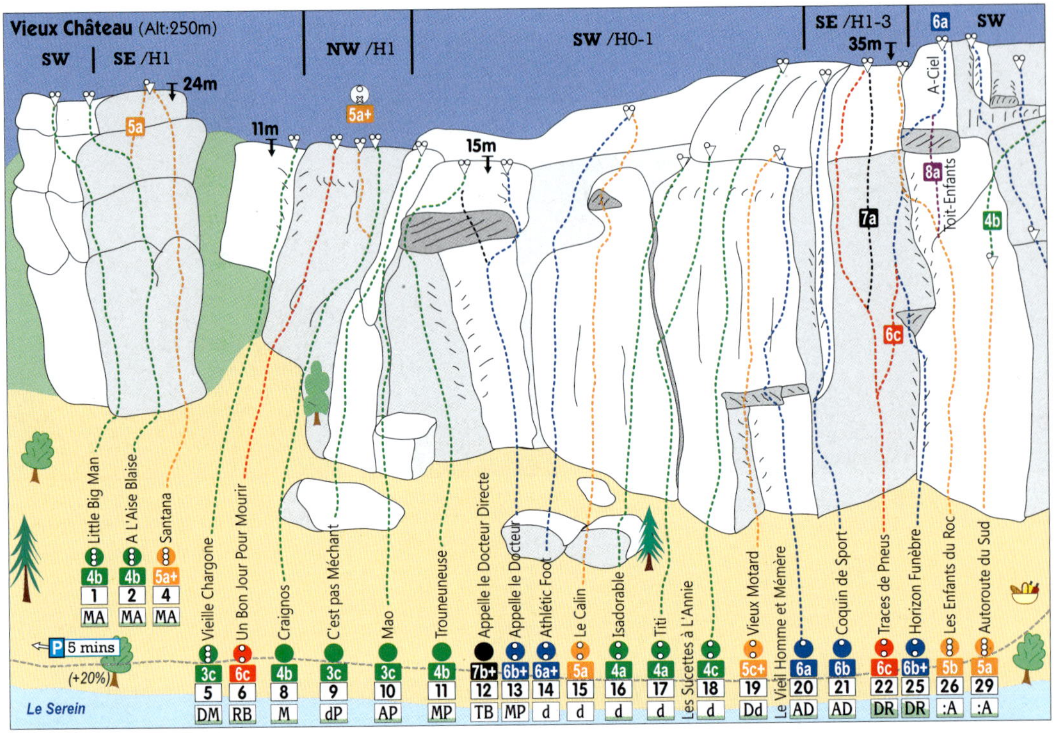

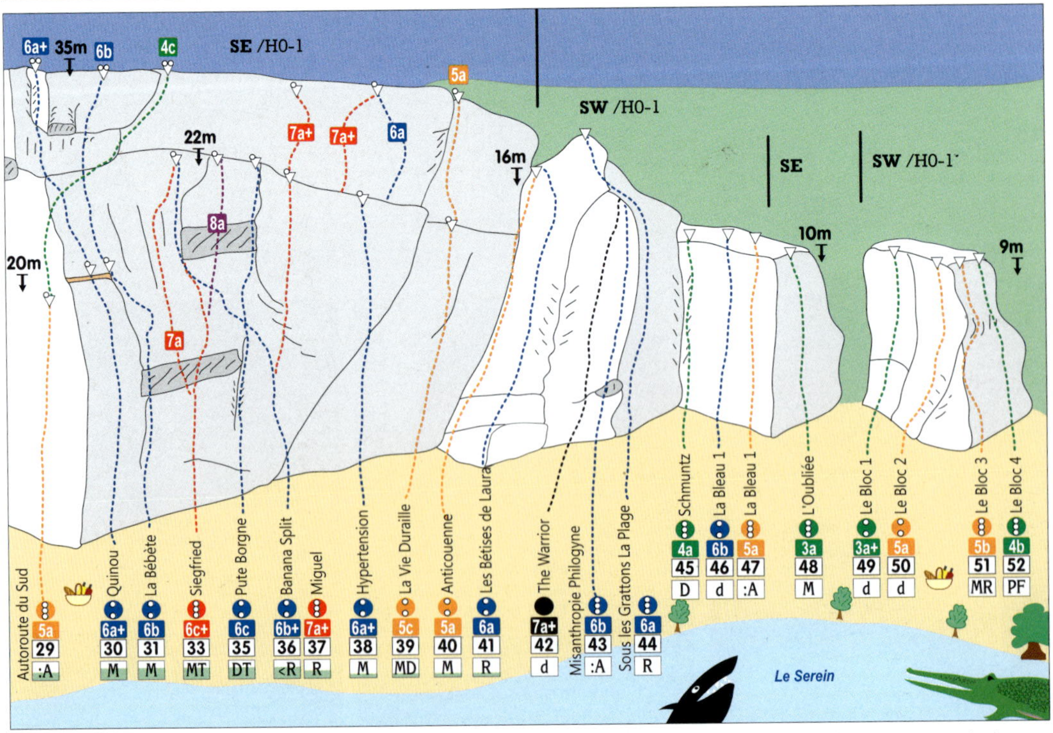

VIEUX CHATEAU (Rocher Sainte-Catherine)

Vieux Château (Alt:250m)

Granite**** A superb cliff with high quality rock and routes. Can get very warm here, but also chilly in the trees at the base.

Most long routes are best done with a mid relais, rope drag is not so good on the rough granite, and nasty ledges too.

VIEUX CHATEAU (Rocher Sainte-Catherine)

Smaller routes in the continuation sector, some friendly slabs, other steep and sustained walls.

Area 3 - AUXOIS - BEAUNE - MACON

Page	Falaise/Cliff		Alt	Arbre-Ori-Séche	Am-Pm	Rocher	Longeur	Numero Voies / Routes					Approche	Ambience
103	D5	Ahuy	310m	S/H1		Cal-Grés	8-12m	3	7	9	3	0	5	Mur, chaud
116	C4	Arcenant 3%	480m	S/H1		Calcaire	11-22m	6	22	49	45	36	8	Mur technique
124	C4	Bouilland After	500m	NW/H3		Calcaire	18-28m	1	1	7	4	7	9	Devers
120	C4	Bouilland Ancien	510m	W/H0-1		Calcaire	10-17m	15	18	26	19	17	3	Mur tecnique
125	C4	Bouilland Cabane	470m	W/H0-1		Calcaire	20-50m	1	6	10	4	3	10	Mini & Grande
126	C4	Bouilland Cloche	500m	NE/H3		Calcaire	13-24m	0	0	6	3	2	14	Raide, Toit
126	C4	Bouilland Dédé	470m	W/H0-1		Calcaire	20-55m	2	3	9	6	5	15	Grande & Awesome
140	C3	Bout-M-Baderne	450m	SE/H0		Calcaire	15-50m	0	0	0	9	35 39	4	Mur,Raide,Toit
141	C3	Bout-M-Reserve	450m	SE/H0		Calcaire	15-20m	0	0	0	5	25 15	6	Mur,Raide
114	C4	Chambolle-M 7%	380m	S&W/H0		Calcaire	6-22m	10	13	13	16	11 1	12	Mur, Pilier, Surp
163	C2	Chardonnay	280m	NW/H0-3		Calcaire	9-14m	0	3	10	7	1 0	4	Mur,Carrière
71	B5	Charrat	245m	S/H0-1		Granit	16-22m	15	3	7	0	0	2	Mur, dalle, Pong
128	C4	Châtelet Nord	480m	NW/H0-1		Calcaire	35-45m	0	0	1	3	0	25	Raide
129	C4	Châtelet Sud	480m	W/H0-1		Calcaire	25-40m	0	8	12	24	46 20	22	Mur, Toit, Zzzz
173	C1	Coche, Roche	430m	S/H0		Calcaire	8-12m	1	2	5	5	5 0	7	Raide,Devers,Vue
134	C4	Combe à la Vieille	480m	W/H0-3		Calcaire	22-40m	0	2	17	33	64 52	17	Raide, Devers
162	C2	Cormatin	230m	E/H1-4		Grés-Cal	8-14m	2	4	4	5	2	4	Mur,Humide
142	C3	Cormot	480m	S/H0-2		Cal-Grés	20-39m	18	28	79	34	12 0	5	Mur,enduro,scary
150	C3	Cormot-Gâteau	520m	W/H0-1		Cal-Grés	11m	13	20	9	4	3 0	5	Mur,Carrière
163	C2	Cruzille	300m	S-SW/H0		Calcaire	12m	0	0	1	3	5 3	4	Devers, Vue
160	C2	Culles-l-Roches	400m	SW/H0-1		Calcaire	7-13m	12	18	8	5	0	0	Mur,Carrière,bon
104	D4	Fixin	510m	SW/H0-1		Calcaire	10-32m	41	35	62	58	38 19	16	Mur tecnicque
102	D4	Fleurey	270m	SW/H0-1		Calcaire	6-19m	8	1	4	13	11 6	1	Raide, bloc
132	C4	Fond de Combe	480m	W/H0-2		Calcaire	30-36m	0	0	9	10	15 5	17	Raide
92	C3	Geligny	480m	NW/H1-3		Calcaire	17-22m	9	8	15	4	2 0	9	Mur,Carrière
172	C1	Grisière	270m	W-N/H0-1		Grés	11-25m	8	23	15	6	0	9	Carrière, Mur
72	C5	Hauteroche-A-B	430m	SW/H1-2		Calcaire	7-22m	38	19	11	6	1	3	Mur,tecnique
72	C5	Hauteroche-C-F	430m	SW/H0-2		Cal-Grés	11-25m	35	34	64	43	5 1	7	Mur,enduro,scary
94	C4	Lantenay-A	500m	SE/H0-1		Calcaire	10-20m	0	4	11	10	6 0	10	Mur,tech,raide
96	C4	Lantenay-C&D	500m	SW/H0-1		Calcaire	16-23m	0	8	14	20	7 4	20	Mur,tech
98	C4	Lantenay-E	500m	W/H0-1		Calcaire	10-16m	16	28	39	28	11 2	15	Mur, Pilier, tech
138	C3	Melin	360m	N/H0-3		Calcaire	10-18m	0	3	5	16	16 5	19	Devers
70	B5	Montbard	250m	S/H0-2		Calcaire	6-19m	6	7	12	13	9 1	2	Mur, Surplomb
152	C3	Mont Rome 10%	520m	Snew/H0		Calcaire	8-19m	21	21	21	28	9 2	3	Mur, ouch, Vent
171	C1	Parvis	310m	S/H0		Cal-Grés	17-20m	4	3	6	2	1 0	7	Tranquil
139	C3	Pas St-Martin	420m	SW/H1		Calcaire	13-20m	0	2	12	12	7 2	3	Mur,surplomb
137	C3	Percée, Roche	440m	NE/H1		Calcaire	19m	0	0	3	3	4 5	5	Raide, Zzzz
156	C3	Remigny	250m	W+N/H0		Calcaire	19-23m	10	23	14	9	6 1	1	Mur,Raide,poche
78	C5	Saffres-Tours	450m	S&N/H1		Calcaire	11-35m	2	12	25	23	4 2	4	Mur,engagée
78	C5	Saffres 7%	460m	SW/H1-2		Cal-Grés	12-30m	46	70	95	102	33 4	3	Mur, engagée
159	C3	Saint Denis	380m	SW/H1		Calcaire	10-16m	18	7	3	2	0	9	dalle,Mur,Pilier
165	C1	Solutré Sud	430m	SE/H0		Cal-Grés	14-21m	10	24	12	11	2 0	14	Rocher moyen
164	C1	Solutré Nord	445m	NW/H1-2		Cal-Grés	20m	0	1	6	2	0	15	Rocher moyen
174	B1	Suin (Bloc)	470m	Wesn/H1		Granit	2-8m	3	39	66	48	52 4	2	Blocs, tranquil
158	C3	Teu (Croix)	370m	S/H0-1		Grés-Cal	20m	0	2	7	3	5 2	13	Devers, Expo
168	C1	Vergisson	430m	SW/H0-1		Cal-Grés	11-30m	13	20	33	30	18 3	8	Expo, Vue, Vent

MONTBARD

P1 47.625875, 4.346262   P2 47.626871, 4.346138

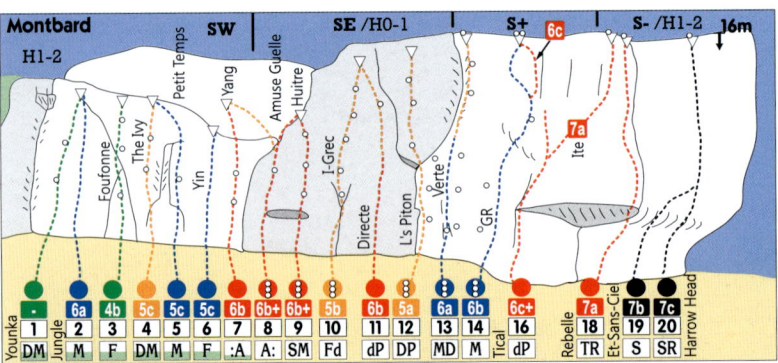
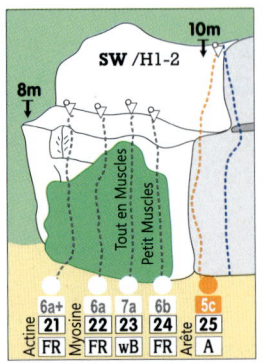
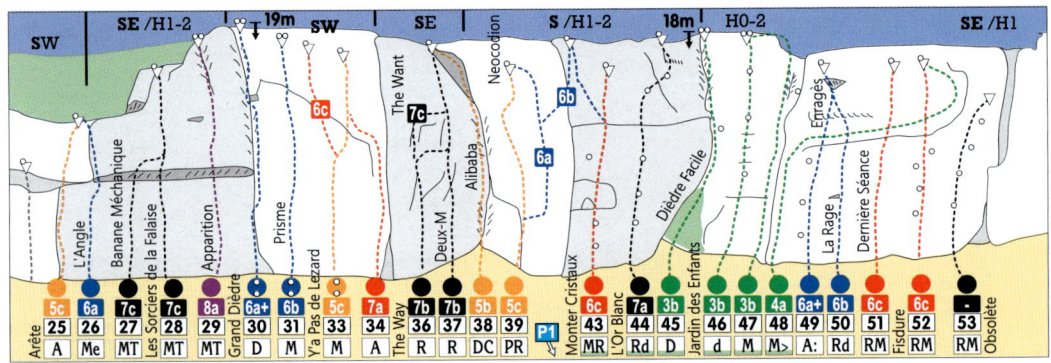

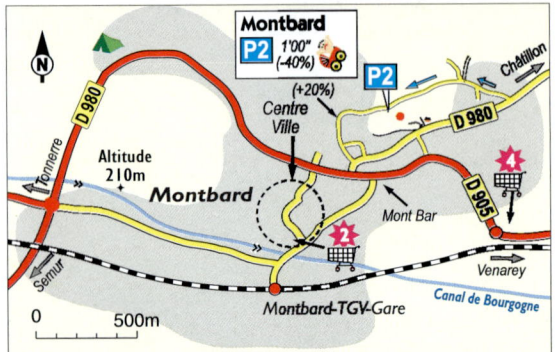
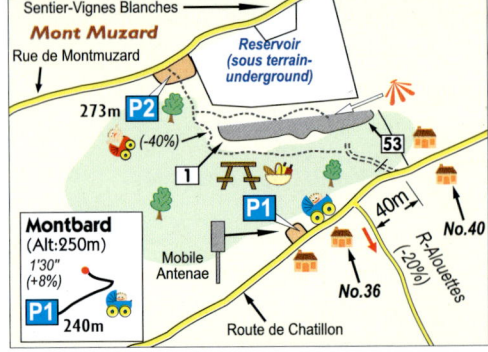

Calcaire** A small cliff overlooking Montbard, entertaining. Can get hot like a cauldron, nice picnic benches in the shade.

LE ROCHER DU CHARRAT

47.497397, 4.334310

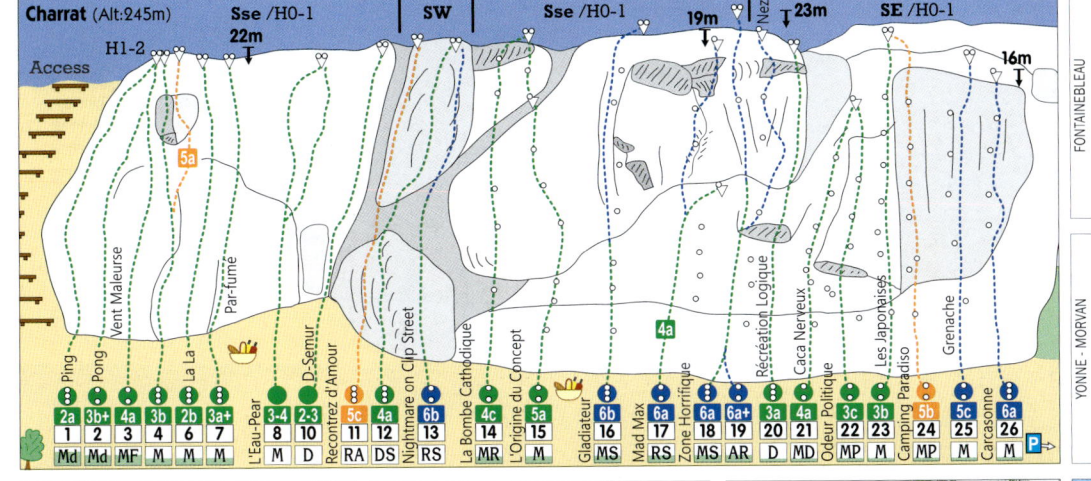

12 — 4a — Le Tapis Rouge

17 6a Mad Max | 18 6a Zone Horrifique | 19 6a+

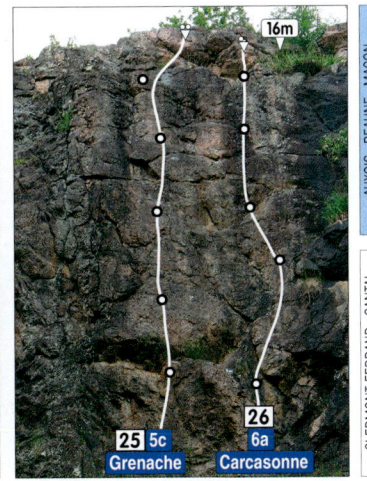

25 5c Grenache | 26 6a Carcasonne

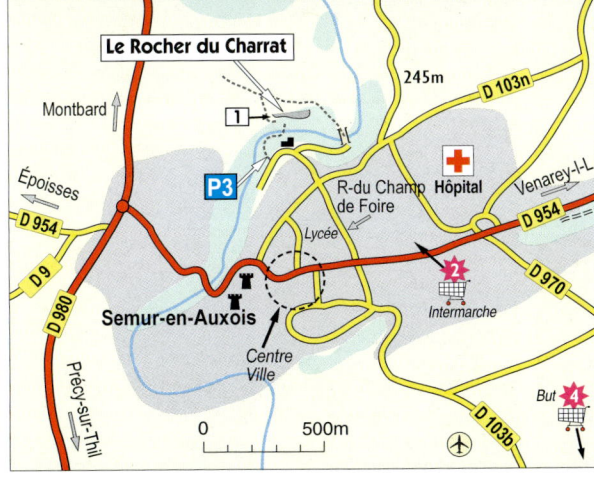

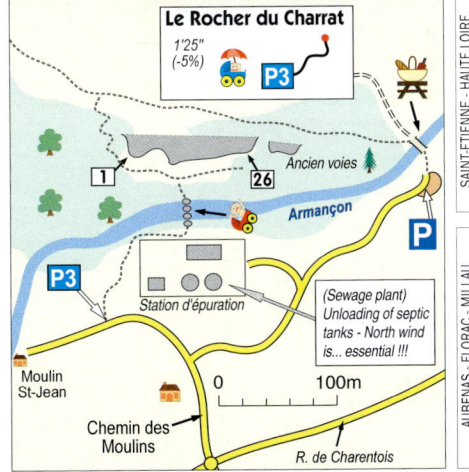

Le Rocher du Charrat — 1'25" (-5%) — P3

(Sewage plant) Unloading of septic tanks - North wind is... essential !!!

Pink Granite**** flat grassy base, sunny - everything is perfect...except for the smell. Avoid sewage unloading days.

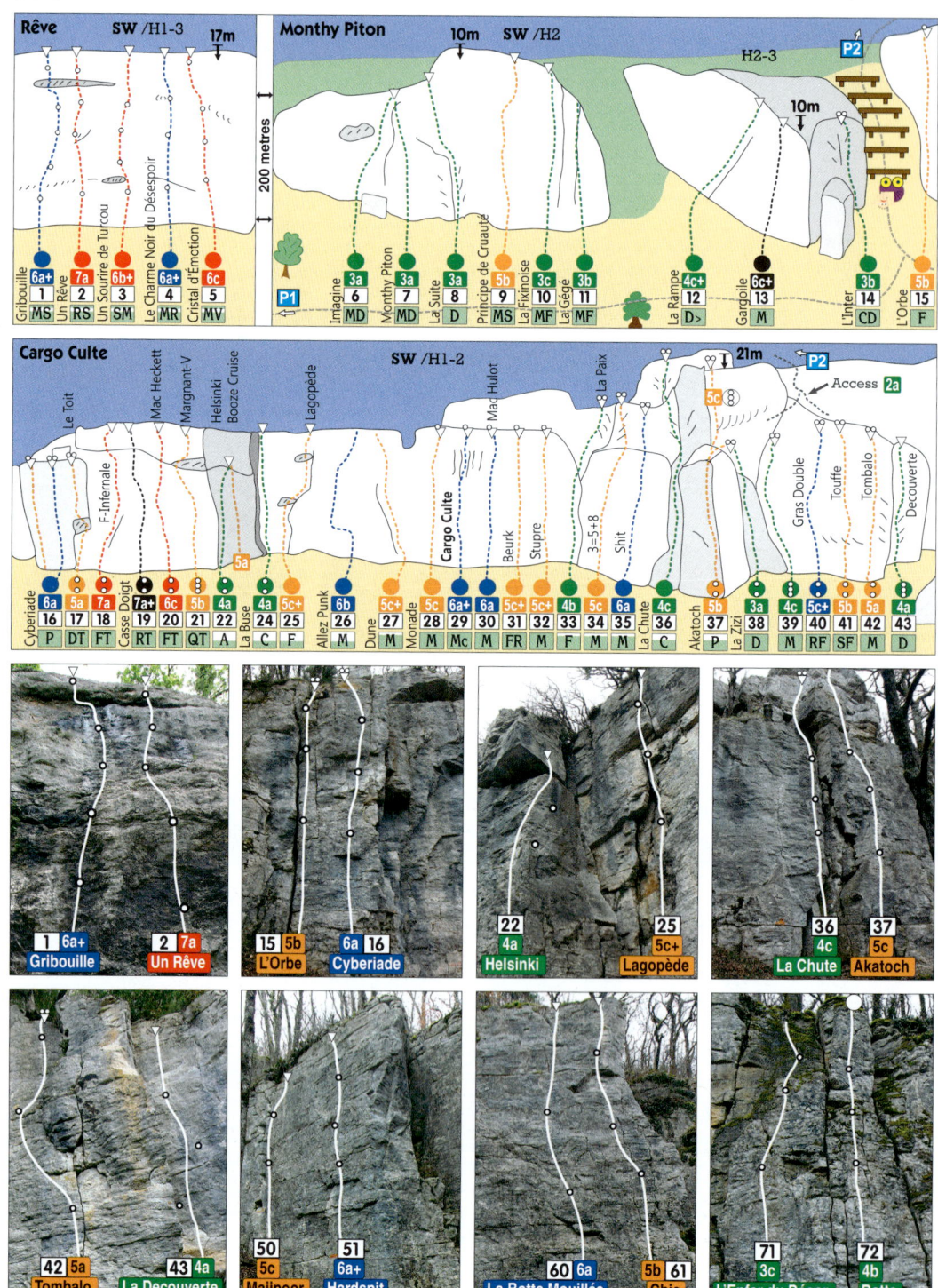

Calcaire** A very long cliff with lots of sectors... some friendly... some big... and some terrifying. Rock is vary variable.

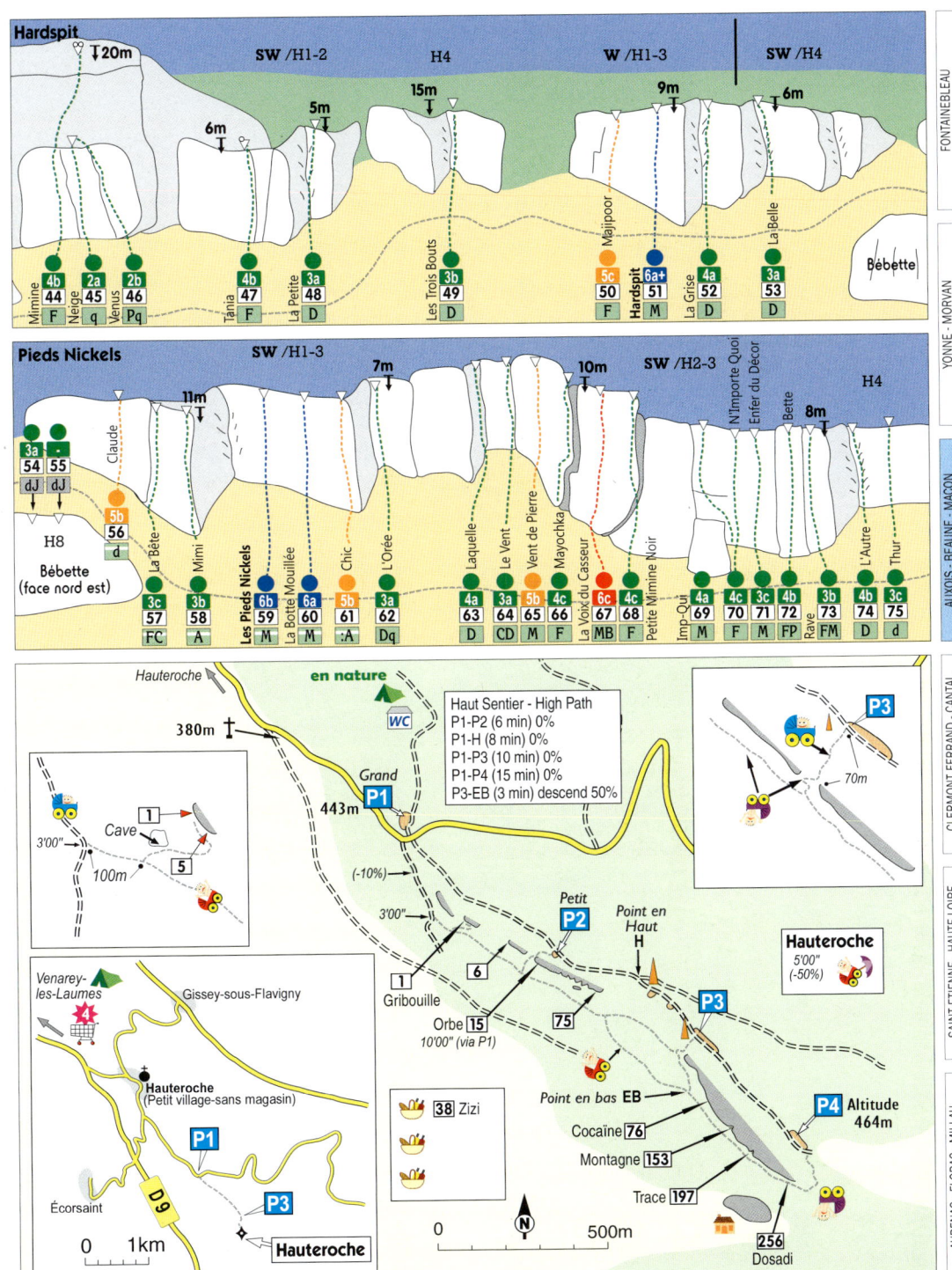

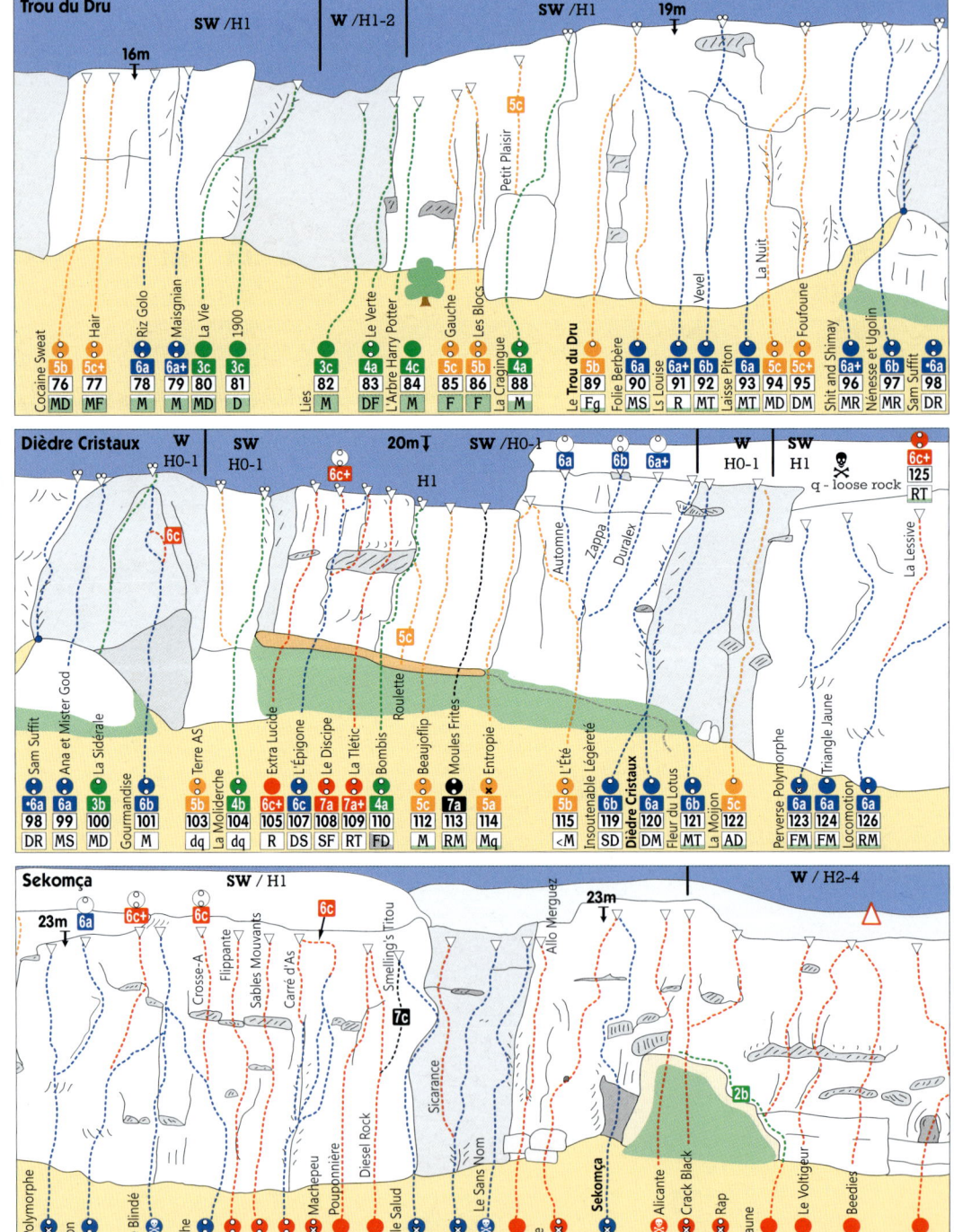

HAUTEROCHE - C

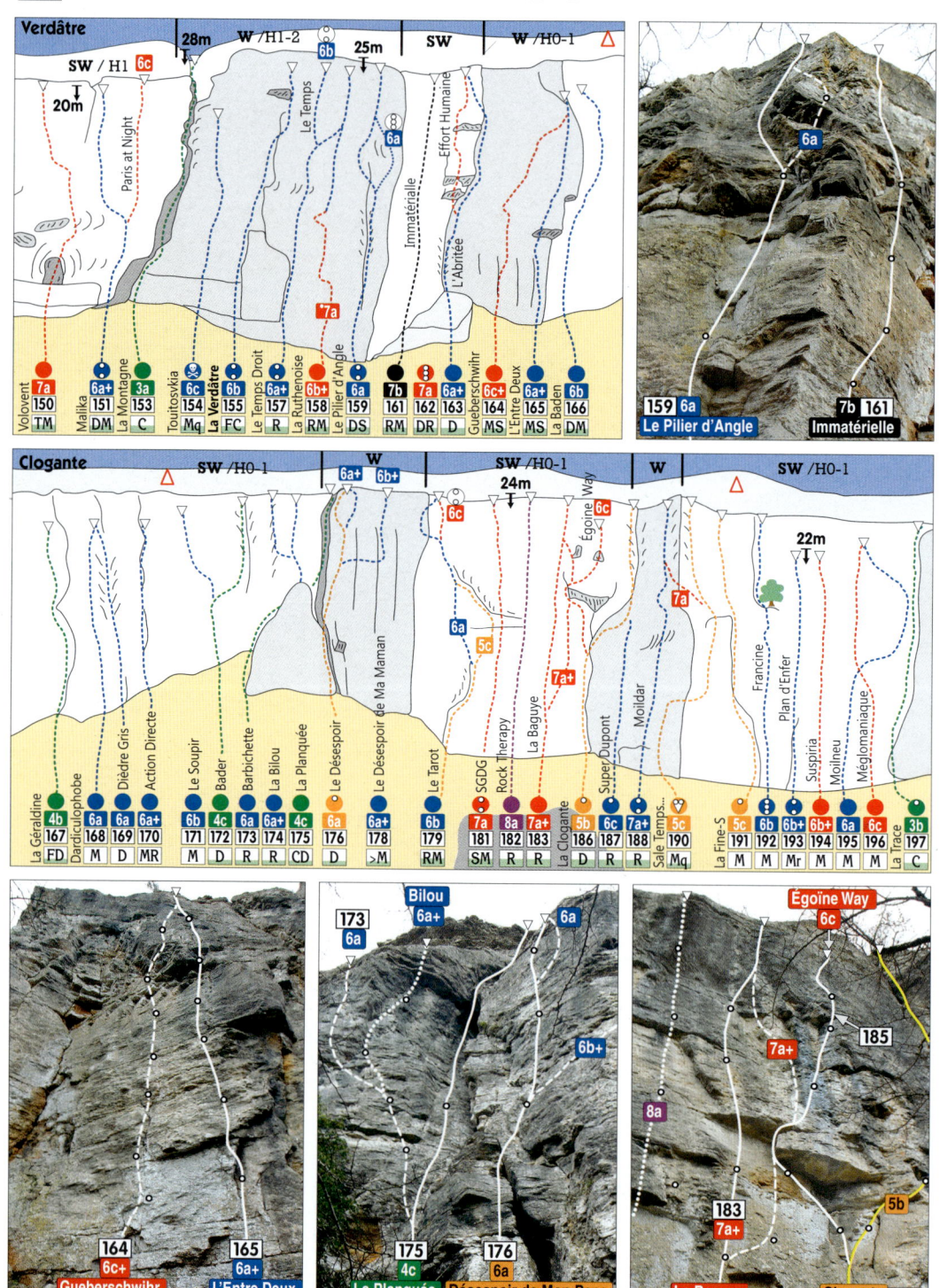

HAUTEROCHE - E - # 02-06

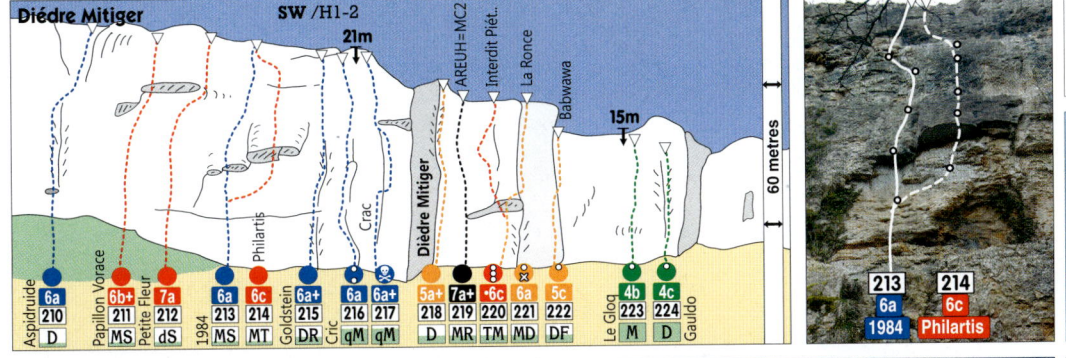
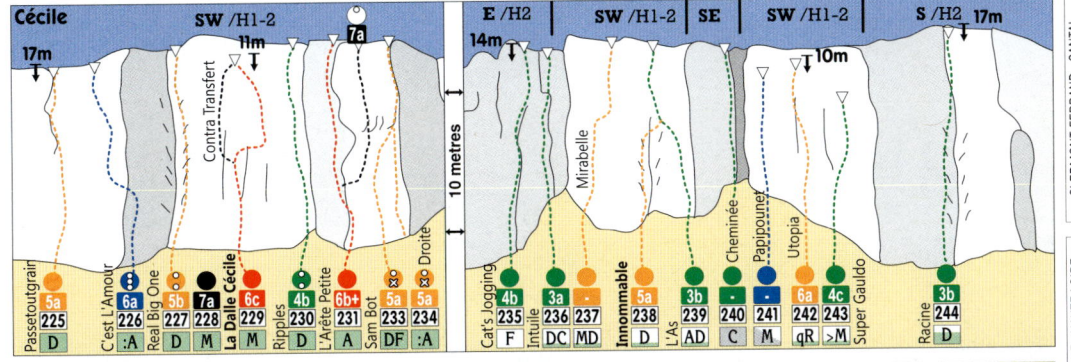
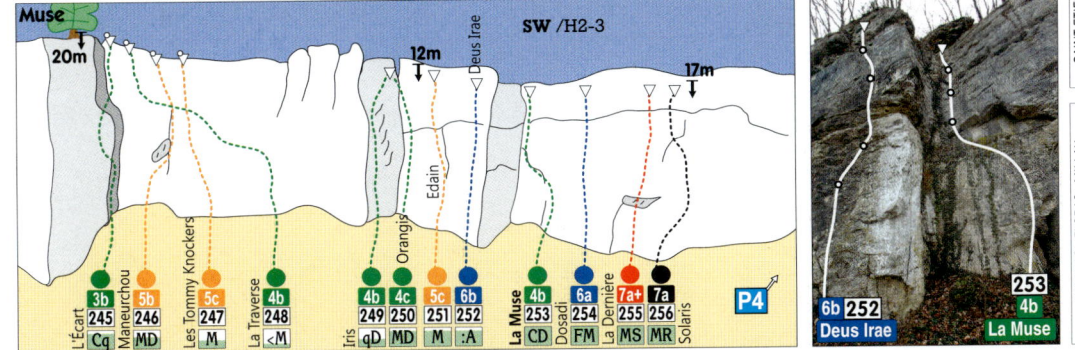

These smaller sectors are often quiet and give less intimidating climbing. Rock quality is 'very' variable.

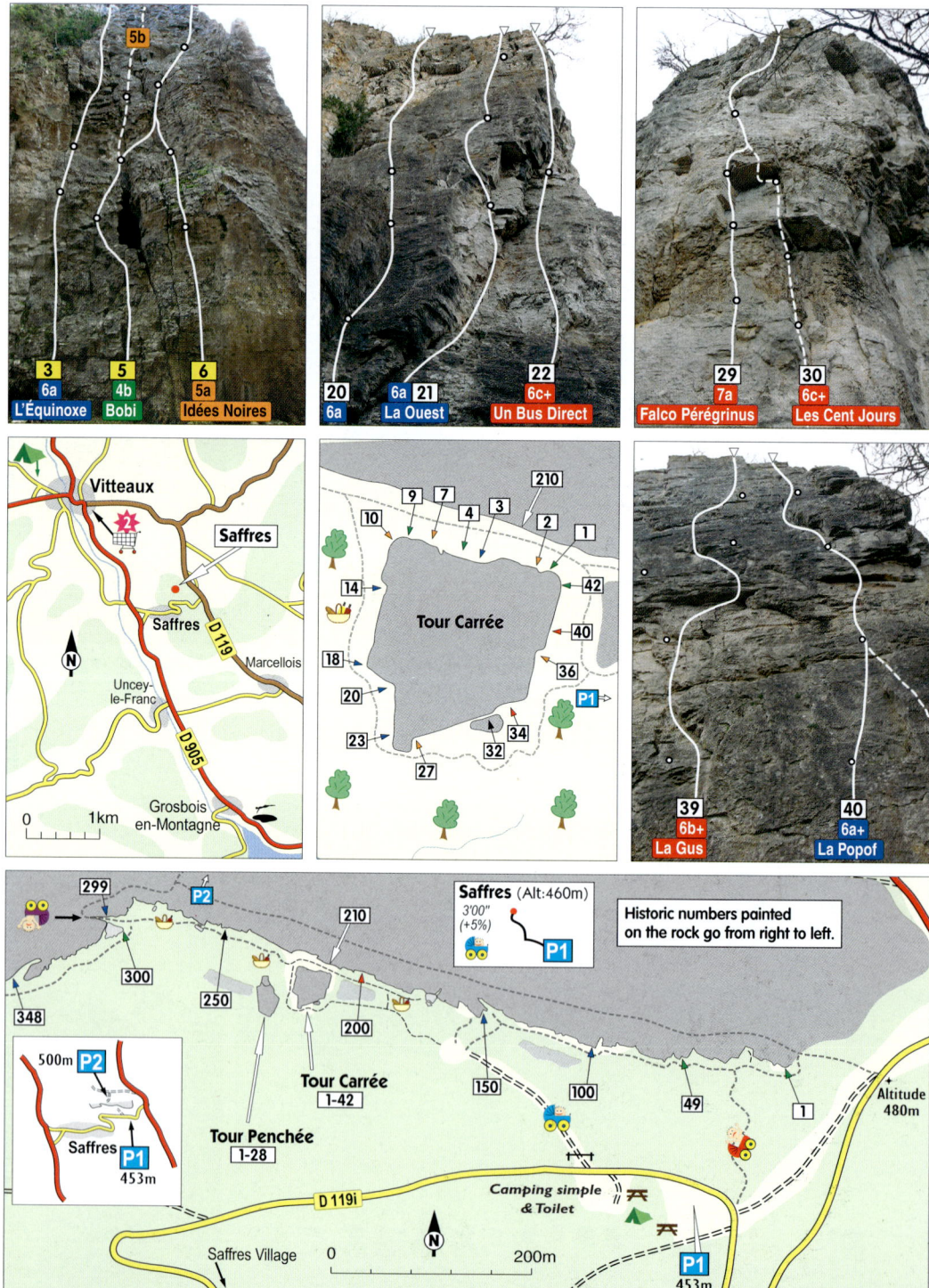

SAFFRES (A-Tour Carrée)

P2 47.373539, 4.581031

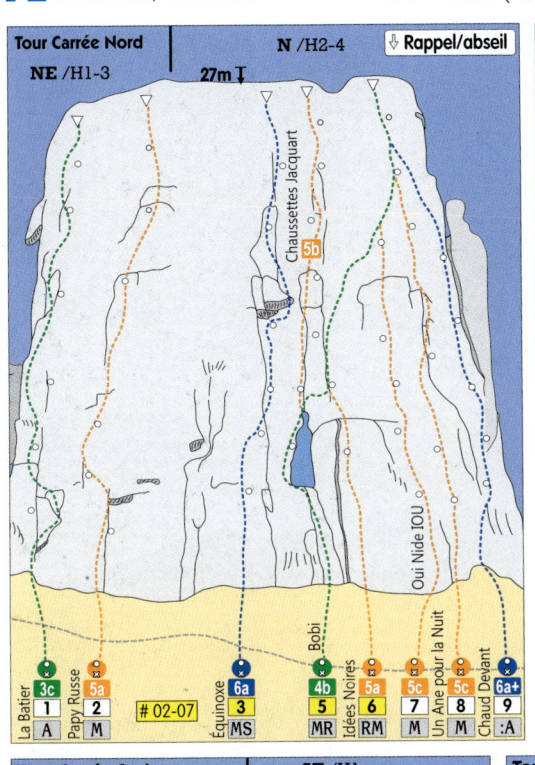

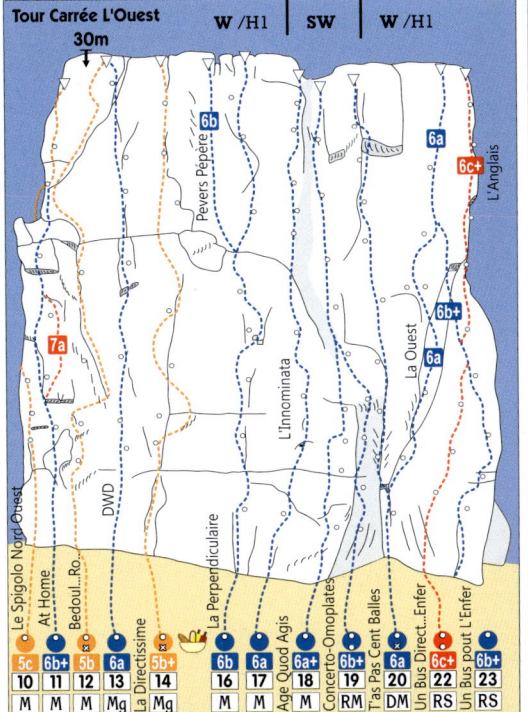

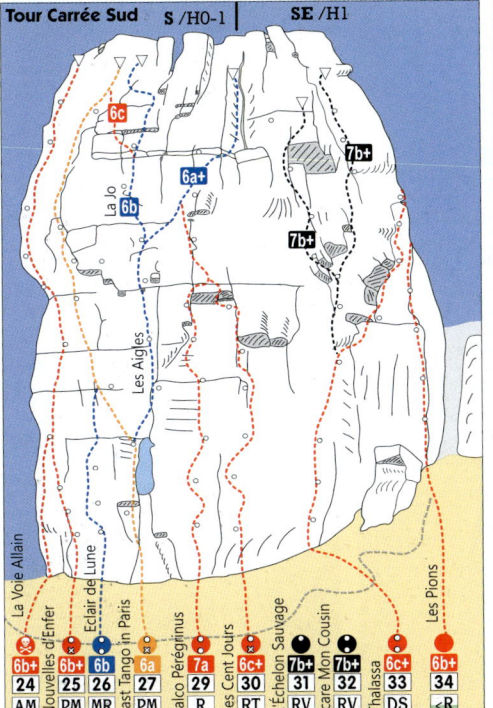

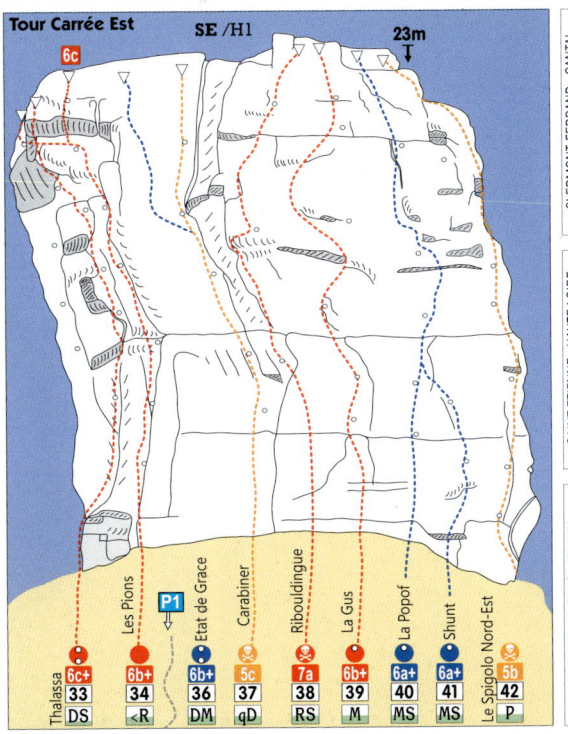

This is a giant isolated boulder with no easy access to the top. Stunning routes in all grades.

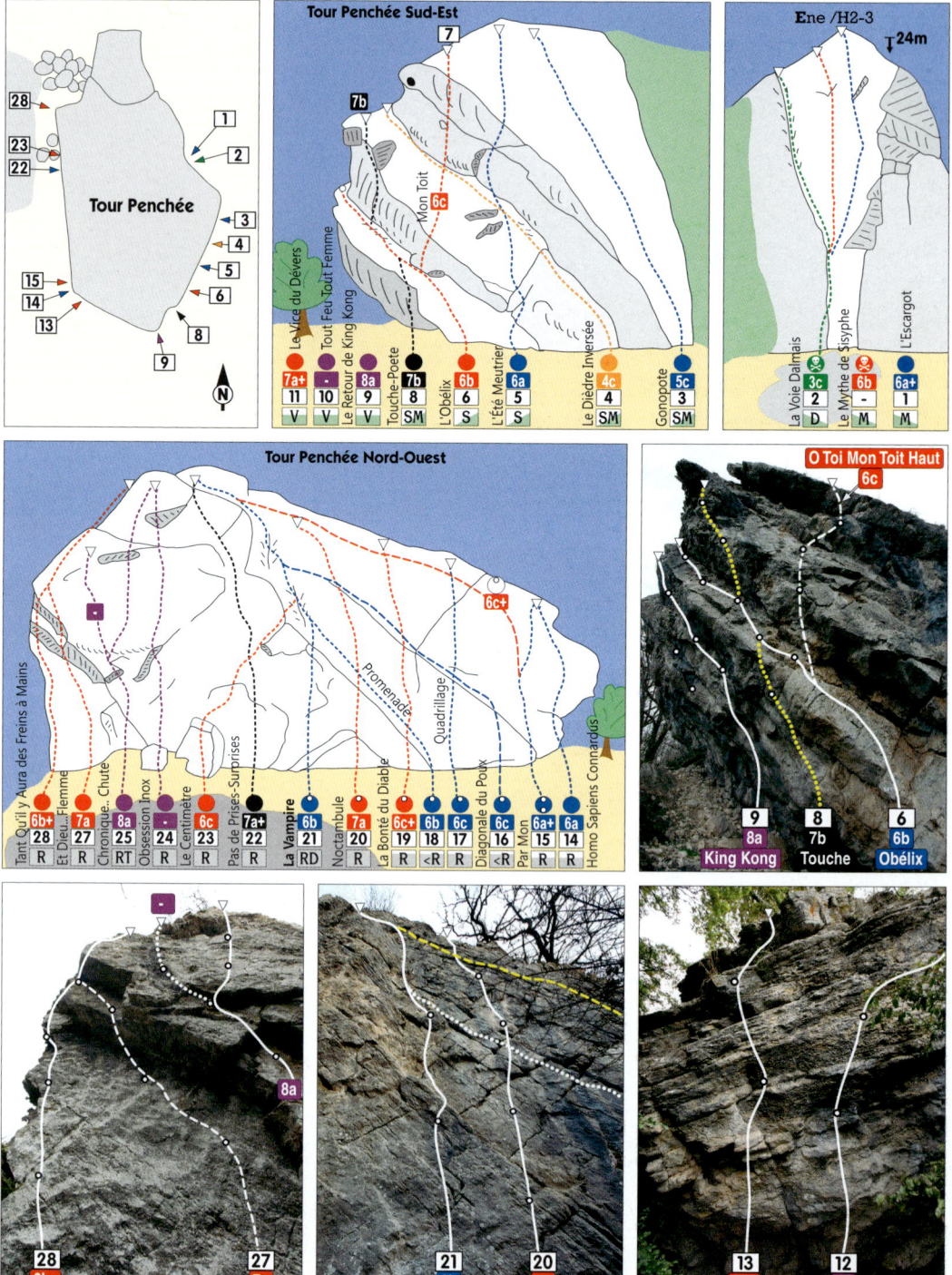

HAUTEROCHE - SAFFRES

AKATOCH 5c, Carrie Aitchison-Jones, Hauteroche (37) ▽

EFFORT HUMAINE 7a, Chris Kestell, Hauteroche (162) △

DWD 6a, David Aitchison-Jones, Saffres - Tour Carrée (13) ▽

LE VILLEBREQUIN 5b, Mitzy Morton, Saffres (123) △

SAFFRES (C-Blattes)

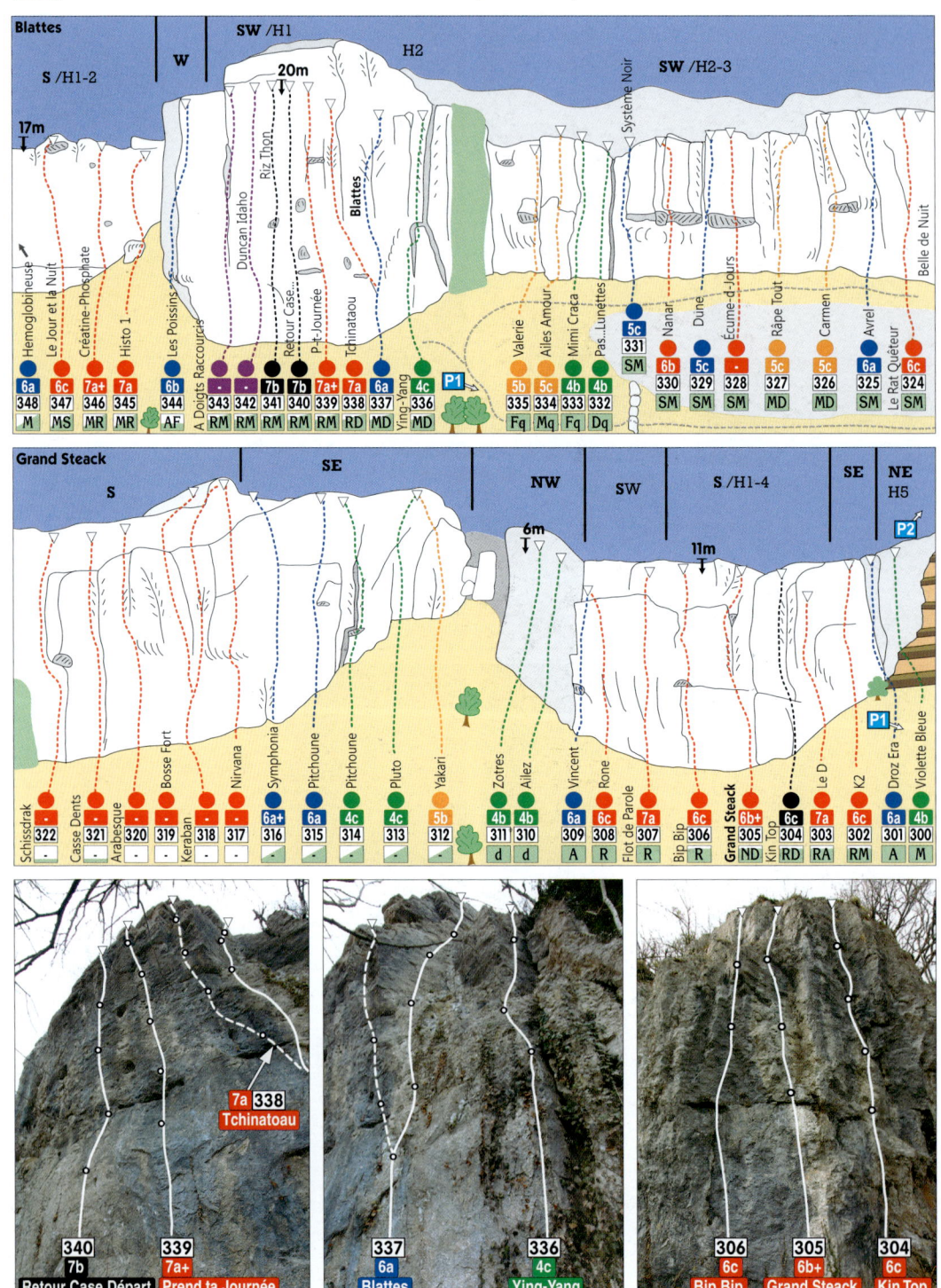

These 2 sectors are the forgotten part of Saffres. Harder climbs on 'hard' rock, softer climbs on 'soft eek' rock.

SAFFRES (D-Gypsy)

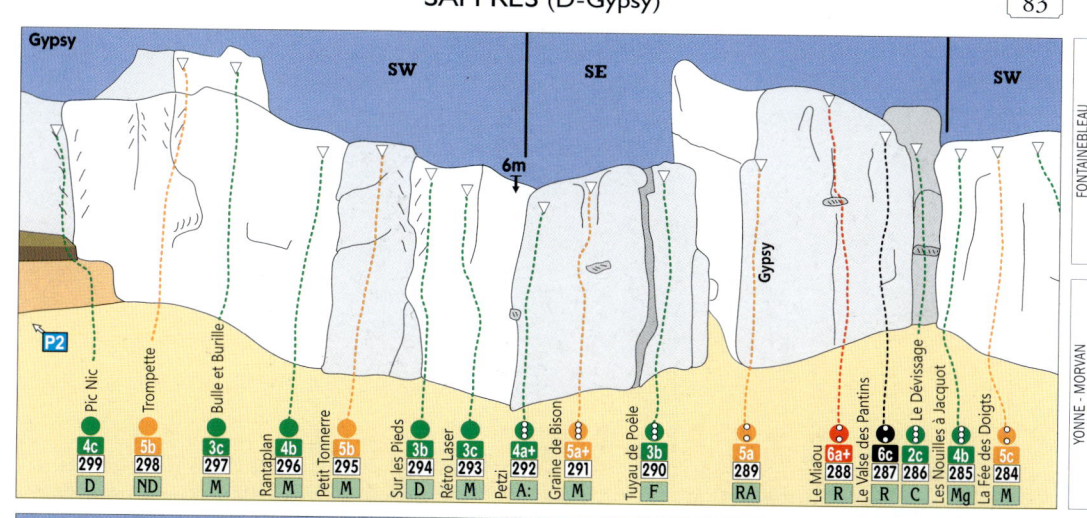
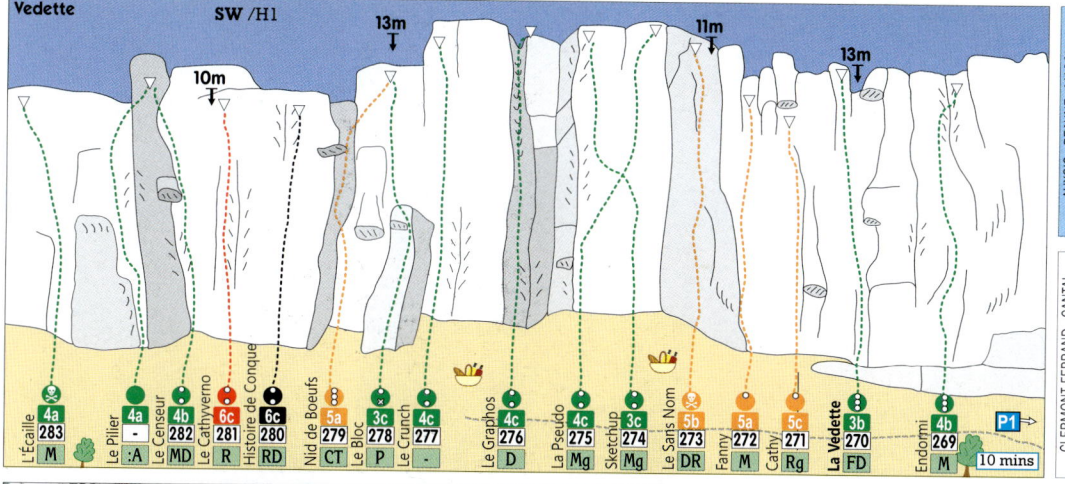

A much smaller sector, ideal for those wanting less intimidating routes. Shady picnic venue, routes pretty polished though.

SAFFRES (F-Piano & Bambino)

85

Piano

#	Name	Grade	Equipper
242	Dalle Orée	5b	Mg
241	Pantoufles	6a+	MR
240	Le Piano à Queue	5b	<D
239	Satyre	6a	-
238	Calinette	7a+	-
237	Bourbons Club	6a	-
236	La Marc	6a+	-
235	Le Mètre Pliant	6a	-
234	—	5b	-
233	Dis L'Auvergne Saoud	6b	-
232	Le Mètre Dépilé	5c	-
231	Les Coups et les Douleurs	6a	-
230	—	6a	x
229	Magie Blanche	6a	FR
228	Tonton Inox / La Pivoine	6c+	FR
227	Edelridissimo	6c	FR
226	Le Caporal	6a	RSCM
225	La Plus Belle Fissure	6a	FD
224	Tintin au Pays des Écailles	7b	R
223	Touche pas..Spit	6c+	-
222	—	6a	FD
221	Inox du Sol	6a	CM
220	La Pépère	5b	
219			

Bambino

#	Name	Grade	Equipper
218	Le Beauf	6a	M
217	Le Aspi	6a	M
216	La Terray Nouvelle	7a	-
215	Robert "Clef de 12"	6c+	-
214	La Quille	6c+	-
213	Ygdrasil	7b+	R
212	Topoverdose	6b+	<R
211	—	6c+	-
210	Splendeur	7c	RS
209	Ben Hur Descend de ton Youpla	6b	Fg
207	La Bambino	6c	FM
206	Radio Chou-Fleur	6b+	MS
204	Ionisation	7c	CM
203	L'Ionisation	6b+	M
202	Bossu Fait Gaffe à l'Orage	7b+	M
201	Gémi Sans Mollir	7b+	M
200	Zargo's Lords	6b+	M
199	Le Chant du Perfodactyle	6c	MT
197	Le Boulevard à Mathieu	6c	Mc
—	Swiss Connection	7a	Mc
195	—	6a+	M
194	—	4b	M

216 La Terray Nouvelle 7a
215 Robert 'Clef de 12' 6c+
216¹ Robert Clef Variante 6c+/7a

203 L'Ionisation 6b+
202 Bossu Fait Gaffe à l'Orage 7b/b+
201 Gémi Sans Mollir 7b/b+

198 Le Pro S'Tate 7c/c+
197 Le Boulevard à Mathieu 7a+

Part of this big wall is shaded at the bottom by the Tour Carrée, very chilly to belay. High quality climbing.

SAFFRES (G-Domino, Zizine & Christine)

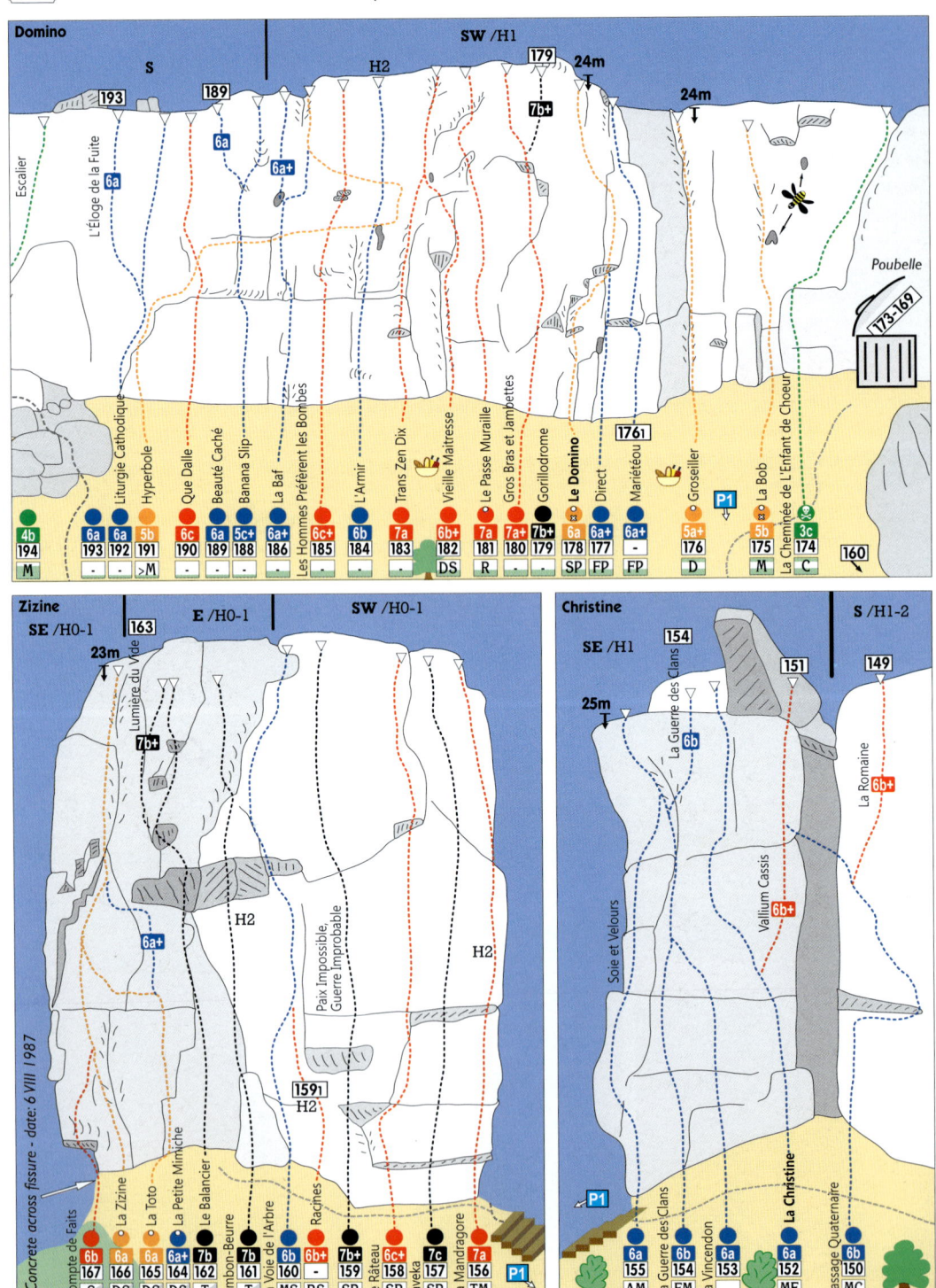

Domino - a very nice sector. Zizine - a wow sector that looks very dodgy, check at base of route 167 though - concrete 1987.

SAFFRES (G-Domino, Zizine & Christine)

These main track from P1 goes to a small grassy bay, continue for Domino, go right for Zizine and routes to right

SAFFRES (H-Éclair, Facteur, Bobologie & Trapco) - 02-07 # 111-131

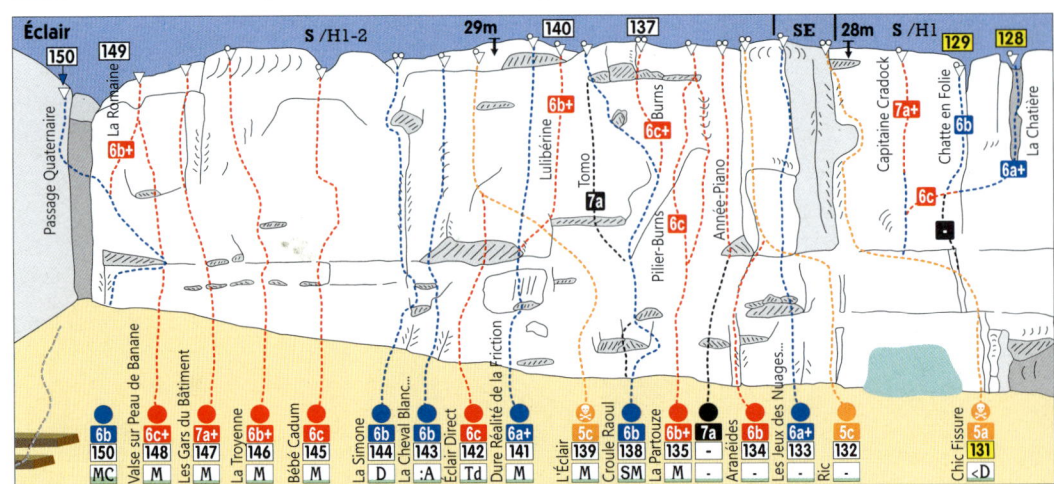
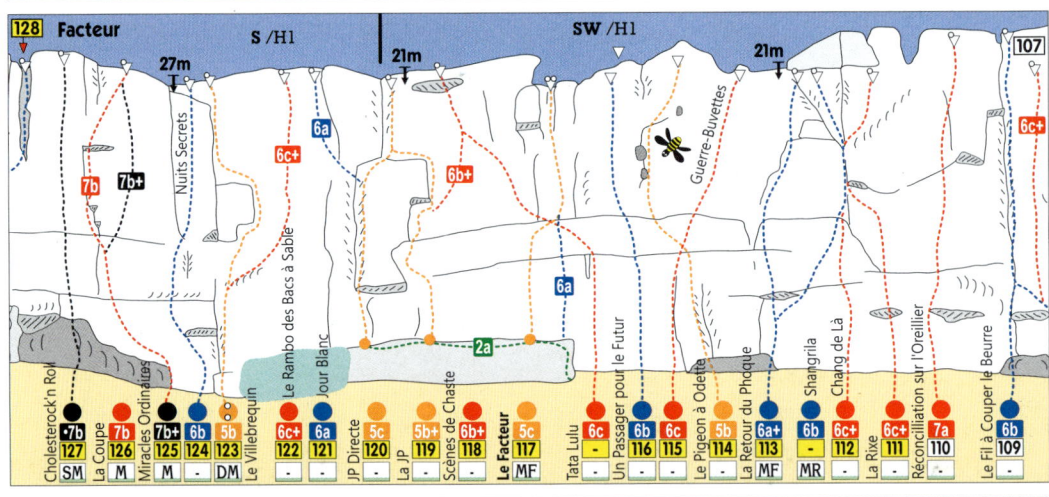
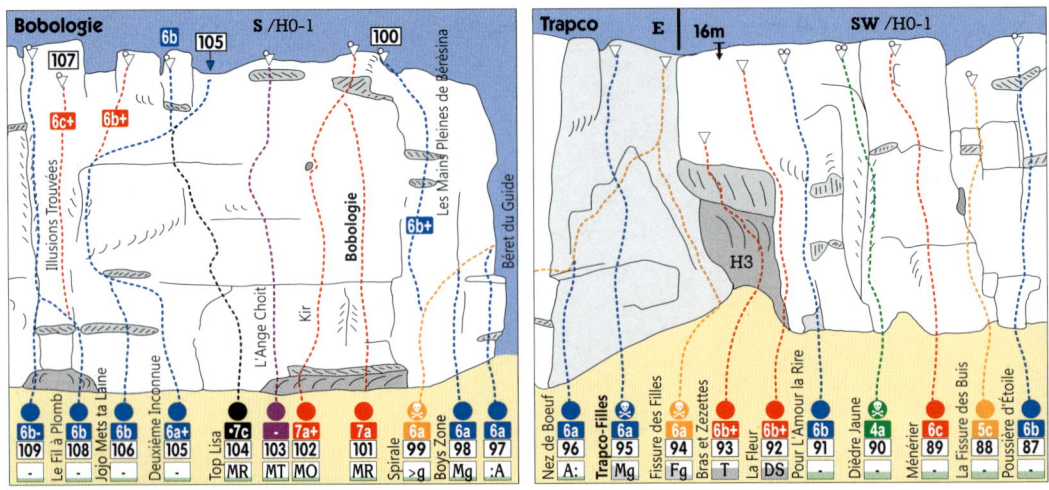

Some fabulous central sections, can be a suntrap. Bird restriciton is variable.

SAFFRES (I-Ondulée)

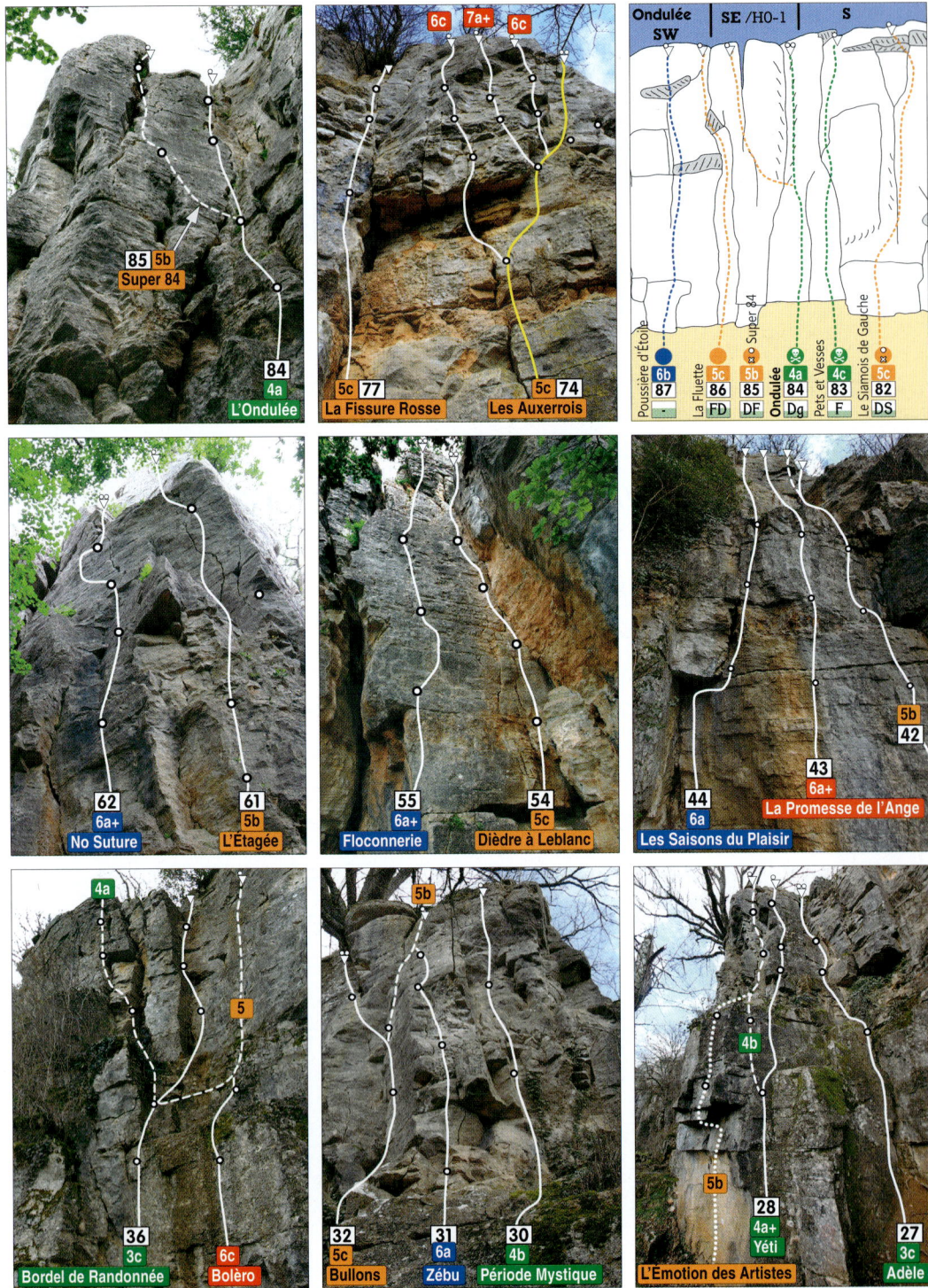

Some nice smaller sectors to the East end of Saffres, some very pleasant easier routes, plus... some unpleasantly equipped.

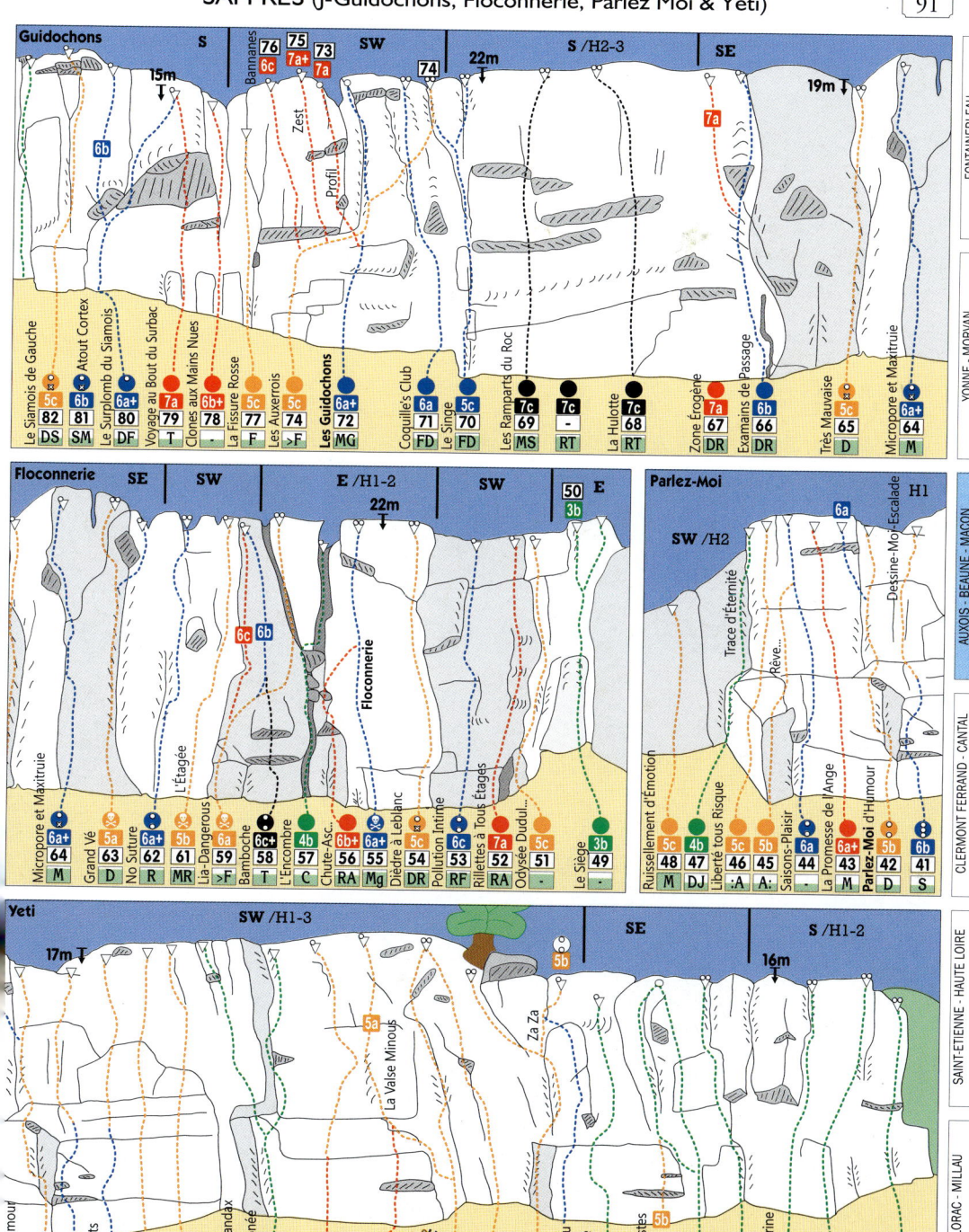

FALAISE DE GELIGNY

P1 47.306356, 4.667342

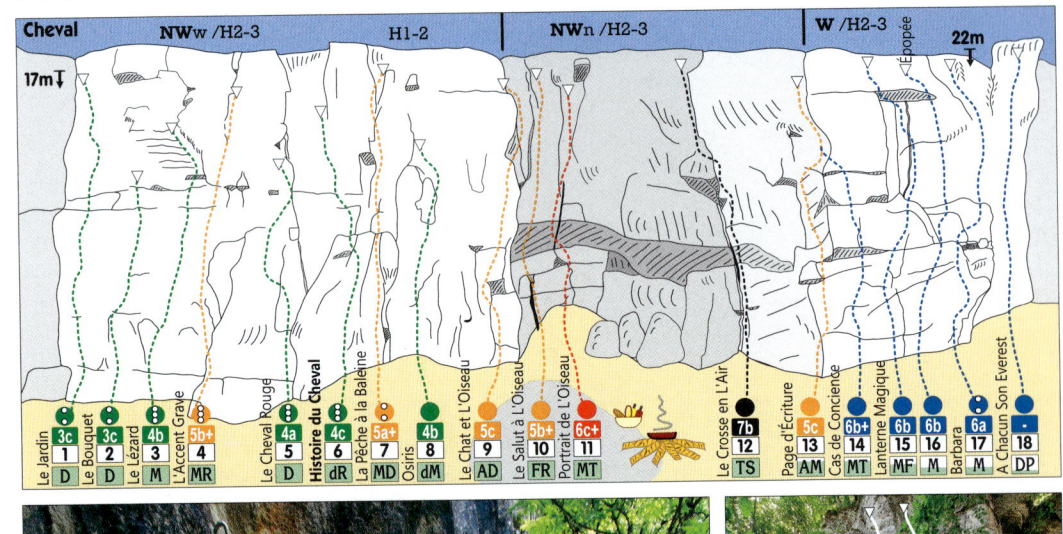

#	Name	Grade	Code
1	Le Jardin	3c	D
2	Le Bouquet	3c	D
3	Le Lézard	4b	M
4	L'Accent Grave	5b+	MR
5	Le Cheval Rouge	4a	D
6	Histoire du Cheval	4c	dR
7	La Pêche à la Baleine	5a+	MD
8	Osiris	4b	dM
9	Le Chat et l'Oiseau	5c	AD
10	Le Salut à L'Oiseau	5b+	FR
11	Portrait de l'Oiseau	6c+	MT
12	La Crosse en L'Air	7b	TS
13	Page d'Écriture	5c	AM
14	Cas de Concience	6b+	MT
15	Lanterne Magique	6b	MF
16		6b	M
17	Barbara	6a	M
18	A Chacun Son Everest	-	DP

CHOCAHOLIQUE 4c. Katie Hopwood, (30) ▷

Calcaire*** An old quarry with a mixture of blank rock and some excellent finger sized tufas. A nice place if dry.

FALAISE DE GELIGNY

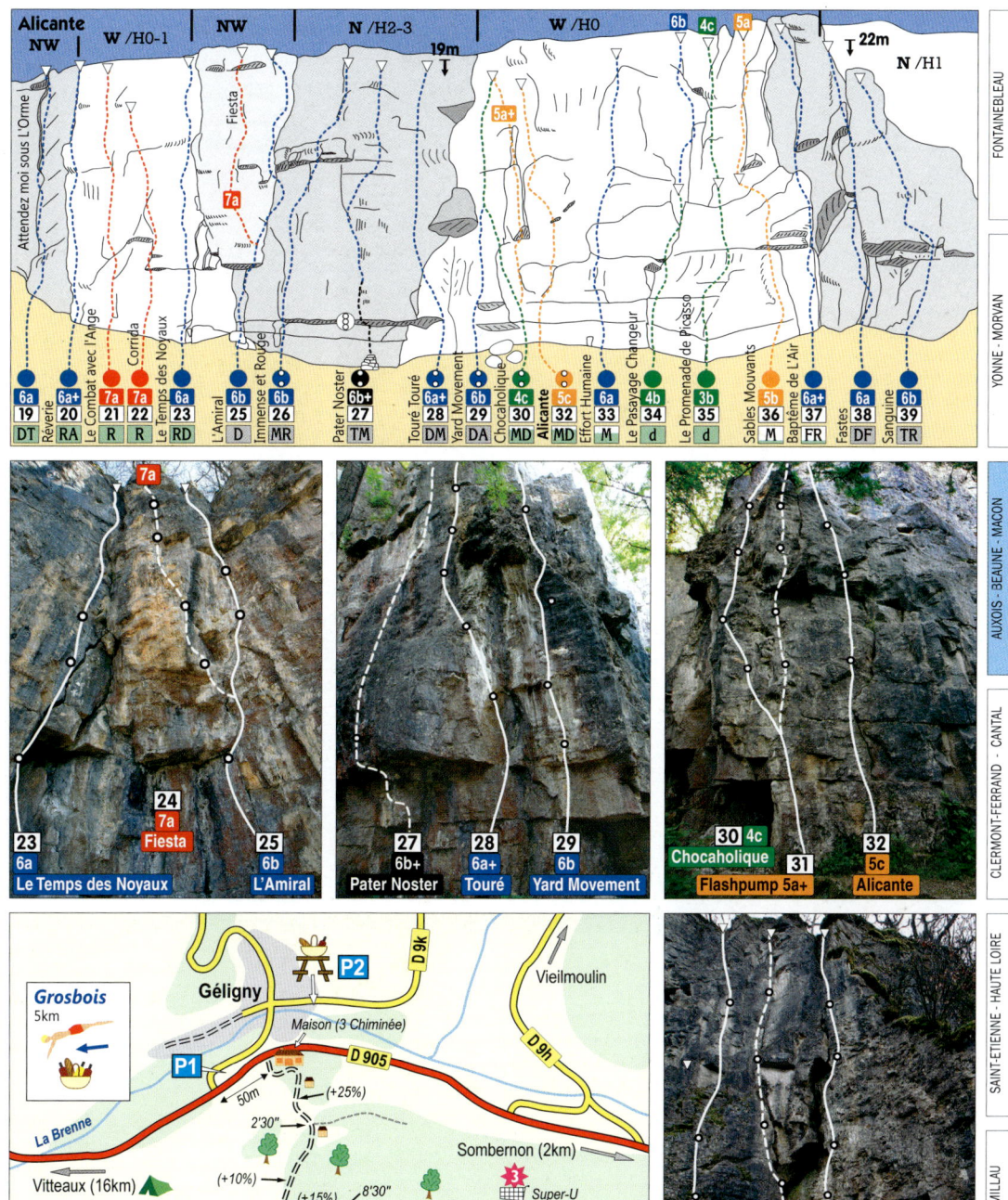

The place to come climbing in hot weather, lots of shade, plus the Grosbois reservoir nearby to go swimming on hot days.

LANTENAY - A (Haute-Charme)

P1 47.352331, 4.849933

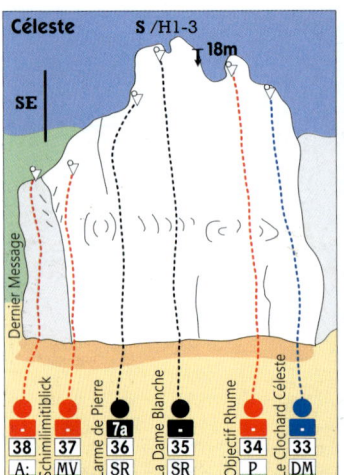

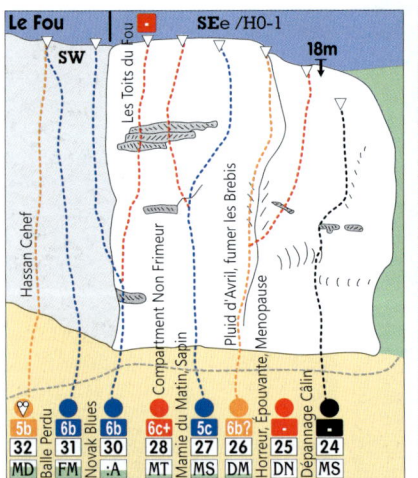

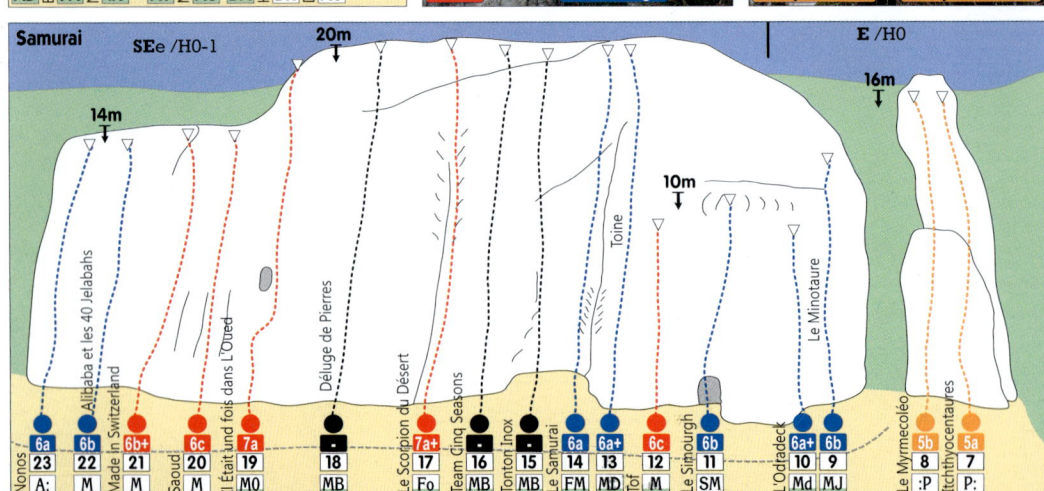

This SE facing sector is very quiet and remote. Nice views and aspect, with plenty of picnic areas on top.

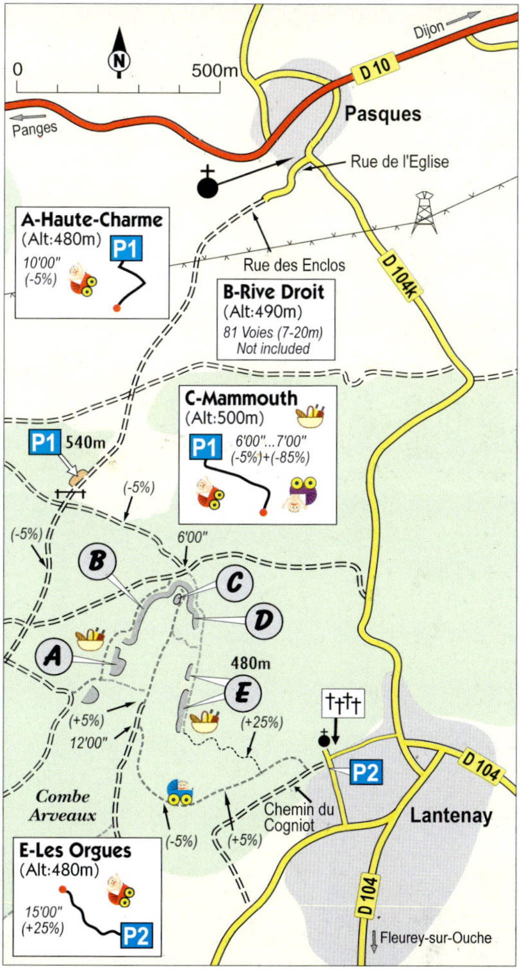

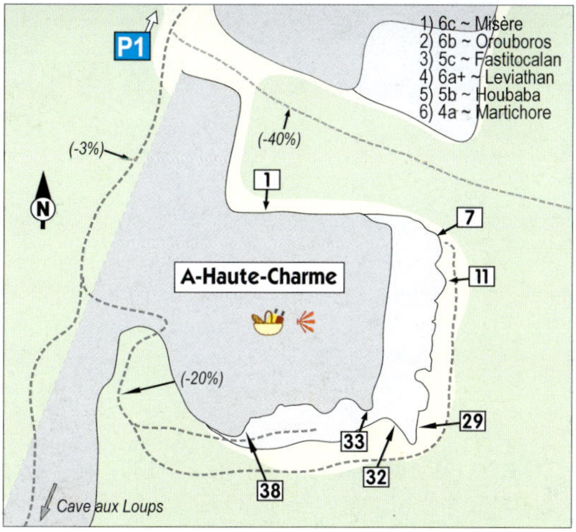

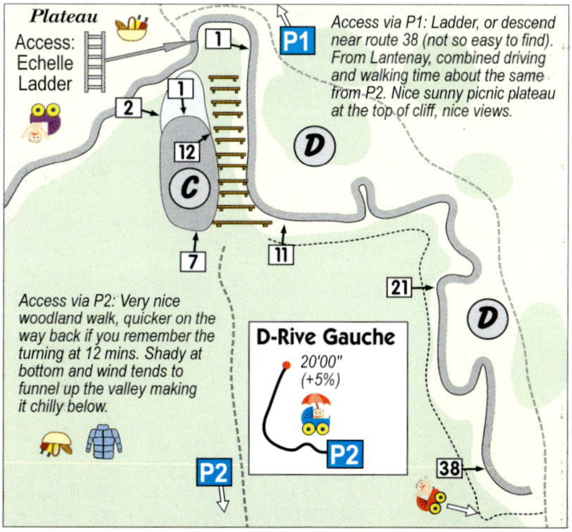

LANTENAY (Cartes-Maps)

P2 47.342896, 4.863565 — 95

Routes (A-Haute-Charme)
1) 6c ~ Misère
2) 6b ~ Orouboros
3) 5c ~ Fastitocalan
4) 6a+ ~ Leviathan
5) 5b ~ Houbaba
6) 4a ~ Martichore

Areas
- **A-Haute-Charme** (Alt: 480m) — 10'00" (-5%)
- **B-Rive Droit** (Alt: 490m) — 81 Voies (7-20m), Not included
- **C-Mammouth** (Alt: 500m) — 6'00"...7'00" (-5%)+(-85%)
- **E-Les Orgues** (Alt: 480m) — 15'00" (+25%)
- **D-Rive Gauche** — 20'00" (+5%)

P1 540m • 6'00" • 480m (+25%) • 12'00" (+5%) • (-5%)

Plateau Access
Echelle Ladder

Access via P1: Ladder, or descend near route 38 (not so easy to find). From Lantenay, combined driving and walking time about the same from P2. Nice sunny picnic plateau at the top of cliff, nice views.

Access via P2: Very nice woodland walk, quicker on the way back if you remember the turning at 12 mins. Shady at bottom and wind tends to funnel up the valley making it chilly below.

Cave aux Loups

Combe Arveaux • Chemin du Cogniot • Lantenay • Fleurey-sur-Ouche • D 104 • D 10 • Pasques • Rue de l'Eglise • Rue des Enclos • D 104k • Panges • Dijon

FONTAINEBLEAU • YONNE - MORVAN • AUXOIS - BEAUNE - MACON • CLERMONT-FERRAND - CANTAL • SAINT-ETIENNE - HAUTE LOIRE • AUBENAS - FLORAC - MILLAU

Calcaire** Rock is very pure giving sharp crimps, but is often shattered with some loose bocks ! Routes numbered at base.

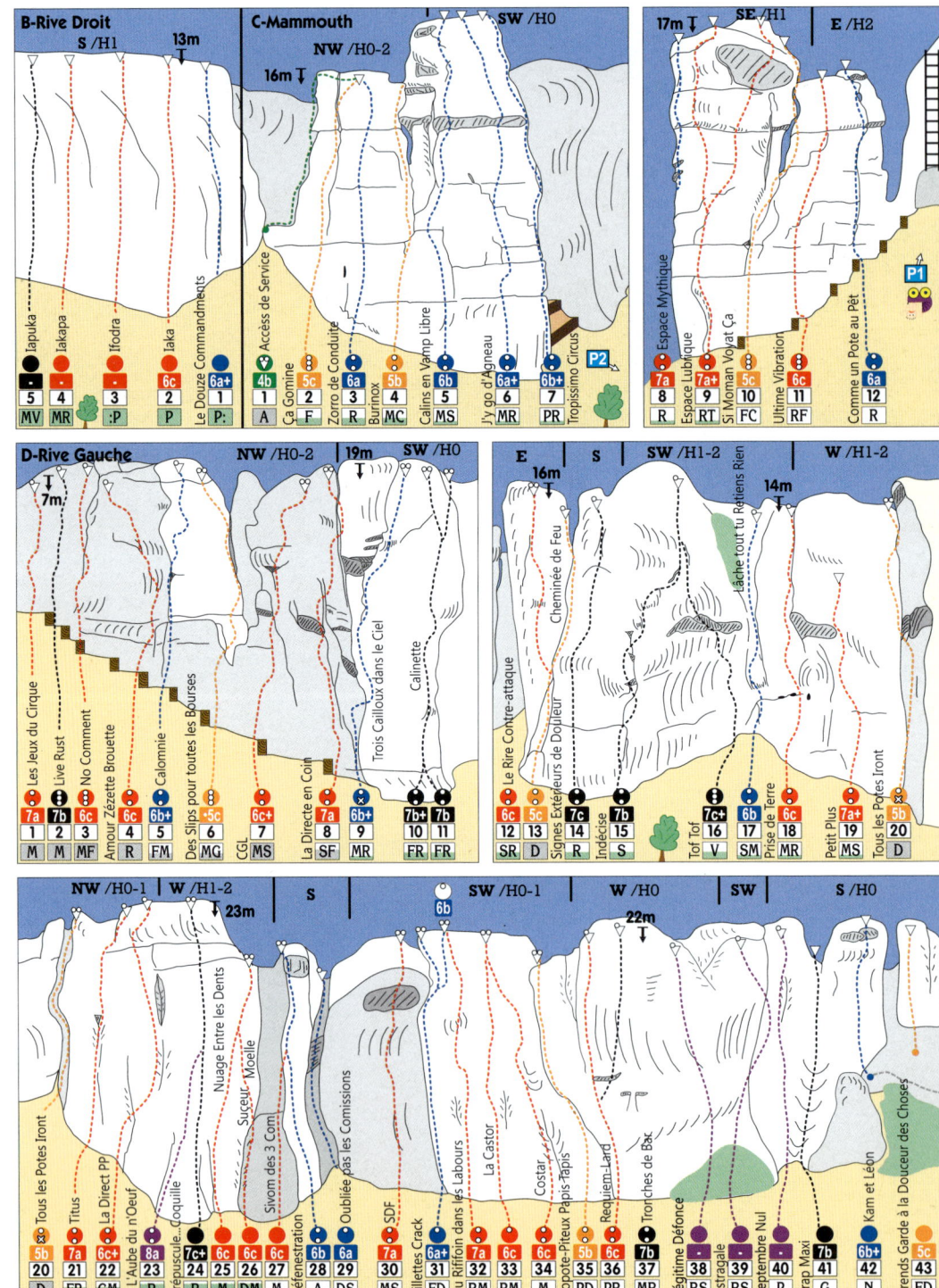

Sector C: A superb free standing tower. Some friable bits, but mostly excellent. Great views and ambience.

LANTENAY C (Mammouth) & D (Rive Gauche)

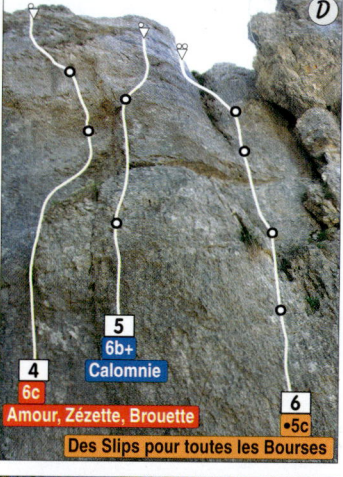
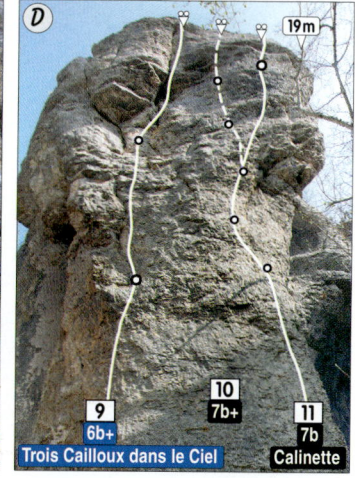

Sector D: Mostly flat walls with highly technical climbing, good footwork essential - bring shoes with good edges.

LANTENAY (E-Les Orgues)

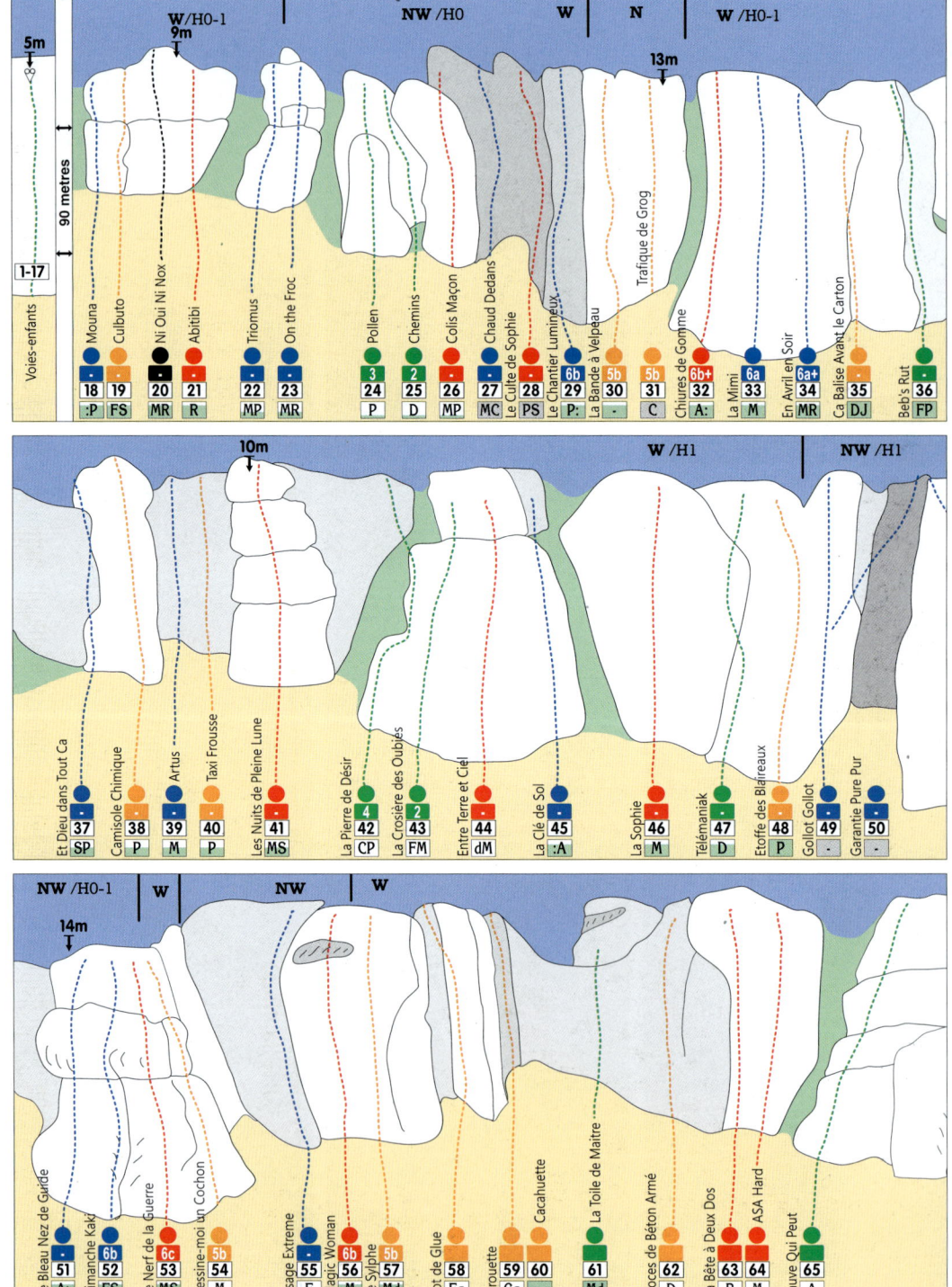

Routes 1-17 are very very short - ideal for very small children on a top rope - moulinette.

LANTENAY (E-Les Orgues)

Medium quality Calcaire and a mixed selection of routes.

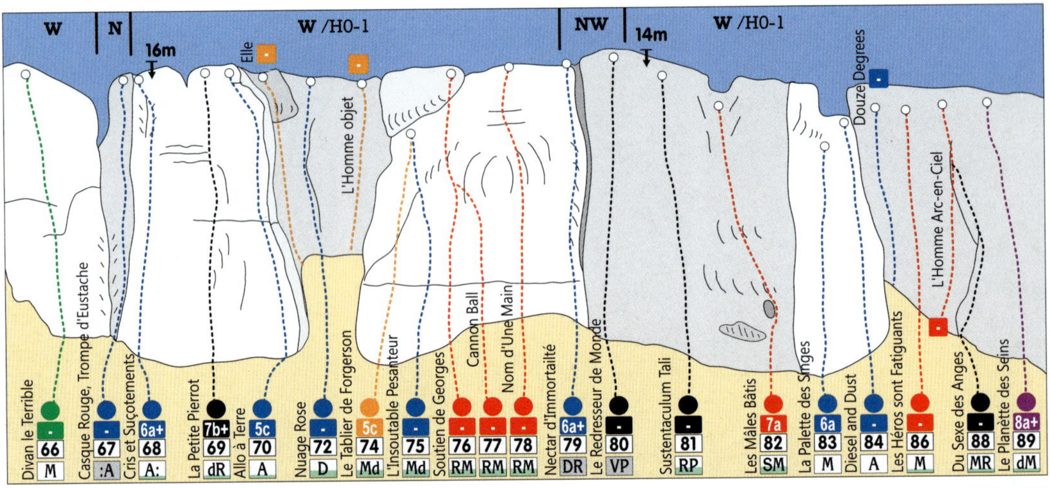

LANTENAY (E-Les Orgues)

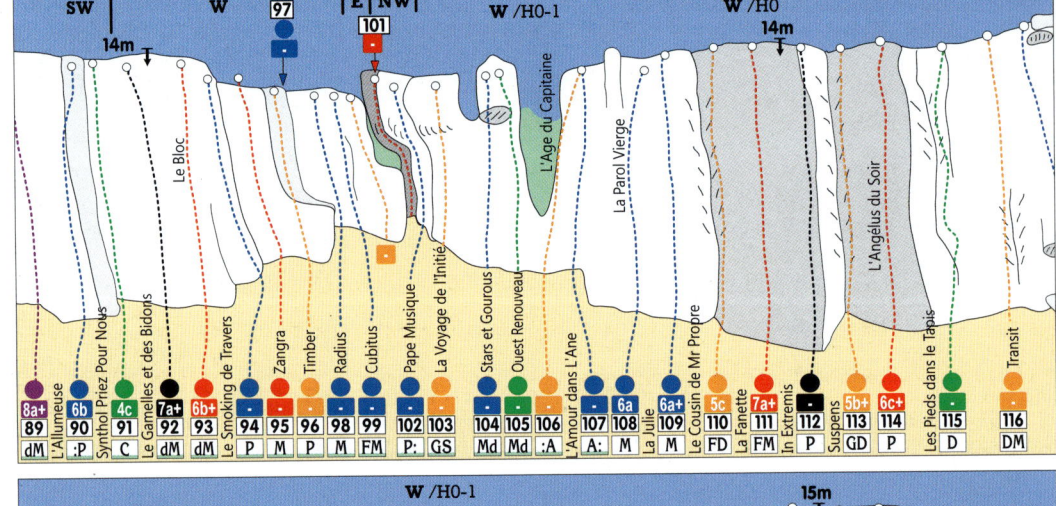
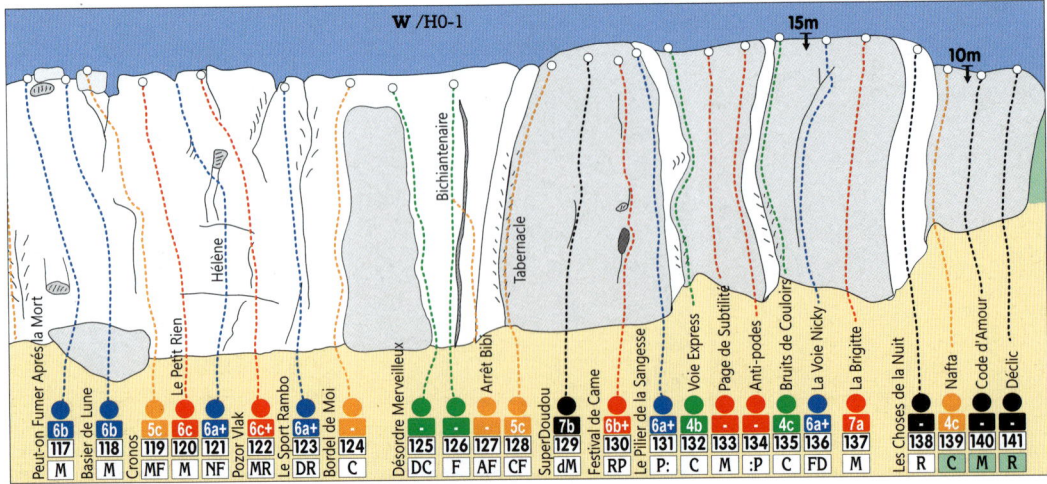

Some very nice short and difficult routes at the far end. Gets the evening sun beautifully.

LANTENAY (E-Les Orgues)

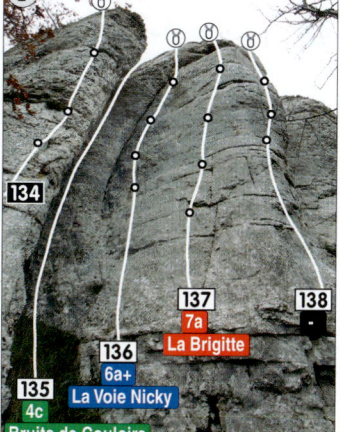

Finding the footpath up through the dense trees direct from Lantenay...is ok if it has been cleared, not ideal after rain.

FLEUREY-SUR-OUCHE (Les Roches d'Orgères)

P1 47.312726, 4.867469

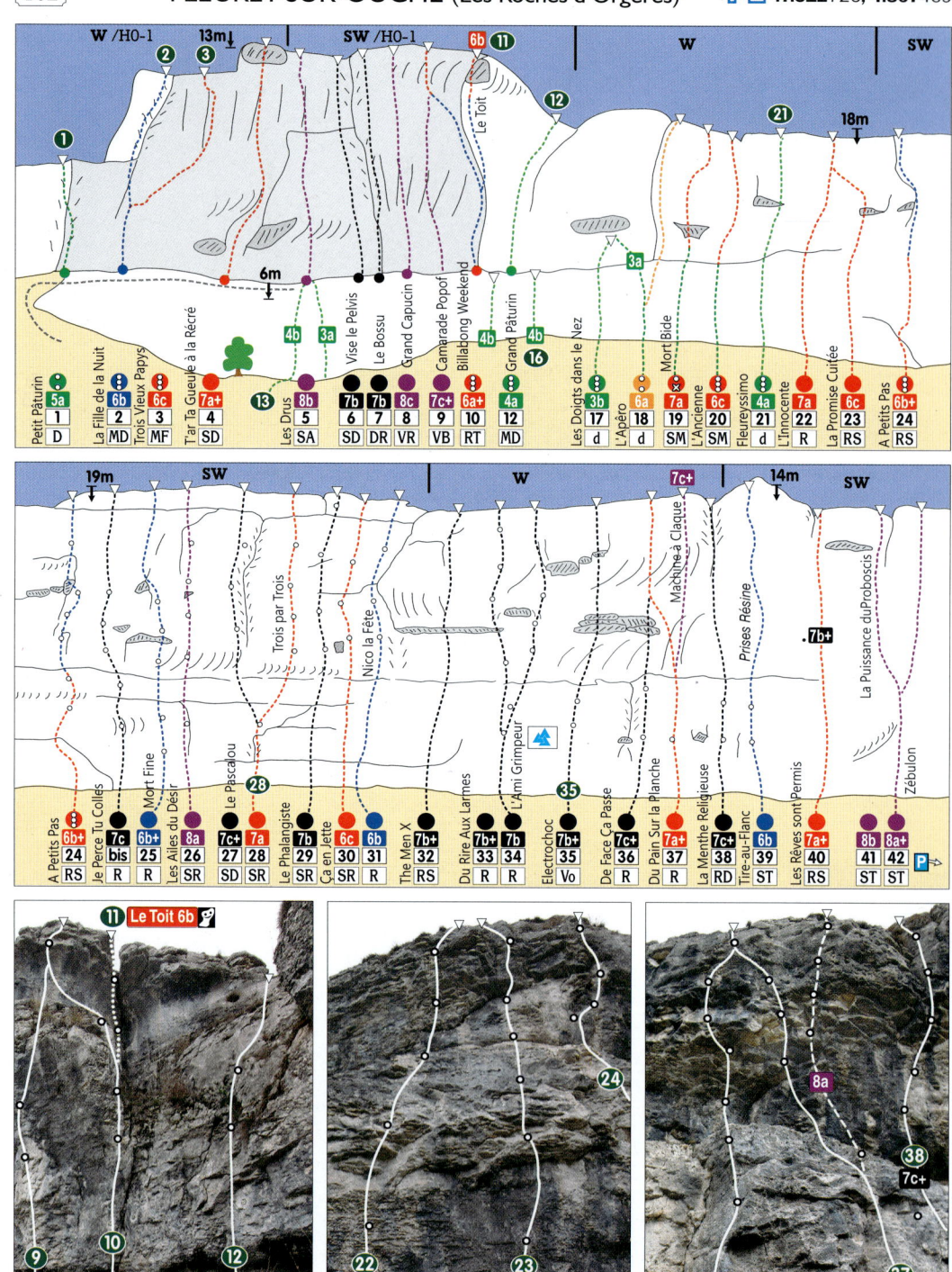

Calcaire**, best rock on the hard routes. A sunny aspect in an open valley bottom. Wind often cools, but the sun can be fierce.

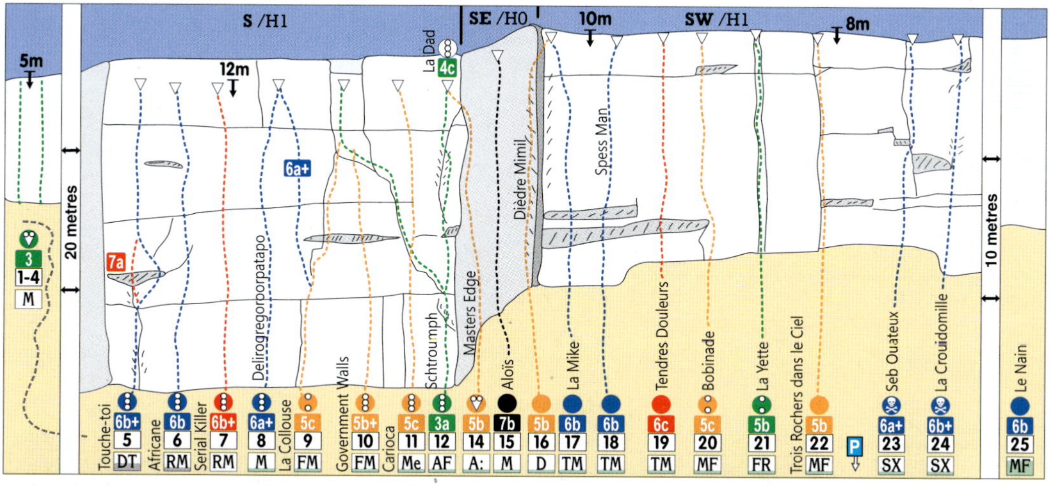

AHUY

#	Name	Grade	Type
1-4	M	3	
5	Touche-toi	6b+	DT
6	Africaine	6b	RM
7	Serial Killer	6c	RM
8	Deli / La Collouse	6a+	M
9	La Collouse	5c	FM
10	Government Walls	5b+	FM
11	Carioca	5c	Me
12	La Schtroumph	3a	AF
13	La Dad	4c	
14	Masters Edge	5b	A:
15	Aloïs	7b	M
16	Dièdre Mimi	5b	D
17	La Mike	6b	TM
18	Spess Man	6b	TM
19	Tendres Douleurs	6c	TM
20	Bobinade	5c	MF
21	La Yette	5b	FR
22	Trois Rochers dans le Ciel	5b	MF
23	Seb Ouateux	6a+	SX
24	La Crouidomille	6b+	SX
25	Le Nain	6b	MF

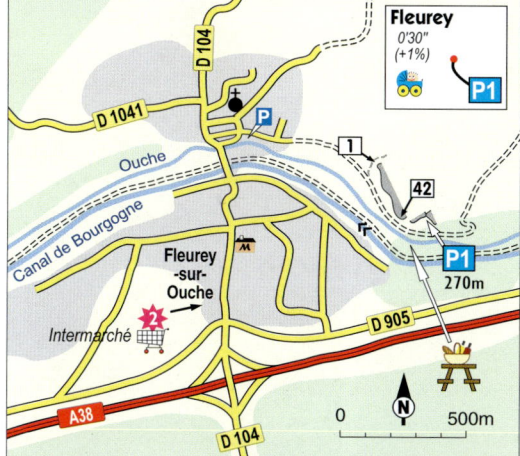
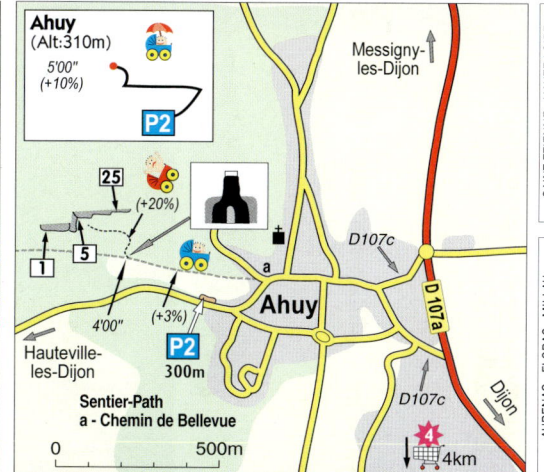

Calcaire* A small cliff only worth visiting if in the area. Rock...not of the highest quality, but fun nevertheless.

FIXIN

P1 47.245747, 4.965467

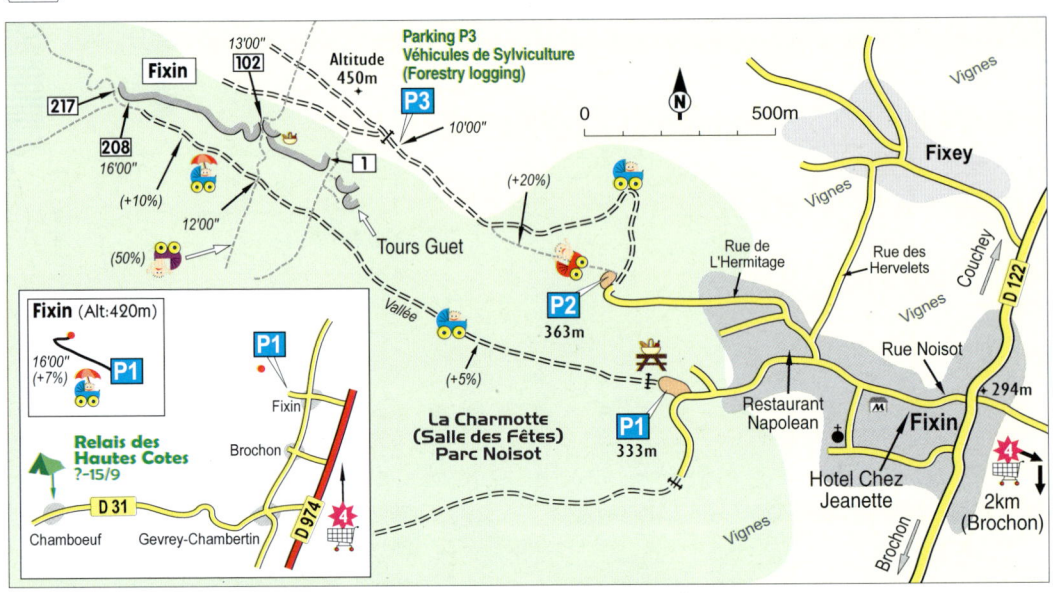

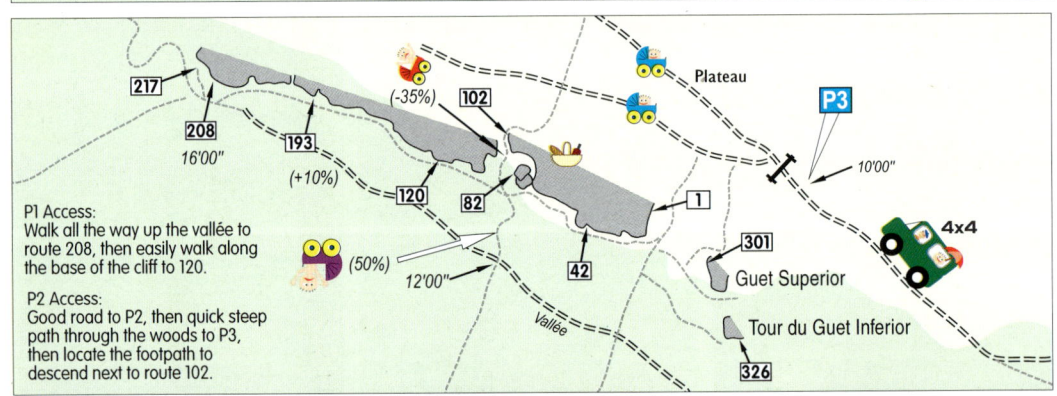

P1 Access:
Walk all the way up the vallée to route 208, then easily walk along the base of the cliff to 120.

P2 Access:
Good road to P2, then quick steep path through the woods to P3, then locate the footpath to descend next to route 102.

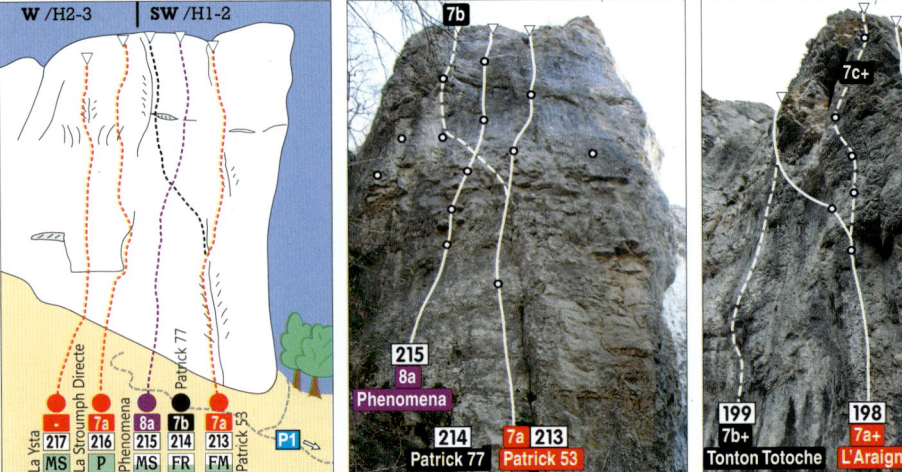

A classic old cliff, routes historically numbered from right end - doh!   Mostly...superb technical vertical wall climbing.

FIXIN (A-Lamentations)

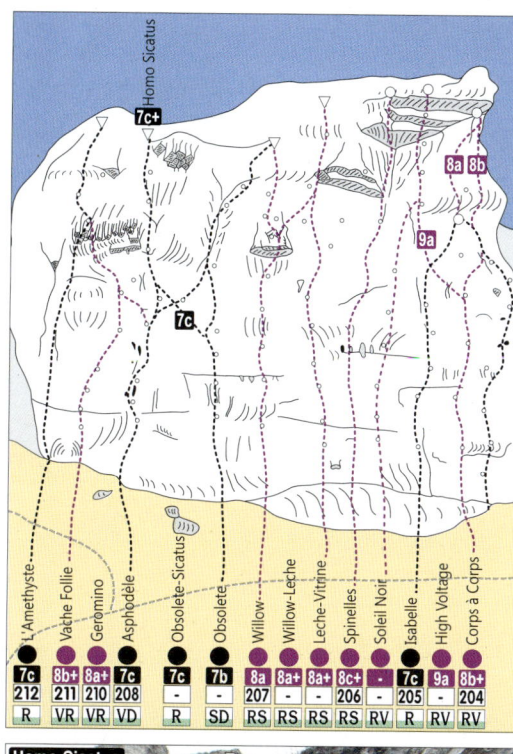
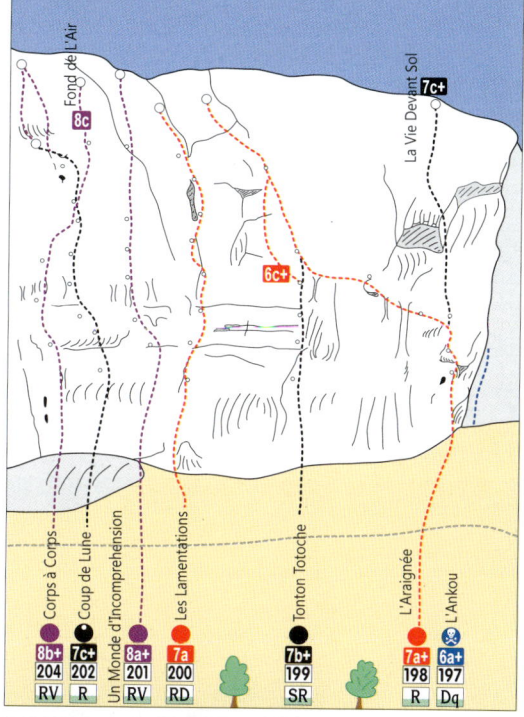

Mur de Lamentations is the classic overhanging wall of the area, powerful and engagée all the way to 9a, flying time - 747 style.

FIXIN - (B-Dièdre Bleu)

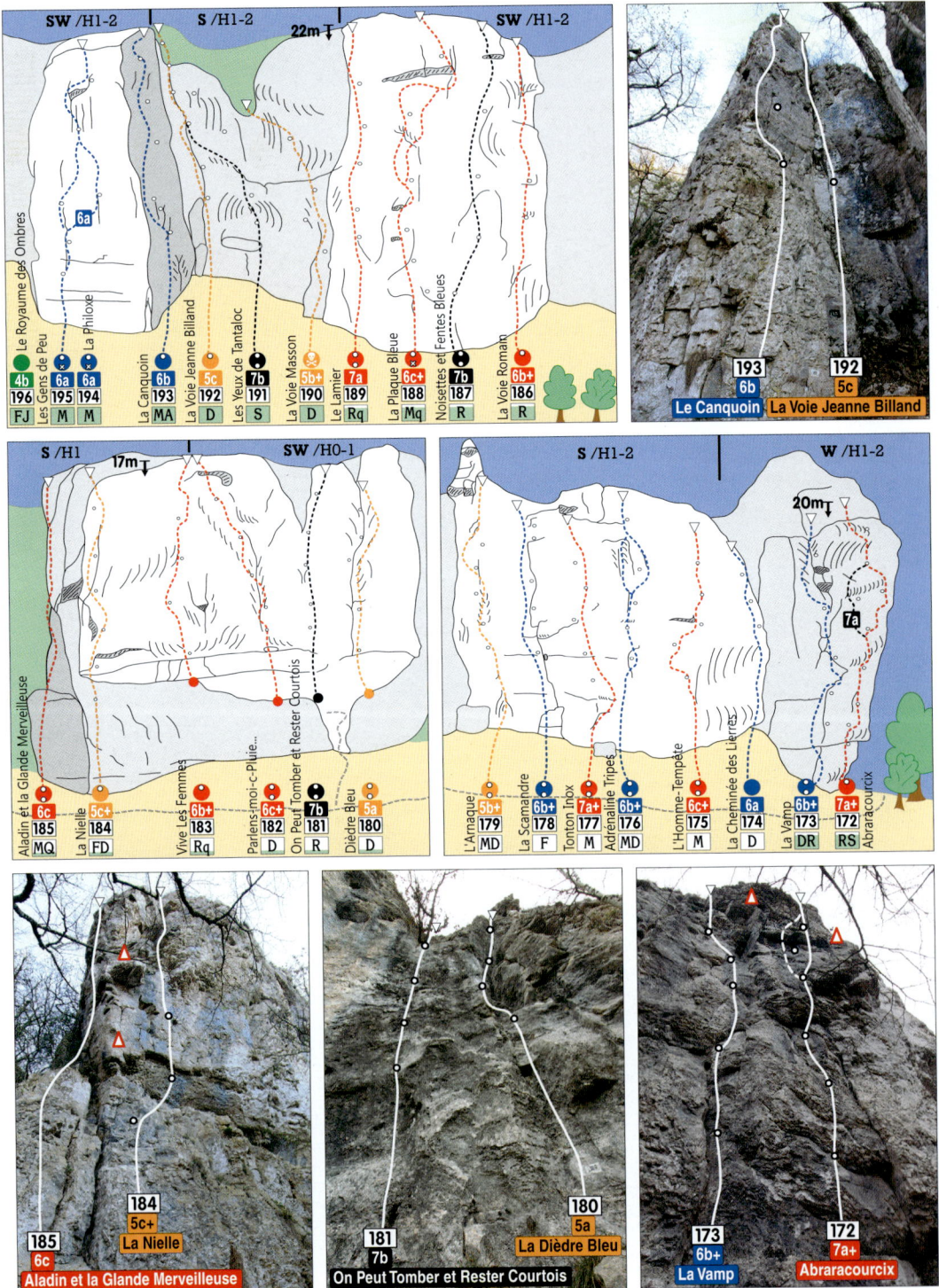

FIXIN (C-Cascade & Batier)

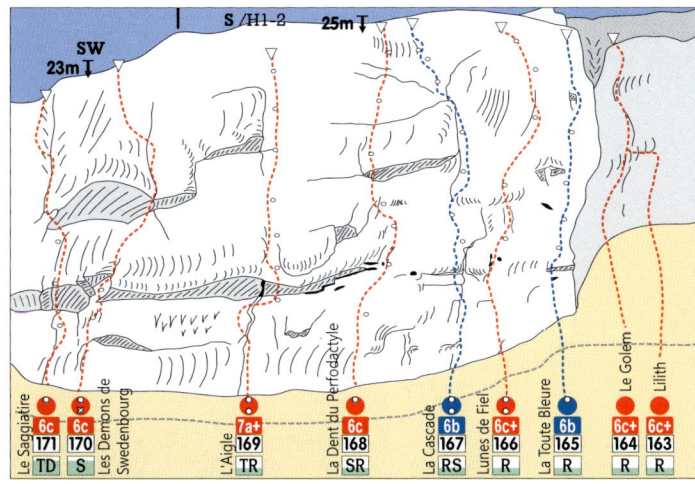

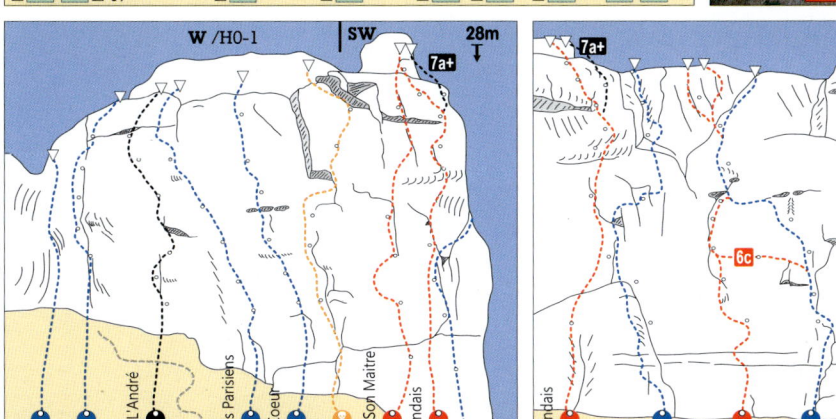
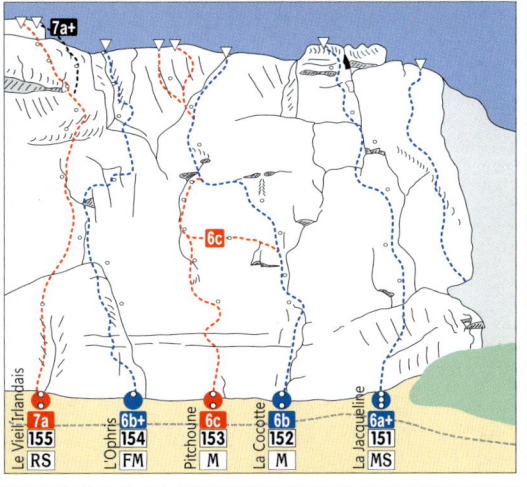

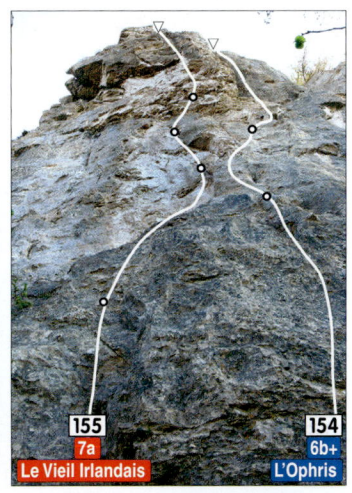

Cascade is a difficult sector to onsight with awkward overhangs. Batier area is easier to onsight - but can get very warm.

FIXIN - (D-Nantet-Beaujolais-Fleur de Lys)

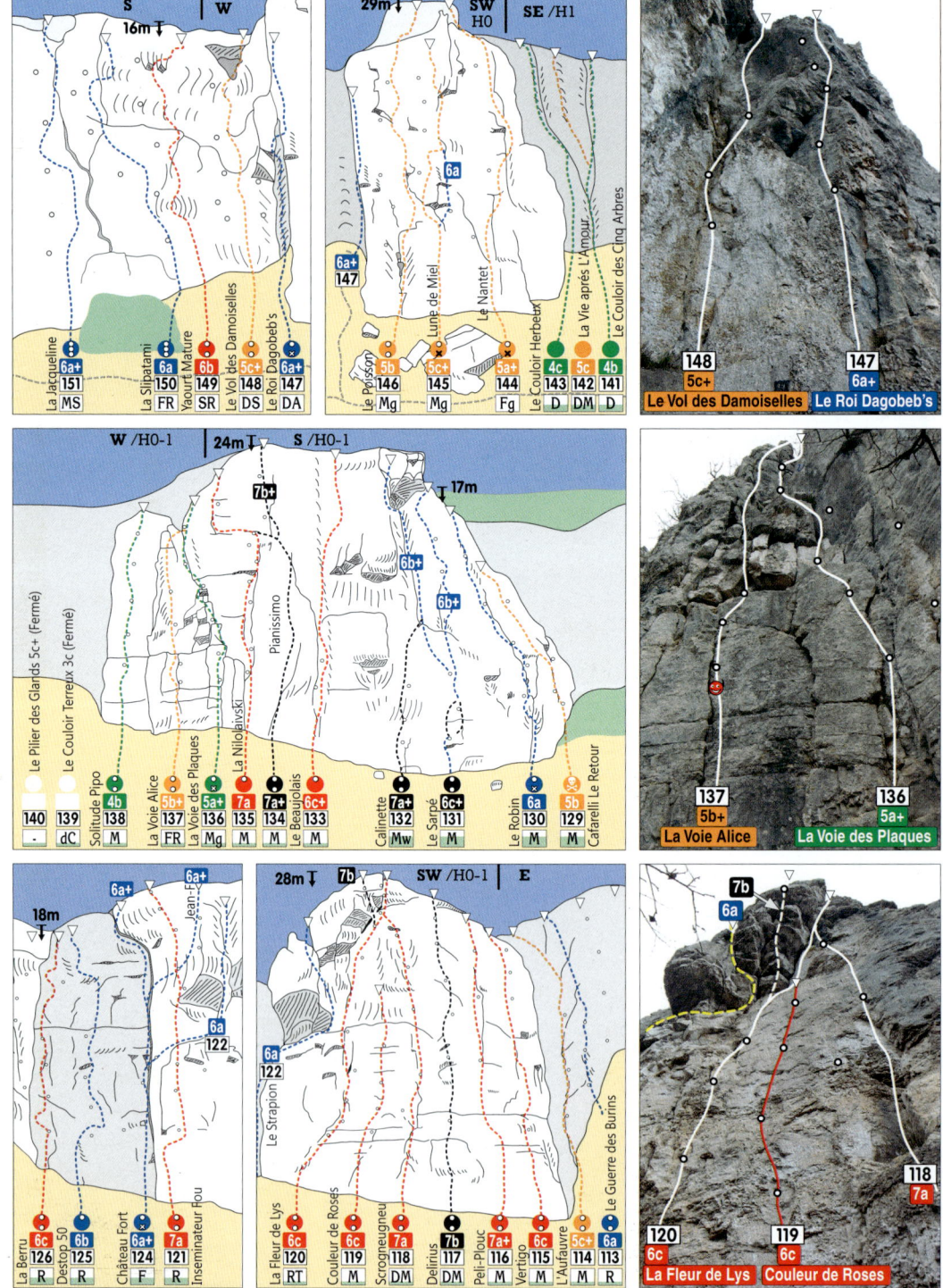

Three of the best sectors at Fixin - top quality.

7a Le Vieil Irlandais (155), Nico Bessenge

FIXIN (E-Dédé - Pic Pontu)

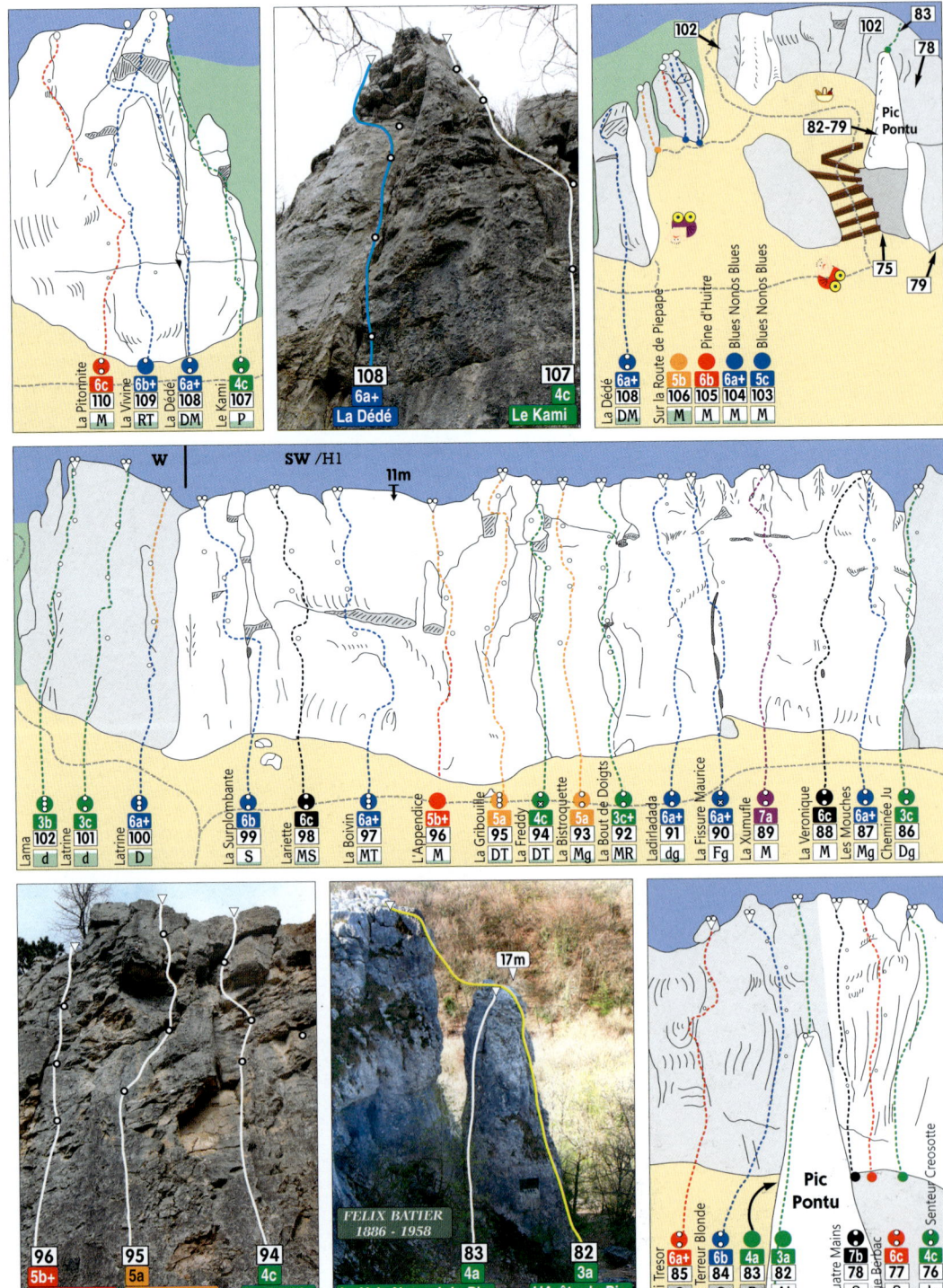

A very well used, popular small sector - polished holds; grades have been adjusted - but they still feel hard.

FIXIN (F-Gégène - Cheminée Oiseaux)

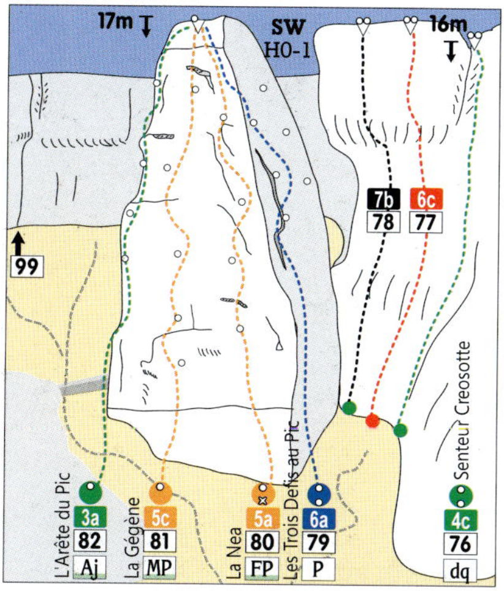

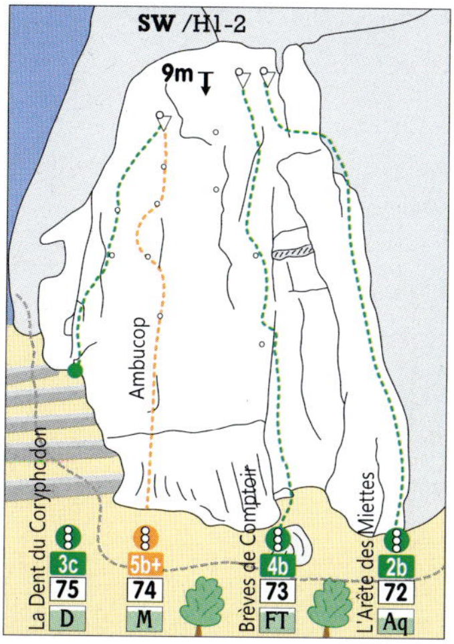

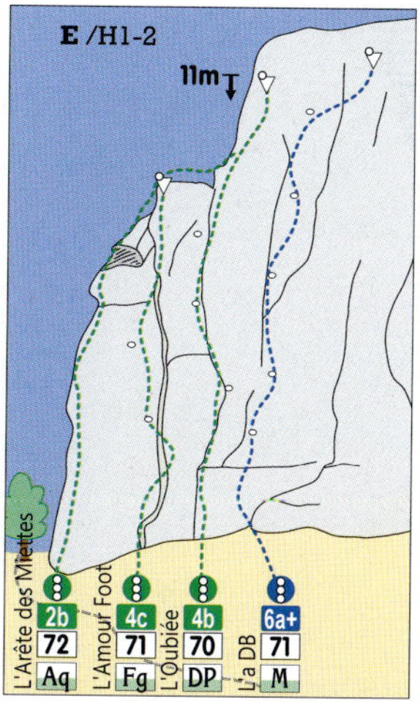

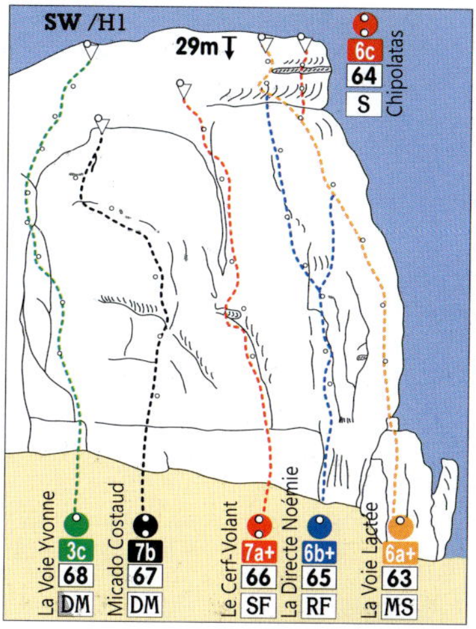

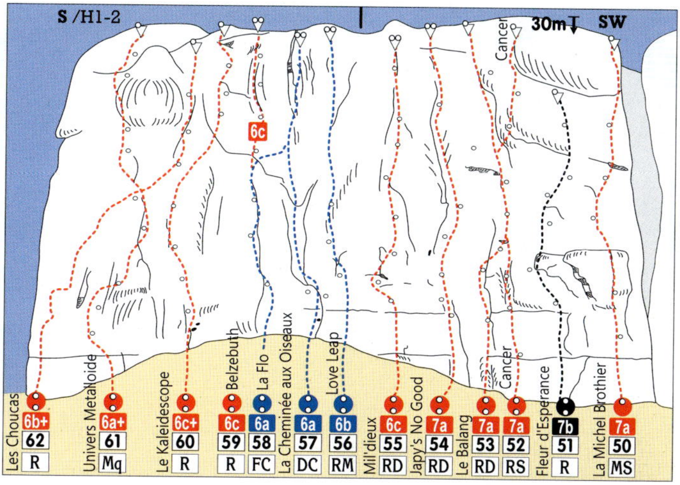

Parking page 104

Sector SW / H0-1 (17m)

#	Name	Grade	Code
82	L'Arête du Pic	3a	Aj
81	La Gégène	5c	MP
80	La Nea	5a	FP
79	Les Trois Defis-au-Pic	6a	P
78	—	7b	—
77	—	6c	—
76	Senteur Creosotte	4c	dq

Sector SW / H1-2 (9m)

#	Name	Grade	Code
75	La Dent du Coryphedon	3c	D
74	Ambucop	5b+	M
73	Brèves de Comptoir	4b	FT
72	L'Arête des Miettes	2b	Aq

Sector E / H1-2 (11m)

#	Name	Grade	Code
72	L'Arête des Miettes	2b	Aq
71	L'Amour Foot	4c	Fg
70	L'Oubliée	4b	DP
—	L'a DB	6a+	M

Sector SW / H1 (29m)

#	Name	Grade	Code
64	Chipolatas	6c / S	—
68	La Voie Yvonne	3c	DM
67	Micado Costaud	7b	DM
66	Le Cerf-Volant	7a+	SF
65	La Directe Noémie	6b+	RF
63	La Voie Lactée	6a+	MS

Sector S / H1-2 (30m)

#	Name	Grade	Code
62	Les Choucas	6b+	R
61	Univers Metaloïde	6a+	Mq
60	Le Kaleidescope	6c+	R
59	Belzebuth	6c	FC
58	La Flo	6a	DC
57	La Cheminée aux Oiseaux	6a	RM
56	Love Leap	6b	—
55	Mill dieux	6c	RD
54	Japy's No Good	7a	RD
53	Le Balang	7a	RD
52	Cancer	7a	RS
51	Fleur d'Esperance	7b	R
50	La Michel Brothier	7a	MS

71 — 4c — L'Amour Foot
70 — 4b — L'Oubliée

67 — 7b — Micado Costaud
66 — 7a+ — Le Cerf-Volant

57 — 6a — La Cheminée aux Oiseaux
56 — 6b — Love Leap
55 — 6c

The historic grades at Fixin have always been regarded as comical - sandbag - Trés dur, only to be taken as a rough guide.

FIXIN (G-Tangentoide-Gaudillot)

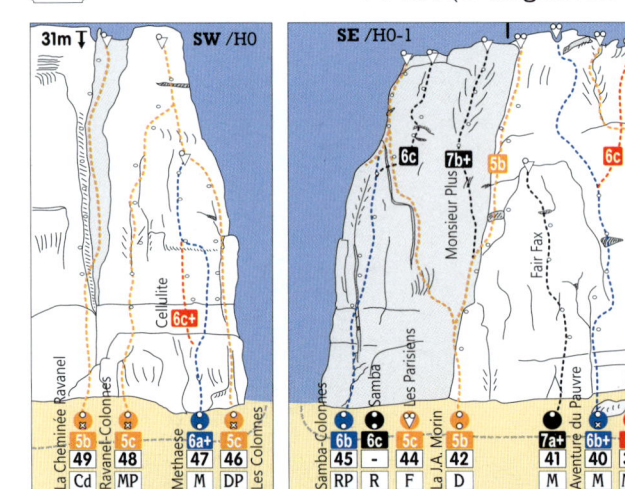
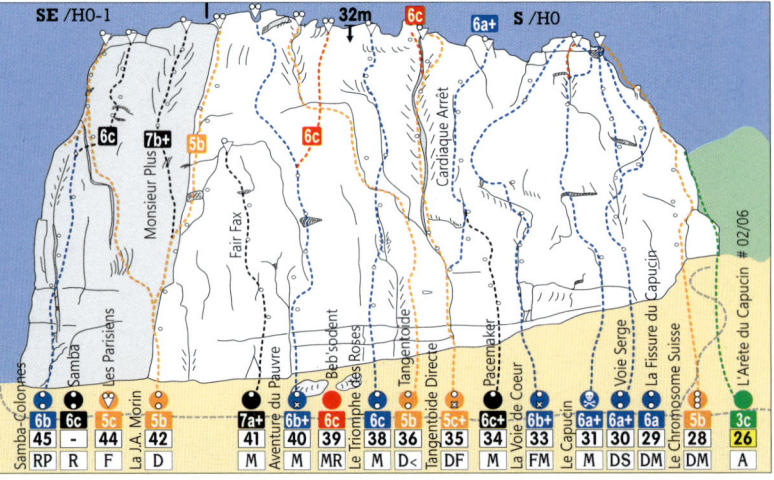

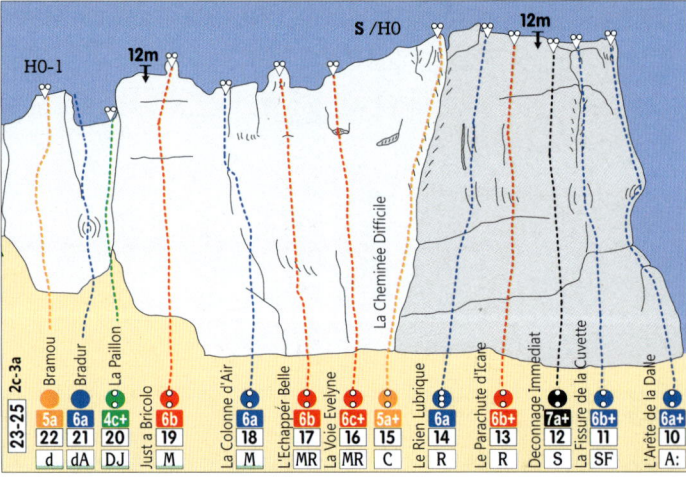
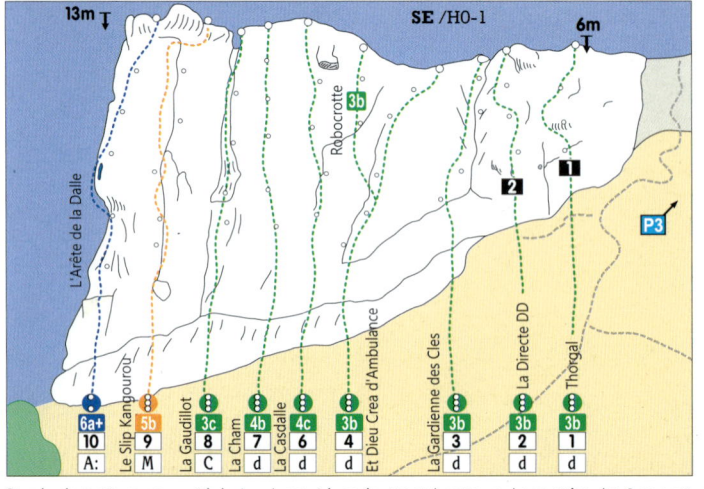
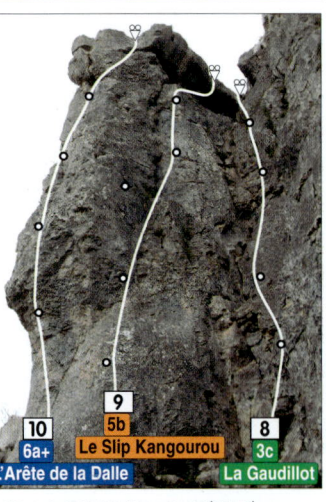

Equipping of routes at Fixin has been historically old style and not friendly. Lots of routes are easy to top rope though.

FIXIN (H-Tours de Guet)

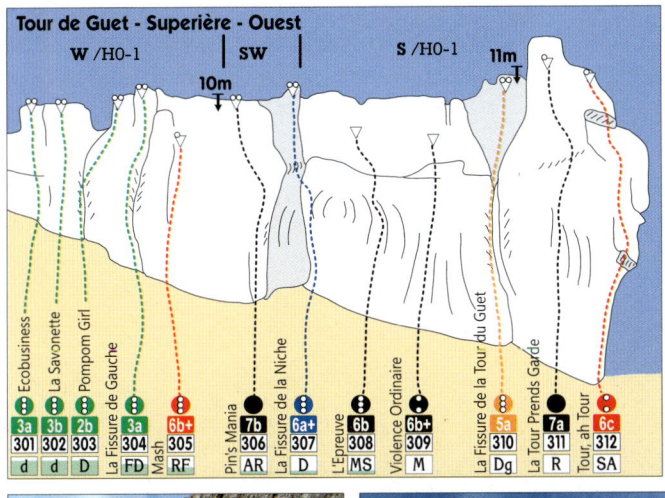

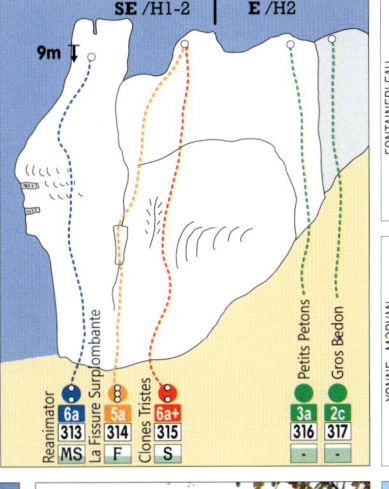

Tour de Guet - Superière - Ouest

W /H0-1 — SW — S /H0-1 — SE /H1-2 — E /H2

#	Name	Grade	Code	Abbr
	Ecobusiness	3a	301	d
	La Savonette	3b	302	d
	Pompom Girl	2b	303	D
	La Fissure de Gauche	3a	304	FD
	Mash	6b+	305	RF
	Pin's Mania	7b	306	AR
	La Fissure de la Niche	6a+	307	D
	L'Epreuve	6b	308	MS
	Violence Ordinaire	6b+	309	M
	La Fissure de la Tour du Guet	5a	310	Dg
	La Tour Prends Garde	7a	311	R
	Tour, ah Tour	6c	312	SA
	Reanimator	6a	313	MS
	La Fissure Surplombante	5a	314	F
	Clones Tristes	6a+	315	S
	Petits Petons	3a	316	-
	Gros Bedon	2c	317	-

306 7b — 307 6a+ La Fissure de la Niche — 308 6b L'Epreuve

310 — 311 7a La Tour Prends Garde — 312 6c Tour, ah! Tour

313 6a Reanimator — 314 5a La Fissure Surplombante — 315 6a+

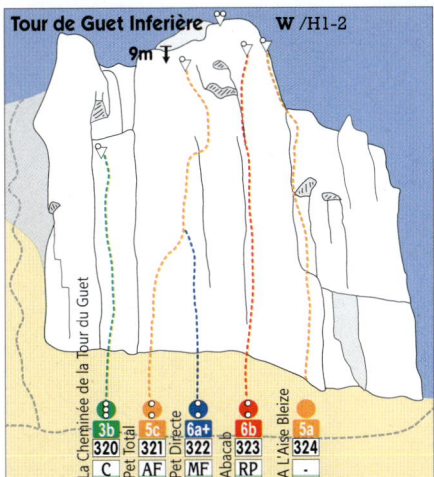

Tour de Guet Inferière

W /H1-2

	Name	Grade	#	Abbr
	La Chéminée de la Tour du Guet	3b	320	C
	Pet Total	5c	321	AF
	Pet Directe	6a+	322	MF
	Abacab	6b	323	RP
	A L'Aise Bleize	5a	324	-

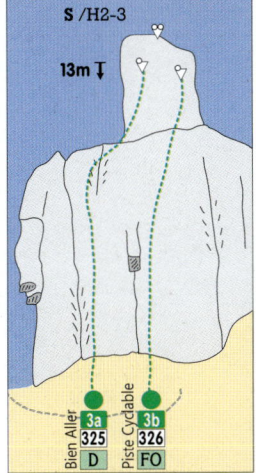

S /H2-3

	Name	Grade	#	Abbr
	Bien Aller	3a	325	D
	Piste Cyclable	3b	326	FO

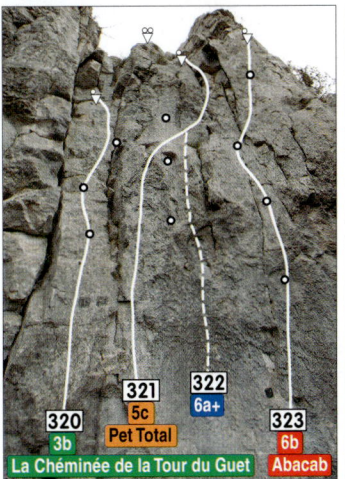

320 3b La Chéminée de la Tour du Guet — 321 5c Pet Total — 322 6a+ — 323 6b Abacab

These two small cliffs give superb rock quality; short, sharp, intense routes - usually quiet.

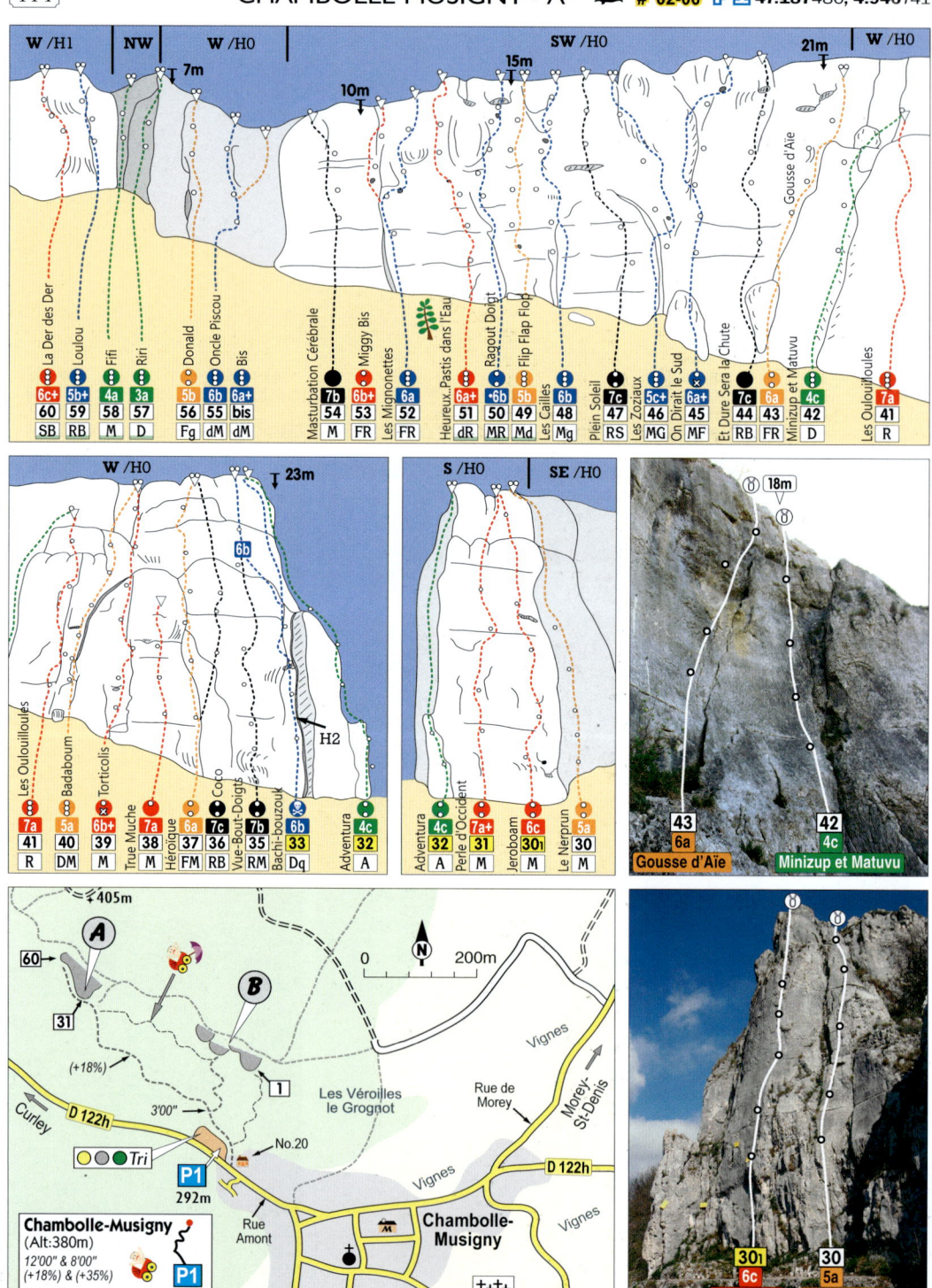

CHAMBOLLE MUSIGNY - B (Combe Ambin)

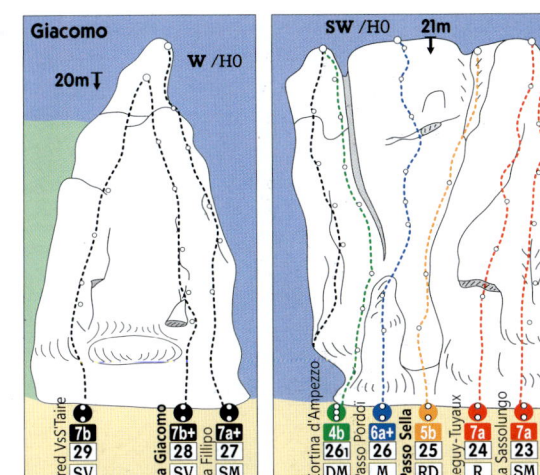
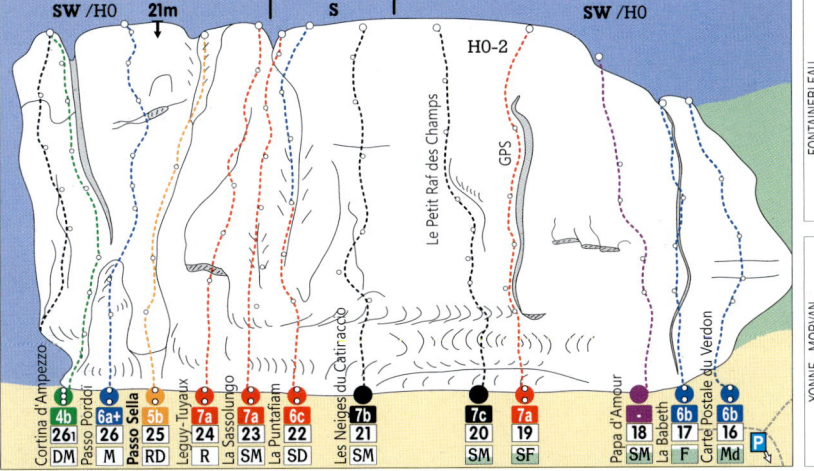
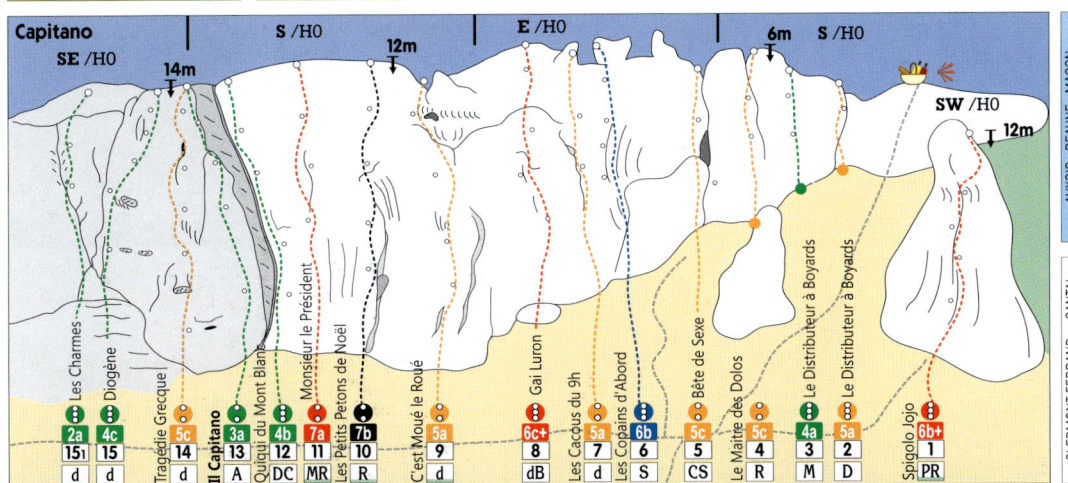
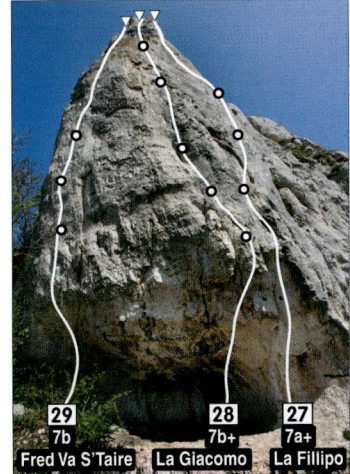

A very variable cliff, some routes polished - some not, some endurance, some bloc style, some good, some not so good.

ARCENANT - A

P1 47.149337, 4.823695

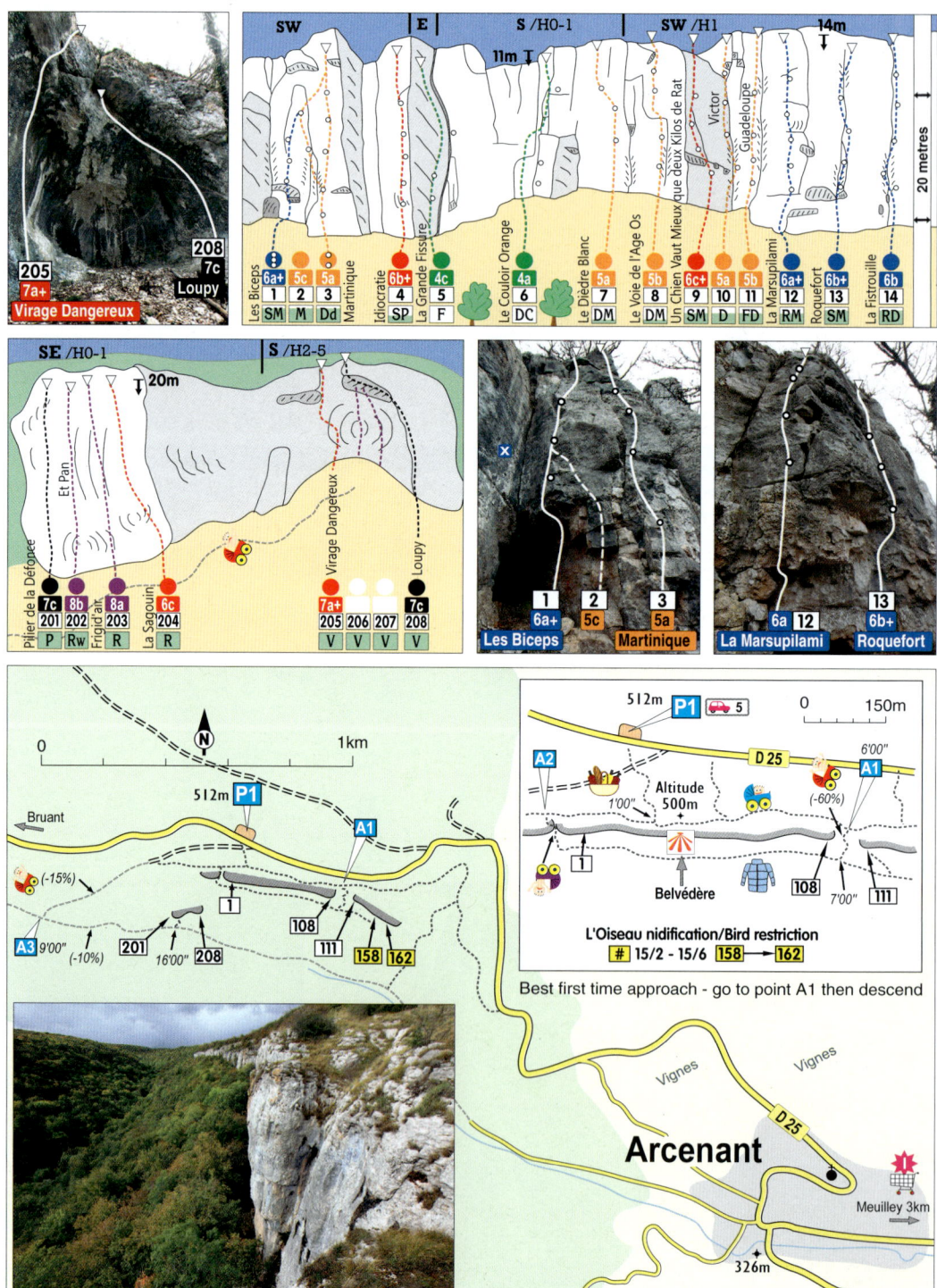

The slope above the cliff gives lot of water run-off. The bottom of the cliff is very shady and cold - even on hot days, brrr-yuk.

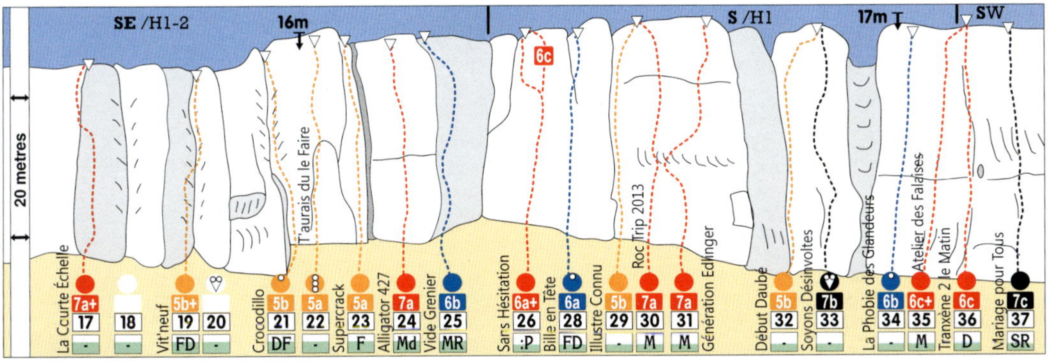

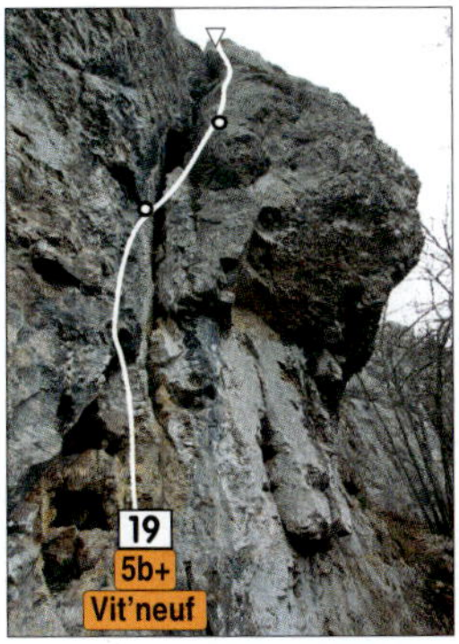

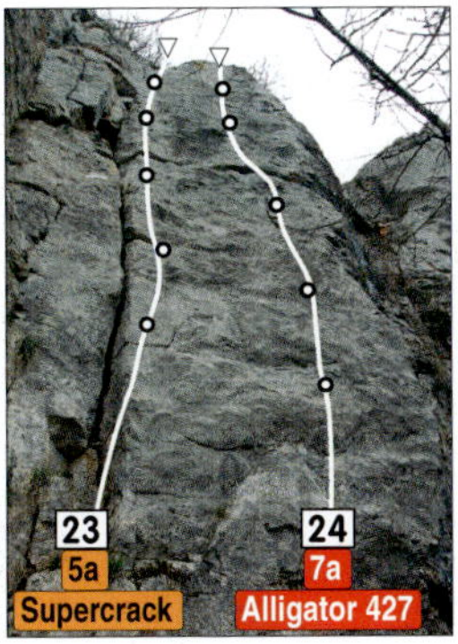

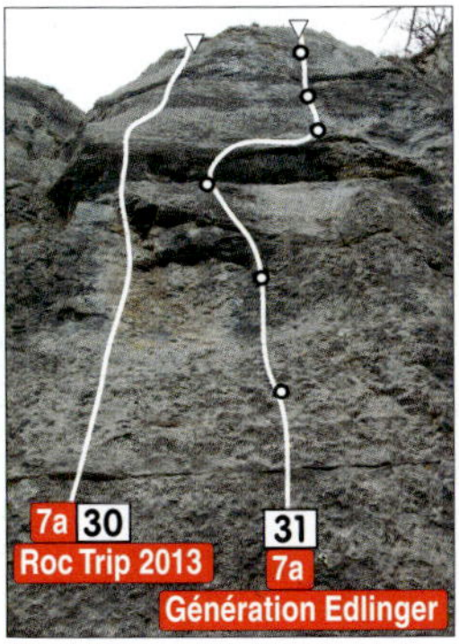

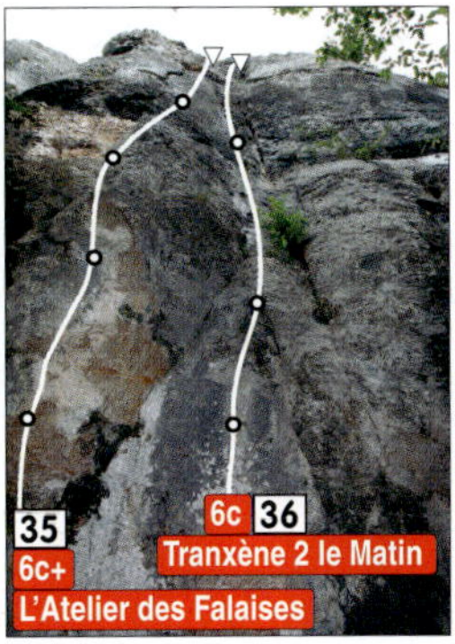

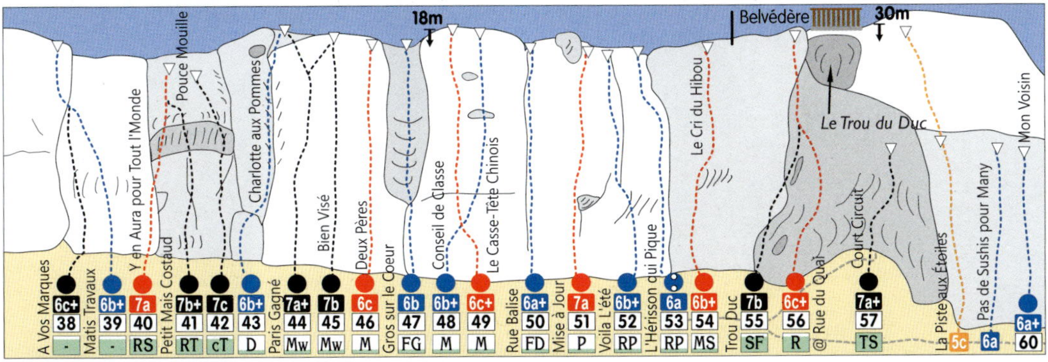

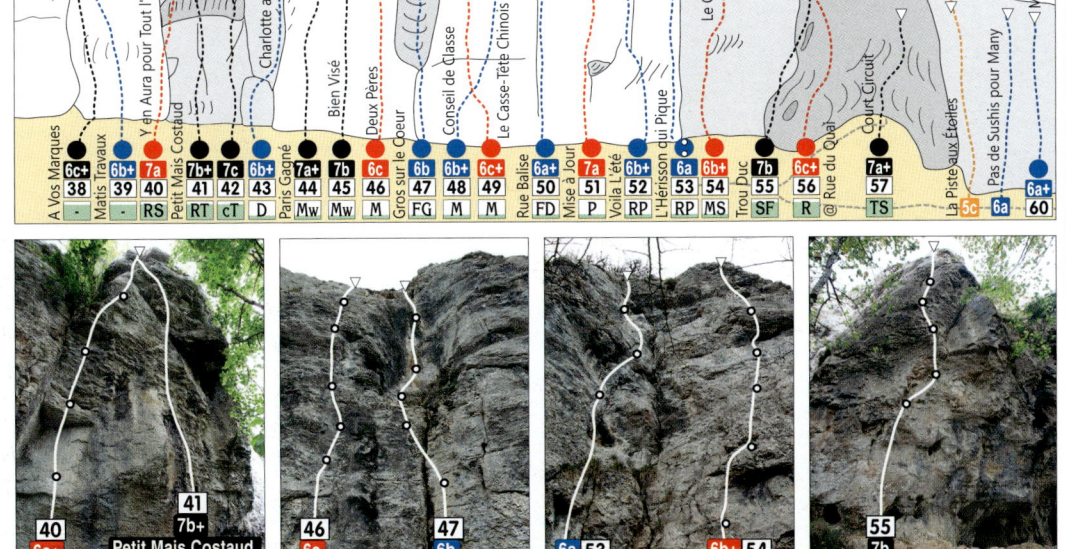

The easier routes at the left end are very worthwhile, even though the best climbing is in the 6-7's.

FONTAINEBLEAU
YONNE - MORVAN
AUXOIS - BEAUNE - MACON
CLERMONT-FERRAND - CANTAL
SAINT-ETIENNE - HAUTE LOIRE
AUBENAS - FLORAC - MILLAU

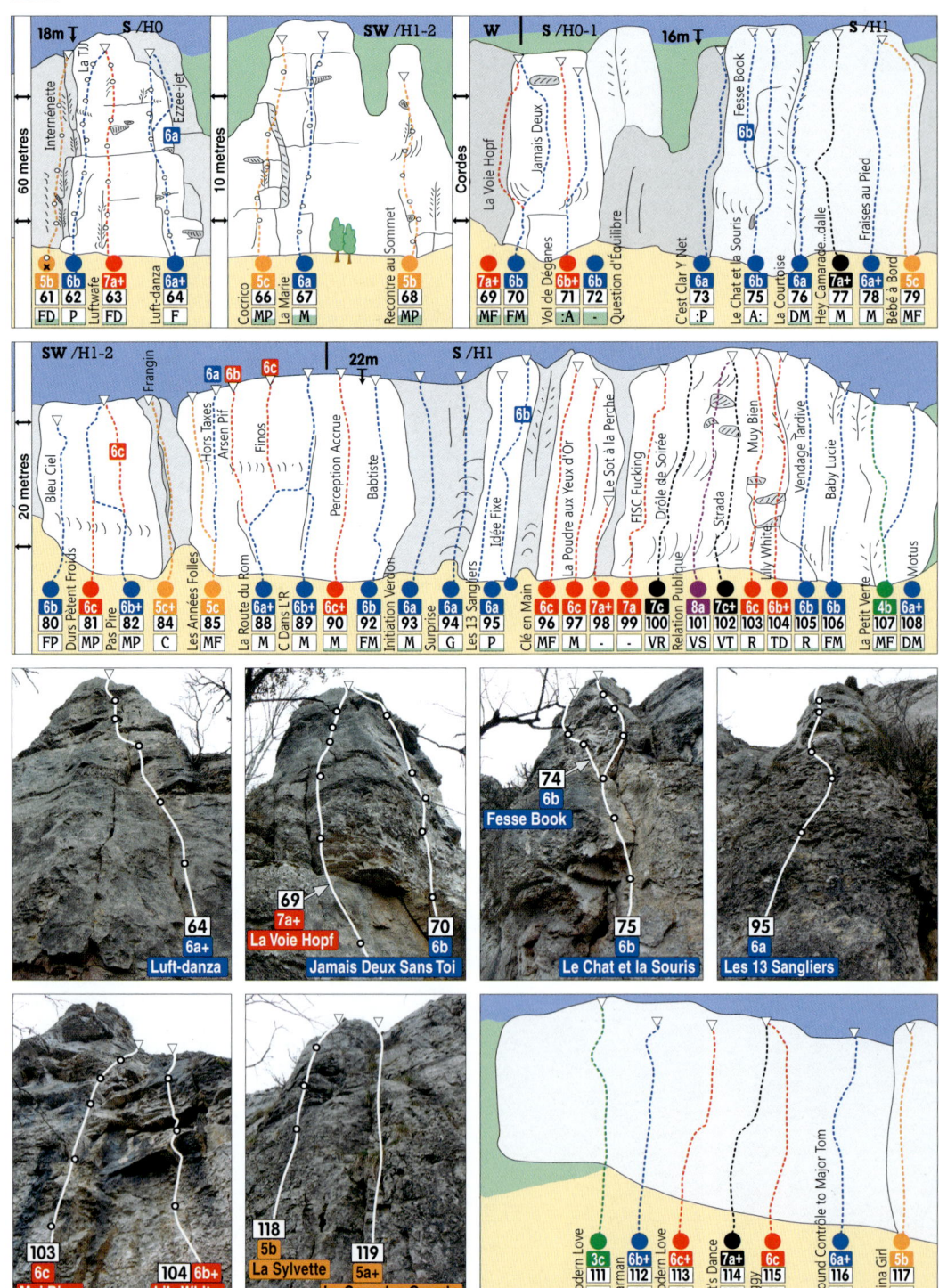

ARCENANT - D - # 157-161

P1 47.149337, 4.823695

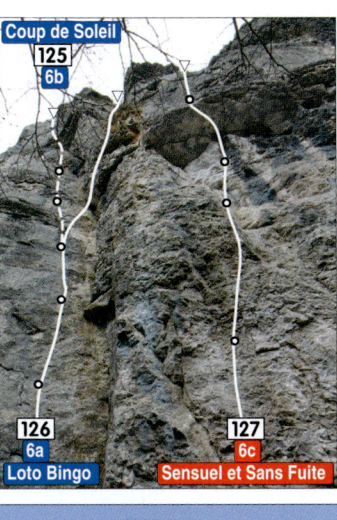

125 Coup de Soleil 6b

126	127
6a	6c
Loto Bingo	Sensuel et Sans Fuite

7c

141	142
7a+	7c
Coupe Franche	Tempête du Désert

Topo schematic (left panel, 50 metres, 16m–22m):

Route	La Sylvette	La Cour des Grands	L'Internationale	Lucky Luke	La Patte Agile	Top Model	Coups de Soleil	Loto Bingo
Grade	5b	5a+	4c+	4c	6a	6a+	6b	6a
#	118	119	120	121	123	124	125	126
	P	D	M	-	-	-	DP	DS

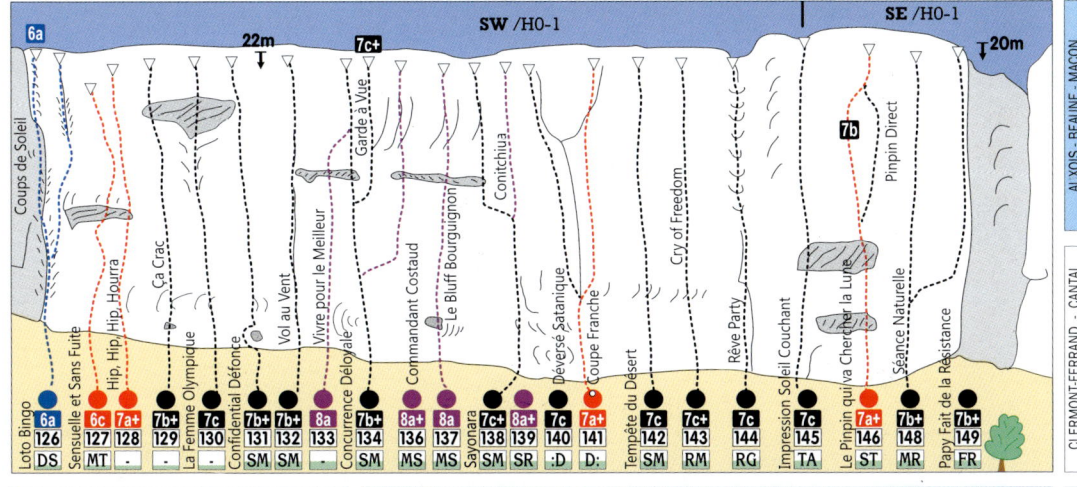

SW /H0-1 — SE /H0-1 — 22m — 7c+ — 20m — 7b — Pinpin Direct

Route	Loto Bingo	Sensuelle et Sans Fuite	Hip, Hip, Hip, Hourra	Ça Crac	La Femme Olympique	Confidentiel Défonce	Vol au Vent	Vivre pour le Meilleur	Commandant Costaud	Le Bluff Bourguignon	Garde à Vue	Concurrence Déloyale	Conitchiua	Sayonara	Déverse Satanique	Coupe Franche	Tempête du Désert	Cry of Freedom	Rêve Party	Impression Soleil Couchant	Le Pinpin qui va Chercher la Lune	Séance Naturelle	Papy Fait de la Résistance
Grade	6a	6c	7a+	7b+	7c	7b+	7b+	8a	7b+	8a+	8a		7c+	8a+	7c	7a+	7c	7c+	7c	7c	7a+	7b+	7b+
#	126	127	128	129	130	131	132	133	134	136	137	138	139	140	141	142	143	144	145	146	148	149
	DS	MT	-	-	-	SM	SM	-	SM	MS	MS	SM	SR	:D	D:		SM	RM	RG	TA	ST	MR	FR

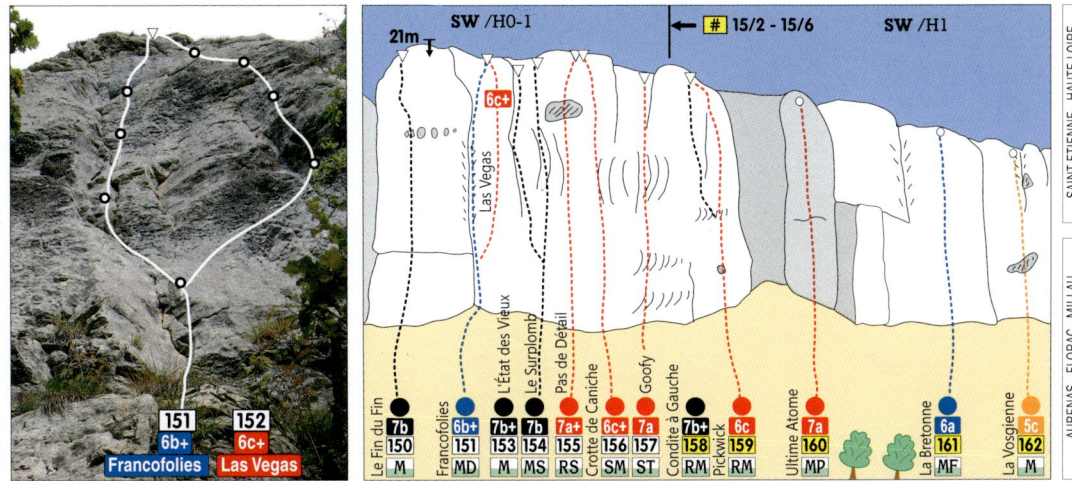

151	152
6b+	6c+
Francofolies	Las Vegas

SW /H0-1 — 21m — 6c+ Las Vegas — ← # 15/2 - 15/6 — SW /H1

Route	Le Fin du Fin	Francofolies	L'État des Vieux	Le Surplomb	Pas de Détail	Crotte de Caniche	Goofy	Condie à Gauche	Pickwick	Ultime Atome	La Bretonne	La Vosgienne
Grade	7b	6b+	7b+	7b	7a+	6c+	7a	7b+	6c	7a	6a	5c
#	150	151	153	154	155	156	157	158	159	160	161	162
	M	MD	M	MS	RS	SM	ST	RM	RM	MP	MF	M

This sector feels big - and the routes keep on going all the way to the top.

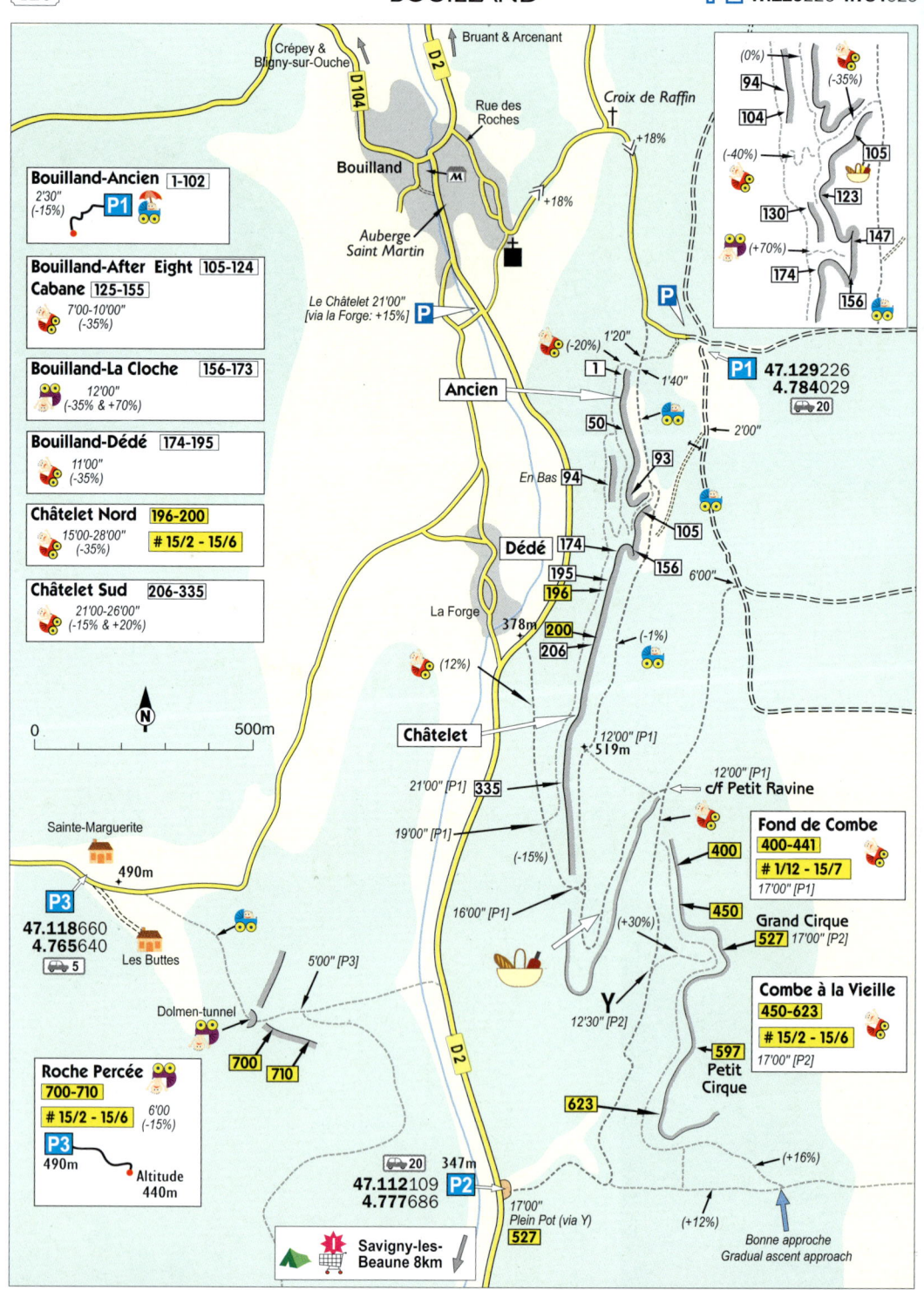

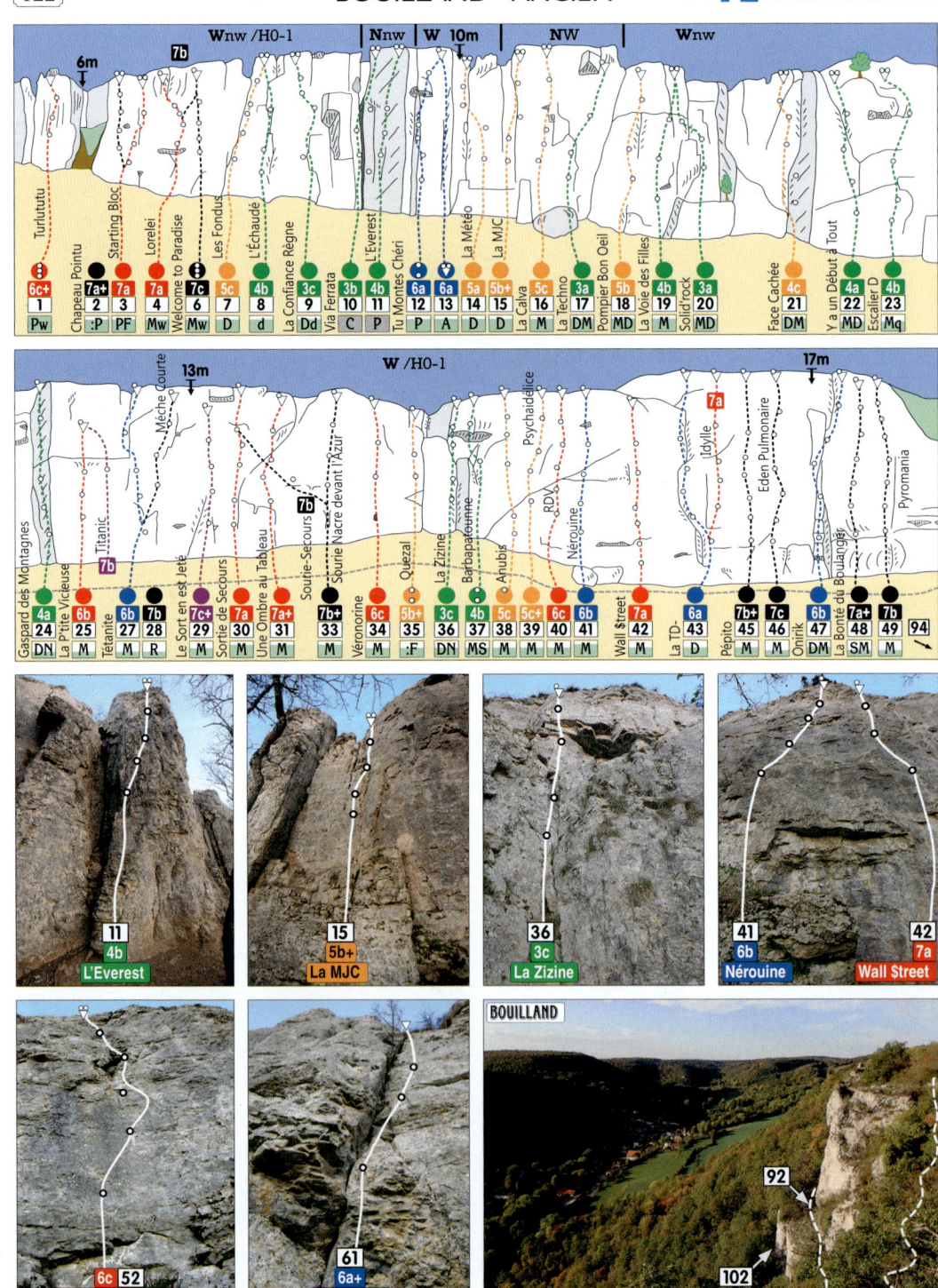

BOUILLAND - ANCIEN

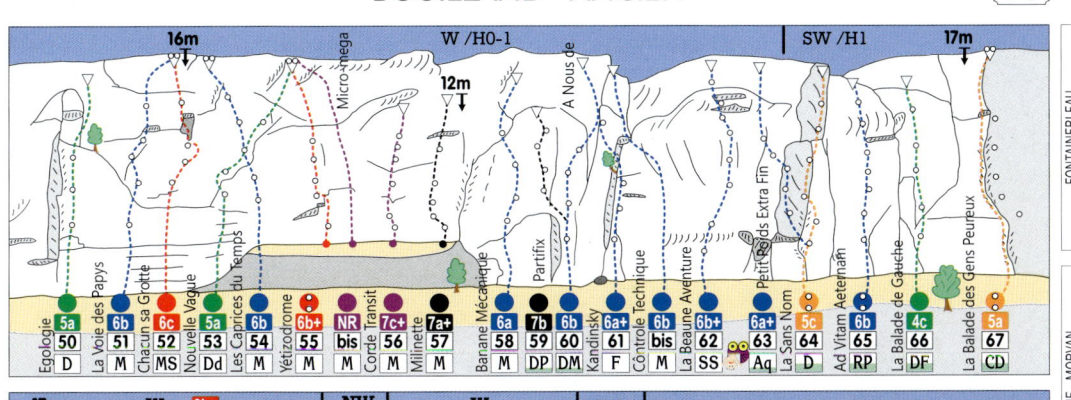

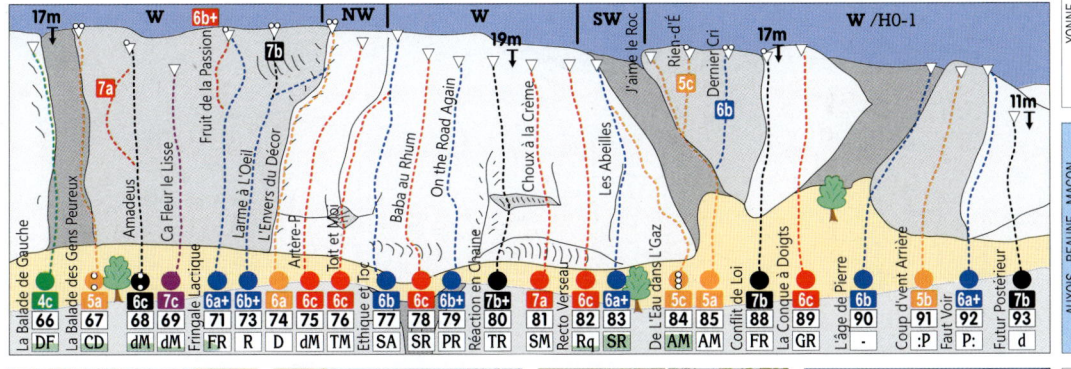

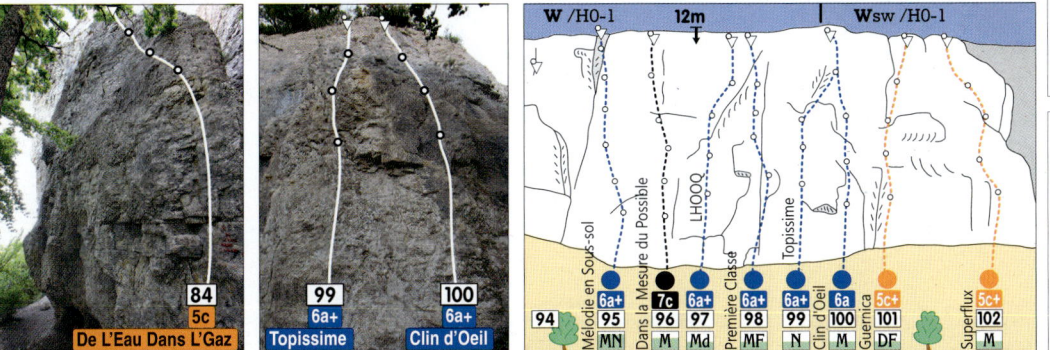

Very variable rock - some amazing... some not so amazing. Lower cliff (95-102) below the path, caution.

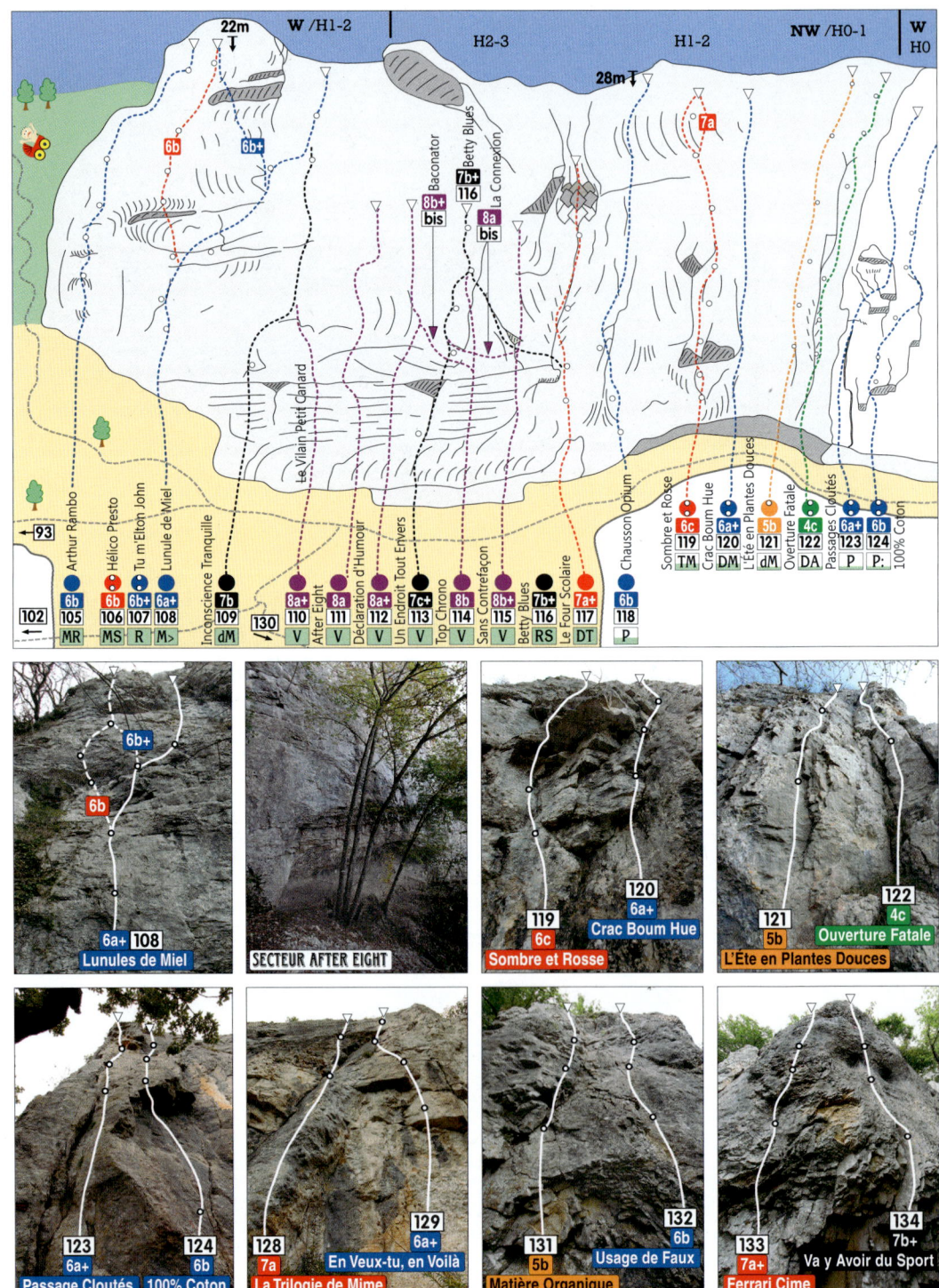

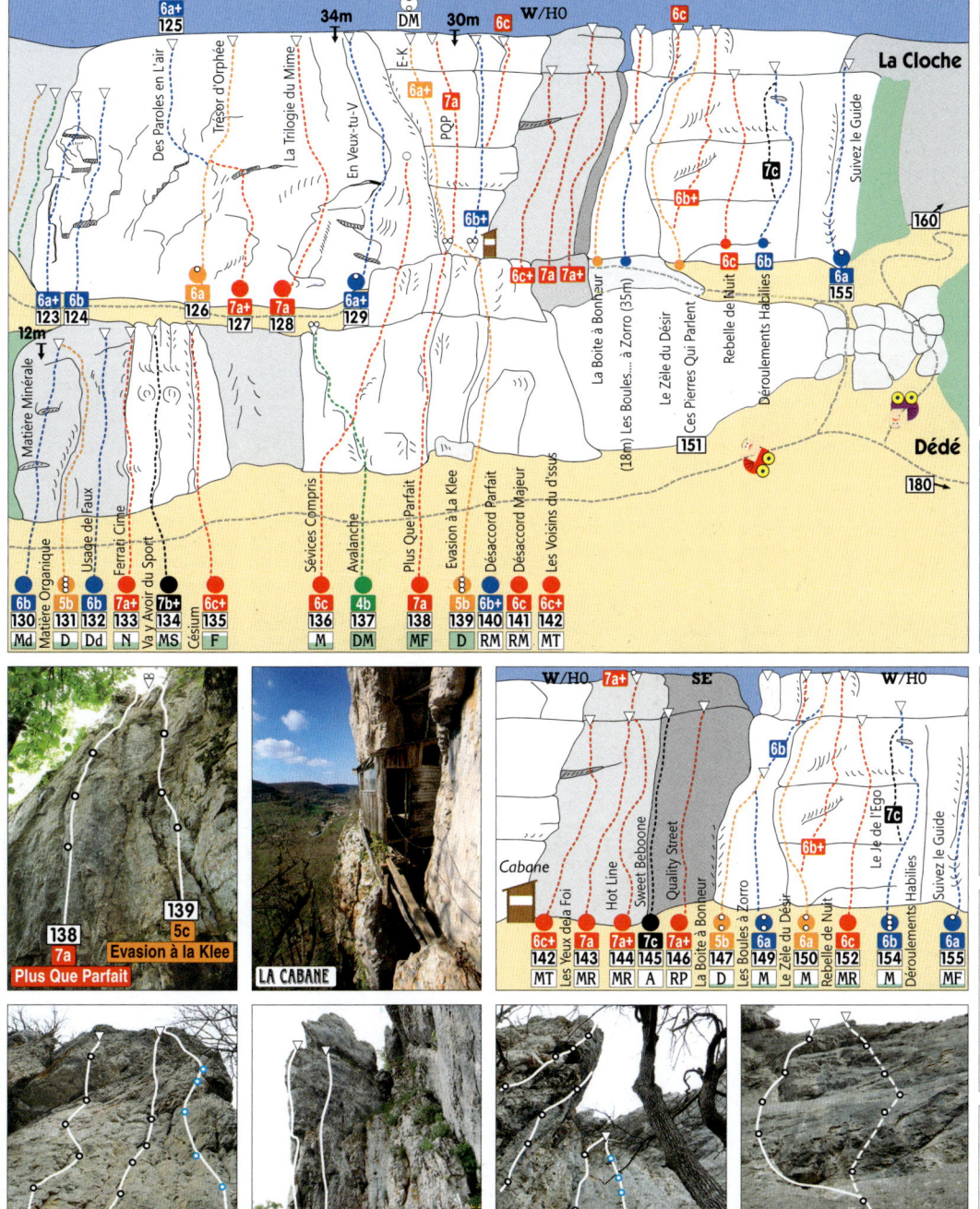

BOUILLAND - CABANE

The cabane sector feels very exposed. The routes are long - and feel very long, mostly stamina tests. Atmospheric.

BOUILLAND - CLOCHE - DÉDÉ

Shorter routes, but still offering good climbing.

Les Pets de Damoclès 6a
6a
4c
6a
4a
5c
5c
5b
6b
Classé X
7c
La Capicopf
7b
Coulis d'Automate
Tombé du Ciel 7c
Majuscule 5c
Minuscule 6a+
Ambre Libertine 7b
7b+
7b+
Pacific Highway 8a
Minimal Impact 8a
Songe et Mensonge 7c
8a
8a
7c
7c
Pacific Highway 7b+
7a+
6b+

6eme degré de Latitude 6c
3 Heures Cool 7a+
Solarium 7a
6b+
Aquarelle 7a

Au Fil du Temps 6b+
Au Fil du Temps 6a

3 Heures Cool 7b
Solarium 7a+

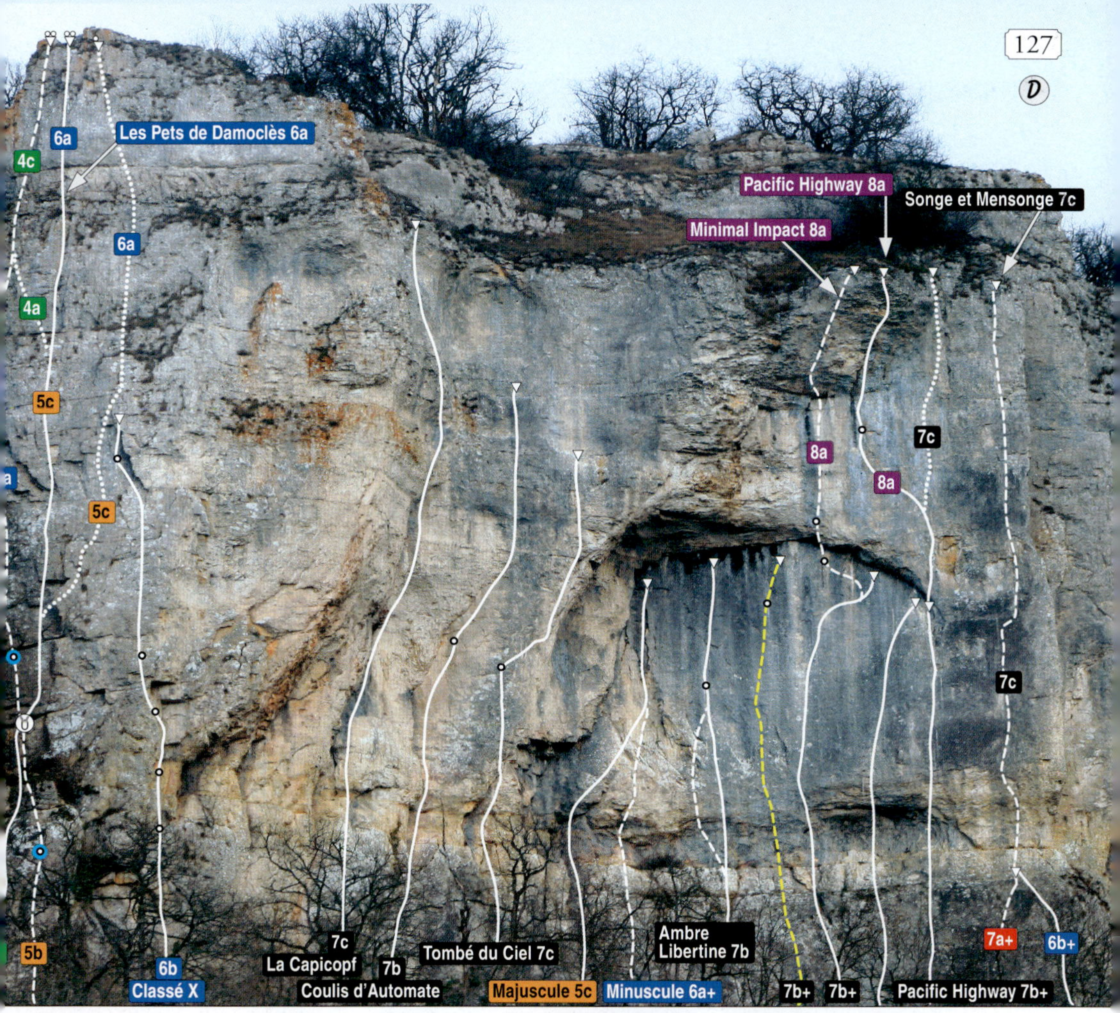

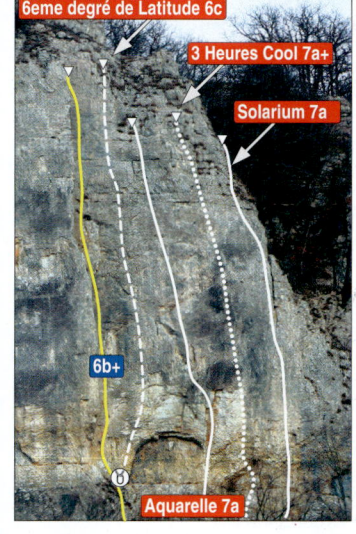

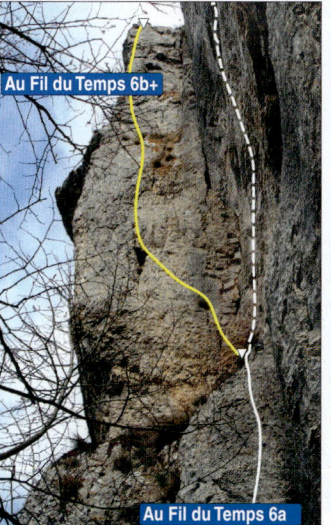

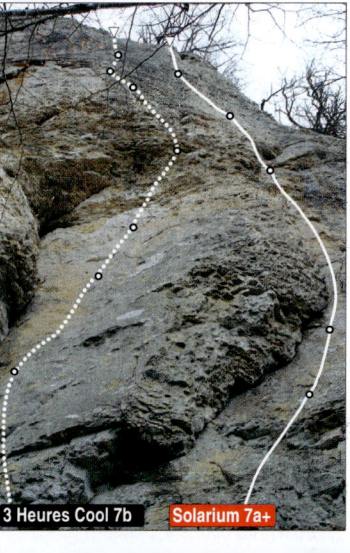

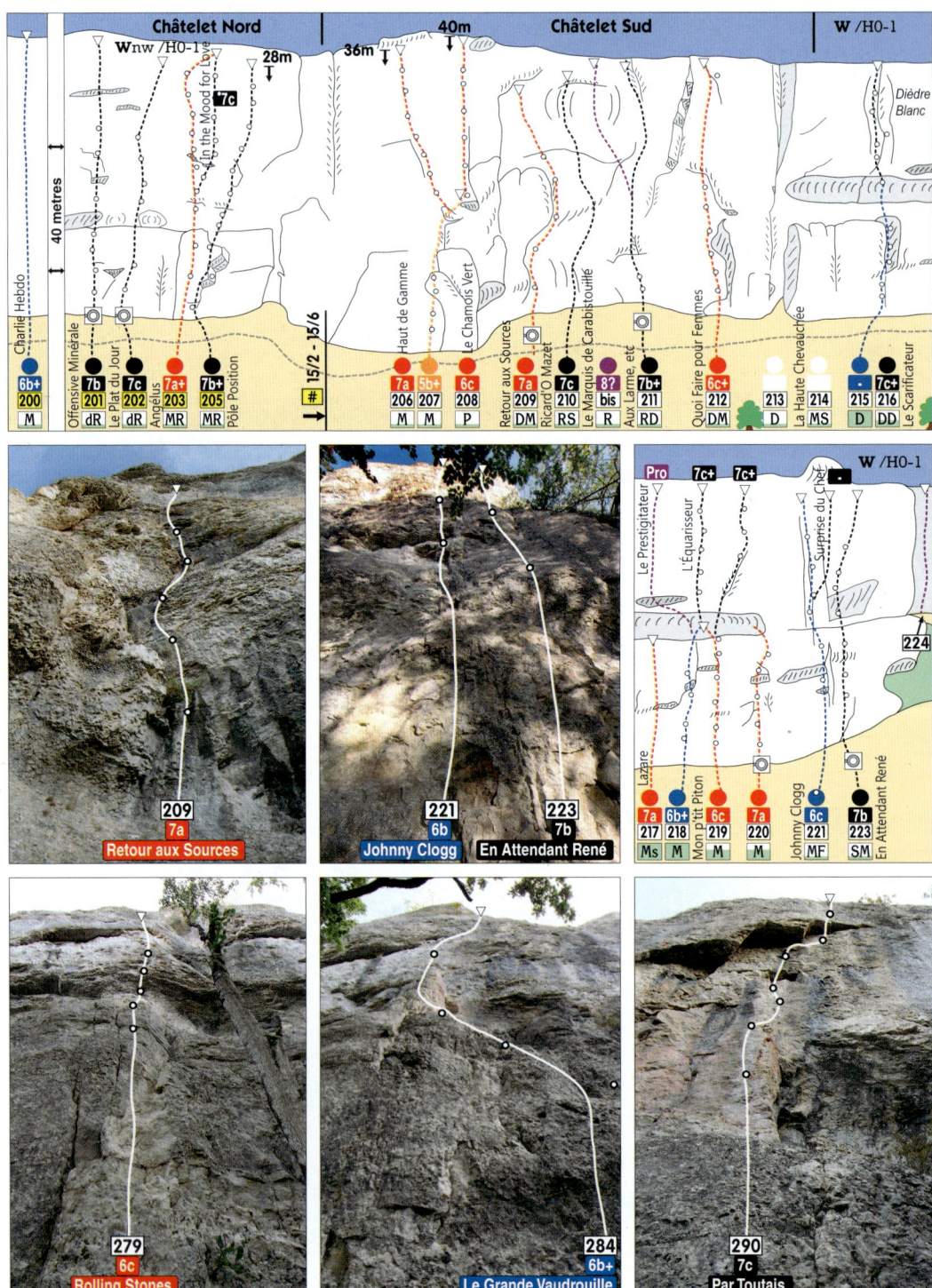

LE CHATELET SUD (La Terrasse)

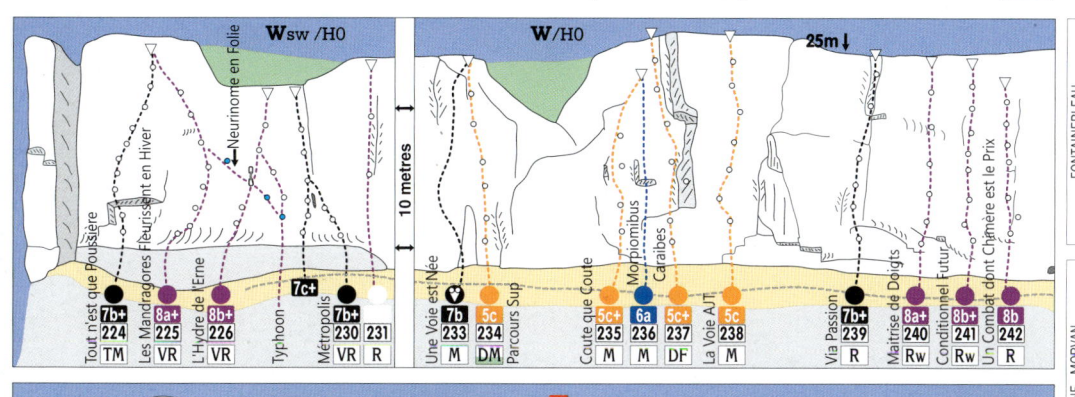
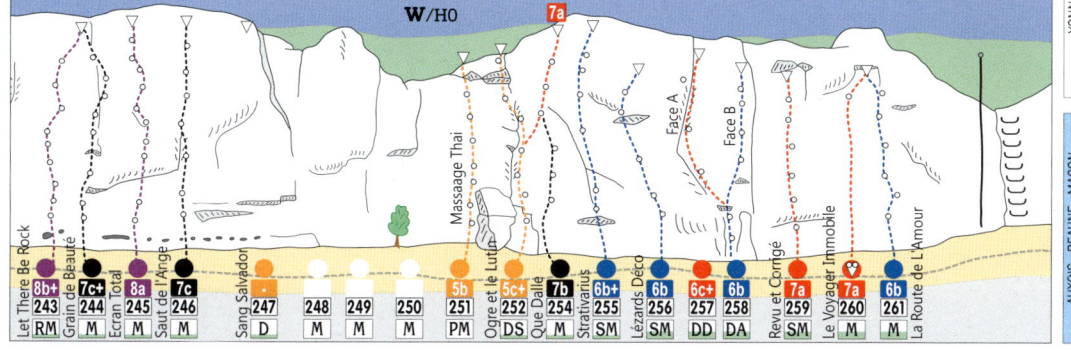
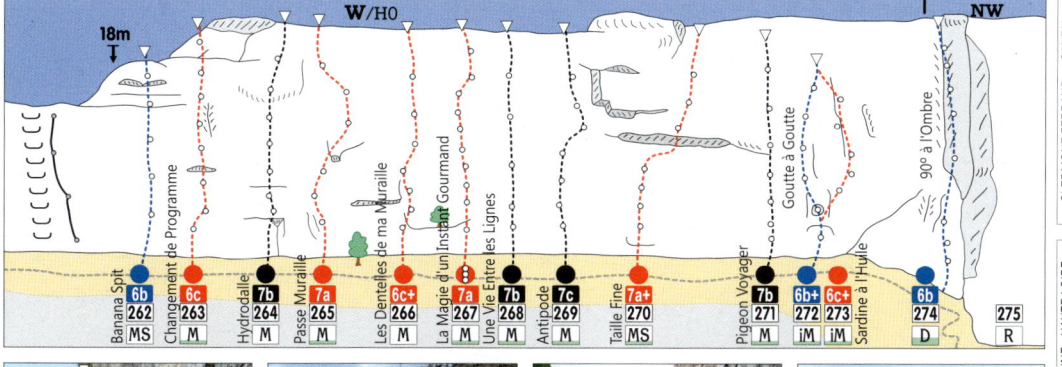

Central section of le Châtelet is situated on a small grassy terrace, gets plenty of belay sunshine; mostly flat technical walls.

LE CHATELET SUD (Grand Surplombs)

Parking page 120

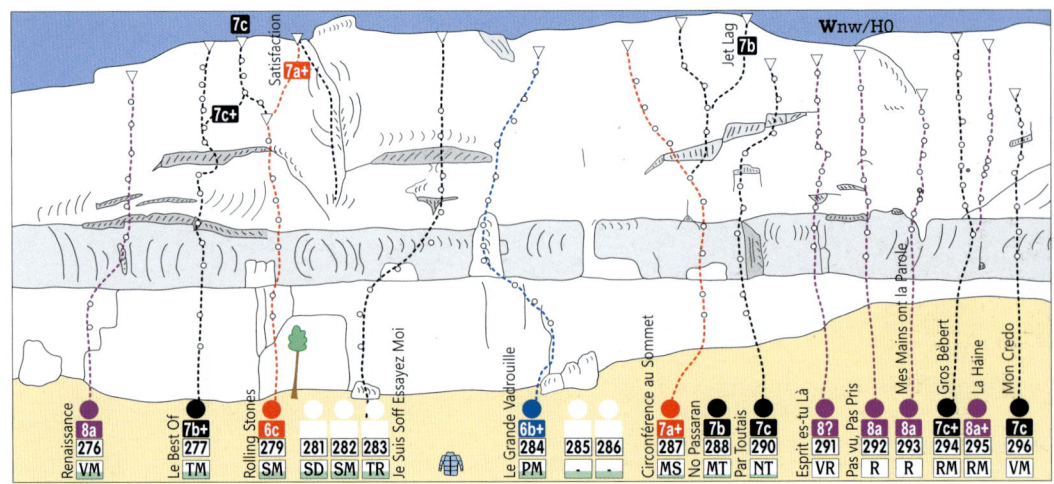

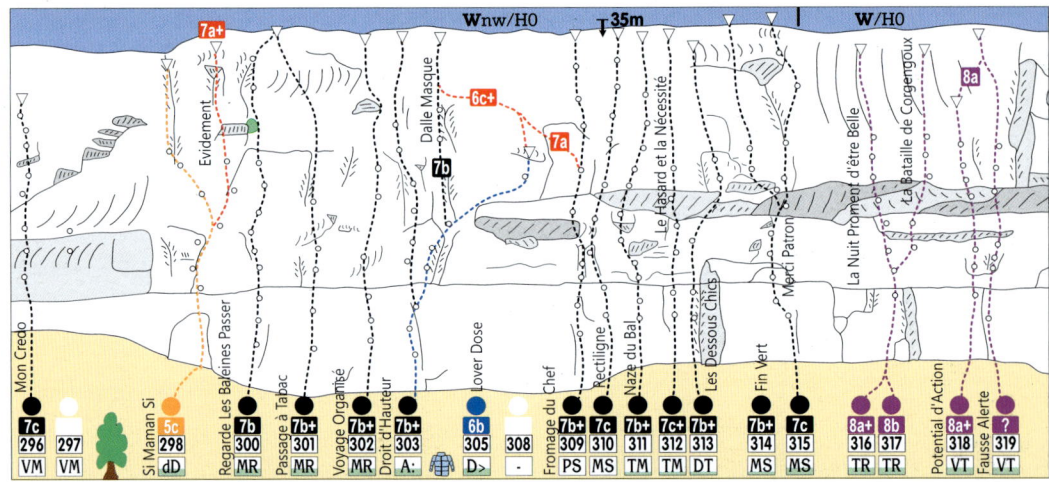

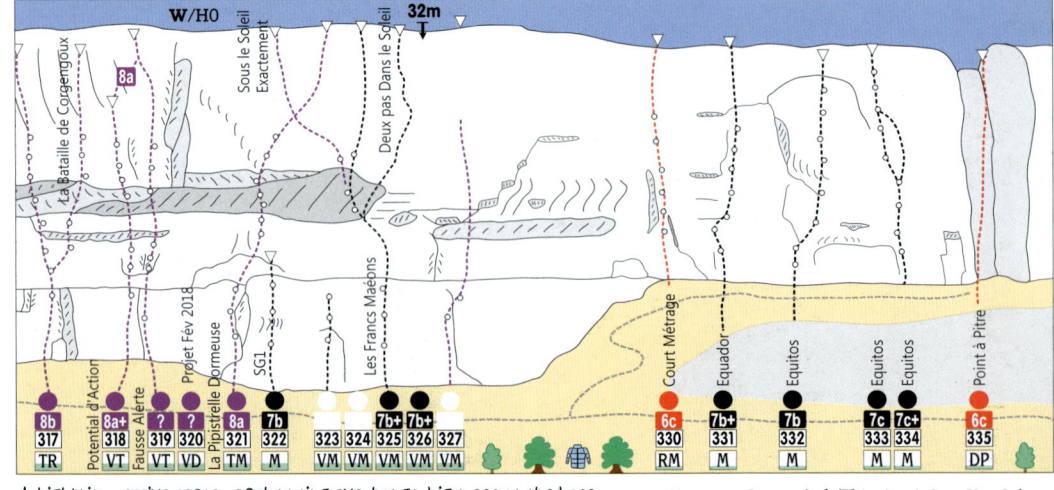

A highly impressive sector of daunting overhangs, big trees at the base.

Voyage Organisé 7b+ *(302), Jean-Yves Salin*

FOND DE COMBE — 1/12–15/7 # 400–441

Parking page 120

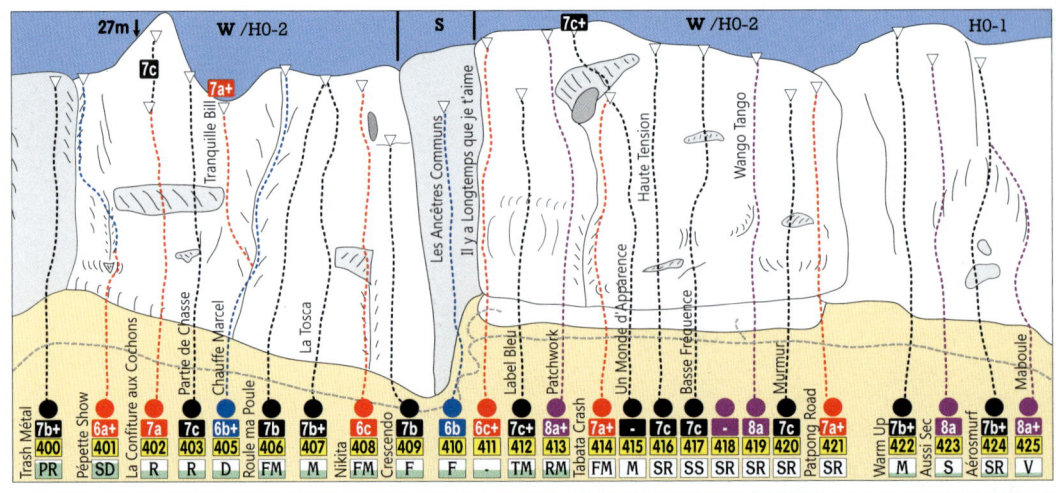

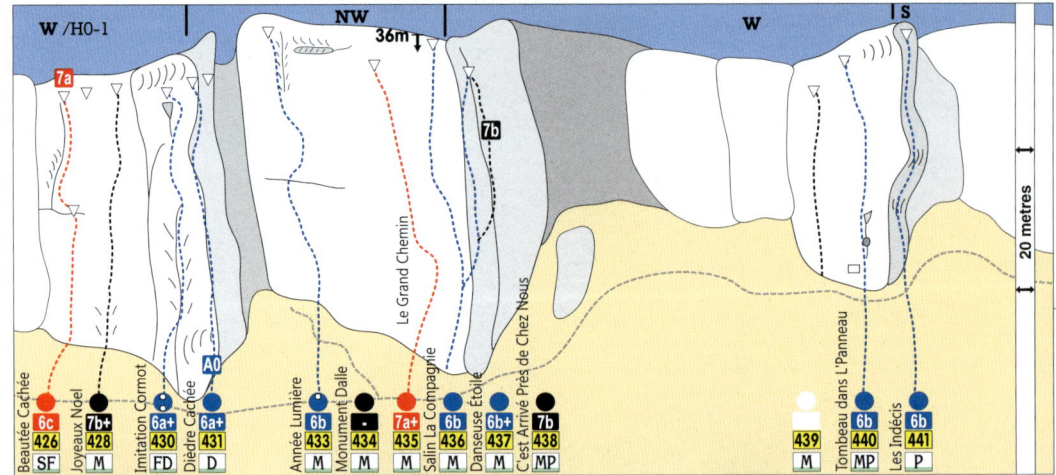

408 — 6c — Nikita

423 — 8a — Aussi Sec   424 — 7b+ — Aerosmurf

430 — 6a+ — Imitation Cormot

The quietest cliff of the Combe, but with some of the best rock.

The Wall 8c+ (518), Brendan Pacquentin ▷

COMBE A LA VIEILLE - 15/2-15/6 # 450-580

Parking page 120

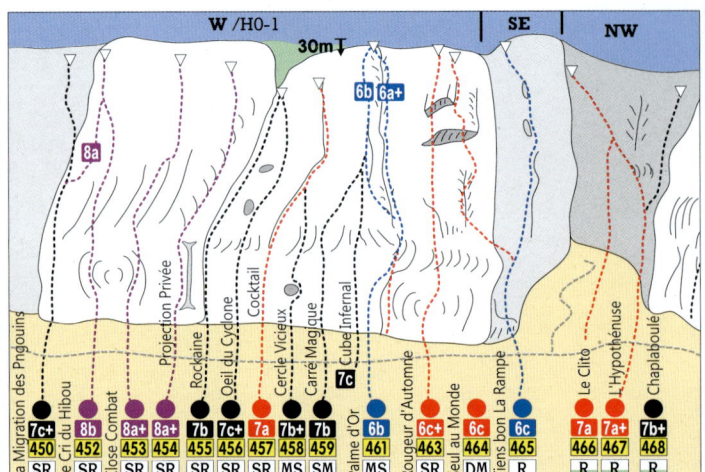

	452	453
	Le Cri de Hibou 8b	Close Combat 8a+

Topo W /H0-1:

Route	La Migration des Pingouins	Le Cri du Hibou	Close Combat		Rockaine	Oeil du Cyclone	Cocktail	Cercle Vicieux	Carré Magique	Cube Infernal	Palme d'Or	Rougeur d'Automne	Seul au Monde	Tiens bon La Rampe		Le Clito	L'Hypothénuse	Chaplaboulé
Grade	7c+	8b	8a+	8a+	7b	7c+	7a	7b+	7b	6b	6c+	6c	6c	7c	7a	7a+	7b+
#	450	452	453	454	455	456	457	458	459	461	463	464	465		466	467	468
	SR	SR	SR	SR	SR	SR	MS	SM	MS	SR	DM	R			R	R	R

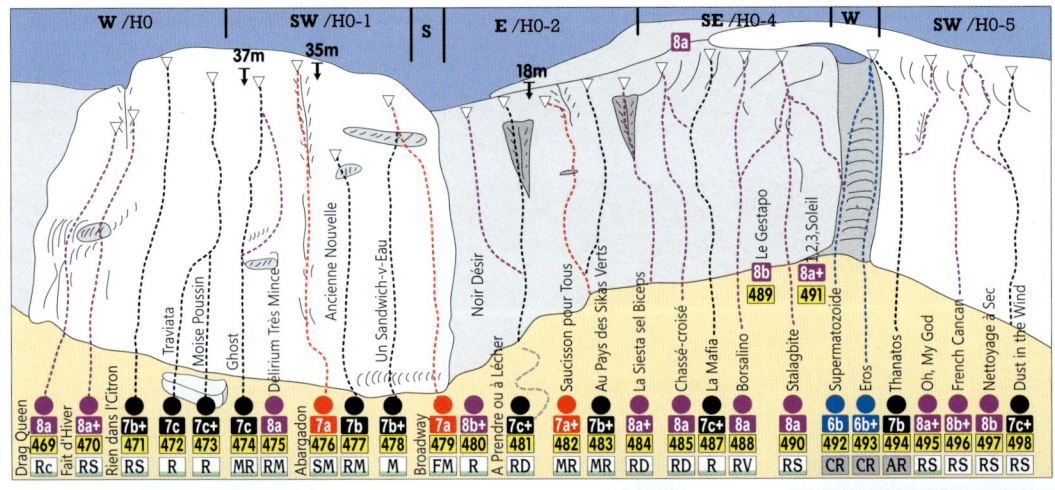

Topos W/H0, SW/H0-1, S, E/H0-2, SE/H0-4, W, SW/H0-5:

Route	Drag Queen	Fait d'Hiver	Rien dans l'Citron	Traviata	Moïse Poussin	Ghost	Délirium Très Mince	Ancienne Nouvelle	Un Sandwich-v-Eau	Noir Désir	Broadway	A Prendre ou à Lécher	Saucisson pour Tous	Au Pays des Sikas Verts	La Siesta sel Biceps	Chassé-croisé	La Mafia	Borsalino	Le Gestapo	Stalagbite	Supermatozoïde	Eros	Thanatos	Oh, My God	French Cancan	Nettoyage à Sec	Dust in the Wind
Grade	8a	8a+	7b+	7c	7c+	7c	7c+	7b+	7b+	7a	7b	8b+	7c+	7a+	7b+	8a	7c+	8a	8a	8b	8a+	6b	6b+	7b	8a	8b+	8b	7c+
#	469	470	471	472	473	474	475		476	477	478	479	480	481	482	483	484	485	487	488	489	491	490	492	493	494	495	496	497	498
	Rc	RS	RS	R	R	MR	RM	SM	RM	M	FM	R	RD	MR	MR	RD	R	RV	RS	CR	CR	AR	RS	RS	RS	RS

6c	464	465
	Seul au Monde	Tiens Bon La Rampe 6c

474	476
Ghost 7c	Abargadon 7a

491 — 8a+
489 — La Gestapo 8b

488	490
Borsalino 8a+	Stalagbite 8a

The quietest cliff of the Combe,

COMBE A LA VIEILLE - 15/2-15/6 # 442-580

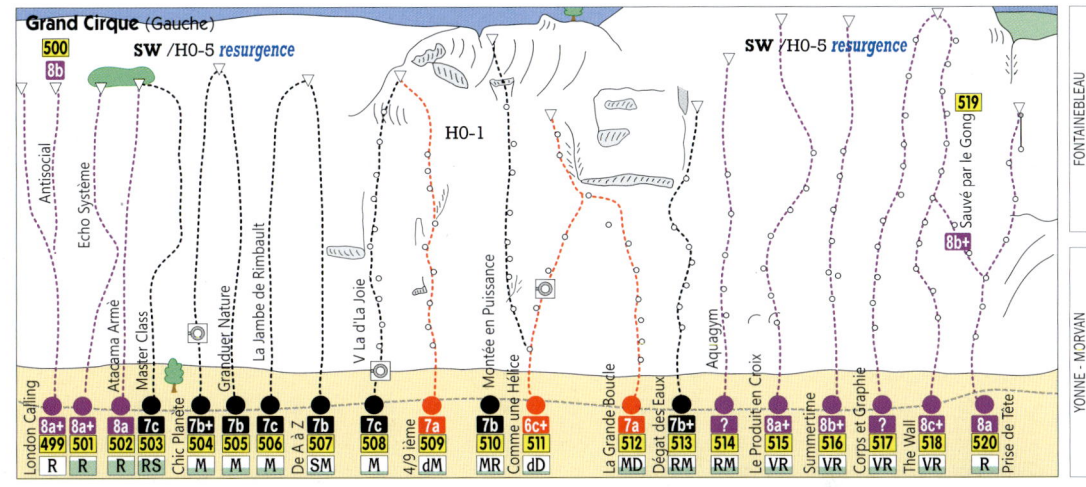

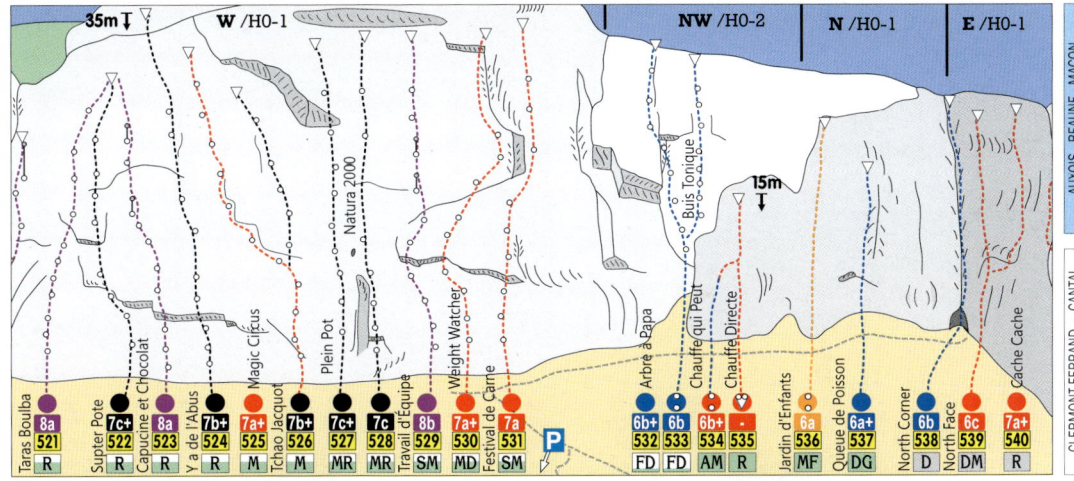

The quietest cliff of the Combe,

COMBE A LA VIEILLE - 15/2-15/6 # 450-623

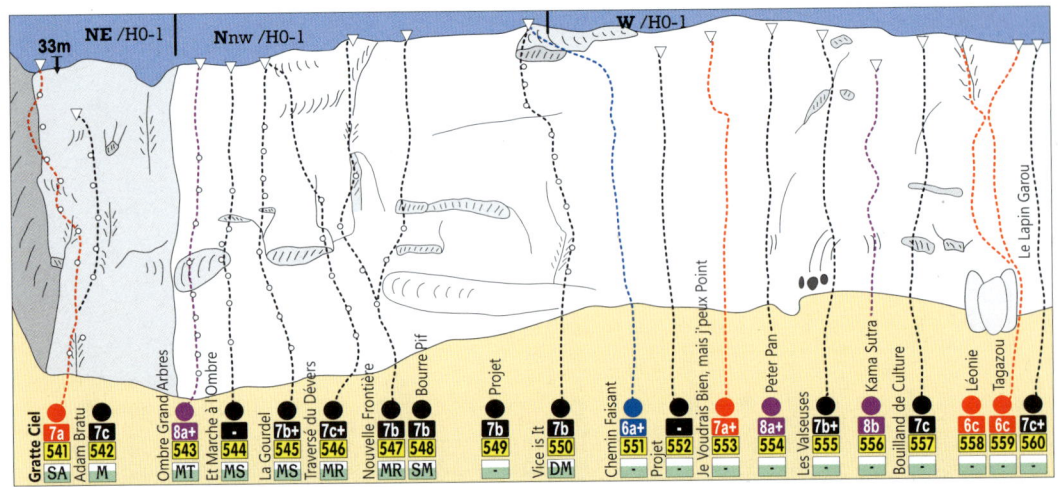
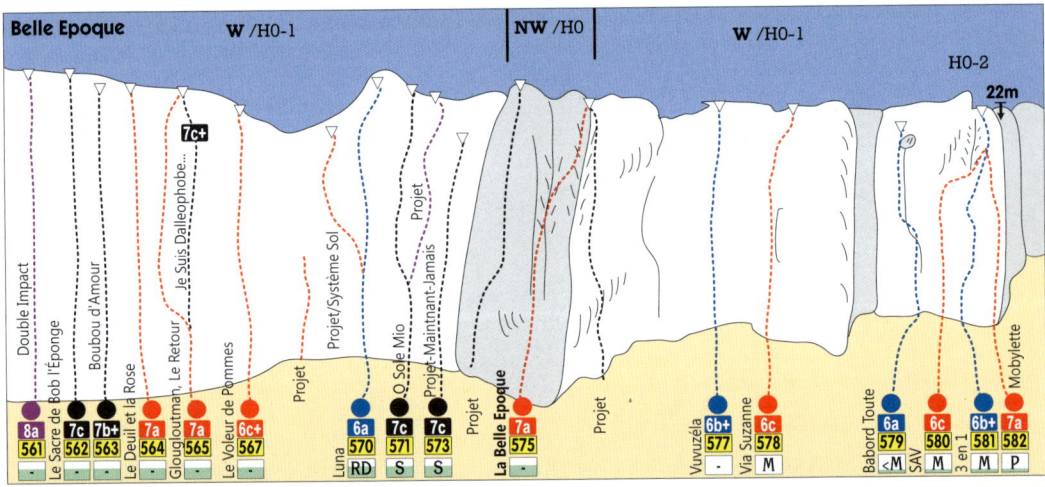
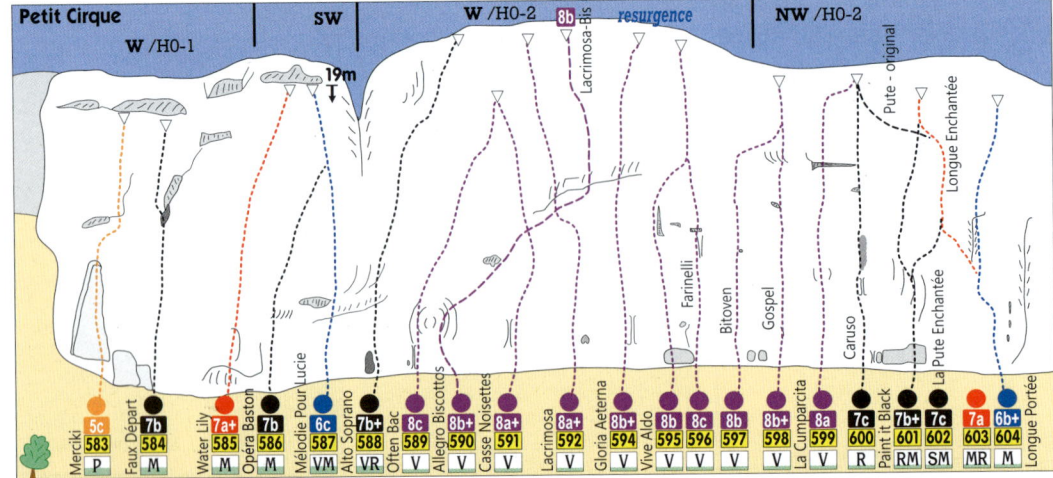

Petit Cirque, as in the name - not so large, but routes are not so easy either. Impressive big blank walls everywhere here.

COMBE A LA VIEILLE & ROCHE PERCEE — 15/2-15/6 #700-710

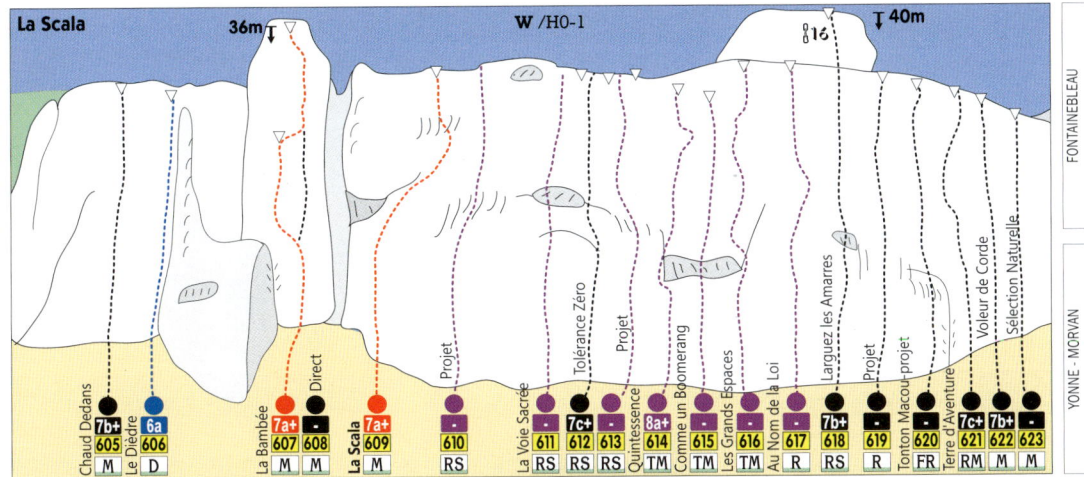

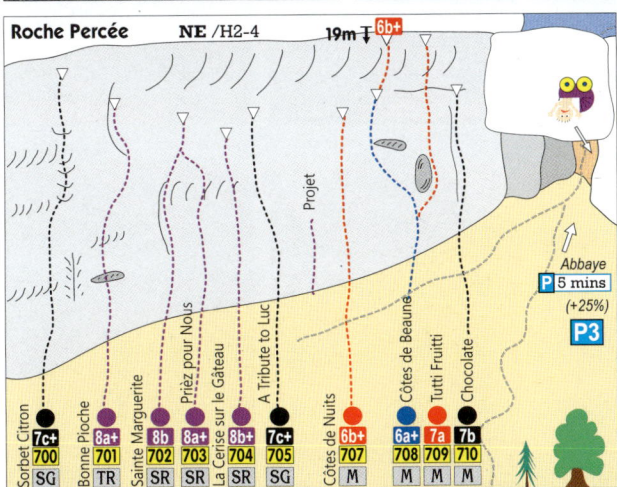

Roche Percée: Calcaire** A very cool and quiet spot, ideal for the very hottest of days.

MELIN

46.982314, 4.712233

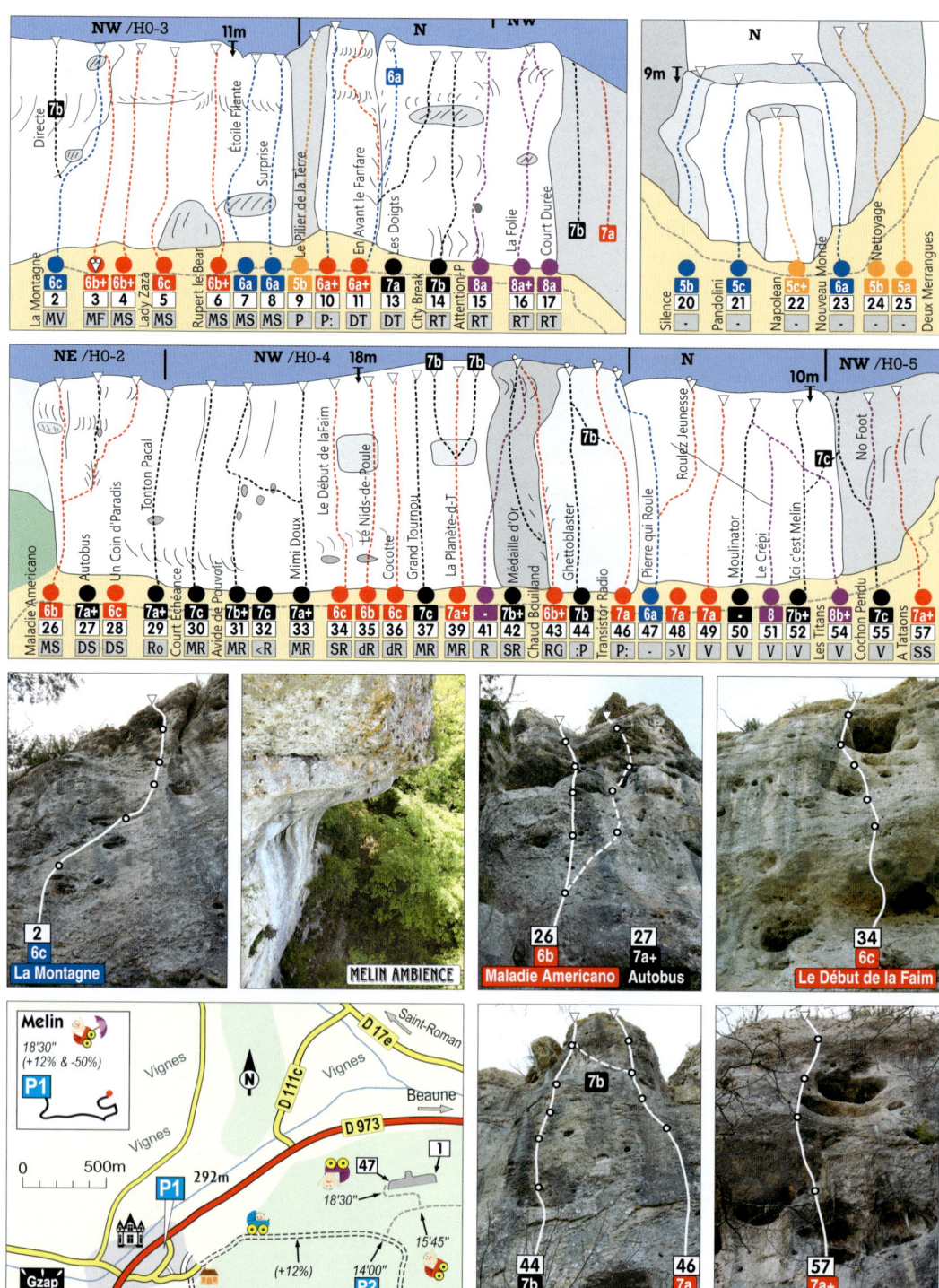

Much steeper than it looks - eek; easy routes are... "not so easy." Too overhanging for easy top roping. Ideal on very hot days.

PAS DE SAINT MARTIN — 15/2-15/6

P3 47.054130, 4.755222 — 139

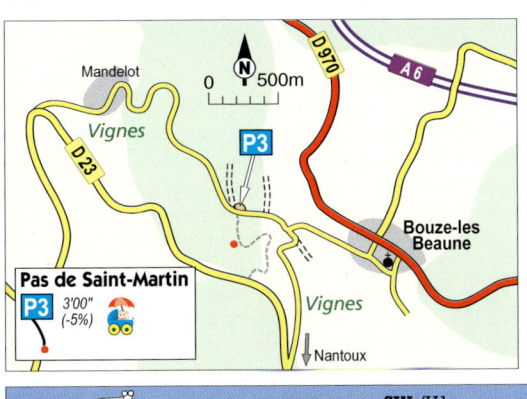
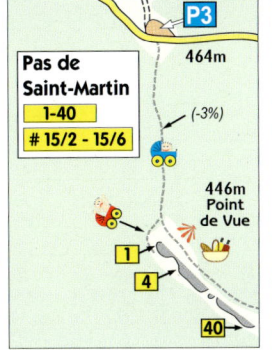
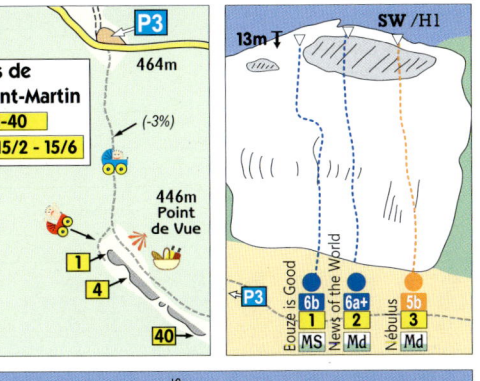
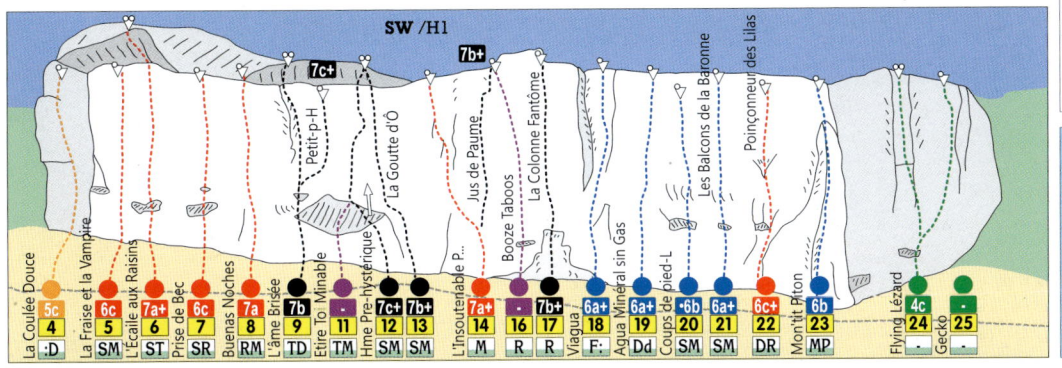
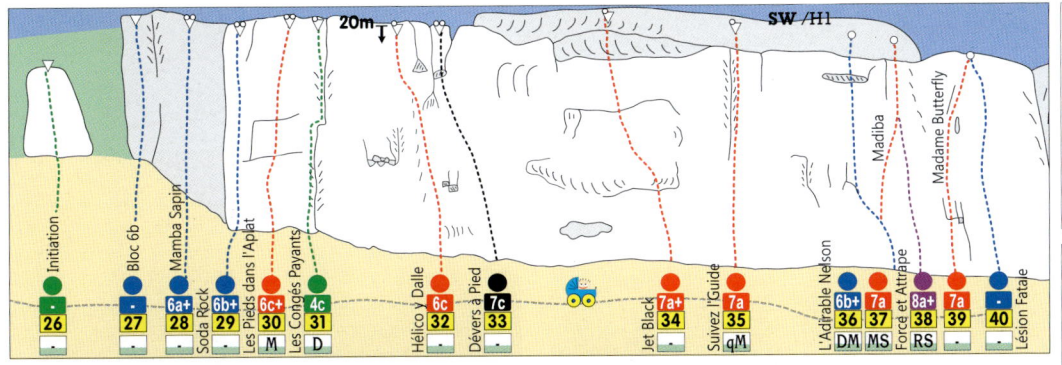

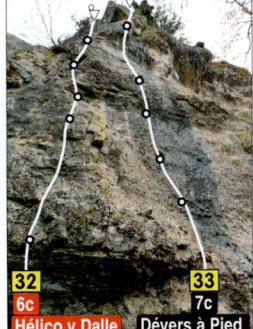

Calcaire-Grés** A warm spot catching the sun. Something on offer for most levels.

BOUT du MONDE - #1-11 1/12 → 15/07 .... #12-68 15/2 → 15/06

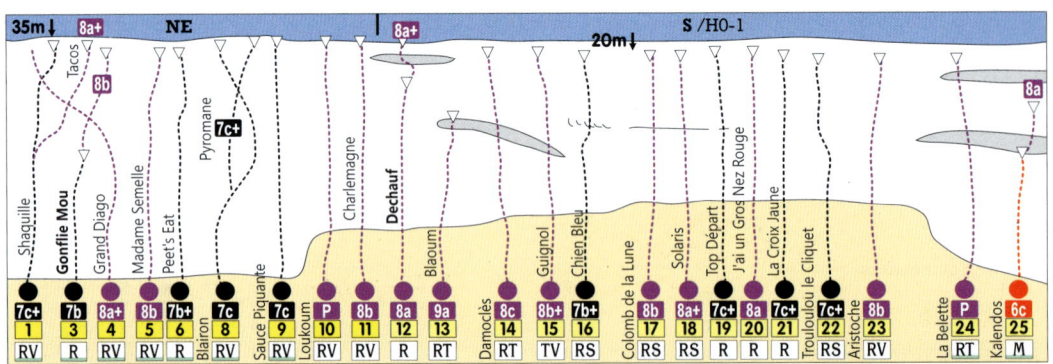
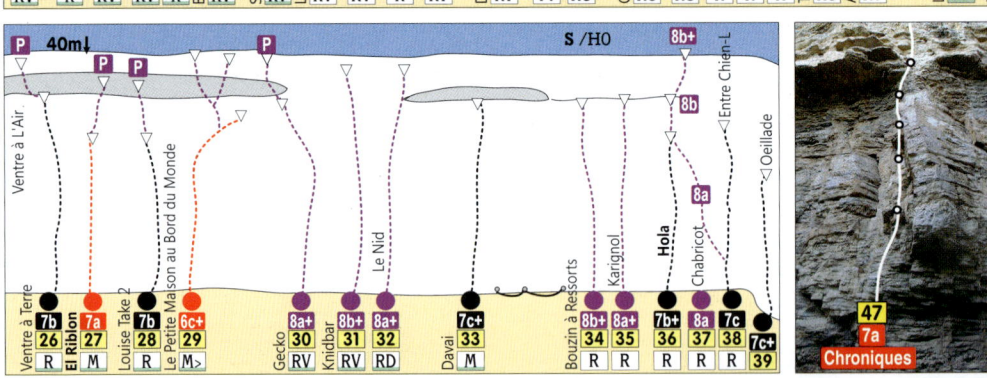

Calcaire* Quite poor rock, so holds can fall off and grades change. Combination of bloc moves, and huge stamina routes.

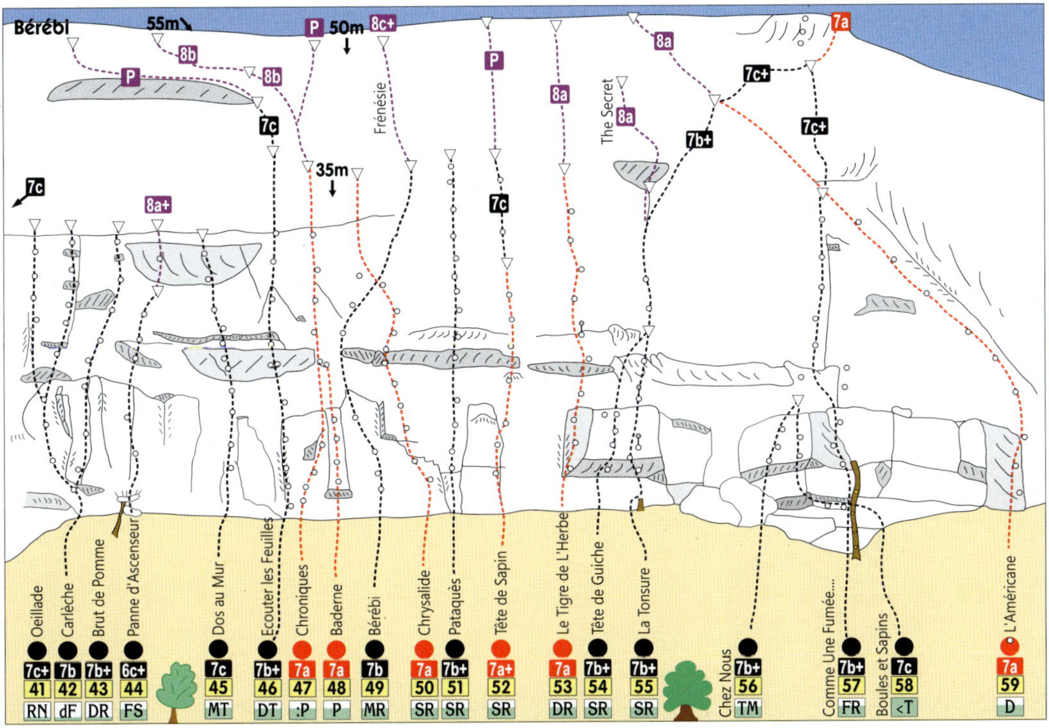

BOUT du MONDE

P1 46.983286, 4.644159 — 141

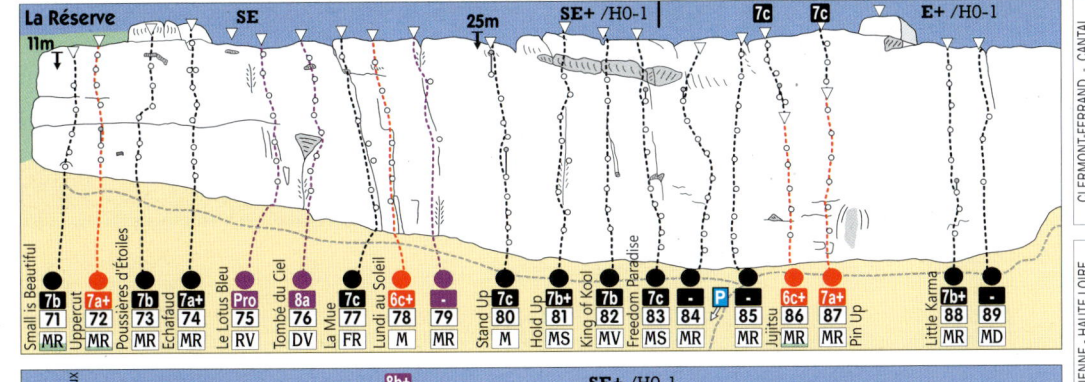

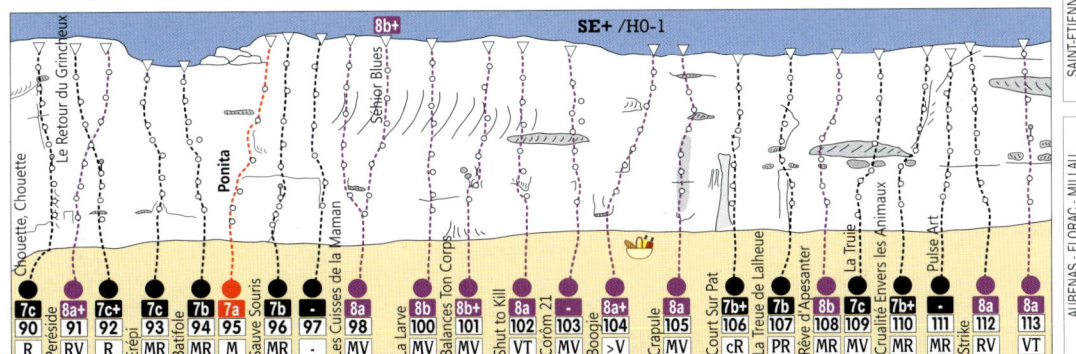

The reserve can be a lovely winter suntrap - forget in summer. Nice mixture of technical Crimps - and steep power.

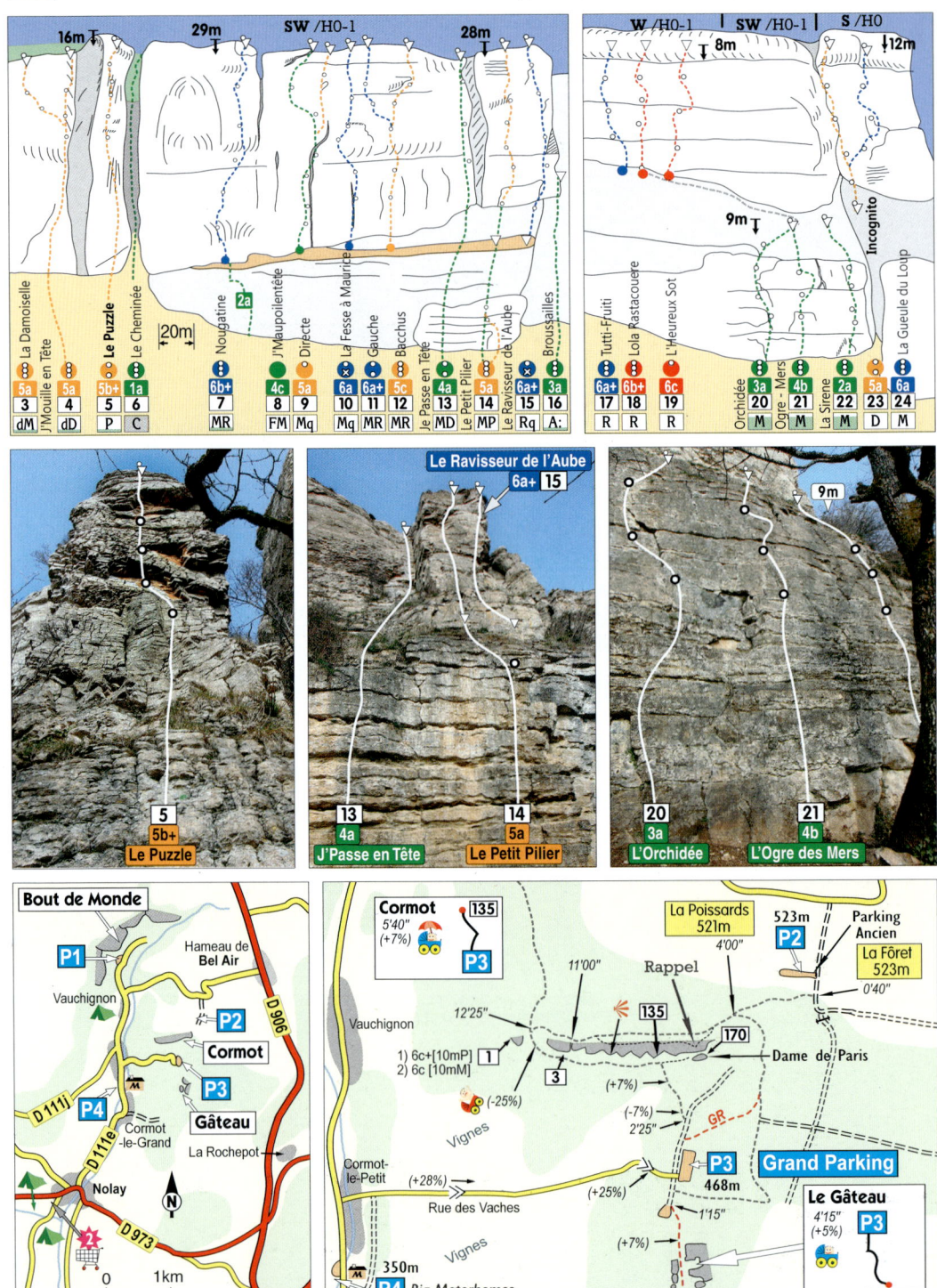

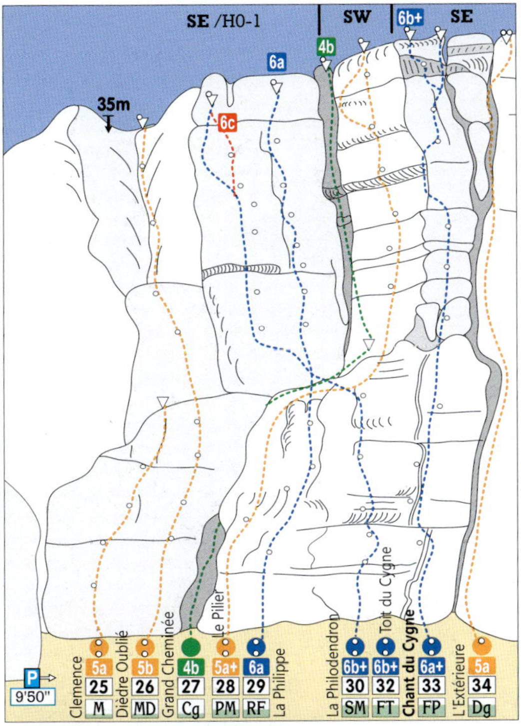

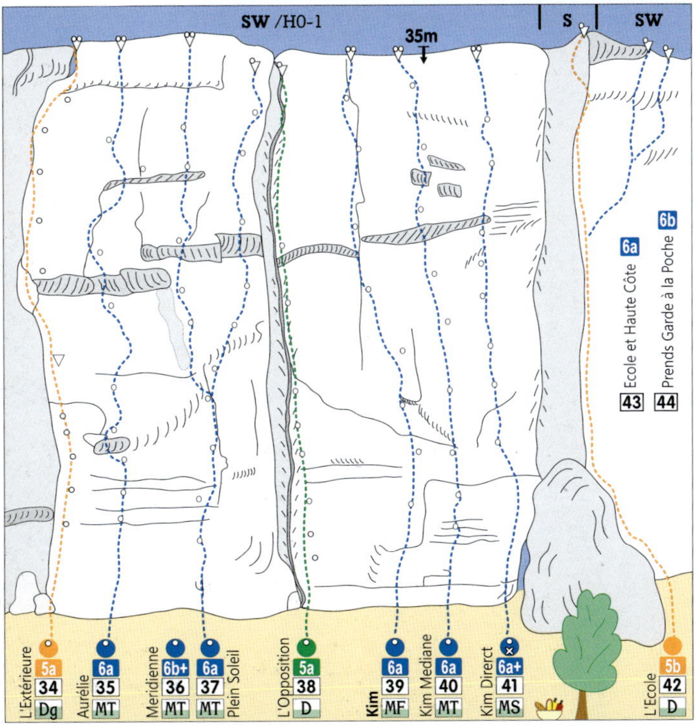

P3 46.968391, 4.653719 CORMOT -AA- (Chant du Cygne-Kim) 143

#	Name	Grade	Code
25	Clemence	5a	M
26	Dièdre Oublié	5b	MD
27	Grand Cheminée	4b	Cg
28	Le Pilier	5a+	PM
29	La Philippe	6a	RF
30	La Philodendron	6b+	SM
32	Toit du Cygne	6b+	FT
33	Chant du Cygne	6a+	FP
34	L'Extérieure	5a	Dg
39	Kim	6a	
40	Kim Médiane	6a	
41	Kim Direct	6a+	
27		4b	
28	Le Pilier	5a+	
29	La Phillipe	6a	
34	Extérieure	5a	
34	L'Extérieure	5a	Dg
35	Aurélie	6a	MT
36	Meridienne	6b+	MT
37	Plein Soleil	6a	MT
38	L'Opposition	5a	D
39	Kim	6a	MF
40	Kim Médiane	6a	MT
41	Kim Direct	6a+	MS
42	L'Ecole	5b	D
43	Ecole et Haute Côte	6a	
44	Prends Garde à la Poche	6b	

This large bay of Kim has a big shady tree at the base, ideal picnic venue for groups. Usually very busy on popular days.

CORMOT -B- (Arc en Ciel-Wally)

A truly superb bay with some classic routes. Most climbers flash Arc-en-Ciel,...most climbers don't flash La Wally !

CORMOT -BB- (Aquallum-Grenouille-President)

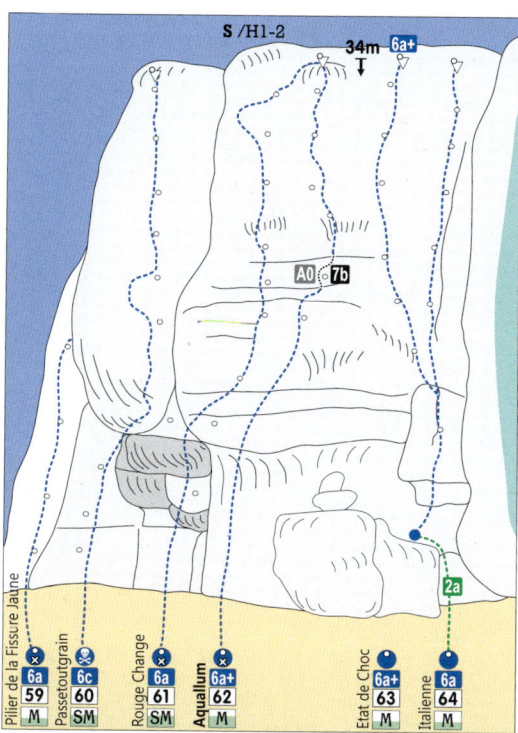

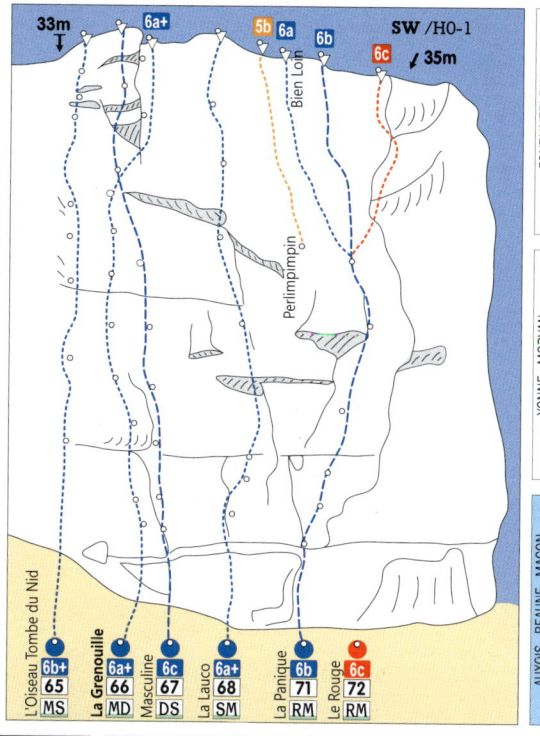

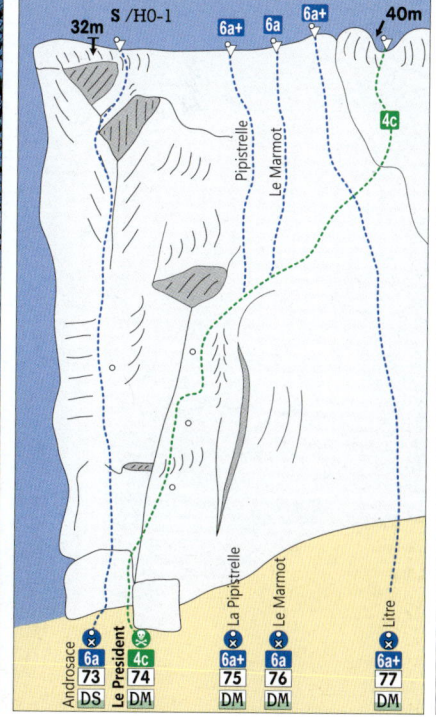

These bays give very nice climbing, but the equipping has been historically awful.

CORMOT -C- (Faille Pourrie-Dièdre Laurent)

Florence, a popular area with long routes... that feel very long, best visit in a quiet time. Very sunny ambience in the afternoon.

CORMOT -CC- (Toit-Bobi-Carmen Cru)

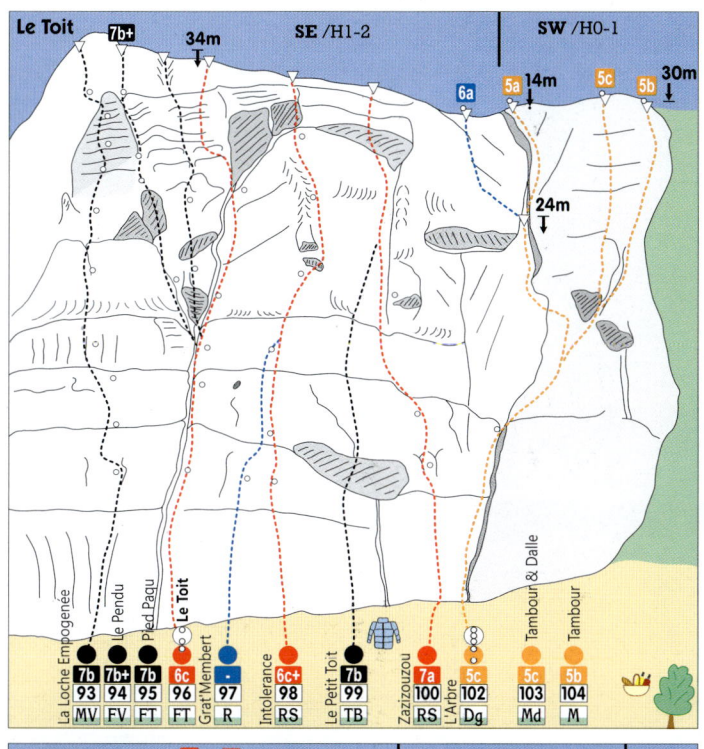

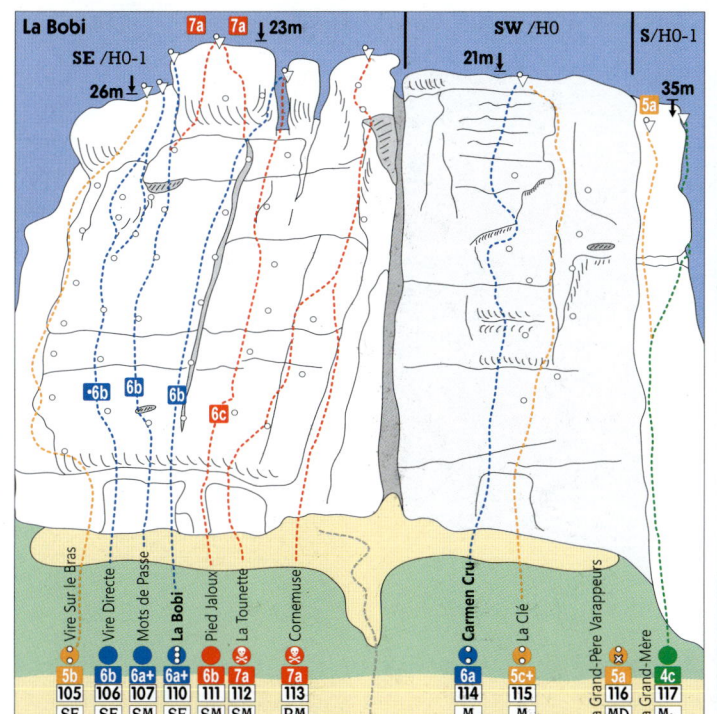

Toit, awesome and overhanging, sustained, chilly on a cold day; Bobi-bakes(cooks) in the morning sun, routes have no warm up.

148 CORMOT -D- (Facteur-Batier-Patrick)

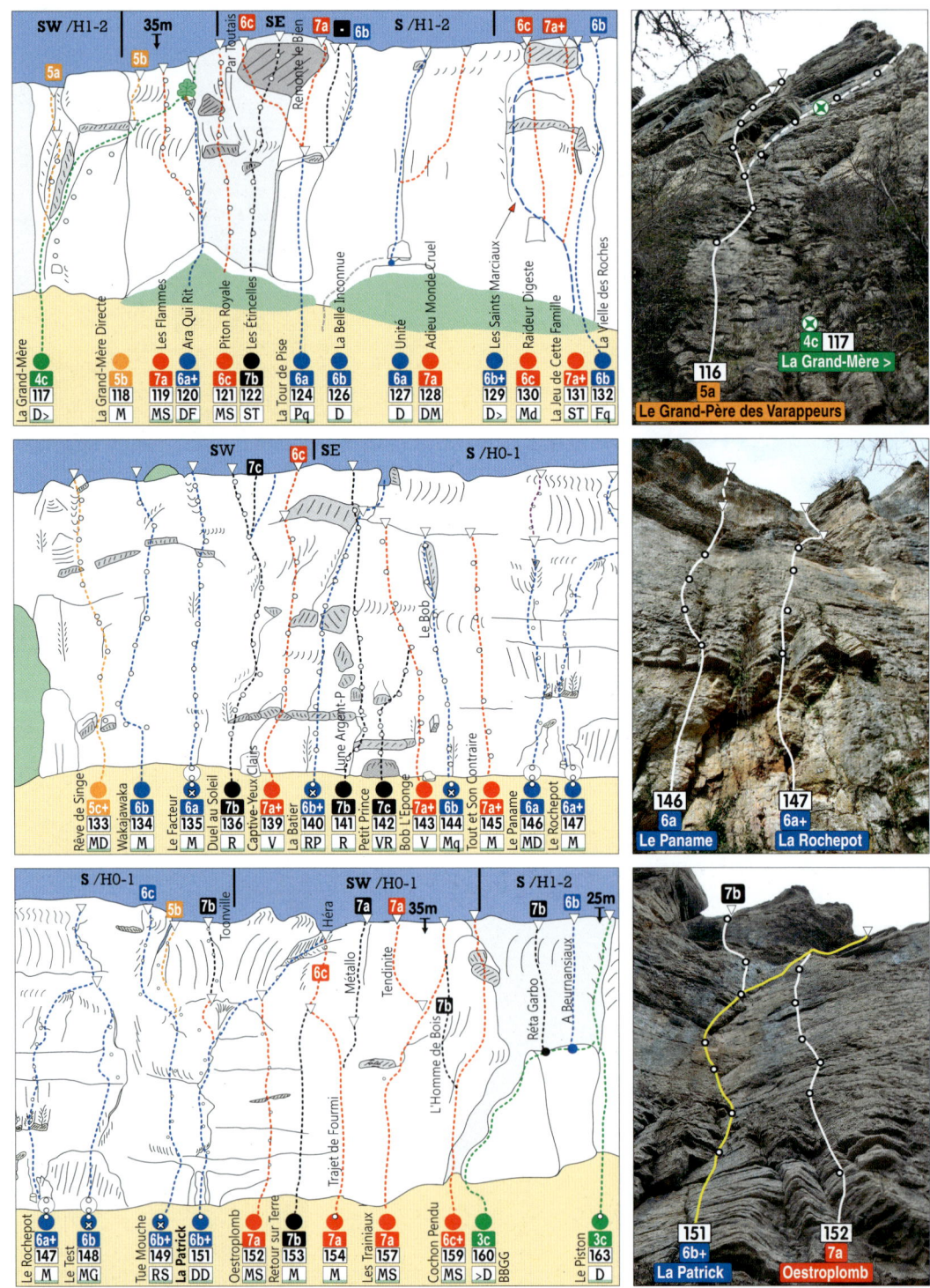

Some big sectors that you first arrive at from P1. Intimidating - be scared !!! Some of the rock here is not good at all !!!

CORMOT -DD- (Gilbert du Moi-Dame de Paris)

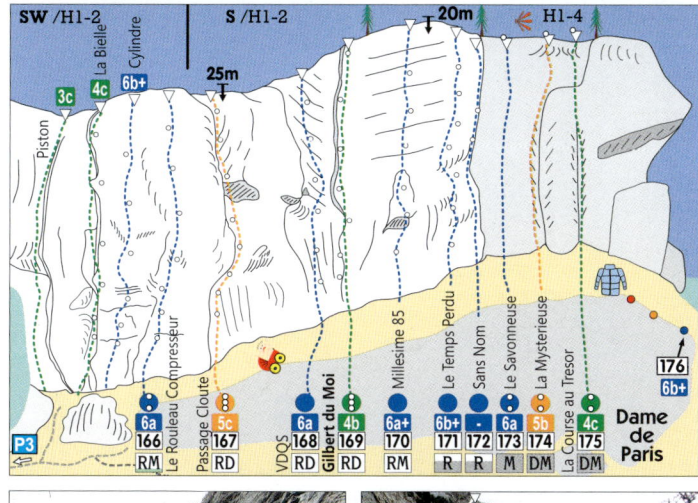
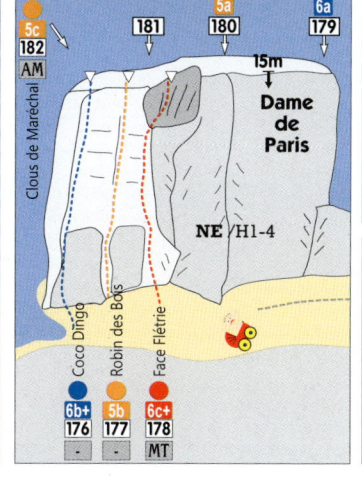

Going to the far end rewards you with a chilly passage and some short routes in the shade, great on hot days. Parking P2 abesil

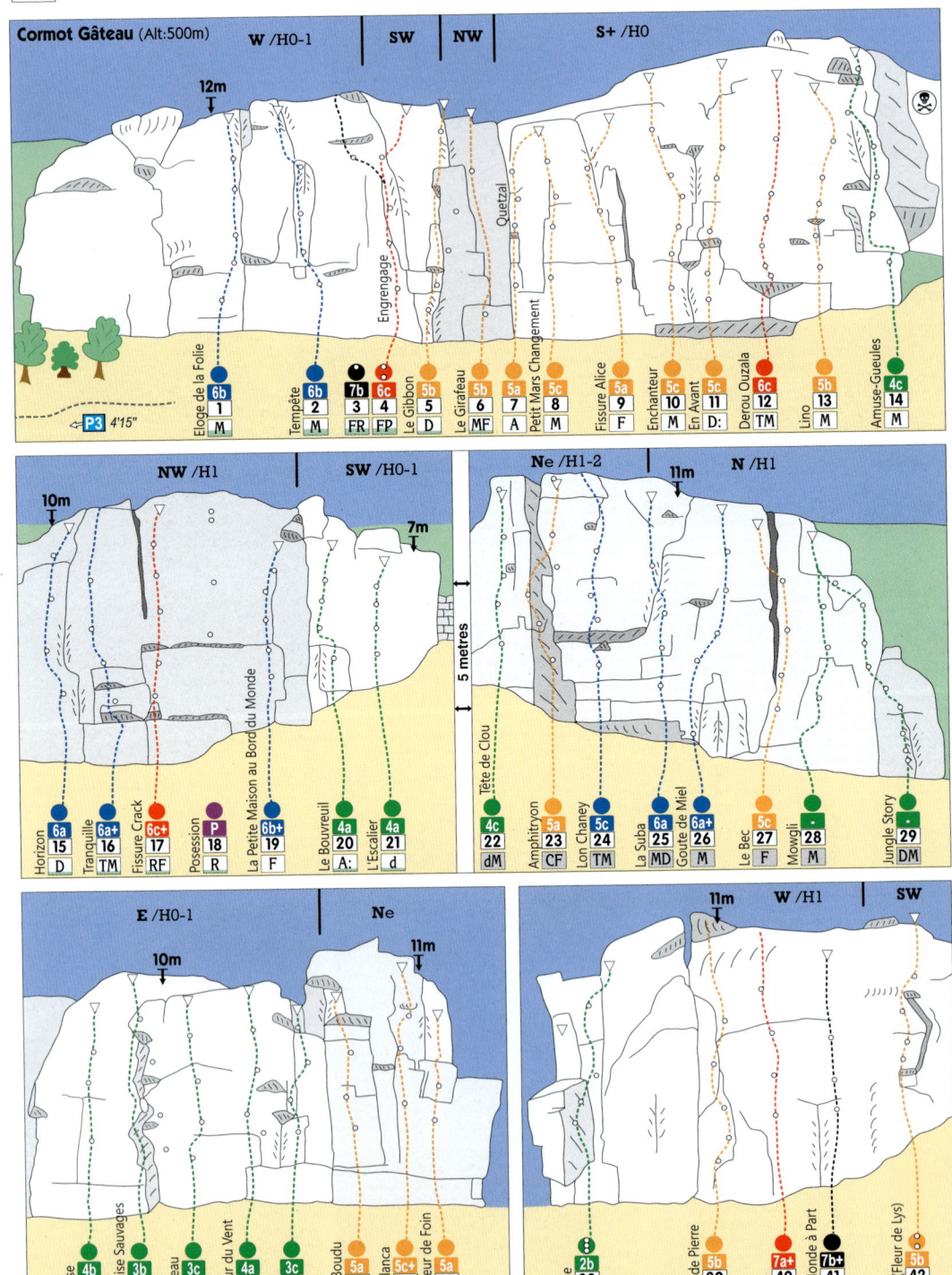

LE GATEAU (Cormot)

P3 46.968391, 4.653719 — 151

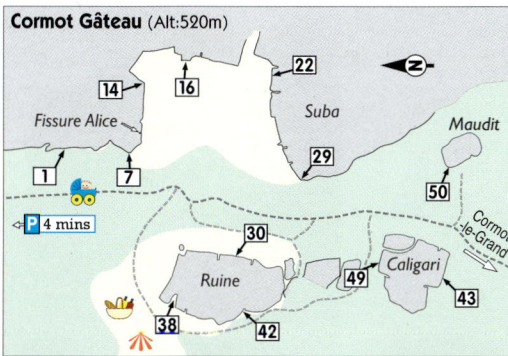

2 — 6b — Têmptete

9 — 5a — Fissure Alice

15 — 6a — Horizon / 16 — 6a+ — Tranquille

26 — 6a+ — Goute de Miel

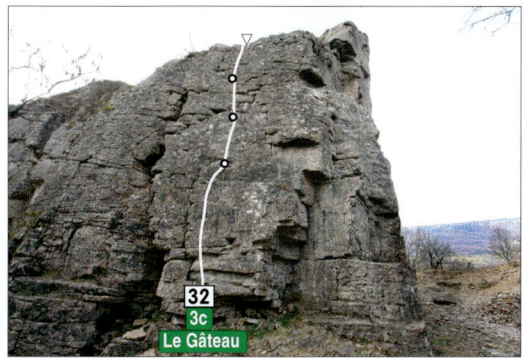
32 — 3c — Le Gâteau

39 — 5b — Fleur de Pierre / 40 — 7a+ — Refus

46 — 5b — Le Parfum de la Dame en Noir

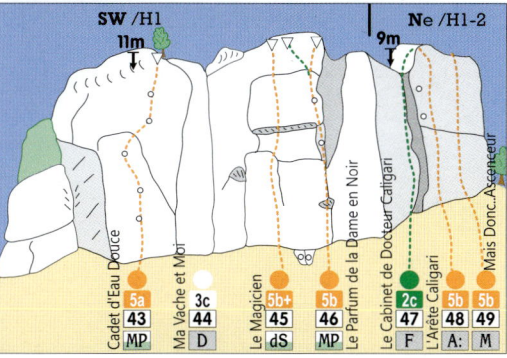

SW /H1 — 11m — Ne /H1-2 — 9m

43	44	45	46	47	48	49
5a	3c	5b+	5b	2c	5b	5b
MP	D	dS	MP	F	A:	M

Cadet d'Eau Douce / Ma Vache et Moi / Le Magicien / Le Parfum de la Dame en Noir / Le Cabinet de Docteur Caligari / L'Arête Caligari / Mais Donc. Ascenceur

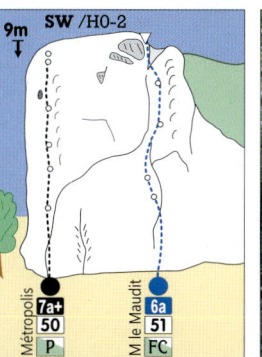

SW /H0-2 — 9m

50	51
7a+	6a
P	FC

Métropolis / M le Maudit

50 — 7a+ — Métropolis / 51 — 6a — M le Maudit

Good climbing, short routes with lots of good moves. Blocs and walls with varying sun and shade. Easy to picnic also.

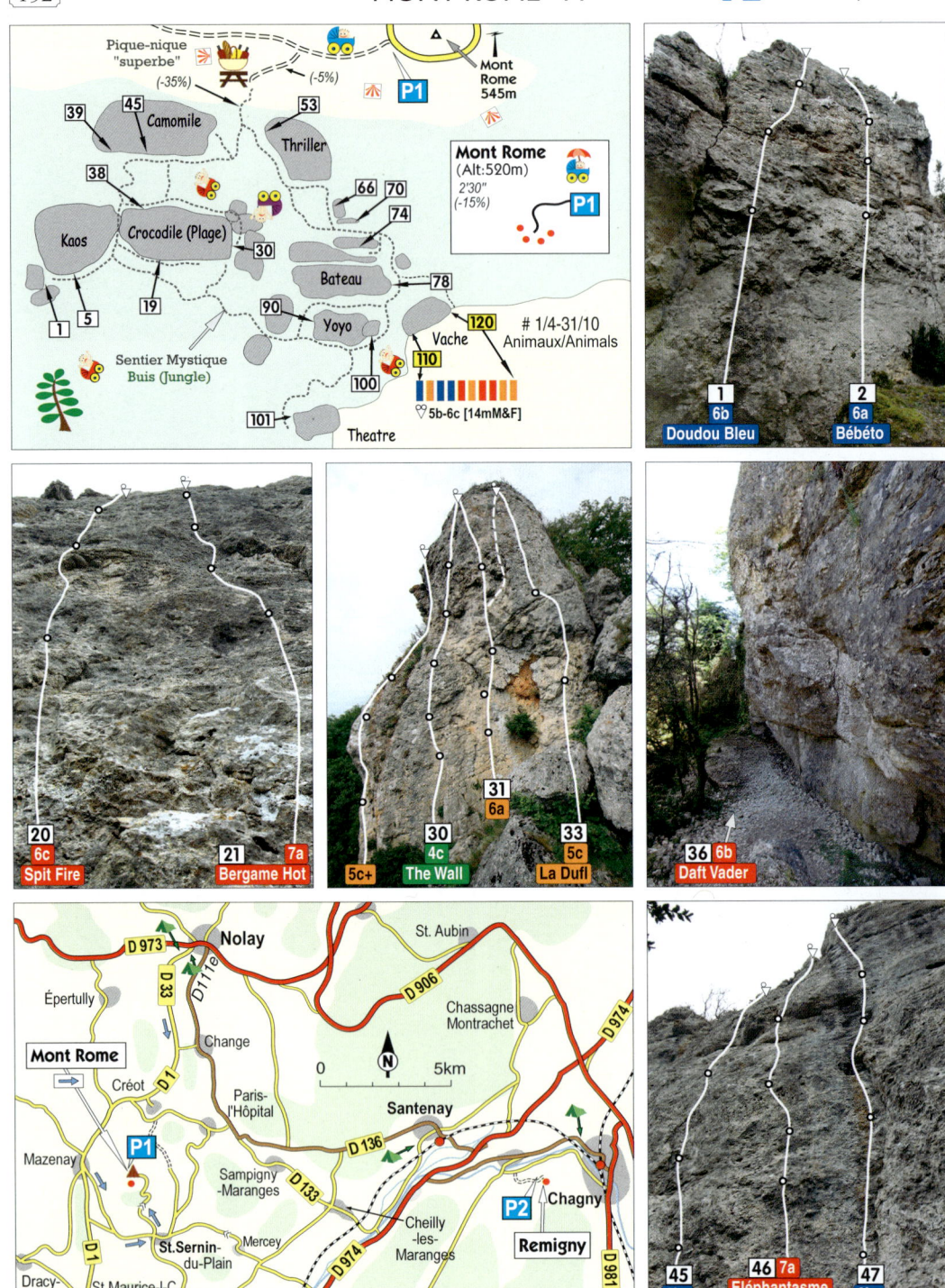

MONT ROME - B

153

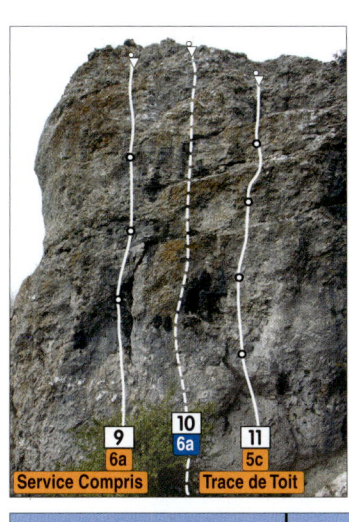
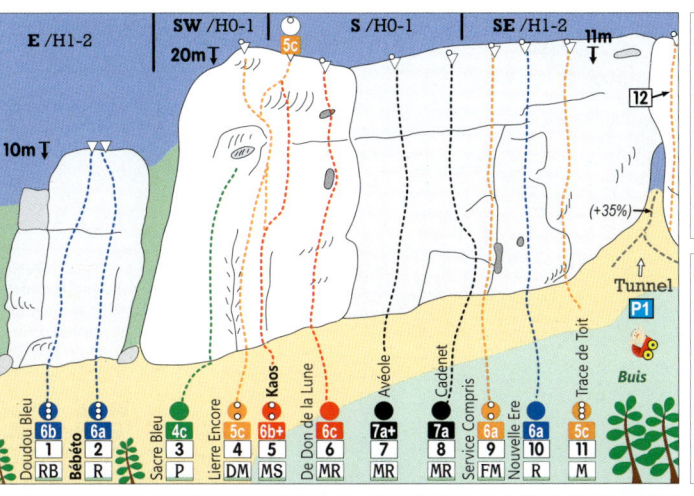
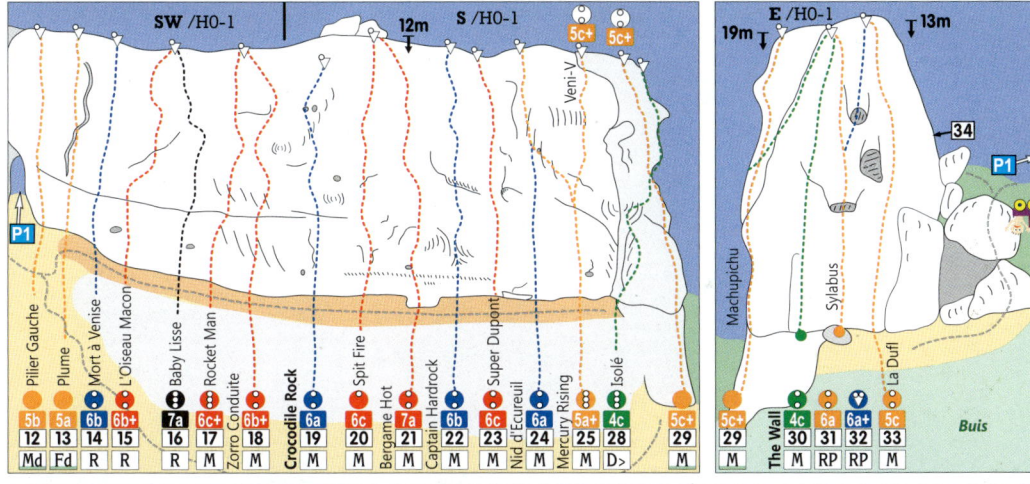
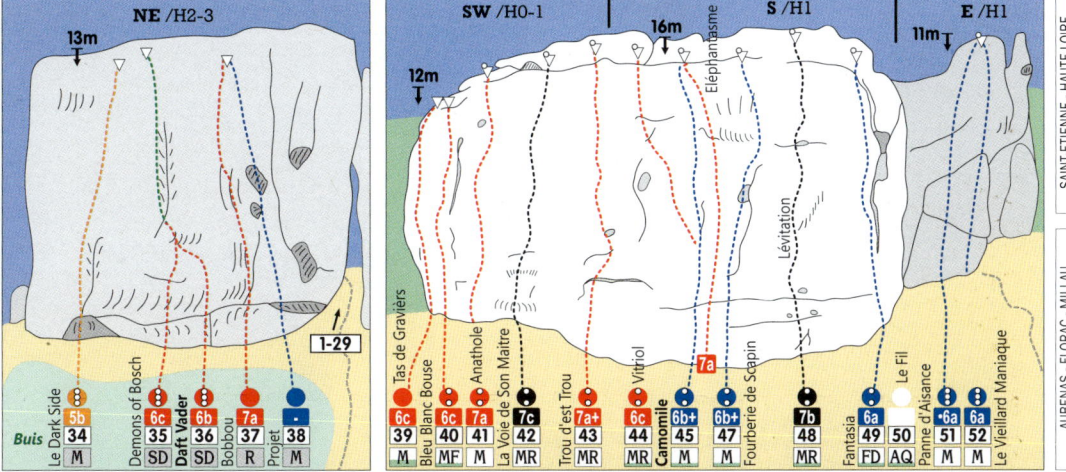

Most of the routes here are short, fingery (ouchy) and bloc style - so grades don't mean much, colours give best indication.

MONT ROME - C

These upper sectors give some good routes for small children with plenty of holds close together. Friendly ambience.

MONT ROME - D

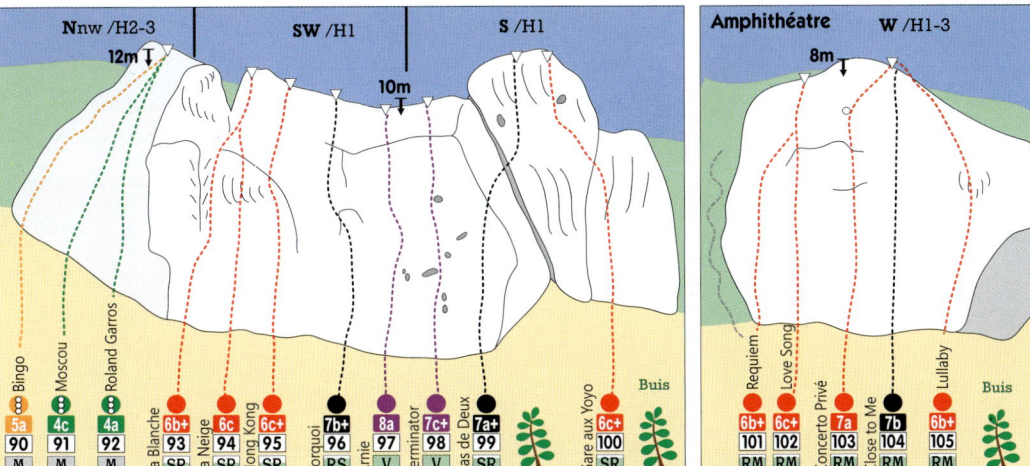

Anyone for steep boulder style routes, head down to the bottom of the rocks in the buis, fierce routes.

REMIGNY - # 10/09 - 01/03

P1 46.904730, 4.732066

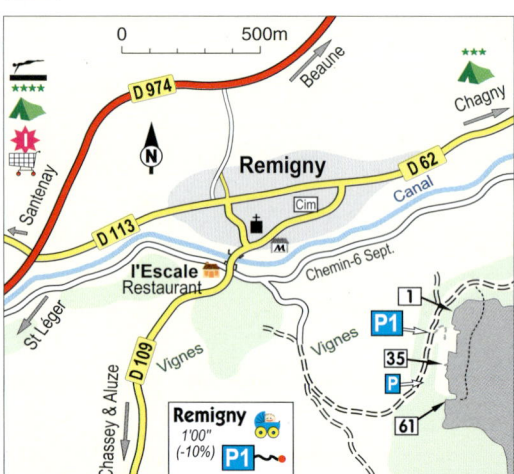

Migration 5b+ [6] Jerome Vielard

18	19
7a+	6c
Carpe Diem	Igzull Wass

27	28	29
7b+	6c+	6c
Chine et Pakistan		Rock'n Roll

35	36	37
4b	5a+	5c+
Petit Pilier	Voie des Buis	

46	5c	47
Fais-Toi du Mouron		6a
	Dans la Gueule de l'Ochre	

50	51	52
4c	5b	4c+
Deb'U	Fond'U	Hell Haut de L'U

56	57
6c+	6b+
Costaud Lulu	Homo Erectus trés Hablis

Calcaire****(**) Variable rock quality, but in general - excellent. An old quarry with a nice open feel and sunny aspect.

LE TEU

P1 46.815978, 4.710313

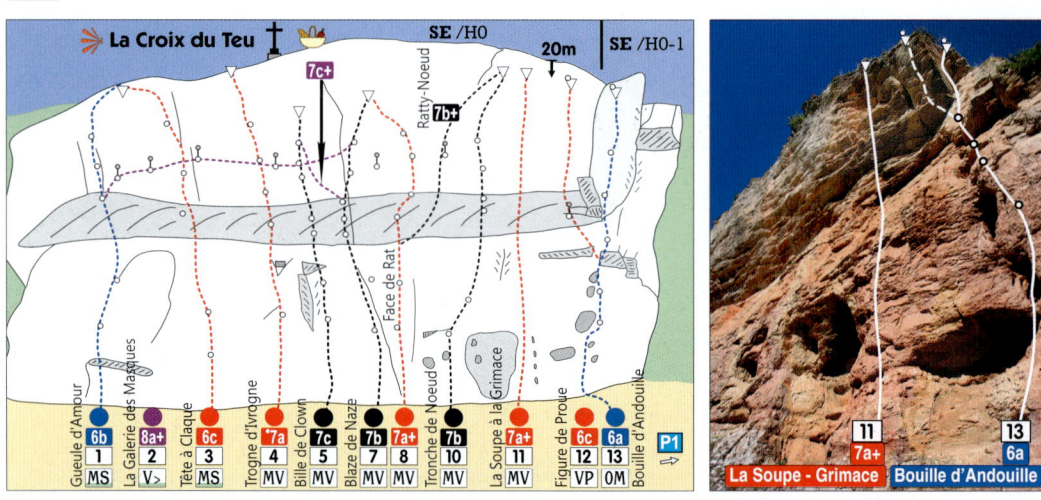

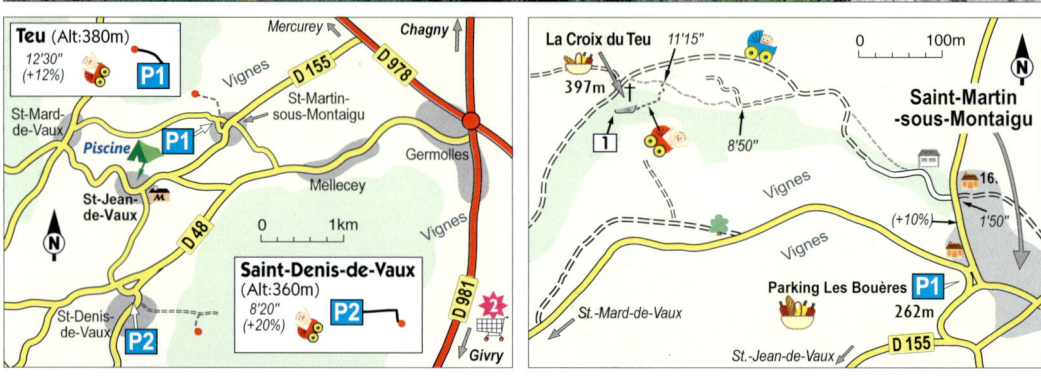

Grés-Calcaire* Quite soft rock. Amazing position with great ambience. Very physical and overhanging. Usually warm (baking).

SAINT-DENIS-DE-VAUX

P2 46.793405, 4.699229 — 159

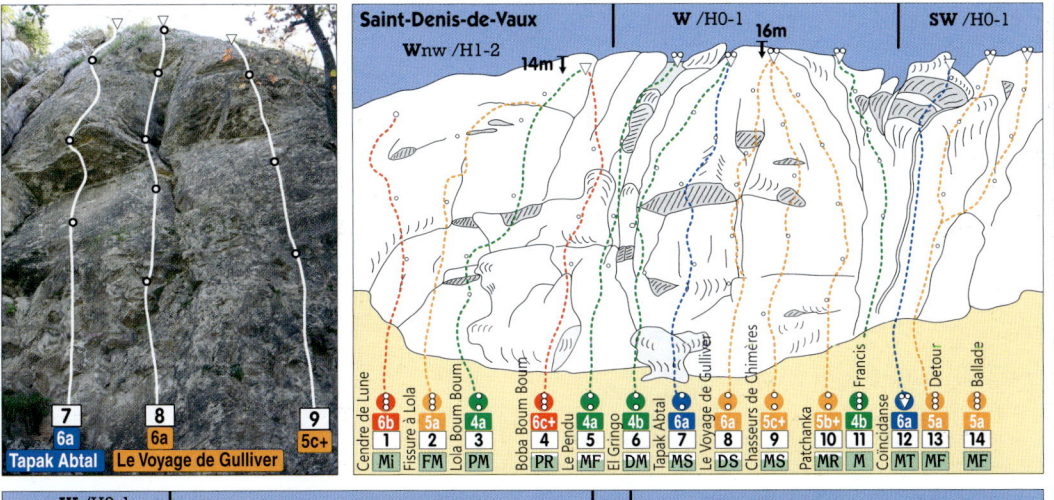

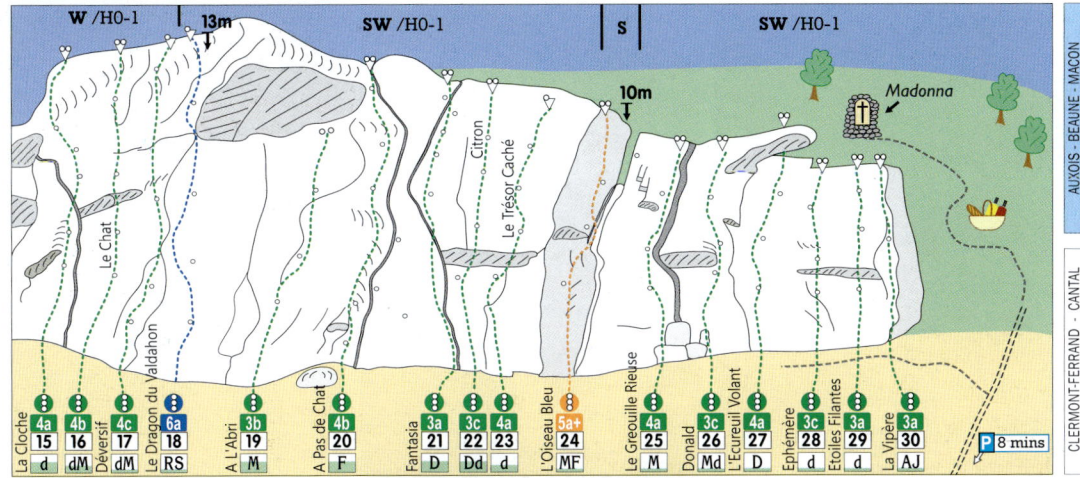

Calcaire*** A very friendly small cliff in the trees, with a nice sunny picnic meadow just behind the cliff.

CULLES LES ROCHES

P1 46.655267, 4.655408

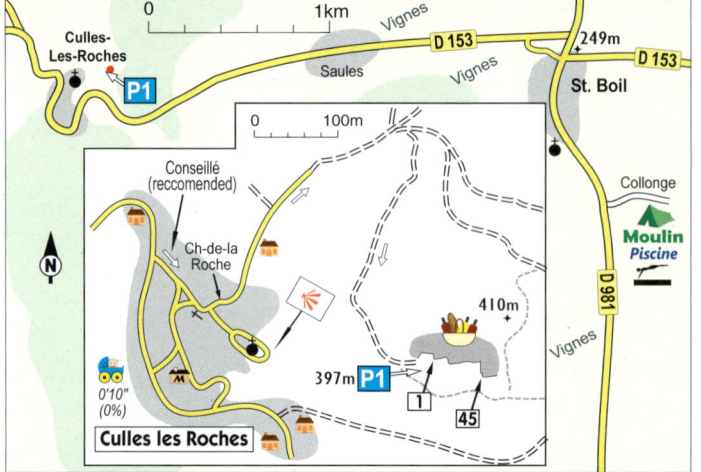

Calcaire*** A small old quarry that is sheltered from the wind and is a rather nice spot... (unlike most old quarries).

CULLES LES ROCHES

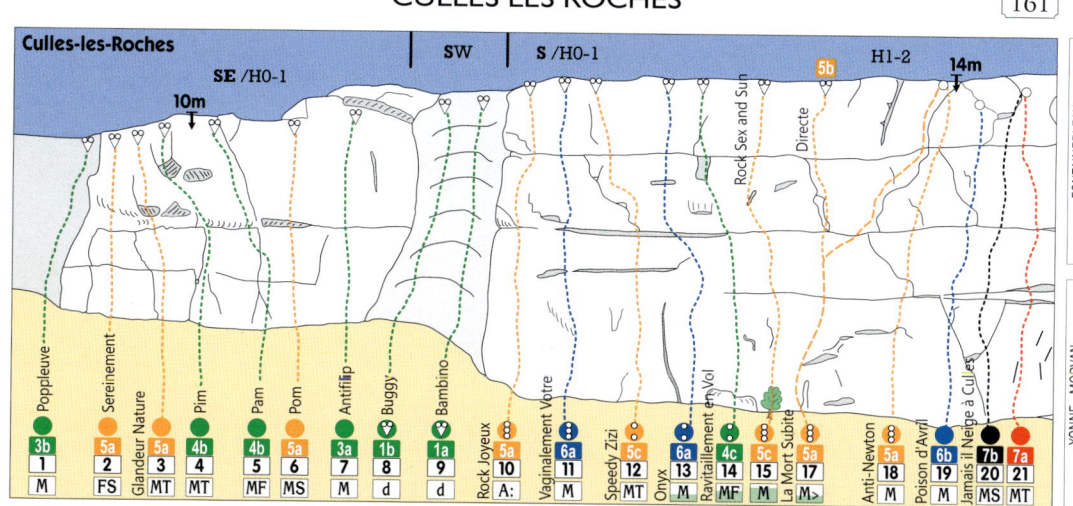
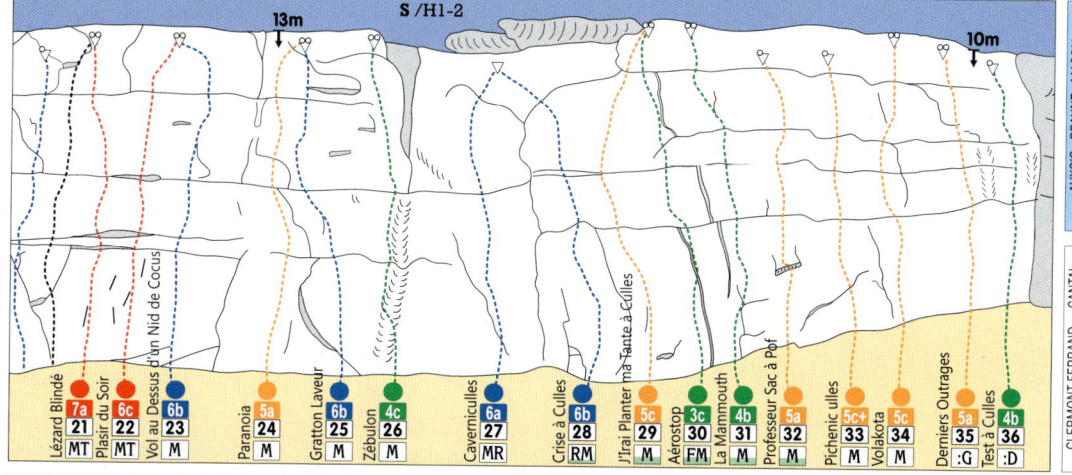
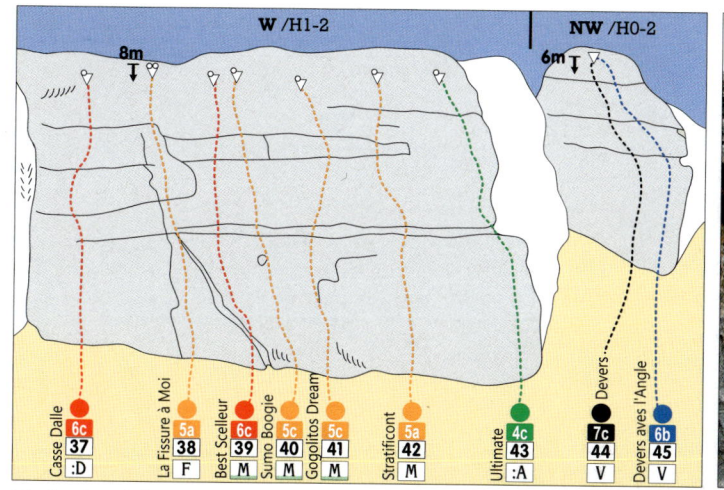

The harder climbs are bloc style. The easier climbs are surprisingly good for their short length. Plenty of picnic spots.

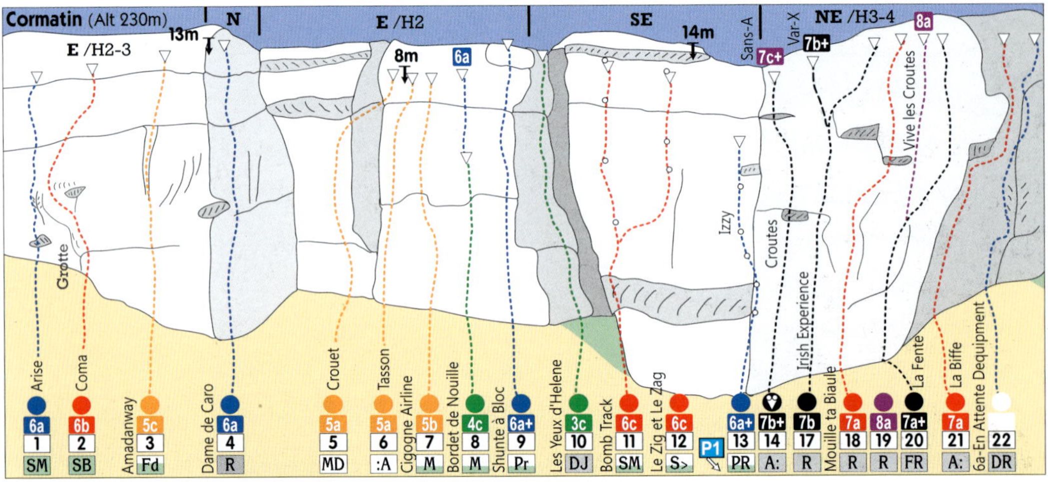

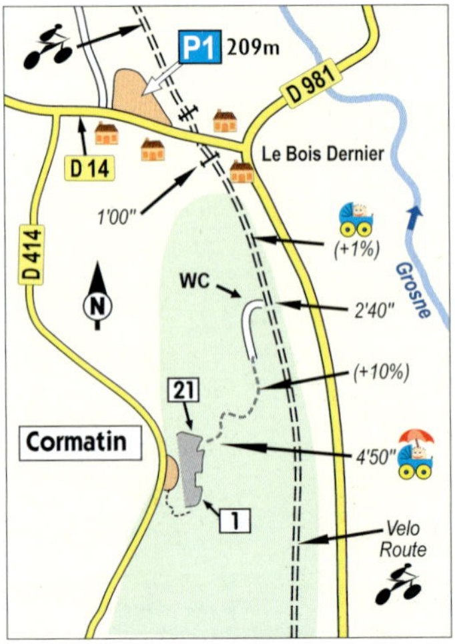

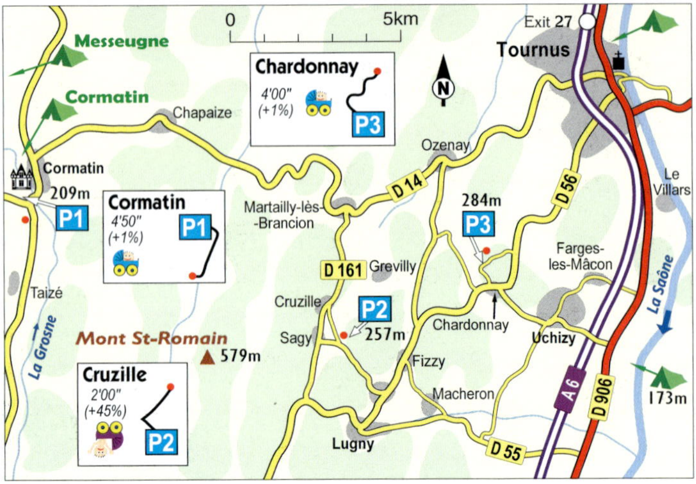

CORMATIN (Les Carrières du Bois Dernier)

P1 46.536194, 4.681984

#	Name	Grade	Type
1	Arise	6a	SM
2	Coma	6b	SB
3	Amadanway	5c	Fd
4	Dame de Caro	6a	R
5	Crouet	5a	MD
6	Tasson	5a	:A
7	Cigogne Airline	5b	M
8	Bordet de Nouille	4c	M
9	Shunte à Bloc	6a+	Pr
10	Les Yeux d'Helene	3c	DJ
11	Bomb Track	6c	SM
12	Le Zig et Le Zag	6c	S>
13		6a+	PR
14		7b+	A:
17	Izzy / Croutes / Irish Experience	7b	R
18	Mouille ta Biaude	7a	R
19		8a	R
20	La Fente	7a+	FR
21	La Biffe	7a	A:
22	6a-En Attente Dequipment		DR

Cormatin** Grés-Calcaire. A damp E facing cliff, needs a good dry spell. Ground at base can be very slippery-muddy.

CRUZILLE (Roche Sainte-Geneviève)

P2 46.494659, 4.802892 — 163

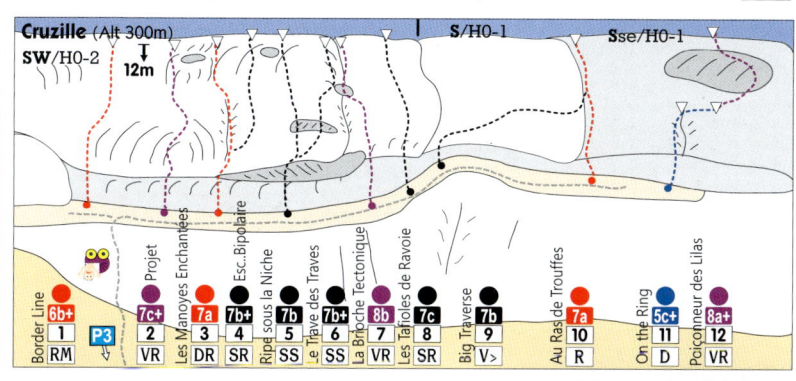

Cruzille (Alt 300m) — SW/H0-2, S/H0-1, Sse/H0-1 — 12m

#	Name	Grade	Code
1	Border Line	6b+	RM
2	Projet	7c+	VR
3	Les Manoyes Enchantées	7a	DR
4	Esc. Bipolaire	7b+	SR
5	Ripe sous la Niche	7b	SS
6	Le Trave des Traves	7b+	SS
7	La Brioche Tectonique	8b	VR
8	Les Tafoles de Ravoie	7c	SR
9	Big Traverse	7b	V>
10	Au Ras de Trouffes	7a	R
11	On the Ring	5c+	D
12	Poiçonneur des Lilas	8a+	VR

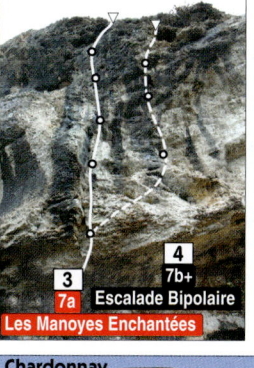

3 — 7a — Escalade Bipolaire — Les Manoyes Enchantées — 4 — 7b+

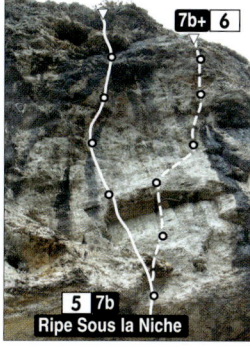

5 — 7b — Ripe Sous la Niche — 7b+ 6

CRUZILLE

Chardonnay

Nw/H0-1, W/H0-2, N/H2-3 — "Moustiques" 10m — 9m

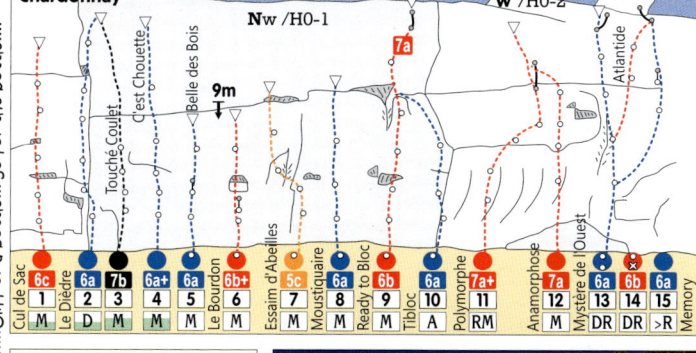

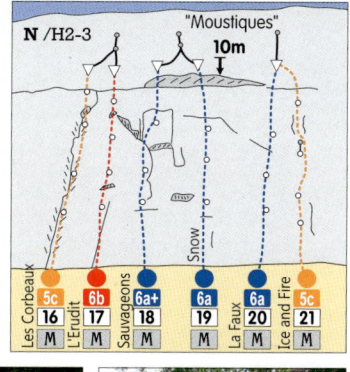

#	Name	Grade	Code
1	Cul de Sac	6c	M
2	Le Dièdre	6a	D
3	Touché Coulet	7b	M
4	C'est Chouette	6a+	M
5	Belle des Bois	6a	M
6	Le Bourdon	6b+	M
7	Essaim d'Abeilles	5c	M
8	Moustiquaire	6a	M
9	Ready to Bloc	6b	M
10	Tibloc	6a	A
11	Polymorphe	7a+	RM
12	Anamorphose	7a	M
13	Mystère de l'Ouest	6a	DR
14	(x)	6a	DR
15	Atlantide	6a	>R Memory
16	Les Corbeaux	5c	M
17	L'Erudit	6b	M
18	Sauvageons	6a+	M
19	Snow	6a	M
20	La Faux	6a	M
21	Ice and Fire	5c	M

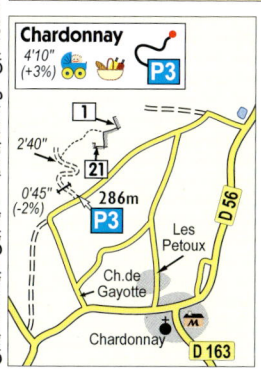

Chardonnay — 4'10" (+3%) — P3 — 286m — Les Petoux — Ch. de Gayotte — Chardonnay — D 163

11 — 7a+ — Polymorphe

18 — 6a+ — Sauvageons

CHARDONNAY

P3 46.515669, 4.857134

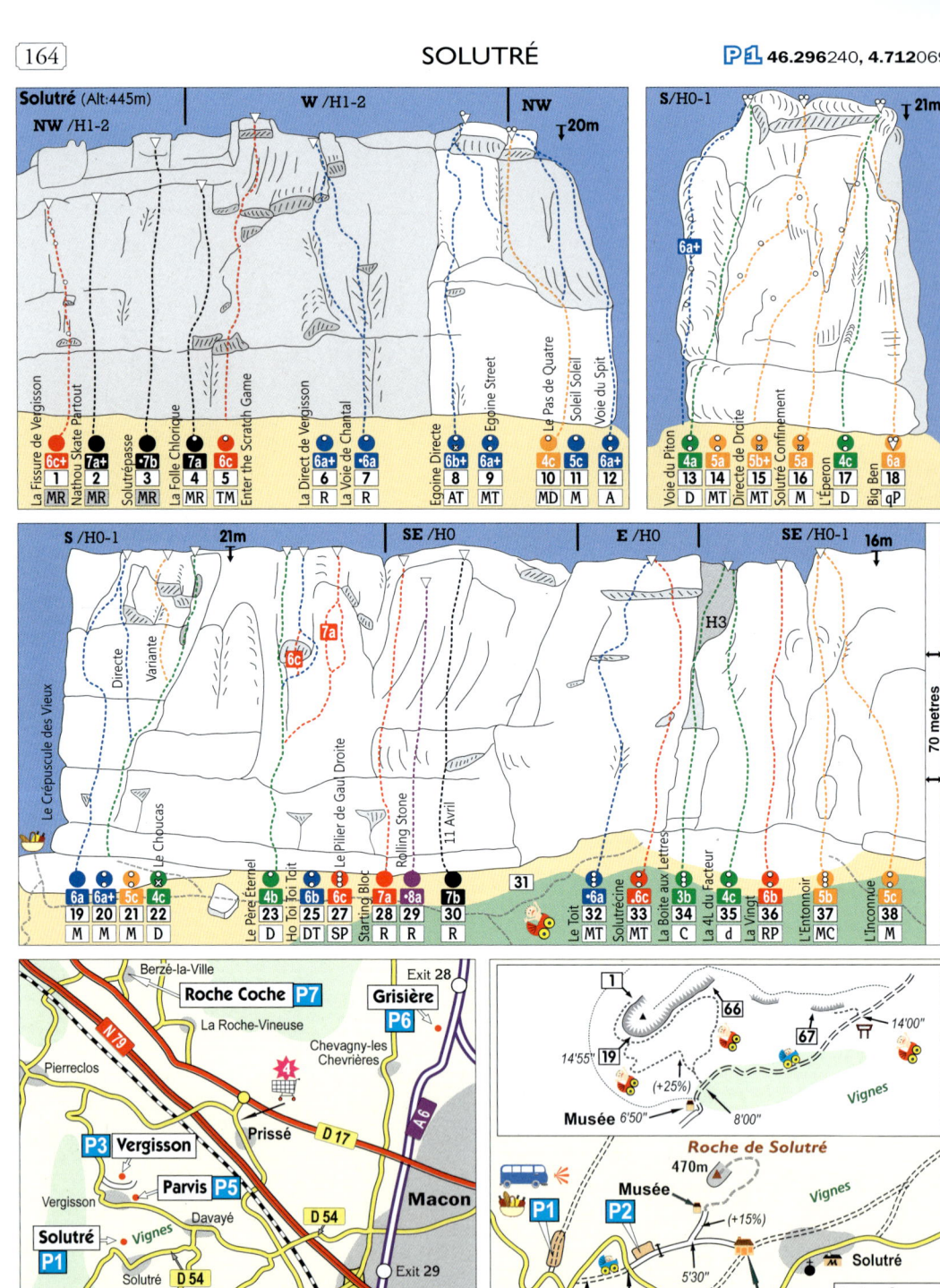

SOLUTRÉ

P2 46.297130, 4.715781 — 165

#	Grade	Name
4	7a	La Folle Chlorique
5	6c	Enter the Scratch Game
8	6b+	Egoïne Directe
9	6a+	Egoïne Street
12	6a+	Voie du Spit
13	4a	Voie du Piton
23	4b	Le Père Éternel
27	—	Le Pilier de Gaul (6c / 6b / 7a / 6c)
32	6a+	Le Toit
33	6c	Solutrécine
34	3b	La Boite aux Lettres
35	4c	—
36	6b	La Vingt
37	5b	L'Entonnoir
38	5c	L'Inconnue

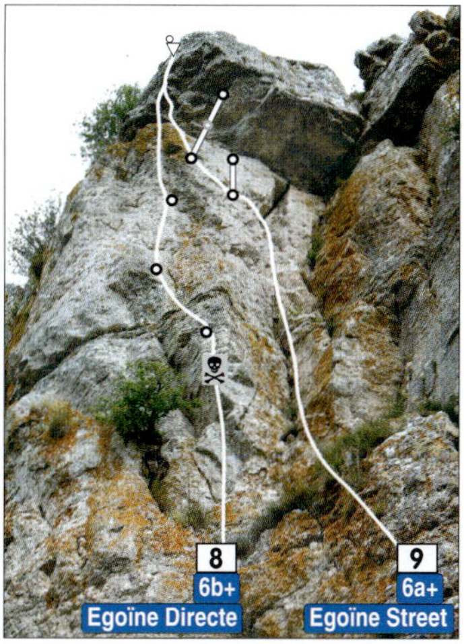

An odd mix of sand and limestone. Gets very windy on the main promontory - and feels totally out there. Space for picnic too.

SOLUTRÉ

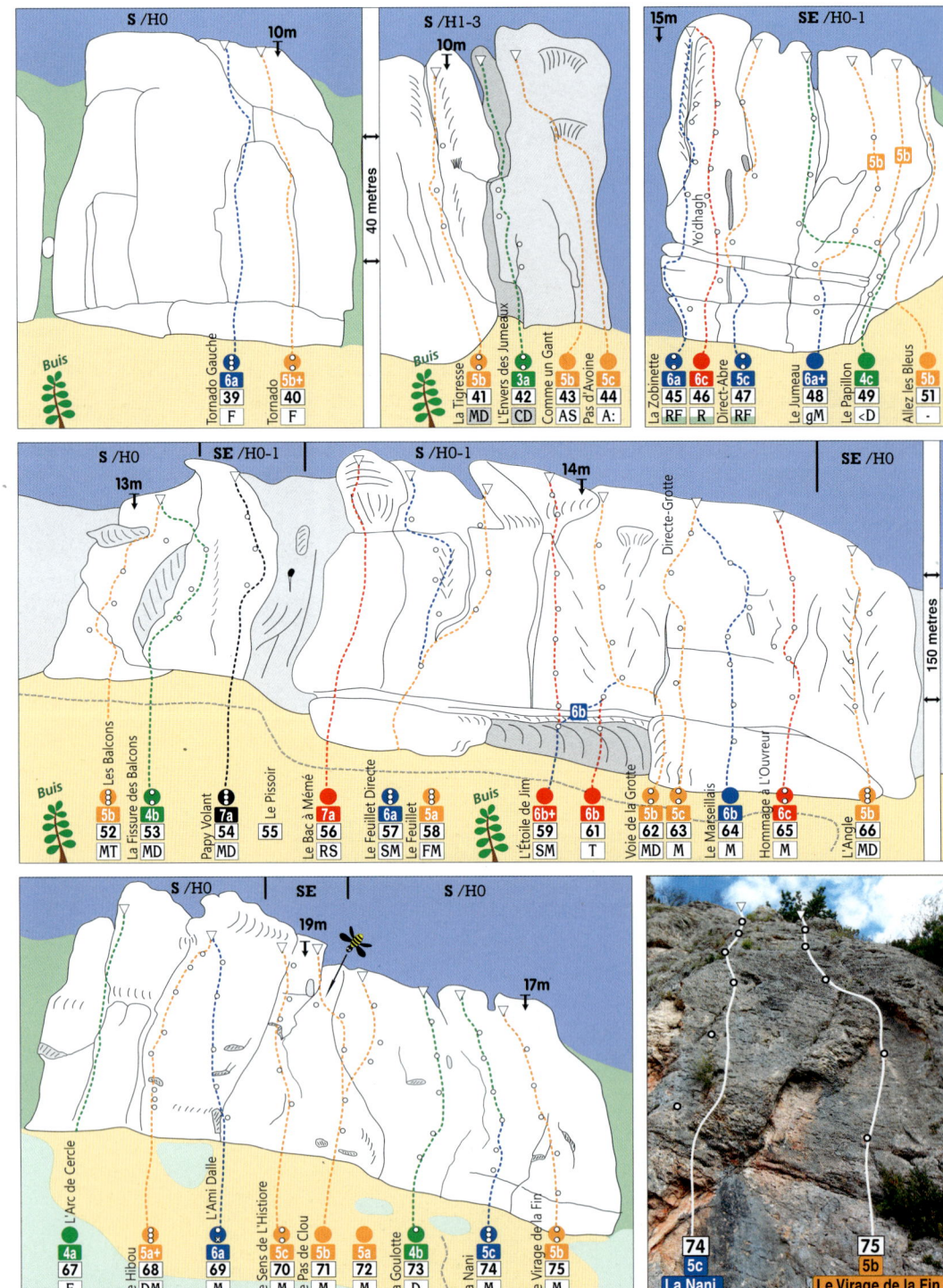

Approach lower sectors from the right - very gnarly buis bushes along the base of the cliff - yuk.

SOLUTRÉ

ROCHE DE SOLUTRE - SUNRISE

Rock is very sketchy in parts, if it's polished - then its solid. Local white wine is fabulous, plenty of tasting to be enjoyed.

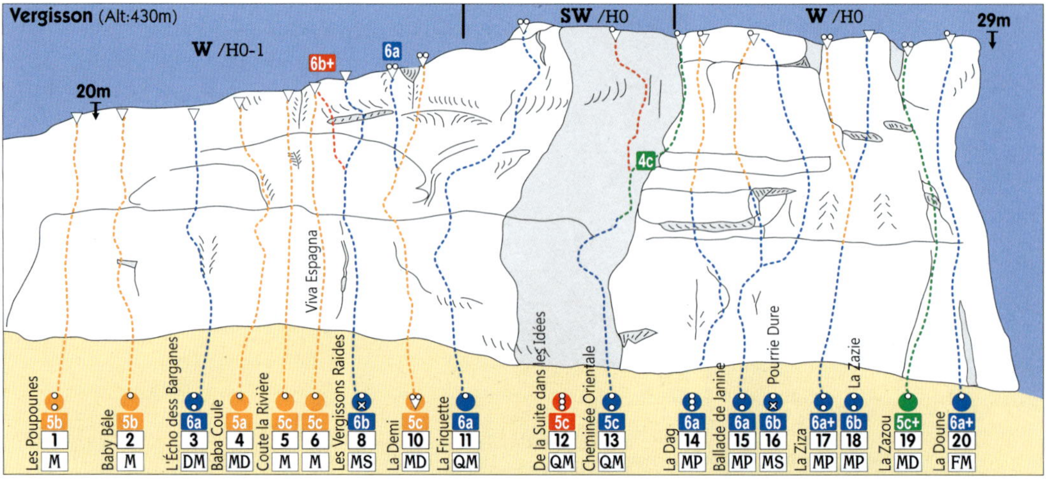

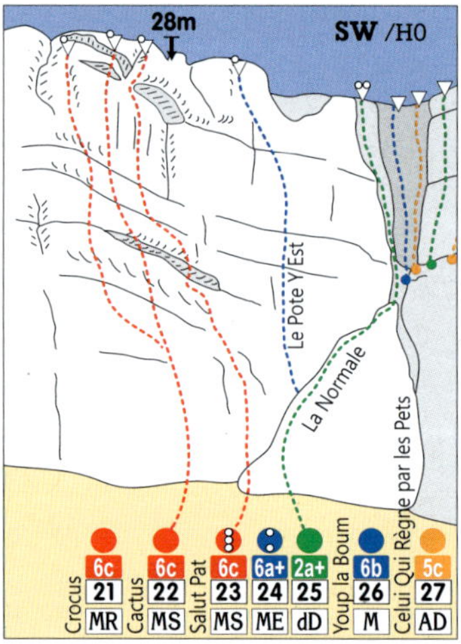

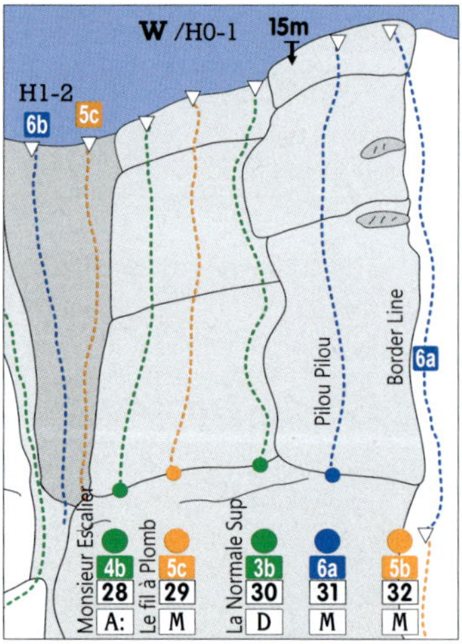

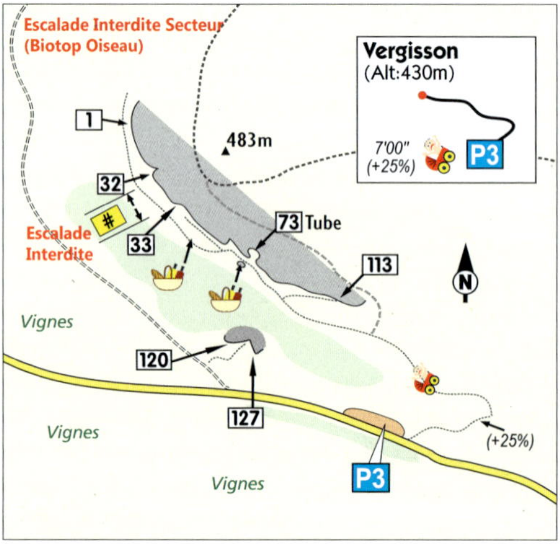

/ # VERGISSON

P3 46.312902, 4.717577

Vergisson (Alt: 430m)

#	Name	Grade	Style
1	Les Poupounes	5b	M
2	Baby Bèle	5b	M
3	L'Écho dess Barganes	6a	DM
4	Baba Coule	5a	MD
5	Coute la Rivière	5c	M
6	Les Vergissons Raides	5c	M
8	—	6b	MS
10	La Demi	5c	MD
11	La Friquette	6a	QM
12	De la Suite dans les Idées	5c	QM
13	Cheminée Orientale	5c	QM
14	La Dag	6a	MP
15	Ballade de Janine	6a	MP
16	—	6b	MS
17	La Zita	6a+	MP
18	Pourrie Dure	6b	MP
19	La Zazou	5c+	MD
20	La Doune	6a+	FM

Les Vergissons Raides — 8 6b
La Demi — 10 5c

#	Name	Grade	Style
21	Crocus	6c	MR
22	Cactus	6c	MS
23	Salut Pat	5c	MS
24	Le Pote Y'Est	6a+	ME
25	—	2a+	dD
26	Youp la Boum	6b	M
27	Celui Qui Règne par les Pets / La Normale	5c	AD
28	Monsieur Escalier	4b	A:
29	Le fil à Plomb	6c	M
30	La Normale Sup	3b	D
31	Pilou Pilou	6a	M
32	Border Line	5b	M

The Cliff has an incredible position, expect wind. Views to Mont Blanc from parking-4.

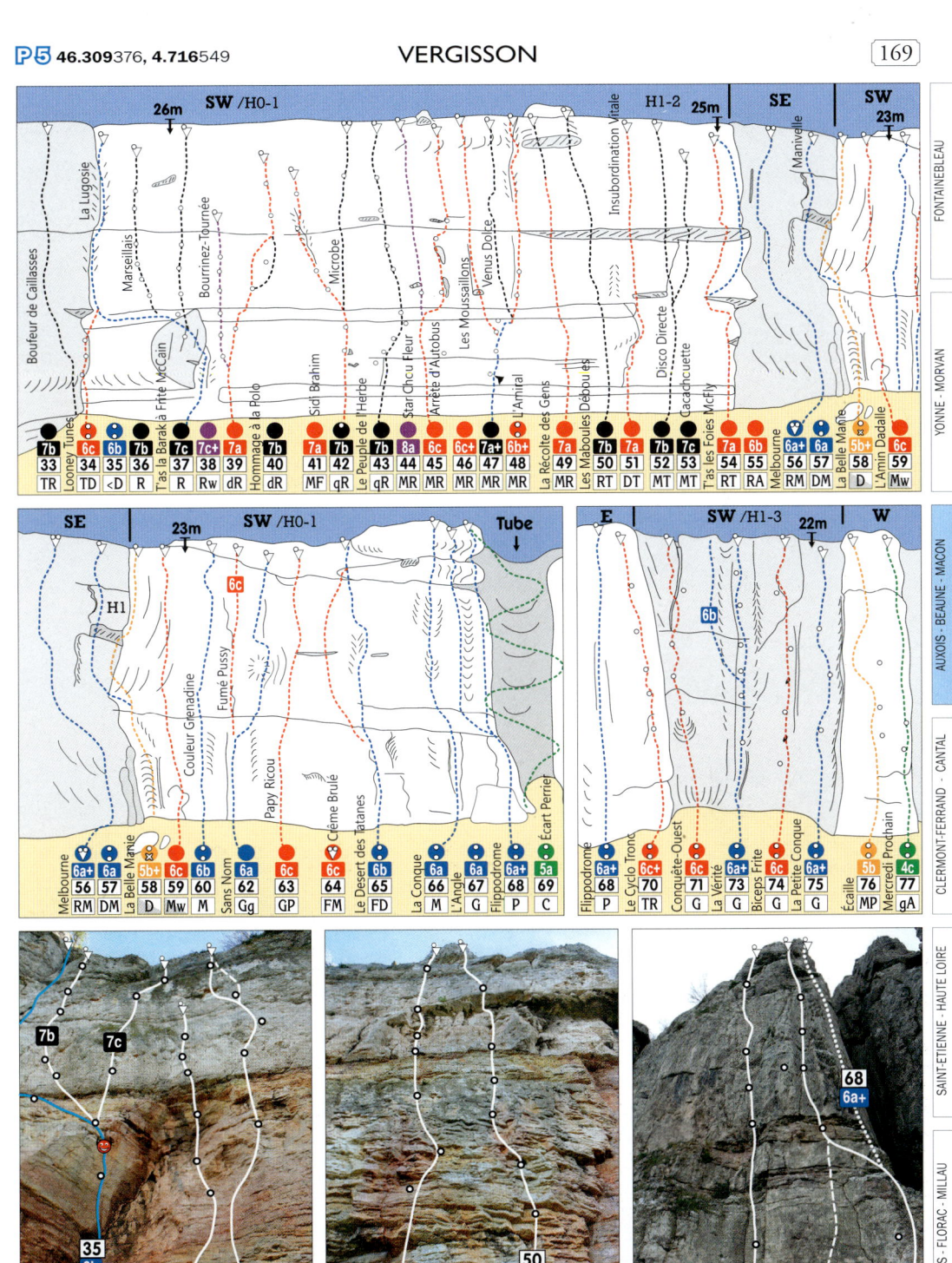

VERGISSON

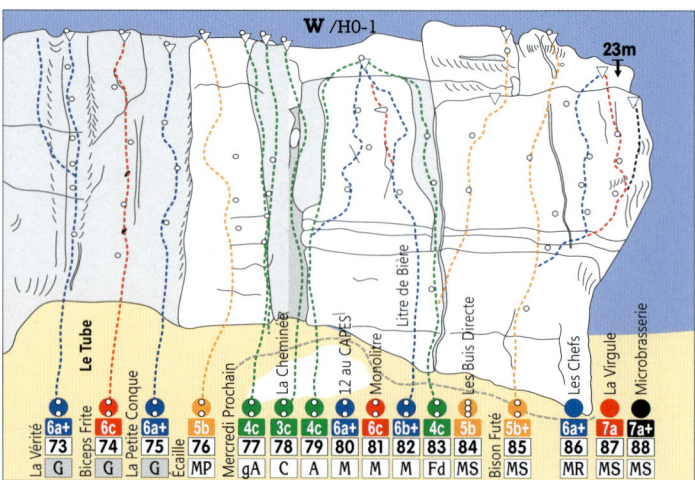

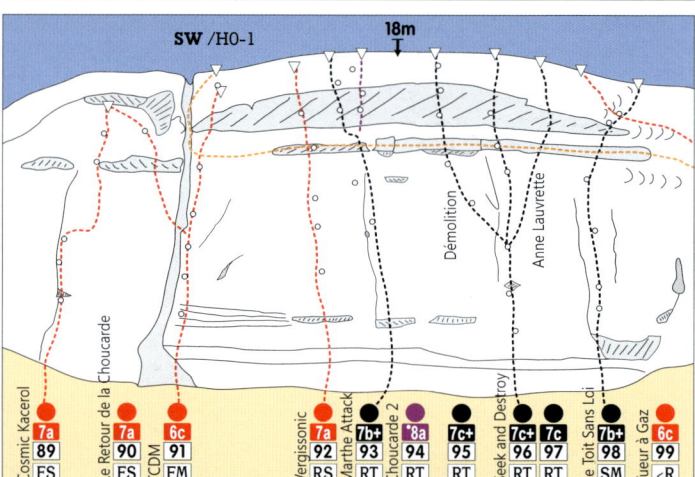
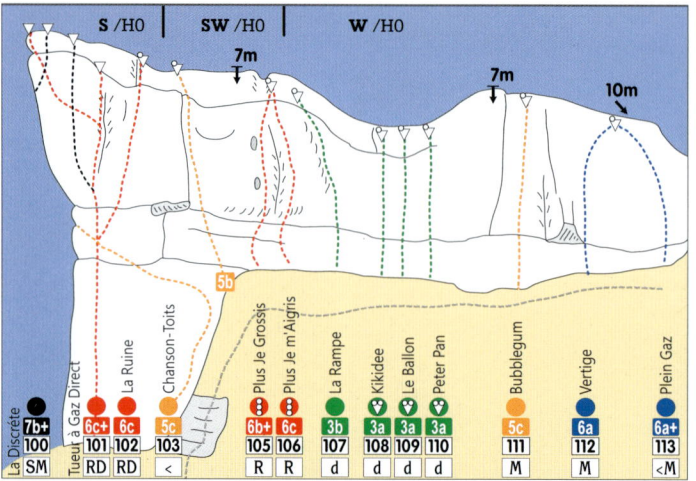

The tube is a classic one-off rock formation, only 30 mins of sun gets in, very technical and cool climbing.

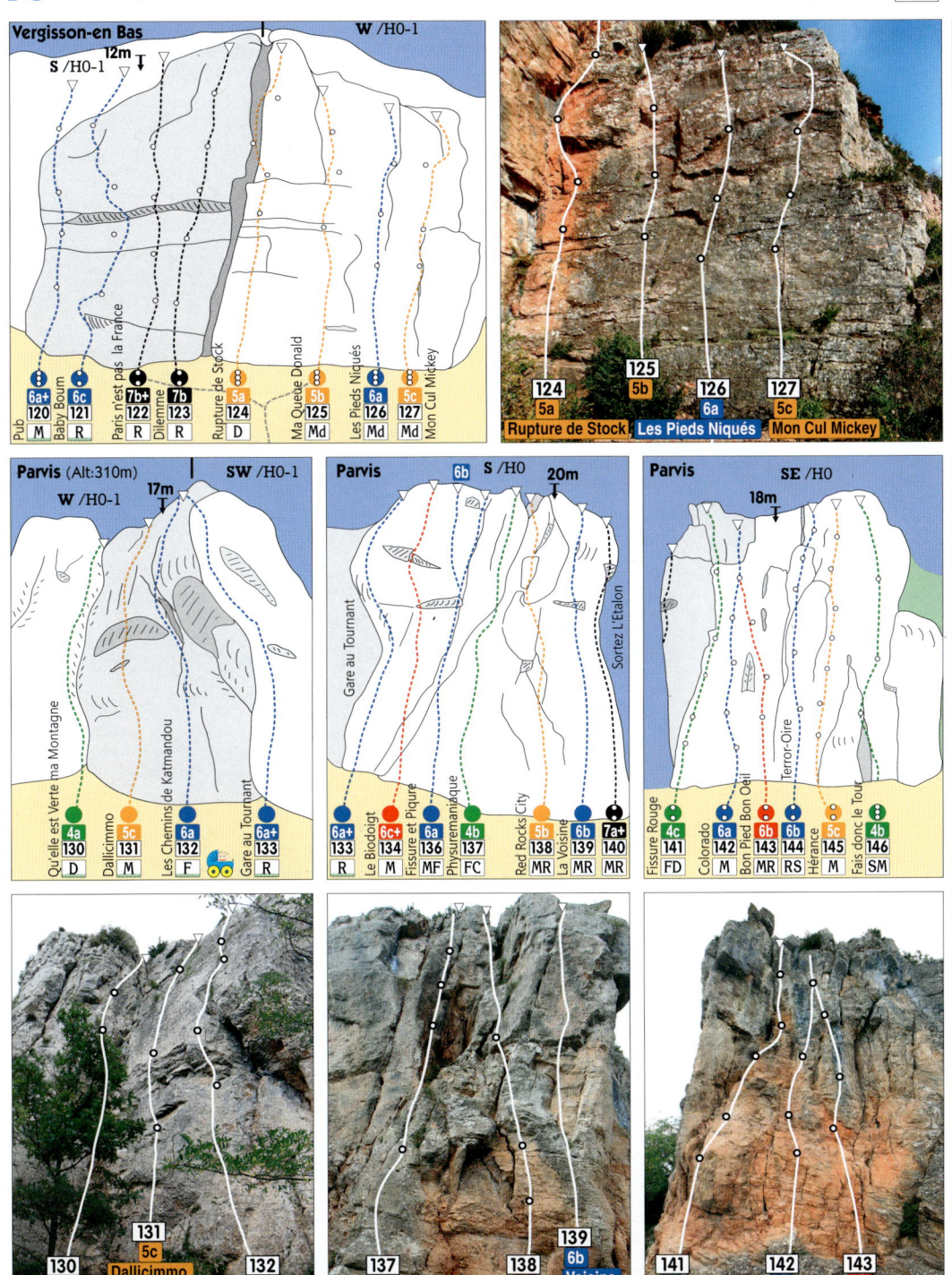

PARVIS

Parvis: A small buttress of rock just by a track, easy family access. Much less intimidating - but still punchy climbing.

LA GRISIÈRE

P6 46.335560, 4.818141

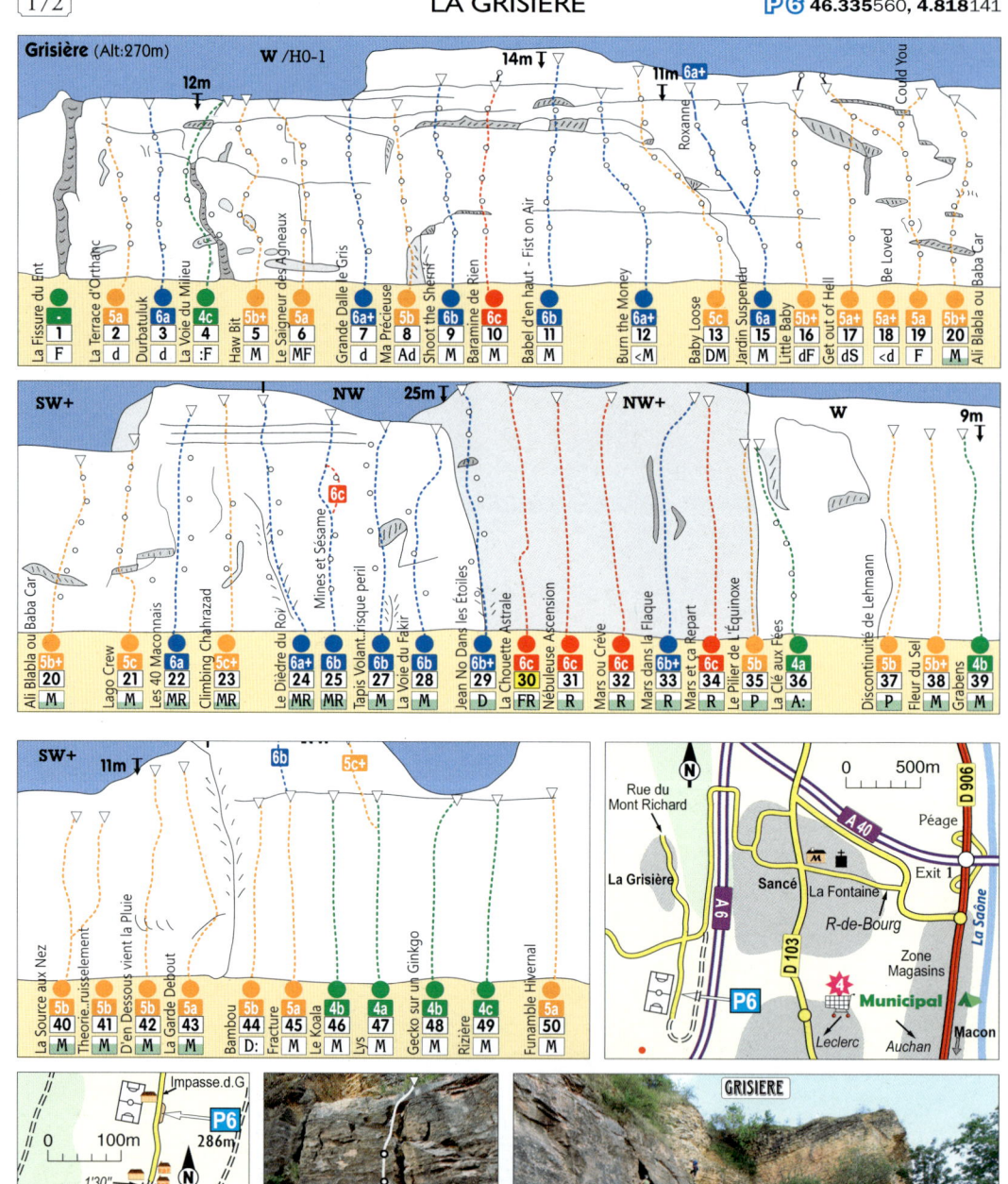

Grés** A quarry very close to the motorway but hidden and a nice afternoon sun spot. Lots of bolts - friendly.

LA ROCHE COCHE (Berzé-la-Ville)

P7 46.366220, 4.706349

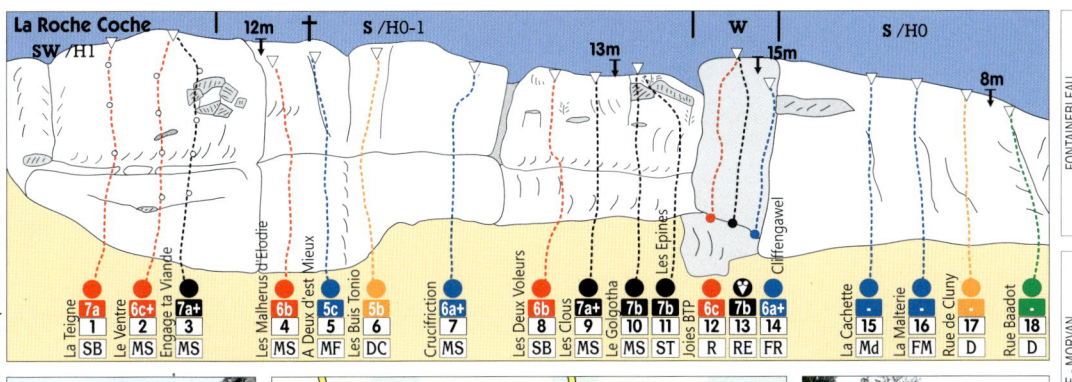

#	Name	Grade	Type
1	La Teigne	7a	SB
2	Le Ventre	6c+	MS
3	Engage ta Viande	7a+	MS
4	Les Malherus d'Elodie	6b	MS
5	A Deux d'est Mieux	5c	MF
6	Les Buis Tonio	5b	DC
7	Crucifriction	6a+	MS
8	Les Deux Voleurs	6b	SB
9	Les Clous	7a+	MS
10	Le Gogotha	7b	MS
11	Les Epines	7b	ST
12	Joies BTP	6c	R
13	Cliffengawel	7b	RE
14	—	6a+	FR
15	La Cachette	·	Md
16	La Malterie	·	FM
17	Rue de Cluny	·	D
18	Rue Baadot	·	D

Calcaire A high position with a lovely view, dries quick, rock is a bit shattered.

La Roche Coche (Alt: 430m) 7'00" (+5-15%)

Vergisson is a quiet village surrounded by excellent vineyards. Very exposed, routes feel very out there. Gets lots of wind.

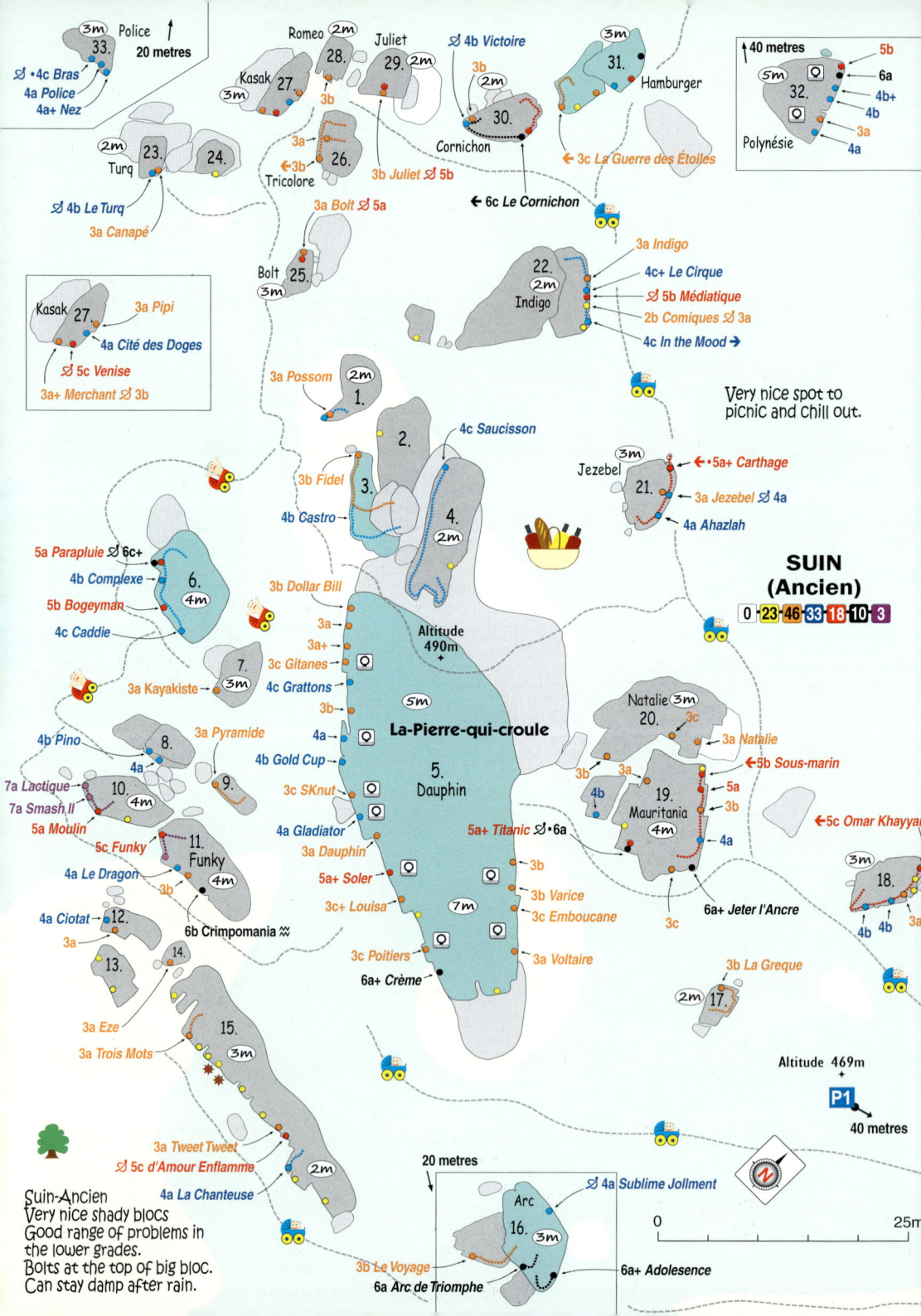

P1 46.442088, 4.466608 — SUIN (Bois de Morphée) — 175

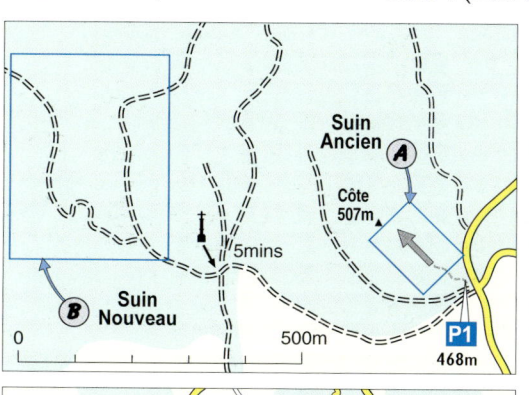

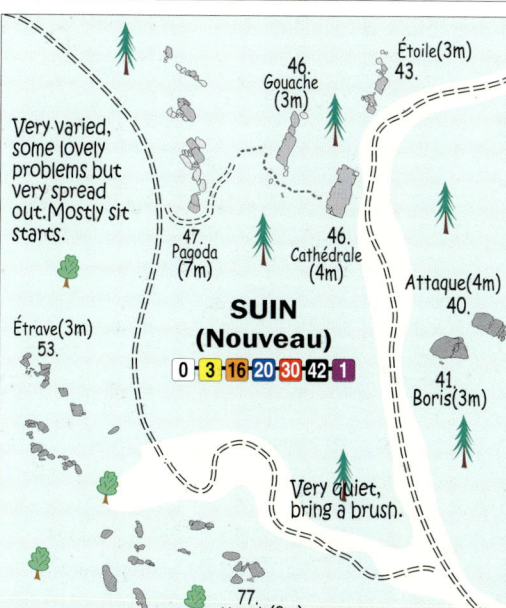

Granit**** Lots of granit blocs in the area. Suin ancien is the best spot for 1st visit. Verosvres, use internet (most high grades).

Area 4 - CLERMONT-FERRAND

Page		Falaise/Cliff		Alt	Arbre-Ori-Séche	Am-Pm	Rocher	Longeur	Numero Voies / Routes						Approche	Ambience
179	B5	Armand, Roc		350m	SW/H0		Granit	17m	1	1	1	1	0	0	0	Pilier
220	A2	Auteroche		780m	NW/H1		Schiste	18-31m	5	3	3	0	0	0	1	Mur-dalle
229	B1	Bès - Gorges		890m	S/H1-3		Granit	17-50m	0	11	17	6	3	1	19	dalle,Mur,zzz
228	C1	Bout du Monde		750m	S/H0-1		Granit	9-15m	4	9	4	2	1	0	1	Mur
210	B3	Capucin		1400m	N/H1-3		Volcanic	21-80m	3	6	14	12	6	0	18	Mur, vue
226	A1	Carlat		840m	N/H2-5		Basalte	7-18m	9	18	21	28	9	5	8	Mur-Raide
194	B3	Ceyrat		580m	SE/H0-1		Granit	19-25m	11	9	4	2	0	0	1	dalle-Toit
214	B3	Chambon-Neiges		1300m	SE/H1-2		Basalte	16-40m	0	1	21	17	2	2	12	Dièdre, Pilier
195	B3	Champeaux		760m	SE/H0		Granit	10-25m	4	5	6	1	0	0	7	dalle-Surplomb
182	B4	Chartreuse		520m	S/H1		Granit	16m	4	5	1	0	0	0	3	Mur
183	B4	Chât-Bains 32%		400m	W/H0-1		Volcanic	16-37m	9	26	21	9	5	1	12	Dièdre, Arête
218	A2	Chât-n-f-Riom		940m	SW/H0-1		Basalte	8-17m	11	26	11	2	1	0	1	Dièdre-Pilier
233	C1	Chazette		870m	SE/H1		Vol-Gra	15m	2	7	0	0	0	0	13	Mur
212	B3	Crête du Coq		1400m	Se/H0-1		Volcanic	35-90m	20	8	12	2	1	0	43	dalle,vue,surplomb
186	D4	Darots		370m	Se/H0		Granit	20-35m	13	13	11	2	0	0	7	Mur
213	B3	Dent Rancune		1350m	Se/H1		Volcanic	30-90m	0	3	19	20	3	0	44	Mur,vue,expo
200	C3	Gournier		360m	E/H0		Granit	22-37m	3	8	12	4	1	0	16	Dièdre,Mur
178	A5	Guillebaud		260m	SE+NW-H1		Schiste	10-18m	15	5	1	0	0	0	12	Mur-humide
222	A1	Hozières-Dévers		1340m	NE/H1-2		Volcanic	35m	0	5	7	1	0	0	12	Dévers
222	A1	Hozières-Grand		1500m	S/SE/H1		Volcanic	32-90m	0	21	7	5	1	0	30	Mur-fragile
224	A1	Lac des Graves		740m	NW/H3		Basalte	11-40m	0	6	5	11	8	1	11	Raide
180	A5	Lignerolles		230m	SE/H0-1		Granit	10-50m	12	9	11	15	12	6	12	Mur-Raide
219	A2	Marchastel		870m	SW/H1-3		Schiste	9-30m	2	7	7	1	0	0	1	Mur-humide
196	B3	Montagne-Perc		670m	N&S/H1		Basalte	10-15m	6	13	11	4	0	0	5	Mur-Vue
201	C3	Orbeil		400m	SW+SE/H0		Granit	20-35m	4	3	5	3	0	0	3	Mur,Raide,Pilier
215	B3	Pavin 25%		1200m	W/H1-2		Basalte	14-21m	1	6	12	5	0	0	6	Dièdre,Pilier,vue
182	B4	Père Rioux		620m	N+S/H0-1		Granit	12-16m	2	4	5	1	0	0	3	Pilier, Mur, Zzz
216	A1	Peyrade-Salers		960m	SE/H1		Basalte	10-19m	11	5	22	3	0	0	5	Dièdres
192	D4	Pierre Châtel		888m	ESW/H1		Granit	9-35m	70	25	12	1	1	0	4	dalle-Mur
188	D4	Pierre Fendue		824m	ENW/H2		Volcanic	12-22m	11	7	6	1	0	0	5	Mur-Raide-Zz
232	C1	Porte des Fées		870m	SW/H0-1		Volcanic	23-50m	0	12	21	5	1	0	5	Mur,Dièdre,Pilier
225	B1	Prés Marty		1430m	W&E/H1		Volcanic	14-25m	3	7	9	4	0	0	22	Mur-dalle-Zzz
223	A1	Puy de la Tourte		1680m	W&N/H1		Volcanic	10-17m	2	8	6	2	0	0	25	Mur-Pilier-Zzz
204	B3	Rivalet		600m	SW/H0-1		Granit	15-50m	25	22	21	6	0	1	3	dalle,Mur,Dièdre
202	C3	Rochettes		350m	SW/H0		Granit	10-21m	5	7	2	2	0	0	0	Mur,Pilier
202	B3	Saint-Floret		490m	NW/H1-2		Granit	10-26m	1	6	6	2	0	0	3	Mur-Raide
179	A5	Saint-Genest		250m	SW/H0-1		Granit	16-22m	4	3	9	6	0	0	15	Mur-Raide
230	B1	Saint-Just		1005m	E+W/H1		Granit	3-7m	5	8	22	25	42	6	2	Blocs, abrasif
208	A3	Saint-Sauves		1005m	W/H0-1		Granit	21-30m	0	1	7	8	13	10	1	Mur,Raide,Devers
189	D4	St-Vincent 30%		880m	WSE/H1		Volcanic	10-37m	32	14	23	12	2	1	4	dalle,Mur,Raide
187	D4	Salette		530m	SE/H0		Granit	7-13m	9	17	18	5	1	0	1	Mur
206	B3	Saurier		600m	SW/H0		Granit	13-45m	6	18	21	6	0	0	6	Mur, Dièdre
198	C3	Sauviat		380m	W,SE/H1		Granit	12-26m	3	6	7	2	0	0	3	dalle, Surplomb
209	B3	Tuillère, Roche		1170m	S/H0		Volcanic	15-80m	21	9	16	7	0	0	18	dalle, Mur
220	A2	Urlande Ouest		860m	SW/H1		Basalte	16m	3	5	7	0	0	0	10	Mur-Dièdre-Zzz
198	D3	Valcivières		1100m	NE/H2		Granit	13-19m	6	6	9	0	0	0	10	dalle,Pilier, Zzz
199	D3	Volpie 100%		950m	SE/H0-1		Granit	25-38m	1	4	3	2	3	0	16	Mur, Raid,vue

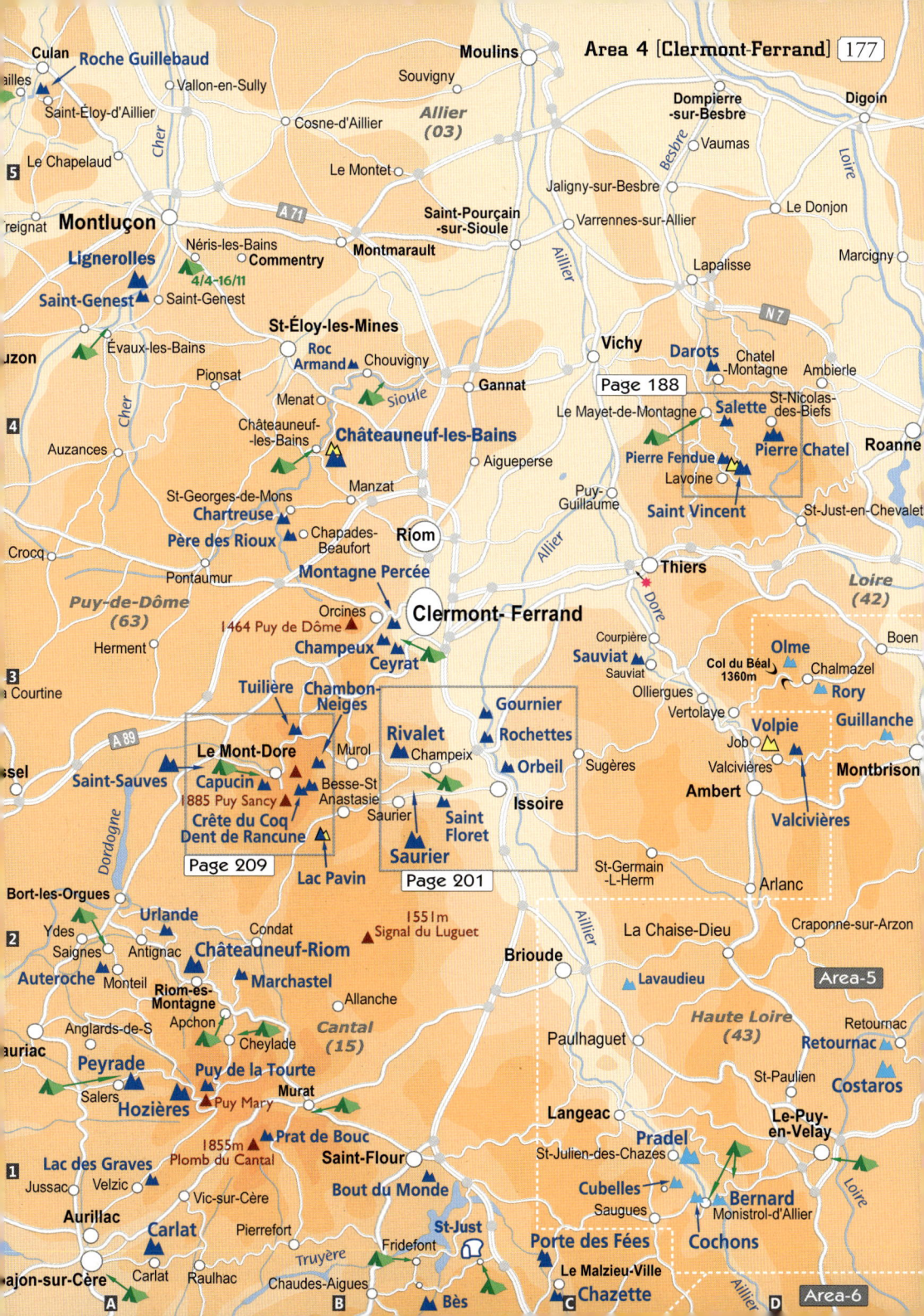

ROCHE GUILLEBAUD

P1 46.489908, 2.326278

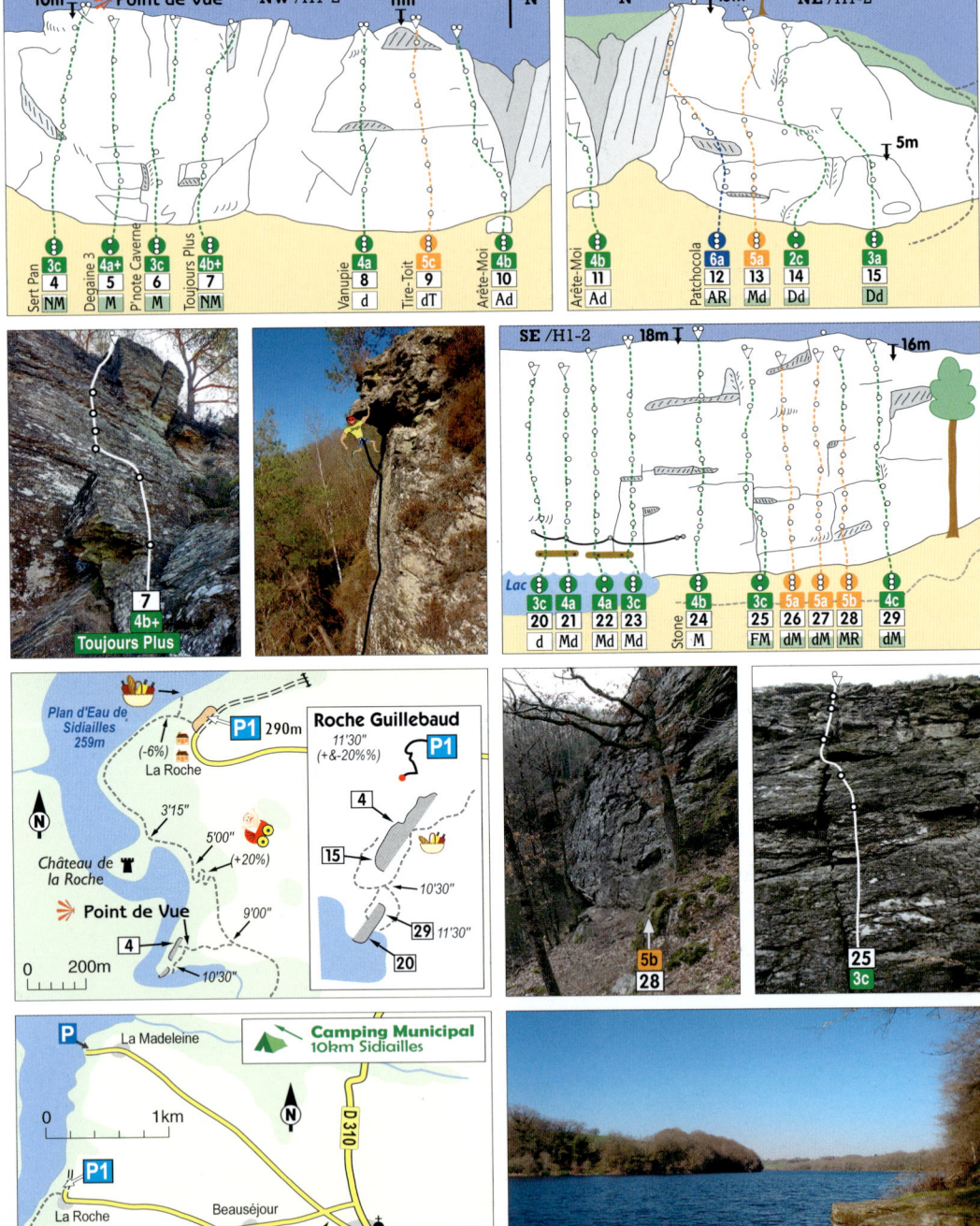

Schiste**: A fun small location by a lovely lake. Rock is quite iffy in parts, but well equipped and easy to set up a moulinette.

SAINT GENEST

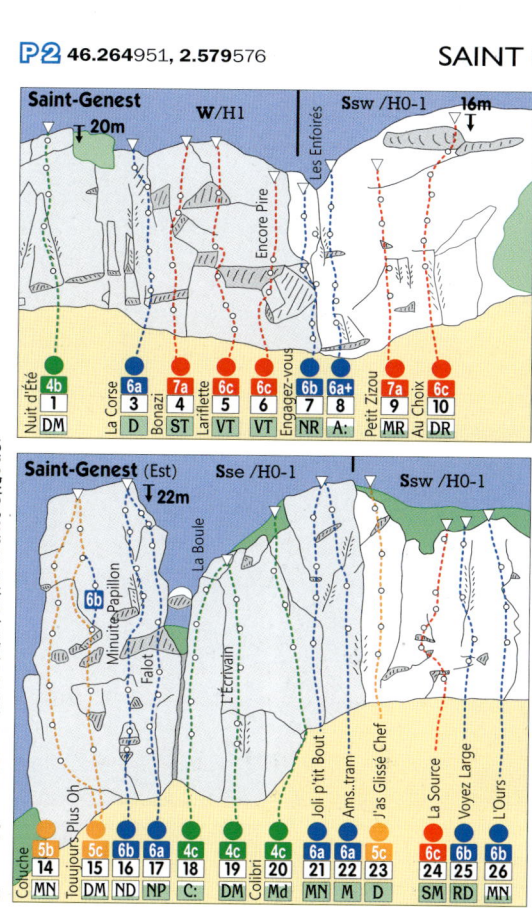

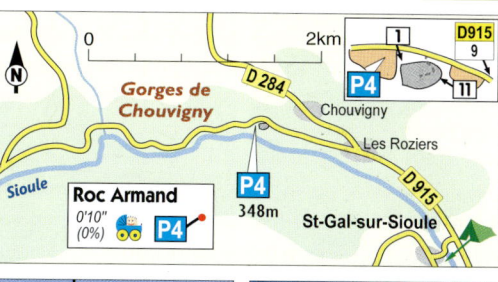
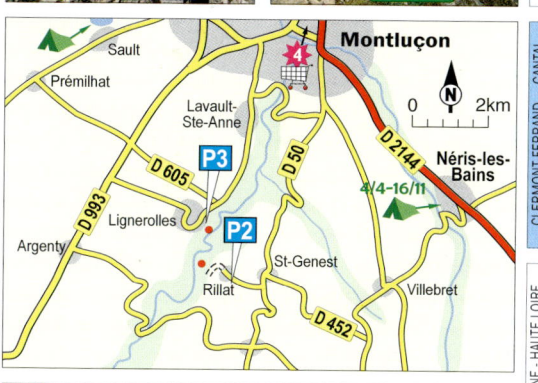
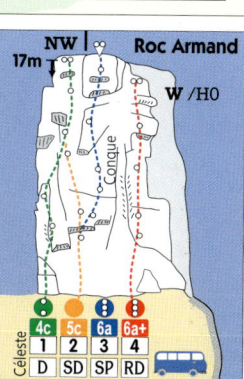

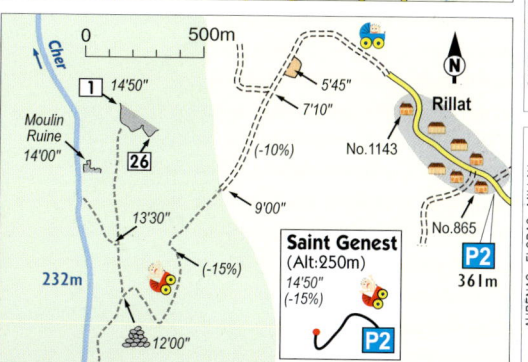

ROC ARMAND

LIGNEROLLES (Rocher du Lion)

Granite*** A deep warm valley where the undergrowth is rampant, other routes are equipped but usually get overgrown.

LIGNEROLLES

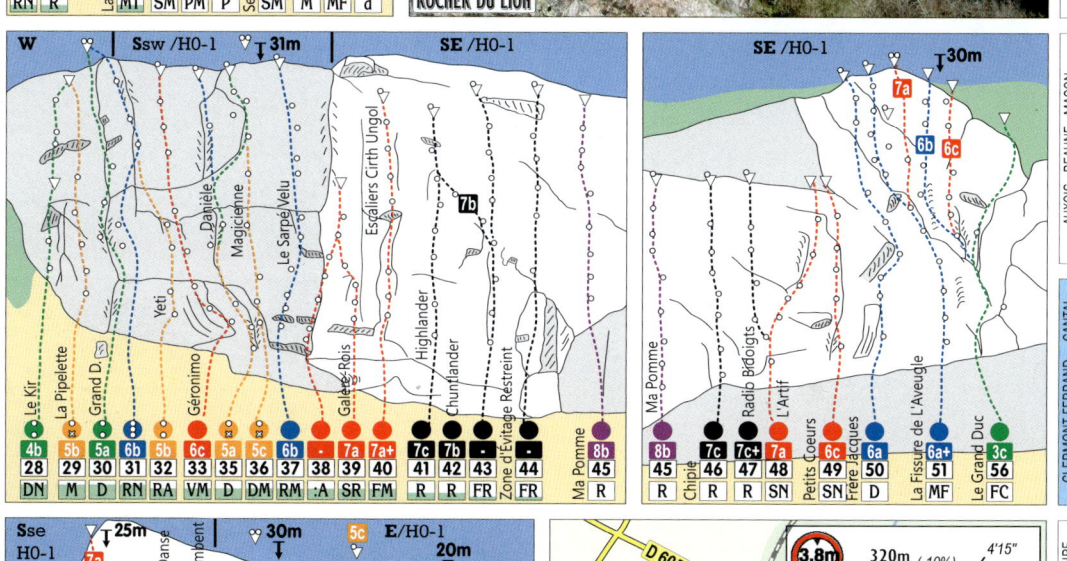

The river Cher gives plenty of opportunity for nice picnics, and some boulder style routes in the shade (Rocher de la Plage).

LA CHARTREUSE

P1 45.908165, 2.801651

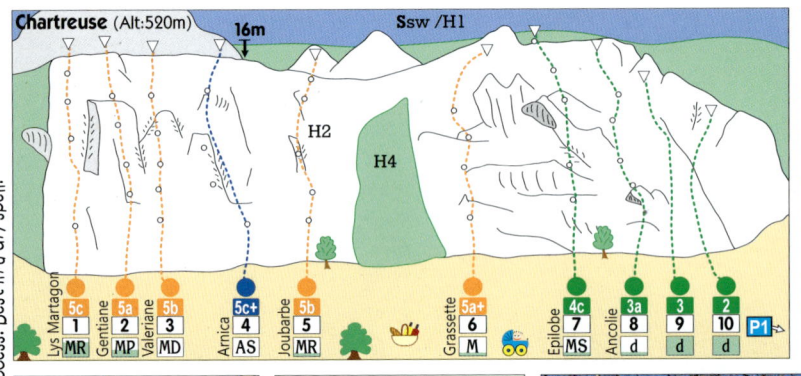

Chartreuse (Alt:520m) — Ssw /H1 — 16m

Granite* Ideal for a riverside picnic, easy access. Best in a dry spell.

	1	2	3	4	5	6	7	8	9	10
Name	Lys Martagon	Gentiane	Valeriane	Arnica	Joubarbe	Grassette	Epilobe	Ancolie		
Grade	5c	5a	5b	5c+	5b	5a+	4c	3a	3	2
	MR	MP	MD	AS	MR	M	MS	d	d	d

Epilobe 7 / 4c

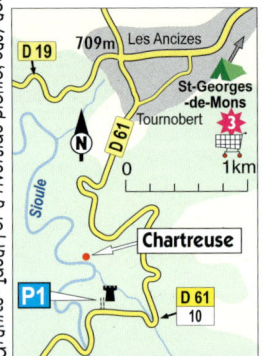
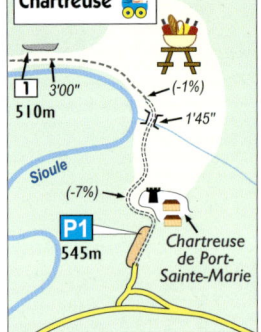

LA CHARTREUSE

4 / 5c+

NE+ /H0 — 12m | W+ /H1 | SW /H0-1 | SW /H0-1 — 16m | SE

Elise et Moi — Xavier Ogliphe — La Voie du Père — Belote — Rebelote — La Mère des Rioux — P'tit Rioux

	1	2	3	4	5	6	7	8	9	10	11	12
Name	Bounette	Tim Oh Leon	Basile de Koch		La Voie du Père		Xavier Ogliphe	Re Mi Fa Sol		Belote	Rebelote	La Mère des Rioux	P'tit Rioux
Grade	6b	6a	6a	5a	5b	5c	7a	.	5a	6b	6a	4b
	A:	R	M	A	D	SM	DA	dF	M	SN	ND	CD

Rebelote 10 / 6b

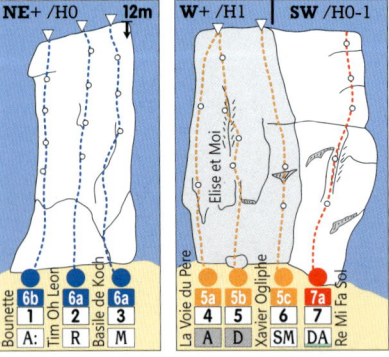
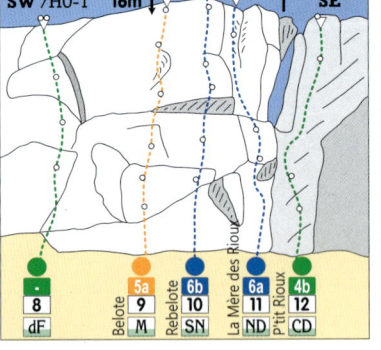

PÈRE DES RIOUX — PÈRE DES RIOUX

Granite** Two nice little quiet cliffs, zzzz

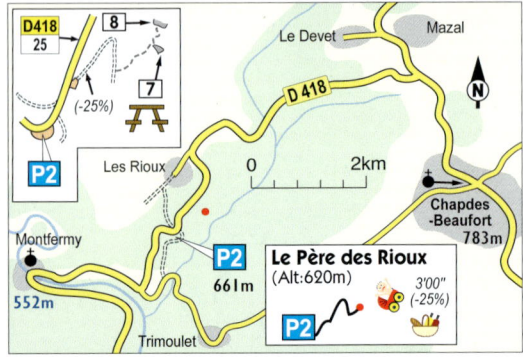

Re Mi Fa Sol 7 / 7a

Le Père des Rioux (Alt:620m)

LE PÈRE DES RIOUX

P2 45.883576, 2.825858

CHÂTEAUNEUF-LES-BAINS

P3 46.038644, 2.903356 # 1/1-14/6 nos 1-36   183

Châteauneuf-Les-Bains (Rocher-Charlemagne - Alt 400m)

NW 35m W /H1+

Wnw /H1   Nnw /H1   Wsw /H0-1

- 5c Afrikaan Bazar
- 5c Osez Joséphine
- H3
- Balai Royal
- In Nomina Schtroumpf
- 16m
- Conjuration des Imbeciles
- 15m
- Jill Bioskop
- La Raie
- Parking

Route	Le Cornafion	Balai Royal	Afrikaan Bazar	Osez Joséphine	Simone	In Nomina Schtroumpf	Tantine	Hot Dog	Année d'Après	Ane Erotique	Manu Cure	Conjuration des Imbeciles	Le Souffle du Diable	Serrez les Cables	Ipanema Girl	Fesse Gauche	Jill Bioskop
Grade	5c	6c	6a+	7a	6a+	6	5c	6b	4c	5a	5b	6a+	5c	5a	5a	5c	4c
№	1	2	3	4	5	6	7	8	9	10	11	12	13	14	15	17	18
Style	D	P	P:	M	P:	J	D	M	DC	FT	DA	M	M	M	D	D	

25m 20m 12m

Route	La Part du Diable	Voodoo Queen		Spaceman Spiff	La Dalle du Cinq		La Pardieu	La Fama Gros Bras	Tu Mousses Ron	Tu Lis Ken
Grade	4c	5c	4c	5c+	5b	5b	4b	6a	4a
№	18	19	20	21	22	23	24	25	26
Style	D	M	F	FR	MD	P	F:	SM	Gd

3 6a+ — Afrikaan Bazar

10 5a — Ane Erotique   **11** 5b — Manu Cure

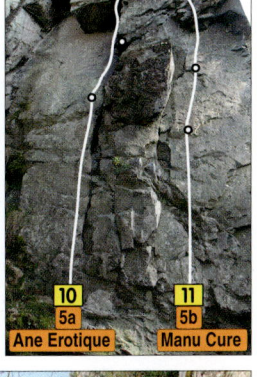

Map

D 99 — Pont de Braynant 379m
D122 10
P3
(-35%) 1'45"
(+1%) 5'15"
Rocher Charlemagne
D 109
9'30"
11'00" 40
Diaspora
Big Bras
Thermes
Châteauneuf-les-Bains
La Sioule

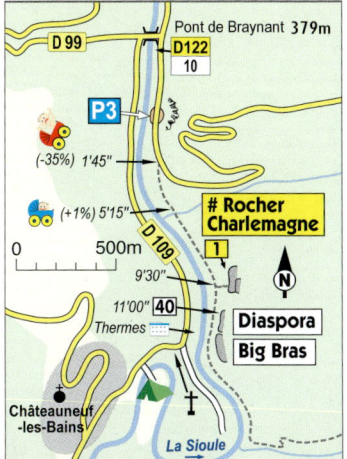

20 4c — Voodoo Queen

23 5b

Volcanic** R-Charlemagne, more old school style, long lonely routes, scary and not so clean. A hidden 15m sector not shown.

CHÂTEAUNEUF-LES-BAINS (Diaspora)

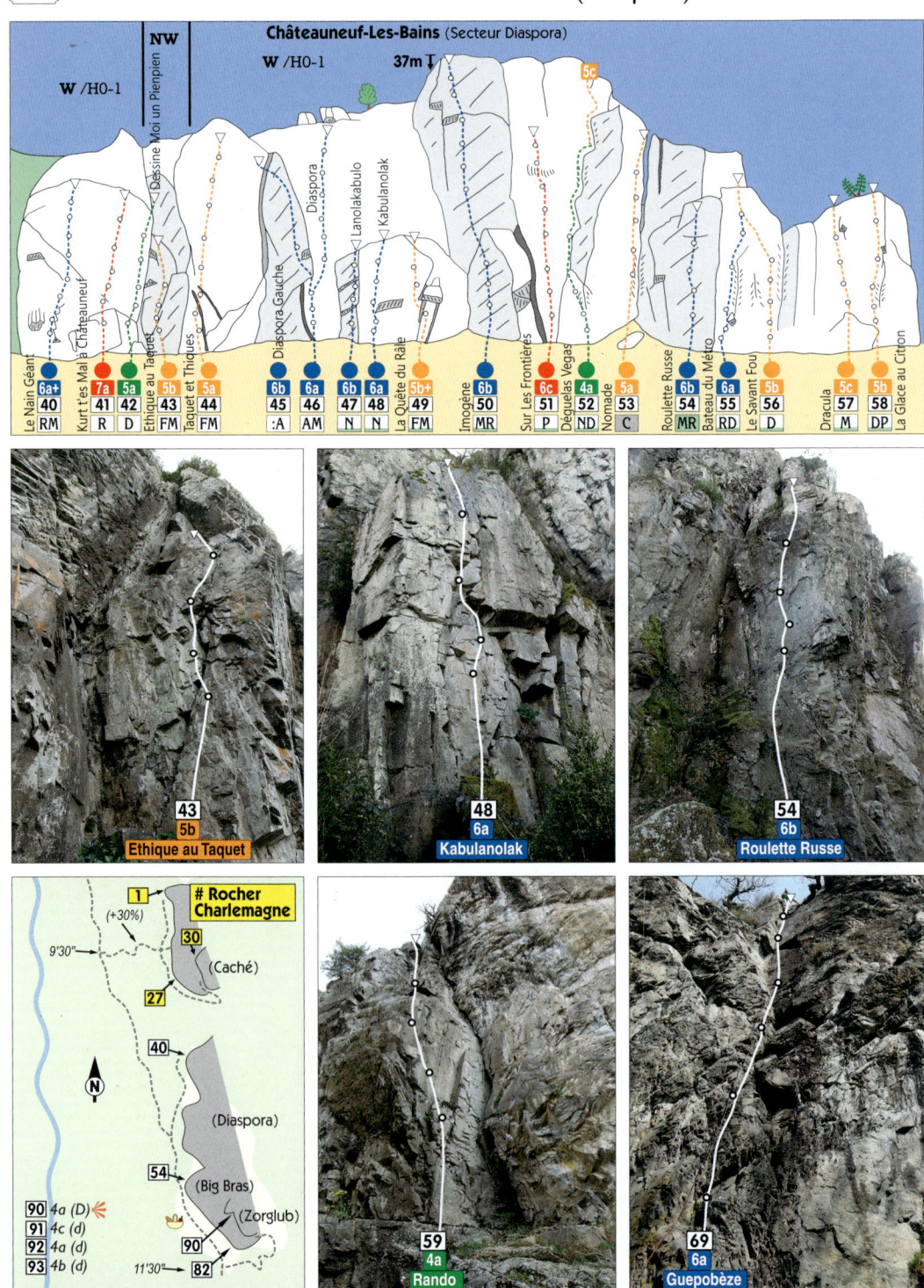

Very nice climbing on slightly leaning rock, a good selection of all types of routes. Grassy belay area - popular for picnics.

CHÂTEAUNEUF-LES-BAINS (Big Bras)

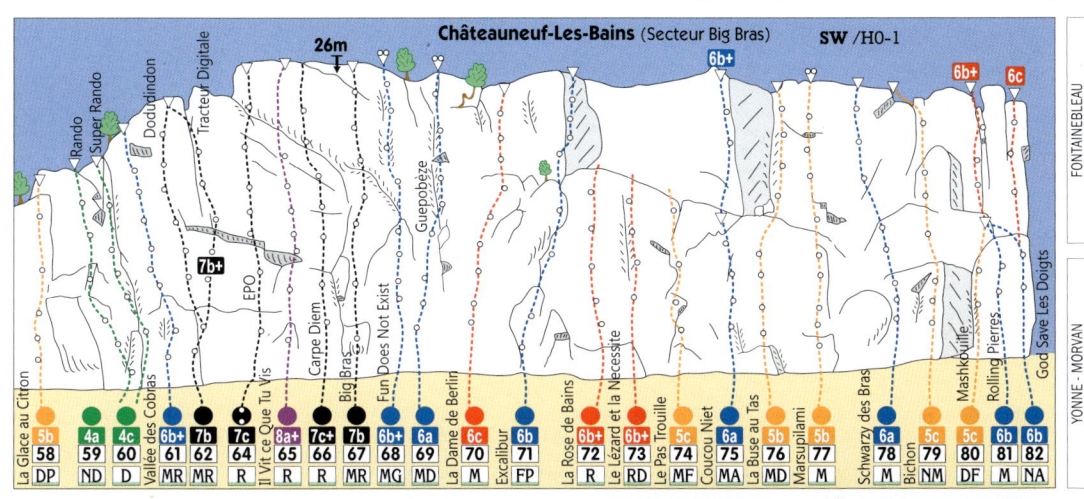

Châteauneuf-Les-Bains (Secteur Big Bras) SW /H0-1

77 — 5b — Marsupilami

80 — 5c — Mashkouille

L'EX TRACTEUR DIGITAL 7b+, *Emilie Sebag*,

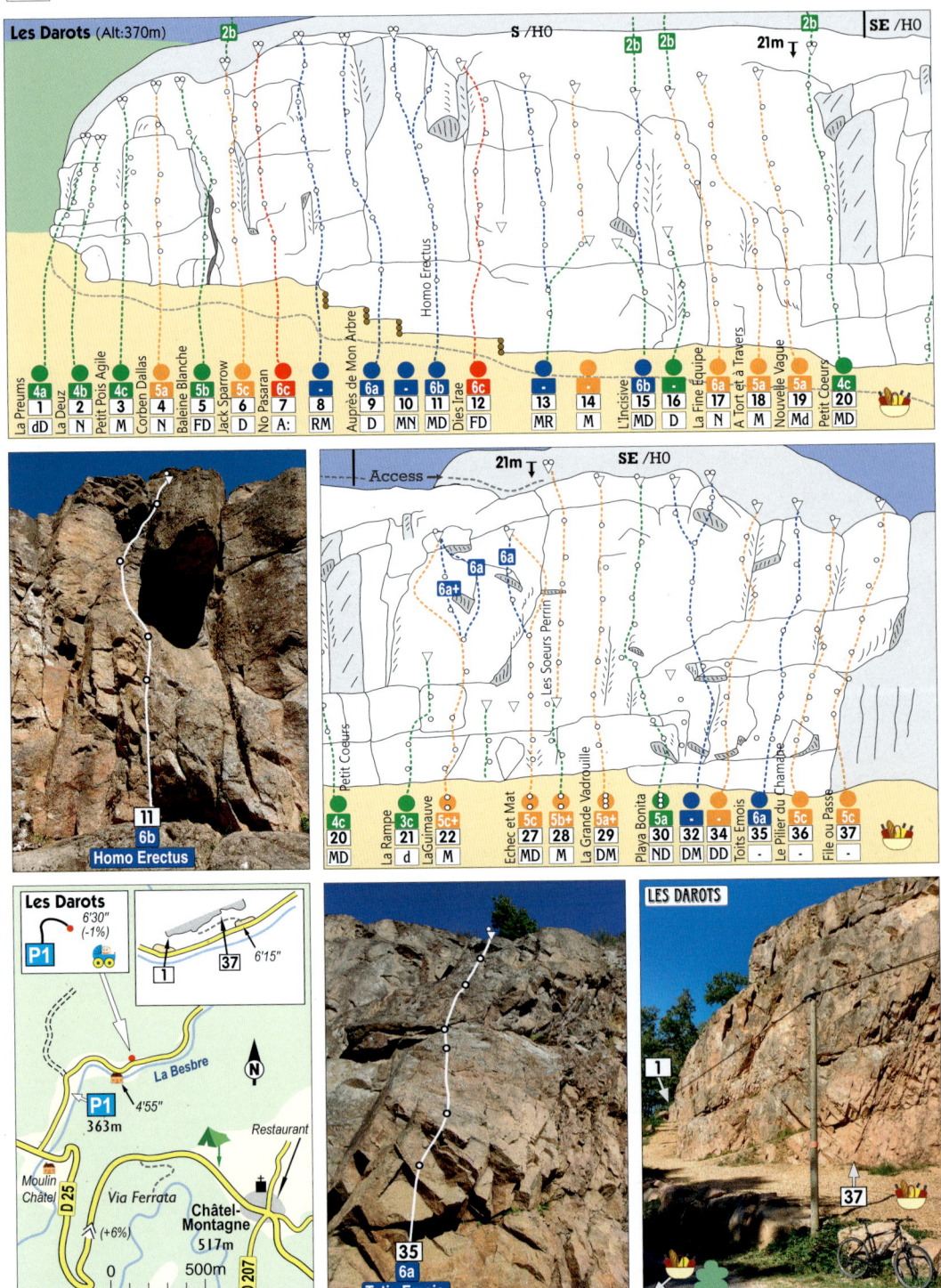

LA SALETTE

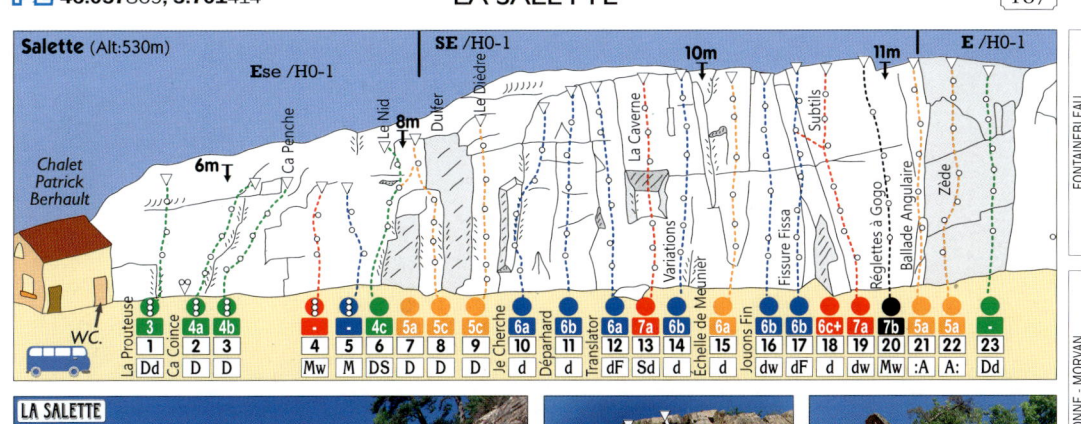

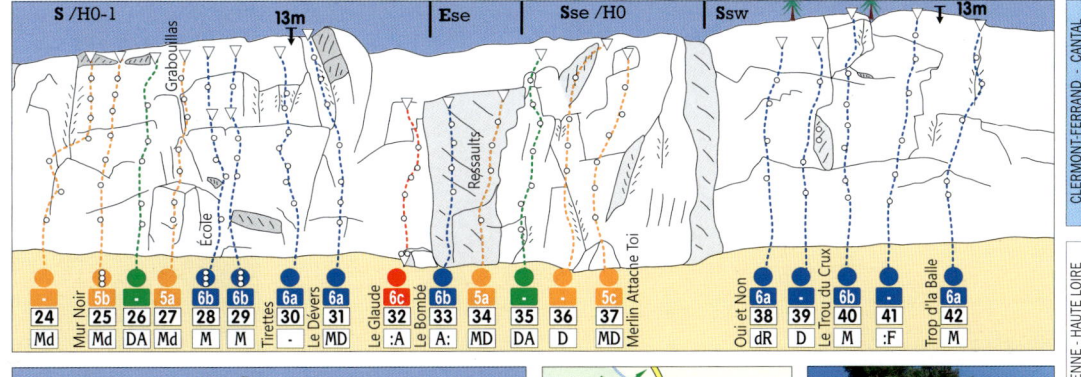

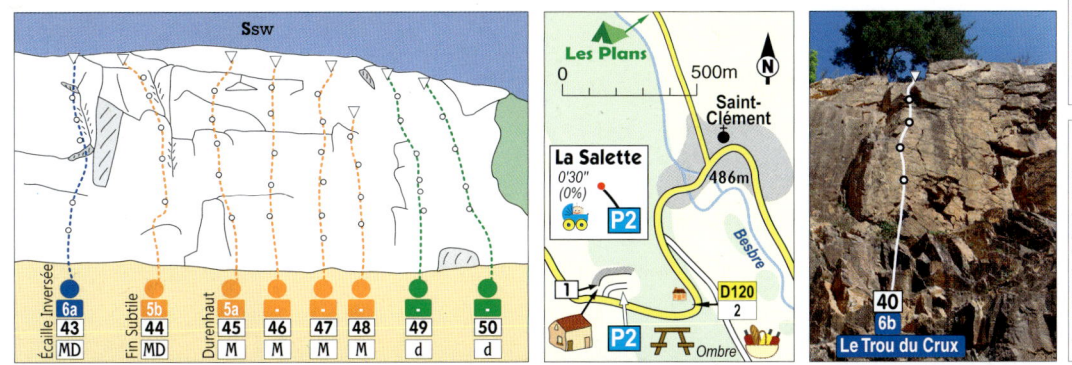

Granite** A small drive in quarry gives warm sunny climbing, plenty of fun for everyone. Picnic table in the shade.

PIERRE FENDUE

P3 45.993331, 3.690680

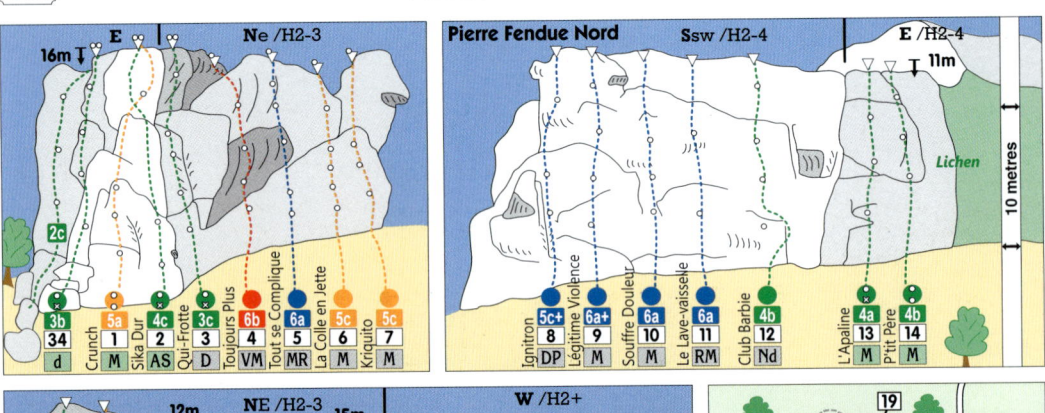

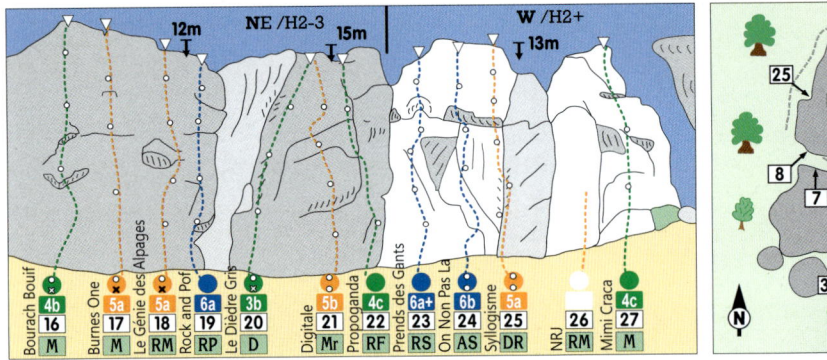

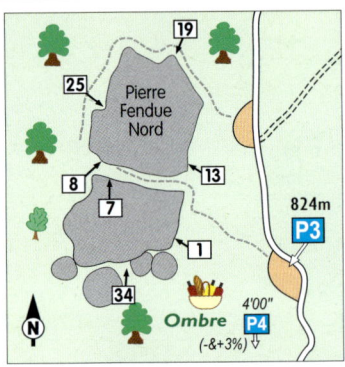

13 3c L'Apaline

24 6b+ Oh Non Pas Là

Volcanic-Andesite** Very shady and damp sector with suffocating trees. Great on a not dry summers day.

ROCHER SAINT VINCENT - A (Rocher Principal) - # 1/3-15/6 nos 1-22 — 189

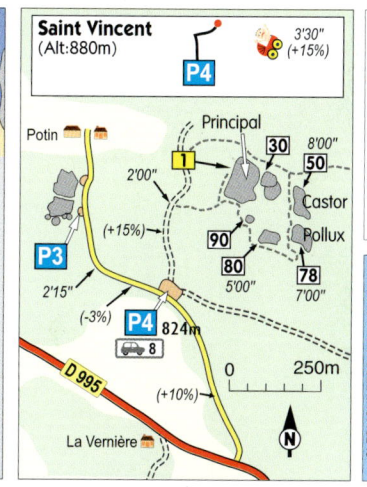

Some spectacular rock and scenery, wonderful climbing and views. Bolting is ancien, so best wait for re-equipping.

7 — 6c — Écriture Émotionnelle

14 — 5c — Petit François

19 — 6a+ — Foufounette

Volcanic-Andesite*** A group of cliffs that give a complete mixed bag of climbing, from friendly....to "not so friendly."

ROCHER SAINT VINCENT - B (Enciente & Greffier)

Photo Pronto 5a [35], Mr. Jingo

Two very nice sectors with fabulous views. Nice place for that mountain style feeling - and picnic if not too hot.

ROCHER SAINT VINCENT - C (Autres)

P4 45.991505, 3.693792 — 191

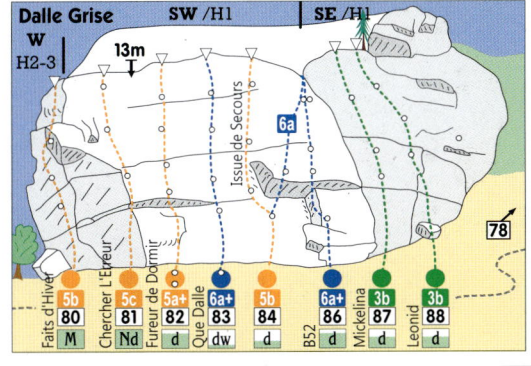

72 — 5a+ — Carpe Diem

87 — 3b — Mickelina

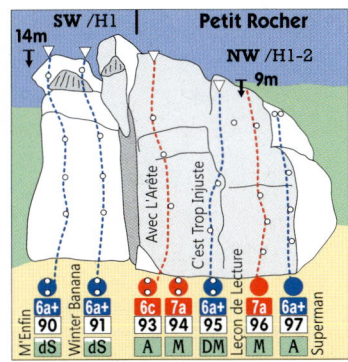

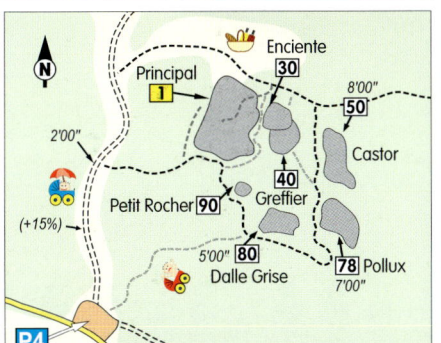

95 — 6a+ — C'est Trop Injuste

Autre sectors: A nice varied selection of small and friendly outcrops. Pleasant picnic possibilities but no views.

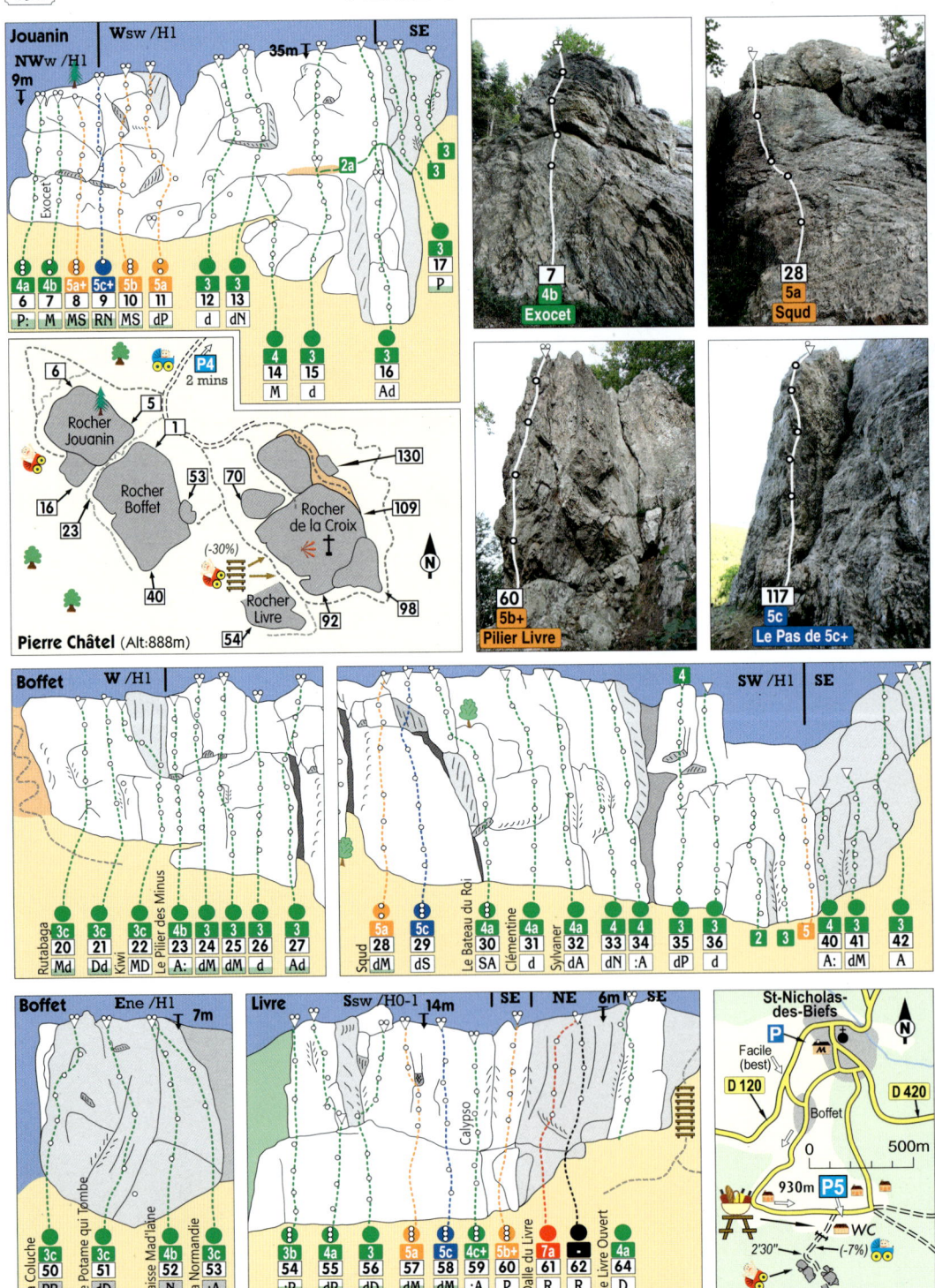

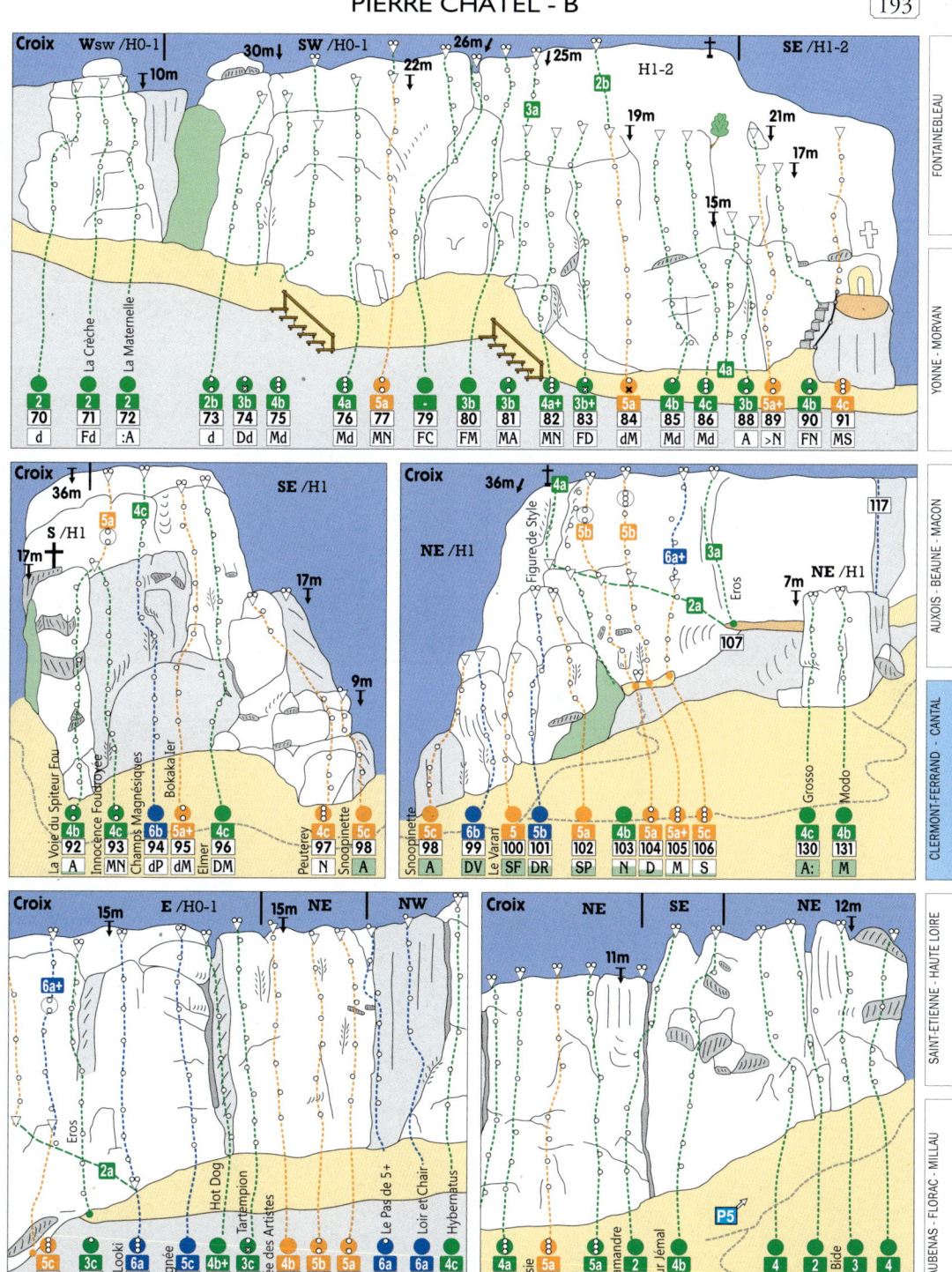

CEYRAT

P1 45.725493, 3.063446

Ceyrat (Alt: 578m) S/H0 19m E/H0 16m NE E

	La Momo	La Ramée	Belle Amie	La Voie du Chemin	Mine de Rien	La Grotte	Alors	La Fissure	La Direct Sous Le Toit	Les Deux Pitons	Amidal	Eperon	Voie Normale	Le Dièdre	Le Z	A Droite du Miroir	Retbur de la Fissure	Pleine Dale	Pas Nôée	Que Dalle	Dereidal	1er Essai
	5a	5c	6b+	6c	5c	6a+	6a	4b	6a+	5c	6a	5a	4a	3b	4b	6a	4c	6b	5c	6a+	5b	5c	3a
#	2	3	4	5	6	7	8	9	12	13	14	15	16	17	18	19	20	21	22	23	24	25	26
	d	dM	M	MR	MN	GD	M	dD	dR	dV	dR	dN	:A	FD	D	d	F	d	d	d	d	d	dN

4 — 6b+ — Belle Amie

7 — 6a+ — La Grotte

16 — 4a — L'Eperon

21 — 4b — Le Z

E 7a 6b SE 25m Ssw /H0-1

Dalle au Soleil — La Voie de L'Arbre — Zaza — Lyly — En Attendant Roro — Ainsi Fond — Haut Syphon

Cool	Dülfer		La Voie de L'Arbre	Zaza	Lyly	En Attendant Roro		Haut Syphon
3a	5c	6b	3a	5c	5a	6a	4b	4c
28	30	31	32	33	34	35	36	37
D	dD	M	D	Md	DM	M	Md	Md

9 — 4b — La Fissure

Ceyrat P1 1'00" (0%) — Av. de la Liberation — No.33 — 37 — 8 — P1 — 578m — Rus-de-St-Genes — P

0   100m

28 — 3a — Cool

30 — 5c — Dülfer

Granite** A highly polished small urban cliff, but still offering some good enjoyable routes. Car break-ins, proabable if enticed.

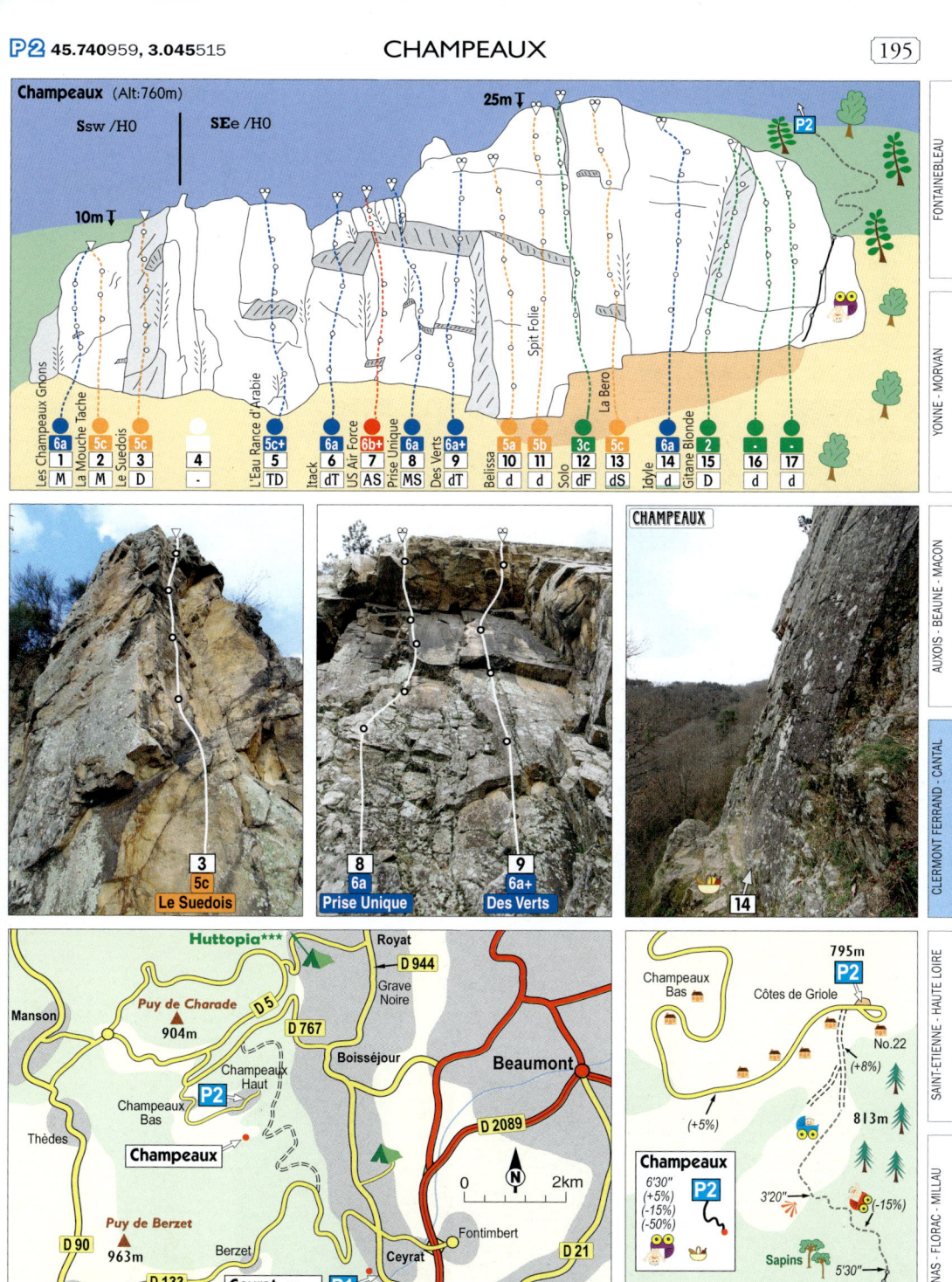

LA MONTAGNE PERCÉE

P3 45.782063, 3.039038

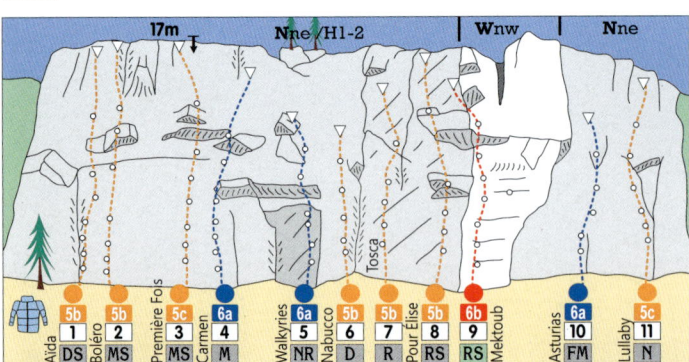
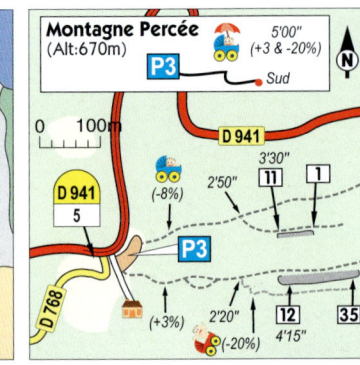

CLERMONT-FERRAND

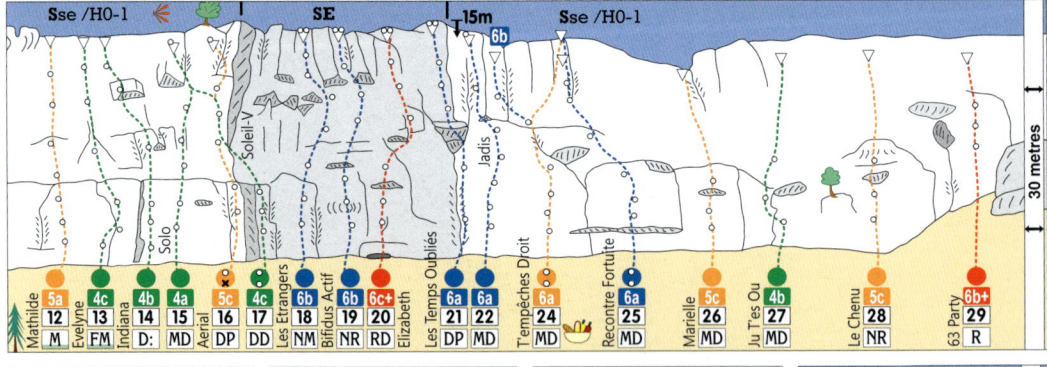

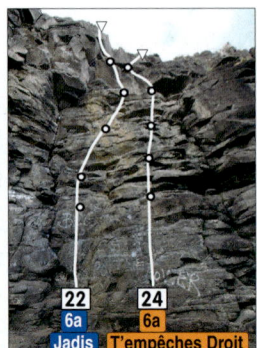

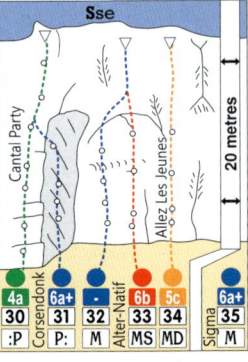

Bassalt: Very nice climbing - 2 sectors completely different in character: Nord, very shady and chilly; Sud, sun trap & views.

VOLPIE - BUNKER PALACE HOTEL

SAUVIAT

198 · P1 45.715175, 3.528456

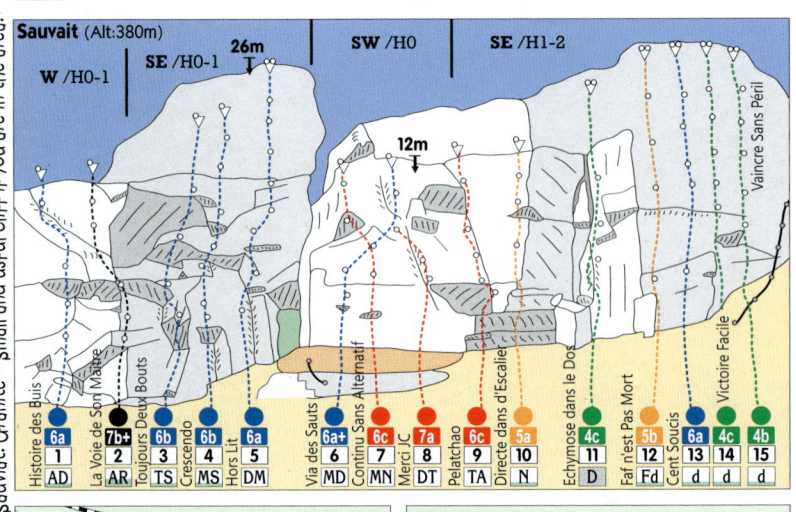

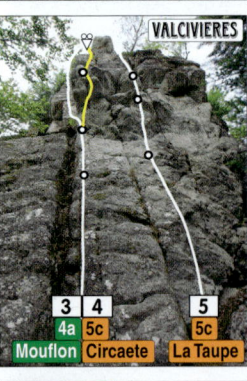

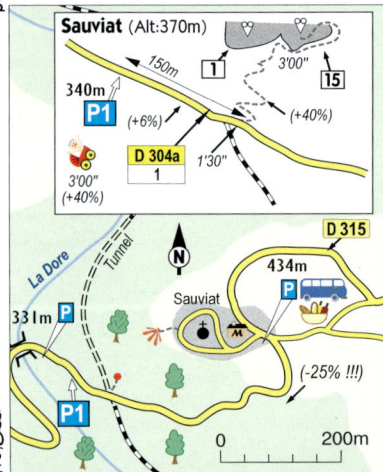
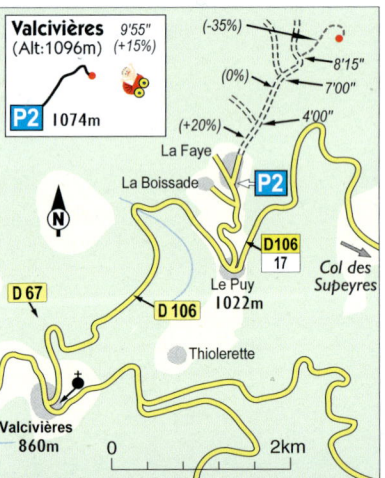
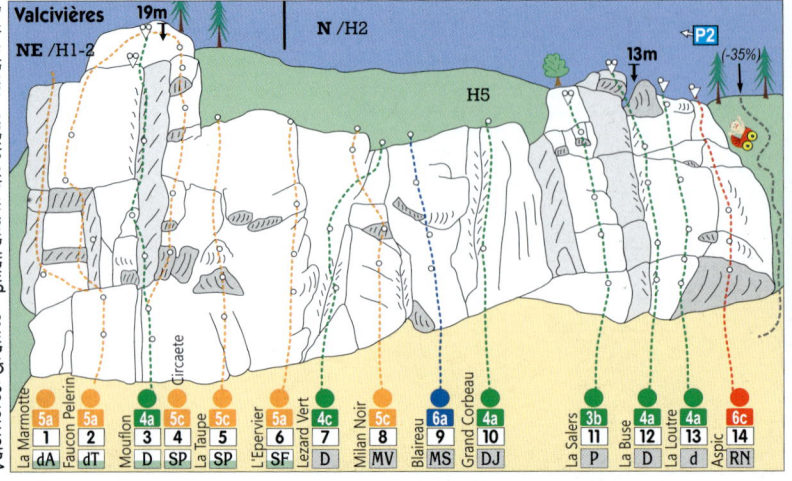

P2 45.601169, 3.808808 — VALCIVIERES

P3 45.619516, 3.760947 — **VOLPIE** — # 1/2-15/5 Total (....15/6) — 199

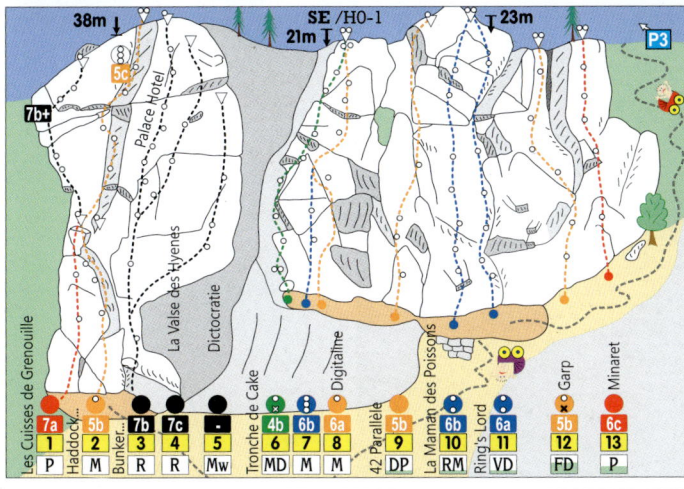

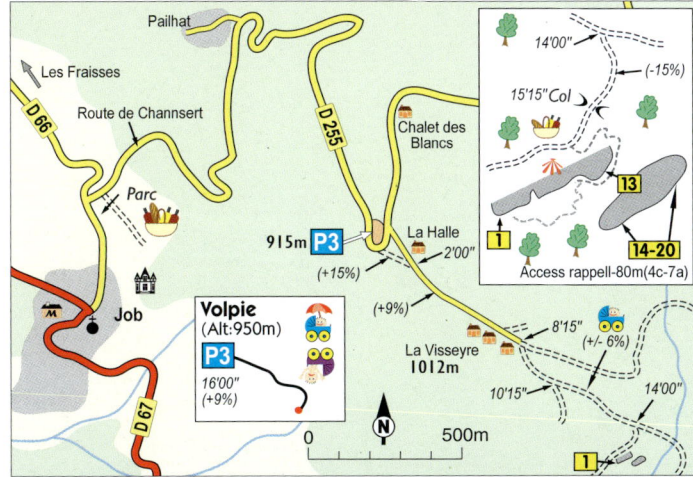

Granite**** A superb small cliff with a wow view. Great aspect. Additional routes on other tower seem less popular - plants.

LA ROCHE GOURNIER

P1 45.643486, 3.204056

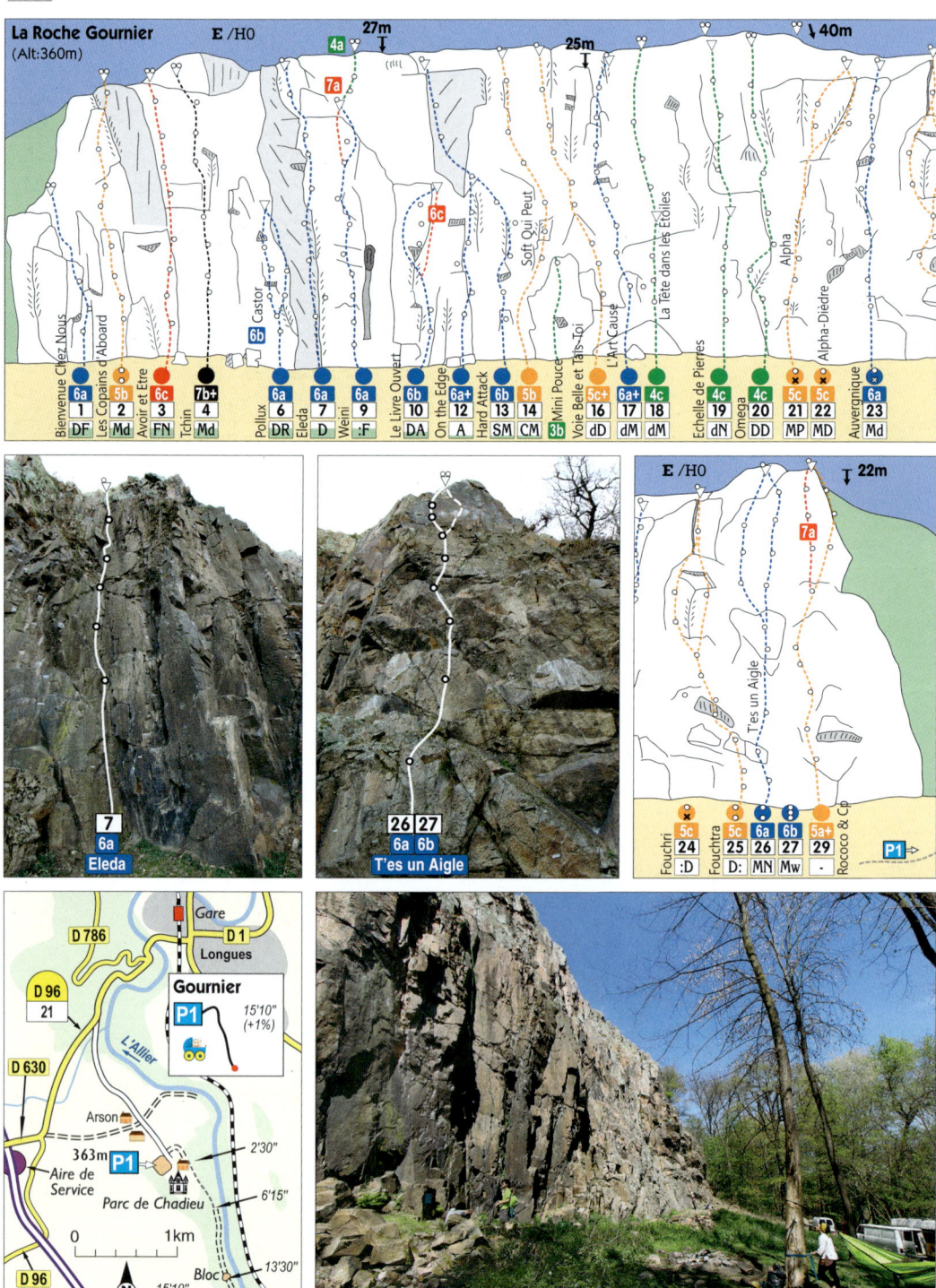

Granite*** Very nice location, looks like Bassalt, but is actually granite. Mostly with more holds than it looks, but not always.

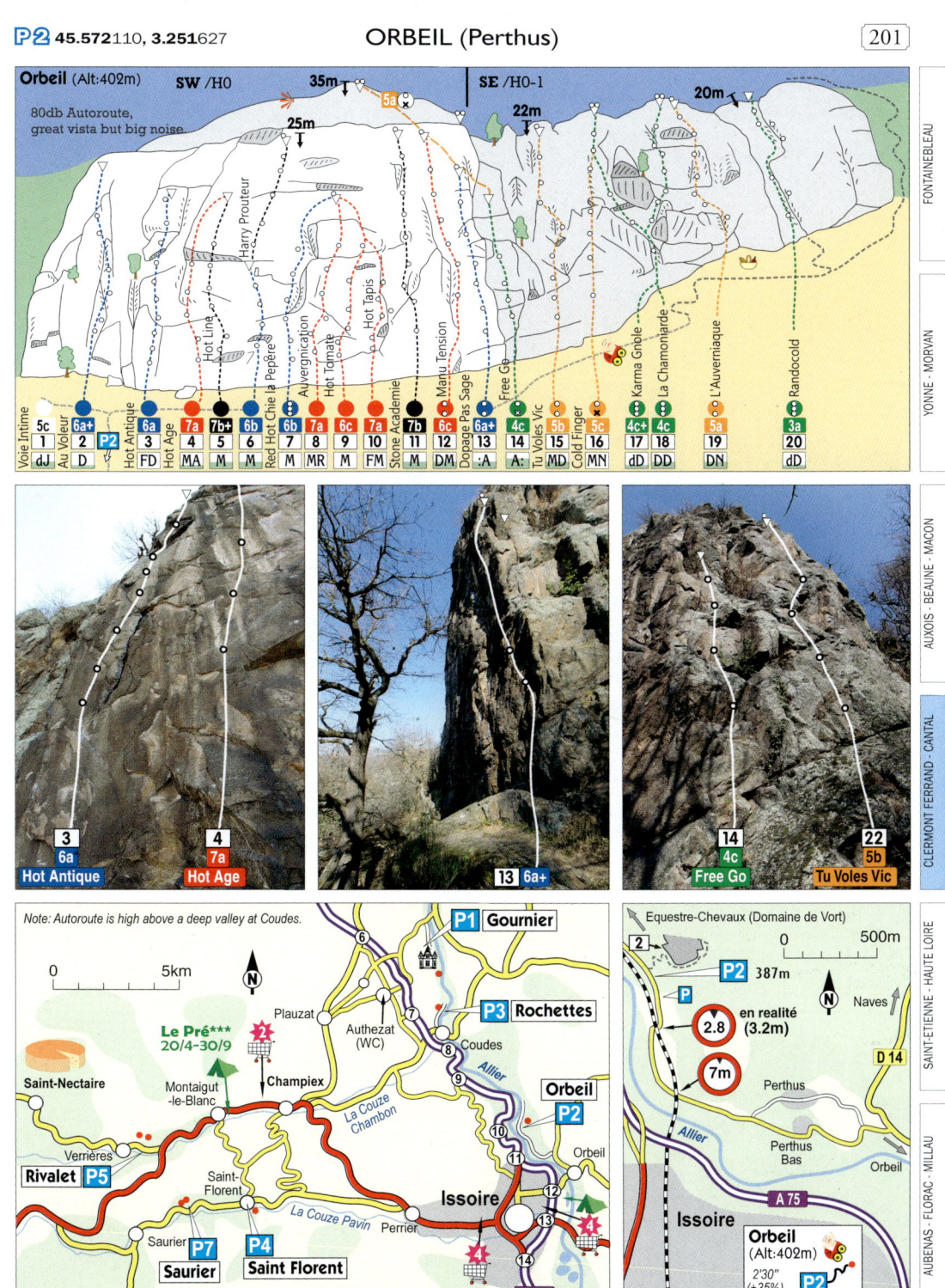

LES ROCHETTES

P3 45.619619, 3.212193

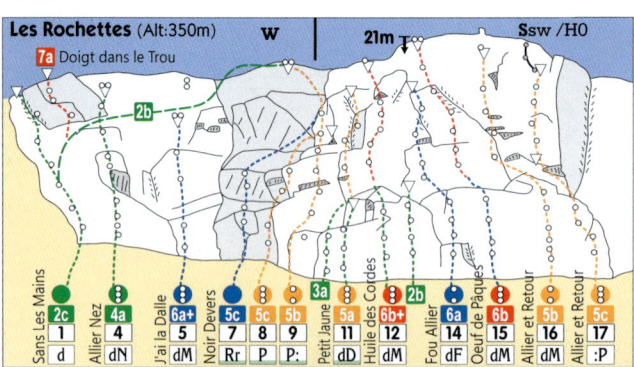
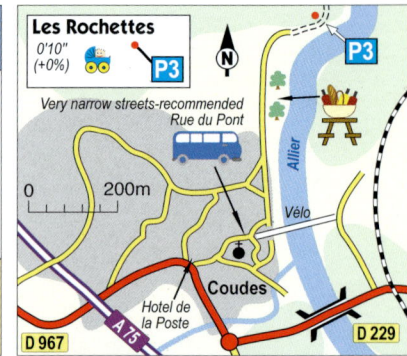

*Granite*** Friendly cliffs don't come much friendlier than this one.*

*Granite** A chilly windy spot, very useful in a heatwave. Bolts not ideally placed.*

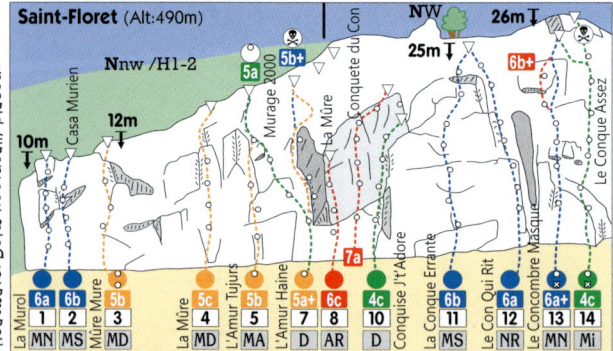
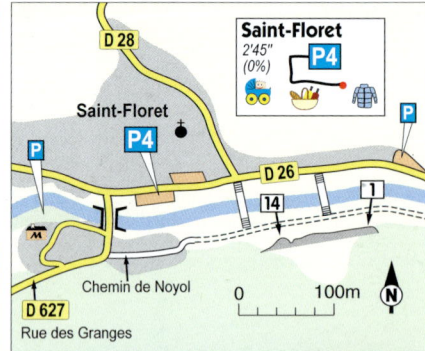

SAINT FLORET

P4 45.550917, 3.109316

Poi Poi Girls 5a, *Marie Marbach. RIVALET*

LE RIVALET - A

P5 45.574060, 3.046089

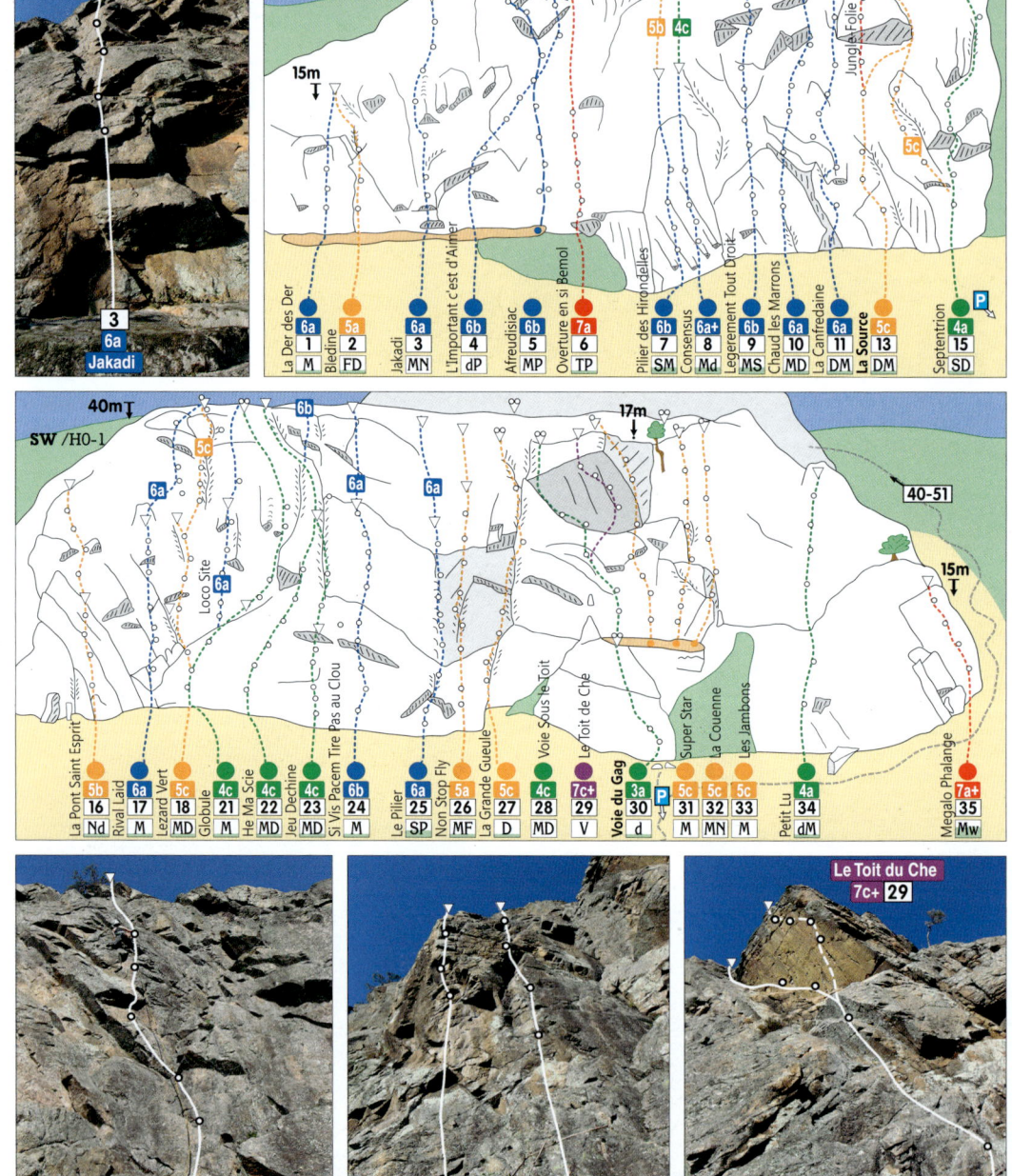

Granite*** (Golden) Rivalet doesn't look impressive from below, but is quite spectacular. Base of the cliff is mostly chaotic.

LE RIVALET - B

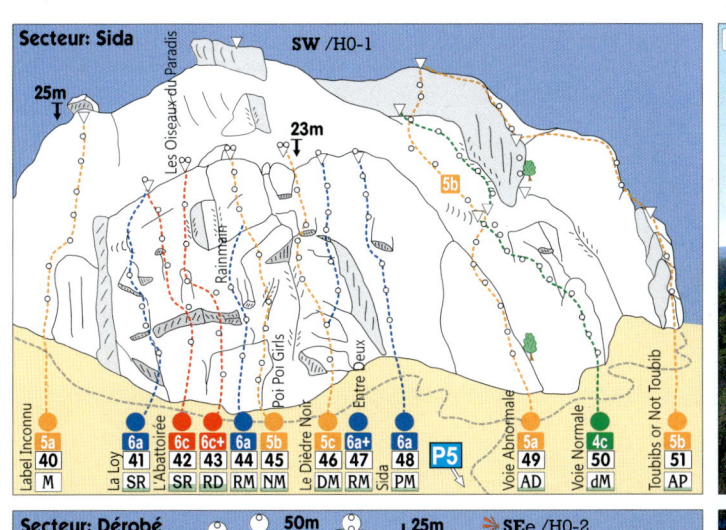

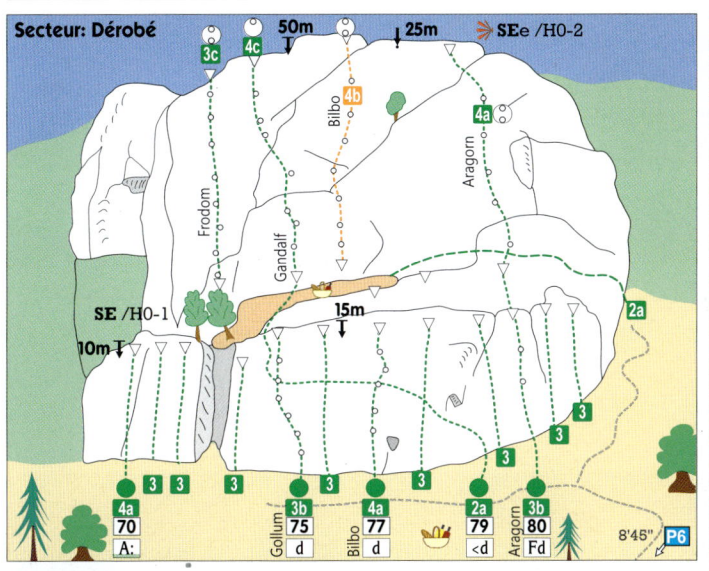

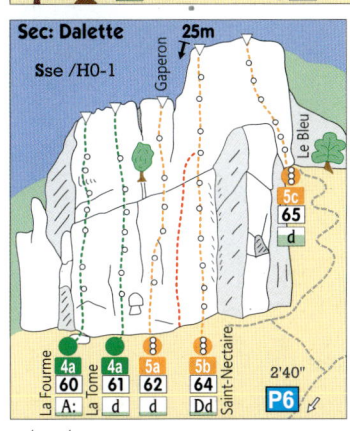
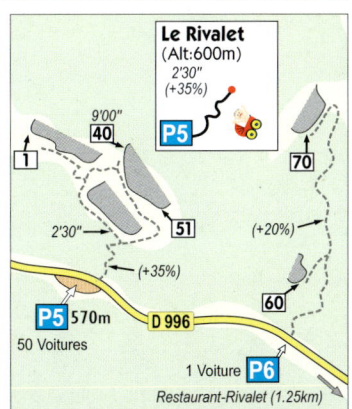

Dérobée: A nice easy angled cliff with great views and is a popular venue for introducing children. Comfortable at bottom.

SAURIER - A

P7 45.545806, 3.070327

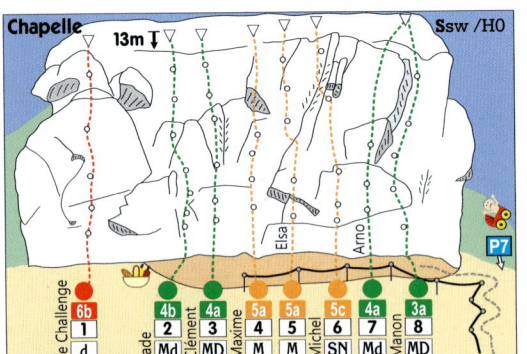
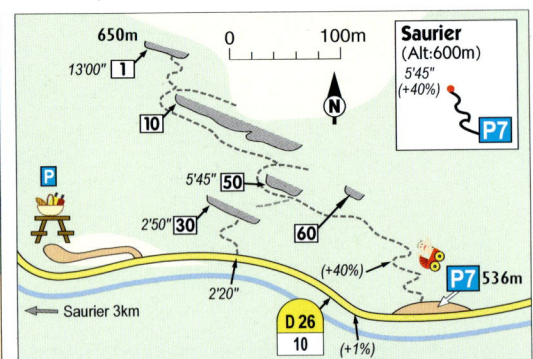
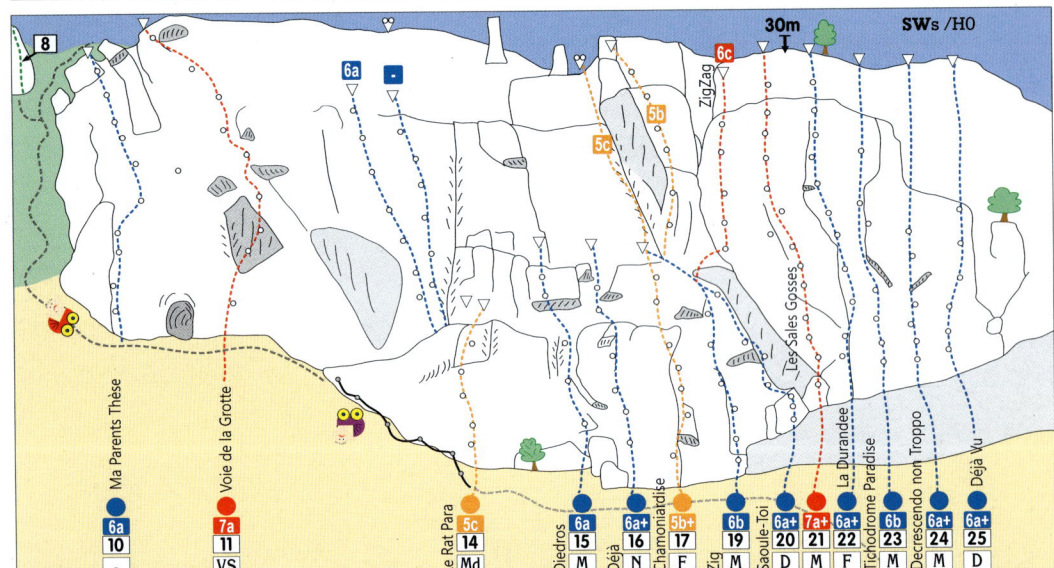
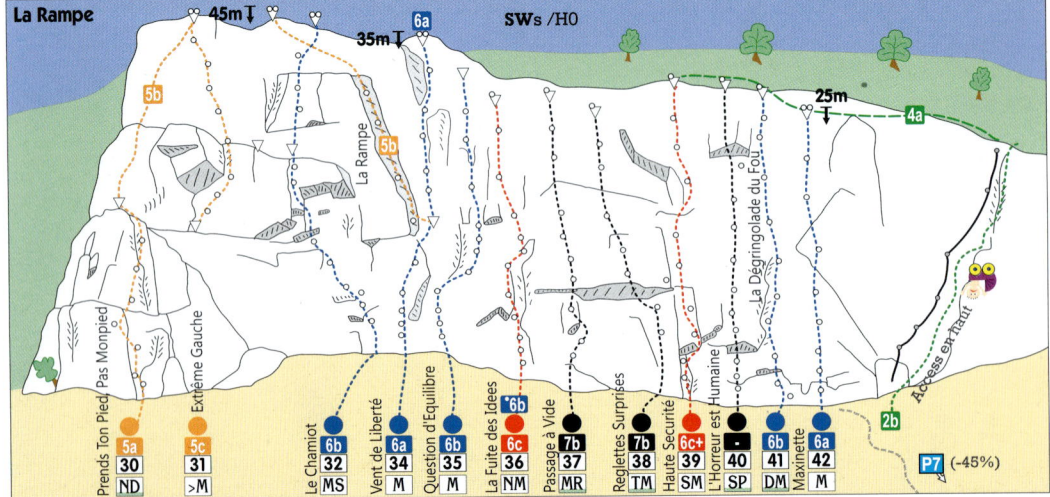

Granite*** A group of mid sized cliffs that gets very warm in the afternoon...but also can stay in shade from mountain clouds.

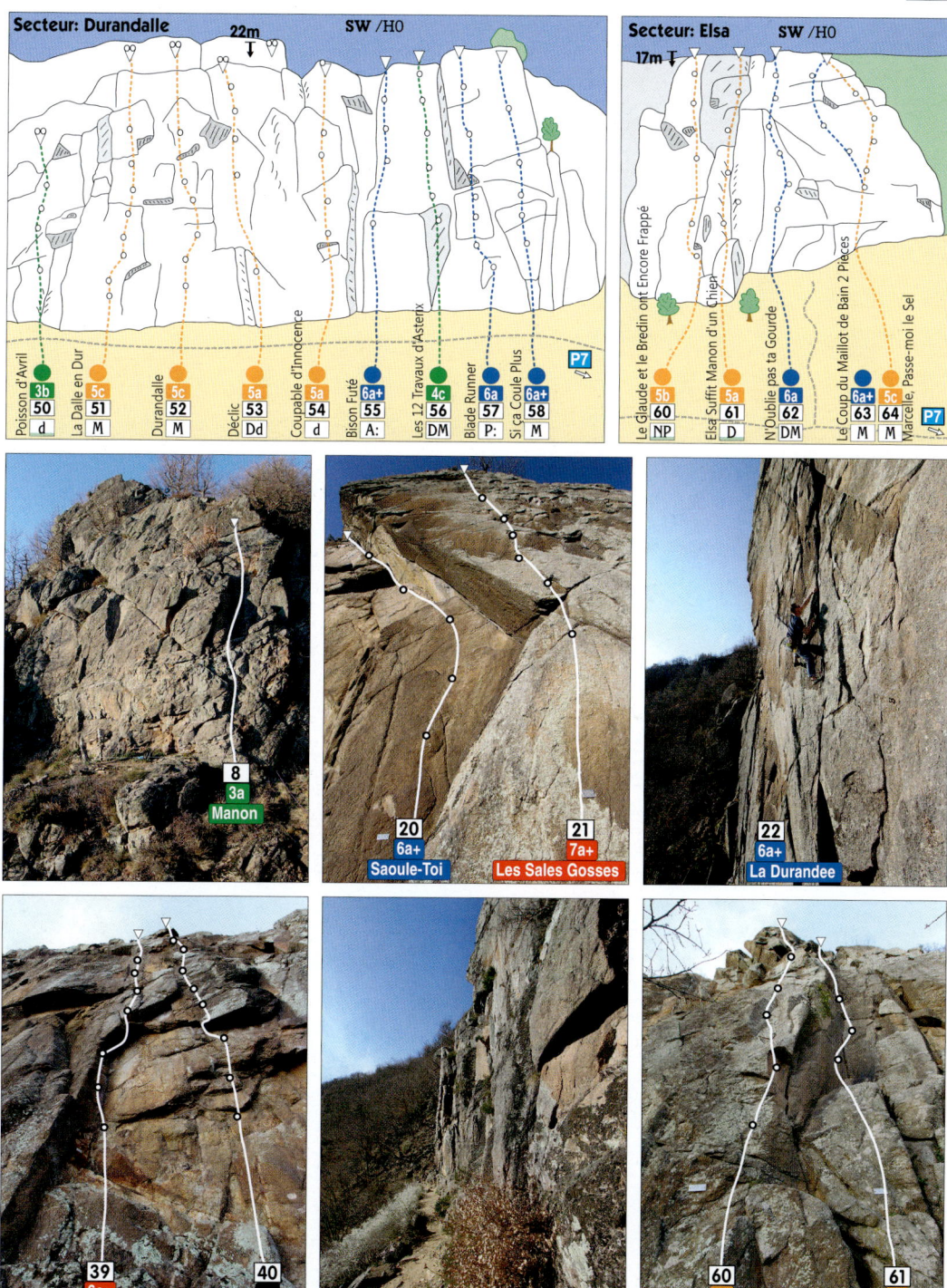

SAINT-SAUVES

P1 45.594154, 2.700169

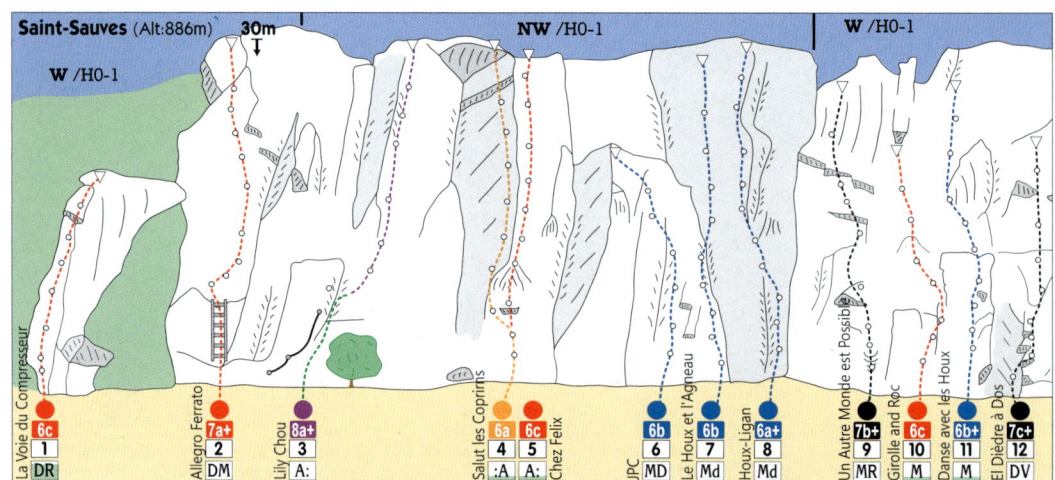

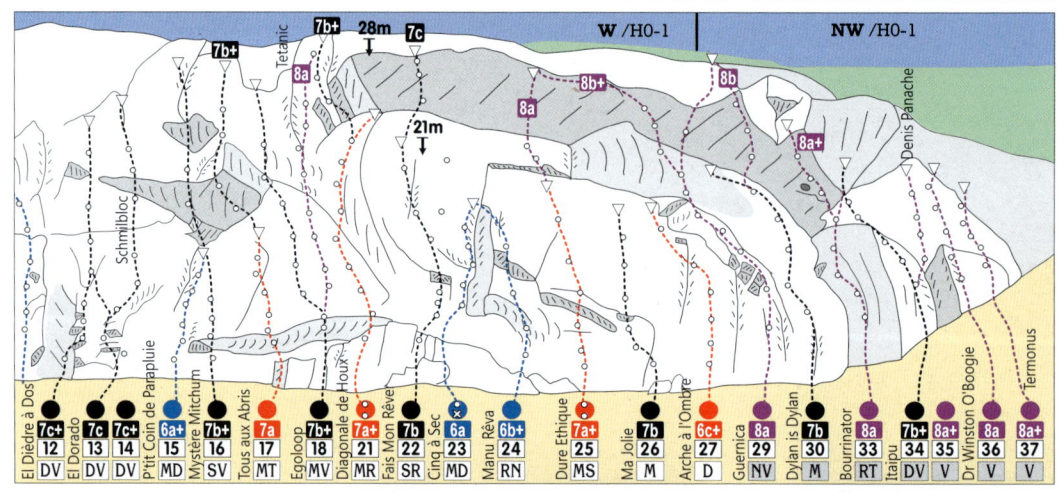

Cinq à Sec — 23 / 6a

Dure Ethique — 25 / 7a+

Diagonale de Houx 7b+, Christophe Martins

Granite**** A very impressive big arch. Situated in a dead end valley - so can get a bit humid.

P2 45.621519, 2.820182   LA ROCHE TUILIERE   209

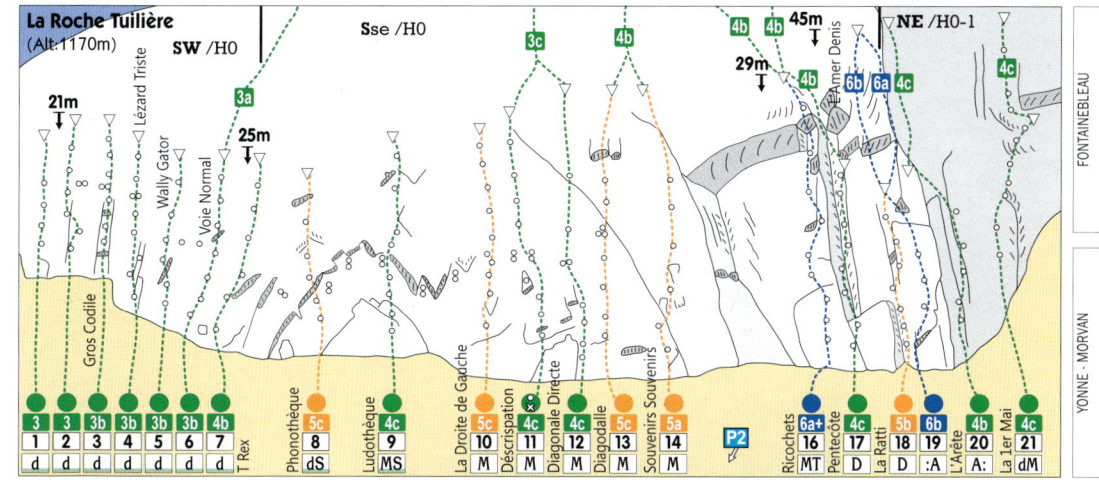

3	3	3b	3b	3b	3b	4b		5c		4c		5c	4c	4c	5c	5a		6a+	4c	4c	5b	6b		4b	4c
1	2	3	4	5	6	7	T Rex	8 Phonothèque	9 Ludothèque	10 La Droite de Gauche	11 Déscrispation	12 Diagonale Directe	13 Diagodalie	14 Souvenirs Souvenirs	P2	16 Ricochets	17 Pentecôte	18 La Ratti	19 L'Arête	20 La 1er Mai	21
d	d	d	d	d	d	d		dS	MS	M		M	M	M		MT	D	D	:A	A:	dM

La Droite de Gauche 5c, Antoine Wallart, Tuilière (10)

LA ROCHE TUILIERE

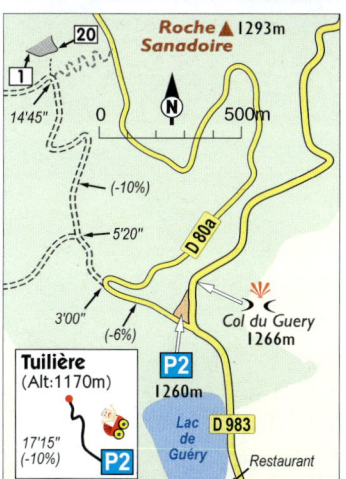

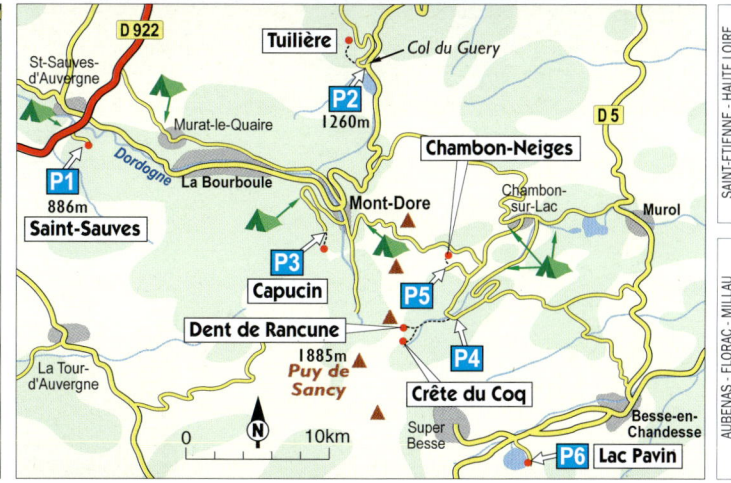

Phonolite*** Popular with groups under instruction on the easier routes. Conical cliff where long routes end up together,

LE CAPUCIN

P3 45.569379, 2.802192

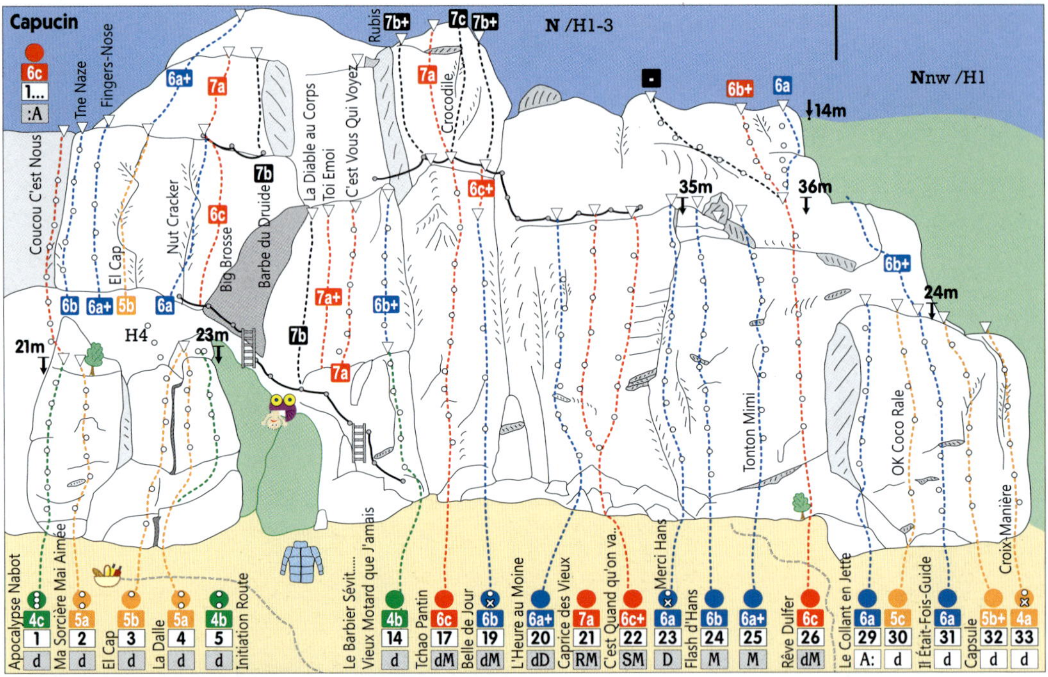

#	Route	Grade	Notes
1	Apocalypse Nabot	4c	d
2	Ma Sorcière Mai Aimée	5a	d
3	El Cap	5b	d
4	La Dalle	5a	d
5	Initiation Route	4b	d
14	Le Barbier Sévit... Vieux Motard que J'amais	4b	d
17	Tchao Pantin	6c	dM
19	Belle de Jour	6b	dM
20	L'Heure au Moine	6a+	dD
21	Caprice des Vieux	7a	RM
22	C'est Quand qu'on va	6c+	SM
23	Flash d'Hans	6a	D
24	Merci Hans	6b	M
25		6a+	M
26	Rêve Dulfer	6c	dM
29	Le Collant en Jette	6a	A: d
30	OK Coco Râle	5c	d
31	Il Était-Fois-Guide	6a	d
32	Capsule	5b+	d
33	Croix Manière	4a	d

1 — 4c — Apocalypse Nabot
2 — 5a — Ma Sorcière

20 — 6a+ — L'Heure au Moine
23 — 6a

29 — 6a — La Collant en Jette
30 — 5c — OK Coco Râle

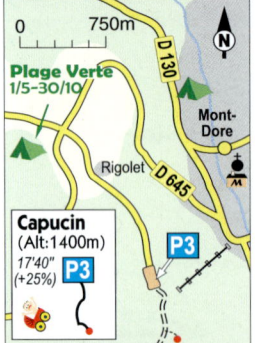

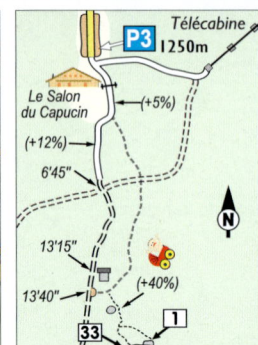

CAPUCIN - VUE

La Dent de la Rancune. Mr fixon en rappel (Voie Normal 9)

Phonolite**** A huge prow, with routes that get exponentially exposed, very chilly place-heatwave. Low routes are friendly.

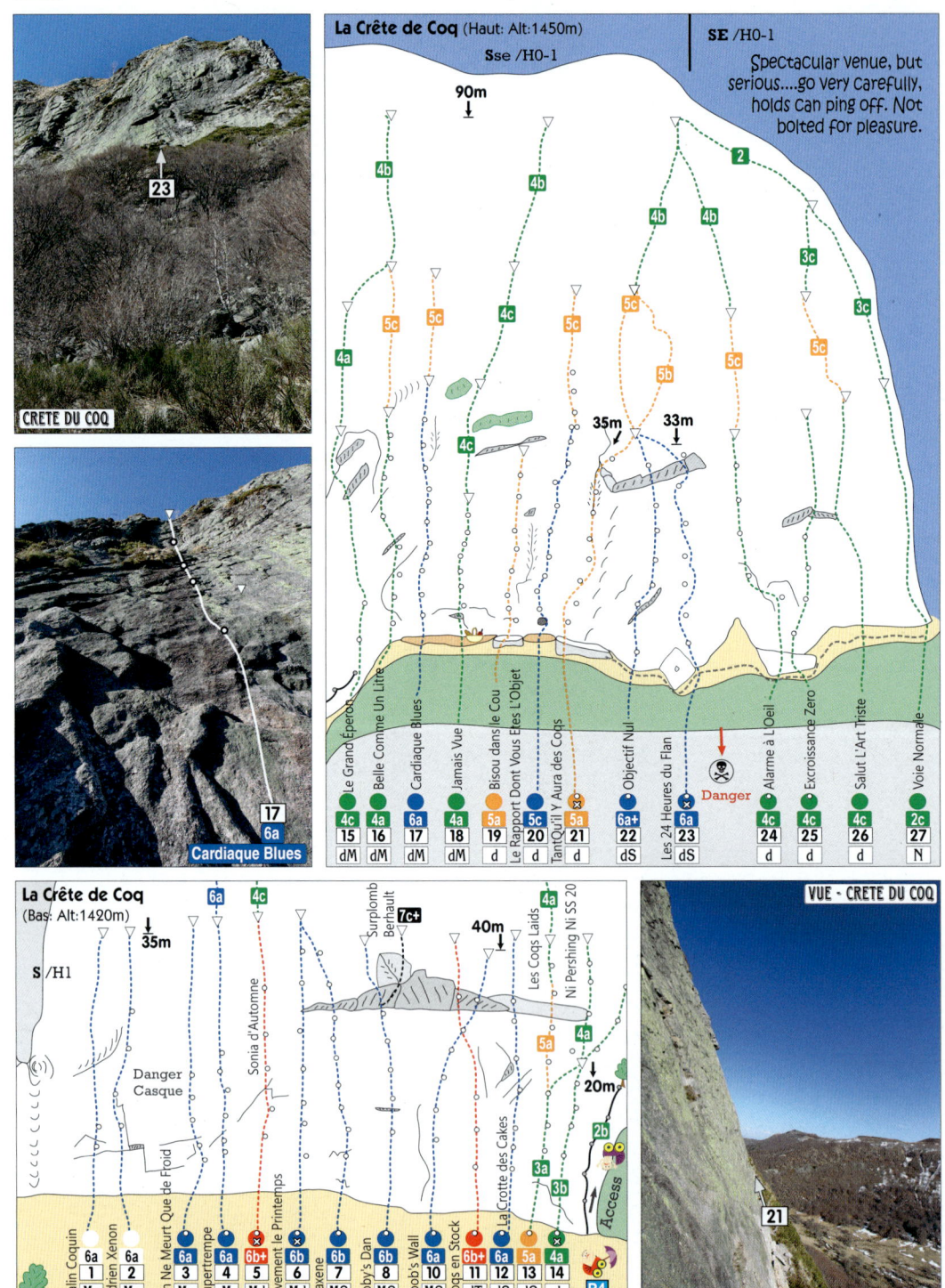

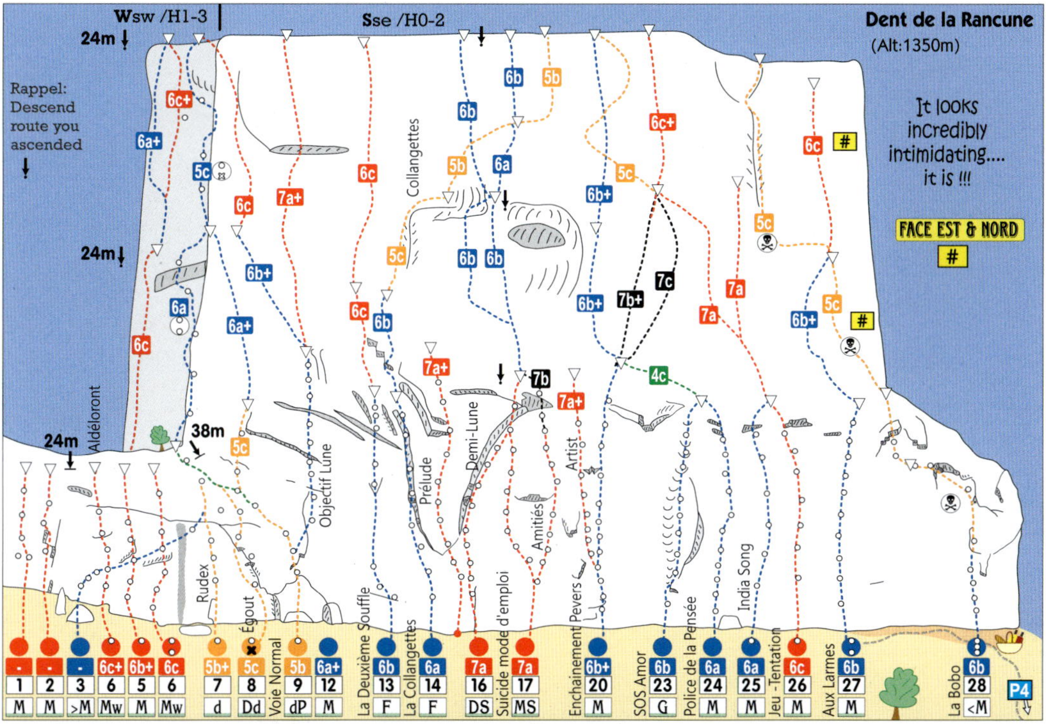

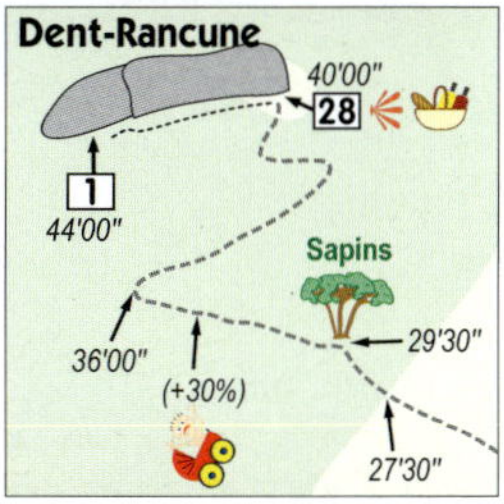

LA DENT DE LA RANCUNE

P4 45.540508, 2.861881 — 213

Dent de la Rancune (Alt: 1350m)

It looks incredibly intimidating.... it is !!!

FACE EST & NORD #

●	●	●	6c+	6b+	6c	6a+	5b+	5c	5b	6a+	●	6b	6a	6a	●	7a	6b+	6b	6a	6a	6a	6c	6b	●
1	2	3	4	5	6	7	8	9	10	11	12	13	14	15	16	17	20	23	24	25	26	27	28	
M	M	>M	Mw	Mw	Mw	d	Dd		dP	M		F	F		DS	MS	M	G	M	M	M	M	<M	

Routes: Aldélaront, Rudex, Égout, Voie Normal, La Deuxième Souffle, La Collangettes, Suicide mode d'emploi, Enchainement Peyers, SOS Amor, Police de la Pensée, India Song, Jeu Tentation, Aux Larmes, La Bobo

Rappel: Descend route you ascended. 24m / 24m / 24m / 38m

Wsw /H1-3 Sse /H0-2

14 6a — La Collangettes

23 6b — SOS Amor

DENT DE LA RANCUNE — 16, 28

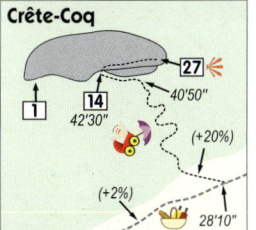

Crête-Coq — 27, 14, 1

Réserve Naturelle de la Vallée Chaudefour — Dent-Rancune, Pont Ste-Anne, Restaurant, P4 1140m, Maison du Parc, Auto & Vélo (VTT), Crête-Coq

Dent-Rancune — 28, 1, Sapins

FONTAINEBLEAU · YONNE - MORVAN · AUXOIS - BEAUNE - MACON · CLERMONT FERRAND - CANTAL · SAINT-ETIENNE - HAUTE LOIRE · AUBENAS - FLORAC - MILLAU

Volcanic lava*** Sunny and out there climbing, always a cool breeze. Equipping is very old school, some mossy decayed routes.

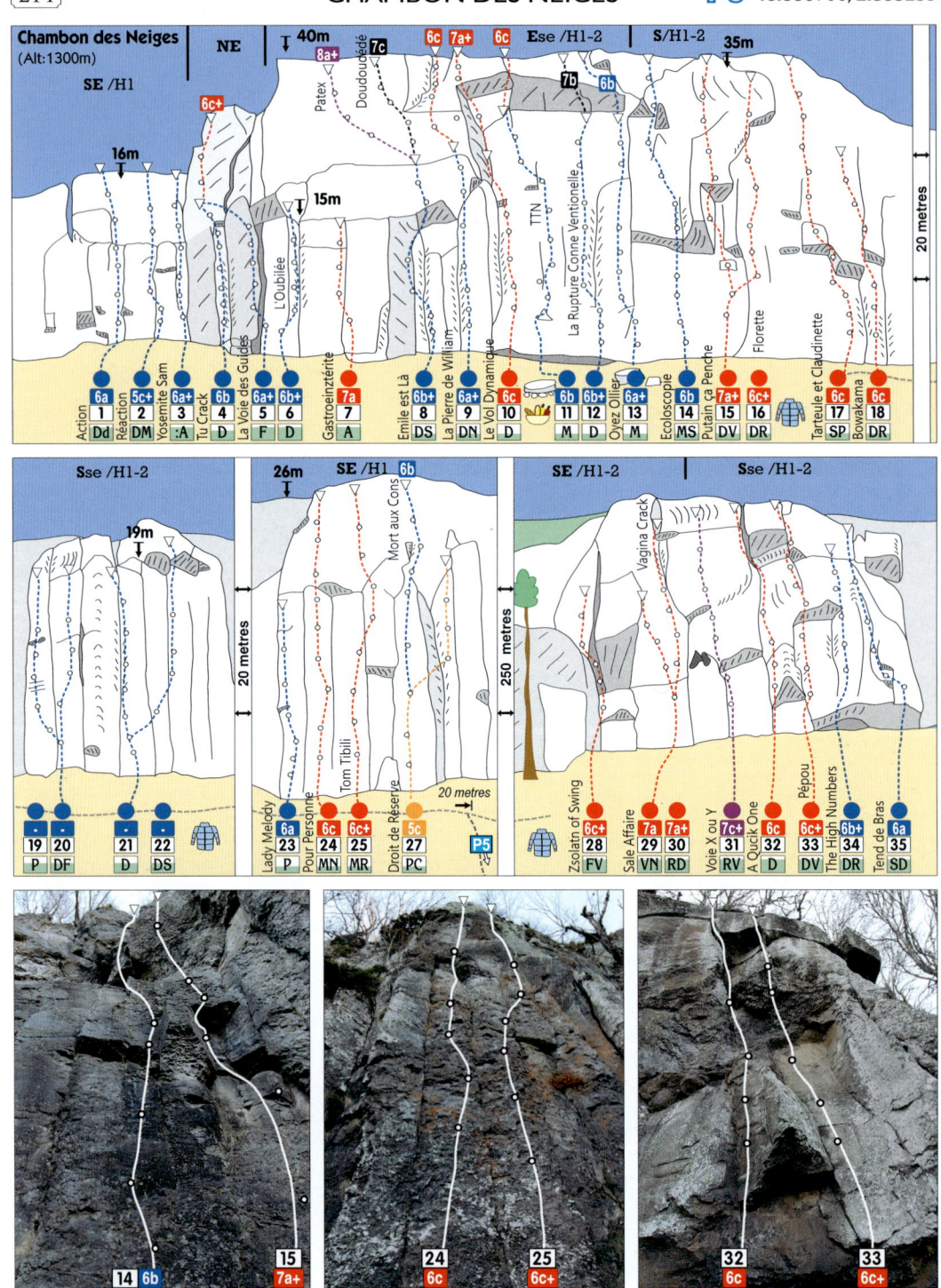

P6 — LE PAVIN 45.496699, 2.893503 # 1-...variable [1/2 - 20/06] 215

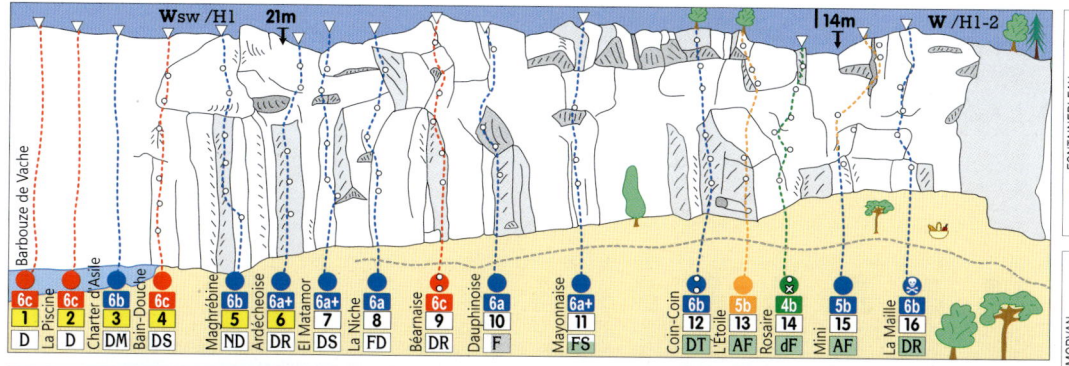

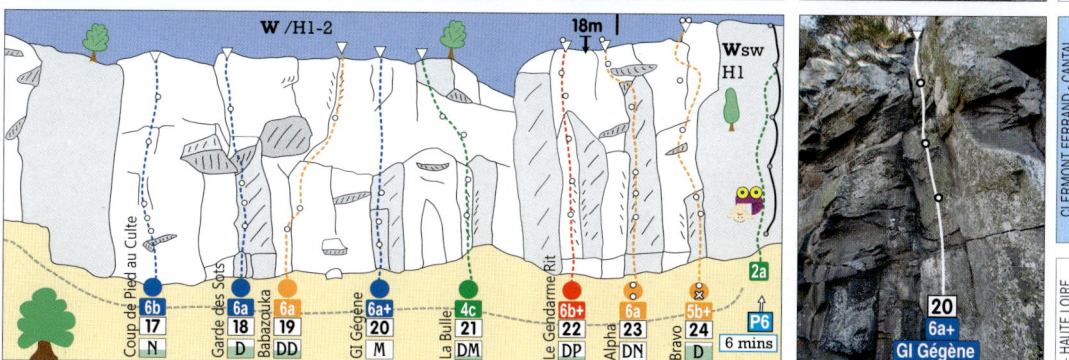
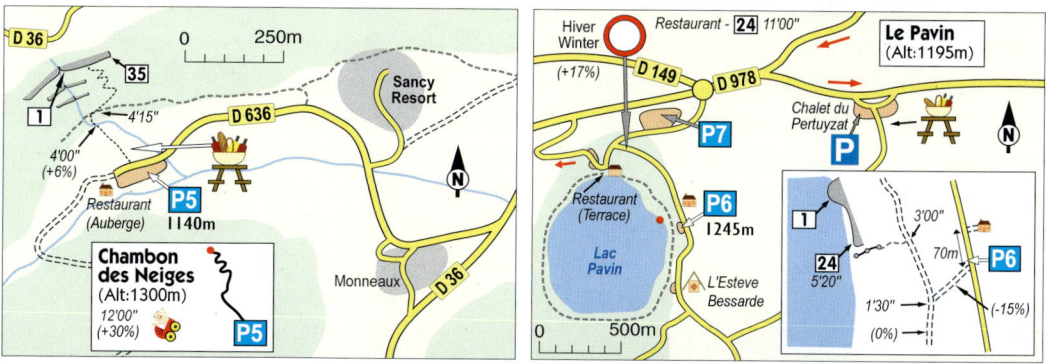

Basalt*** Superb lake setting, picnic sites everywhere, very busy tourist spot - however, cliff is quiet and isolated.

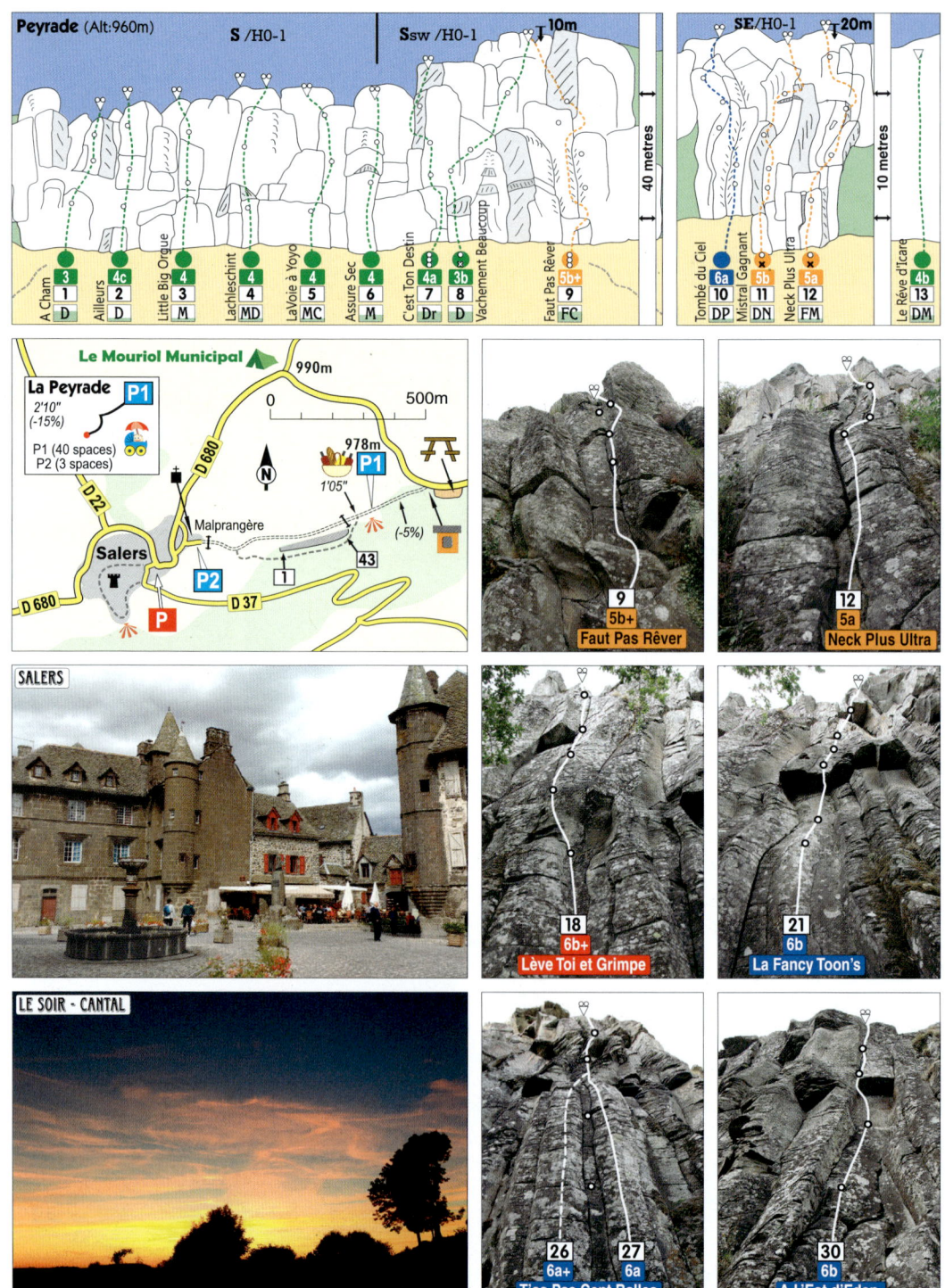

LA PEYRADE - B

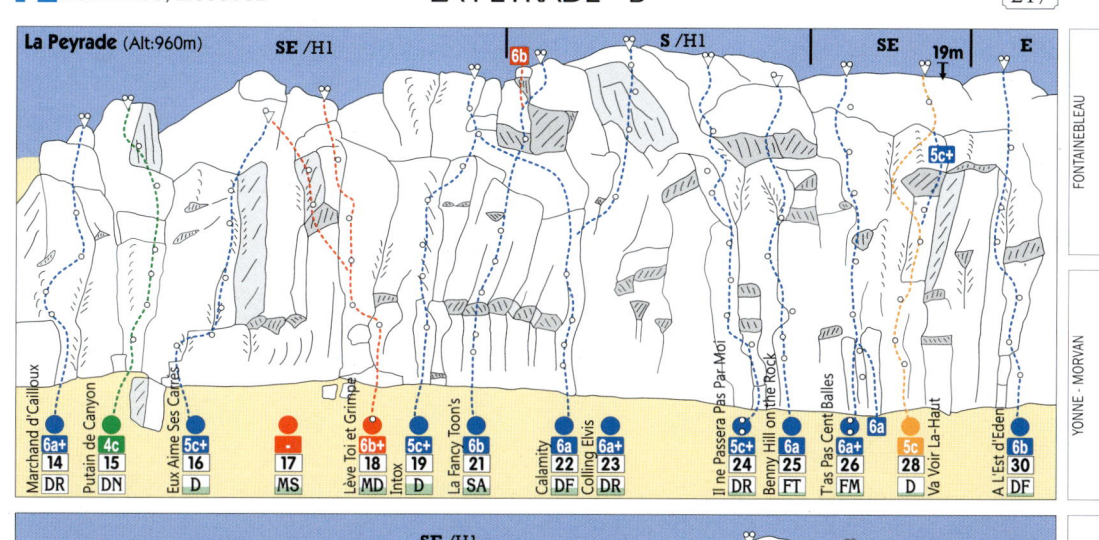

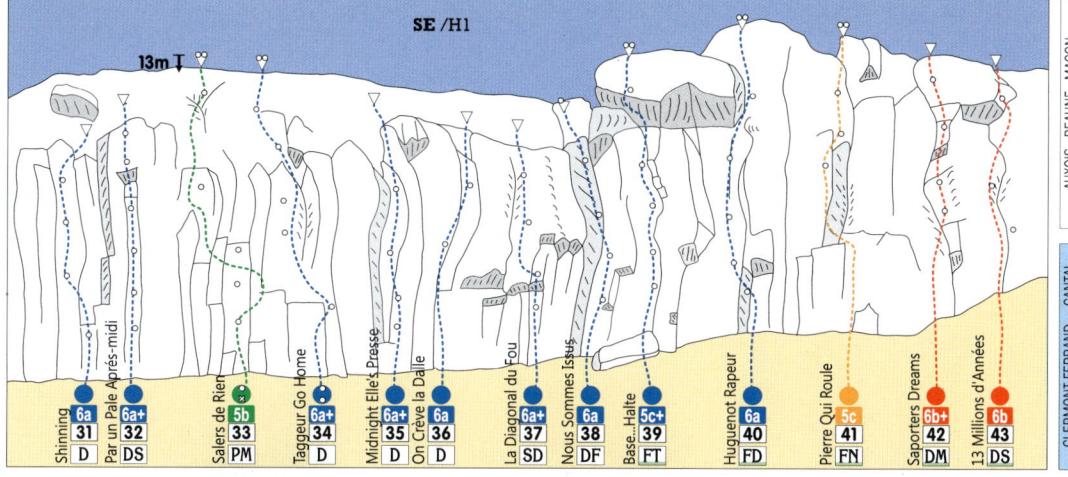

Peyrade: Bassalt***: Classic grooves that are harder than they look. Fabulous small venue. Best pic-nic venue at parking 1.

CHÂTEAUNEUF-RIOM

P1 45.304471, 2.640398

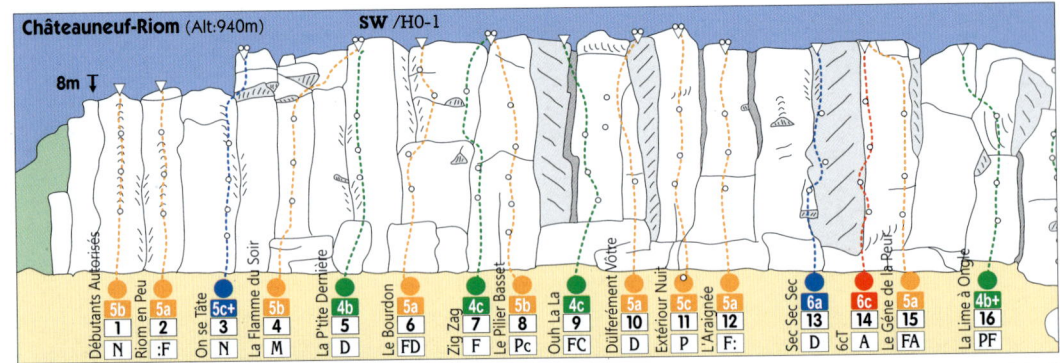
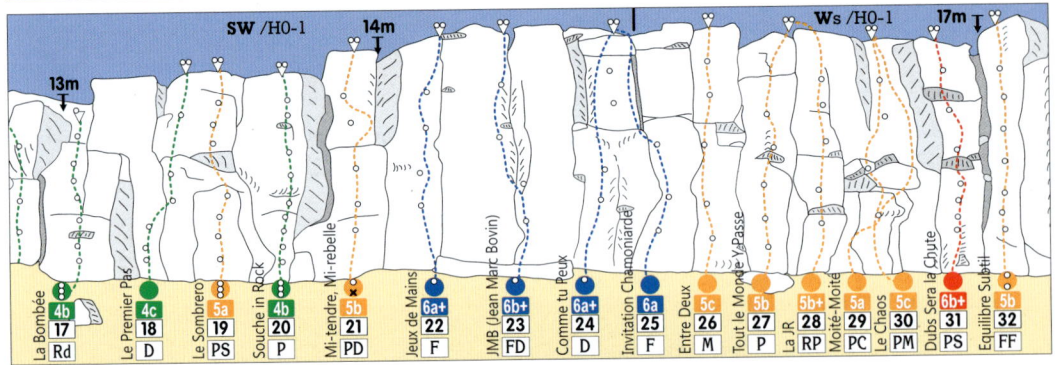
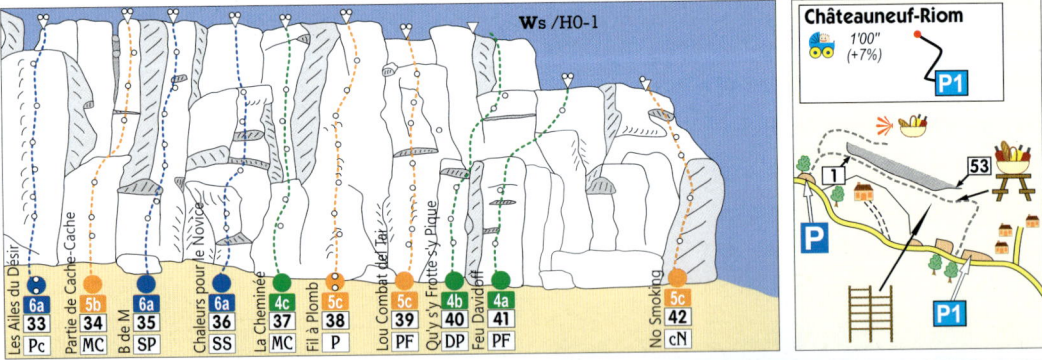
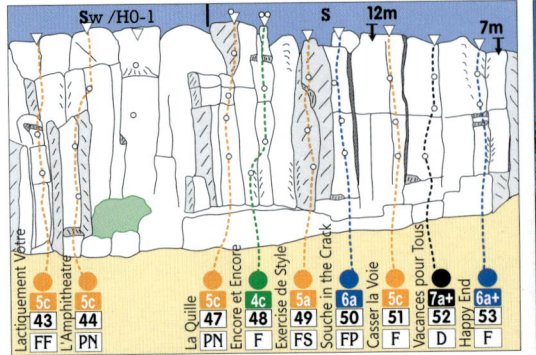

Chateauneuf-Basalt*** A superb small cliff with wonderful Basalt columns, great afternoon sunshine, extensive views, yum.

MARCHASTEL

P2 45.283030, 2.724343 — 219

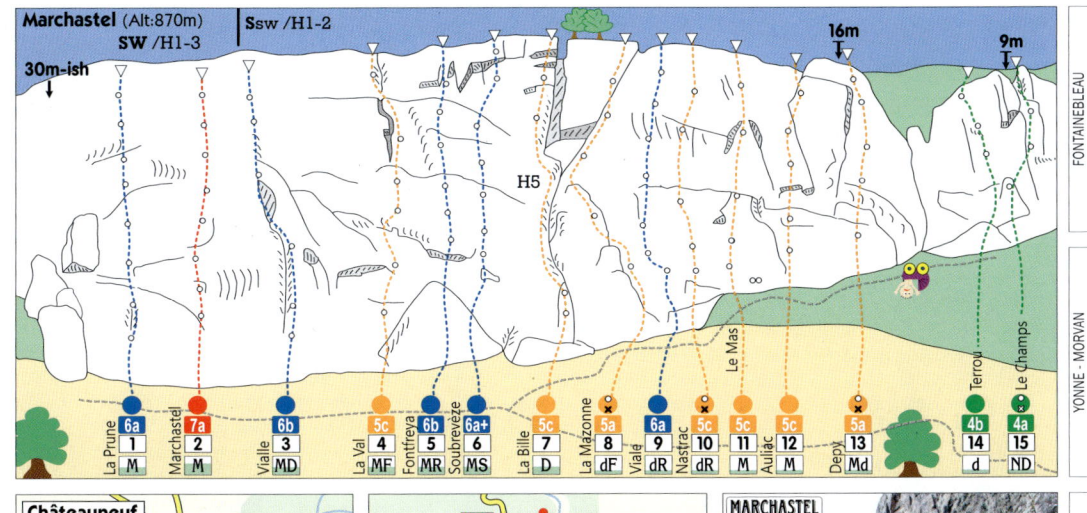

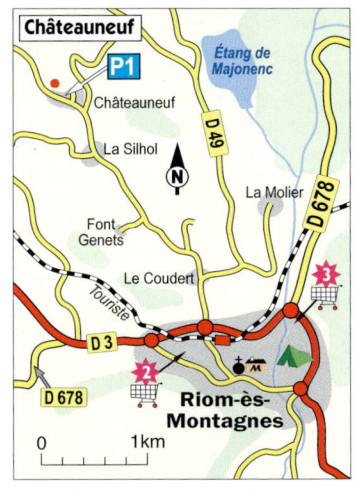

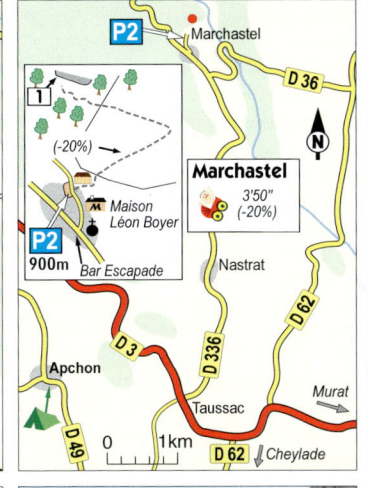

17 — 4b — La Bombée

31 — 6b+ — Dubs Sera La Chute

43 — 5c — Lactiquement Vôtre

Marchastel: Schiste - iffy rock, challenging routes. Deep down in trees, can stay damp, mosquitos, not ideal for a picnic.

AUTEROCHE

P1 45.304463, 2.471085

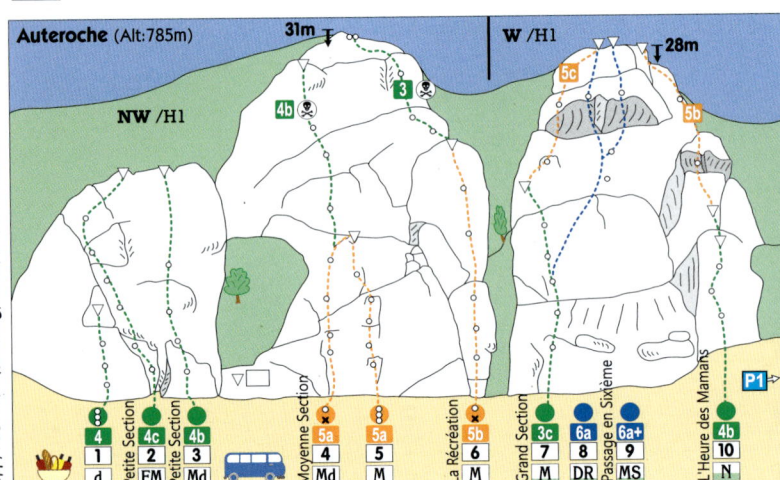
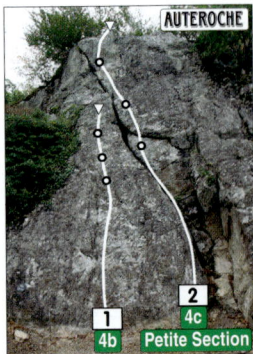

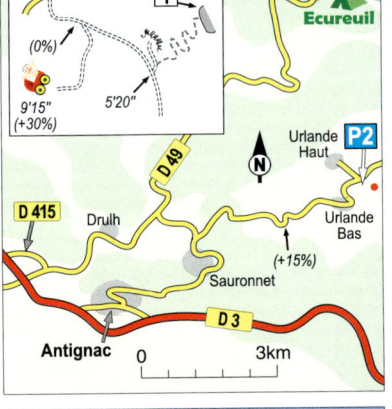

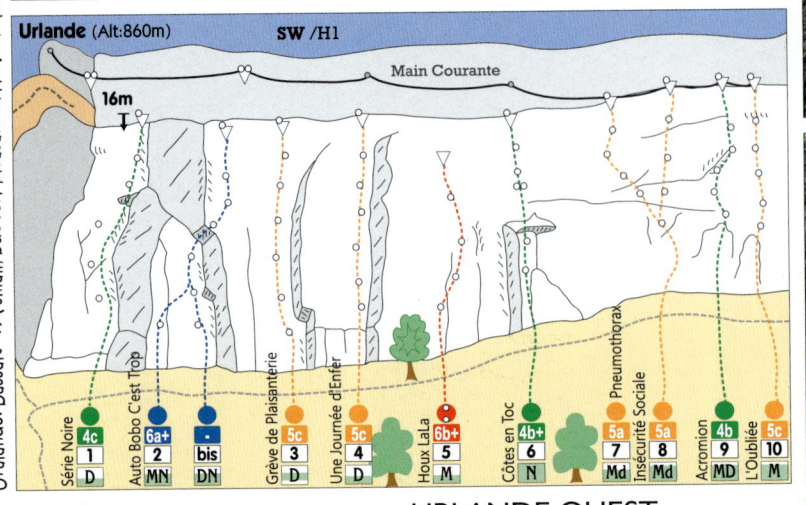

Auteroche: Schiste: Drive in cliff, rock on the dodgy side, bolts variable.

Urlande: Basalt***. A small, but very pleasant cliff. Very quiet situation.

P2 45.350919, 2.578898

▲ **6a LES MARMOTTES** 7 , *Carrie Atchison-Jones, Roc d'Hozières (Descending 'Fono'-lite...Hands Free)*

ROC D'HOZIÈRES

P1 45.114829, 2.648669 **P2** 45.104429, 2.662173

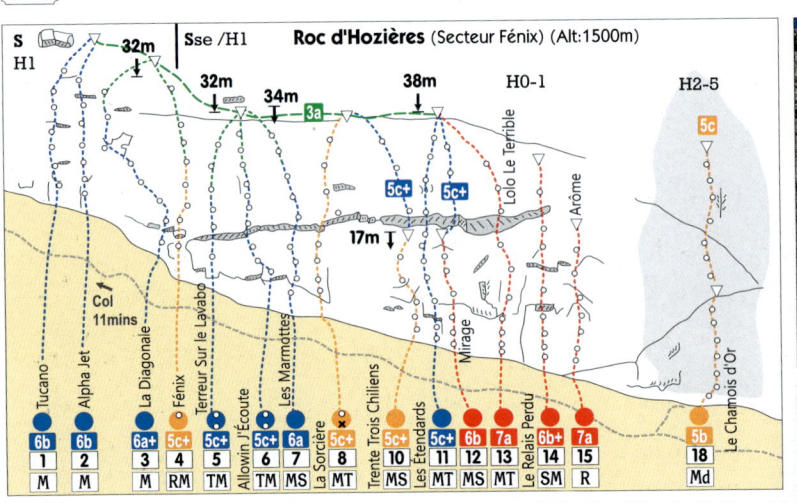

Roc d'Hozières (Secteur Fénix) (Alt:1500m)

#	Name	Grade	Style
1	Tucano	6b	M
2	Alpha Jet	6b	M
3	La Diagonale	6a+	M
4	Fénix	5c+	RM
5	Terreur Sur le Lavabo	5c+	TM
6	Allowin J'Écoute	5c+	TM
7	Les Marmottes	6a	MS
8	La Sorcière	5c+	MT
10	Trente Trois Chiliens	5c+	MS
11	Les Étendards	5c+	MT
12	Mirage	6b	MS
13	Lolo Le Terrible	7a	MT
14	Le Relais Perdu	6b+	SM
15	Arôme	7a	R
18	Le Chamois d'Or	5b	Md

14 6b+ Le Relais Perdu

Roc d'Hozières (Secteur Bulle)

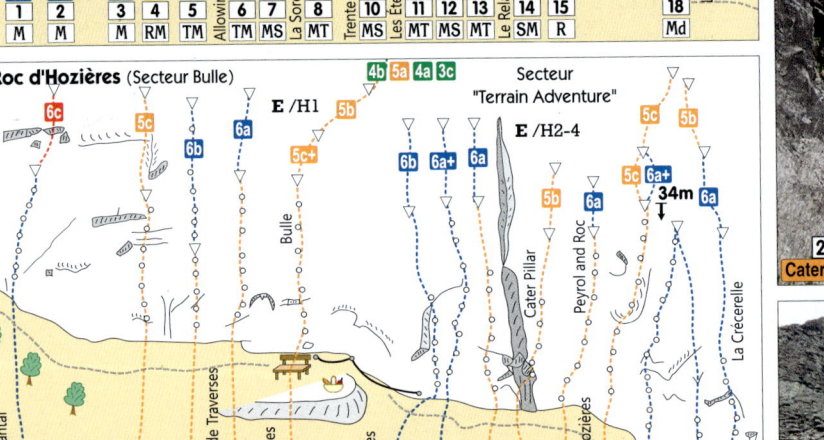

Secteur "Terrain Adventure"

#	Name	Grade	Style
21	Supplice du Cantal	6a	MT
22	Intifada	5b	dS
23	Capucine	5b	MR
24	Les Chemins de Traverses	5c	M
24	Bulle d'Hozières	5b	M
25	Les Hirondelles	6a+	MD
26	Tichodromes	6b	M
27	La Noire	5c+	AR
28	Peyrol and Roc	5c	M
29	Cater Pillar	5c+	M
30	Le Magicien d'Hozières	5b	RM
32	Milan Royal	6a	RM
33	Milan Noir	5b	RM
34	La Crécerelle	6a+	MR

28 5c Cater Pillar

30 5b Le Magicien d'Hozières

Roc d'Hozières (Secteur Dévers) NEe /H1-2

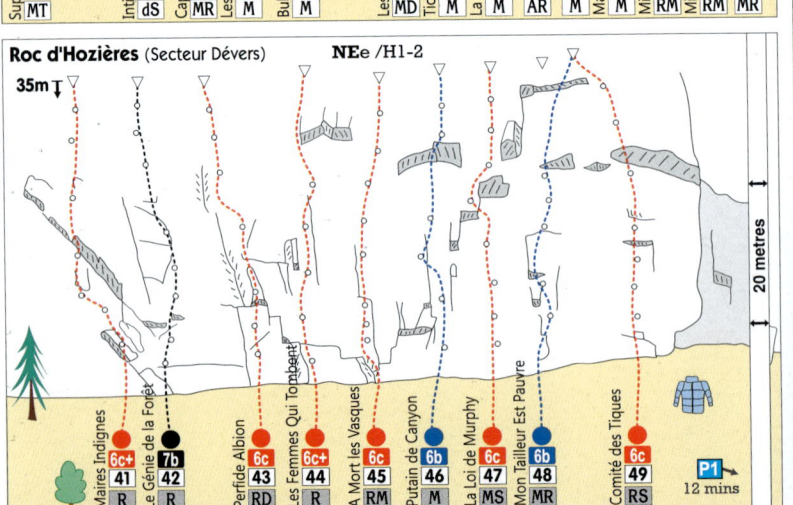

#	Name	Grade	Style
41	Maires Indignes	6c+	R
42	Le Génie de la Forêt	7b	R
43	Perfide Albion	6c+	RD
44	Les Femmes Qui Tombent	6c+	R
45	A Mort Les Vasques	6c	RM
46	Putain de Canyon	6b	M
47	La Loi de Murphy	6c	MS
48	Mon Tailleur Est Pauvre	6b	MR
49	Comité des Tiques	6c	RS

P1 12 mins

HOZIERS DEVERS

Volcanic lava - Phonolite; Like a crocodile back, sounds hollow - and is ! Impressive venue, great views, go carefully.

PUY DE LA TOURTE

P3 45.115090, 2.670746 — 223

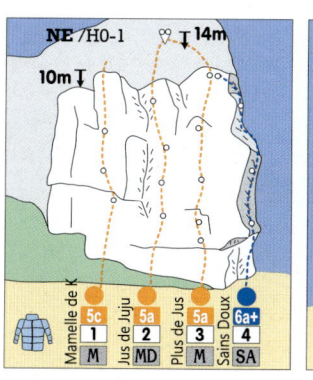
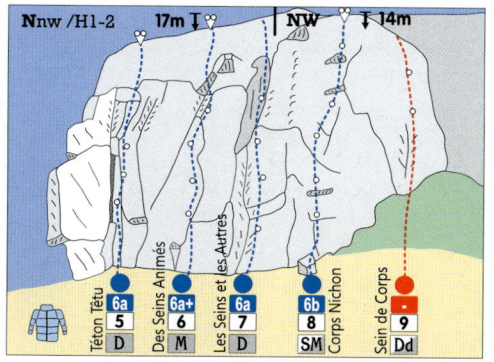

#	Name	Grade	
1	Mamelle de K	5c	M
2	Jus de Juju	5a	MD
3	Plus de Jus	5a	M
4	Sains Doux	6a+	SA
5	Téton Têtu	6a	D
6	Des Seins Animés	6a+	M
7	Les Seins et les Autres	6a	D
8	Corps Nichon	6b	SM
9	Sein de Corps	-	Dd
4	Sains Doux	6a+	

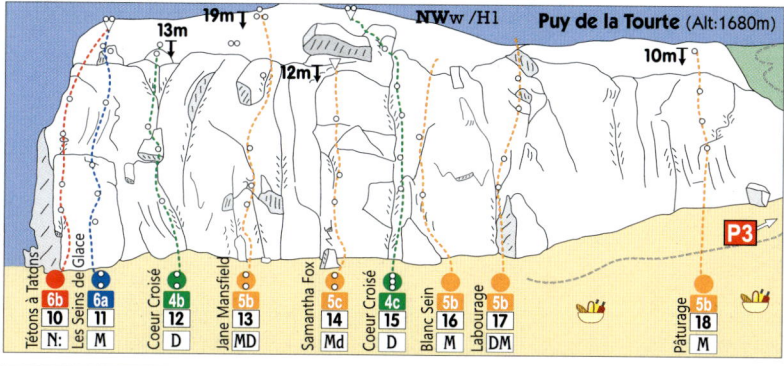

#	Name	Grade	
10	Tétons à Tatons	6b	N
11	Les Seins de Glace	6a	M
12	Coeur Croisé	4b	D
13	Jane Mansfield	5a	MD
14	Samantha Fox	5c	Md
15	Coeur Croisé	4c	D
16	Blanc Sein	5b	M
17	Labourage	5b	DM
18	Pâturage	5b	M
14	Samantha Fox	5c	
15	Coeur Croisé	4c	

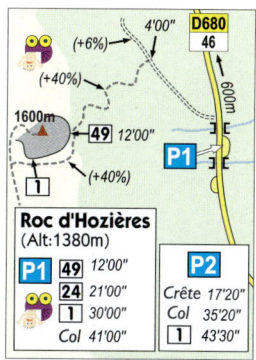

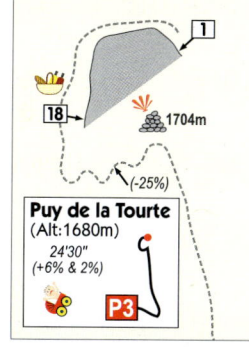

Roc d'Hozières (Alt: 1380m)

P1	49	12'00"
	24	21'00"
	1	30'00"
	Col	41'00"

P2	Crête	17'20"
	Col	35'20"
	1	43'30"

Puy de la Tourte (Alt: 1680m) — 24'30" (+6% & 2%)

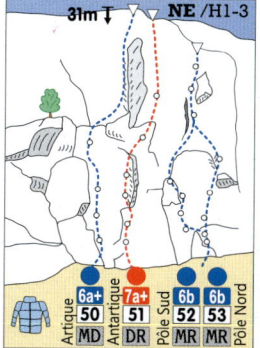

#	Name	Grade	
43	Perfide Albion	6c	
50	Artique	6a+	MD
51	Antartique	7a+	DR
52	Pôle Sud	6b	MR
53	Pôle Nord	6b	MR

Puy: Volcanic lava*** great friction, wonderful place on a hot sunny day, chilly on North face. Great for picnic, wow views.

LAC DES GRAVES

P1 45.015118, 2.557964

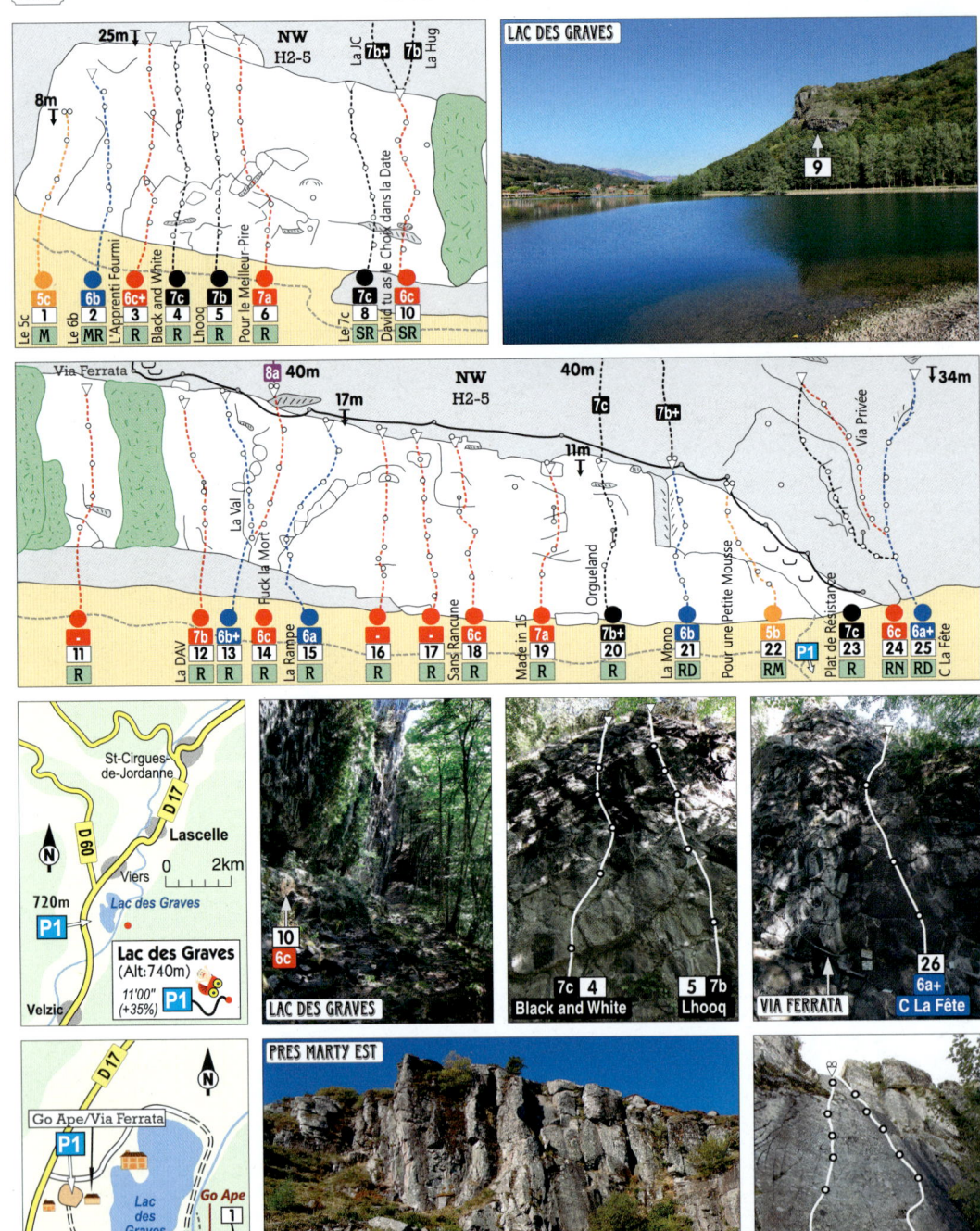

Dark black slippery Basalt, overhanging and constantly pushes you off. Climbing mostly on lower the section in trees (humid).

PRÉS MARTY

P2   45.052647, 2.793674   225

10 — 5c

11 — 6c — Mixmit

16 — 6c+ — La Pep   19 — 6b — Auxerre

Superb location, incredible views...on a nice sunny day. Volcanic lava, most parts excellent quality, but some iffy bits.

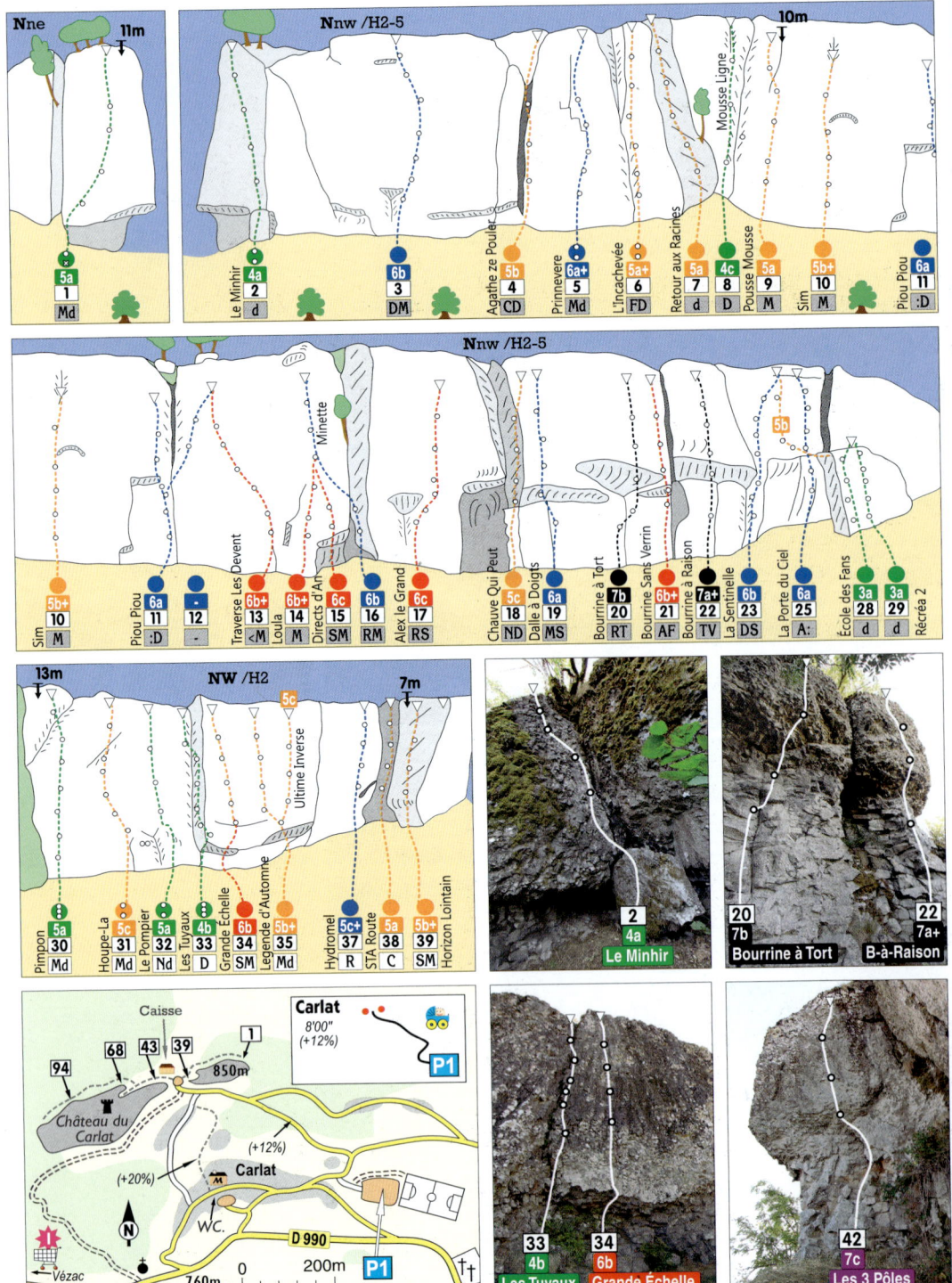

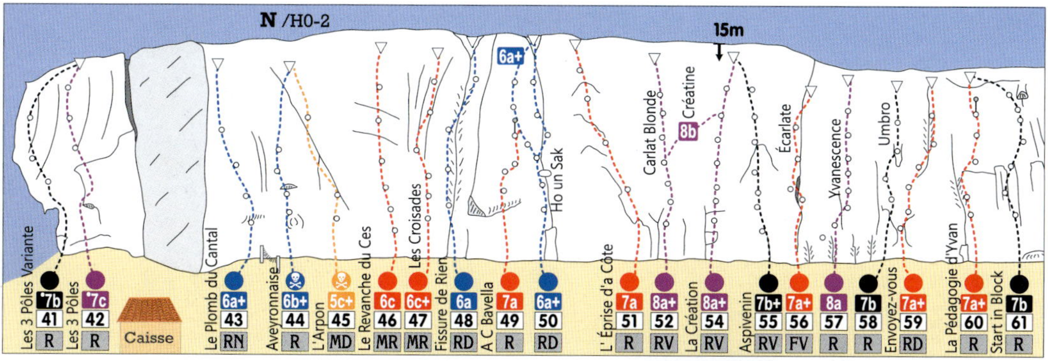

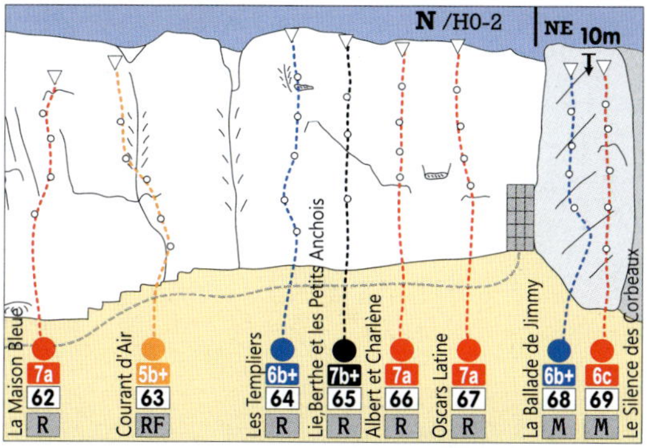

CARLAT - B

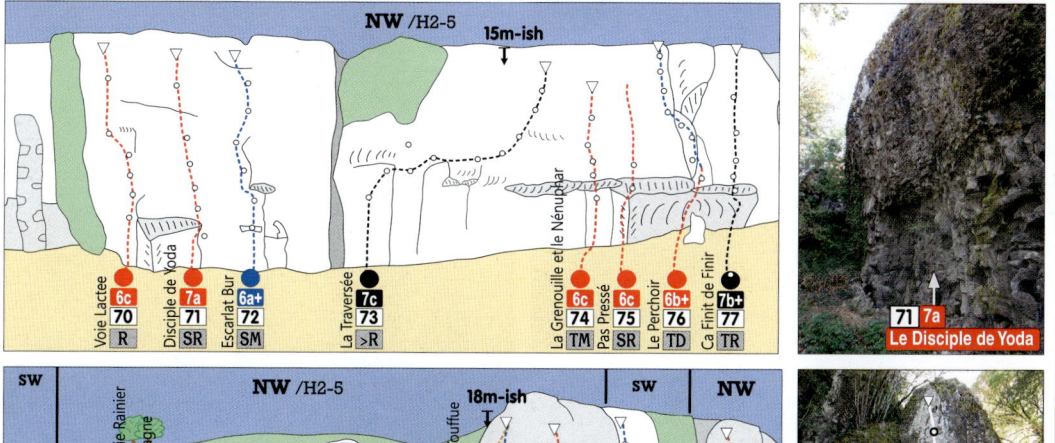

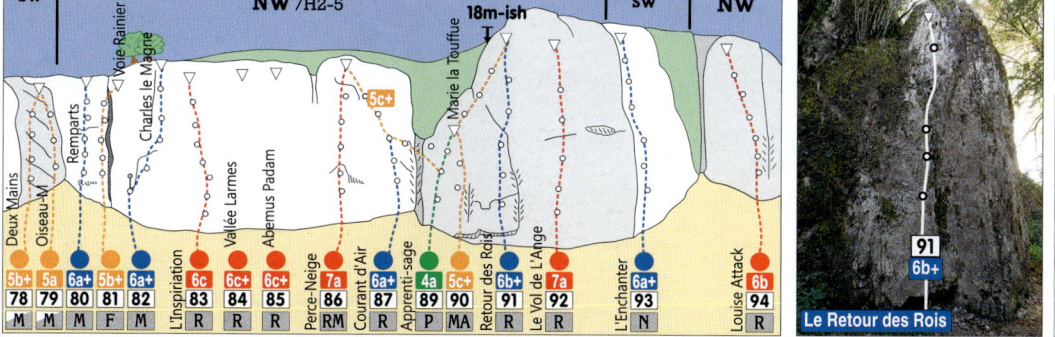

Basalt: Very good short climbs, a nice variety of styles requiring good energy, packs plenty of punch for the distance.

LE BOUT DU MONDE (Saint-Flour)

P1 45.009370, 3.137378

Orange Granit** A mega sun trap in a very dry valley, the cliff feels mediteranean. Nice for a few hours.

GORGES DU BÈZ

A2 44.861048, 3.092952 — 229

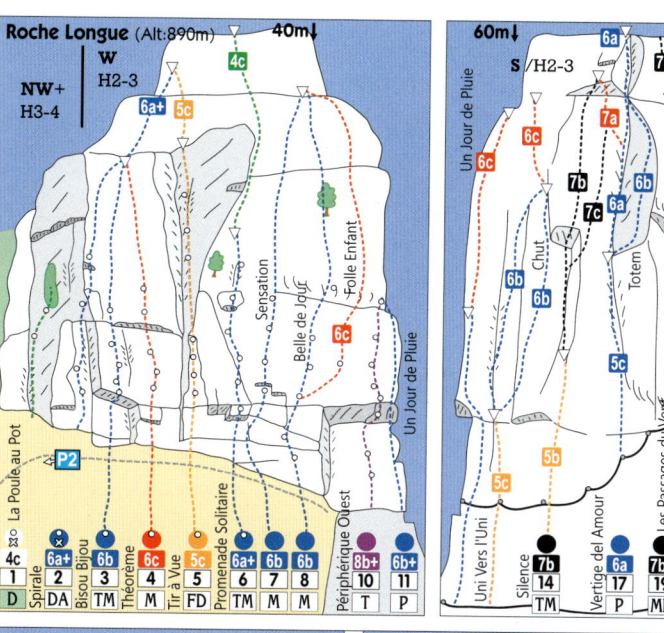

Spirale — 2 — 6a+

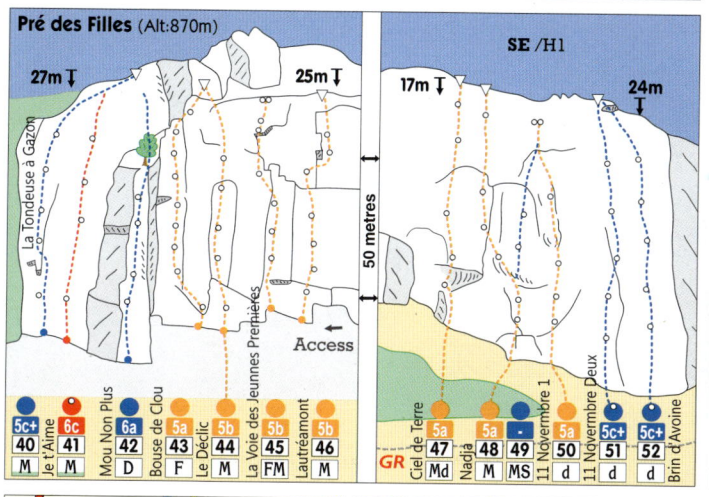

Lautréamont — 46 — 5a

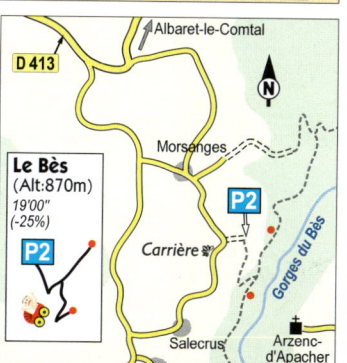
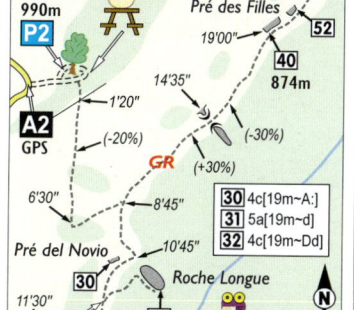

Granite*** Lots of rock, deep down in a valley - lichen grows quickly. Often too hot or too cold. For the adventureous!

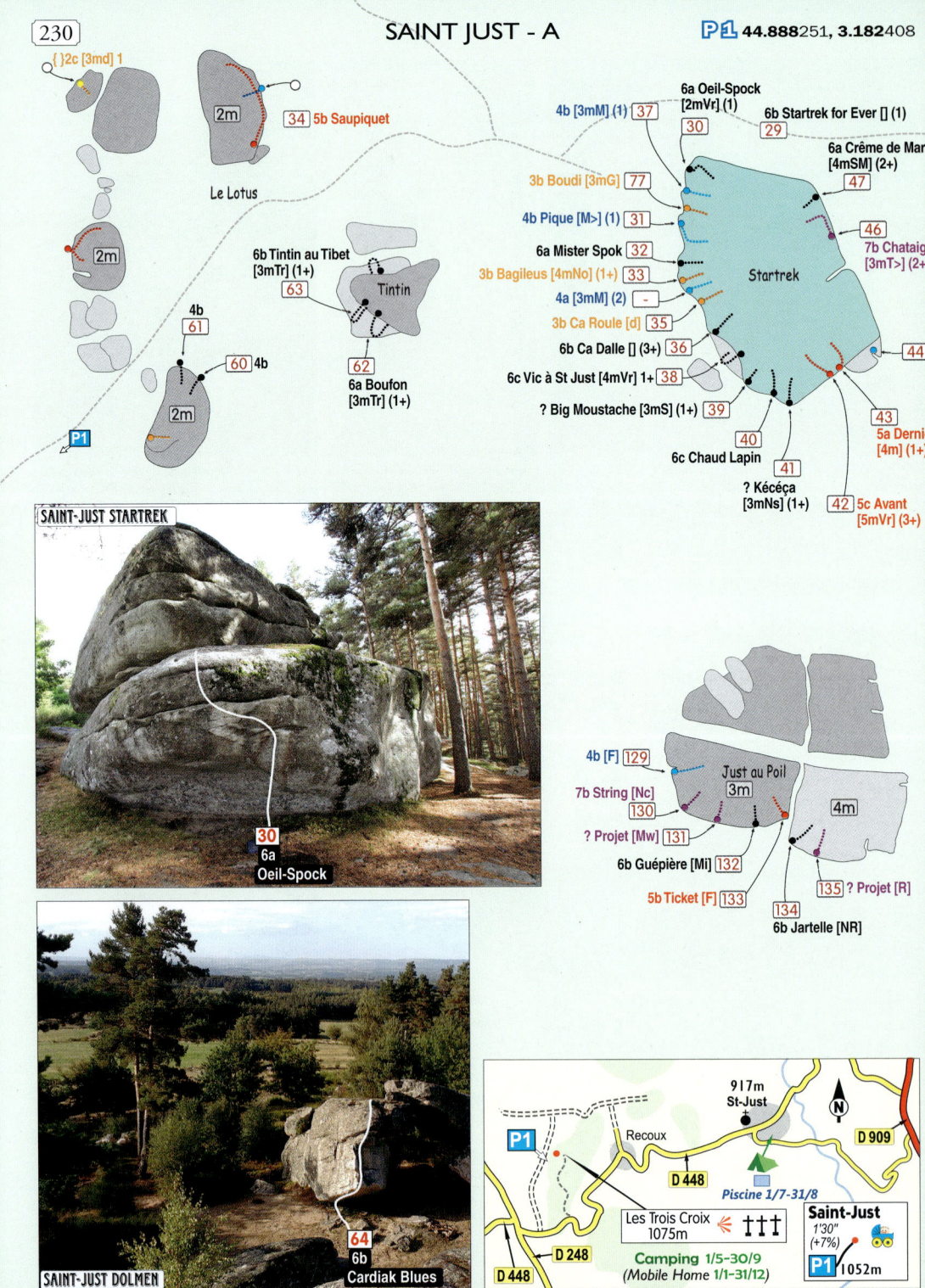

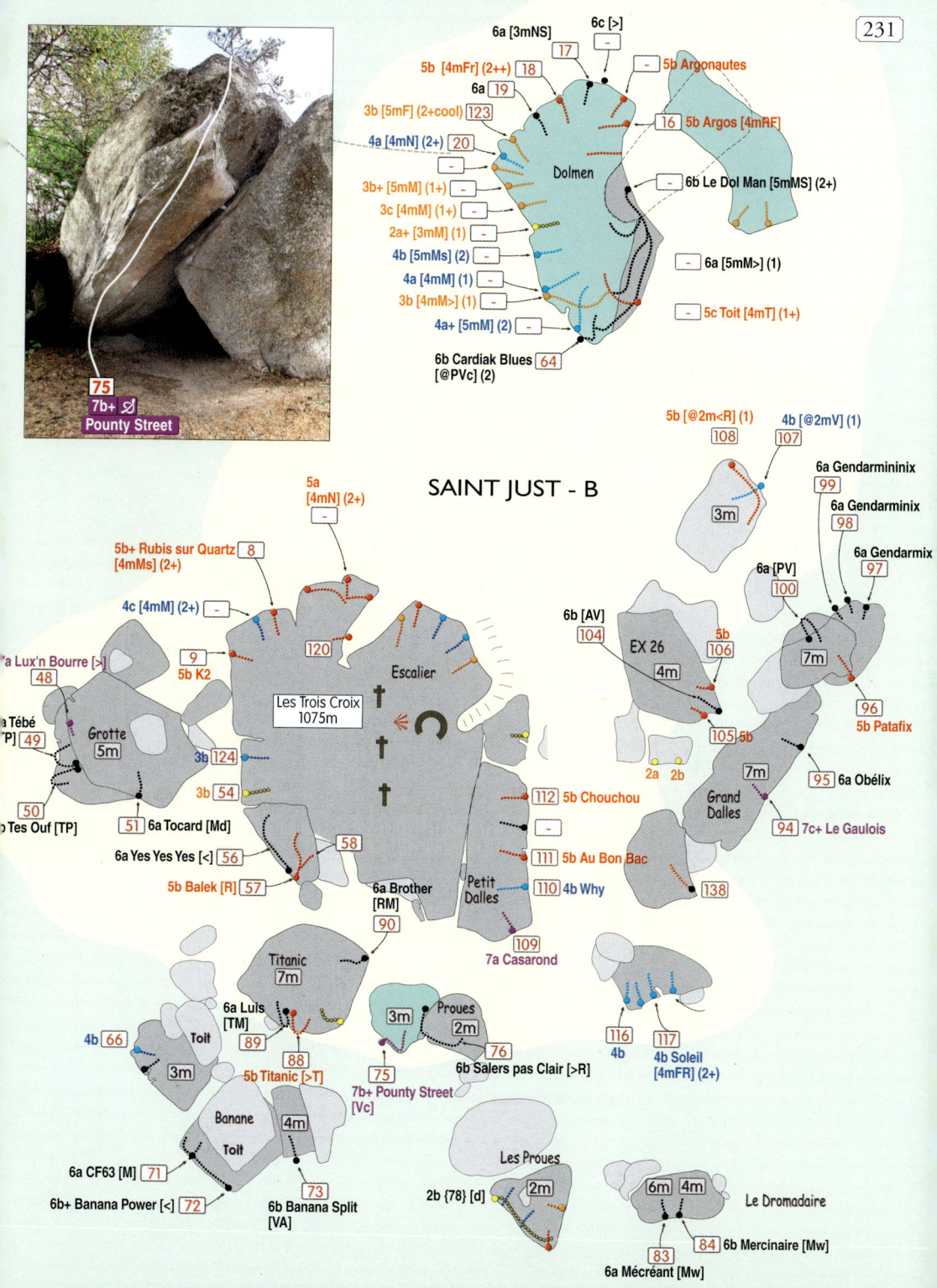

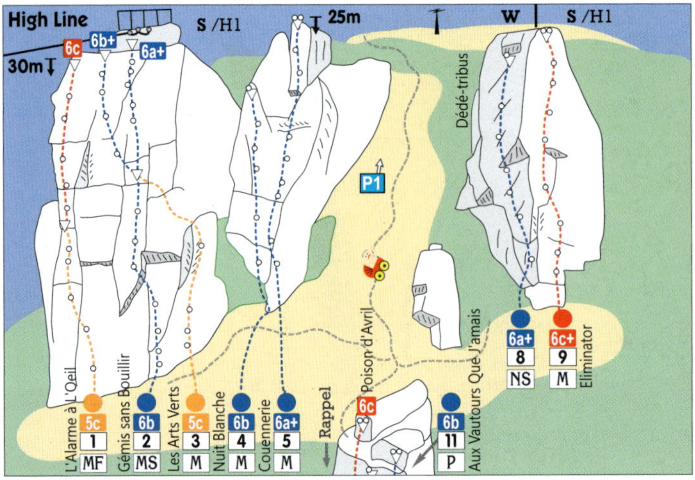

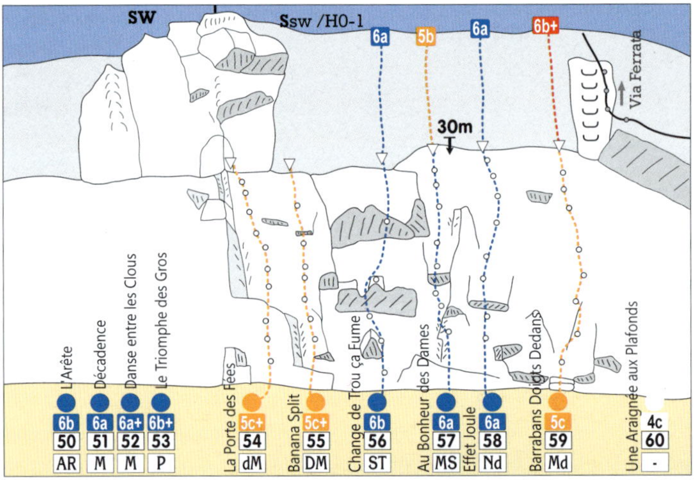

LA PORTE DES FÉES

P1 44.862870, 3.323729

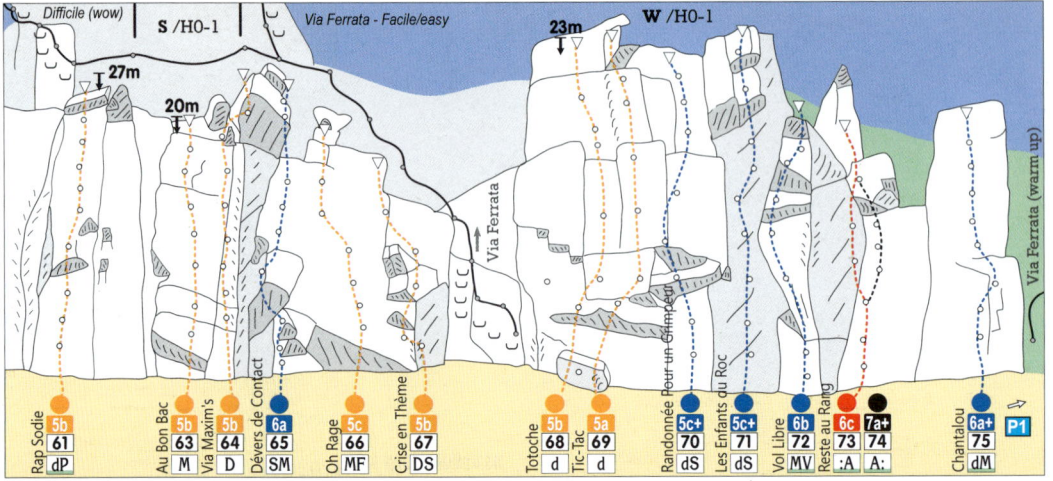

Orange Granit** A large chaotic gorge with some excellent climbing. Complicated central area to access, not featured.

CHAZETTE

P3 44.846875, 3.342011 — 233

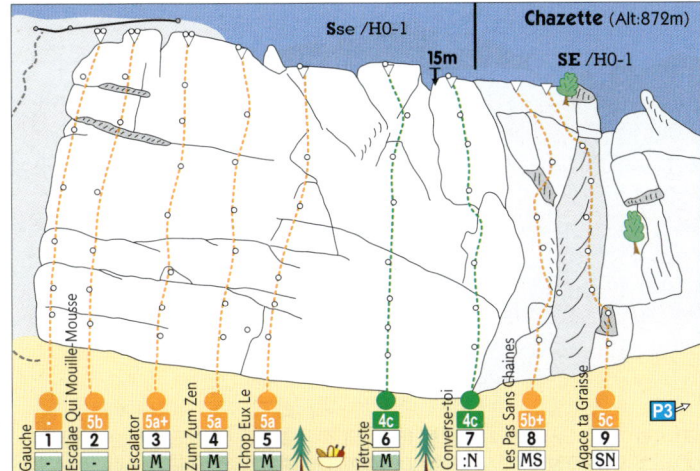

	Gauche	Escalae Qui Mouille-Mousse	Escalator	Zum Zum Zen	Tchop Eux Le		Tétryste	Converse-toi	Les Pas Sans Chaines	Agace ta Graisse
Grade	-	-	5b	5a+	5a	5a		4c	4c	5b+	5c
#	1	2	3	4	5	5		6	7	8	9
								M	:N	MS	SN

Chazette (Alt:872m) — Sse /H0-1 — 15m — SE /H0-1

Zum Zum Zen — 4 / 5a

VIA FERRATA - DIFFICILE

LA PORTE DES FEES - HIGH LINE (MOAI)

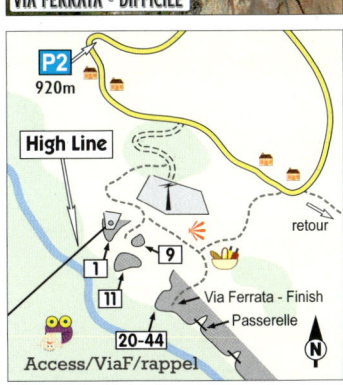
P2 920m — High Line — Via Ferrata - Finish — Passerelle — 20-44 — Access/ViaF/rappel

P2 Verdezun — Porte des Fées — P1 860m Parking Via Ferrata (Dog poo) — Via Ferrata - intro — Le Malzieu-Ville — 75 5'00" — 3'00" — 500m

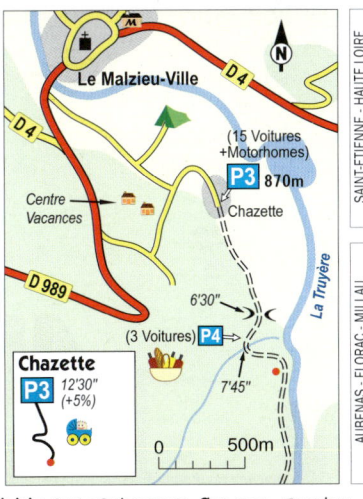
Le Malzieu-Ville — (15 Voitures +Motorhomes) — P3 870m — Centre Vacances — Chazette — D 989 — La Truyère — 6'30" — (3 Voitures) P4 — 7'45" — Chazette P3 12'30" (+5%) — 500m

2 popular via ferrata's...pretty steep and very out there. Useful to do - to get a good initial feel of the gorge. Sun trap - gets hot.

Area 5 - ST-ÉTIENNE - HAUTE LOIRE

Page	Falaise/Cliff	Alt	Arbre-Ori-Sèche	Am-Pm	Rocher	Longeur	2	4	6	3	1	0	Approche	Ambience
260	D2 Auvergnat	370m	NW/H1-2		Granit	26m	2	4	6	3	1	0	3	Dièdre, Raide
268	D1 Beaumiral	230m	SE/H0		Calcaire	10-20m	1	6	16	16	8	0	13	Mur, Raide
250	A2 Bernard, Rocher	610m	S&W/H1		Granit	9-35m	8	12	4	0	0	0	3	dalle, multi
264	D1 Cabannes, Les	300m	SW/H0-1		Granit	13-25m	12	19	15	5	2	0	8	Mur, Fissure
266	D1 Chat Gourmand	360m	Sw/H0-1		Calcaire	10-15m	1	21	27	13	7	0	21	Dièdre,Mur
263	C1 Chevillère, R	430m	NW/H1-2		Granit	35m	0	8	6	2	2	1	0	2	Mur, Dièdre
269	D1 Chomérac-Carr	190m	S/H0		Calcaire	14-24m	5	18	20	17	4	0	4	Mur,Carrière
269	D1 Chomérac-Vialet	200m	NE/H0		Calcaire	7-8m	6	8	3	0	0	0	1	Mur, Surplomb
251	A2 Cochons	650m	E&N/H0		Basalte	15-35m	0	0	5	4	22	5	0	Devers, Raide
244	C3 Corbière, R 10%	750m	W&E/H1		Volcanic	15-60m	15	27	32	15	16	4	7	Mur,Expo,multi
246	B2 Costaros, R 100%	870m	S/H0-1		Schiste	30-65m	0	15	31	13	2	0	13	Mur,Toit,Expo
257	C1 Coux, Les	1450m	SW/H0-1		Lava	15-22m	5	8	7	2	1	0	28	Mur,Dièdre, Zzz
251	A2 Cubelles	870m	E/H1		Granit	31m	3	7	4	1	0	0	7	dalle,Mur
241	D5 Curis	290m	S/H0-1		Calc-Gr	10-26m	4	16	10	0	0	0	2	Mur, Carrière
241	D3 Doisieux	810m	SE/H0-2		Volcanic	10-50m	19	47	44	17	3	0	6	Mur,Pilier,Dièdre
254	C2 Fay-sur-Lignon	1250m	S/H0-1		Lava	12-49m	16	23	27	6	1	5	9	Mur,Pilier,Dièdre
252	B2 Grazac	680m	SE/H2-3		Granit	20-35m	3	8	12	4	1	0	10	Mur,Toit,Zzz
237	B4 Guillanche	480m	S-NW/H2		Volcanic	14-20m	4	9	12	0	0	0	7	Dièdre,Raide
256	B1 Issarlés	1040m	NE/H1-3		Granit	10-35m	13	16	8	5	3	0	11	dalle,Mur
257	A3 Lavaudieu	480m	NE/H2-3		Volcanic	16m	3	4	1	0	0	0	7	Mur,Surplomb
240	D5 Limas	300m	W&n/H1		Gré-con	7-12m	15	17	6	5	0	0	3	Mur, Carrière
259	D2 Mer de Glace	420m	S/H0-1		Granit	10-18m	5	17	13	7	4	1	3	Mur, Surplomb
236	B4 Olme 40%	1170m	SE/H0-1		Volcanic	15-30m	2	15	6	0	0	0	7	Mur,Expo
260	A2 Péréandre, R	240m	S&E/H1-3		Granit	40m	0	7	15	7	2	0	6	Dièdre,Mur,Toit
253	B1 Pointue	1500m	Se/H0-1		Lava	17-39m	11	10	3	1	0	0	2	dalle,Mur,Vue
262	C1 Pont-Fromentières	580m	SW/H1-2		Granit	10-30m	8	28	9	3	3	1	4	Mur, Surplomb
248	A2 Pradel	520m	SE/H0-1		Basalte	12-40m	5	18	30	14	4	0	15	Dièdre, Toit
247	B2 Retournac	520m	NE/H1-4		Granit	16-23m	4	4	11	3	2	0	9	dalle, Raide
236	B4 Rory	660m	SE/H1		Volcanic	14-32m	2	7	7	4	3	2	16	Mur,Raide
238	C4 St-Symp-Coise	520m	N&S/H1-2		Granit	19m	7	20	11	5	0	0	6	dalle, Carrière
238	C5 St-Symp-Lay	390m	NW/H1-3		Calcaire	10-35m	2	5	10	6	4	1	3	dalle,Raide, Carrière
258	D2 Thorrenc	320m	S/H0-2		Granit	8-25m	1	13	13	9	5	1	11	Mur, Surplomb
267	D1 Top Secret	300m	SW/H0		Calcaire	6-19m	1	8	8	7	3	1	13	Mur, Carrière
253	B2 Tortue	1230m	NW/H0-1		Lava	19-32m	6	2	4	0	0	0	6	Mur,Pilier,Vue
265	D1 Tour, La	310m	S&N/H2		Granit	17-35m	6	5	5	3	1	0	10	Mur,Fissure,Raide
261	D1 Tournay	420m	S/H1-2		Granit	8-22m	8	9	10	5	3	2	12	Mur,Devers, Zzz
239	D4 Yzeron blocs	480m	SW/H1-2		Volcanic	3-9m	6	11	15	14	7	1	24	Blocs, abrasif

RORY

P1 45.695566, 3.927040

Rory (Alt:664m) — Saint Georges en Couzan

32m • E+/H1 • S • SE • S/H1 • E+/H1-2

*Rory-Granite*** A good little spot, hidden away down the hill - steep & intense.

#	1	2	3	4	5	6	7	8	9	10	11	12	13	14	15	16	17	18	19	20	21
Grade	5a+	5a+	6b+	5a	6a	6a+	6b+	5b	5b+	7a	4c	6a+	7b	8a	6a	6c	5a	5b	4c
Name	A Livre Ouvert	Dalle qui Peut	Et au Milieu Coule le Lignon	Une Mousse Biery Fraîche	Sous la dalle...Le'Bloc	Que Dalle	Adhérence Précaire	J'Préfère la Dalle		Vol d'Icare	La Faille	La Dalle Engagée	Grit Experiment	Grit Theory	Corsica Roac	RD 42	Couzan ou Pas	Sur les Terres de Jean	Bienvenu à Rory
	D	d	MA	d	Md	Md	D	M		RA	D	Md	VP	TR	SM	M	F	F	N

Astrée ou d'Ailleurs 7a • Alonge 7b • La Grand Dièdre 6c • Rororyry Horologe 8a 7c+ • Lichen 6a

14m • 10m

Rory — 12 Vol d'Icare 7a

Rory — 14 La Dalle Engagée 6a+ P1

OLME — 2 Tango 5b *Carrie Atchison-Jones*

Roc de l'Olme

Vierge • 35m • 30m • 5b • 6b • 5c • 6a • 5a • # 2 Longeur • SE/H0-1 • 5b • 15m

*Olme-Granite** A very nice spot with a lovely view. Doing 2 pitch routes here is fun.

Via Ferrata

#	P2	2	3	4	5	6	7	8	9	10	11	12	13	14	15	16
Grade		5b	5b	4c	5c	5a	5b	5b	5b	6b	5b	5b	5a+	5b	5b	5b
Name	Pin Up	Tango		Les Amants de J	Giboiin		Café	FM	La Couillonnade			Chocrane	Violette		Figlou
	dD	dS	Normale FD	:F	MS	Mc		MR	dC	MA	MN	Mw	M	MG		

Luca Ramel • Cactus • Calimero • Crac

OLME — 4 Normale 4c

OLME — # 2 Longeur — A2 45.694520, 3.820152

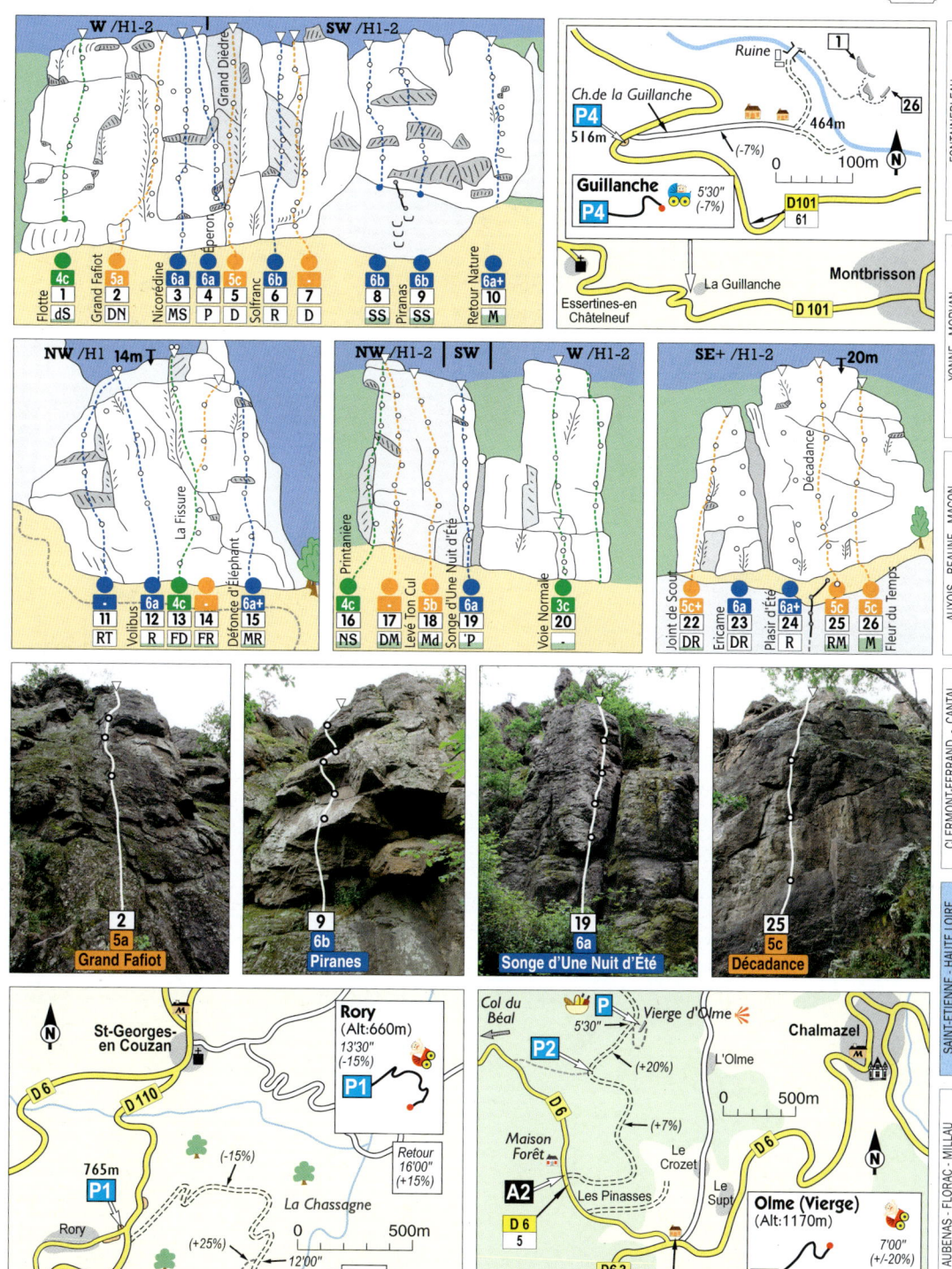

SAINT-SYMPORIEN-DE-LAY

P1 45.942871, 4.204926

St-S-Lay: Calcaire** An old large quarry. Not so many holds.

St-S-Coise: Granite*** An old small group of quarries. In a valley but quite open and airy.

P2 45.631534, 4.451488

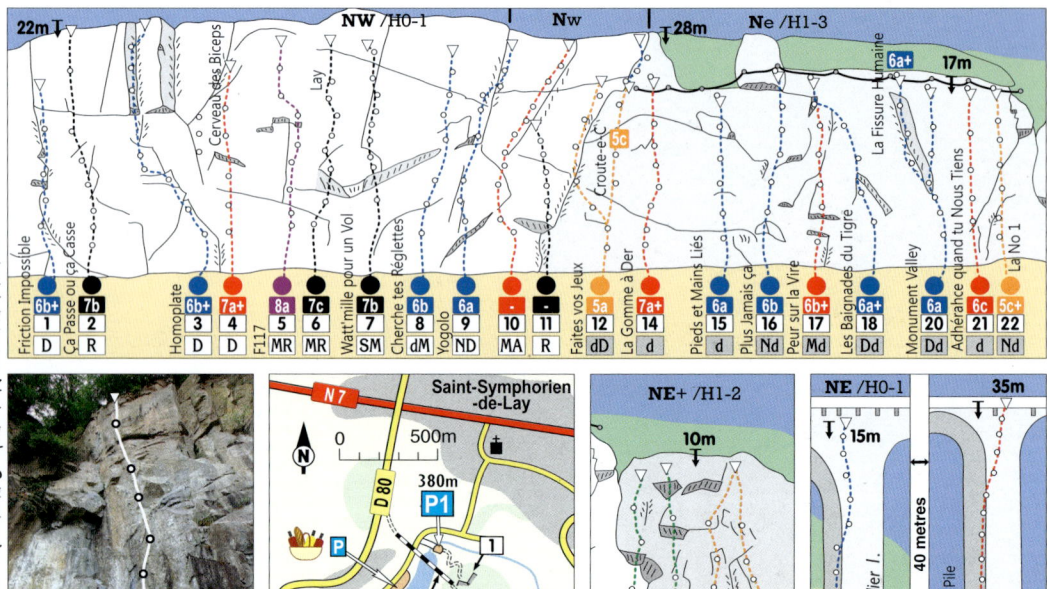

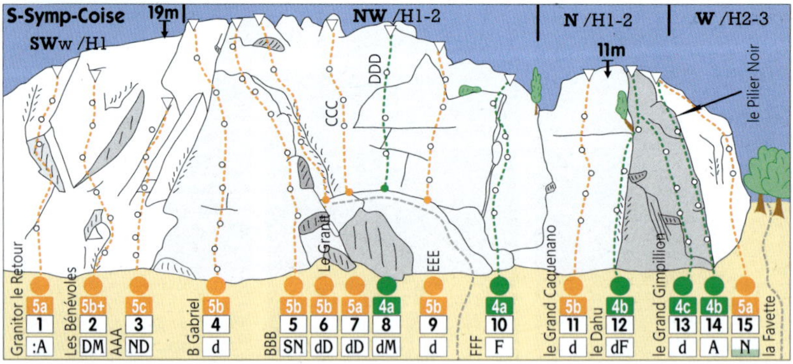

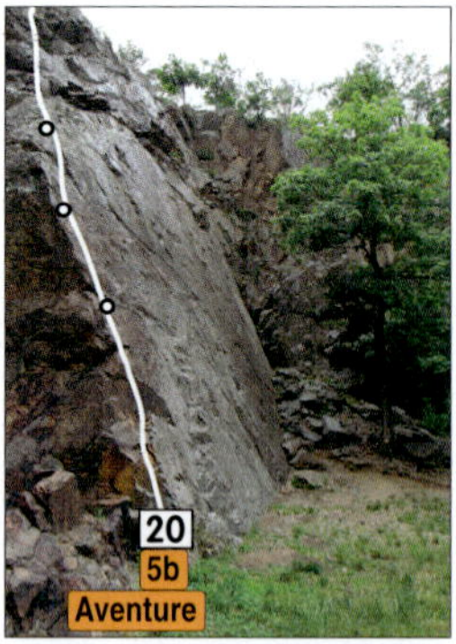

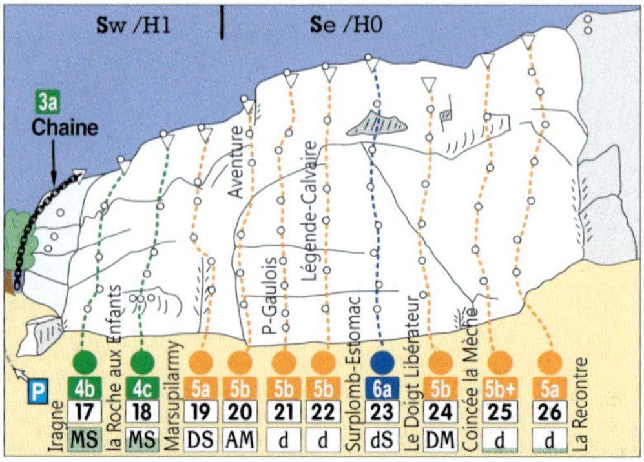

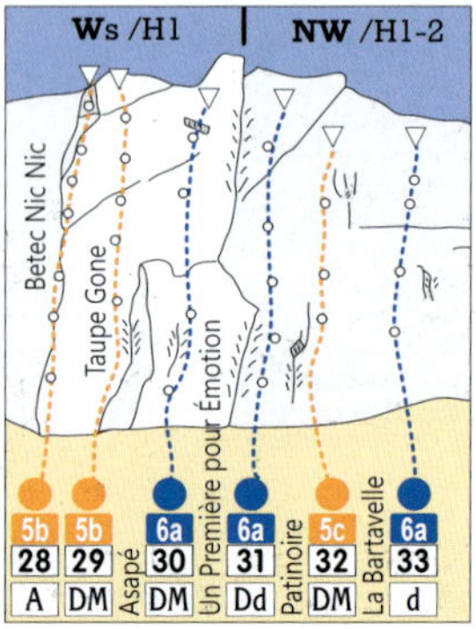

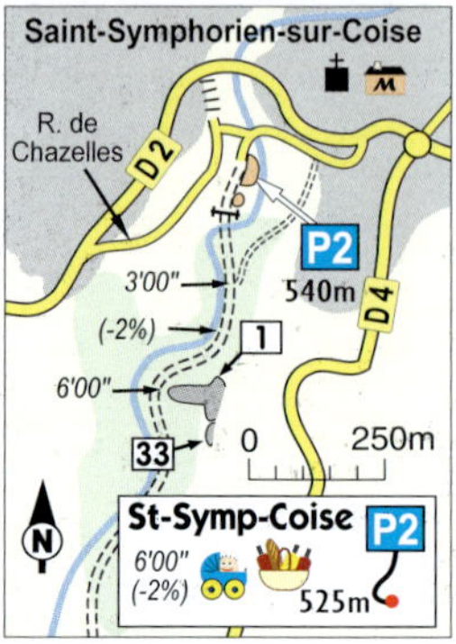

YZERON (Font cotation/grades)

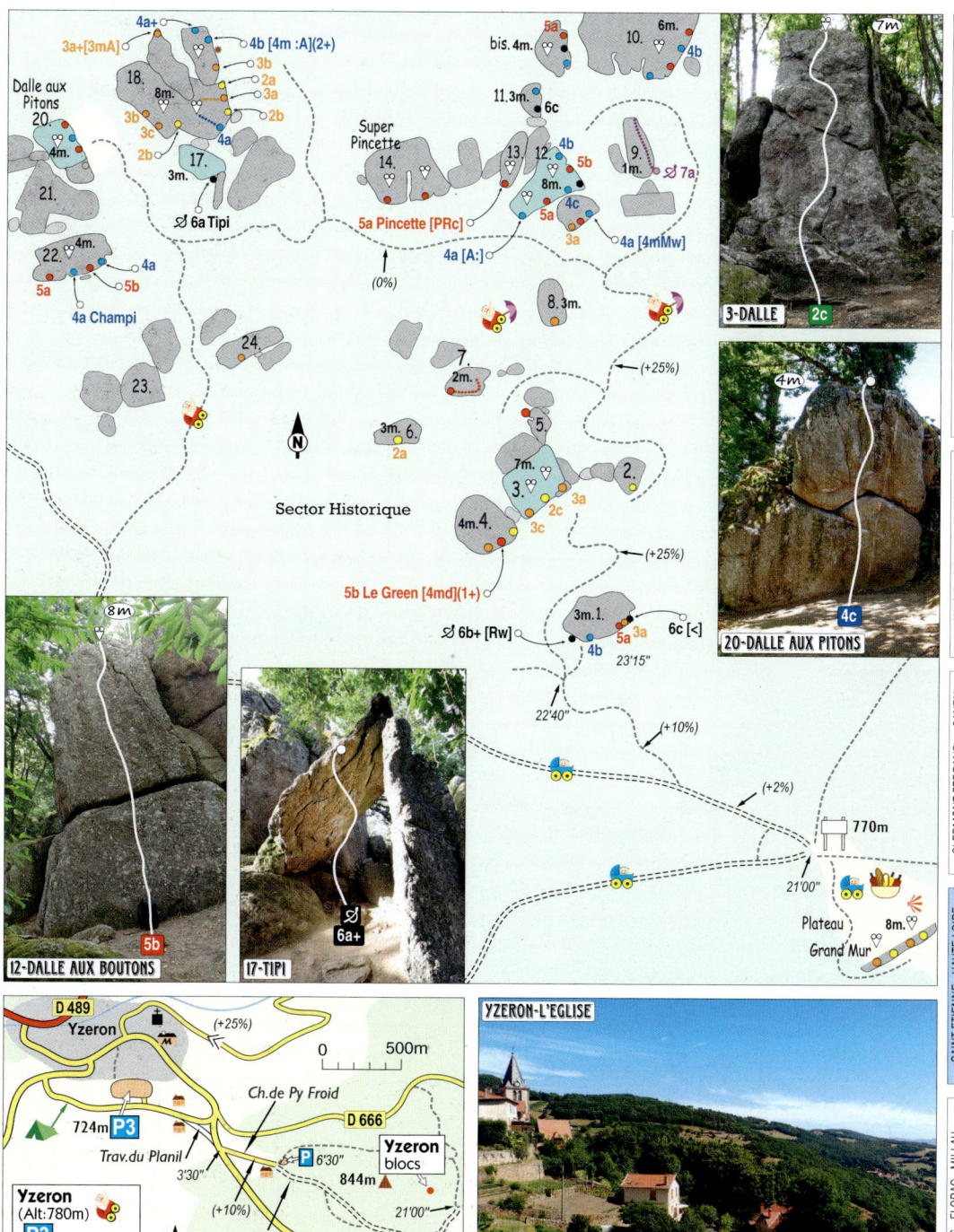

Gneiss**** Very abrasive, and "very large boulders" on a steep hill. Top rope more useful and fun than crash pads. Nice spot.

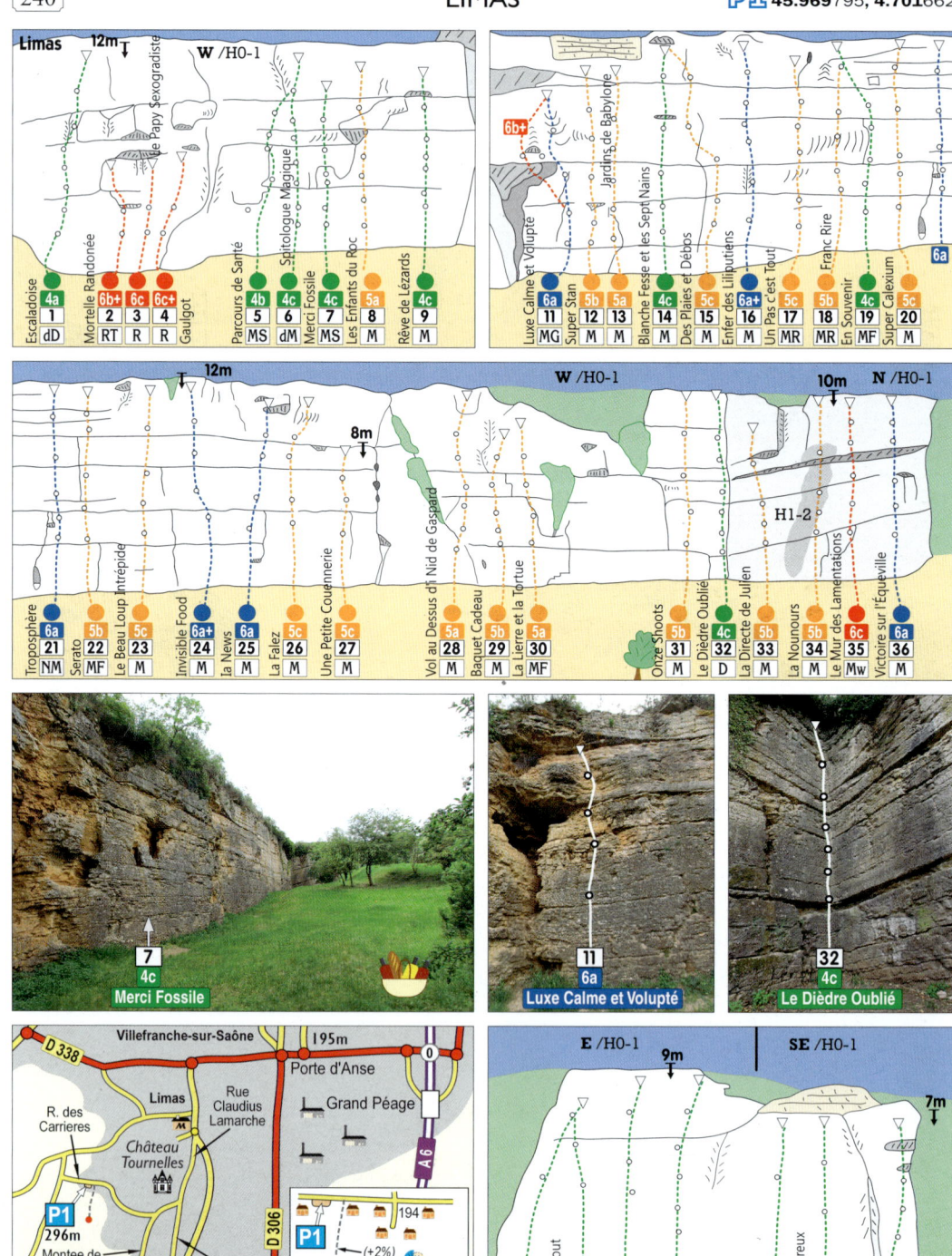

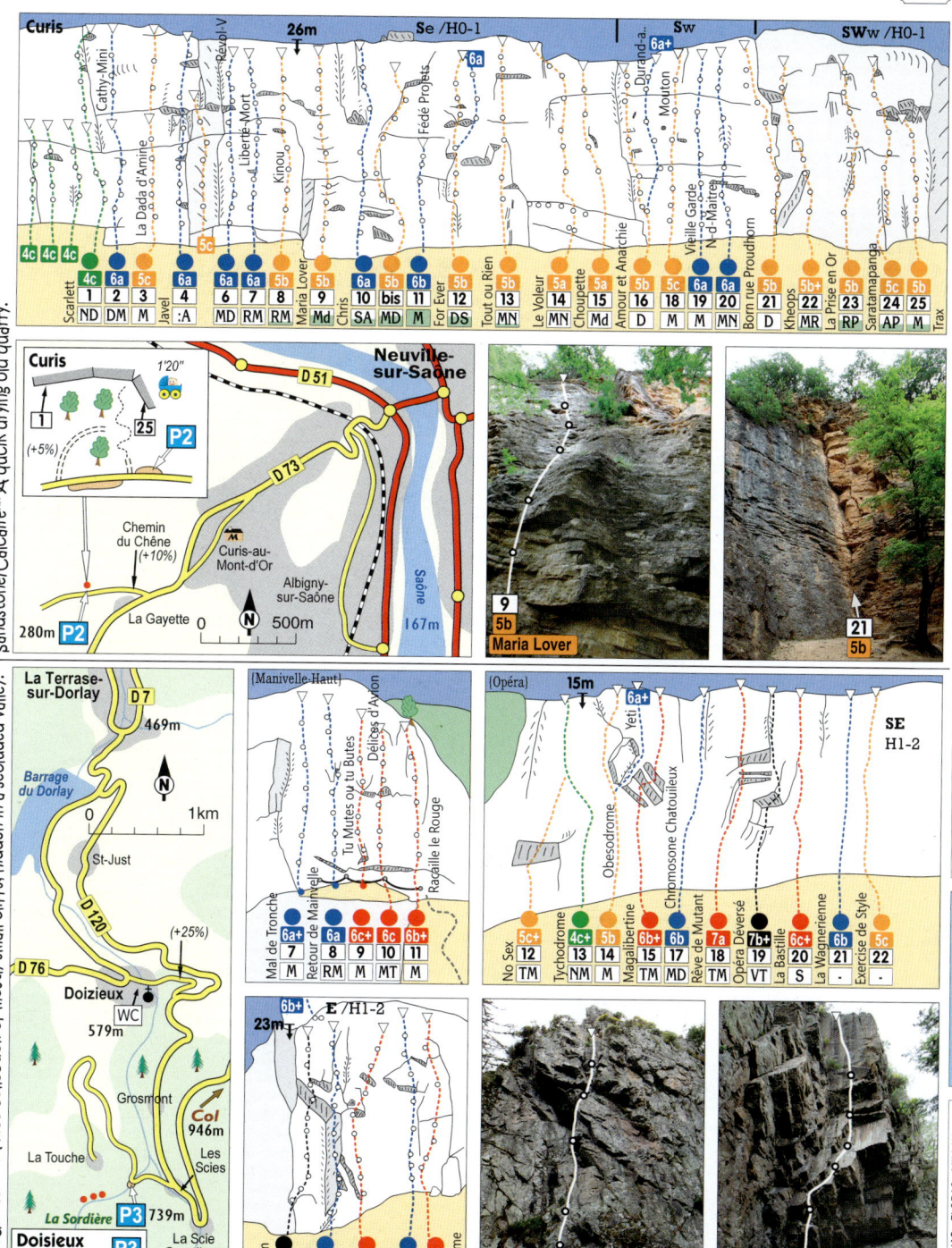

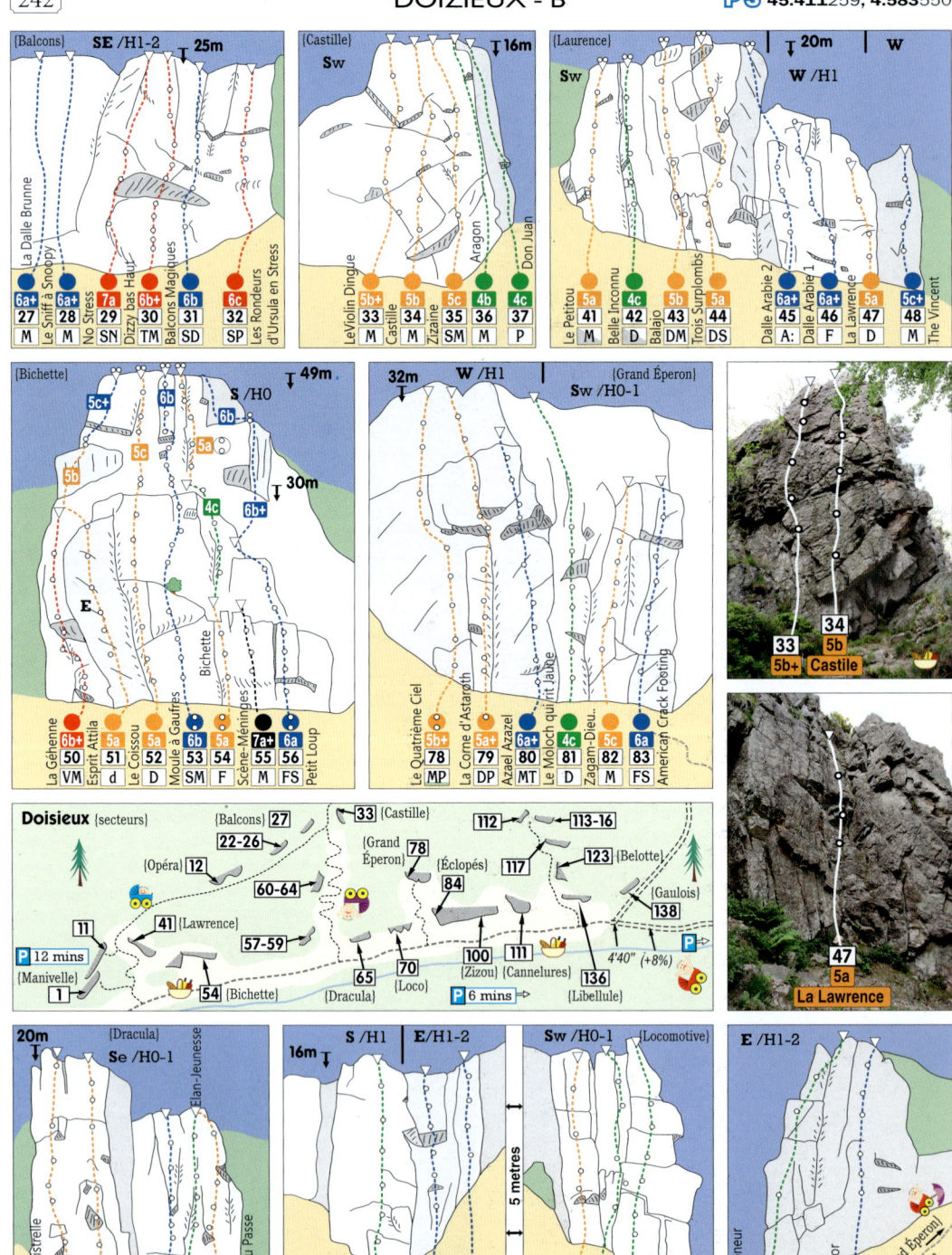

DOIZIEUX - C

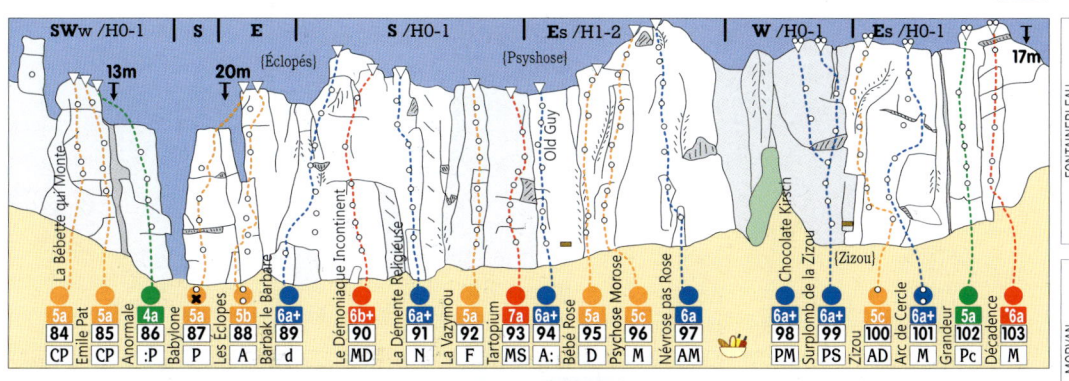

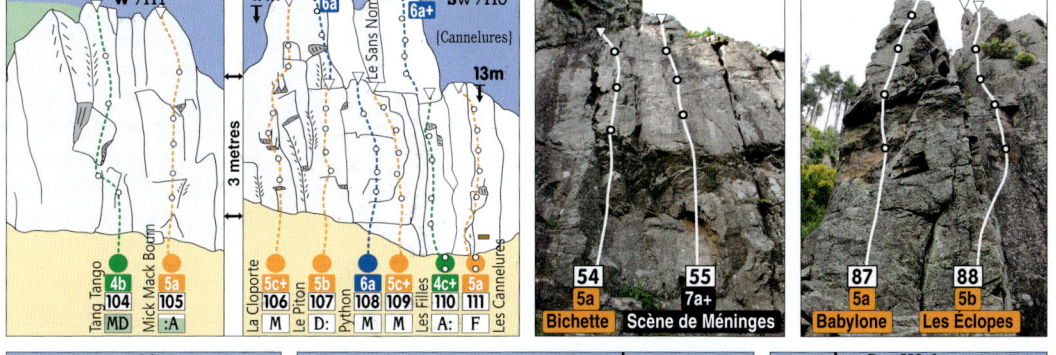

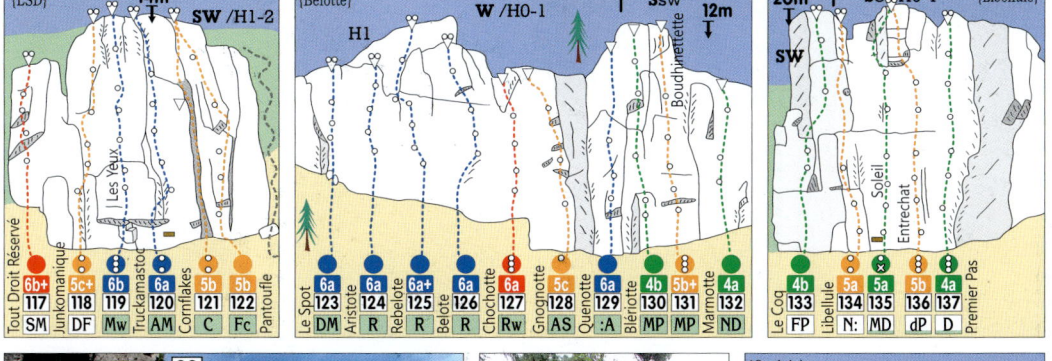

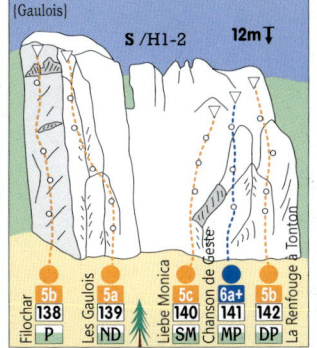

The valley tends to be very sheltered from the west winds, and its easy to find sun or shade at most times of the day.

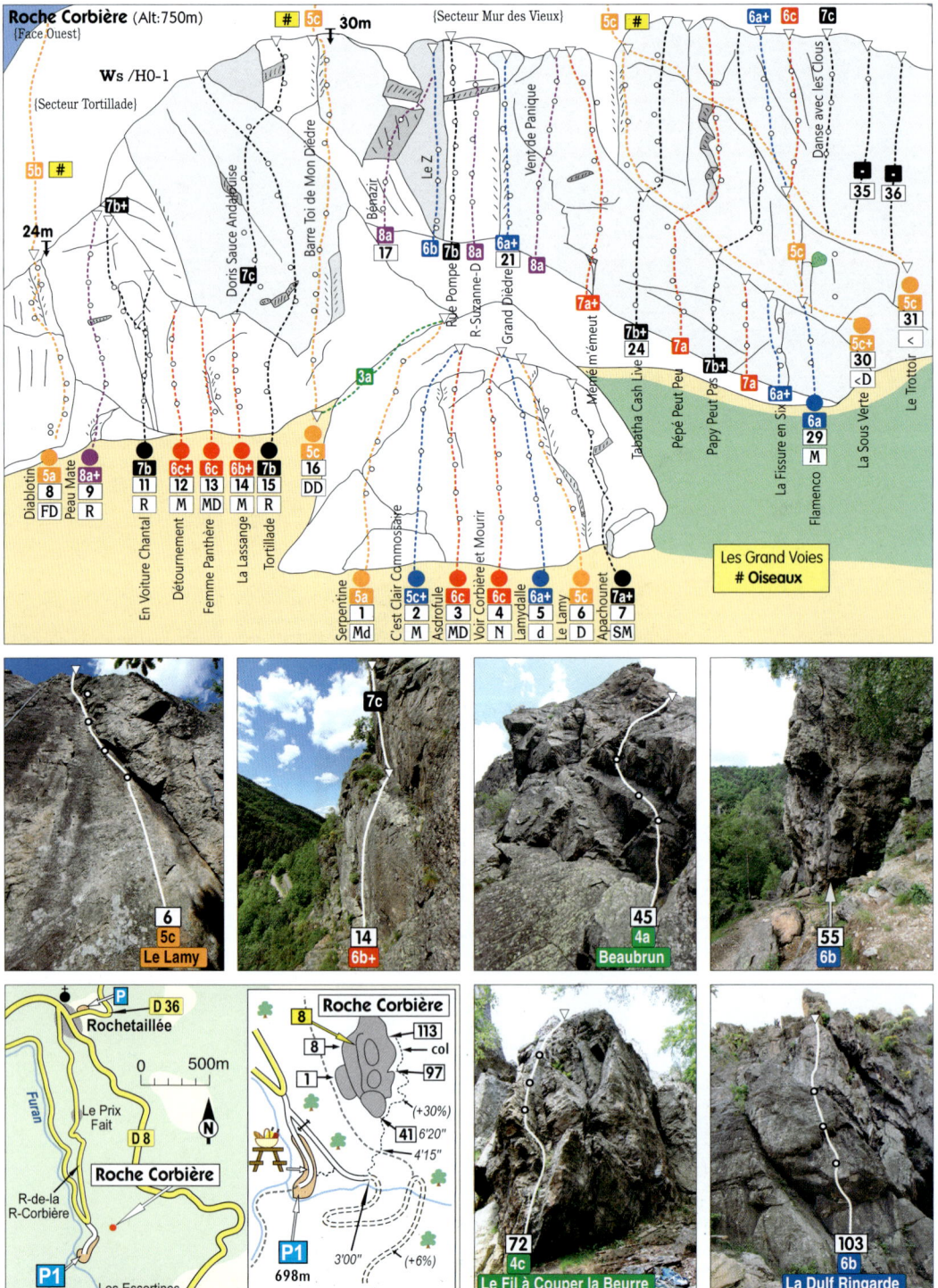

Volcanic**** Climbing on all sides of this "GIANT" lump of rock: wild west & easier east. Follow the sun or the shade all day.

ROCHE CORBIÈRE - B

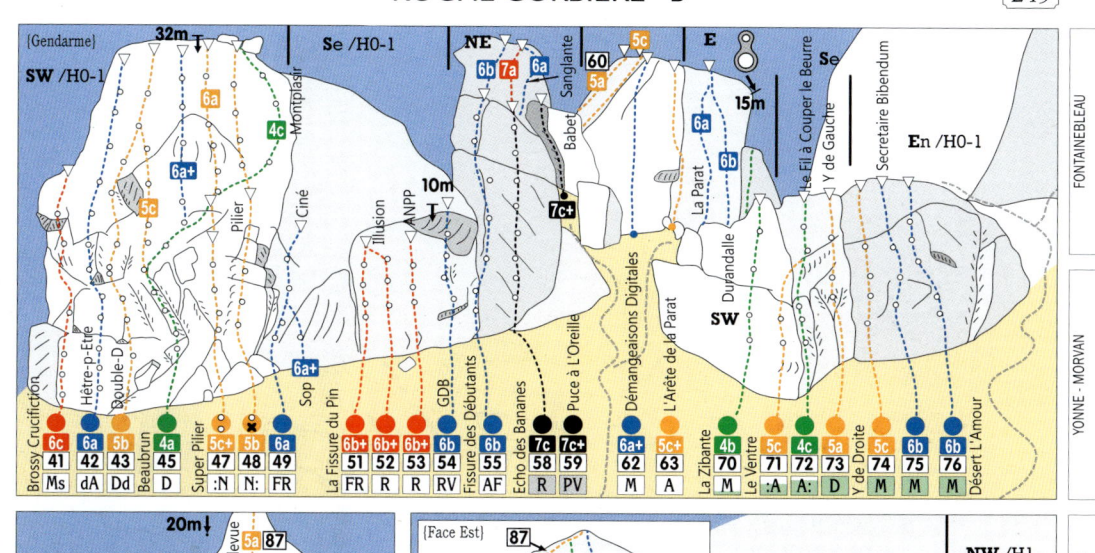
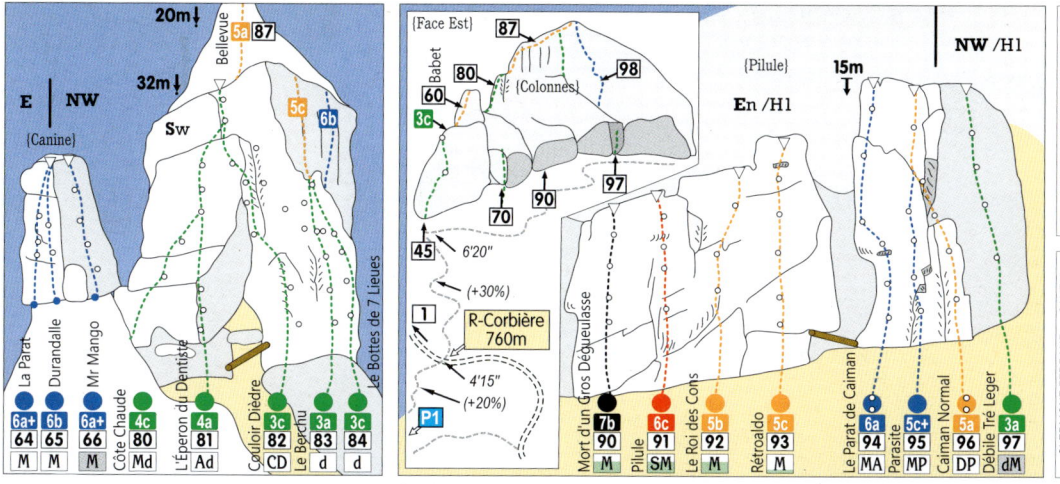
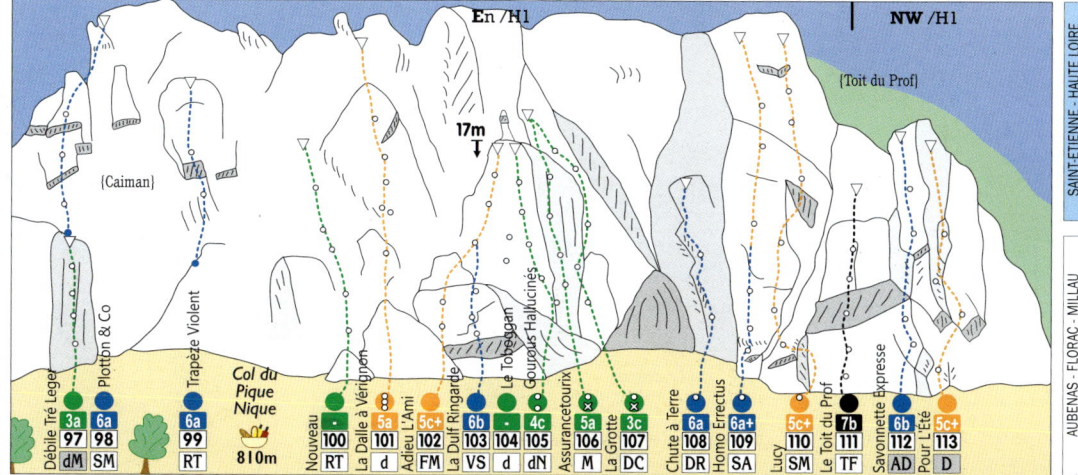

COSTAROS — # 31/03-30/06 P1 45.175948, 3.967507

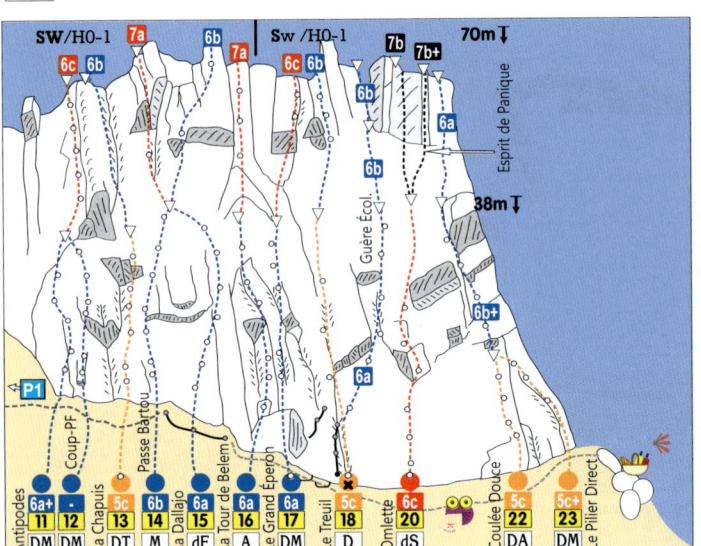

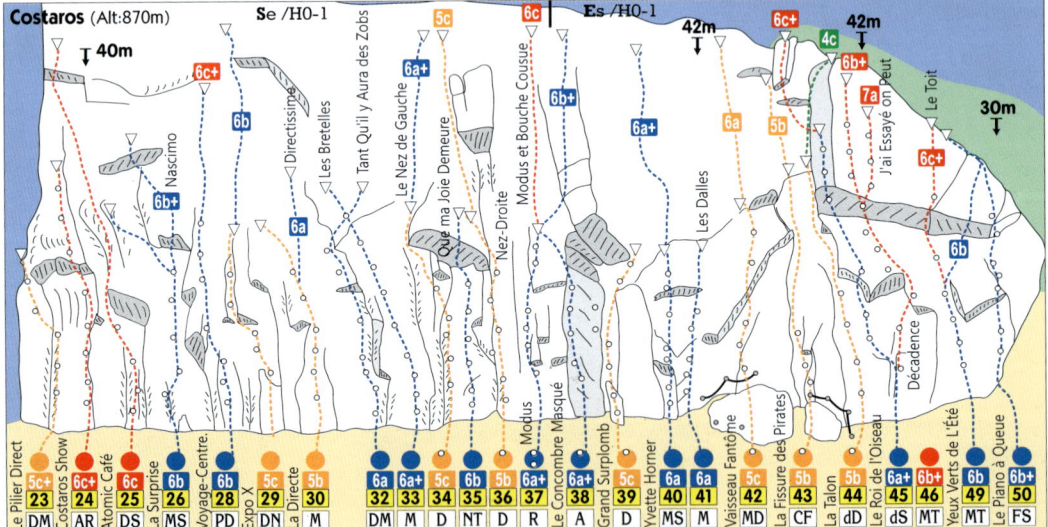

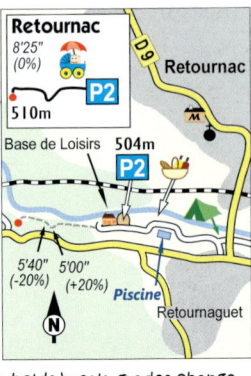

Volcanic lava - Phonolitic schiste** An impressive cliff, not so many bolts. Equipped - old school, holds break, grades change.

RETOURNAC (Rocher de la Base)

P2 45.200089, 4.028085 — 247

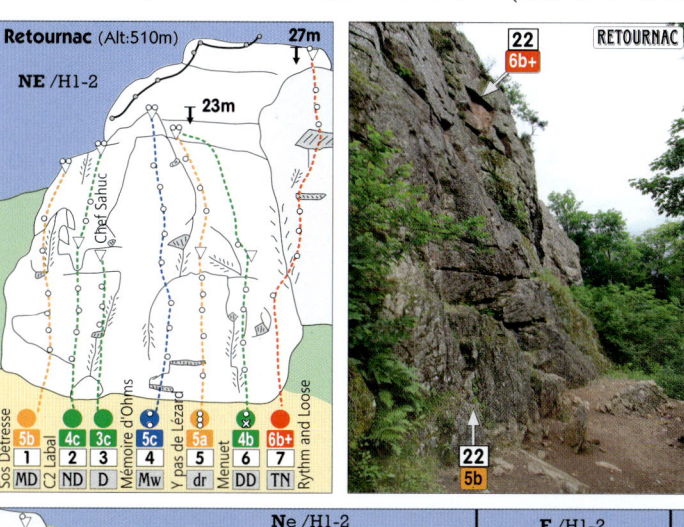

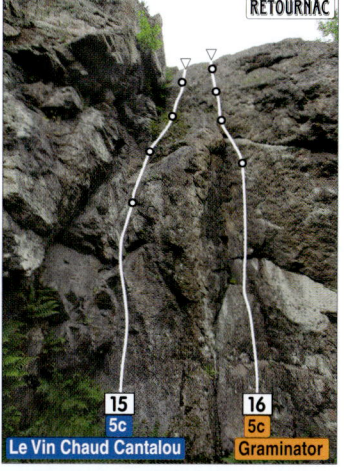

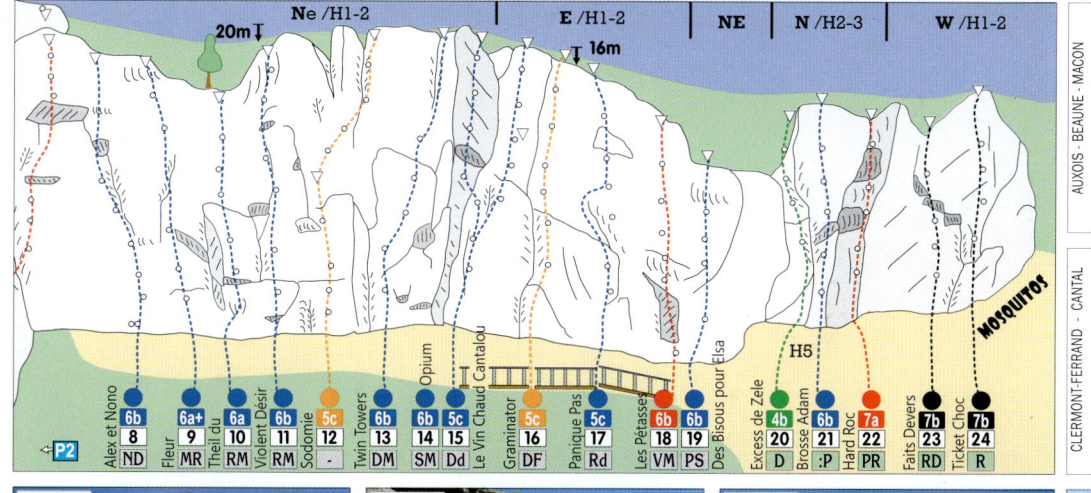

Granite** Some very good climbing, some very-very dodgy rock, some very-very-very hungry mosquitos. In shade and sheltered.

PRADEL-A (St-Julien-des-Chazes)

P1 45.044989, 3.591770

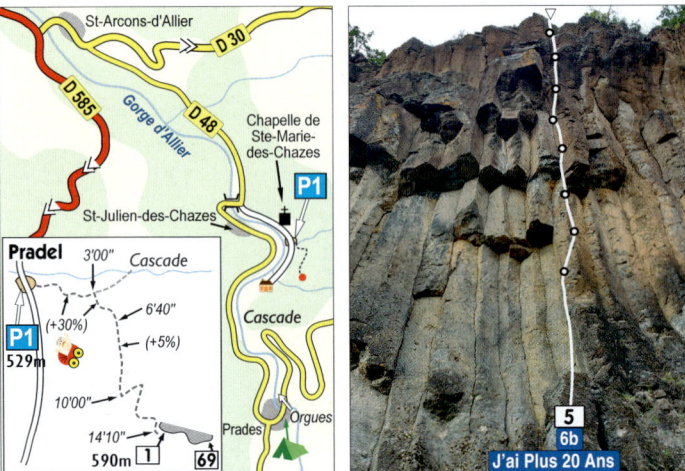

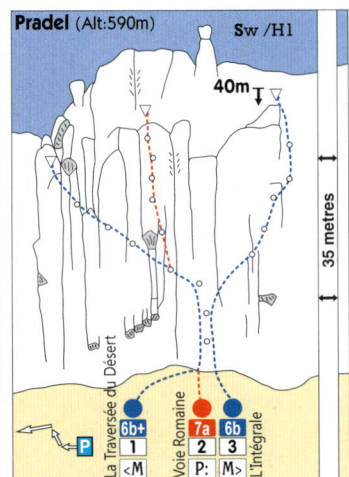

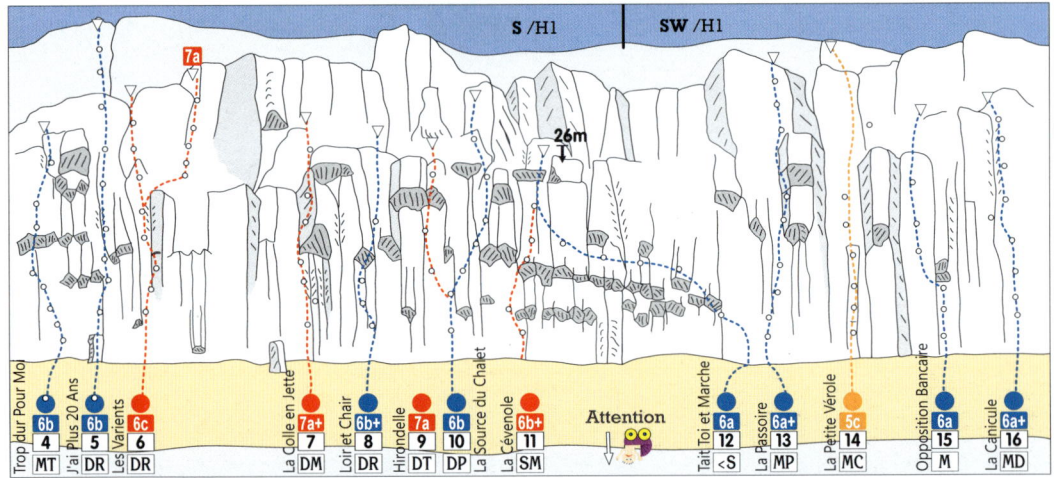

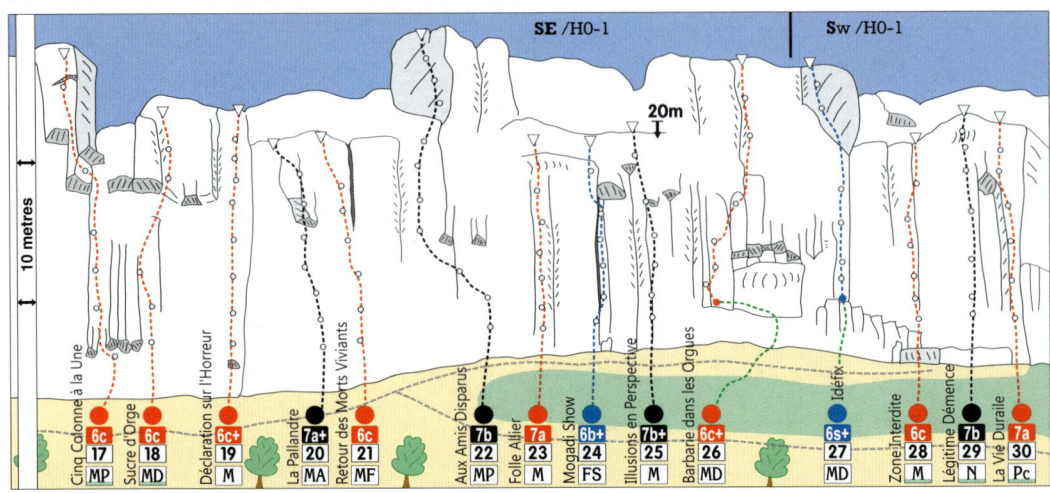

Bassalt****. Very sunny cliff, old school bolting on most routes (bring clip stick). Lots of Dièdres, but face crimping actually.

PRADEL-B (St-Julien-des-Chazes)

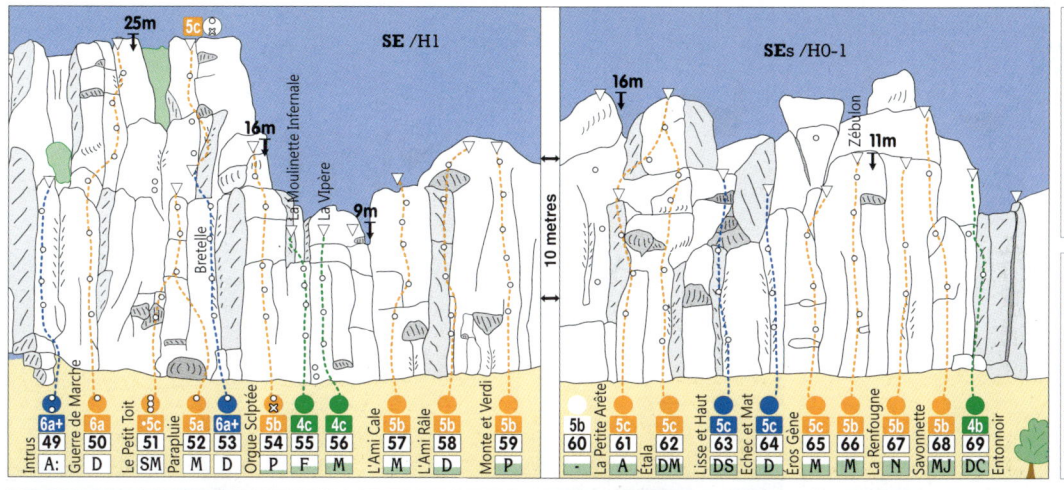

#	Name	Grade	Code
31	Ca Plane Pour Moi	6b	DT
32	Orgues Défuntes	7a	PS
33	Moi et Toits	6a+	MD
34	La Palagr-hot	6a+	MS
35	Double Jeu	6a	DM
36	Emile Franc	6b	SM
37	Roger Langeac	6a	M
38	Fundy Dead	6a	AD
39	Obélix et Cie	5c	MN
40	Nous n'Irons Plus au Bois	6a+	Mr
41	Si Tu Vas à Rio	6b+	DF
42	Débils Towers	5b	AC
43	Préméditation	5b	SP
44	Sur Bac à Bac	6b+	TP
45	Bloc en Stock	4b	DF
46	Terre Yfic	5b	DF
47	L'Age de la Terre	5b	FD
48	Incognito	6a	DD
49	Intrus	6a+	A:
49	Intrus	6a+	A:
50	Guerre de Marche	6a	D
51	Le Petit Toit	5c	SM
52	Parapluie	5a	M
53	La Moulinette Infernale	6a+	D
54	Orgue Sculptée	5b	P
55	L'Ami Cale	4c	F
56	L'Ami Râle	4c	M
57	La Vipère	5b	M
58	Monte et Verdi	5b	D
59		5b	P
60	La Petite Arête	-	-
61	Etala	5c	A
62	Lisse et Haut	5c	DM
63	Echec et Mat	5c	DS
64	Eros Gène	5c	D
65	La Renfougne	5b	M
66	Savonnette	5b	M
67	Zébulon	5b	N
68	Entonnoir	5b	MJ
69		4b	DC

26 6c+ Barbarie dans les Orgues

44 6b+ Sur Bac à Bac
45 4b Bloc en Stock

53 6a+ La Bretelle
54 5b Orgue Sculptée

A very steep initial approach, then a scenic traverse in the trees. Nice vistas for a picnic, plus some tree shade in parts.

LES COCHONS

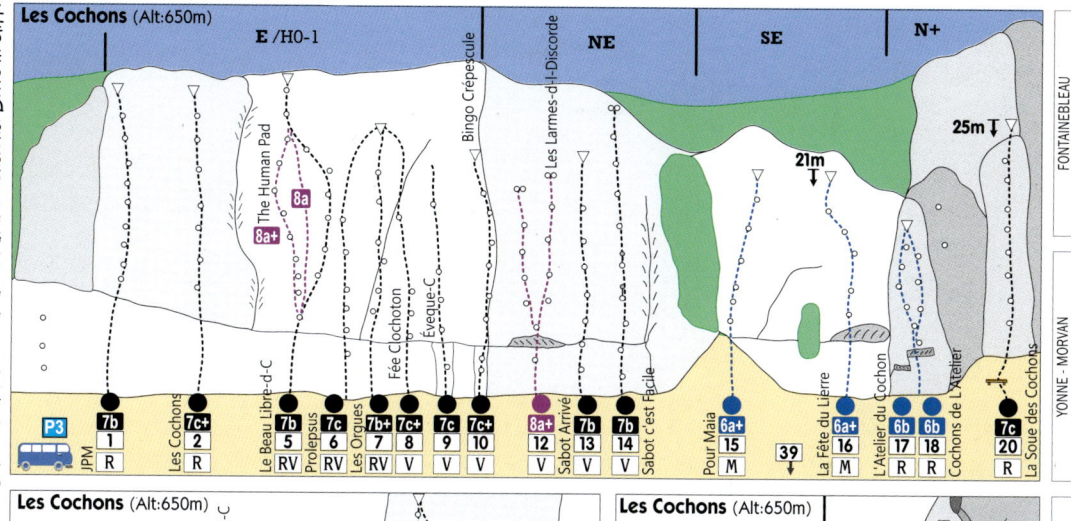

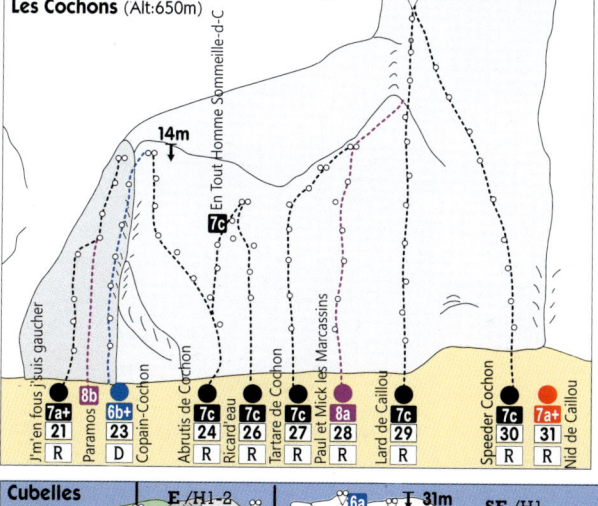

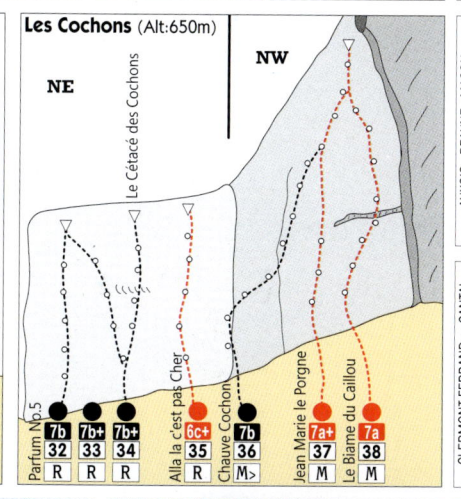

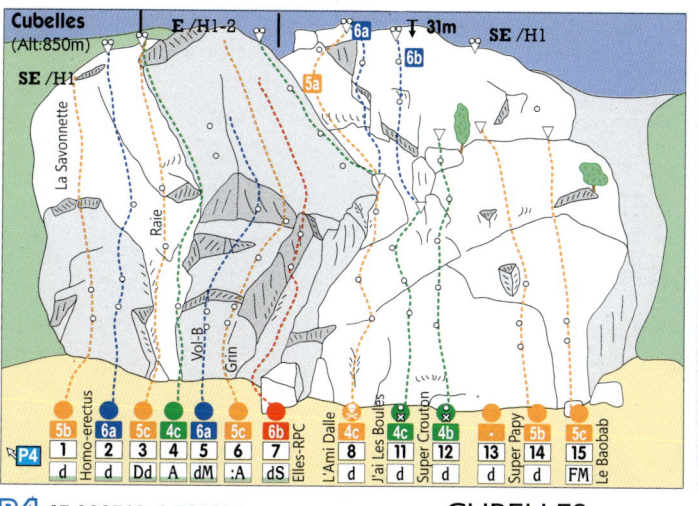

CUBELLES

GrazaC: Granite*** Deep down in the trees, best in a dry period for all the normal reasons.

LA TORTUE — LA ROCHE POINTUE

P3 44.924969, 4.189332 — 253

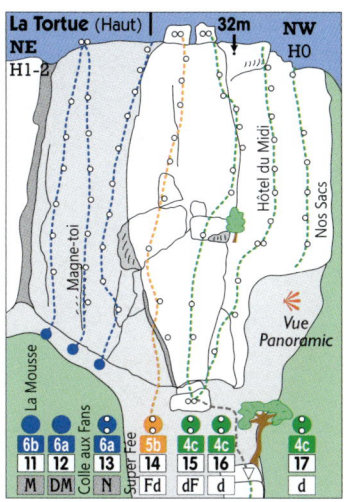
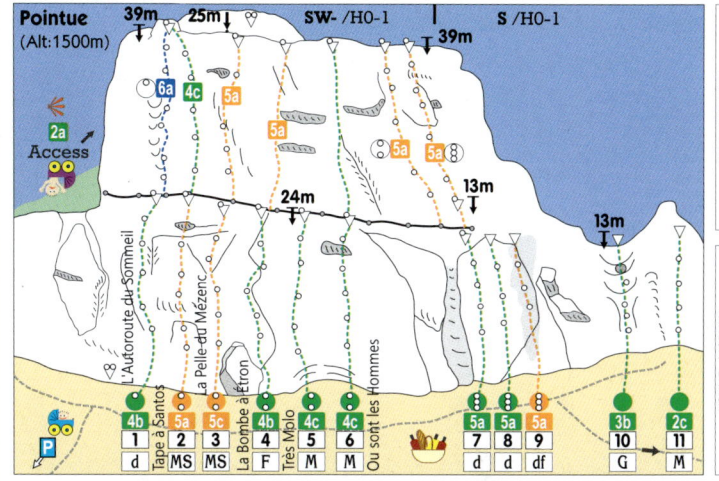

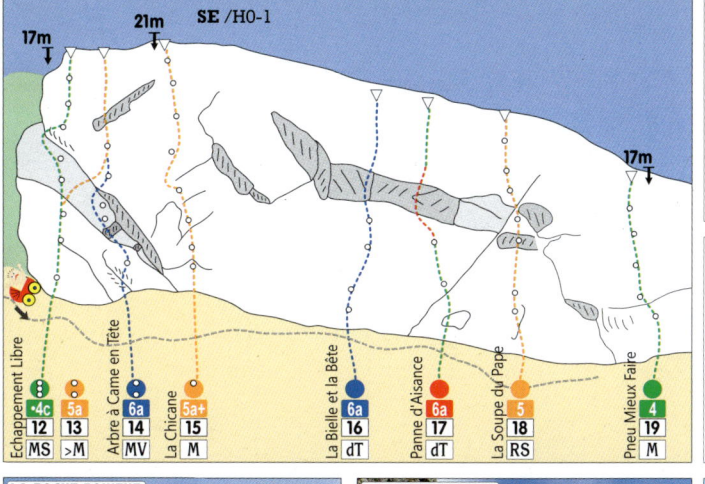
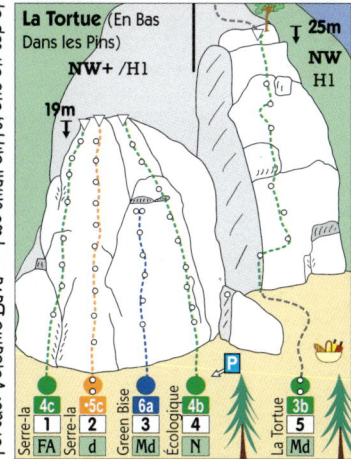

Pointue: Lava*** A volcanic plug, on a nice day.... is the most perfect situation.

P2 45.027032, 4.113897

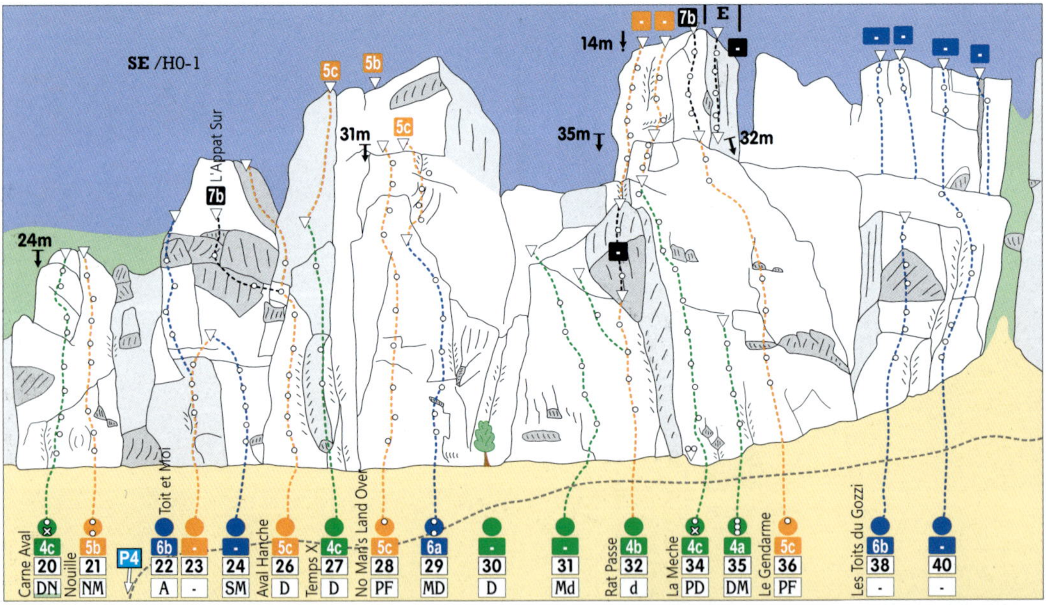

FAY-SUR-LIGNON - A

P4 44.977575, 4.196141

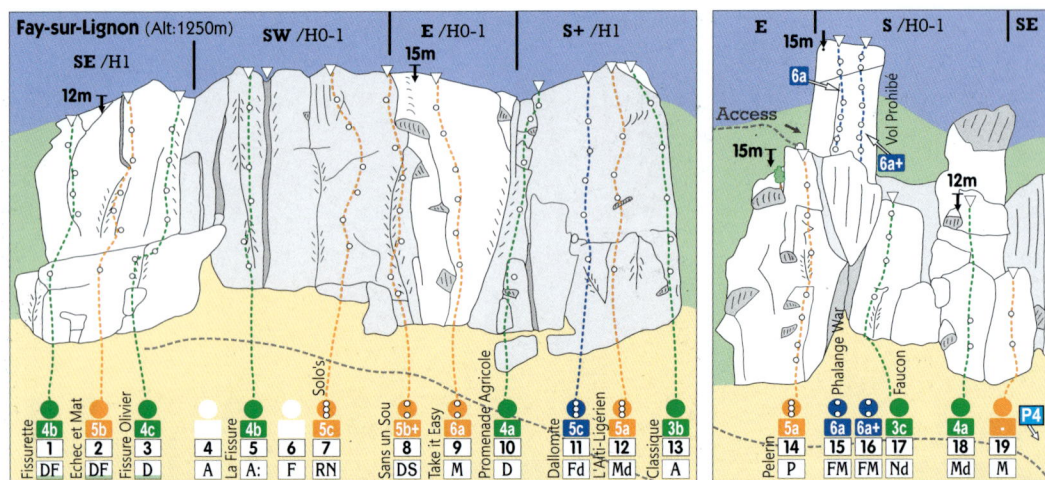

Volcanic Lava-Phonolite**** A very good location with a fine assortment of routes, both small and large. Great views.

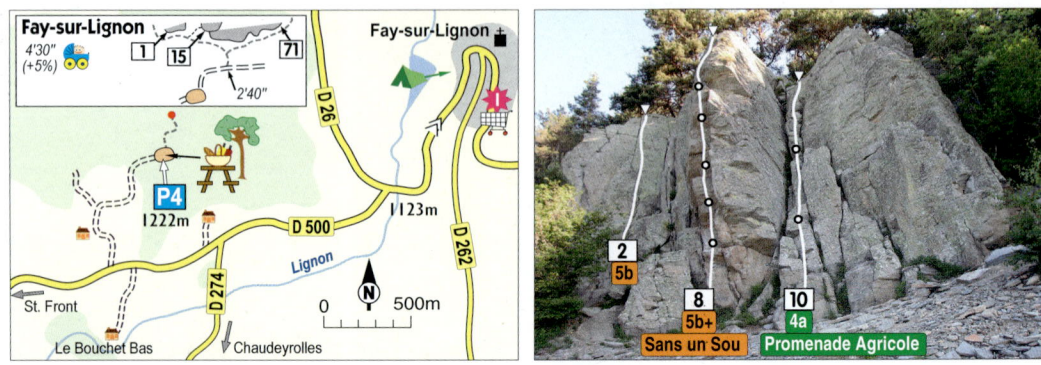

FAY-SUR-LIGNON - B

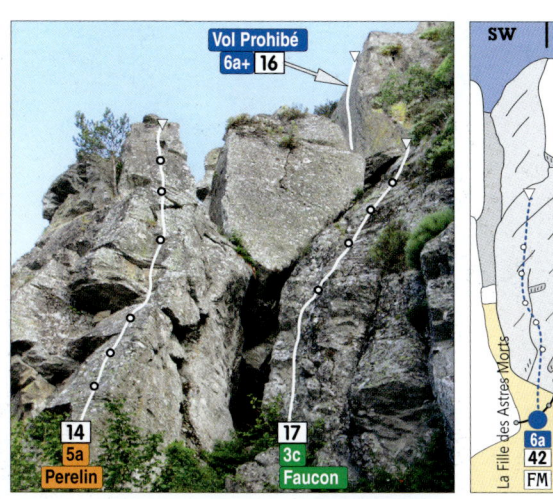
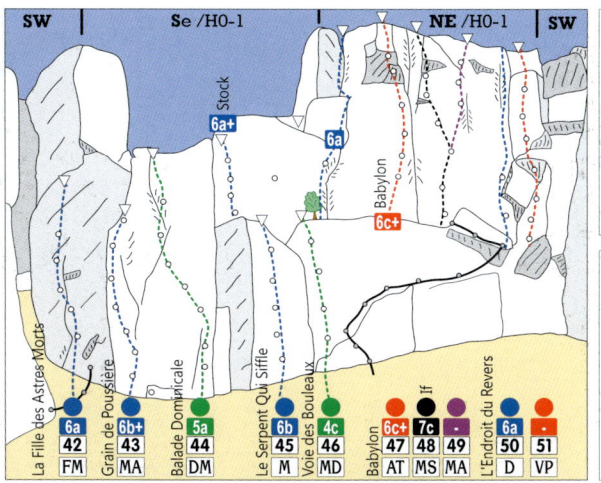
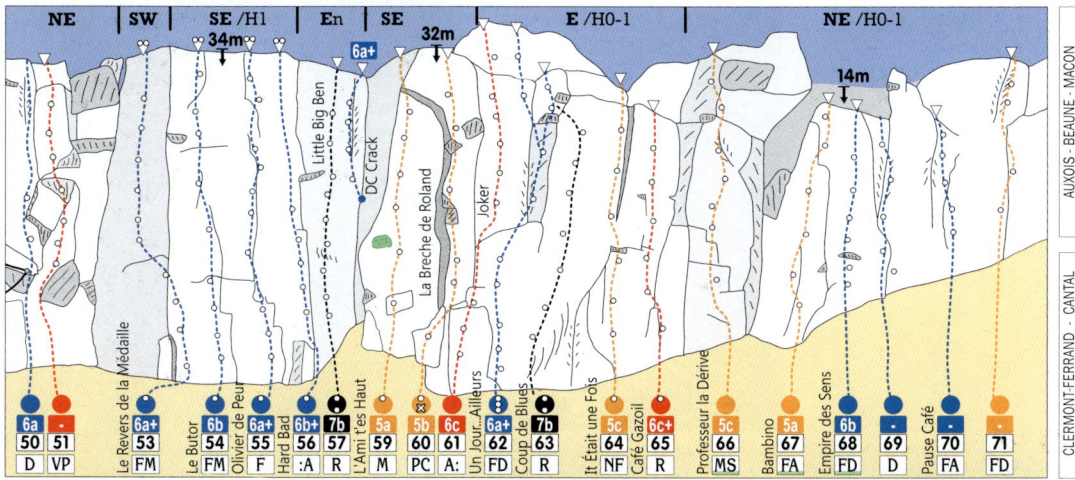

Some of the bigger routes are very old style equipped. Top can generally be accessed. Nice spot for a picnic.

Granite** Some nice climbing in the trees, close to the beautiful lac d'Issarles (popular in summer).

LES COUX

P2 44.824918, 4.229495   257

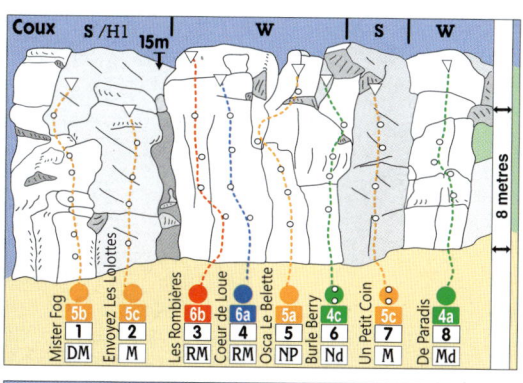

LES COUX

Coux S/H1   15m   W   S   W   8 metres

5b	5c	6b	6a	5a	4c	5c	4a
1	2	3	4	5	6	7	8
Mister Fog	Envoyez Les Lolottes	Les Rombières	Cœur de Loue	Osca Le Belette	Burje Berry	Un Petit Coin	De Paradis
DM	M	RM	RM	NP	Nd	M	Md

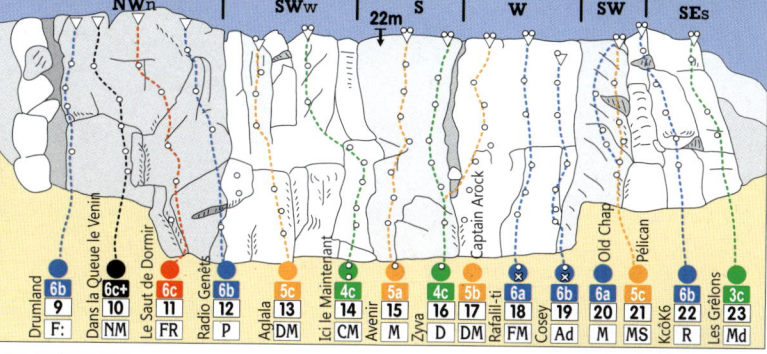

COUX — Le Saut du Dormeur 11 6c

NWn   SWw   22m   S   W   SW   SEs

6b	6c+	6c	6b	5c	4c	5a	4c	5b	6a	6b	6a	5c	6b	3c
9	10	11	12	13	14	15	16	17	18	19	20	21	22	23
Drumland	Dans la Queue le Venin	Le Saut de Dormir	Radio Genêts	Aglala	Ici Le Maintenant	Avenir	Zyva	Cosey	Rafalli-ti	Cosey	Old Chap	Pélican	KcoK6	Les Grélons
F:	NM	FR	P	DM	CM	M	D	DM	FM	Ad	M	MS	R	Md

Les Coux (Alt:1450m) P2

COUX — 12 6b Radio Genêts
COUX — 20 6a Old Chap   21 5c Pélican

LAVAUDIEU

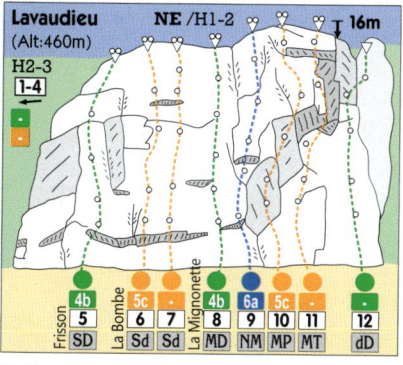
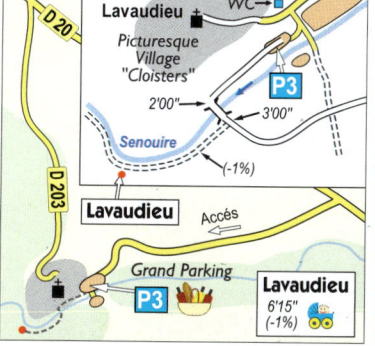

Lavaudieu NE /H1-2 (Alt:460m) 16m
H2-3 1-4

4b	5c	—	4b	6a	5c	—	—
5	6	7	8	9	10	11	12
Frisson	La Bombe	—	La Mignonette	—	—	—	—
SD	Sd	Sd	MD	NM	MP	MT	dD

Lavaudieu P3 6'15" (-1%)

LAVAUDIEU — 12

P3 45.262734, 3.455818

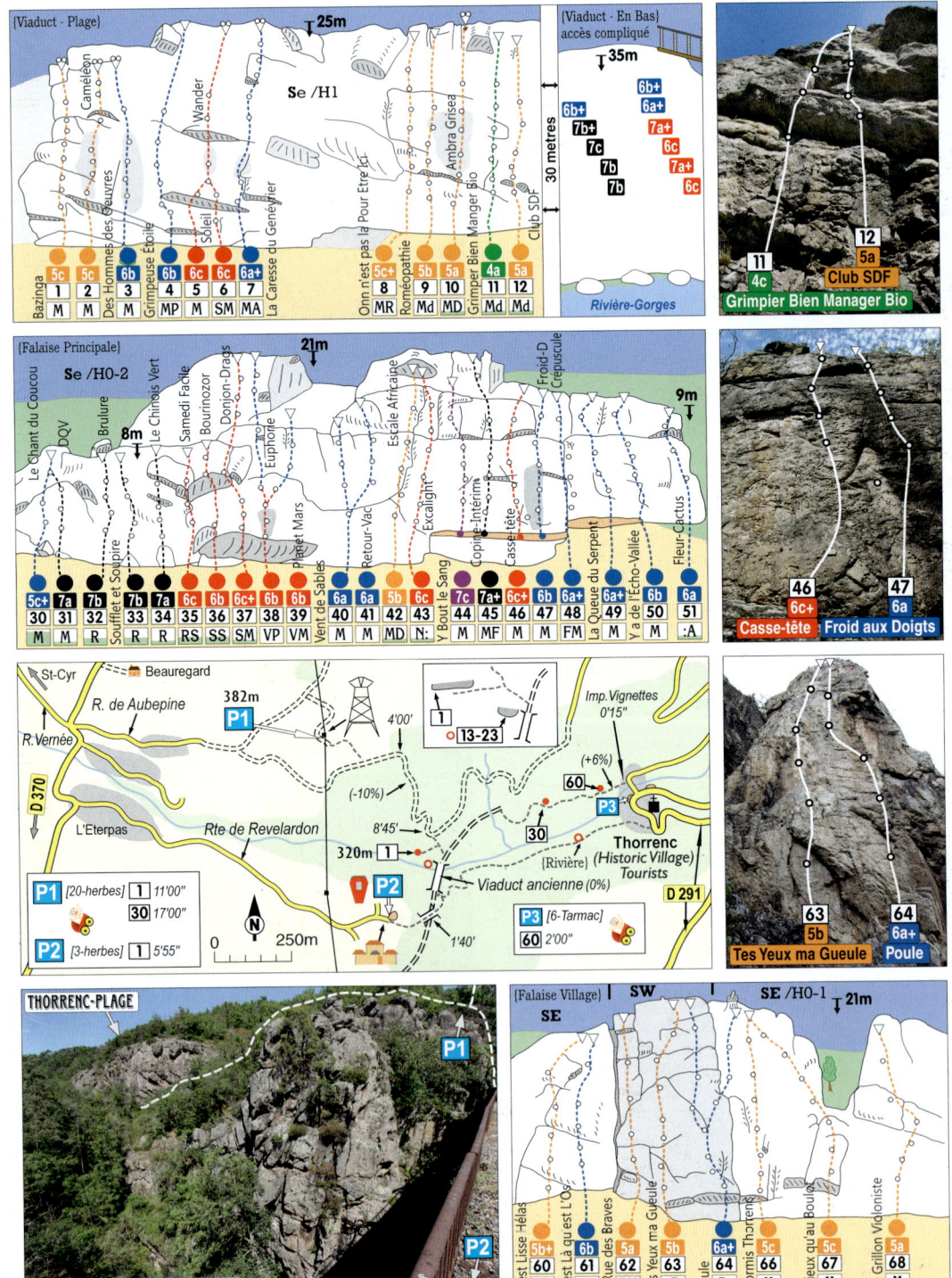

MER DE GLACE

P4 45.238510, 4.600675 | 259

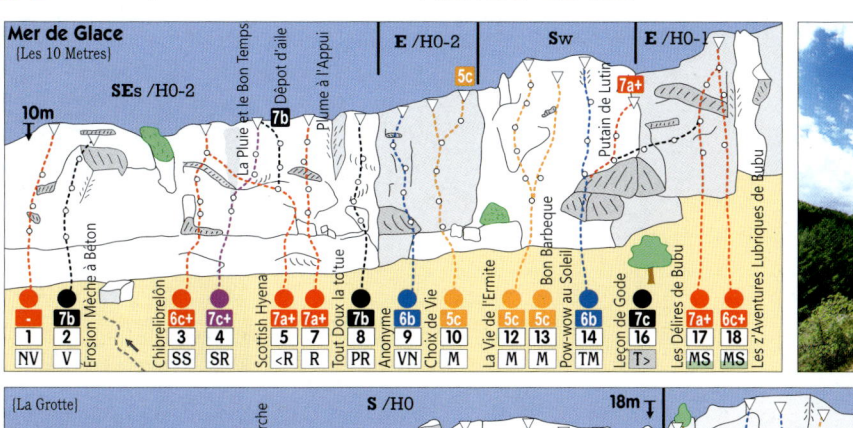

Mer de Glace (Les 10 Metres) — SEs /HO-2 — 10m

#	Grade	Name	Code
1	-		NV
2	7b		V
3	6c+	Chibreli/brelon	SS
4	7c+		SR
5	7a+	Scottish Hyena	<R
6	7a+		R
7	7b	Tout Doux la td'tue	PR
8	-	Anonyme	
9	6b		VN
10	5c	Choix de Vie	M
12	5c	La Vie de l'Ermite	M
13	5c		M
14	6b	Bon Barbeque / Pow-wow au Soleil	TM
16	7c	Lecon de Gode	T>
17	7a+	Les Délires de Bubu	MS
18	6c+	Les z'Aventures Lubriques de Bubu	MS

9 — 6b — Anonyme

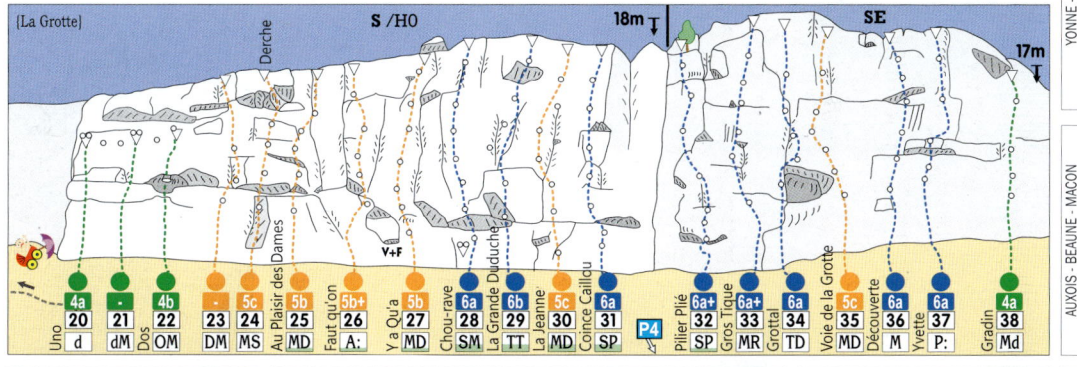

(La Grotte) — S /HO — 18m — SE — 17m

#	Grade	Name	Code
20	4a	Uno	d
21	-		dM
22	4b	Derche	OM
23	5c	Dos Dames	DM
24	5b	Au Plaisir des Dames	MS
25	5b+		MD
26	5b+	Faut qu'on	A:
27	5b	Y a Qu'a	MD
28	6a	Chou-rave	SM
29	6b	La Grande Duduche	TT
30	5c	La Jeanne	MD
31	6a	Coince Caillou	SP
32	6a+	Pilier Plié	SP
33	6a+	Gros Tique	MR
34	6a	Grottal	TD
35	5c	Voie de la Grotte	MD
36	6a	Découverte	M
37	6a	Yvette	P:
38	4a	Gradin	Md

29 — 6b — La Grande Duduche

41 — 5a — La Boite aux Lettres

53 — 5c

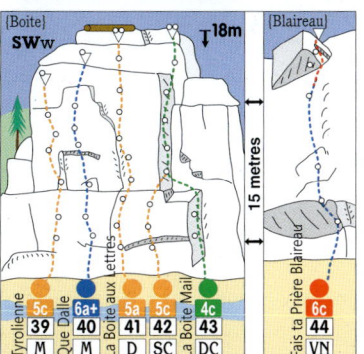

(Boite) — SWw — 18m — (Blaireau) — 15 metres — (Crépuscule) — Se /HO-1 — 11m

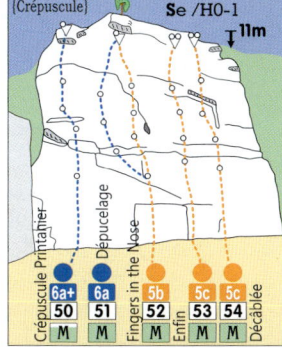

#	Grade	Name	Code
39	5c	Tyrolienne	M
40	6a+	Que Dale	M
41	5c	La Boite aux Lettres	D
42	5c		SC
43	4c	La Boite Mail	DC
44	6c	Fais ta Prière Blaireau	VN
50	6a+	Crépuscule Printanier	M
51	6b	Dépucelage	M
52	5b	Fingers in the Nose	M
53	5c		M
54	5c	Enfin	M
		Décâblée	

Mer de Glace (Alt:425m) — P4 — 416m

Granite* A good mixture of small Cliffs, most with a riverside/picnique setting. Gets quite warm, bring sun tan lotion.

AUVERGNAT

A1 45.242021, 4.657597

Auvergnat: Granite*** Big giant corners, impressive.

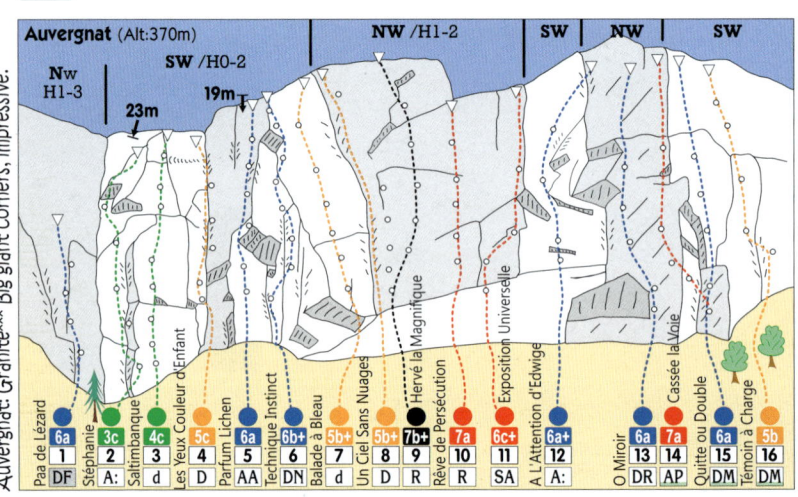

AUVERGNAT — 3 / 4c Saltimbique

AUVERGNAT — 13 / 6a Ô Miroir

Péréandre: Granite*** A very impressive monolite. Access can be interesting, river height and flow - variable !!!

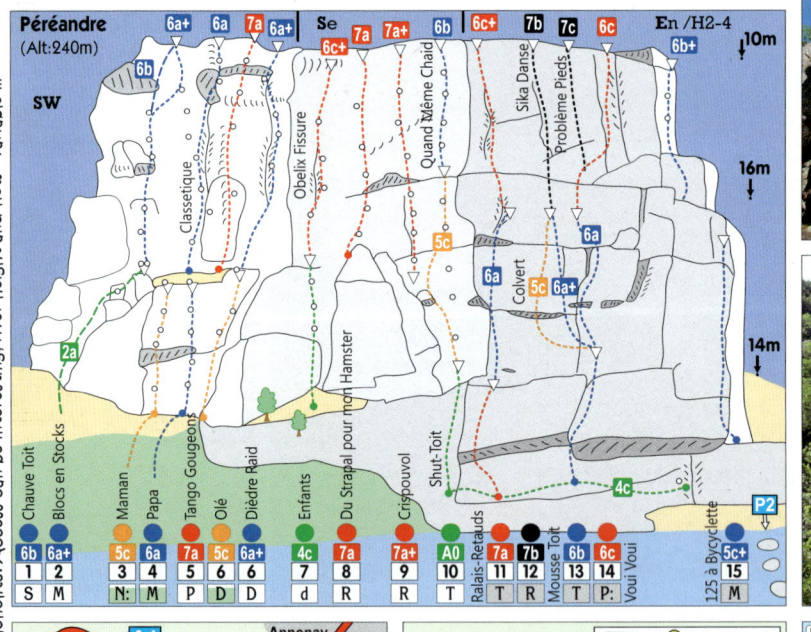

PEREANDRE

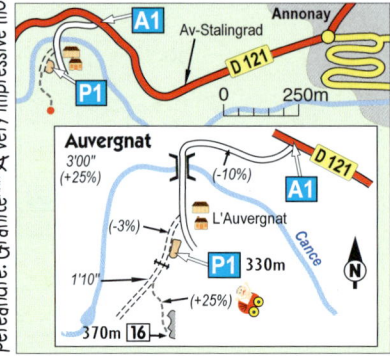

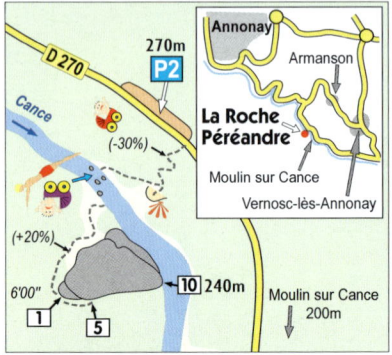

PEREANDRE — 4 / 6a Classetique

PÉRÉANDRE

P2 45.214505, 4.701055

TOURNAY

P3 44.875288, 4.527908   261

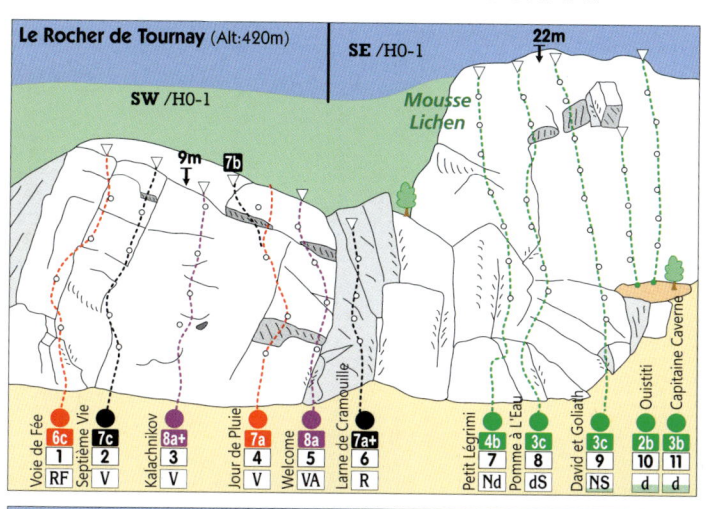

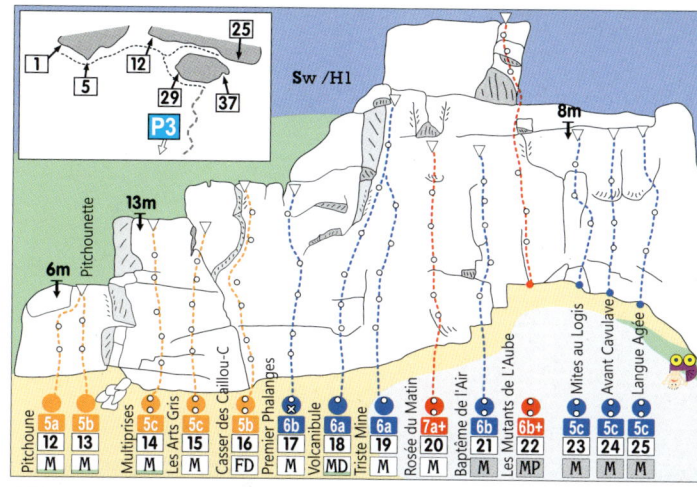

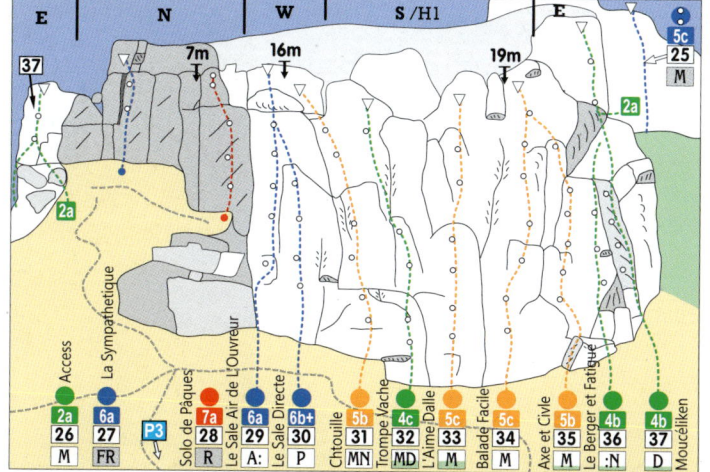
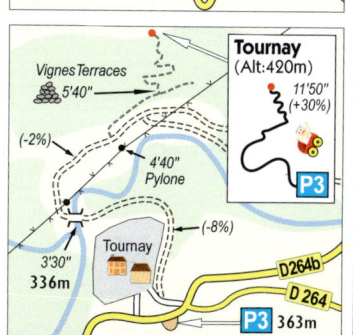

Granite: A complete mixture of styles - usually quiet. Quite old school equipping. Nice setting, but gets hot and lichen grows.

LE PONT DE FROMENTIÈRES (Mariac)

P1 44.876705, 4.367785

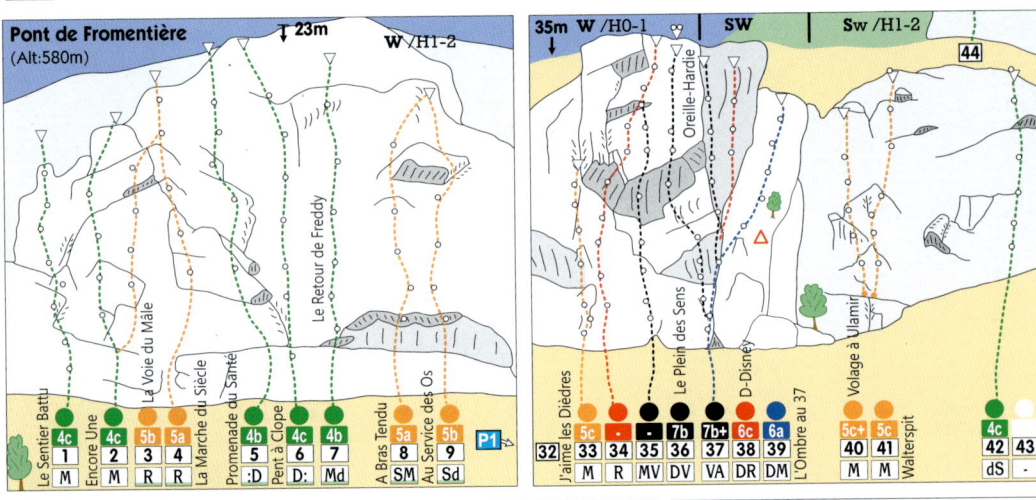

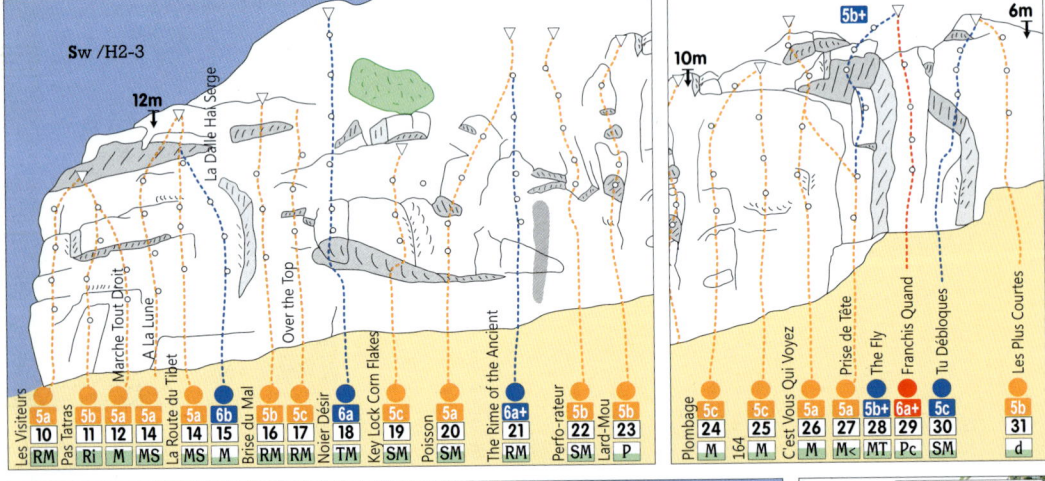

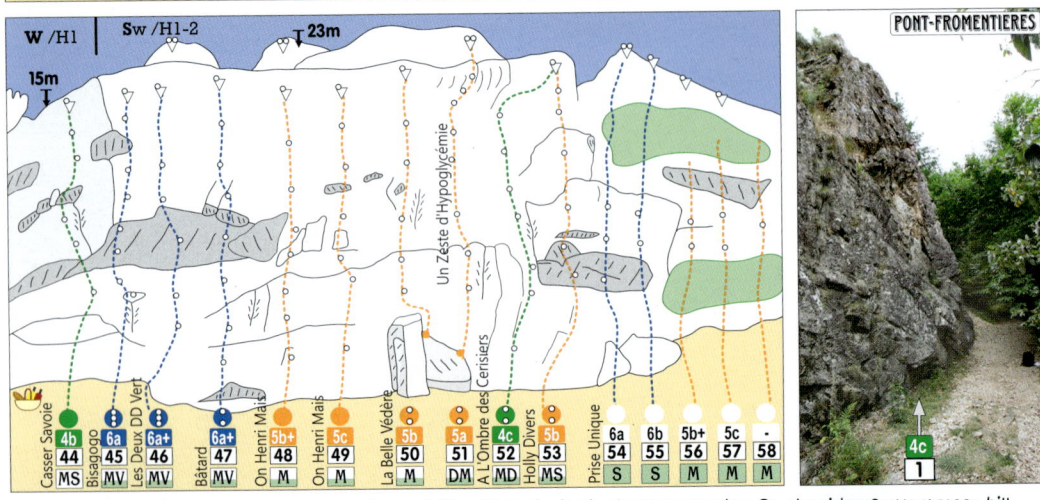

Granite*** Something for everyone, mostly nice and friendly equipping in the lower grades. On the side of a very steep hill.

LE ROCHER DE LA CHEVILLÈRE

P2 44.905189, 4.424511 — 263

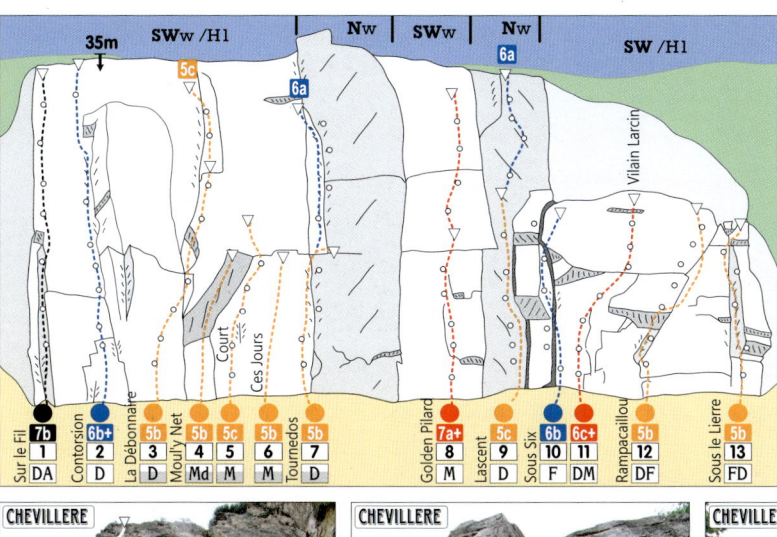

#	1	2	3	4	5	6	7	8	9	10	11	12	13
Grade	7b	6b+	5b	5b	5c	5b	5b	7a+	5c	6b	6c+	5b	5b
Name	Sur le Fil	Contorsion	La Débonnaire	Mou'ly Net	Court	Ces Jours	Tournedos	Golden Pilard	Lascent	Sous Six	Rampacaillou	Vilain Larcin	Sous le Lierre
	DA	D		Md	M	M		M	D	F	DM	DF	FD

CHEVILLERE — 2 — 6b+ — Contorsion

CHEVILLERE — 9 / 10 — 5c Lascent / 6b Sous Six

CHEVILLERE — 13 — 5b

PONT-FROMENTIERES — 21 — 6a+ — The Rime of the Ancient

PONT-FROMENTIERES — 37 / 38 — 7b+ / 6c — L'Oreille est Hardie / Devine Qui Vient Disney

Chevillere: Granite*** A town centre cliff, ideal for cranking and shopping, plus lunch in a nice café. (dog poo - beware).

LES CABANNES

P1 44.838227, 4.578284

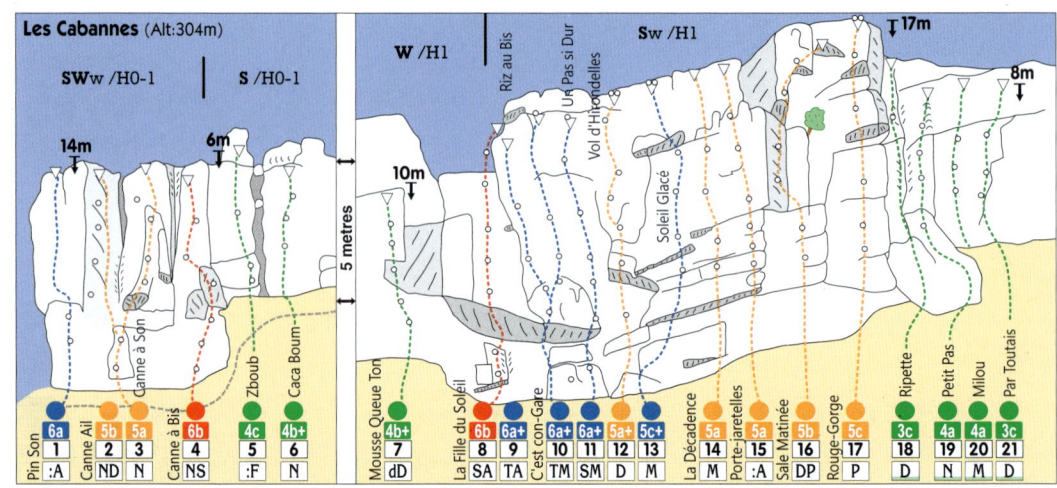

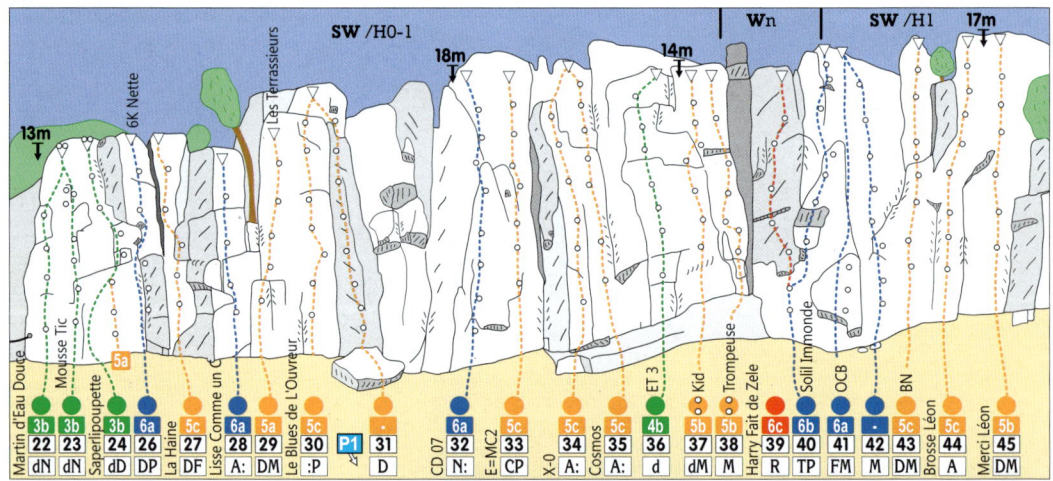

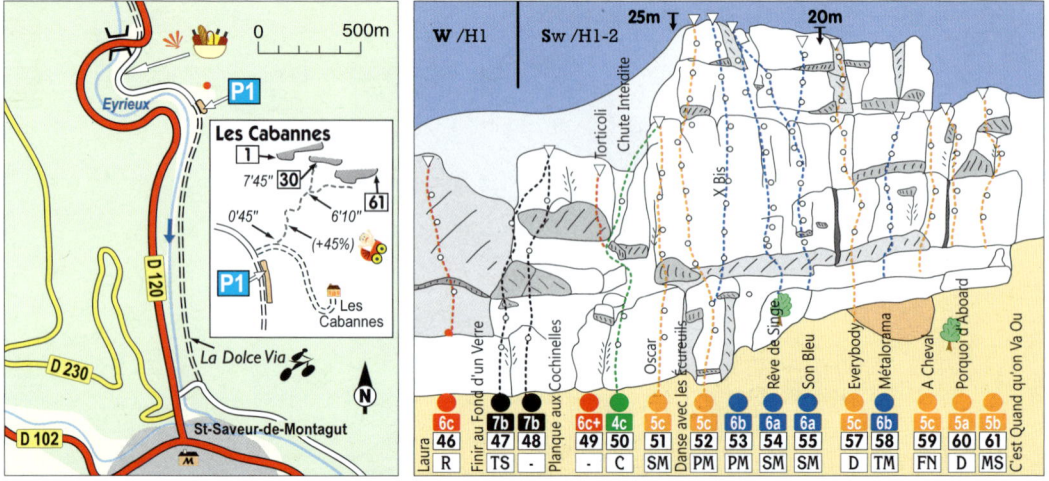

Granite*** Set in a very sheltered position, gets very warm. Situated above a very popular cycle route with nice picnic spots.

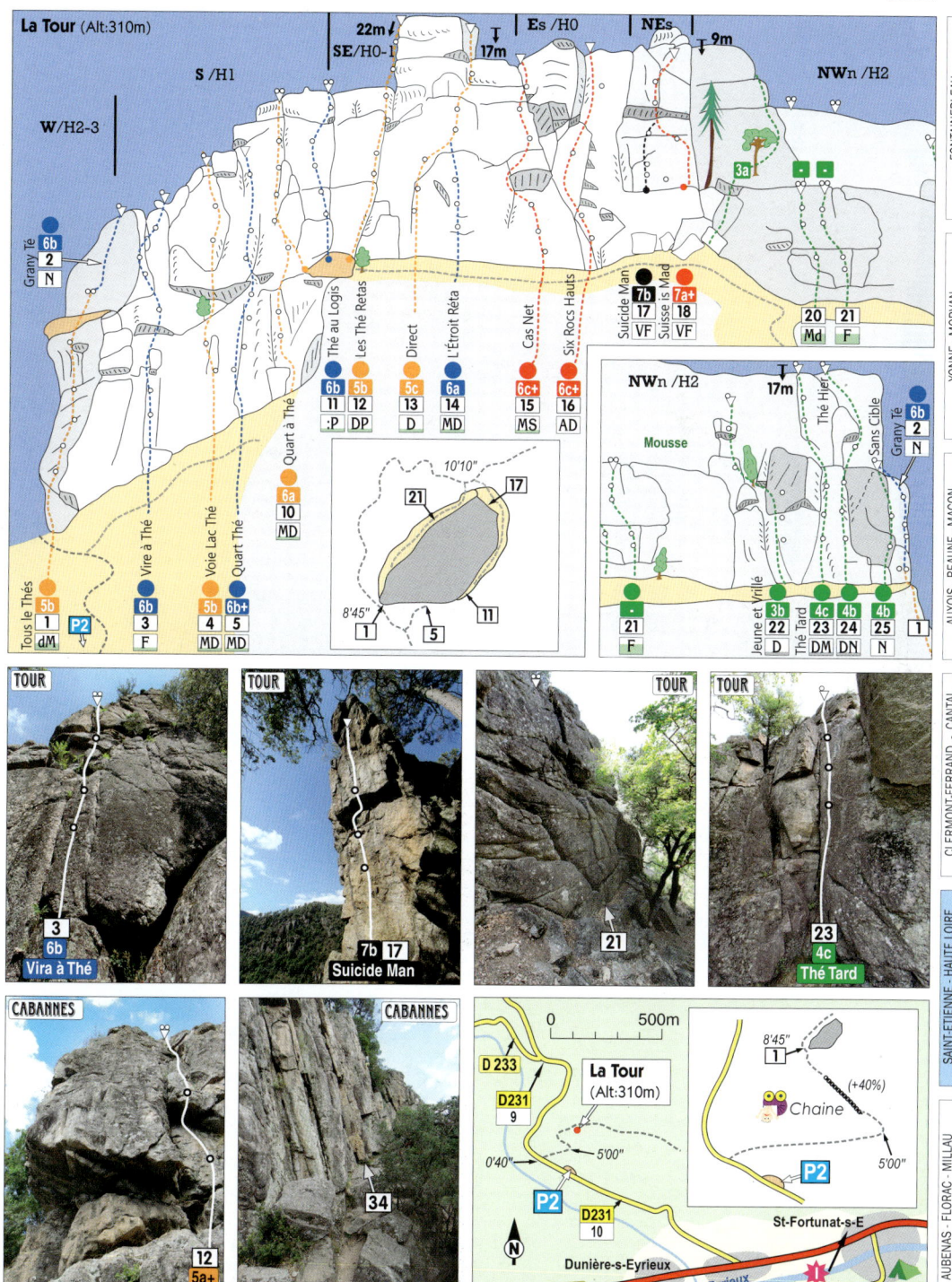

LE CHAT GOURMAND (Rompon)

P1 44.773144, 4.730162

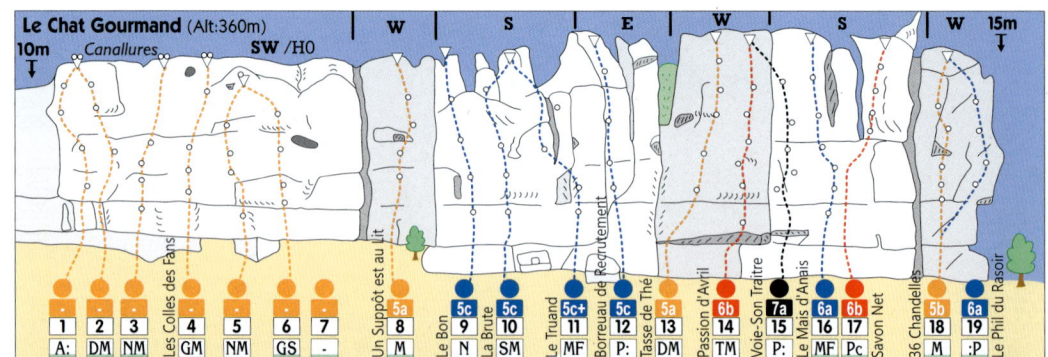

Le Chat Gourmand (Alt: 360m)

#	1	2	3	4	5	6	7	8	9	10	11	12	13	14	15	16	17	18	19
Name	Canallures	Les Colles des Pans		Les Colles des Pans				Un Suppôt est au lit	Le Bon	La Brute	Le Truand	Borreau de Recrutement	Tasse de Thé	Passion d'Avril	Voie-Son Traître	Le Mais d'Anaïs		Savon Net	36 Chandelles	Le Phil du Rasoir
Grade	A:	DM	NM	GM	NM	GS	-	5a / M	5c / N	5c / SM	5c+ / MF	5c / P:	5a / DM	6b / P:	7a / TM	6a / MF	6b / Pc	5b / P:	6a / :P

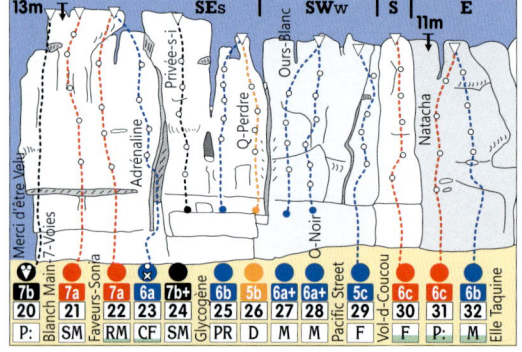

Le Truand 11 5c+ — Bourreau-R 12 5c

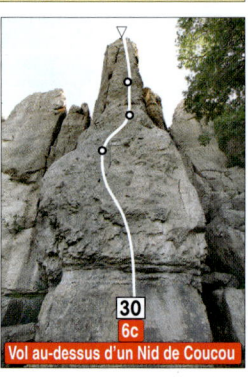

Vol au-dessus d'un Nid de Coucou 30 6c

#	20	21	22	23	24	25	26	27	28	29	30	31	32
Name	Blanch Main / 7-Voies	Faveurs-Sonja	Adrénaline	Privée-s-i	Glycogène	Q-Perdre	Ours-Blanc	O-Noir	Pacific Street	Vol-d-Coucou	Natacha		Elle Taquine
Grade	7b / P:	7a / SM	6a / RM	6a / CF	7b+ / SM	6b / PR	6a+ / D	6a+ / M	5c / M	6c / F	6c / F	6c / P:	6b / M

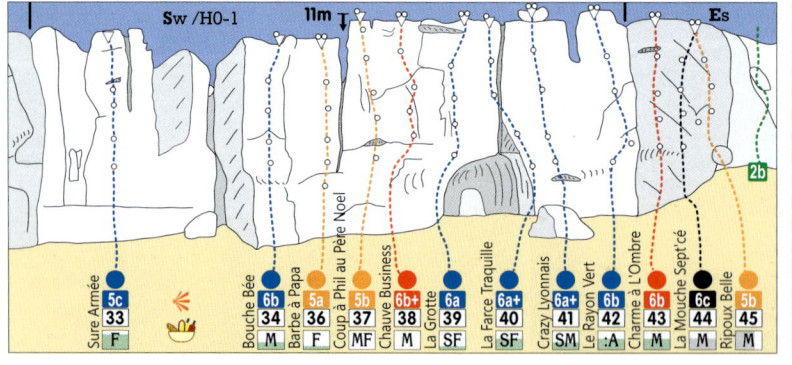

La Fracture du Myocarde 53 6b

#	33	34	35	36	37	38	39	40	41	42	43	44	45
Name	Sure Armée	Bouche Bée	Barbe a Papa	Coup à Phil au Pépé Noel	Chauve Business	La Grotte	La Farce Traquille	Crazy Lyonnais	Le Rayon Vert	Charme à L'Ombre	La Mouche Sept'cé	Ripoux Belle	
Grade	5c / F	6b / M	5a / F	5b / MF	6b+ / M	6a / SF	6b / SF	6a+ / SM	6b / F	6c / :A	6c / M	6a / M	2b

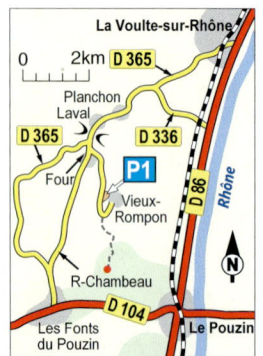
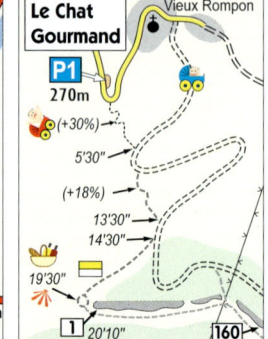

Le Chat Gourmand P1 270m (+30%) 5'30" (+18%) 13'30" 14'30" 19'30" 20'10" 160

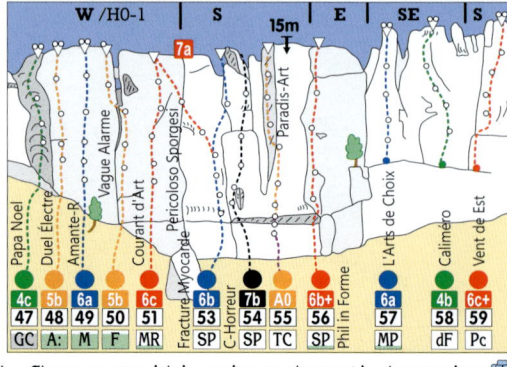

#	47	48	49	50	51	52	53	54	55	56	57	58	59
Name	Papa Noel	Duel Électre	Amante-R	Courant d'Art	Vague Alarme	Pericoloso Sporgesi	Fracture Myocarde	C-Horreur	Paradis-Art	Phil in Forme	L'Arts de Choix	Caliméro	Vent de Est
Grade	4c / GC	5b / A:	6a / M	5b / F	6c / MR	6b / SP	7b / SP	A0 / TC	6b+ / SP	6b / MP	6b / dF	4b / SP	6c+ / Pc

Calcaire-polished**** One of the best views in the lower Ardèche. Short routes with intensity, can be cool in the morning.

TOP SECRET (Crussol)

P2 44.941122, 4.848071 267

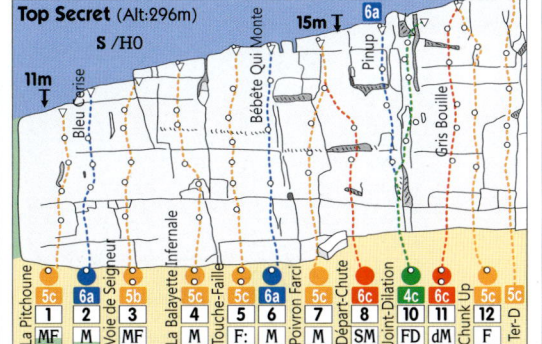

Top Secret (Alt: 296m) — S/H0

	La Pitchoune	Bleu Cerise	Voie de Seigneur	La Balayette Infernale	Touche-Faille	Bébête Qui Monte	Poivron Farci	Départ-Chute	Joint-Dilation	Pinup	Chunk Up	Gris Bouille	Ter-D
Grade	5c	6a	5b	5c	5c	6a	6a	6c	4c	6a	6c	5c	5c
#	1	2	3	4	5	6	7	8	10	9	11	12	
Type	MF	M	MF	M	M	F:M	SM	FD	dM		F		

Le Joint de Dilation — 10 / 4c

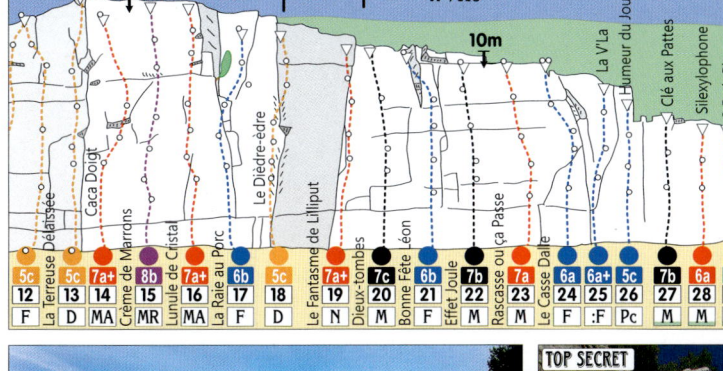
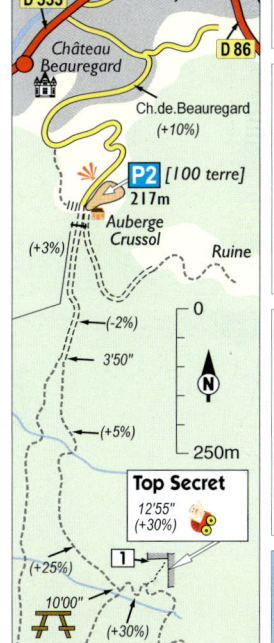

	La Terreuse Délatsée	Caca Doigt	Crème de Marrons	Lunule de Cristal	La Raie au Porc	Le Diédre-èdre		Le Fantasme de Lilliput	Dieux-tombés	Bonne Fête Léon	Effet Joule	Rascasse ou ça Passe	La Casse Dalle	La V'La	Humeur du Jour	Clé aux Pattes	Silexylophone	3 Petit Pitons
Grade	5c	5c	7a+	8b	7a+	6b	5c	7a+	7c	6b	7b	7a	6a	6a+	5c	7b	6a	5b
#	12	13	14	15	16	17	18	19	20	21	22	23	24	25	26	27	28	29
Type	F	D	MA	MR	MA	D		N	M	M	M	F	M	F:F	Pc	M	M	M

VUE CHAT GOURMAND

Le Fantasme de Lilliput — 19 / 7a+

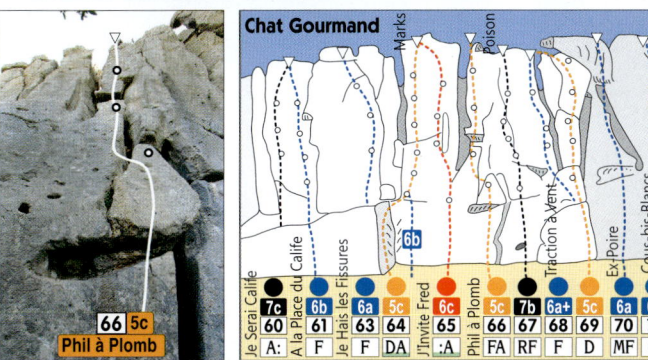

Phil à Plomb — 66 / 5c

Chat Gourmand

	Je Serai Calife	A la Place du Calife	Je Hais les Fissures	Marks	J'invite Fred	Poison	Phil à Plomb	Traction à Vent	Ex Poire	Cous-bis-Blancs	Échappée Belle
Grade	7c	6b	6a	5c	6c	7b	6a+	6a	5c	6b	5c-7a
#	60	61	63	64	65	66	67	68	69	70	71	73	74-159
Type	A:	F	F	DA	:A	FA	RF	F	D	MF	M	DM	

L'Échappée Belle — 73 / 6a

Top Secret: Calcaire-polished**** A very hidden old quarry up a steep path. Bolts positioned oddly - clip stick essential.

BEAUMIRAL

P1 44.746685, 4.742701

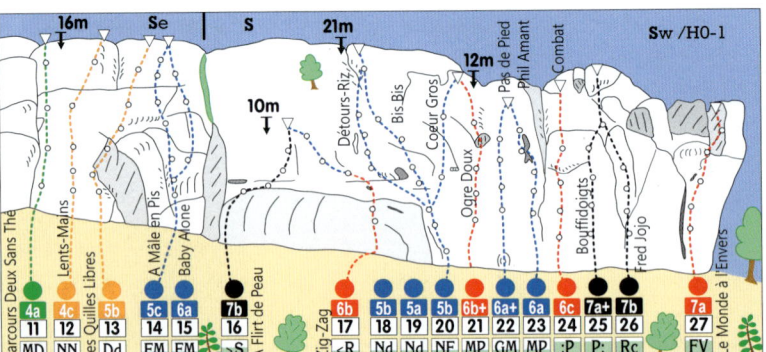
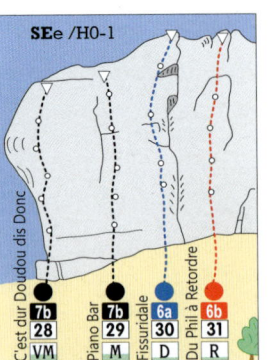
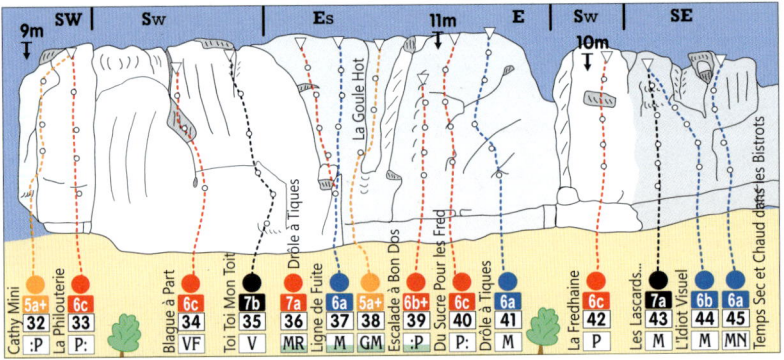

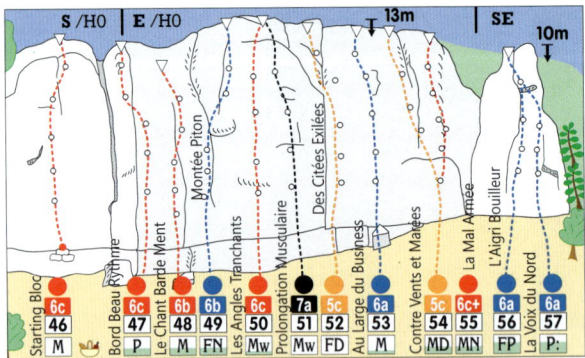
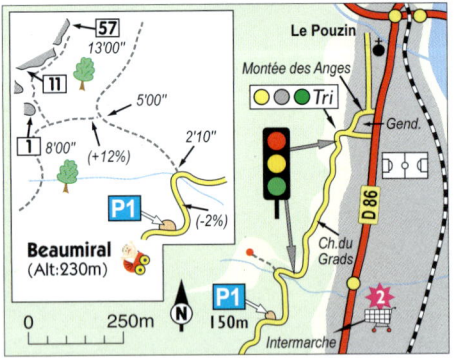
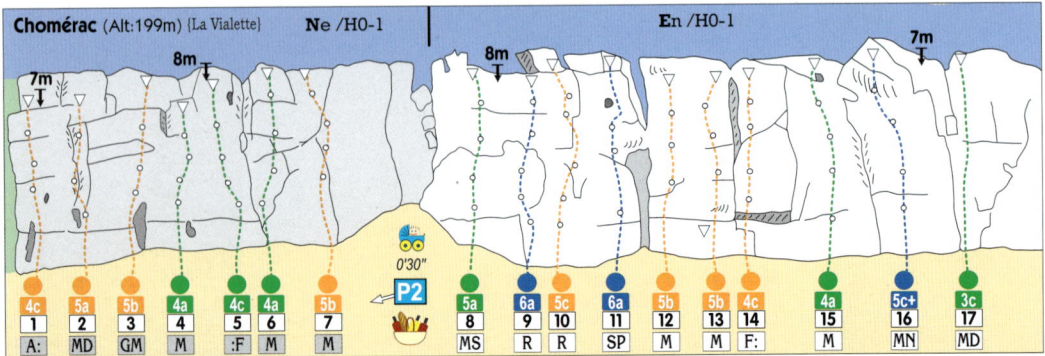

Beaumiral: Calcaire**** Short boulder style routes, very in your face. Pockets and powerful. Often, Hot and sunny.

CHOMÉRAC

P2 44.709962, 4.655735 — 269

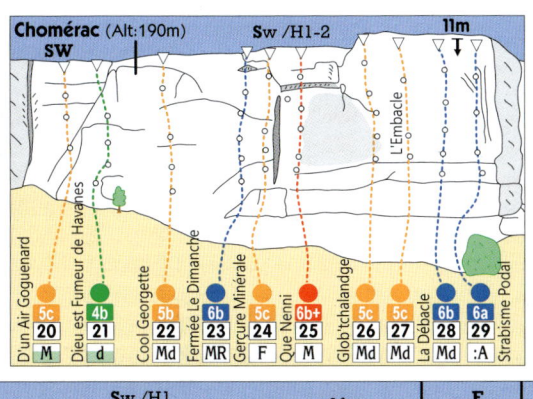

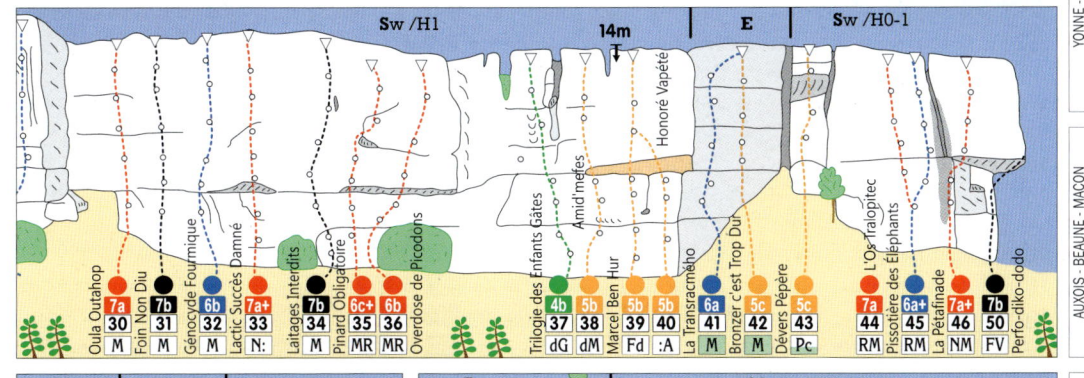
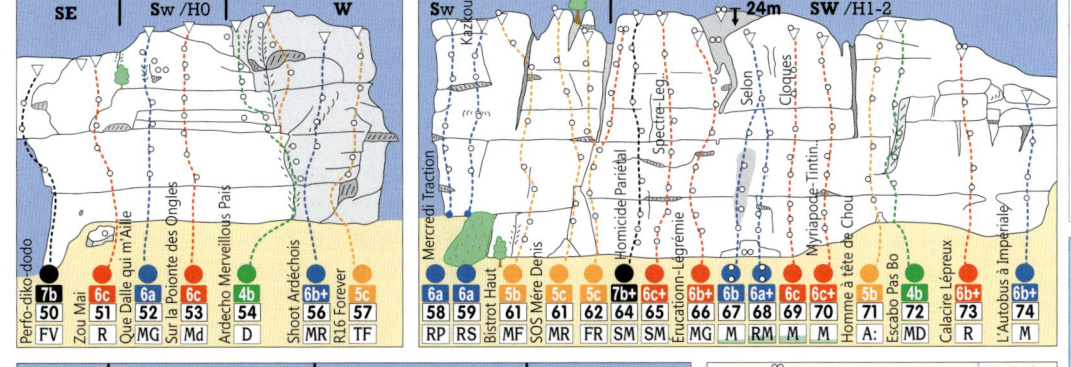
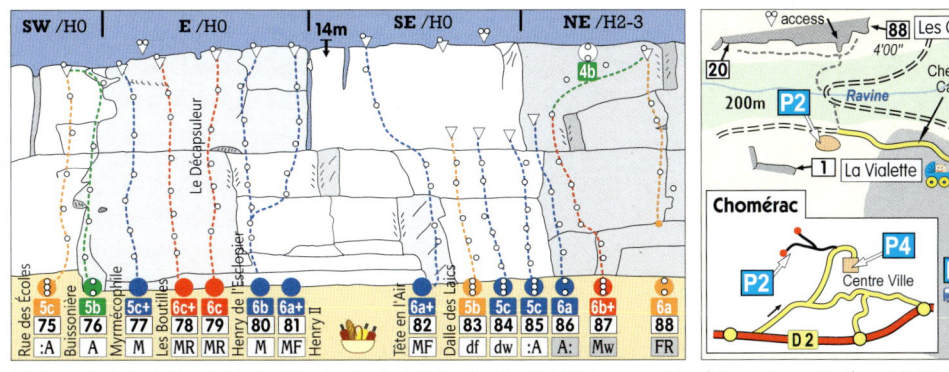
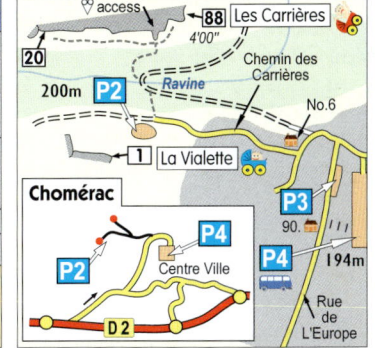

Chomerac: Calcaire*** Some very good quarried walls. A lot of variety, some easy - some not so easy. A good sun trap.

Area 6 - AUBENAS - FLORAC - MILLAU

Page		Falaise/Cliff	Alt	Arbre-Ori-Séche	Am-Pm	Rocher	Longeur	\multicolumn{5}{c}{Numero Voies / Routes}	Approche	Ambience
298	C3	Actinidias	110m	NE/H0-2		Calcaire	7-35m	0	0	2	8	15	23	11	Raide,Surplomb
298	C3	Agachou	180m	SW/H0-1		Calcaire	13m	8	2	2	0	0	0	3	Dalle, Mur
277	D4	Barasses, Les	185m	Se /H0		Calcaire	9-17m	14	17	20	10	5	2	10	Mur,glissant
318	A2	Boffi	720m	S,SE/H0		Calcaire	22-38m	3	10	24	30	18	4	34	Mur, Raide
276	D4	Bourdary	250m	SE /H0-1		Calcaire	7-16m	8	9	8	3	1	0	14	Mur, Dièdre
317	A2	Cantobre	520m	S /H0-1		Calcaire	20-35m	0	1	5	9	31	24	21	Mur,Devers
279	D4	Chamtadu	165m	SE /H0		Calcaire	7-13m	9	8	7	4	1	0	5	Mur
292	C3	Chaulet	120m	Sw/H0-2		Calcaire	23-40m	5	28	28	29	21	6	7	Mur,Dièdre
280	D3	Cirque des Gens	160m	ESW /H0		Calcaire	20-40m	9	18	78	138	71	4	12	Mur, Raide
273	D4	Courpatas	640m	W&N/H0		Calcaire	11-23m	3	19	33	39	12	3	7	Mur,Pilier,Zzz
288	D3	Fontgarnide	206m	NW/H0-2		Calcaire	20-35m	6	18	24	32	12	8	18	Mur, trous
303	B3	Forgette	860m	SW/H0-1		Granit	11-35m	3	11	13	3	0	0	10	Pilier,Surplomb
290	D3	Grd-Charmasson	270m	NW/H0-1		Calcaire	20-35m	5	9	33	35	9	0	2	Mur,raide
272	C4	Horologe	565m	SW/H0-1		Granit	15m	2	5	3	0	0	0	5	dalle, Dièdre
298	C3	Jardin-Endie-Bloc	180m	N&S/H1		Calcaire	3-9m	50	50	50	50	30	0	10	Blocs,Surplomb
300	C4	Jardin Jouqueirou	600m	S/H0-2		Granit	12-26m	12	8	8	2	0	0	32	Pilier,Mur, Zzzz
312	A3	Jonte-A-Capluc C	630m	Wn/H0-1		Calcaire	35-50m	0	0	12	17	22	12	24	Mur, Endurance
313	A3	Jonte-B-Patates	610m	SW/ H0-1		Calcaire	16-23m	1	1	7	5	0	0	17	Mur, Raide
314	A3	Jonte-C-Reverend	600m	SW/H0-1		Calcaire	30+m	1	6	14	6	23	2	19	Mur, Raide
315	A3	Jonte-H-Gogol	710m	S/ H1		Calcaire	30+m	7	11	1	0	0	0	24	dalle, Mur
315	A3	Jonte-Body Build	475m	S /H0		Calcaire	10-16m	0	0	0	2	4	0	2	Devers
316	A2	Laumet	440m	S /H0-1		Calcaire	10-50m	4	14	14	12	12	8	8	Mur, Raide
276	D4	Lavilledieu Blocs	280m	SE /H1-2		Calcaire	3-6m	30	30	30	30	30	5	6	Blocs-Circuits
296	C3	Mazet	110m	W/H1		Calcaire	15-40m	21	22	25	31	18	0	2	Mur,Dièdre
301	C4	Moulin-Garde-G	820m	NE/H1-2		Granit	10-23m	12	0	4	2	0	0	3	dalle, Raide
299	C4	Pourtalas	330m	S/H0-1		Granit	22-35m	4	9	11	8	0	0	1	Mur, Dièdre
302	B4	St-Julien-Tournel	970m	NE/H1-2		Schiste	10-19m	2	12	5	1	0	0	5	Mur, Surplomb
304	A3	Tarn-A-Aiguille	620m	E /H0		Calcaire	150m	0	2	0	1	0	0	16	Grand Voies,Vue
305	A3	Tarn-AA-Noir Désir	530m	E /H0		Calcaire	15-30m	0	0	10	12	2	0	10	Mur,Raide,Vue
305	A3	Tarn-AA-Cancer	490m	NE /H0		Calcaire	14-19m	0	0	0	8	4	1	5	Raide,Devers
306	A3	Tarn-B-Foetus	460m	SW /H0		Calcaire	13-35m	0	5	7	7	8	1	5	Mur, Raide
306	A3	Tarn-B-Face Fig	440m	N /H1		Calcaire	21m	2	4	0	0	0	2	2	Mur
308	A3	Tarn-C-Fas Aqui	450m	Es/H0-1		Calcaire	20-50m	1	1	14	24	14	7	1	Mur, Raide
309	A3	Tarn-CC-Figues-C	440m	SW /H1		Calcaire	20m	1	2	6	3	3	0	1	Mur
309	A3	Tarn-CC-Tennesse	450m	Se /H0		Calcaire	15-70m	0	1	4	5	14	14	3	Raide, Wow
309	A3	Tarn-CC-Calmez-v	490m	E /H0		Calcaire	20-25m	0	0	1	13	6	0	4	Raide
310	A3	Tarn-D-Trésor-Zeb	500m	SW /H0		Calcaire	20-35m	0	0	6	8	5	3	7	Pilier, Raide
310	A3	Tarn-D-Club House	510m	W /H0		Calcaire	17-19m	0	1	9	7	0	0	8	Mur, Raide
310	A3	Tarn-D-Güllich	470m	E /H0		Calcaire	20-28m	0	0	0	2	3	7	6	Devers,Surplomb
311	A3	Tarn-DD-Oasif-Pla	450m	S /H0		Calcaire	11-38m	0	0	2	18	24	5	1	Raide
272	C4	Tras les Baumes	470m	SW/H0-1		Granit	13-35m	16	3	2	4	2	0	6	dalle-Raide
278	D4	Viel Audon, Le	185m	Se /H0		Calcaire	12-35m	3	15	17	21	2	0	20	Mur,glissant

TRAS LES BAUMES (JAUJAC)

A1 44.619436, 4.228305

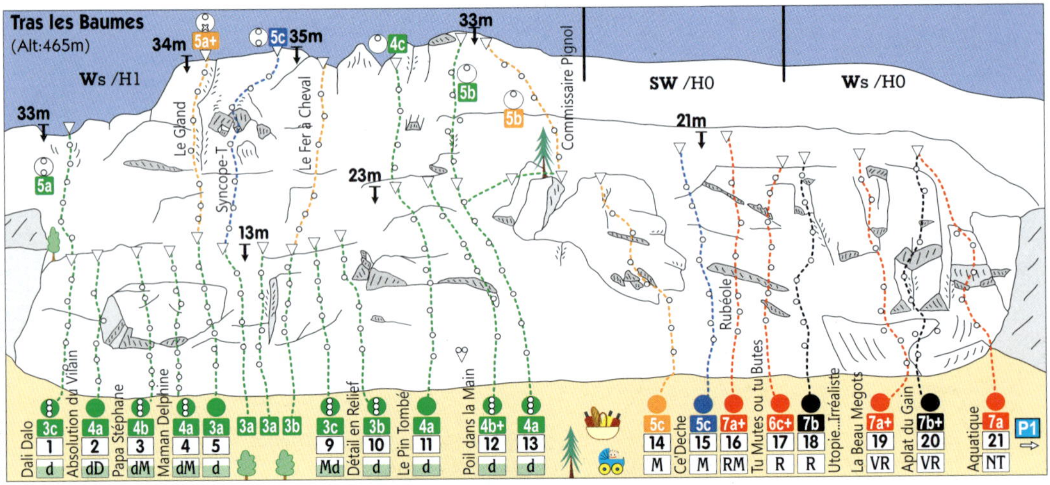

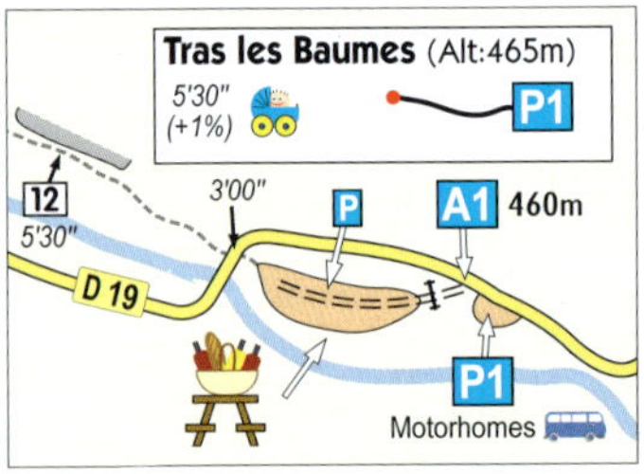

Tras les Baumes (Alt:465m)
Ws /H1 — SW /H0 — Ws /H0

Tras-Baumes: Granite** Variable rock. Rope drag on long climbs, split into 2 lengths. Nice shade at bottom.

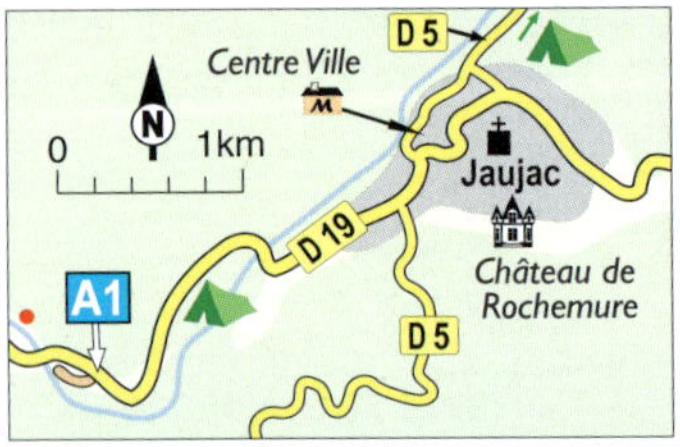

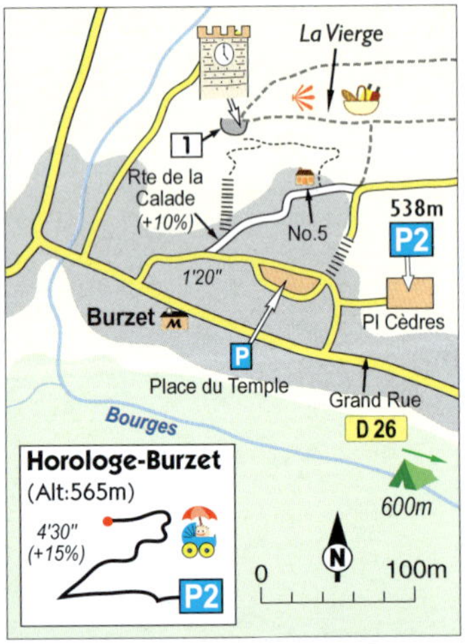

#	Name	Grade	Style
1	Dali Dalo	3c	d
2	Absolution de Vilain	4a	dD
3	Papa Stéphane	5a	dM
4	Maman Delphine	4a	dM
5	Le Grand	5a+	d
6	Syncope-T	3a	
7	Le Fer à Cheval	3a	
8	—	3b	
9	—	3c	Md
10	Détail en Relief	3b	d
11	Le Pin Tombé	4a	
12	Poil dans la Main	4b+	d
13	Commissaire Pignol	4c	d
14	Ce Dêche	5c	M
15	Rubéole	5c	M
16	Tu Mutes ou tu Butes	7a+	RM
17	—	6c+	R
18	Utopie...Irréaliste	7b	R
19	La Beau Megots	7a+	VR
20	Aplat du Gain	7b+	VR
21	Aquatique	7a	NT

P1

Horloge: Granite*** Nice little cliff, fun ambience.

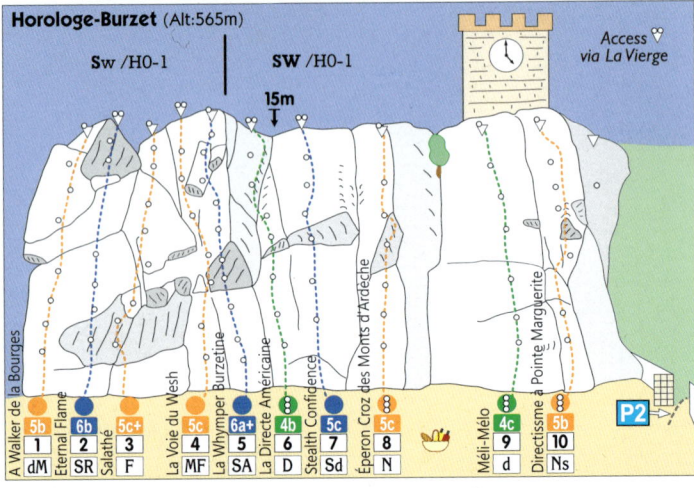

Horloge-Burzet (Alt:565m)
Sw /H0-1 — SW /H0-1

#	Name	Grade	Style
1	A Walker de la Bourges	5b	dM
2	Eternal Flame	6b	SR
3	Salathé	5c+	F
4	La Voie du Wesh	5c	MF
5	A Whymper Burzetine	6a+	SA
6	La Directe Américaine	4b	D
7	Stealth Confidence	5c	Sd
8	Eperon Croz des Monts d'Ardèche	5c	N
9	Méli-Mélo	4c	d
10	Directissime à Pointe Marguerite	5b	Ns

HORLOGE - BURZET **P2** 44.739811, 4.246066

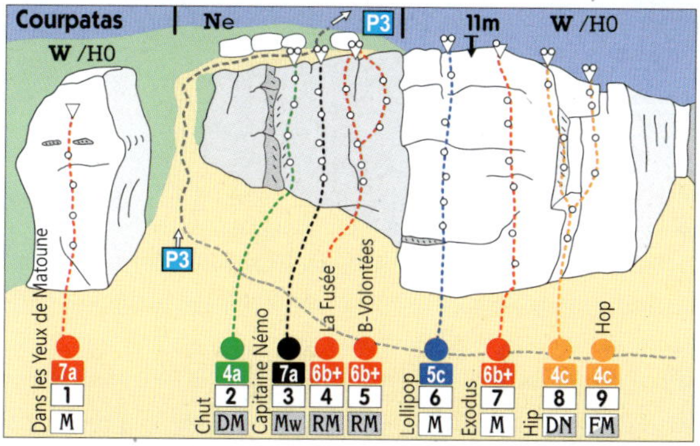

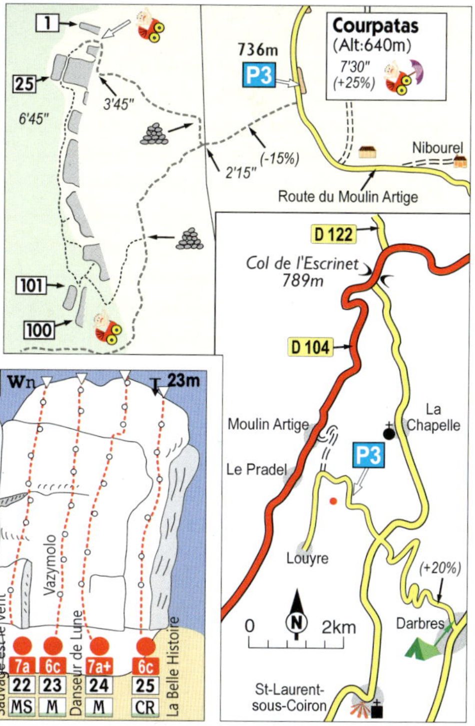

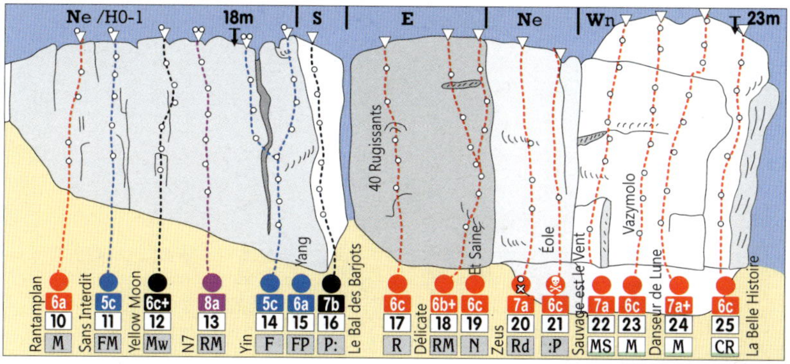

COURPATAS - A

	7a	4a	7a	6b+	6b+	5c	6b+	4c	4c
Name	Dans les Yeux de Matoune	Chut Capitaine Némo	La Fusée	B-Volontées		Lollipop	Exodus	Hip	Hop
#	1	2	3	4	5	6	7	8	9
	M	DM	Mw	RM	RM	M	M	DN	FM

	6a	5c	6c+	8a	5c	6a	7b	6c	6b+	6c	7a	6c	7a	6c	7a+	6c
Name	Rantamplan	Sans Interdit	Yellow Moon	N7	Yin		Le Bal des Barjots	Délicate		Zeus	Éole	Sauvage est le Vent	Vazymolo		Danseur de Lune	La Belle Histoire
#	10	11	12	13	14	15	16	17	18	19	20	21	22	23	24	25
	M	FM	Mw	RM	F	FP	P:	R	RM	N	Rd	:P	MS	M	M	CR

7 — 6b+ — Exodus

14 — 5c — Yin ; 19 — 6c — Et Saine

22 — 7a — Sauvage est le Vent

26 — 7c — Nuit d'Amour

Courpatas: Calcaire**** A classic cliff. Great views and position, slightly NE facing so chilly long mornings, then an oven.

COURPATAS - B

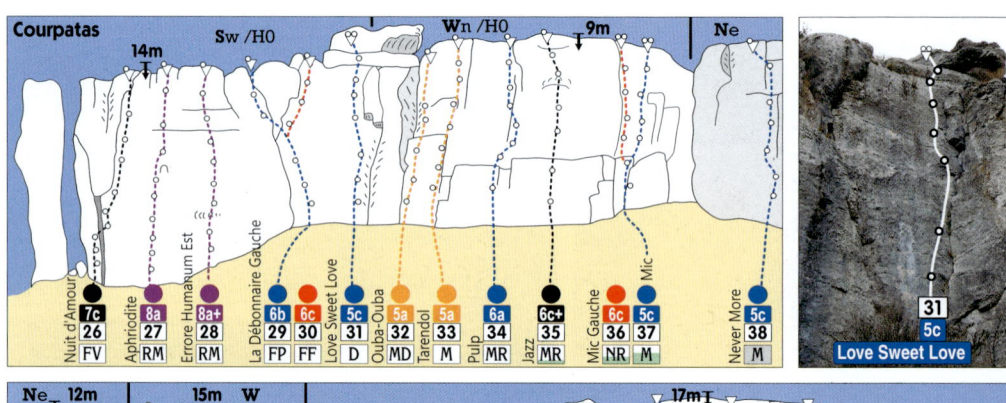

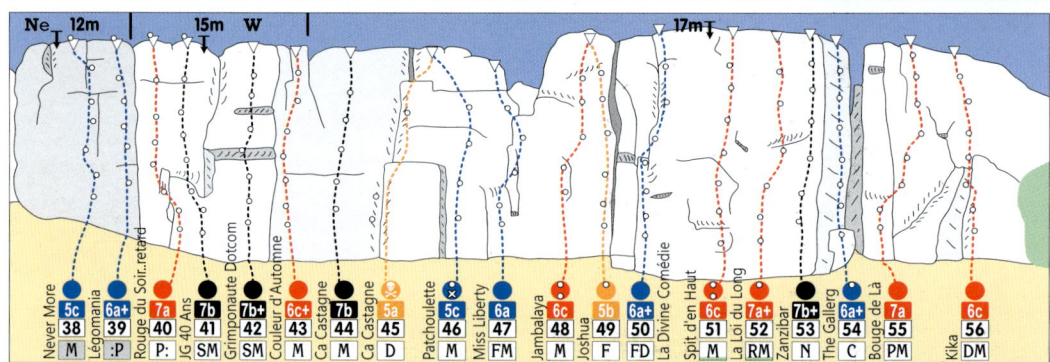

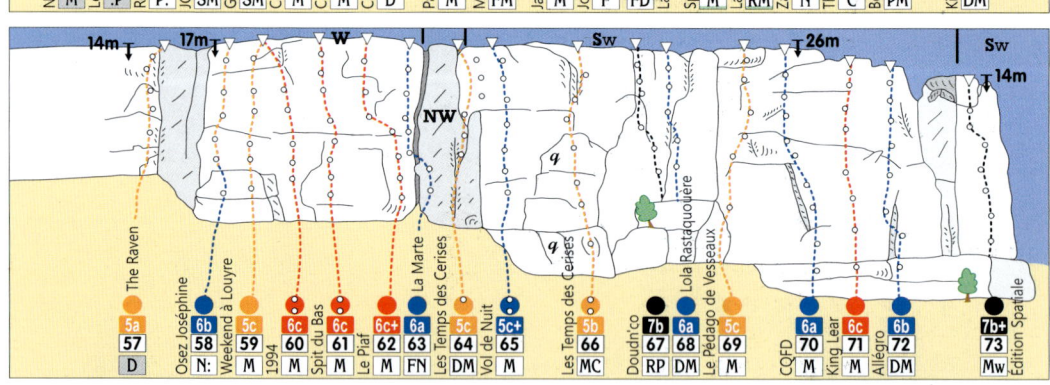

Rouge du Soir la Cuite - Retard — 40 — 7a

Joshua — 49 — 5b

The Gallerg — 54 — 6a+

Le Roi Lear — 71 — 7a

Not very high, but certainly packs a lot in over the distance, constantly entertaining. Base of cliff is very up and down.

COURPATAS - C

P3 44.676126, 4.480258 — 275

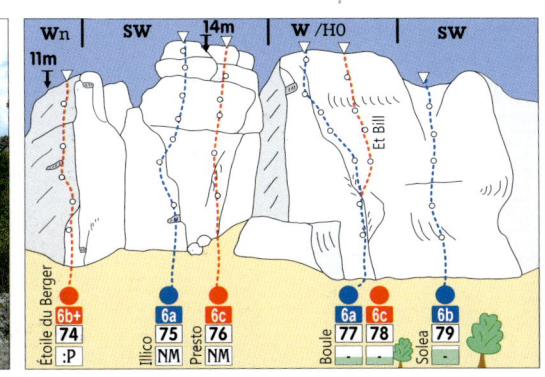

#	Name	Grade
73	Édition Spatiale	7b+
74	Étoile du Berger	6b+ :P
75	Illico	6a NM
76	Presto	6c NM
77	Boule	6a
78	Et Bill	6c
79	Solea	6b
75	Illico	6a

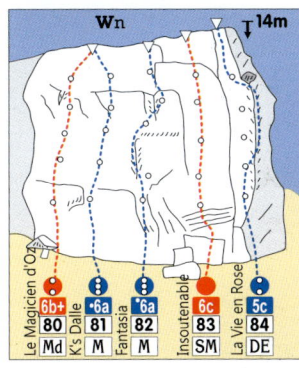
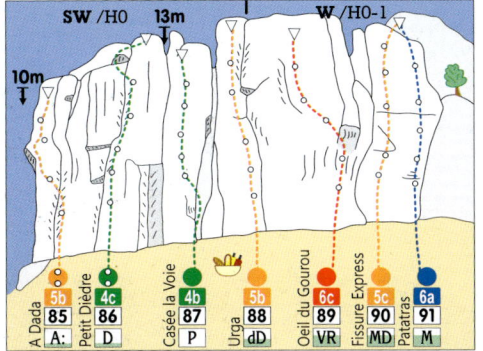

#	Name	Grade
80	Le Magicien d'Oz	6b+ Md
81	K's Dalle	*6a M
82	Fantasia	*6a M
83	Insoutenable	6c SM
84	La Vie en Rose	5c DE
85	A Dada	5b A:
86	Petit Dièdre	4c D
87	Casse la Voie	4b P
88	Urga	5b dD
89	Oeil du Gourou	6c VR
90	Fissure Express	5c MD
91	Patatras	6a M
83	Insoutenable Légèreté de l'Age	6c

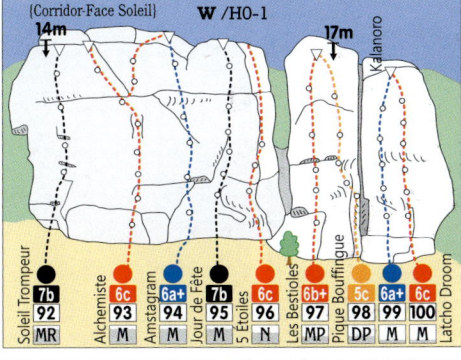
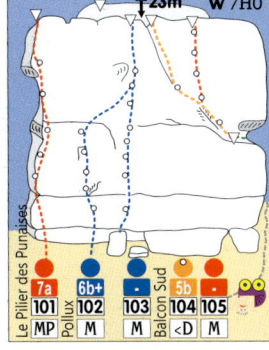
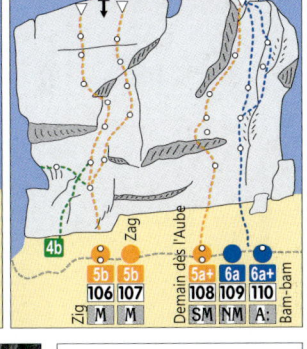

#	Name	Grade
92	Soleil Trompeur	7b MR
93	Alchemiste	6c M
94	Amstagram	6a+ M
95	Jour de Fête	7b T
96	5 Etoiles	6c N
97	Les Bestioles	6b+ MP
98	Pique Bouffigue	5c DP
99		6a+ M
100	Latcho Droom	6c M
101	Le Pilier des Punaises	7a MP
102	Pollux	6b+
103		6a M
104	Balcon Sud	5b <D
105		* M
106	Zig	5b SM
107	Zag	5b NM
108	Demain dès l'Aube	5a+ A:
109		6a
110	Bam-bam	6a+

#	Name	Grade
88	Urga	5b
89	L'Oeil du Gourou	6c
92	Soleil Trompeur	7b
93		6c
108		5a+
106	Zig	5b
107	Zag	5b

The far end sector is best approached from the South. Very useful corridor with good shade (wind tunnel too).

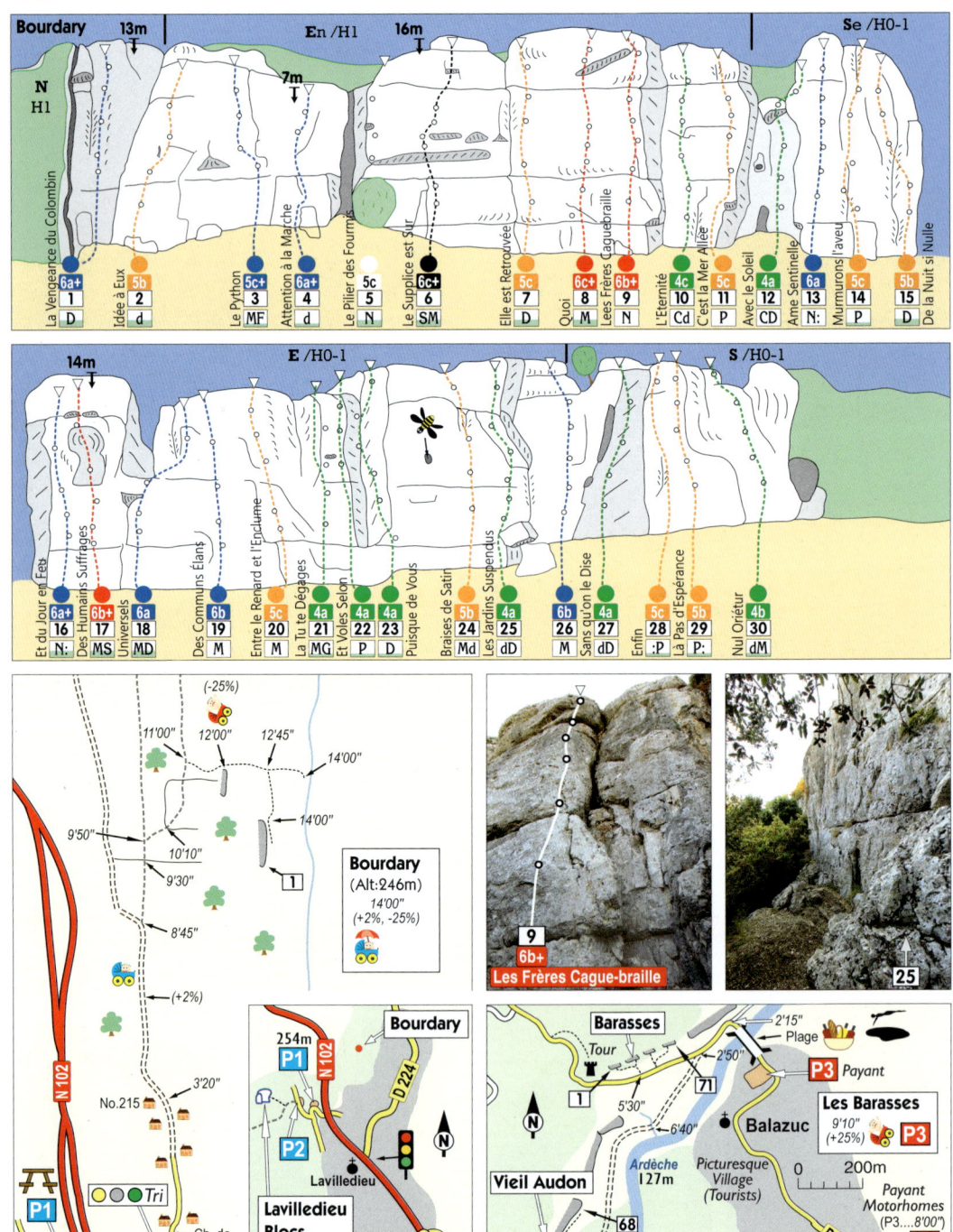

LES BARASSES (Balazuc)

P3 44.510506, 4.372433 — 277

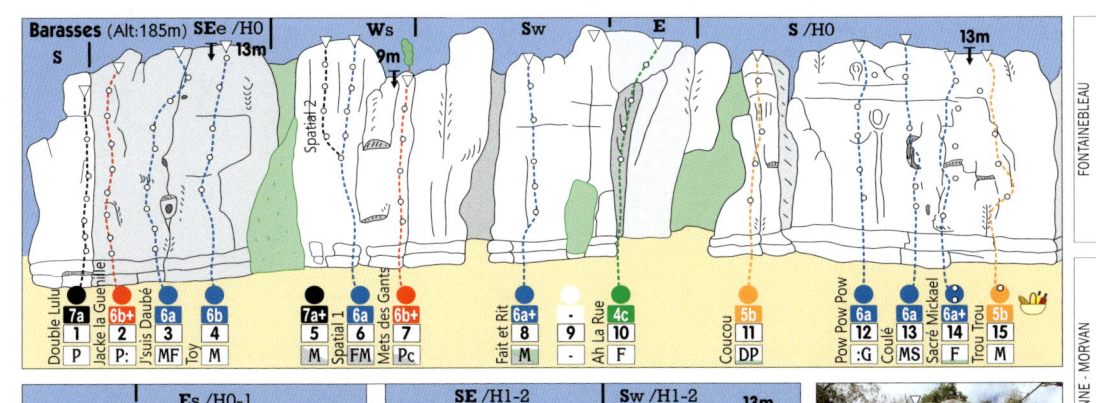
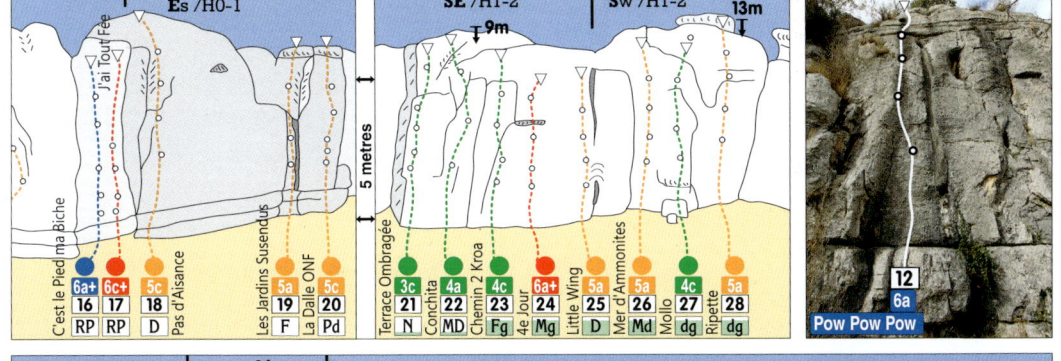
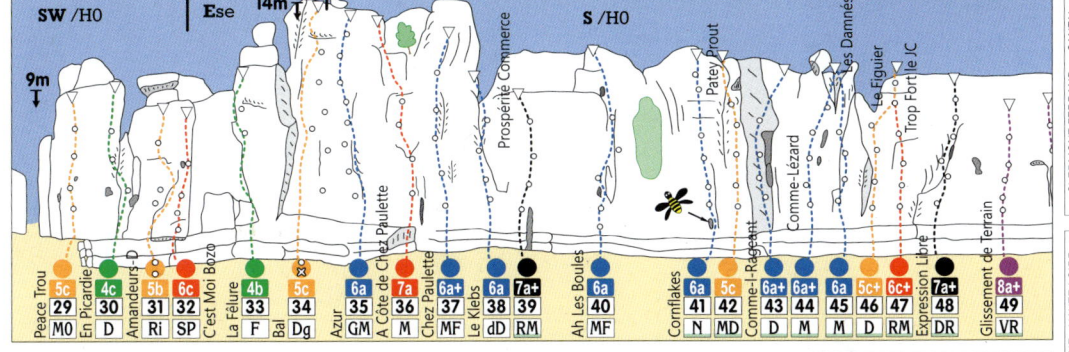
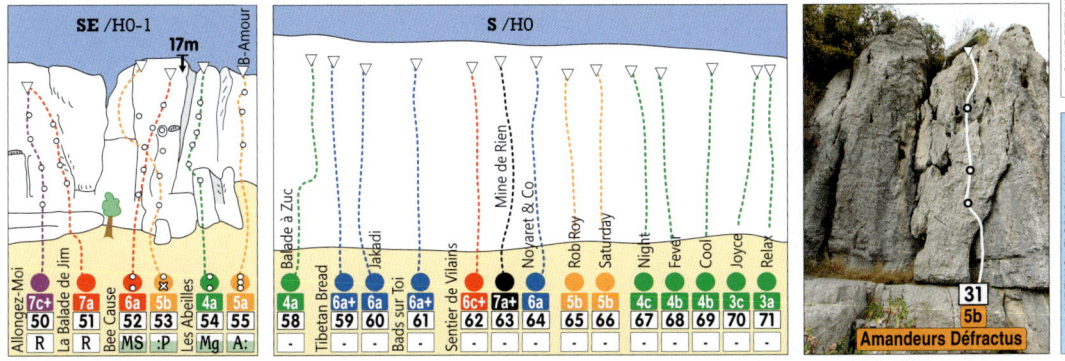

Barasses**** A sunny aspect with lovely views to Balazuc and Ardeche river (easy swimming point). Short - polished routes.

LE VIEL AUDON

P4 44.506269, 4.373417

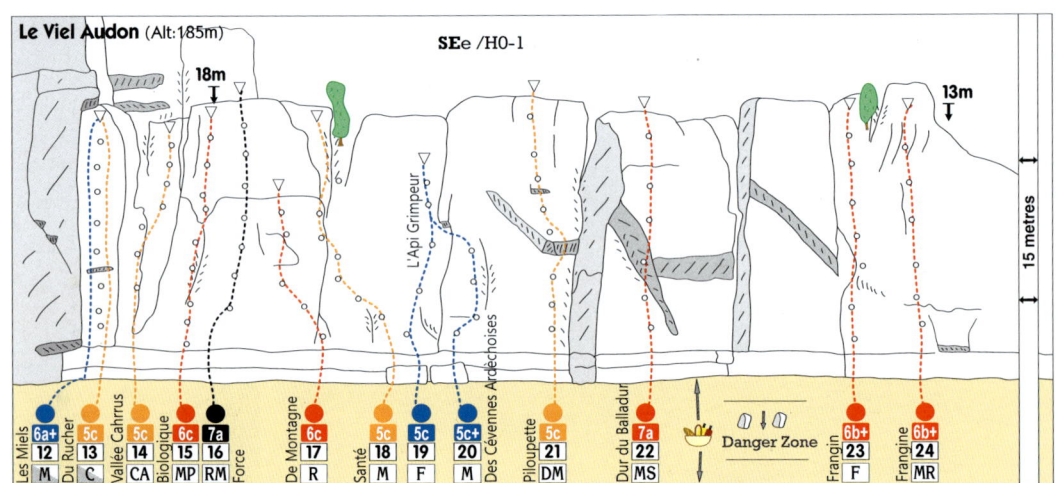

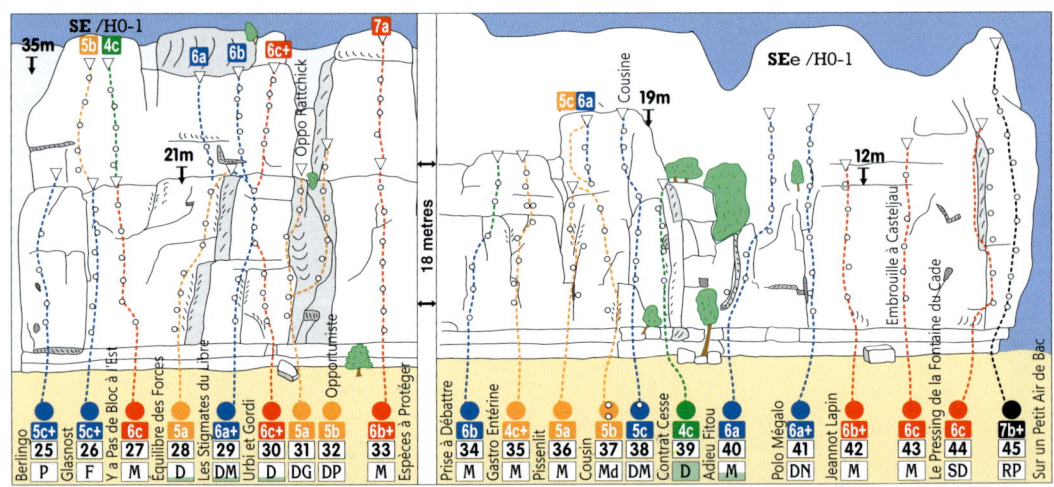

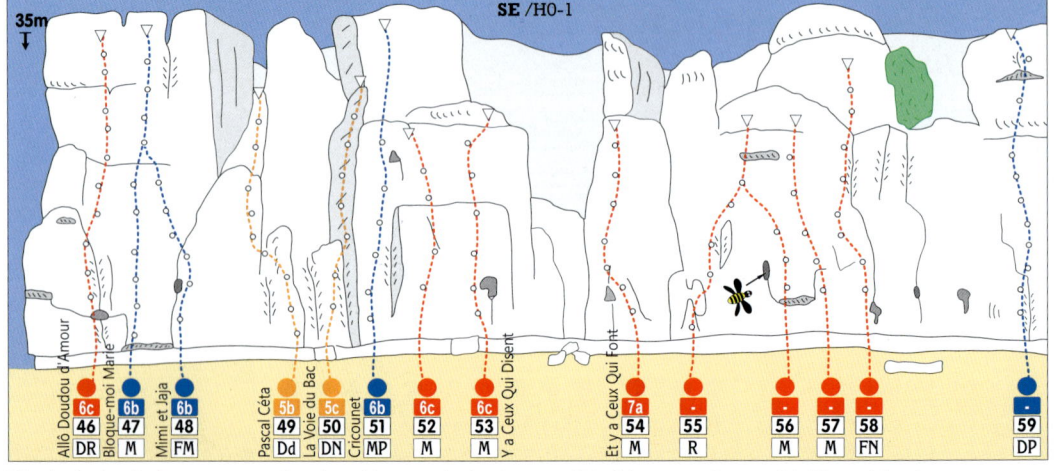

Viel Audon*** A nice terrace at the cliff with some shade. A large cliff with plenty of potential, iffy rock in places.

CHAMTADU (Lanas)

P5 44.523421, 4.392825 — 279

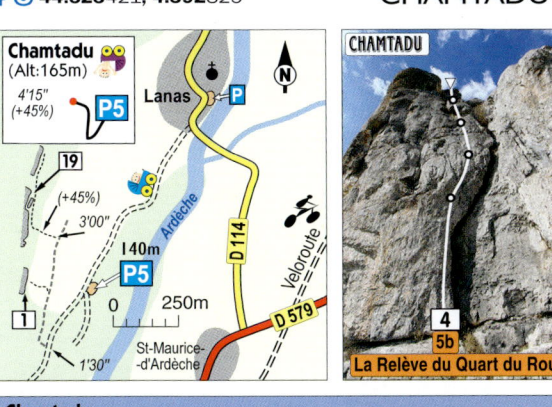
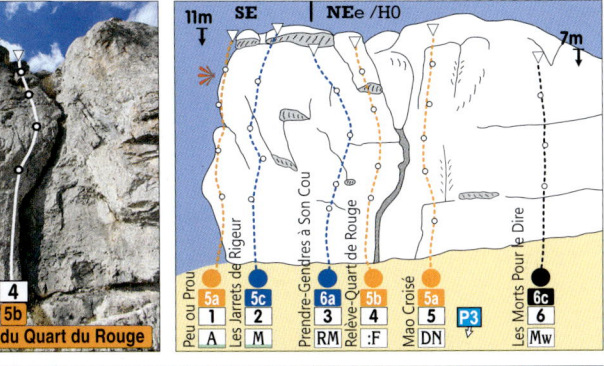
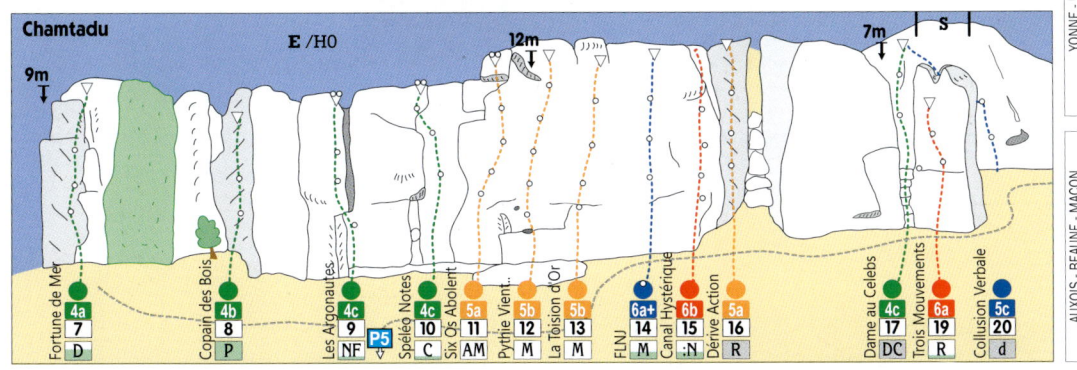
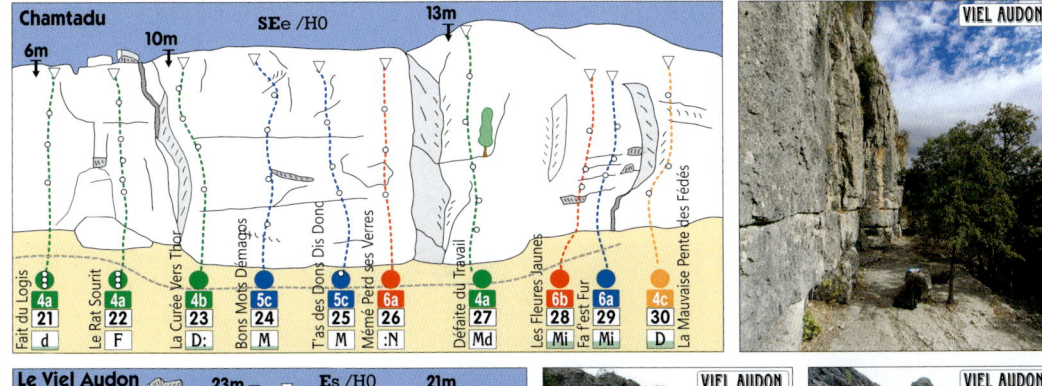
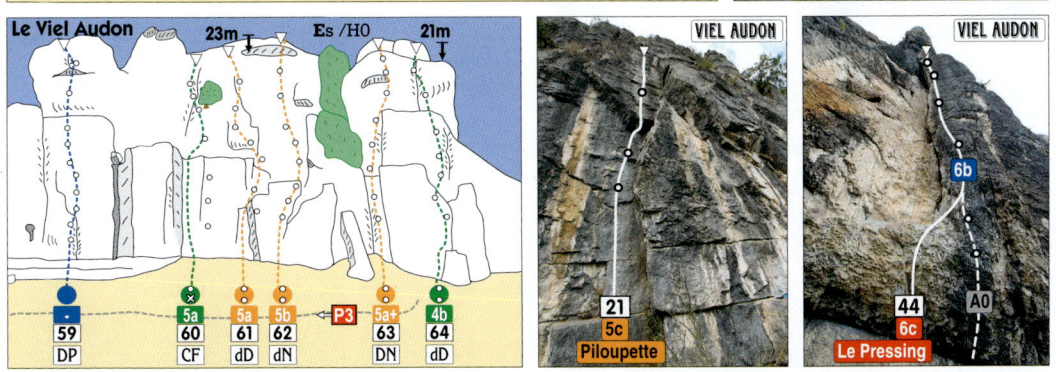

Chamtadu**** A selection of very small cliffs. Short routes, but good quality rock with a lovely sunny aspect.

CIRQUE DES GENS - A

P1 44.475397, 4.351306

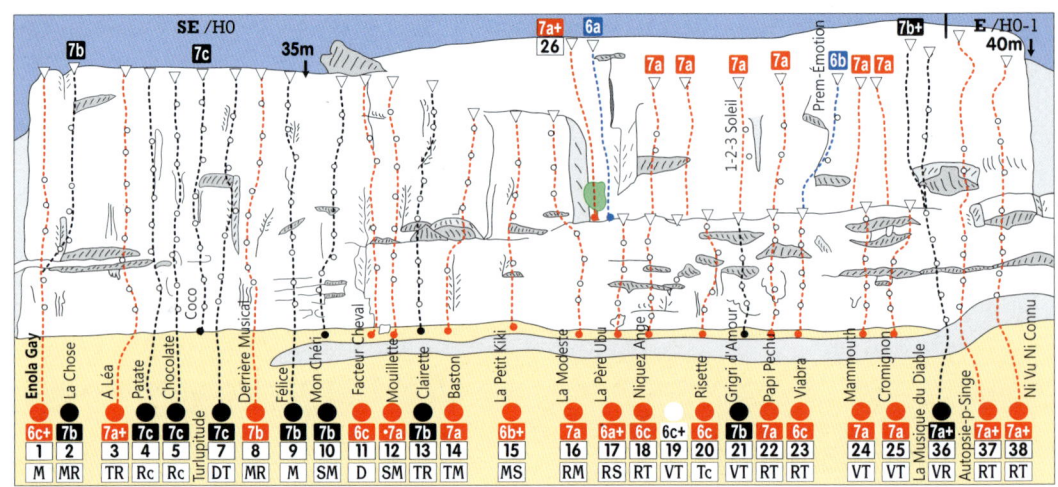
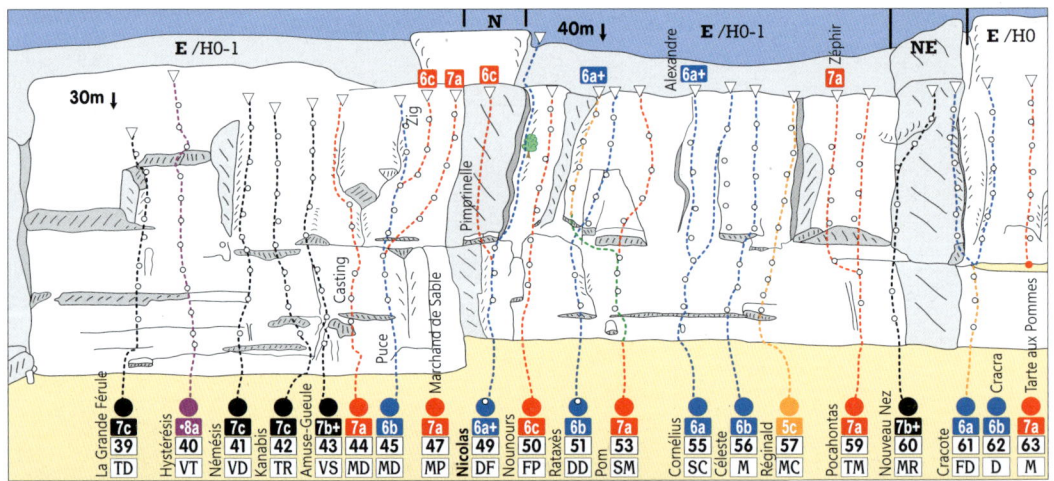

6 / 7c — Coco

22 / 7a — Le Papi Pêchu

49 / 6a+ — Nicolas

Calcaire ***: A giant cliff with a huge variety in rock quality and styles of routes; big and overhanging sector & long walk in.

CIRQUE DES GENS - B

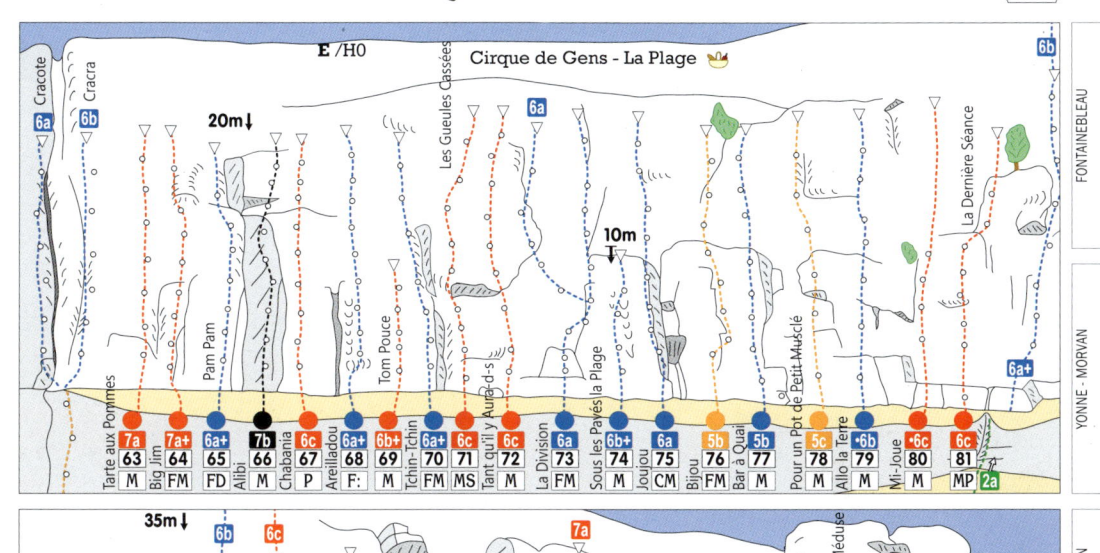
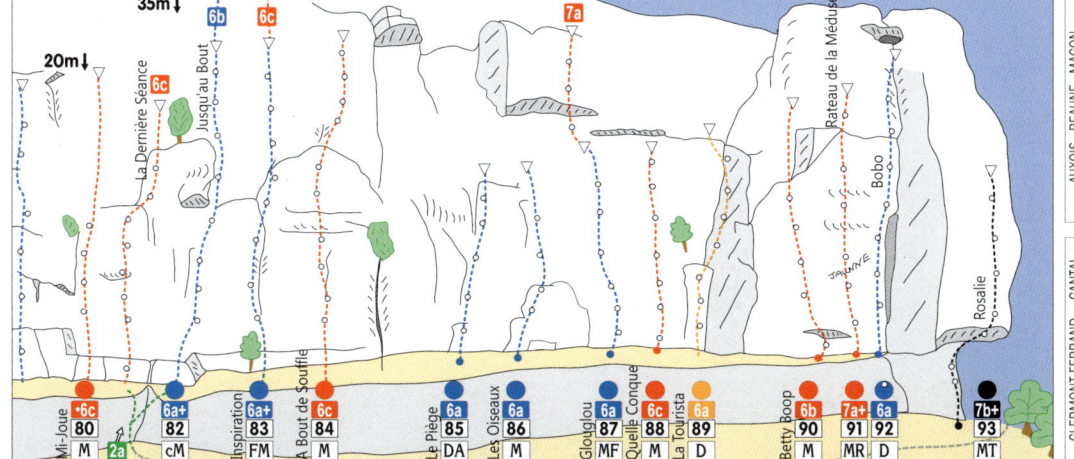

To help cross use of guidebooks on this big cliff, the route numbering used is the historic, and is not always continuous.

CIRQUE DES GENS - C

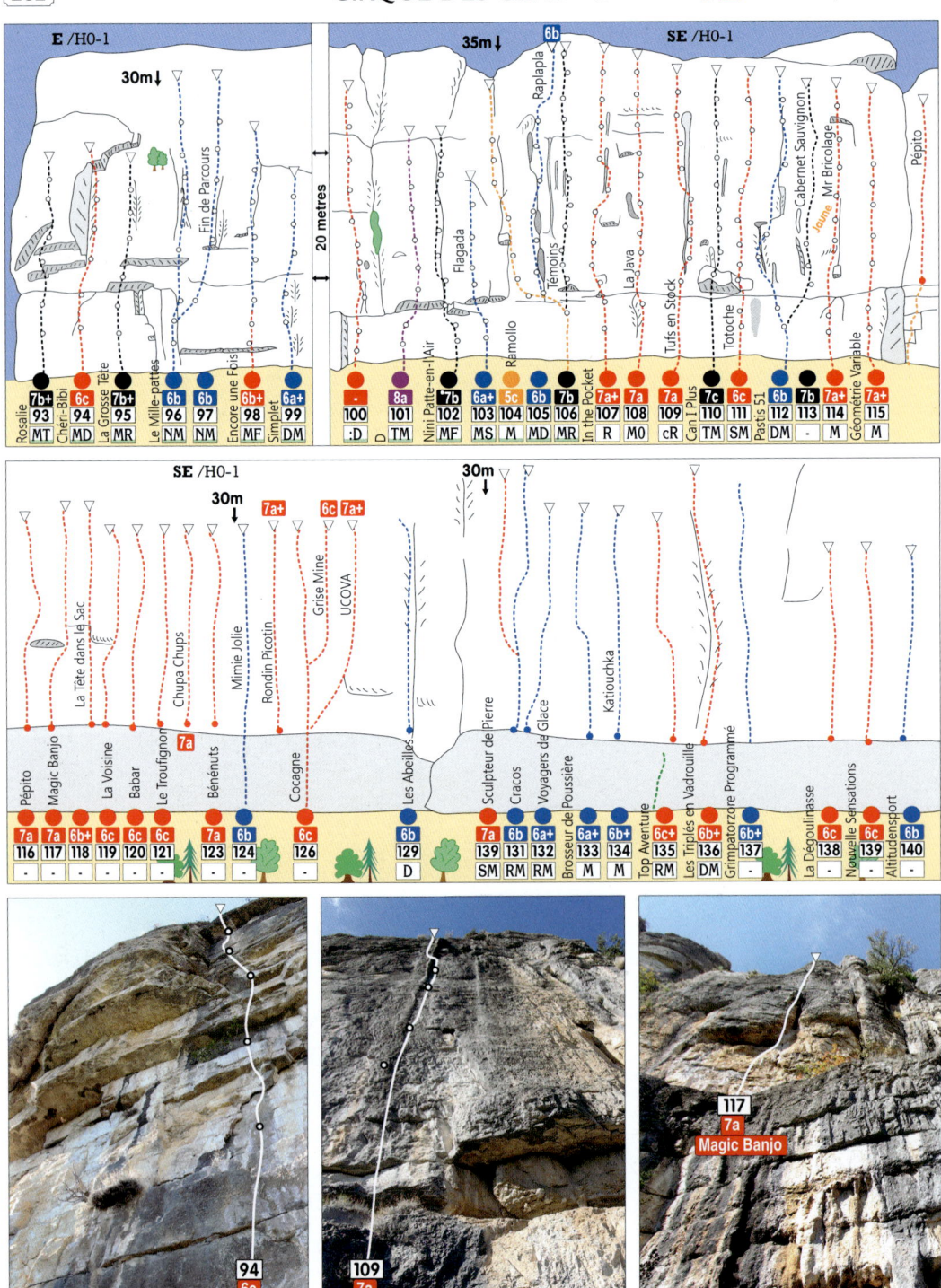

This cliff is equipped for a grade 7 leader, don't expect anything friendly on the lower grades! (Routes 116-153 on a higher tier)

CIRQUE DES GENS - D

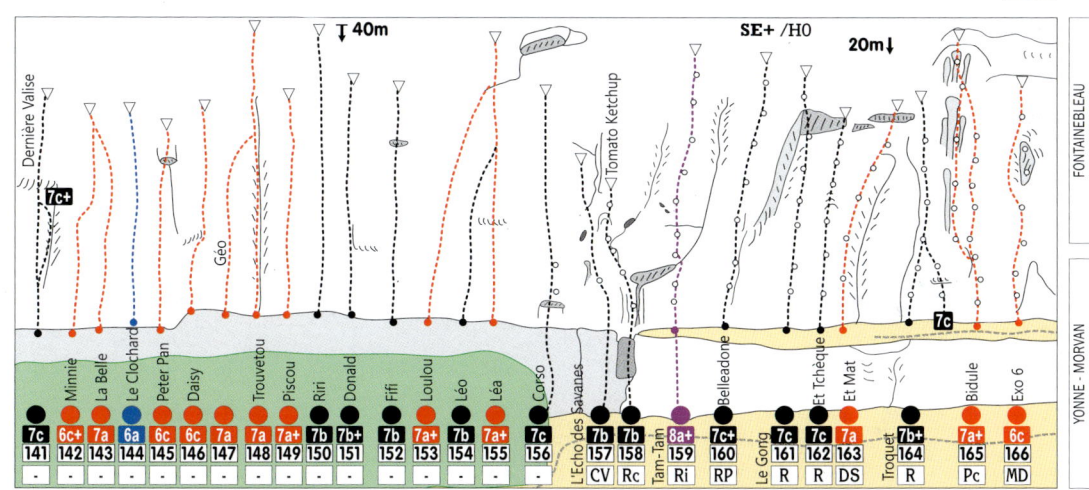

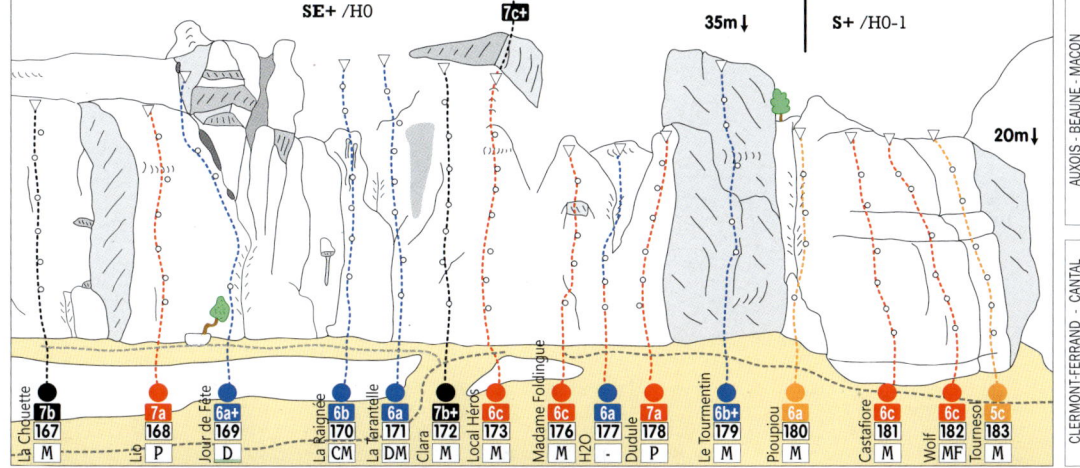

159 — 8a+ — Tam-Tam

168 — 7a — Lio

179 — 6b+ — Le Tourmentin
180 — 6a — Pioupiou

Routes 154-183, very impressive sector, can get very hot even in cold weather.

CIRQUE DES GENS - E

P1 44.475397, 4.351306

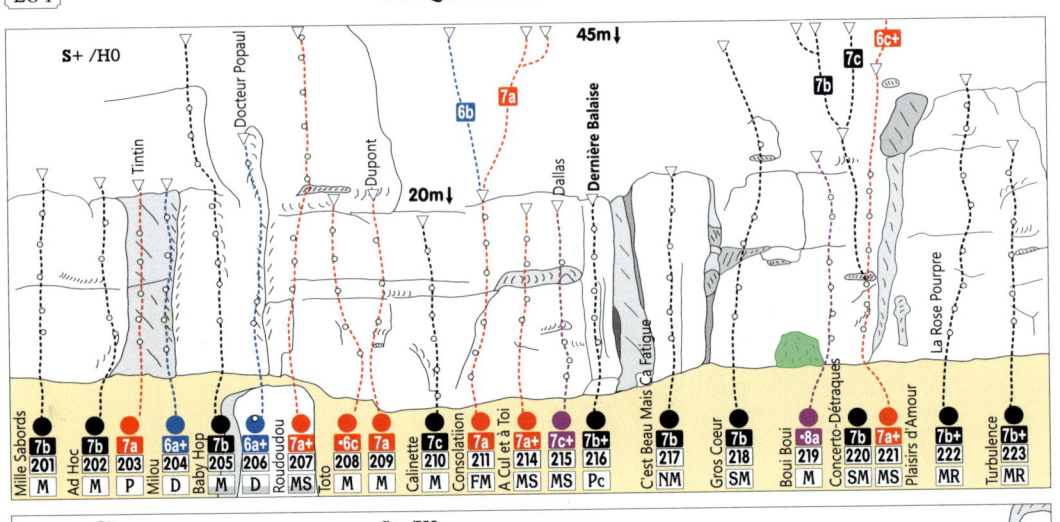
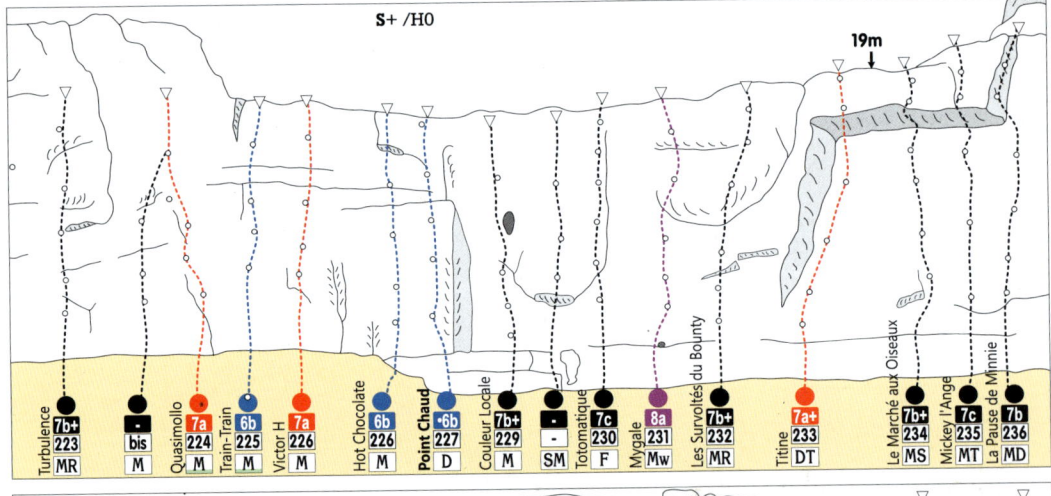
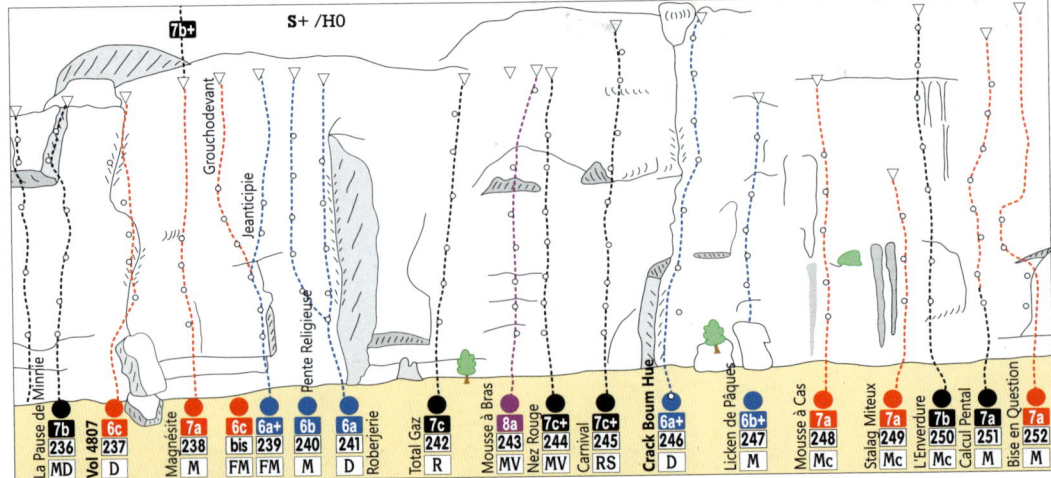

The centre part of the cliff is very tall and intimidating, best for high grade Climbers.

Calcaire**** Many of the easier routes are exceptionally polished, don't expect an easy time here.

CIRQUE DES GENS - G

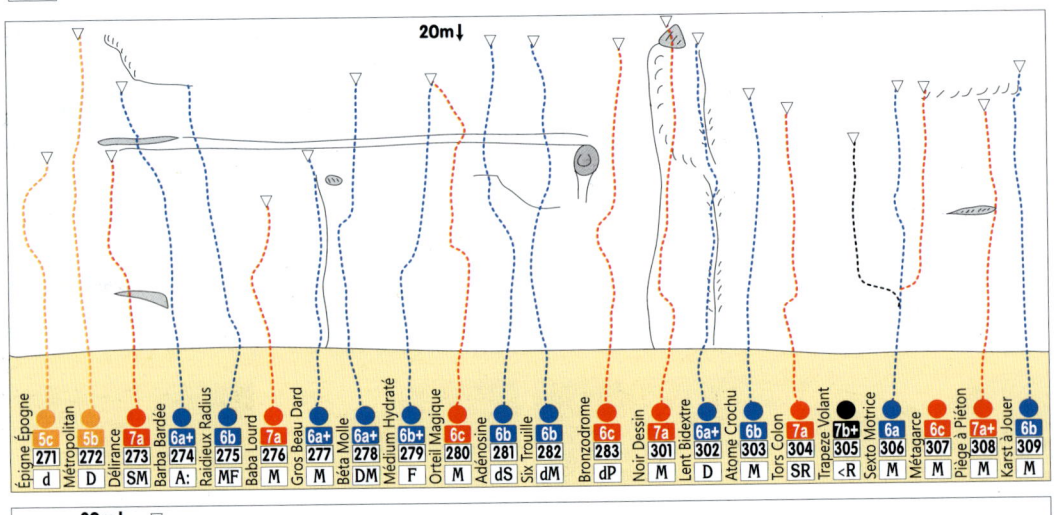
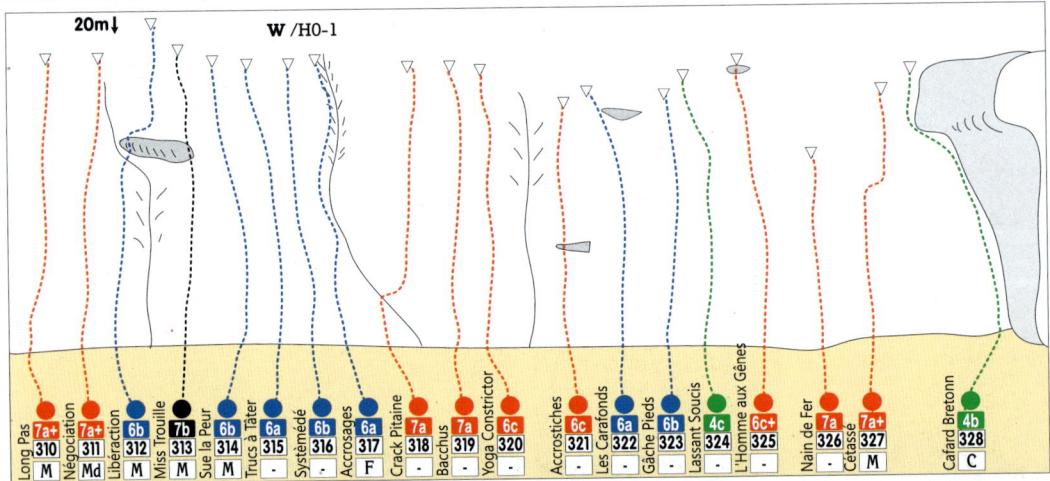
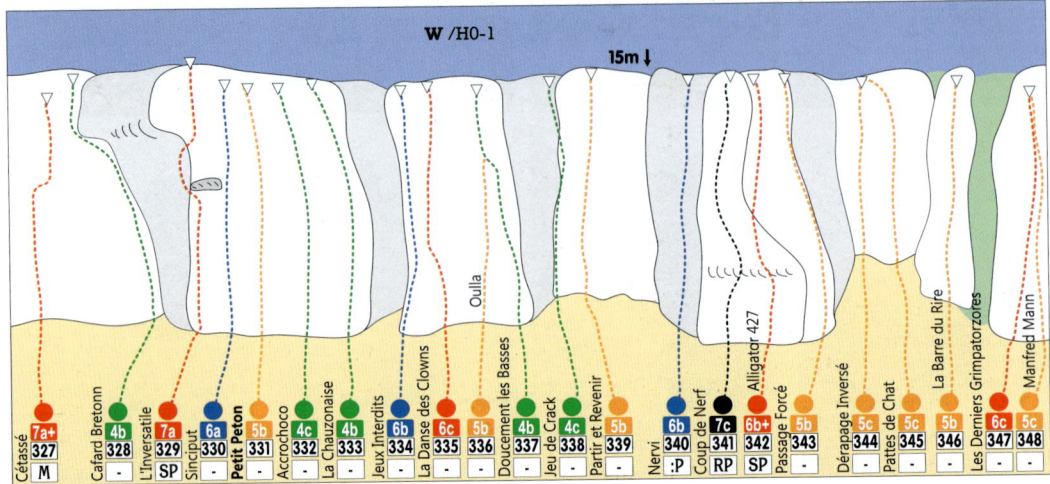

Base of routes is generally comfortable with good shade for belayer in central section. (No actual routes 284-299)

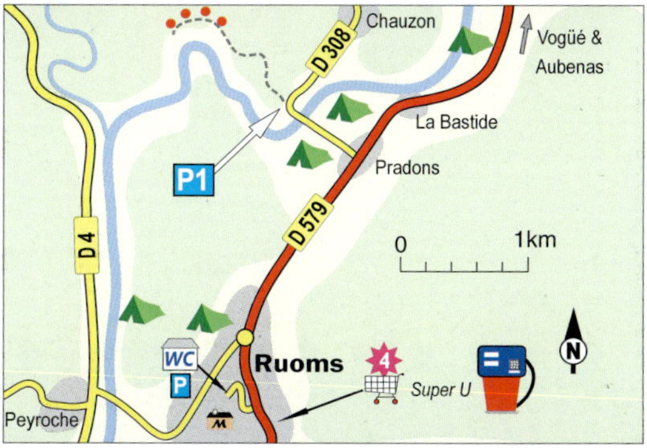

CIRQUE DES GENS (Chauzon)

#	Grade	Name
271	5c	Épigne Épogne
272	5c	Métropolitain
301	7a	Noir Dessin
302	6a+	Lent Bidextre
308	7a+	Piège à Piéton
311	7a+	Négociation
312	6b	Libéraction
317	6a	Accrosages
321	6c	Accrostiches
329	7a	L'Inversatile
334	6c	La Danse des Clowns
341	7c	Coup de Nerf

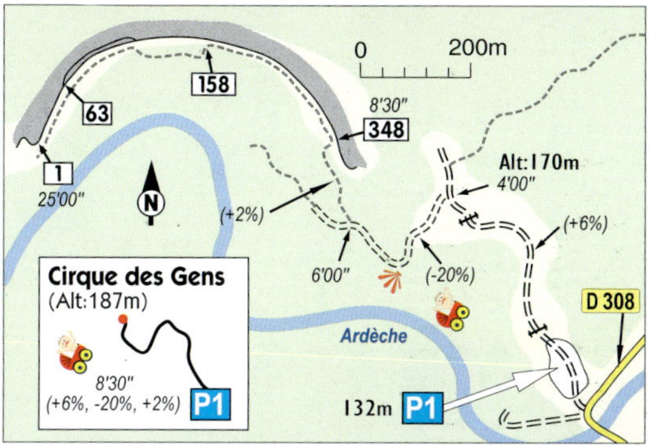

P1 44.475397, 4.351306 — 287

FONTAINEBLEAU — YONNE - MORVAN — AUXOIS - BEAUNE - MACON — CLERMONT-FERRAND - CANTAL — SAINT-ETIENNE - HAUTE LOIRE — AUBENAS - FLORAC - MILLAU

Parking: the road up has disintegrated big time over the years. Now, 5 mins walk up to a nice viewpoint and picnic spot.

FONTGARNIDE - A - (Salavas)

P1 44.397691, 4.369751

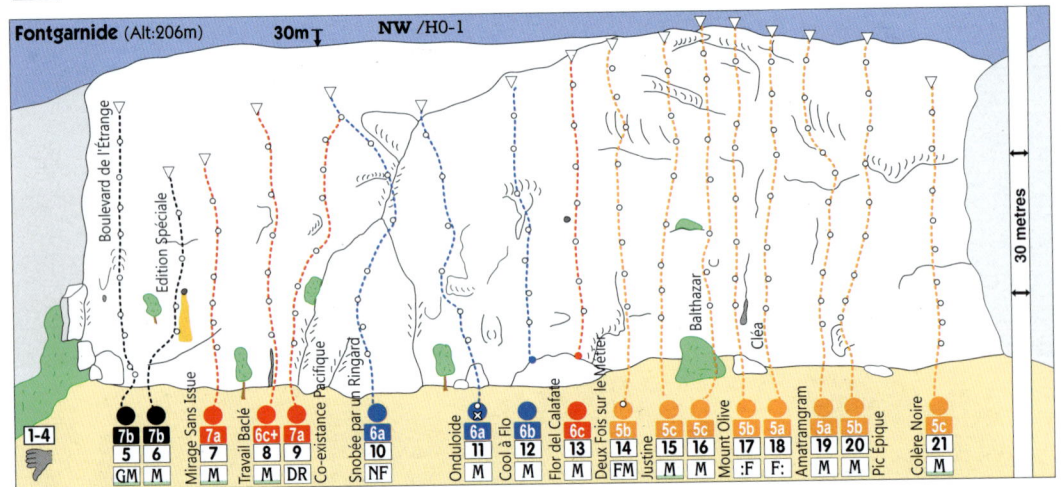
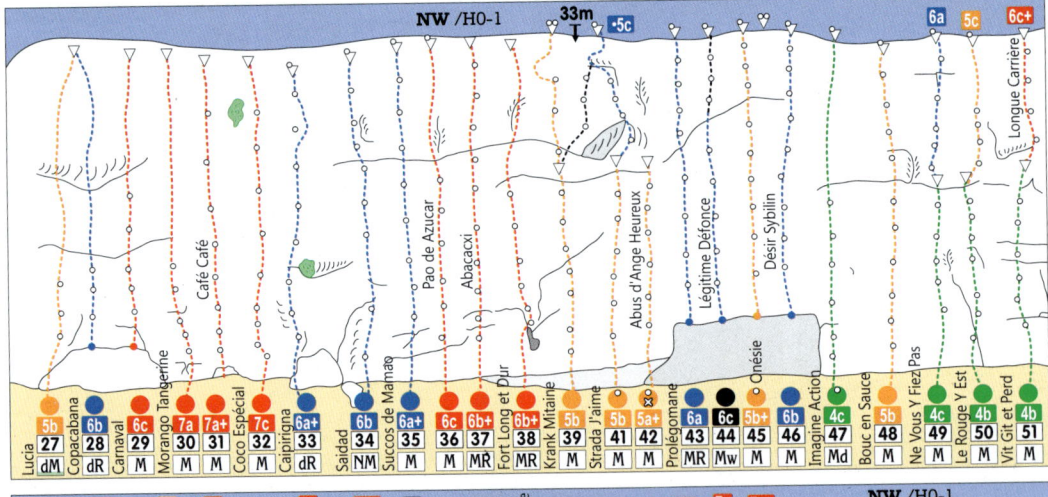
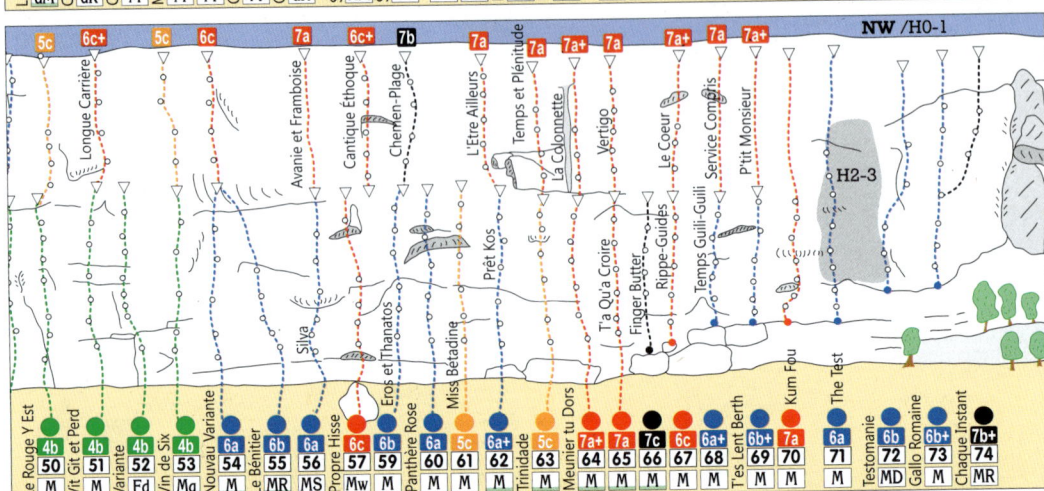

Calcaire***** Perfect pocketed rock. Follow the pockets and not the bolts, enjoyable for experienced 6b and above climbers.

GRAND CHARMASSON

A2 44.381604, 4.443579

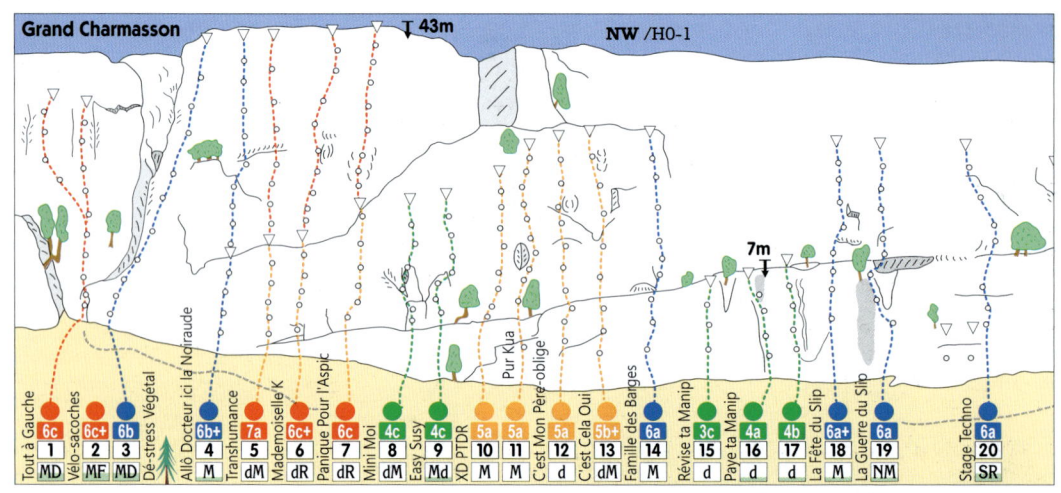
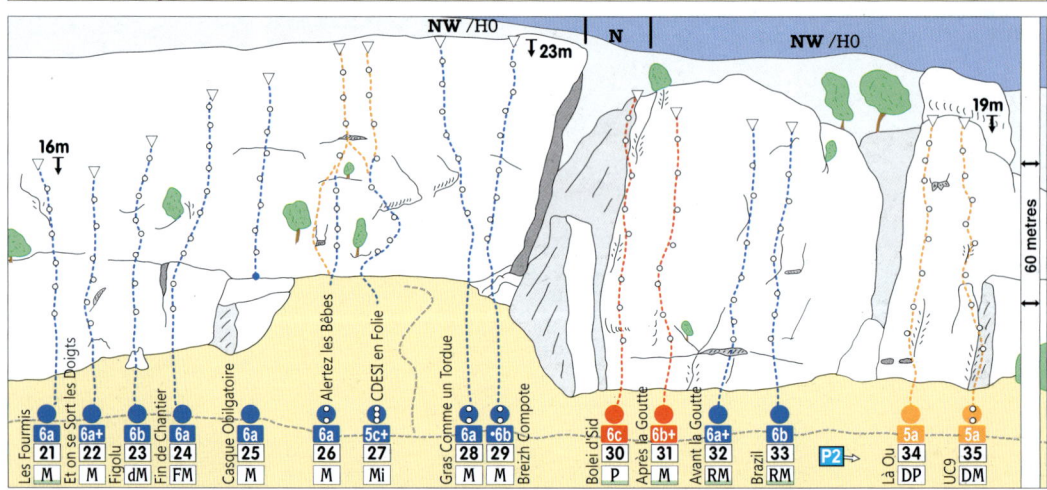
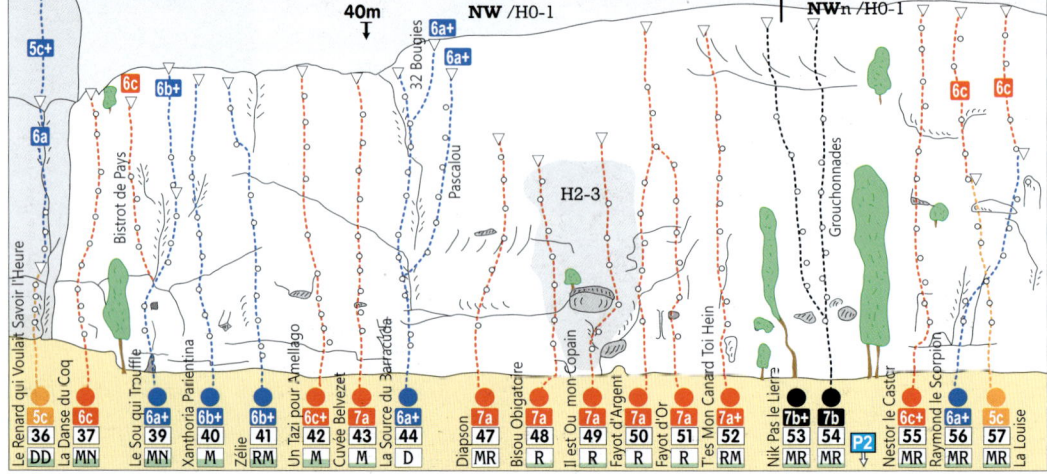

Calcaire*** A very quiet part of the Ardèche, shade, wow views. Rock variable but generally good. A new cliff on the scene.

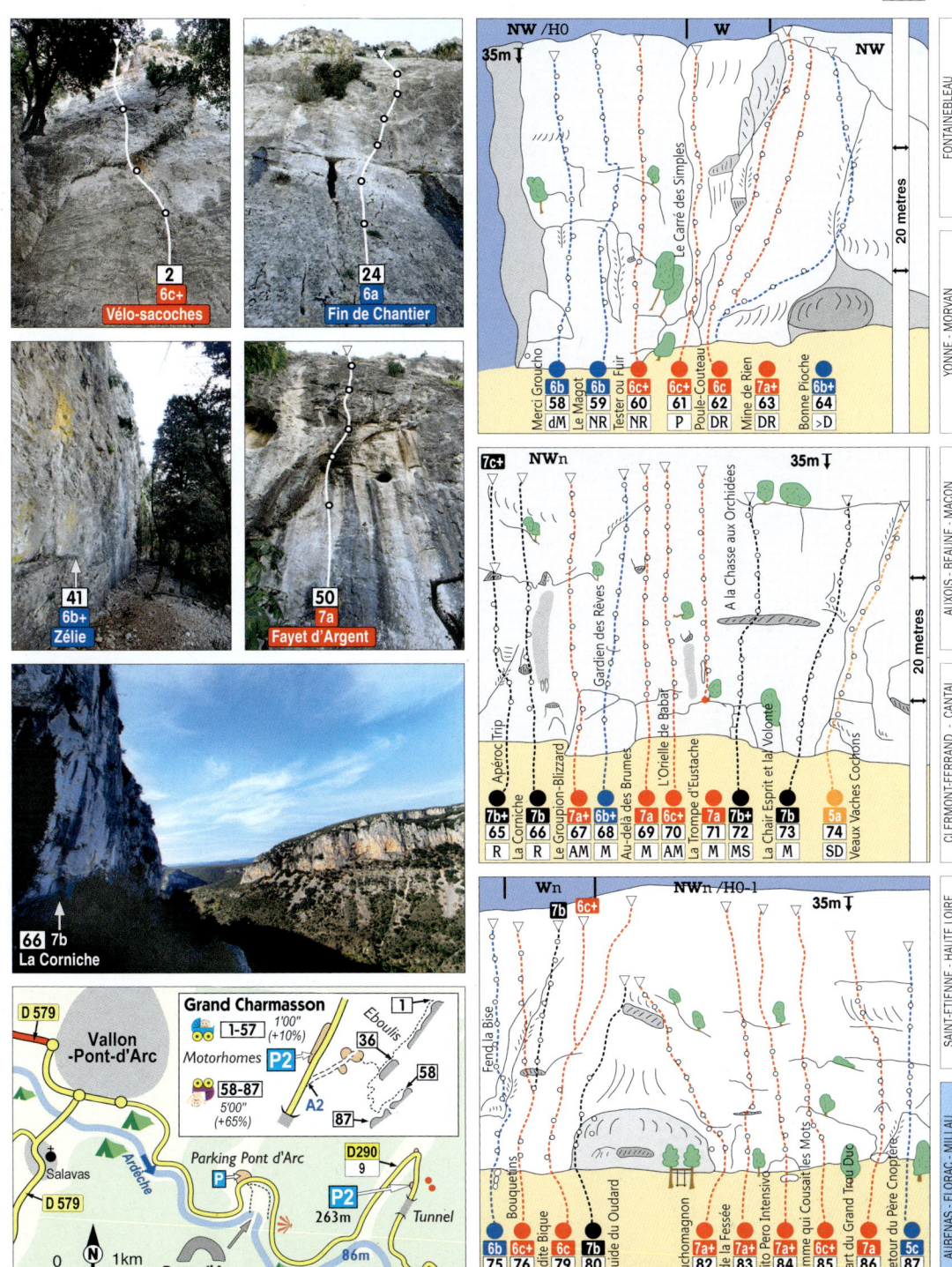

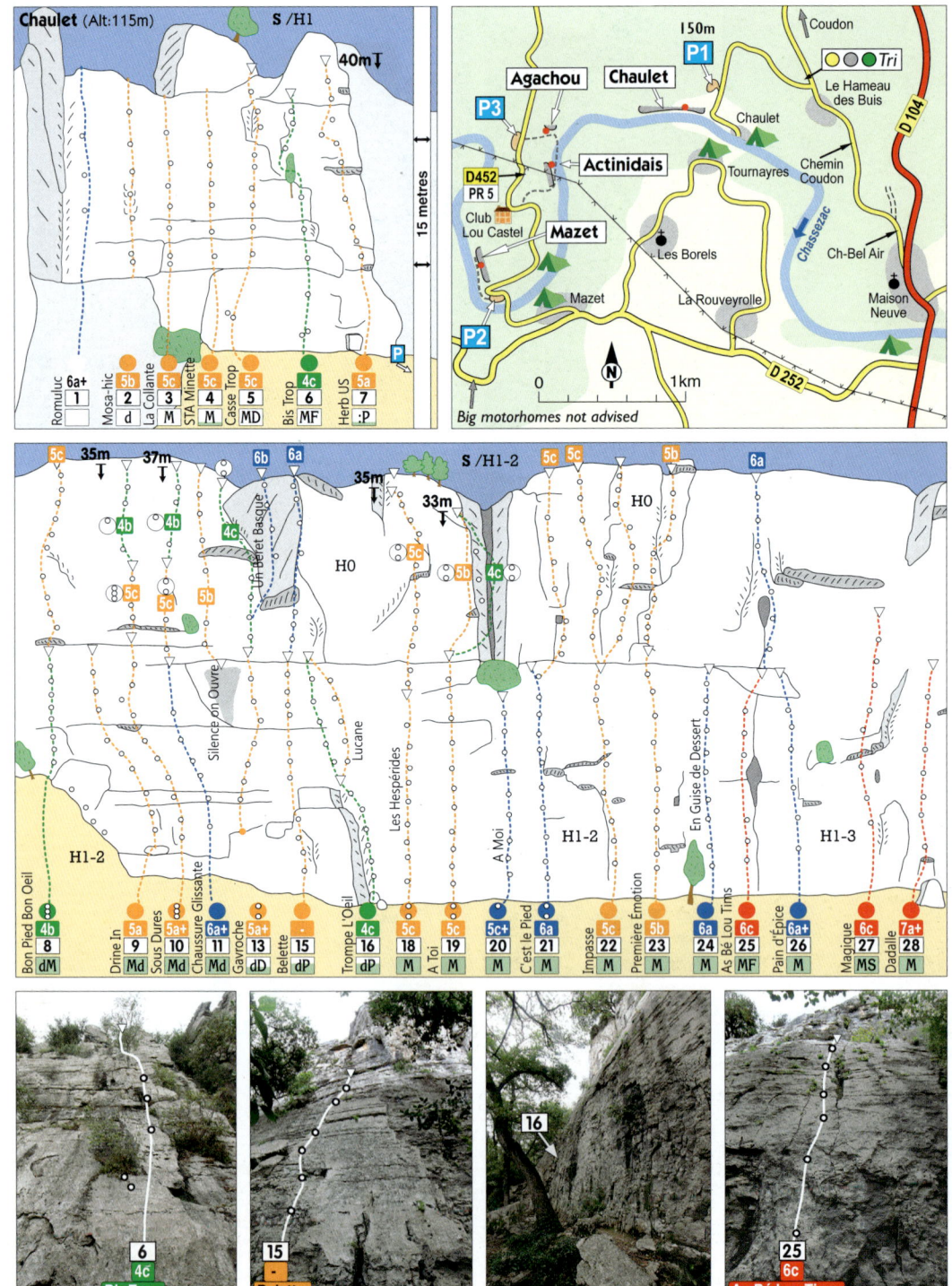

CHAULET - VOIE 22

CHAULET - B

A1 44.408451, 4.216583

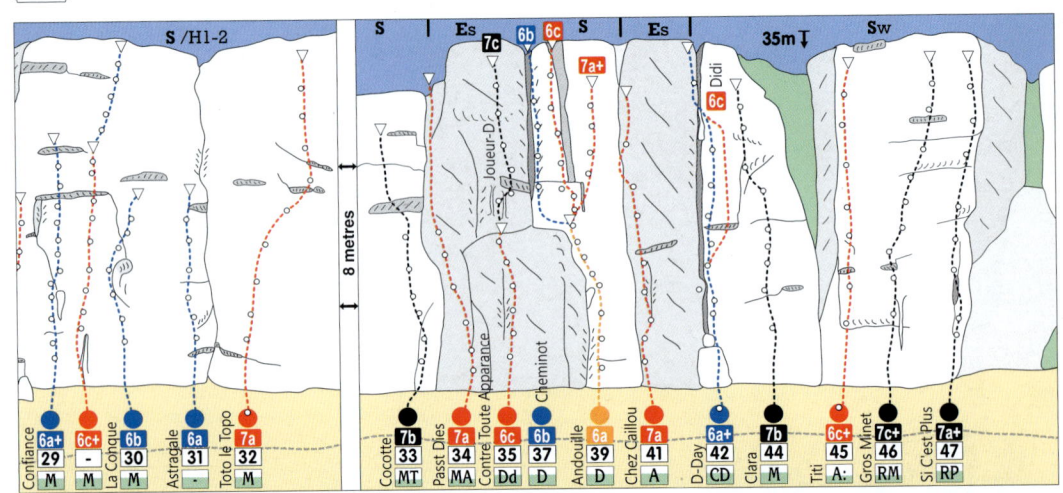

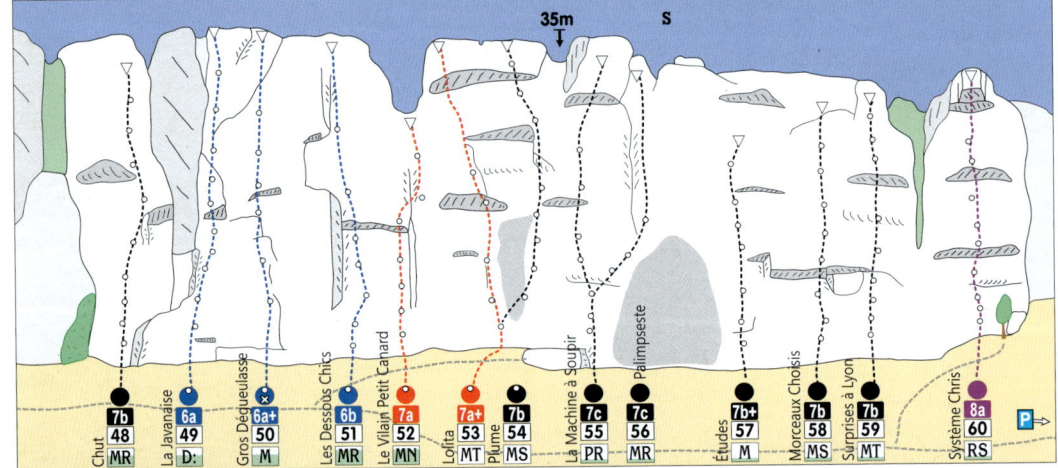

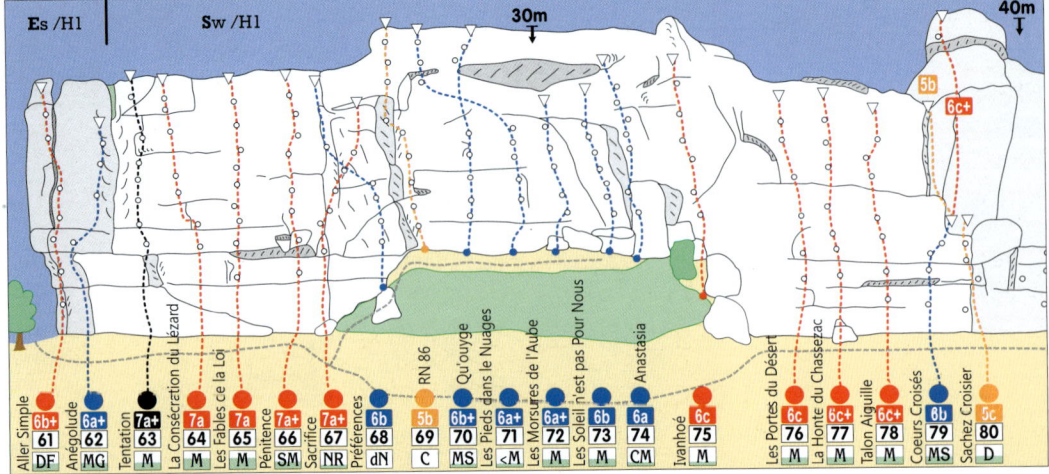

This middle sector in the trees is less frequented and hence less polished - atmospheric.

CHAULET - C

295

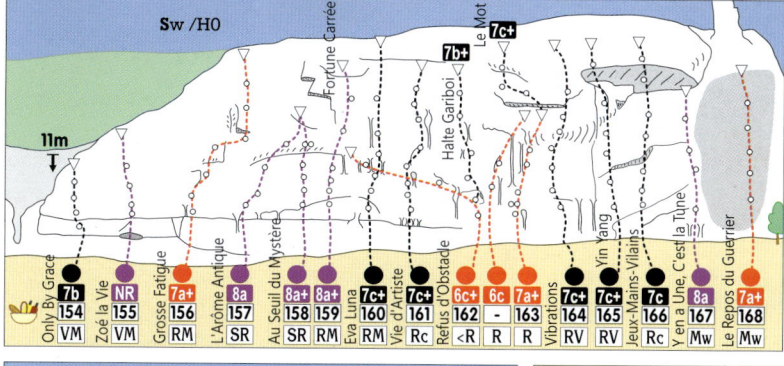

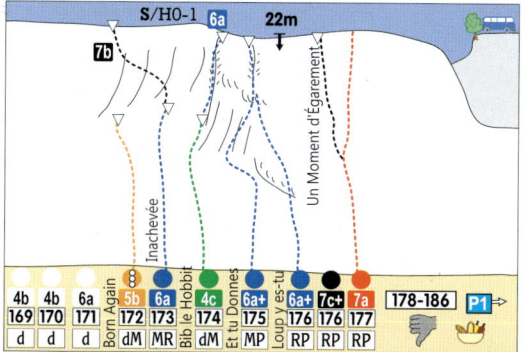
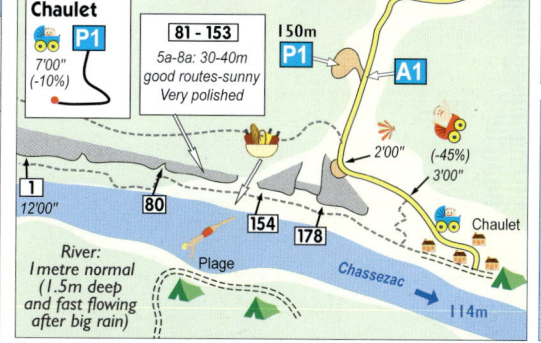

80-153**** Fine routes, technical walls and overhangs, very popular (online info) - but not in summer - too hot.

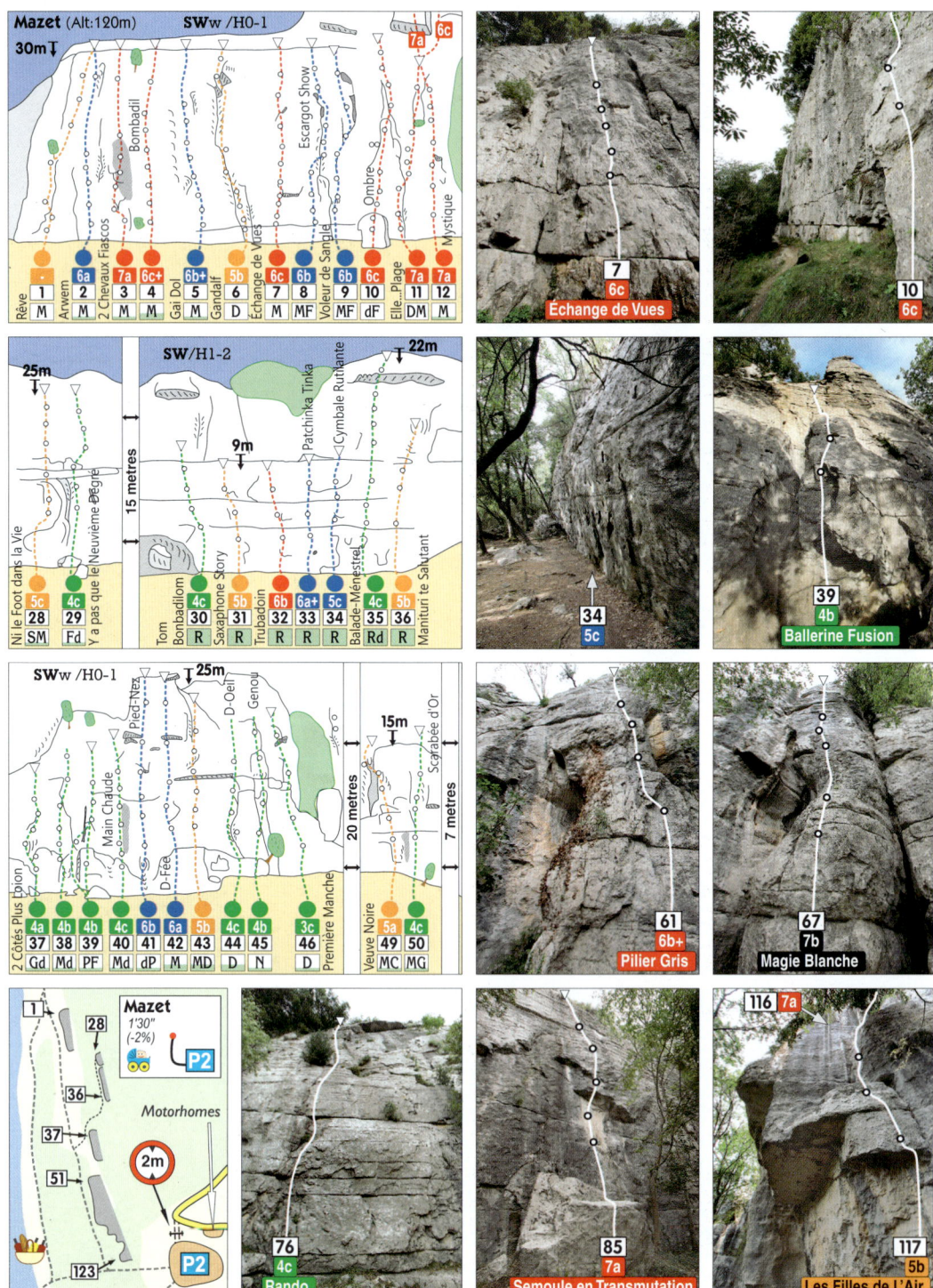

MAZET - B

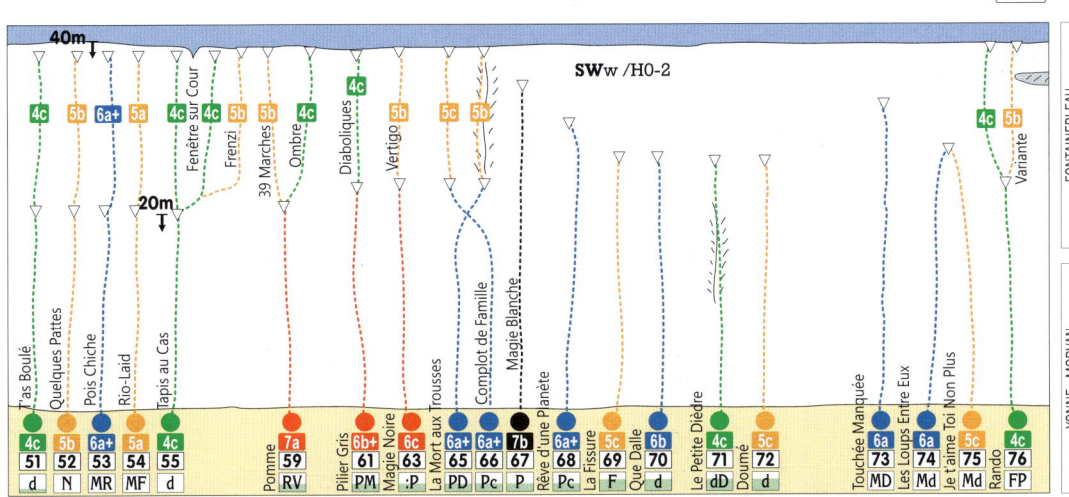
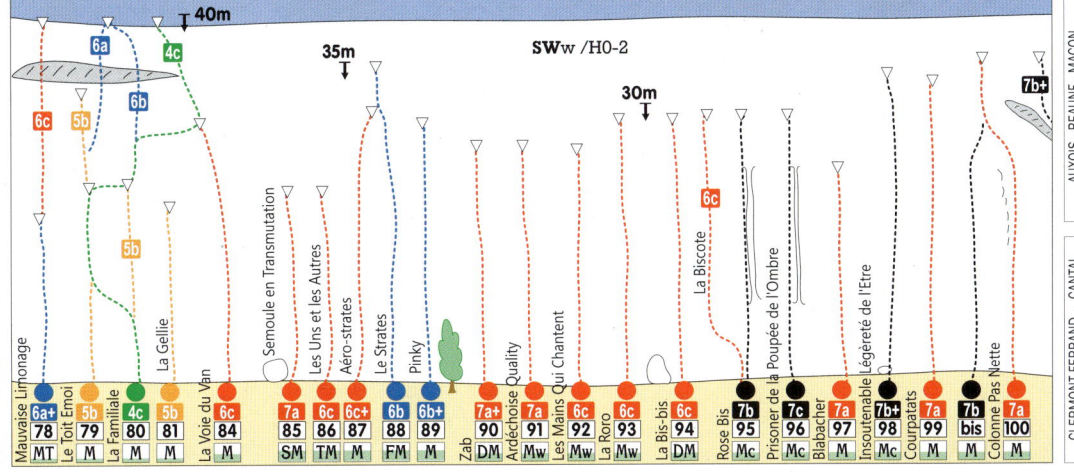
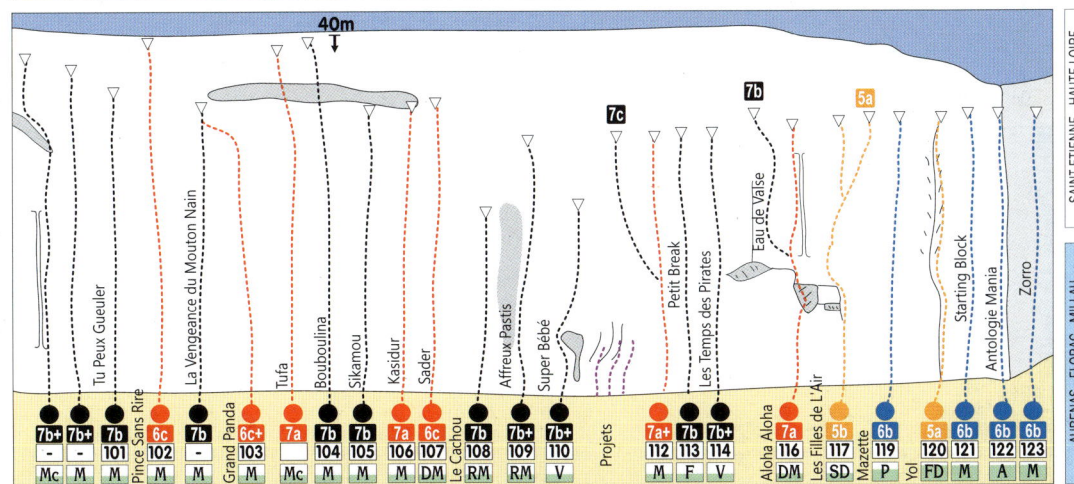

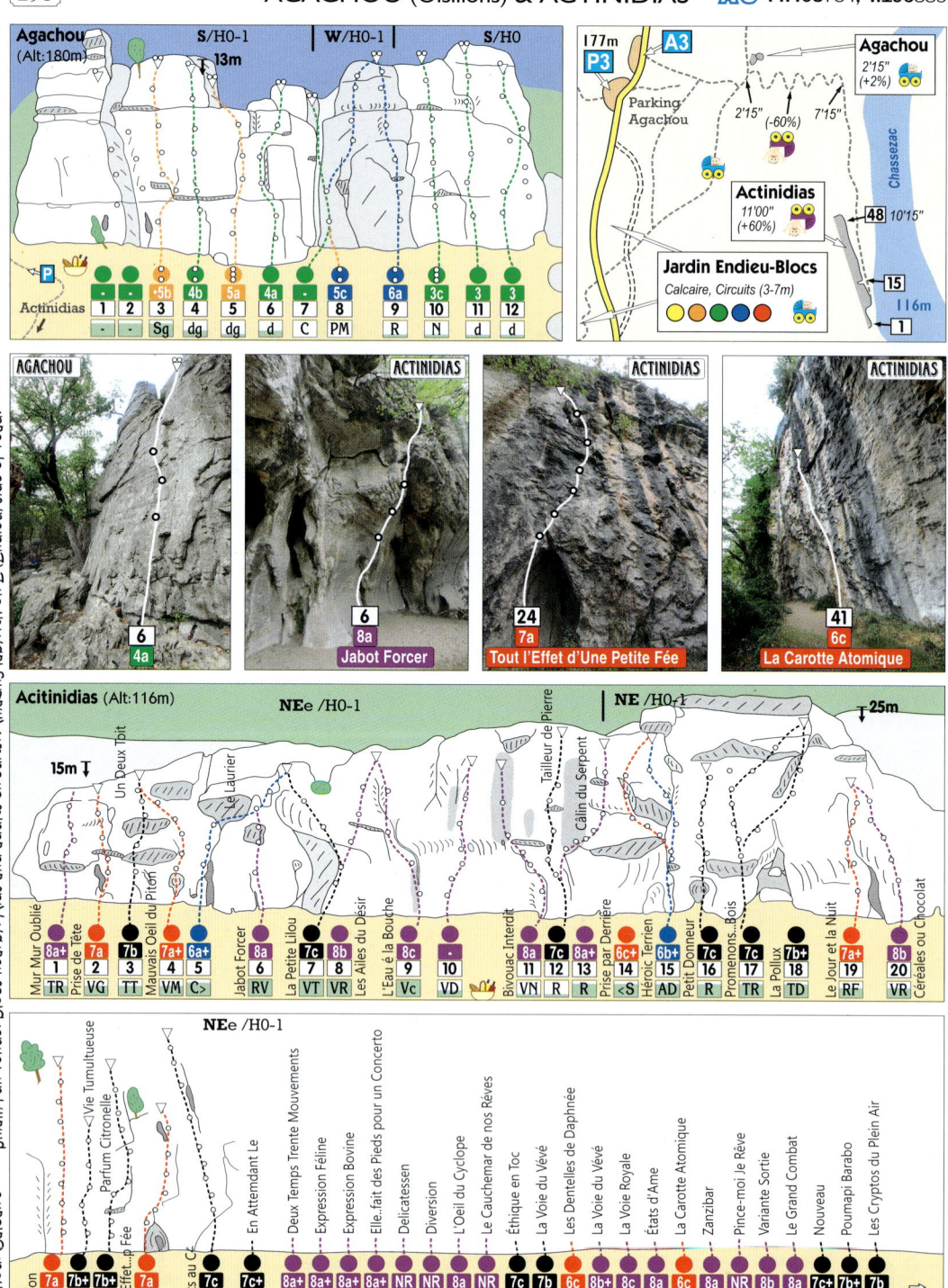

POURTALAS (Pied-de-Borne)

P4 44.476652, 3.985549   299

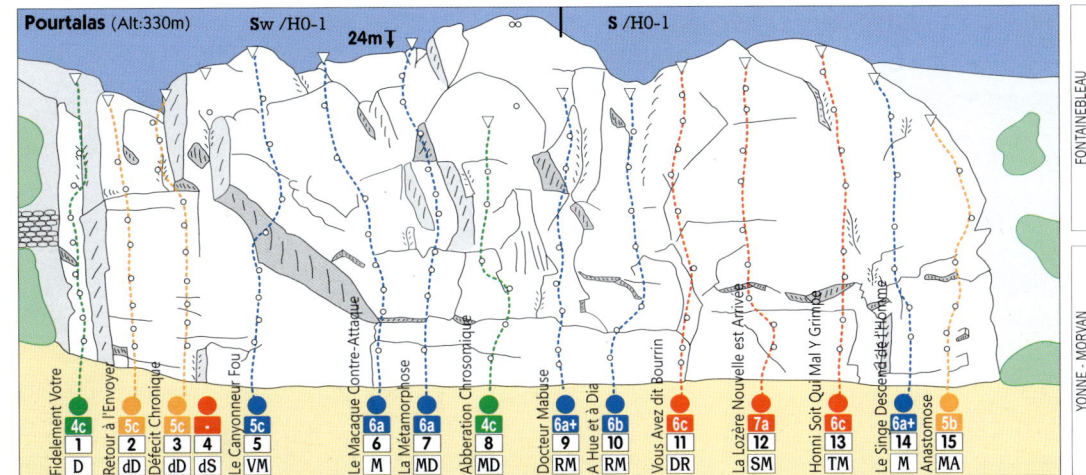

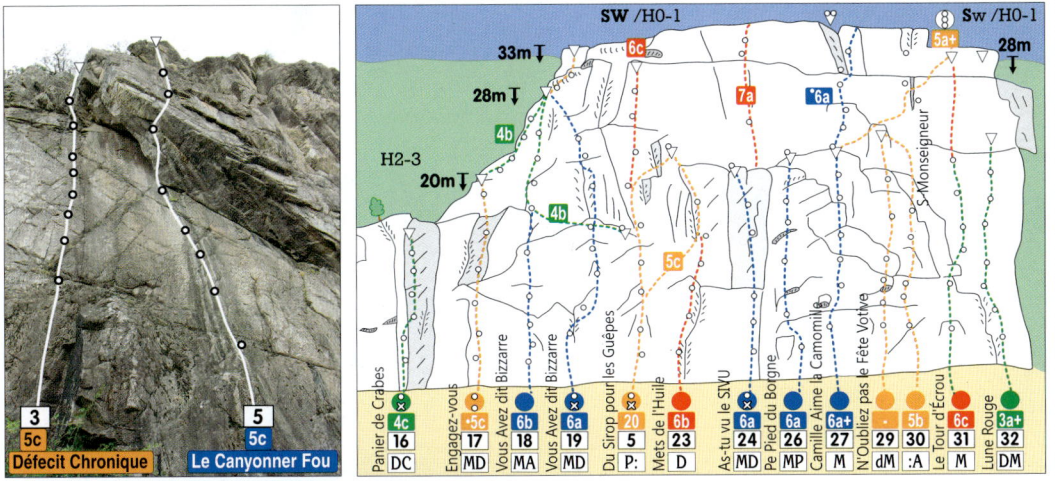

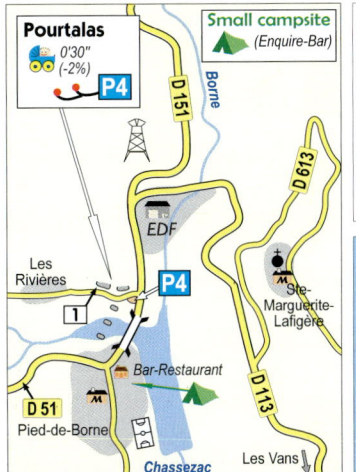

Granite** Rock and routes are very variable - bloc style. Something different. A quiet little village, with a very friendly bar.

JARDIN DU JOUQUEIROU - (Garde Guérin)

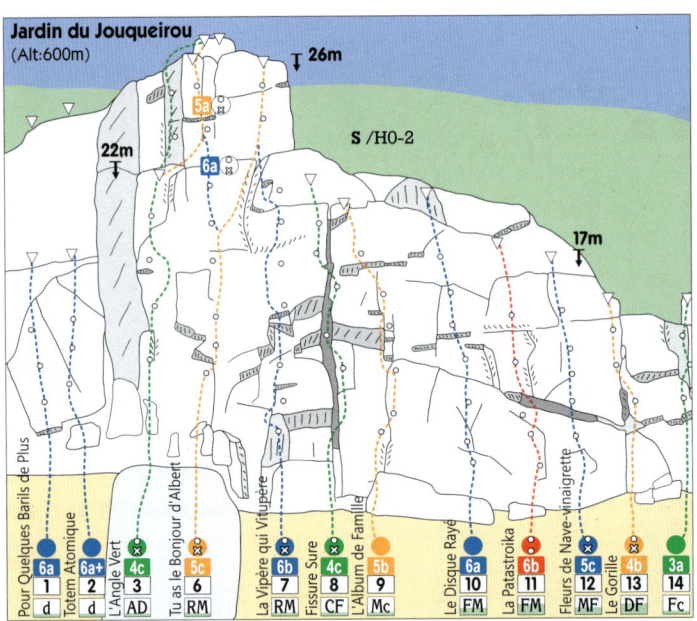

Jardin du Jouqueirou (Alt: 600m)

S /H0-2

26m, 22m, 17m

#	Name	Grade	Style
1	Pour Quelques Barils de Plus	6a	d
2	Totem Atomique	6a+	d
3	L'Angle Vert	4c	AD
4	Tu as le Bonjour d'Albert	x	
5		5a	
6		6a	RM
7	La Vipère qui Vitupère	6b	RM
8	Fissure Sure	4c	CF
9	L'Album de Famille	5b	Mc
10	Le Disque Rayé	6a	FM
11	La Patastroika	6b	FM
12	Fleurs de Nave-vinaigrette	5c	MF
13	Le Gorille	4b	DF
14		3a	Fc

JARDIN-AMBIENCE

↙ 27

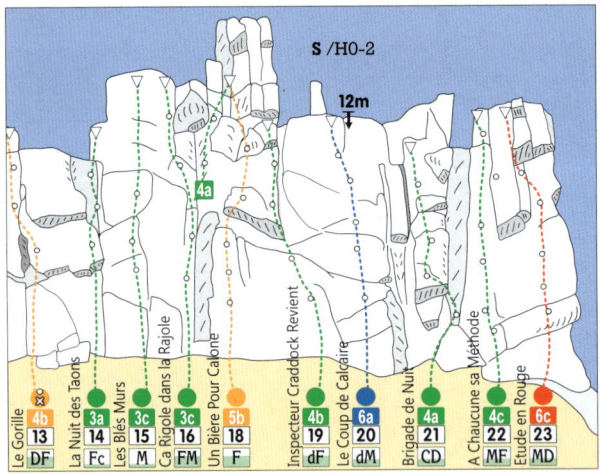

S /H0-2   12m

E /H0-1   14m   Ne /H0-1

#	Name	Grade	Style
13	Le Gorille	4b	DF
14	La Nuit des Taons	3a	Fc
15	Les Blés Murs	3c	M
16	Ça Rigole dans la Rajole	3c	FM
17			
18	Un Bière Pour Calone	5b	F
19	Inspecteur Craddock Revient		dF
20	Le Coup de Calcaire	6a	dM
21	Brigade de Nuit	4a	CD
22	A Chaucune sa Méthode	4c	MF
23	Etude en Rouge	6c	MD
24	Emboîte Gazeuse	5a	A:
25	Histoire Parallèle	6a	DS
26	Les Pieds dans l'Eau	3b	D
27	Aux Frais de la Princesse	4c	Md
28	La Couenne et le Jambon	4b	Fd
29	Ramon le Ramoneau	5c	M
30	Haut les Mains	5b	M

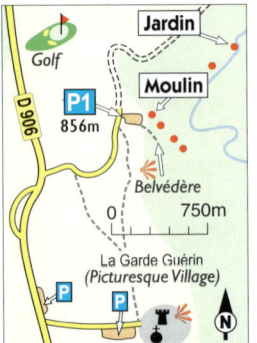

Jardin, Golf, P1 856m, Moulin, Belvédère, 750m, La Garde Guérin (Picturesque Village)

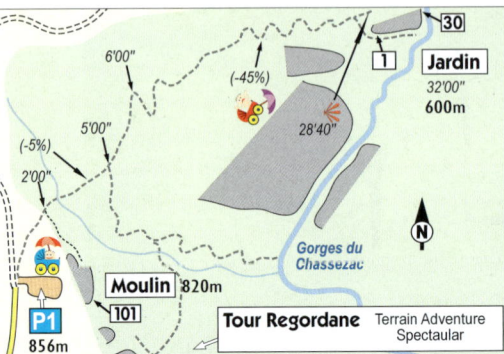

P1 856m, Moulin 820m, Jardin 32'00" 600m, Tour Regordane — Terrain Adventure Spectacular, Gorges du Chassezac

21

Granite**** A worthwhile cliff at the bottom of a deep gorge, stays coolish with constant cool wind and some trees.

P1 44.483257, 3.934160 ROCHER DU MOULIN - (Garde Guérin) 301

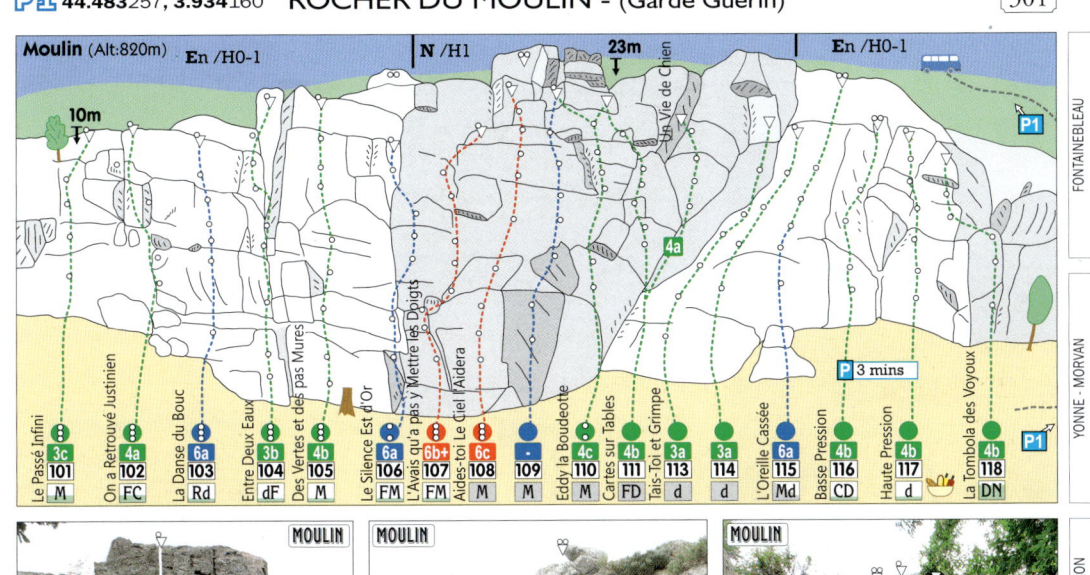

105 – 4b – Des Vertes et des Pas Mures

111 – 4b / 112 – 4a

116 – 4b – Basse Pression / 117 – 4b – Haute Pression

7 – 6b – La Vipère qui Vitupère / 8 – 4c – Fissure Sure

23 – 6c – Etude en Rouge

27 – 4c – Aux Frais de la Princesse

Granite***** Easy access, lovely climbing. Popular little spot with groups. (Also big terrain adventure cliffs above the gorge.)

SAINT-JULIEN-DU-TOURNEL

P1 44.501106, 3.698924

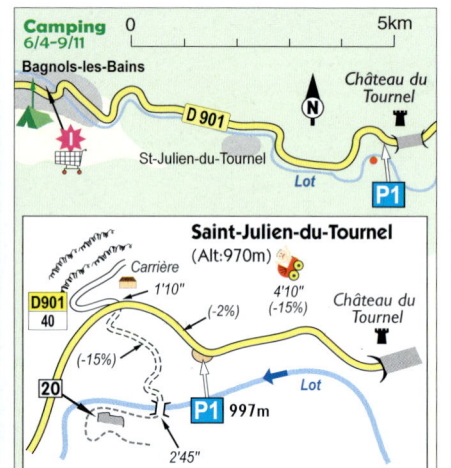

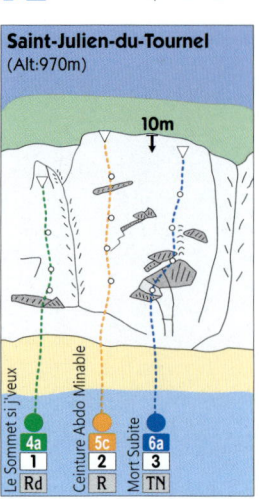

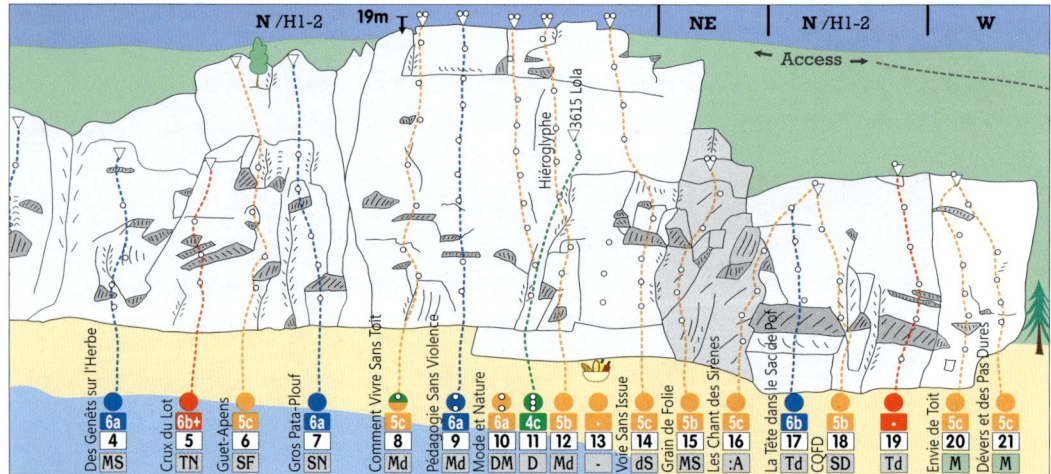

Schiste*** A very quiet part of the upper Lot. Mostly good holds with some punchy overhangs. Lovely setting by river.

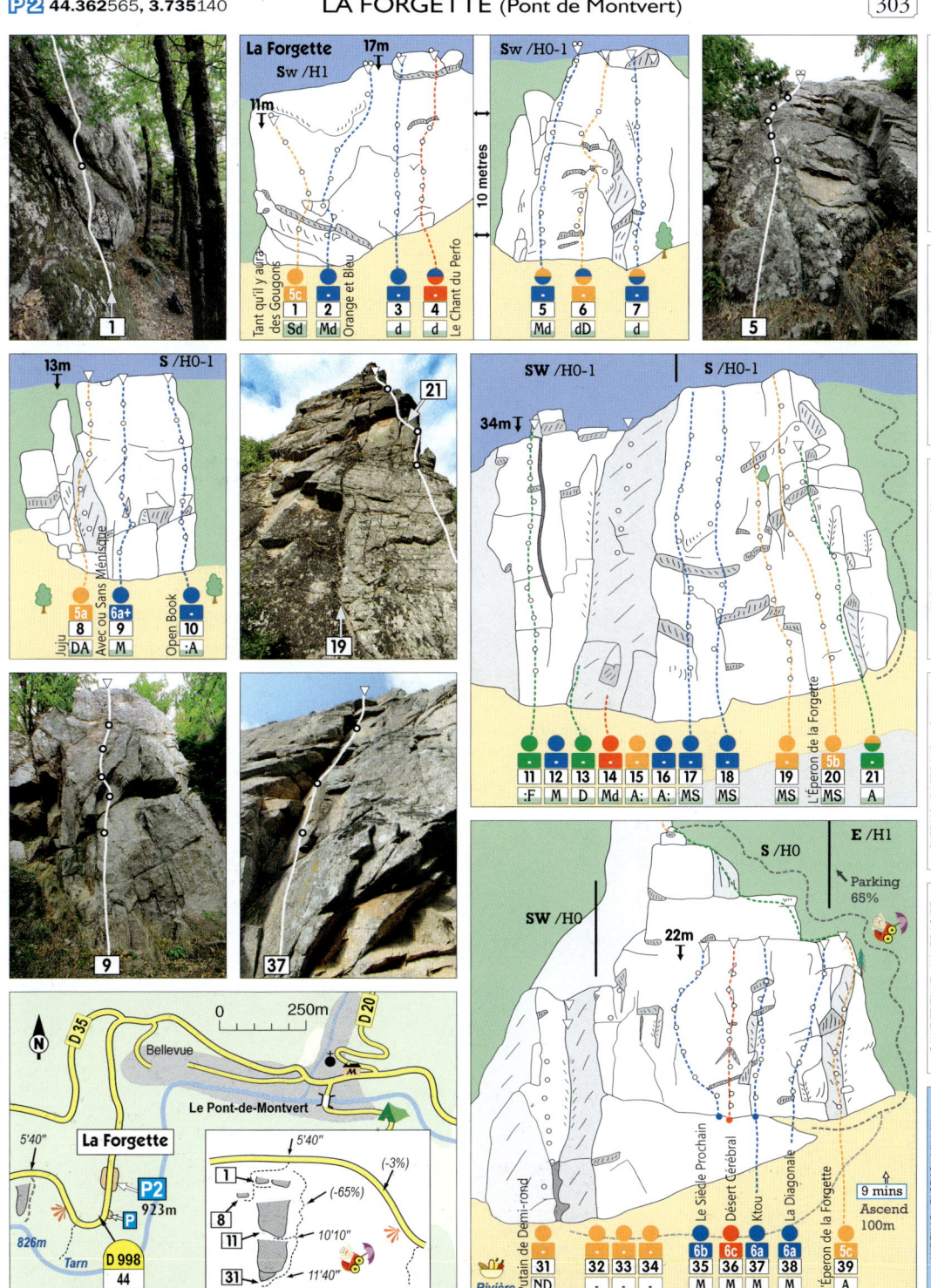

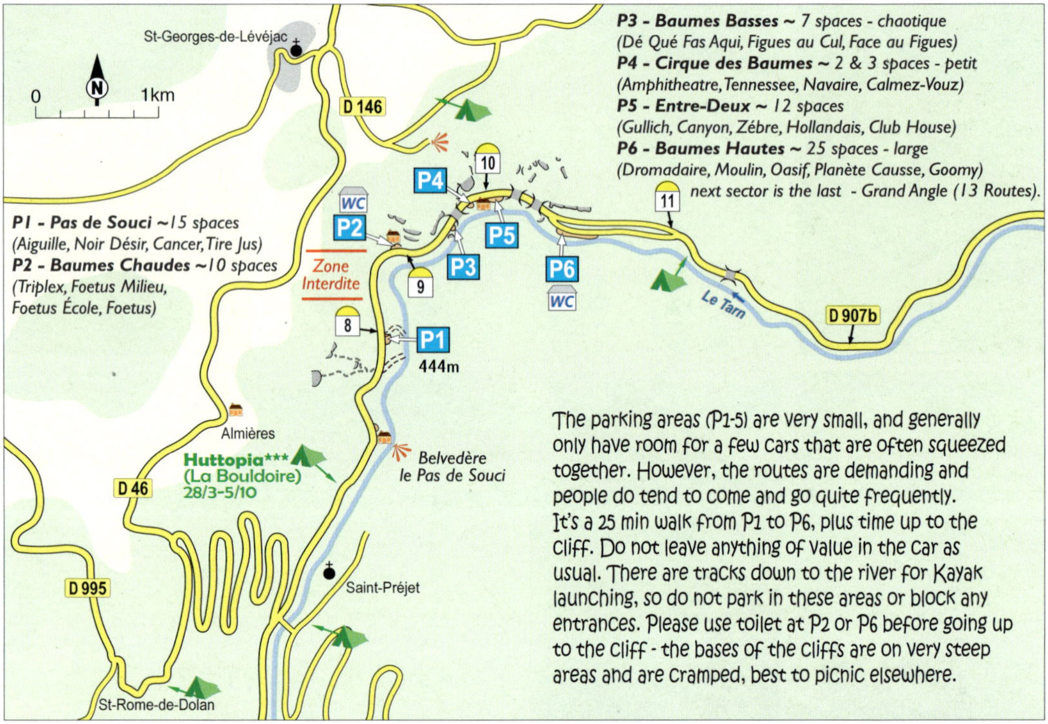

TARN (A) - (P1) PAS DU SOUCY

P1 44.297206, 3.238773

P1 - Pas de Souci ~ 15 spaces
(Aiguille, Noir Désir, Cancer, Tire Jus)

P2 - Baumes Chaudes ~ 10 spaces
(Triplex, Foetus Milieu, Foetus École, Foetus)

P3 - Baumes Basses ~ 7 spaces - chaotique
(Dé Qué Fas Aqui, Figues au Cul, Face au Figues)

P4 - Cirque des Baumes ~ 2 & 3 spaces - petit
(Amphitheatre, Tennessee, Navaire, Calmez-Vouz)

P5 - Entre-Deux ~ 12 spaces
(Gullich, Canyon, Zébre, Hollandais, Club House)

P6 - Baumes Hautes ~ 25 spaces - large
(Dromadaire, Moulin, Oasif, Planète Causse, Goomy)
next sector is the last - Grand Angle (13 Routes).

The parking areas (P1-5) are very small, and generally only have room for a few cars that are often squeezed together. However, the routes are demanding and people do tend to come and go quite frequently. It's a 25 min walk from P1 to P6, plus time up to the cliff. Do not leave anything of value in the car as usual. There are tracks down to the river for kayak launching, so do not park in these areas or block any entrances. Please use toilet at P2 or P6 before going up to the cliff - the bases of the cliffs are on very steep areas and are cramped, best to picnic elsewhere.

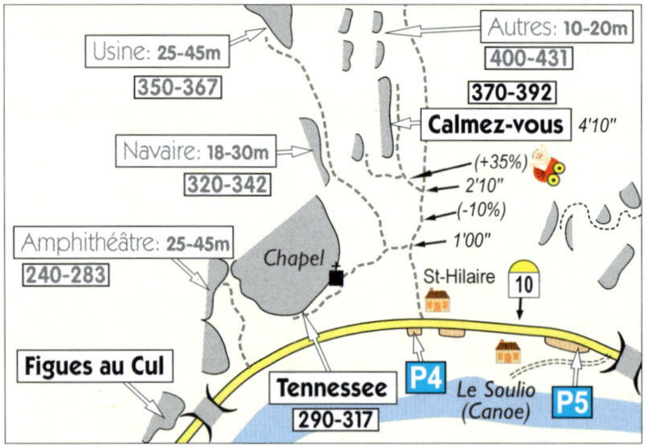

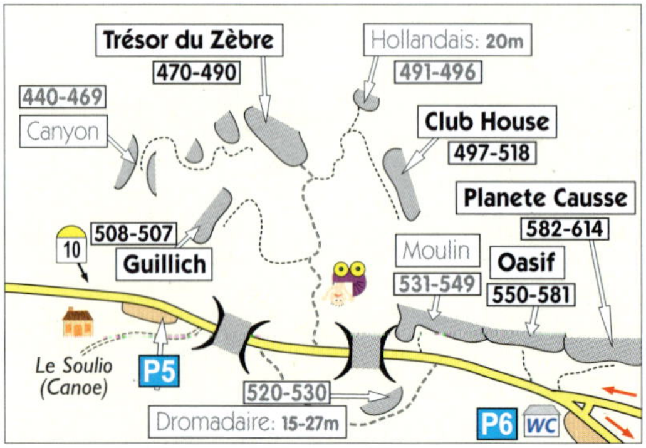

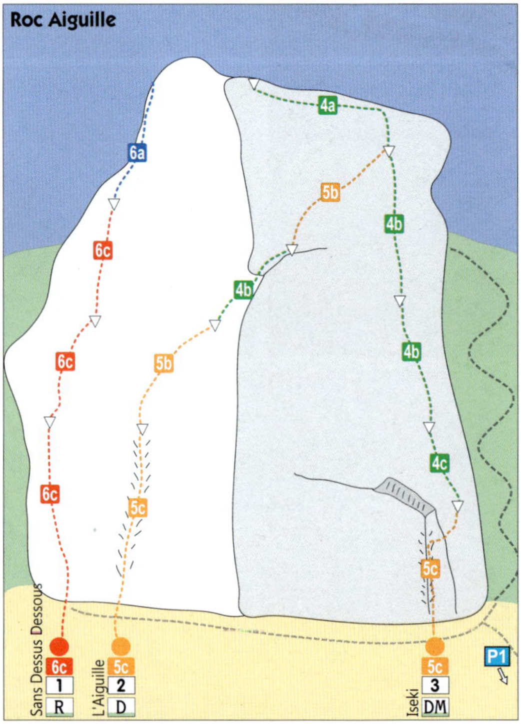

Roc Aiguille

99% of the cliffs in the Gorges du Tarn are reserved for wildlife, or are very inaccessable. The 1% bolted, is of high quality.

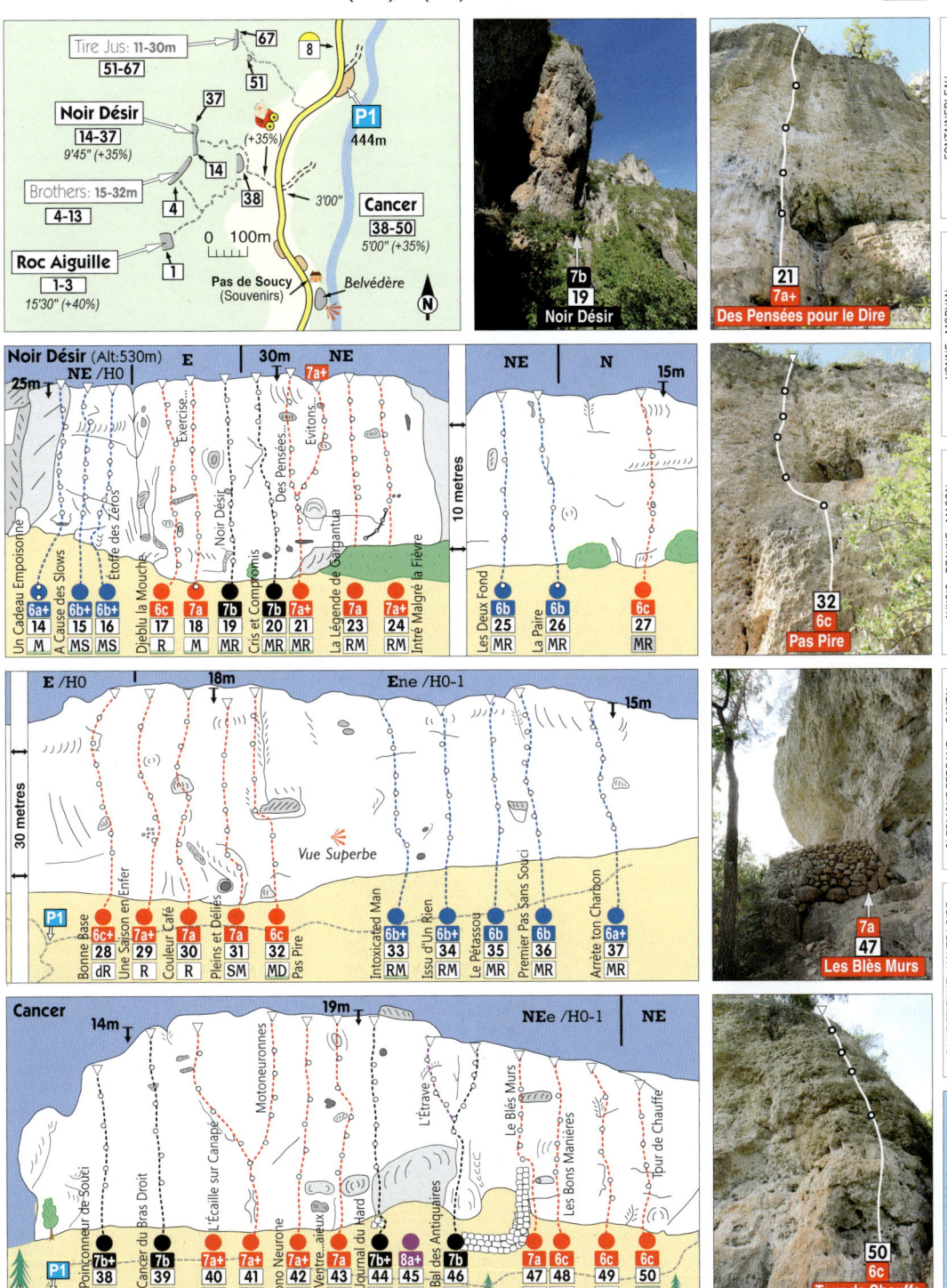

TARN (B) - (P2) BAUMES CHAUDES

P2 44.304177, 3.239523

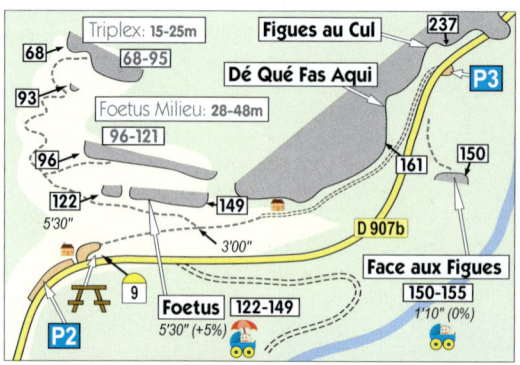

123 5b **Petit Rond**

Foetus: S/H0

	Si Trouille	Petit Rond	Par Devant en Finesse	Et d'Jip	La Grosse Papaille	Le 6b	Just for Fun		Oeil du Sphinx	Poussière d'Or	Huit Dehors	Orage o des Dehors	La Fin du Début	Hue Pony	
Grade	5b	5b	5c	5c	6a	6c+	7c+	7b	7b+	7b	7a	5c+	6a	6a	6c
No.	122	123	124	125	126	127	128	129	130	131	132	133	134	135
	M	MS	DS	:P	M	MS	RS	R	dR	MR	DR	R	FM	RA

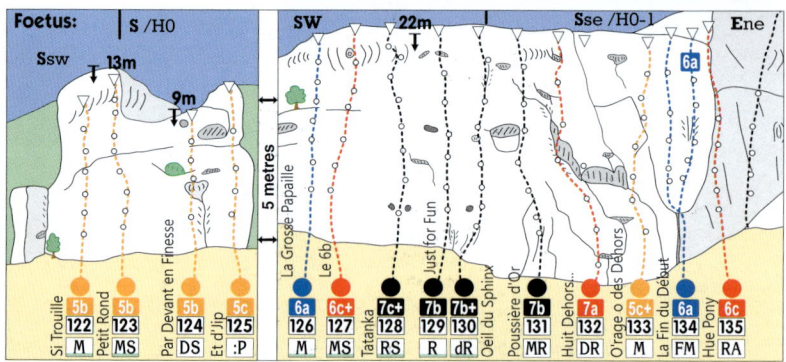

	Tripoux n'Trufàde	Du Côte du Coeur	Big Babadoum	Directe	Honneur aux Dames	Vive le Weekend	Gold Rush	Mousse le Houx Blond	Un Éternal Amour	Le Bug	Peur aux Tafioles	Equiper ce n'est pas Donné	Que des Matmores	Pieds, Mains	Passage de Témoin	Contre Courant	Beau Geste	Face aux Fiques	Pompe-Couillons	Face de Fique	One Man Chaud
Grade	7b+	6b+	6a+	6b+	6a+	6b	7a	7a+	7a	7c	8a	7b+	7a+		7c+	4c+	4c+	6a	5b+	5b+	5b
No.	136	137	138	139	140	141	142	143	144	145	146	147	148		149	150	151	152	153	154	155
	R	M	M	M	M	M	RM	RM	RV	MR	RV	RV	MT		MT	dN	Mo	Mo	Mo	Mo	Mo

Face aux Fiques

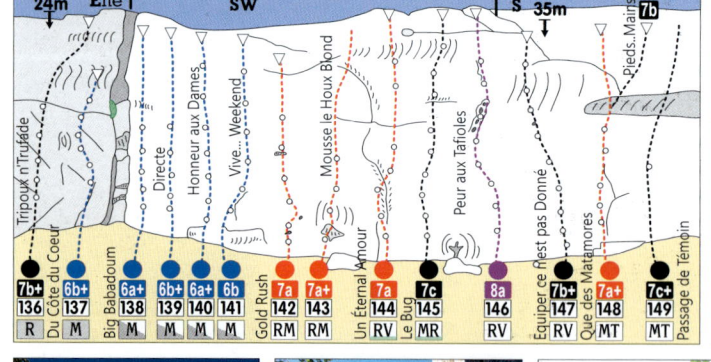
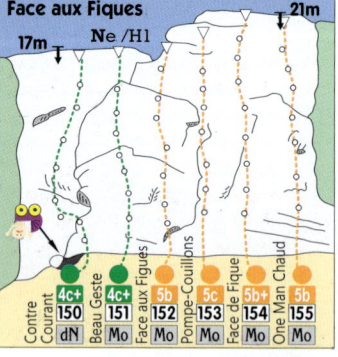

130 7b+ **L'Oeil du Sphinx**

135 6c **Hue Pony**

150 4c+ **Court Courante**

FACE AUX FIGUES

155 5b **One Man Chaud**

The selection in this guide, is to the easier routes/sectors of the gorge. Cliffs not featured - are generally 7b-8c.

Souvenir de Bleau 6c, *Carolin Otzelberger*

TARN (C) - (P3) BAUMES BASSES

P3 44.306690, 3.245379

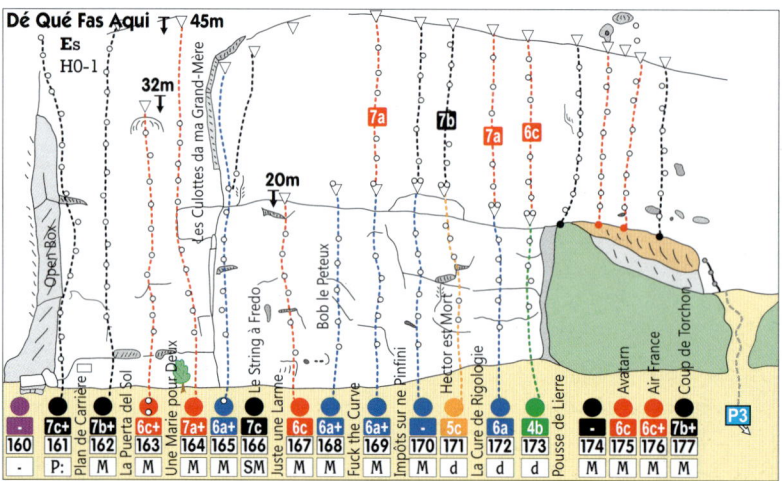

182 7a+ Australopitèque du Samedi

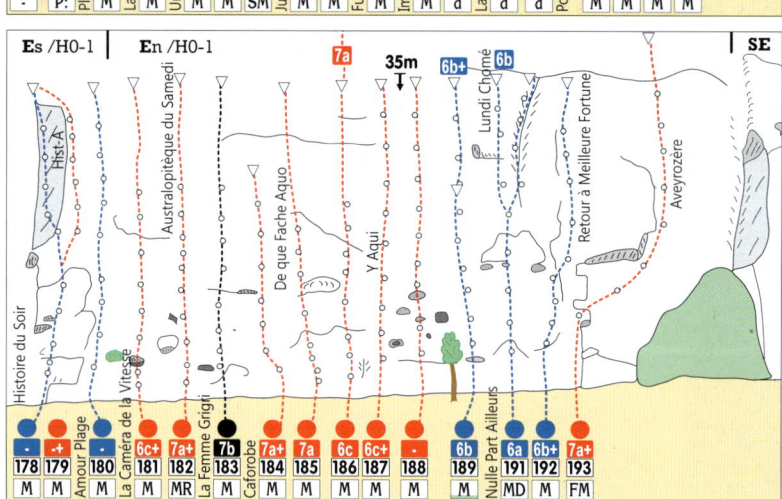

205 7a Farniente

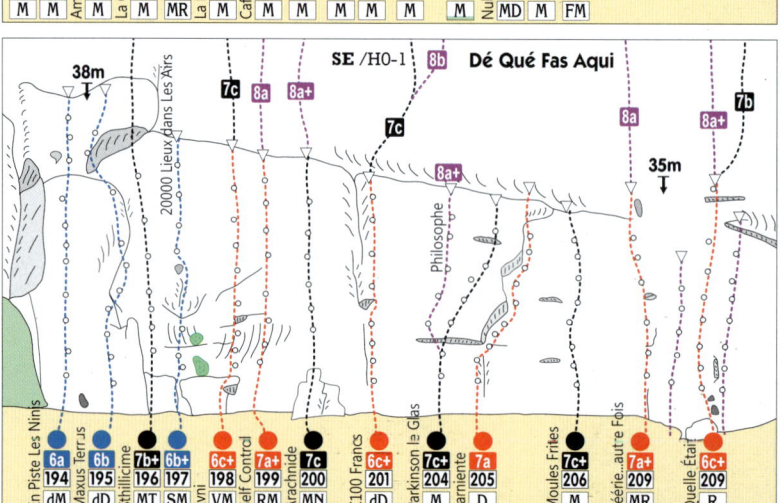

237 6b+ Le Vieux Raphiot

373 7c Arnaque

This is the most popular big wall in these parts, plenty of good long routes and cool afternoon shade - wind whips through too.

TARN (CC) - (P4) CIRQUE DES BAUMES

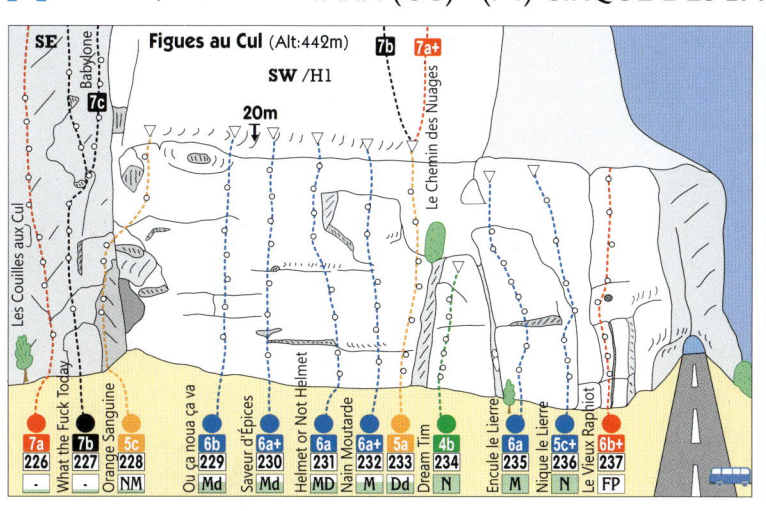

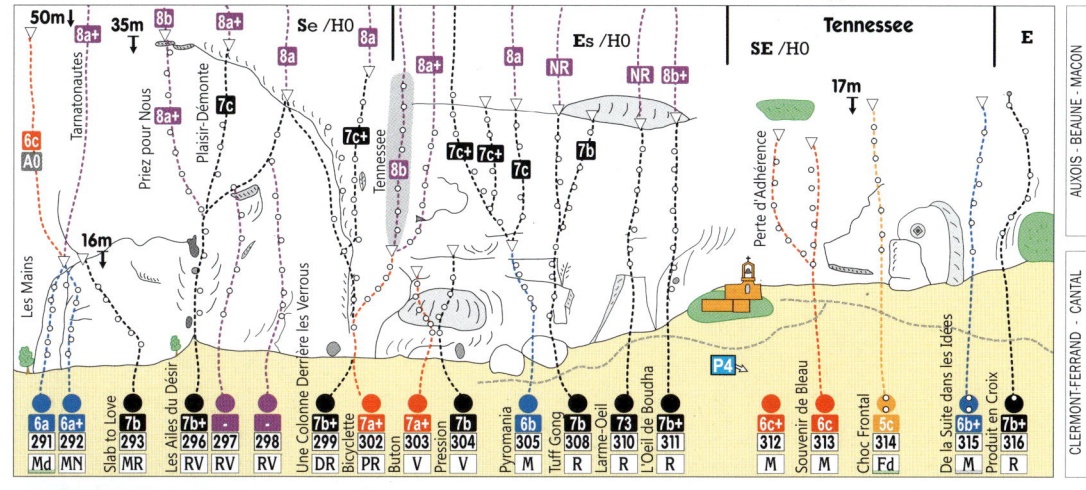
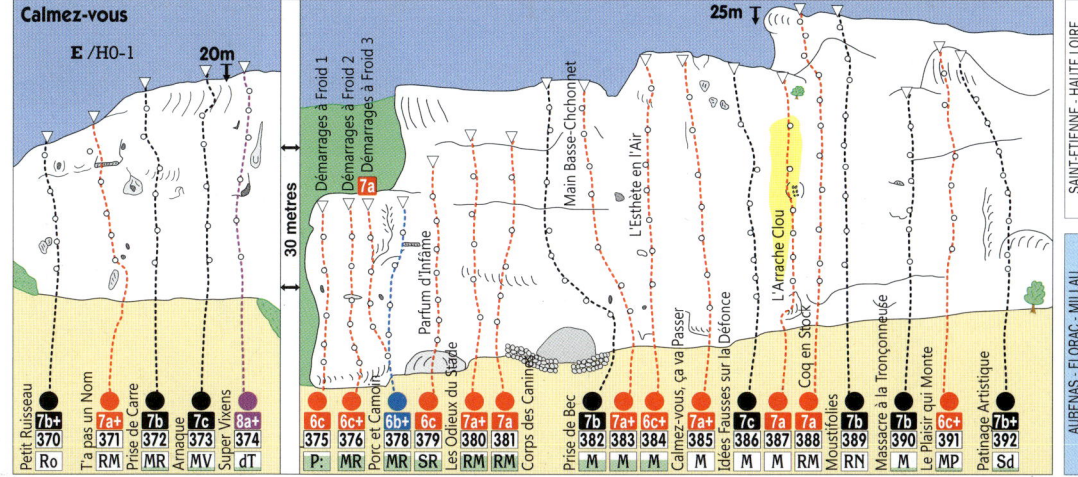

Tennessee is the most dramatic sector of the gorge. Most other sectors are small and scattered up the hillside.

TARN (D) - (P5) ENTRE DEUX

P5 44.307861, 3.251897

Trésor du Zèbre

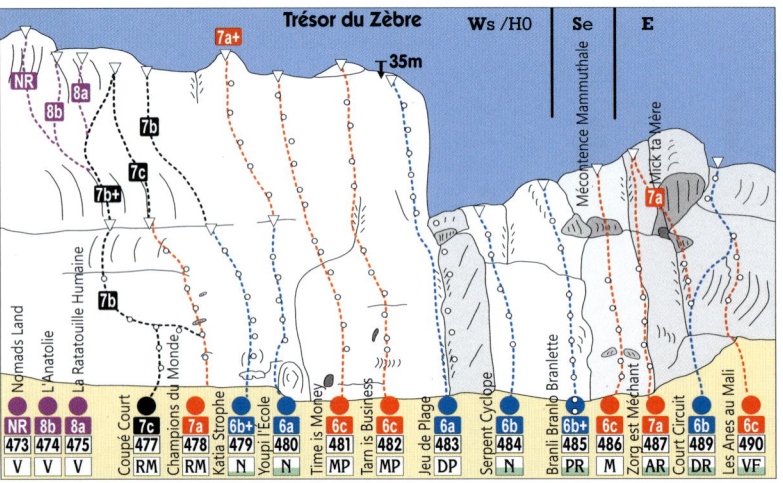

483 6a Jeu de Plage

NR	8b	8a	7c	7a+	6b+	6a	6c	6c	6a	6b	6b+	6c	7a	6b	6c
473	474	475	477	478	479	480	481	482	483	484	485	486	487	489	490
V	V	V	RM	RM	N	N	MP	MP	DP	N	PR	M	AR	DR	VF

Routes: Nomads Land, L'Anatolie, La Ratatouille Humaine, Coupé Court, Champions du Monde, Katia Strophe, Youpi l'École, Time is Money, Tarn is Business, Jeu de Plage, Serpent Cyclope, Branli Branlo Branlette, Jeu est Méchant, Zorg est Méchant, Court Circuit, Les Ânes au Mali

Club House

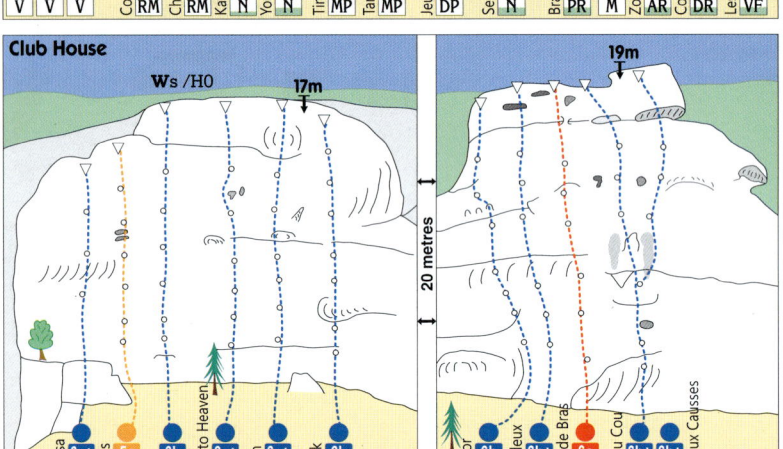

499 6b Trix

6a+	5c	6b	6a+	6a+	6b	6b	6b	6c	6b+	6b+
497	498	499	500	501	502	503	504	505	506	507
MS	M	Trix	M	M	M	dN	dR	MR	RR	RR

Routes: Luna Rosa, Oh Lands, Trix, Starway to Heaven, Caldéron, Glispstick, Fatal Error, D2 Merdeux, Footing de Bras, Lapine au Cou, Lapine aux Causses

506 6b+ 507 Lapine au Cou

Güllich

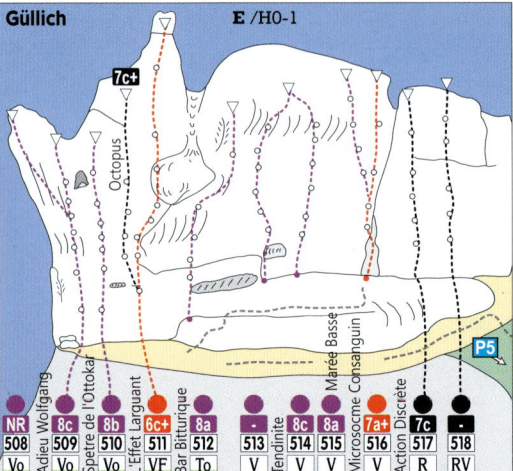

509 8c Adieu Wolfgang

NR	8c	8b	6c+	8a	-	8c	8a	7a+	7c	-
508	509	510	511	512		514	515	516	517	518
Vo	Vo	Vo	VF	To	V	V	V	R	RV	

Routes: Adieu Wolfgang, Spectre de l'Ottokar, L'Effet Larguant, Bar Bitturique, Tendinite, Microsocme Consanguin, Marée Basse, Action Discrète

Spectre de l'Ottokar 8b. Thibault Pawlas

510

Individual small sectors. Quite a scramble up the side of the gorge to locate each sector. Warm and sunny.

TARN (DD) - (P6) BAUMES HAUTES

P6 44.306253, 3.254651

Oasif (droite)

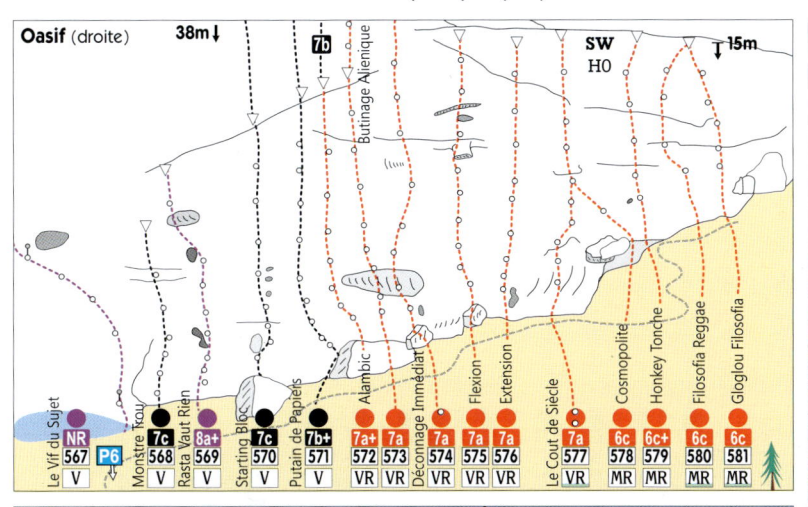

#	567	568	569	570	571	572	573	574	575	576	577	578	579	580	581
Name	Le Vif du Sujet	Monstre Trou	Rasta Vaut Rien	Starting Bloc	Putain de Papiers	Alambic	Butinage Alienique	Déconnage Immédiat	Flexion	Extension	Le Cout de Siècle	Cosmopolite	Honkey Tonche	Filosofia Reggae	Gloglou Filosofia
Grade	NR	7c	8a+	7c	7b+	7a+	7a	7a	7a	7a	7a	6c	6c+	6c	6c
Style	V	V	V	V	V	VR	VR	VR	VR	VR	VR	MR	MR	MR	MR

Planete Causse

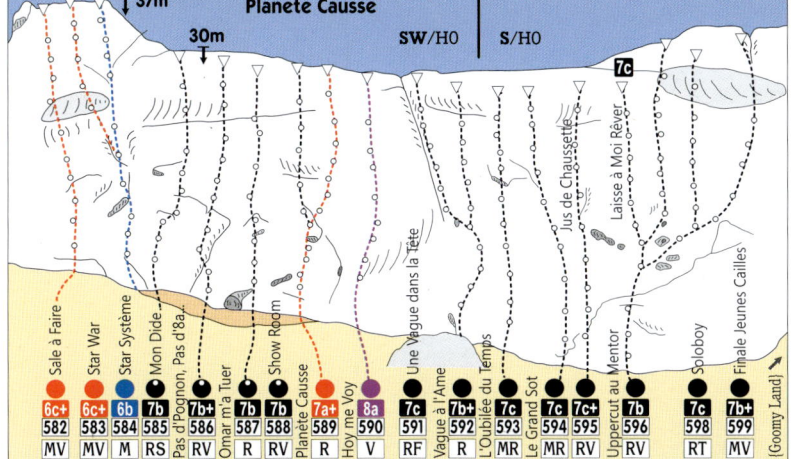

#	582	583	584	585	586	587	588	589	590	591	592	593	594	595	596	597	598	599
Name	Sale à Faire	Star War	Star Système	Mon Dide	Pas d'Pognon, Pas d'8a..	Omar m'a Tuer	Show Room	Planete Causse	Hoy me Voy	Une Vague dans la Tête	Vague à l'Ame	L'Oubliée du Temps	Le Grand Sot	Jus de Chaussette	Uppercut au Mentor	Laisse à Moi Rêver	Sploboy	Finale Jeunes Cailles
Grade	6c+	6c+	6b	7b	7b+	7b	7b	7a+	8a	7c	7b+	7c	7c	7c+	7b	7c	7c	7b+
Style	MV	MV	M	RS		R	RV	R	V	RF	MR	MR	MR	RV	RV	RT		MV

Goomy Land

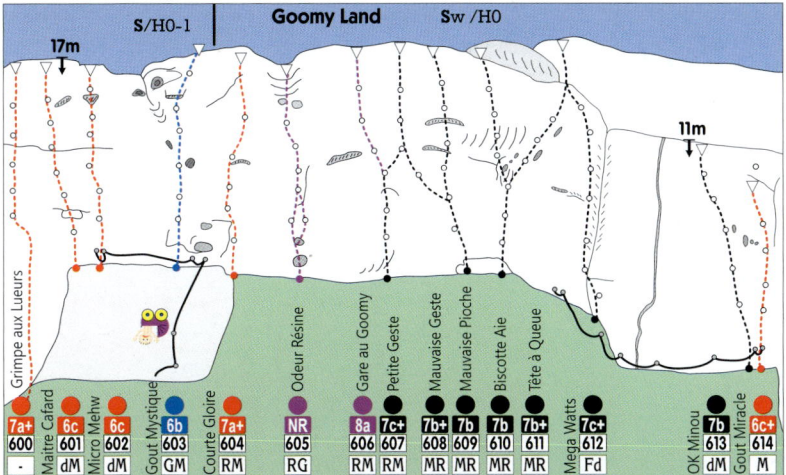

#	600	601	602	603	604	605	606	607	608	609	610	611	612	613	614
Name	Grimpe aux Lueurs	Maitre Cafard	Micro Mehw	Gout Mystique	Courte Gloire	Odeur Résine	Gare au Goomy	Petite Geste	Mauvaise Geste	Mauvaise Pioche	Biscotte Aie	Tête à Queue	Mega Watts	OK Minou	Gout Miracle
Grade	7a+	6c	6c	6b	7a+	NR	8a	7c+	7b+	7b	7b	7b+	7c+	7b	6c+
Style	-	dM	dM	GM	RM	RG	RM	MR	MR	MR	MR	MR	Fd	dM	M

Le Cout de Siècle 6c, *Karolina Gurba* — 577

587 7b — Omar m'a Tuer

603 6b — Gout Mystique

A good place to start exploring the gorge, the big parking and route access is very obvious...so is the angle and difficulty.

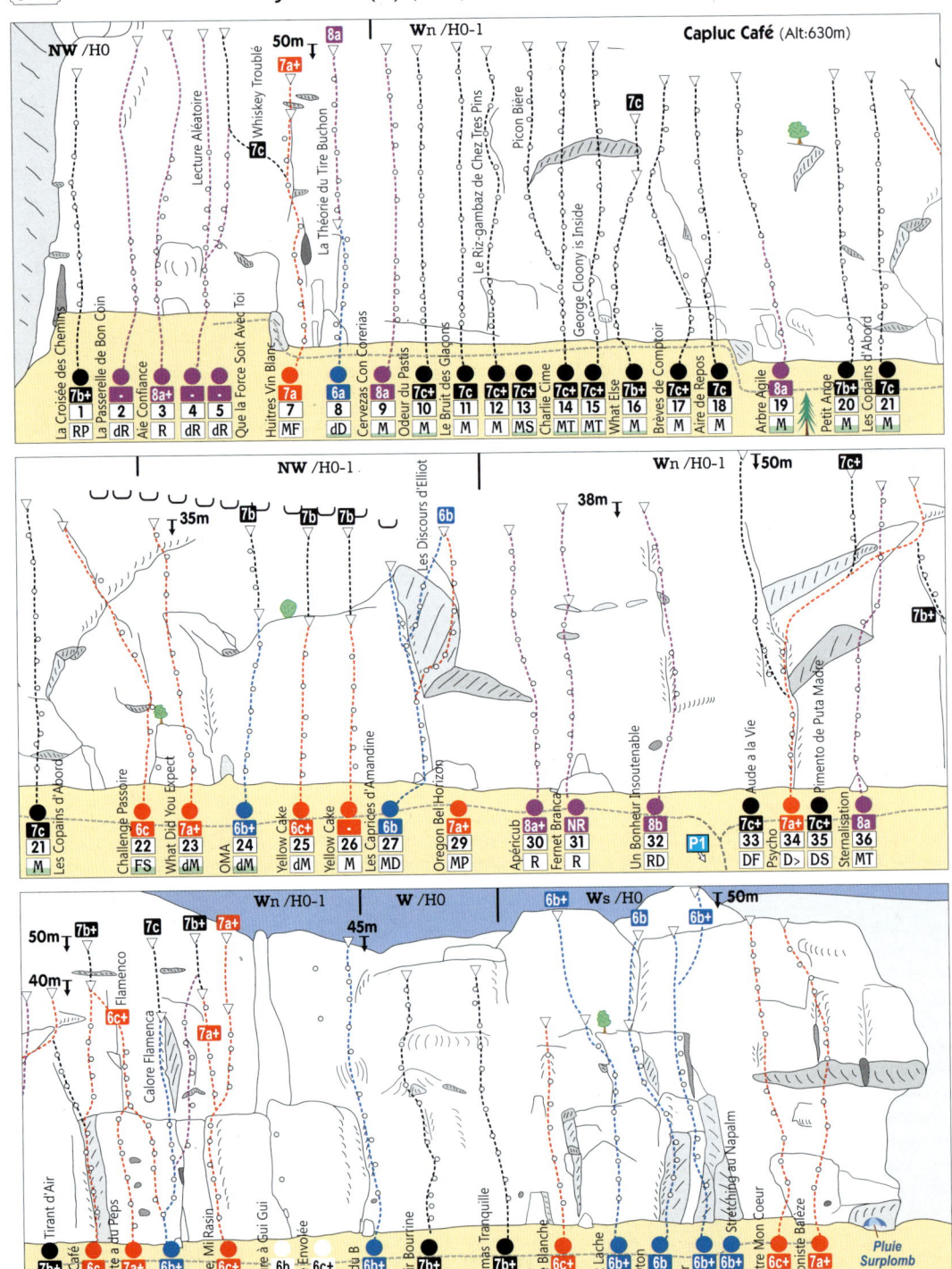

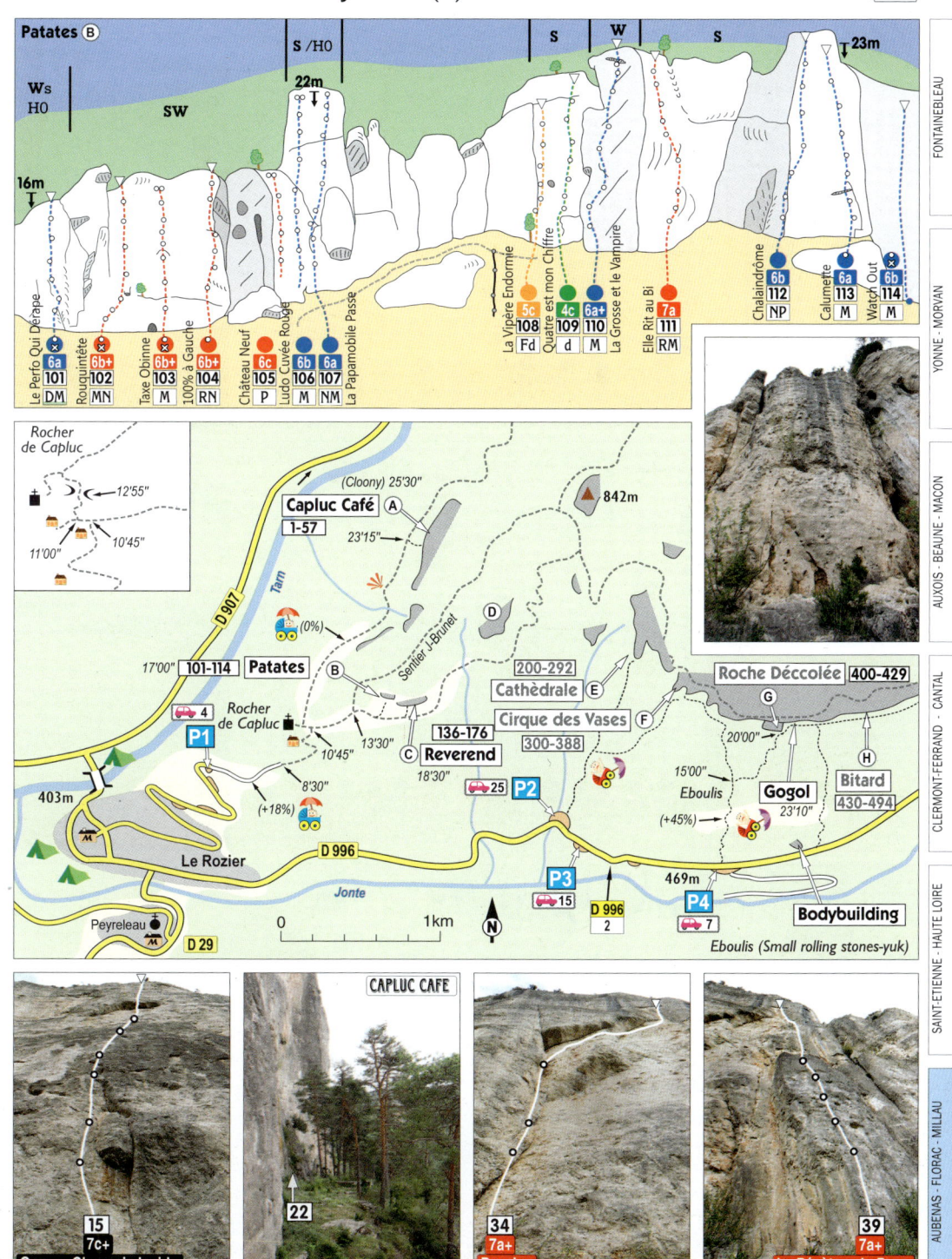

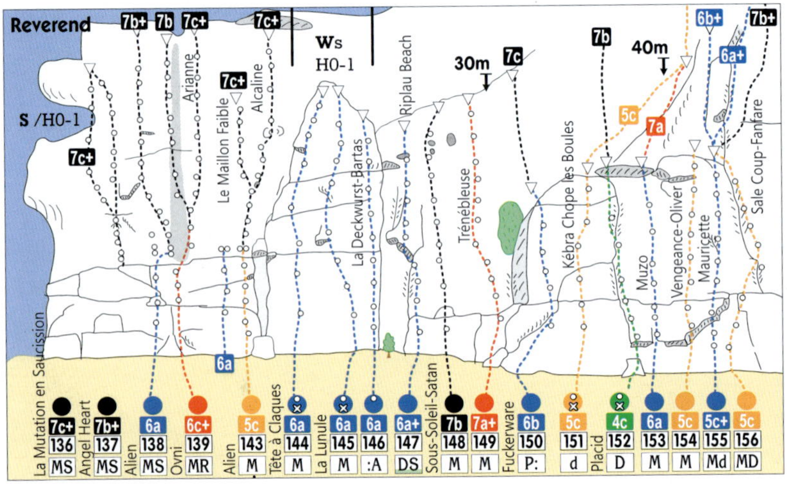

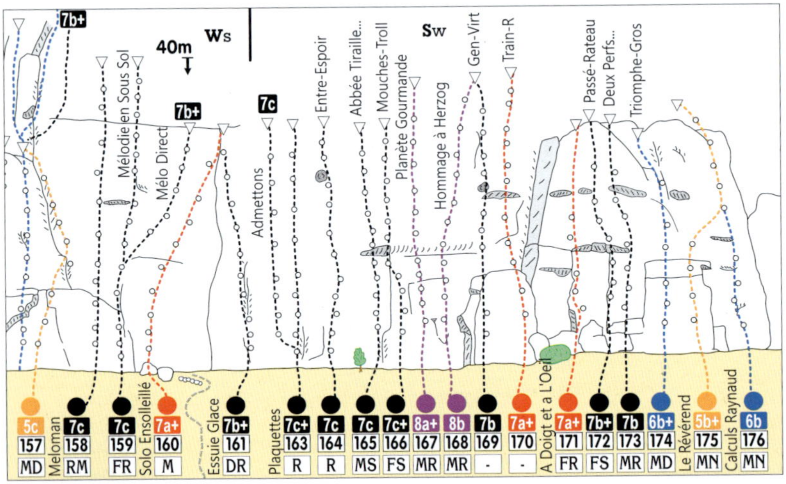

JONTE (C) - REVEREND

P1 44.192440, 3.211241

Route	Grade	#	Type
La Mutation en Saucission	7c+	136	MS
Angel Heart	7b+	137	MS
Alien	6a	138	MS
Ovni	6c+	139	MR
Ariane	7b		
Le Maillon Faible	7c+		
Alcaline	7c+		
Tête à Claques	5c	143	M
La Lunule	6a	144	M
La Deckwurst-Bartas	6a	145	:A
Riplau Beach	6a+	146	DS
Trénébleuse	6a	147	M
Sous-Soleil-Satan	7b	148	M
Fuckerware	7a+	149	M
Muzo	6b	150	P:
Kébra Chope les Boules			d
Placid	4c	151	Placid
Vengeance-Oliver	6a	152	D
Mauricette	5c	153	M
Sale Coup-Fanfare	5c+	154	M
	5c	155	Md
	5c	156	MD

Route	Grade	#	Type
	5c	157	MD
Meloman	7c	158	RM
Mélodie en Sous Sol	7c	159	FR
Melo Direct	7a+	160	M
Essuie Glace		161	DR
Admettons	7b+		
Plaquettes	7c+	163	R
Entre-Espoir	7c	164	R
Abbée Tiraille...	7c	165	MS
Mouches-Troll		166	FS
Planète Gourmande	8a+	167	MR
Hommage à Herzog	8b	168	MR
Gen-Virt	7b	169	-
Train-R	7a+	170	-
Passé-Rateau	7a+	171	FR
Deux Perfs...	7b+	172	FS
Triomphe-Gros	7b	173	MR
	6b+	174	MD
Le Reverend	5b+	175	MN
Calculs Raynaud	6b	176	MN

144 — 6a

139 — 7b — Ovni

171 — 7a+ — A Doigt et a L'Oeil

151 — 6a+ — Kébra Chope Les Boules

Calcaire** There are a lot of spectacular rock formations in the gorge, some will no doubt fall down over time, be carefull.

JONTE (H) - GOGOL - BODY BUILDING

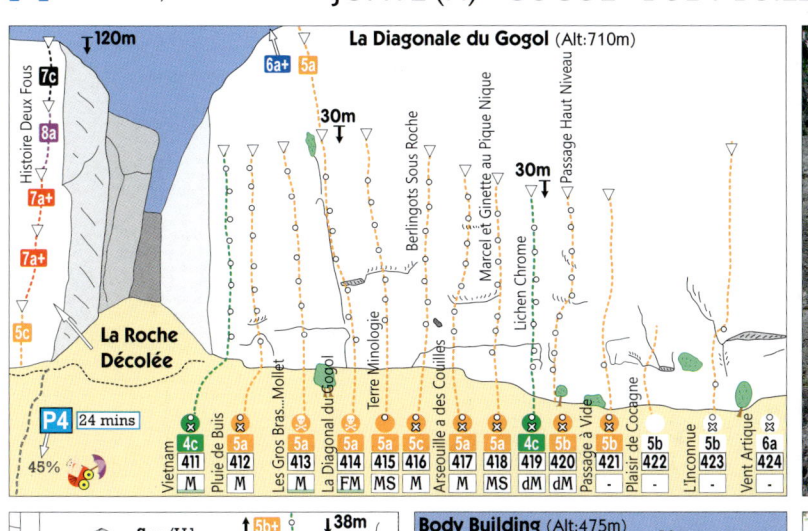

La Diagonale du Gogol (Alt:710m)

	Vietnam	Pluie de Buis	Les Gros Bras...Mollet	La Diagonal du Gogol	Arsenouille à des Couillés	Marcel et Ginette au Pique Nique	Lichen Chrome	Passage à Vide	Plaisir de Cocagne	L'Inconnue	Vent Artique
Grade	4c	5a	5a	5a	5a	5a	5c	4c	5b	5b	5b	6a
#	411	412	413	414	415	416	417	418	419	420	421	422	423	424
	M	M	M	FM	MS	M	MS	dM	dM	-	-	-

414 - La Diagonal du Gogol (5a)

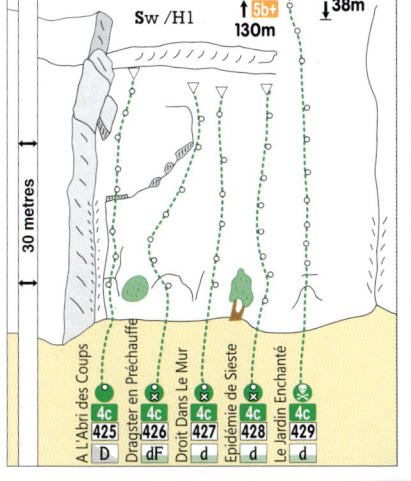
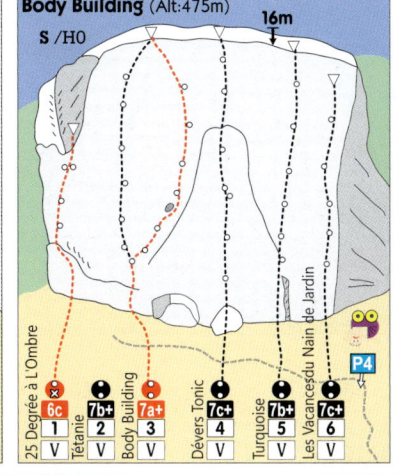

Body Building (Alt:475m) — S/H0 — 16m

	A L'Abri des Coups	Dragster en Préchauffe	Droit Dans Le Mur	Epidémie de Sieste	Le Jardin Enchanté	25 Degrée à L'Ombre	Tétanie	Body Building	Dévers Tonic	Turquoise	Les Vacances du Nain de Jardin
Grade	4c	4c	4c	4c	4c	6c	7b+	7a+	7c+		7c+
#	425	426	427	428	429	1	2	3	4	5	6
	D	dF	d	d	d	V	V	V	V	V	V

425 - L'Abri des Corps (4c)

406 - Pierrot Y Mondino (5c)

412 - GOGOL

3 - Body Building (7a+)

Gogol: A giant dalle (slab), shaded in the afternoon by the giant Roche Décollée. Body Building - roadside - says it all !!!

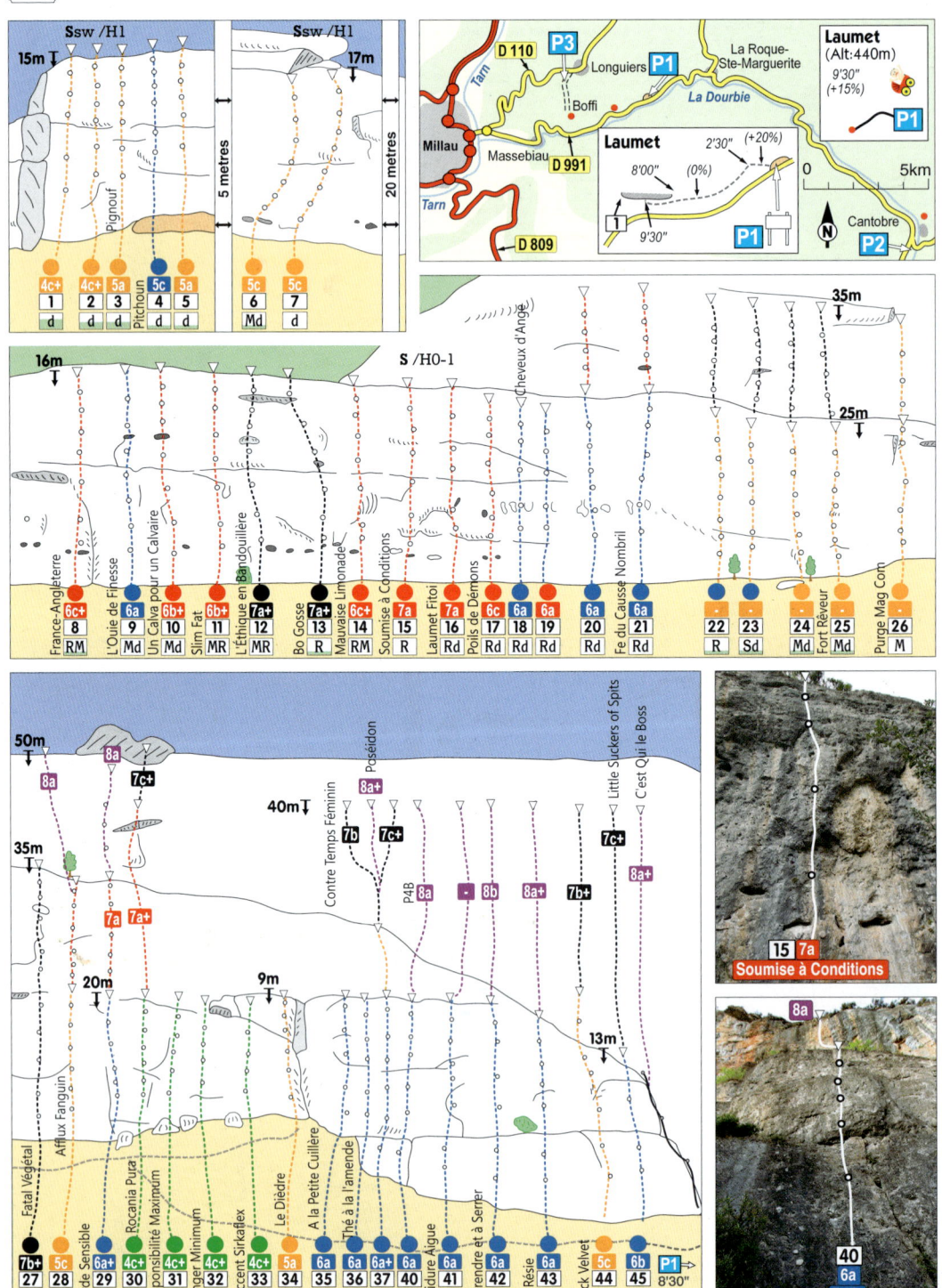

Calaire*** A recently developed cliff with easy access from Millau. A complete assortment of routes.

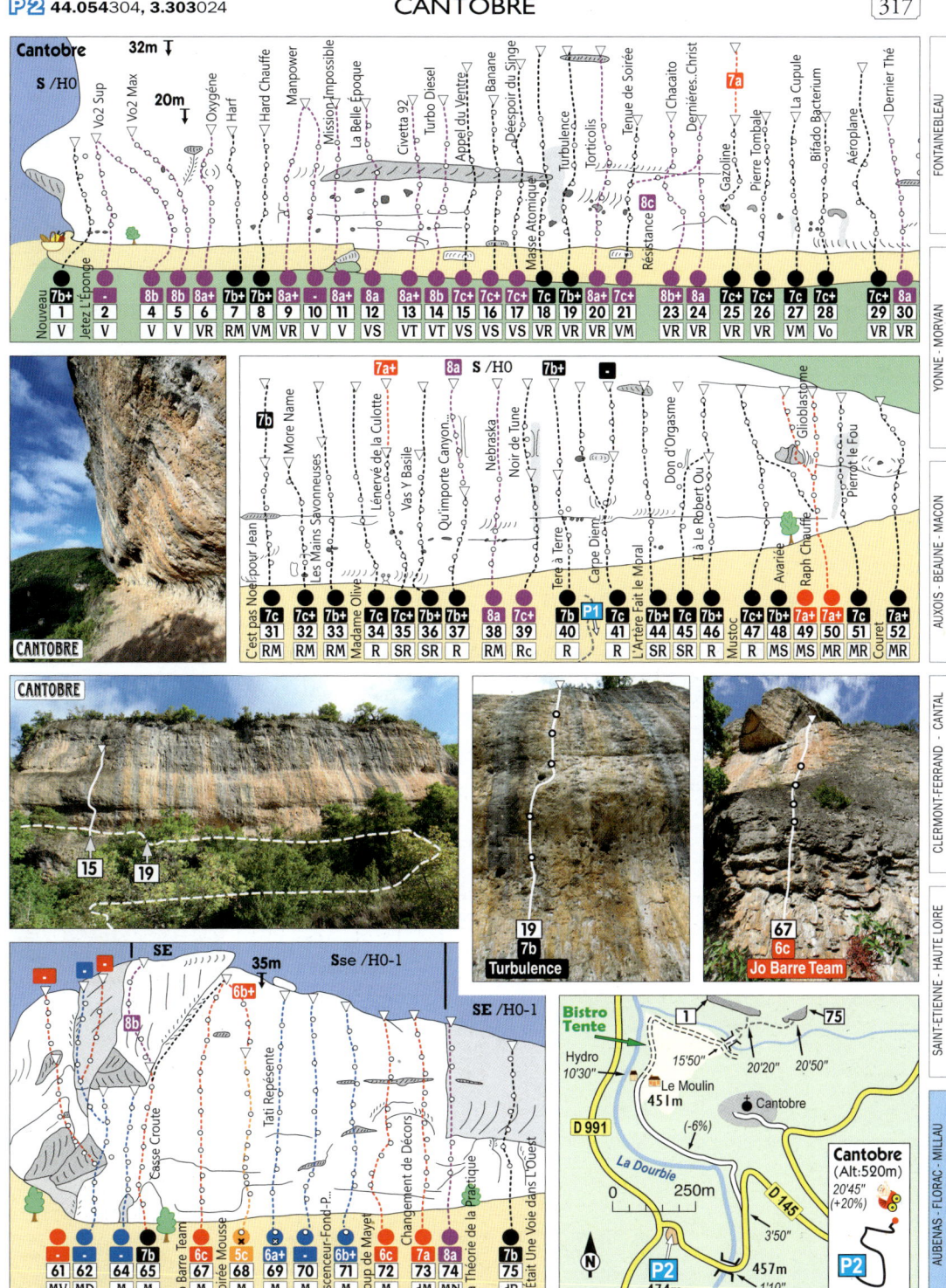

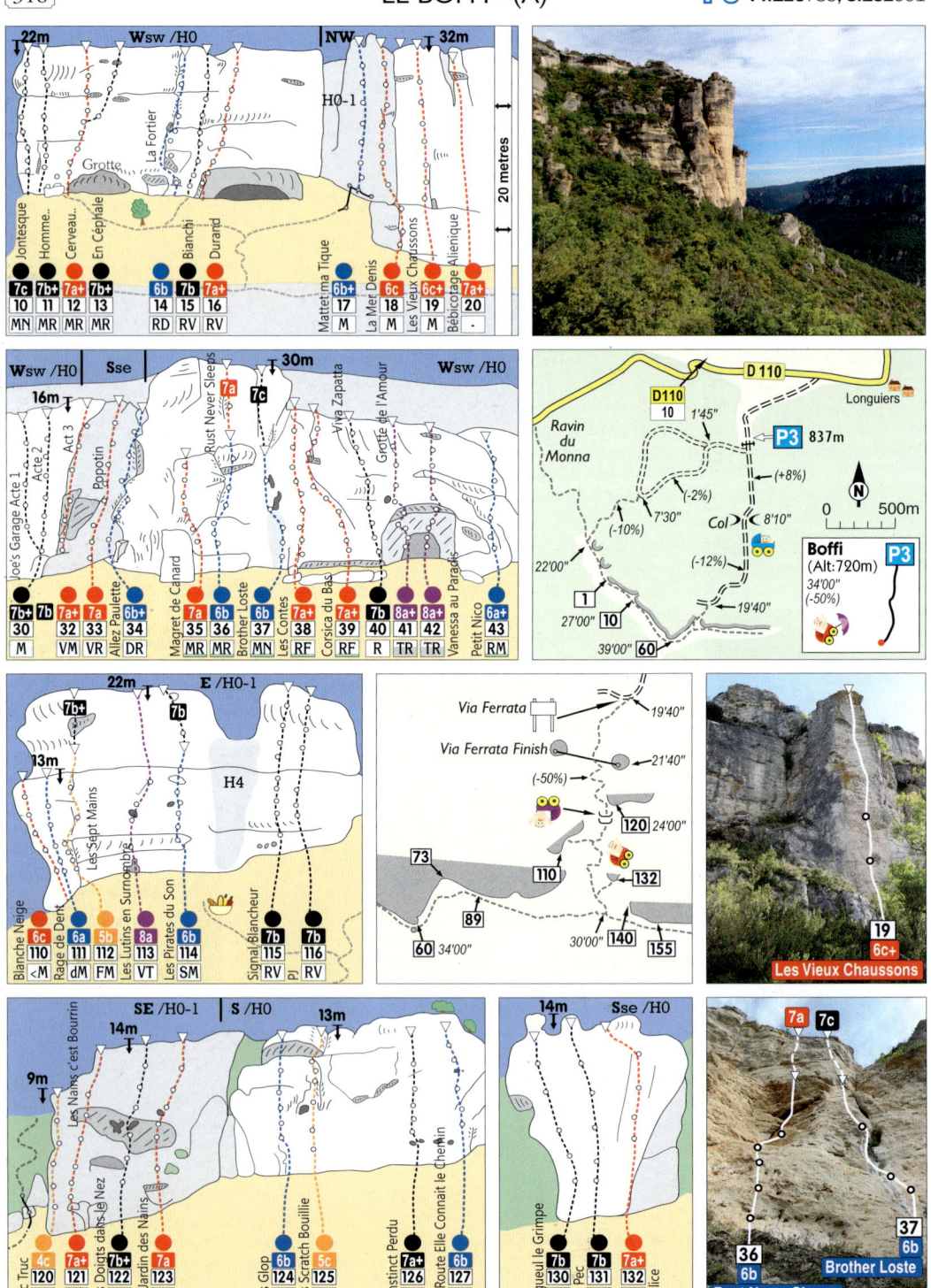

LE BOFFI - (B)

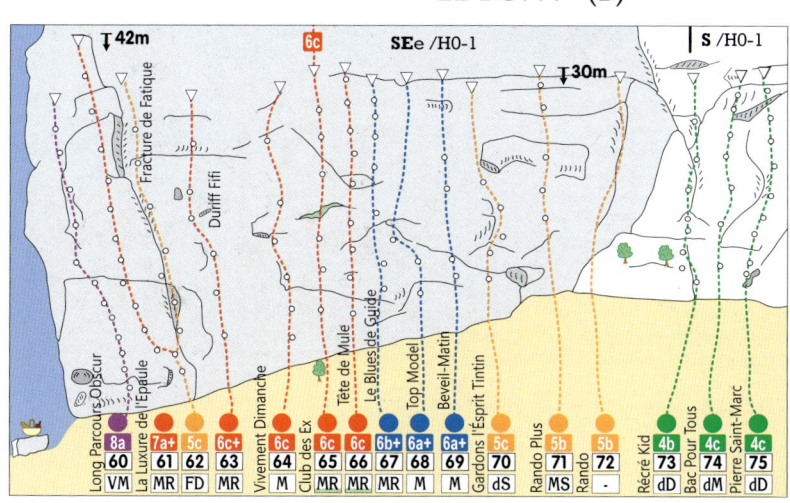
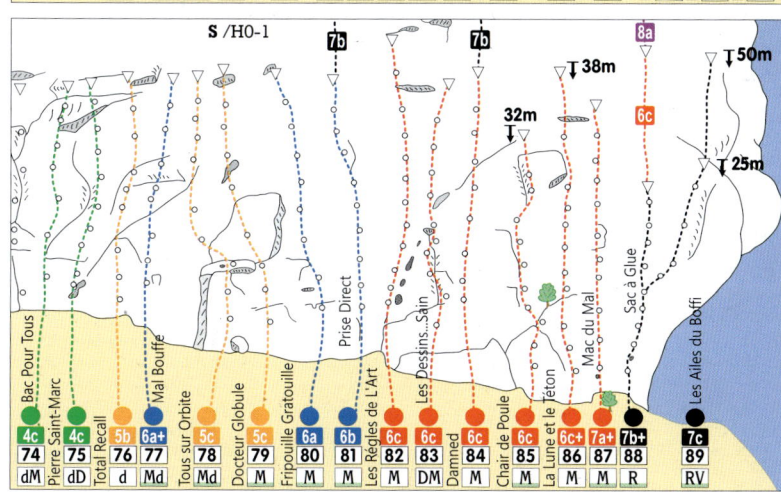
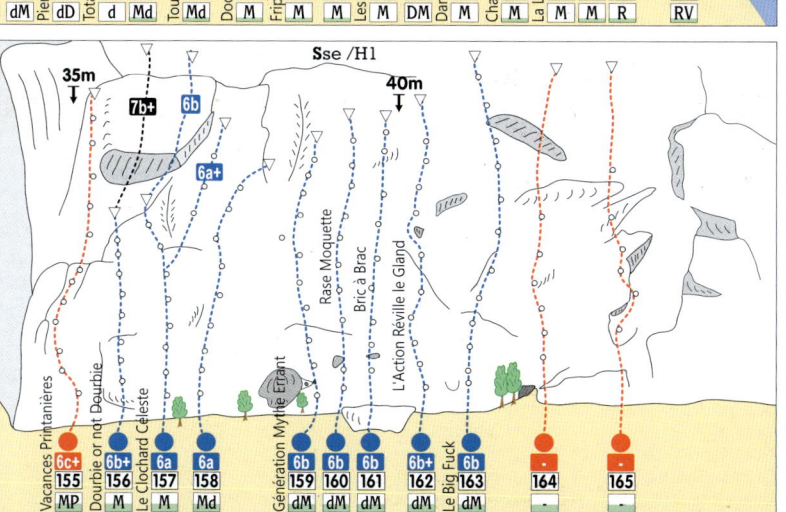

60 — 8a — Long Parcours Obscur

115 — 7b — Signal Blancheur

122 — 7b+ — Les Doigts dans le Nez

159 — 6b — Génération Mythe Errant
160 — 6b — Rase Moquette

These 3 sectors offer the best climbing here at Boffi, a good sun trap and stay pretty dry in winter. High up, above the gorge.

INDEX

91.1, page 16
95.2, page 16
Actinidias, 298
After Eight, 124
Agachou, 298
Aiguille-Roc-Tarn, 304
Apremont Dames, 15
Apremont Gorges, 15
Apremont Ouest, 15
Arcenant, 116
Armand-Roc, 179
Auteroche, 220
Auvergnat, 260
Avallon, 52
Baderne, 140
Balazuc, 277
Barasses, 277
Baumes Basses, 308
Baumes Chaudes, 306
Baumes Hautes, 311
Beaumiral, 268
Beauvais - Hameau, 14
Beauvais - Nainville, 14
Beauvais - Télégraphe, 14
Bernard-Rocher, 250
Bèz-Gorges, 229
Body Building-Jonte, 315
Boffi, 318
Bois Rond, 16
Bouilland, 120
Bourdary, 276
Bout de Monde/Nolay, 140
Bout-Monde/St-Flour, 228
Burzet, 272
Buthiers Canard, 17
Buthiers Coccinelle, 17
Buthiers Piscine, 17
Cabane, 125
Cabannes, 264
Cailleau, 16
Calmez-vous-Tarn, 309
Cancer-Tarn, 305
Canche aux Merciers, 16
Canon, Rocher, 15
Cantobre, 317
Capluc Café-Jonte, 312
Capucin, 210
Carlat, 226
Ceyrat, 194
Chambolle-M, 114
Chambon des Neiges, 214
Champeaux, 195
Chamtadu, 279
Chardonnay, 163
Charrat, 71
Chartreuse, 182
Chat Gourmand, 266
Chatalet, 128
Châteauneuf-Bains, 183
Châteauneuf-Riom, 218
Chaudefour, 209
Chaulet, 292
Chauzon, 280
Chazette, 233

Chevillère, 263
Chien-Rocher, 62
Chomérac, 269
Cirque des Gens, 280
Clermont-Ferrand, 177
Cloche, 126
Club House-Tarn, 310
Coche-Roche, 173
Cochons, 251
Combe-Vieille, 134
Corbière, 244
Cormatin, 162
Cormot, 142
Costaros, 246
Courpatas, 273
Cousin, 52
Coux, 257
Crête-de-Coq, 212
Crussol, 267
Cruzille, 163
Cubelles, 251
Cuisinière, 15
Cul de Chien, 16
Culles-les-Roche, 160
Curis, 240
Cuvier - Bas, 14
Cuvier - Rempart, 14
Dame de Lac, 256
Dame Jouanne, 17
Darots, 186
Dé Qué Fas Aqui, 308
Décollée-Roche, 315
Dédé, 126
Dent de la Rancune, 213
Doizeaux, 242
Eléphant, 17
Entre-Deux-Tarn, 310
Face-Figues-Tarn, 306
Fay-sur-Lignon, 254
Fées, 57
Figues au Cul-Tarn, 309
Fixin, 104
Fleurey, 102
Foetus-Tarn, 306
Fond de Combe, 132
Fontainebleau, 12
Fontgarnide, 288
Forgette, 303
Franchard, 15
Garde Guerin, 301
Gateau-Cormot, 150
Geligny, 93
Gogol-Jonte, 315
Goomy Land-Tarn, 311
Gorges de la Jonte, 312
Gorges du Bèz, 229
Gorges du Tarn, 304
Gournier-Roche, 200
Grand Charmasson, 290
Grazac, 252
Grisière, 172
Gués de Dun, 60
Guichot, Rocher, 16
Guillanche, 237

Guillebaud, 178
Guillich-Tarn, 310
Hauteroche, 73
Horloge, 272
Hozières-Roc, 222
Isatis, 15
Issarles, 256
Issoire, 201
JA Martin, 16
Jarden de Jouqueirou, 300
Jaujac, 272
Jonte-Gorges, 312
Lac de Graves, 224
Lantenay, 95
Laumet, 316
Lavilledieu Blocs, 276
Lavudieu, 257
Lignerolles, 180
Limas, 240
Lormes, 54
Malzieu Ville, 232
Marchastel, 219
Mariac, 262
Maunoury, 17
Mazet, 296
Melin, 138
Mer de Glace, 259
Moai, 233
Monistrol-Allier, 250
Mont Rome, 152
Montagne Percée, 196
Montal, 58
Montbard, 70
Mont-Bourbonnaise, 188
Morvan, 56
Moulin-Garde Guerin, 301
Moulins d'Yonne, 53
Noir Désir-Tarn, 305
Oasif-Tarn, 311
Oisillons, 298
Olme, 236
Orbeil, 201
Padole, 14
Parc, Rochers, 20
Parvis, 17
Pas de St-Martin, 139
Patates-Jonte, 313
Pavin-Lac, 215
Percee-Roche, 137
Père des Rioux, 182
Péréandre, 260
Petit Bois, 17
Peyrade, 216
Pied-de-Borne, 299
Pierre Fendue, 188
Pierre-Châtel, 192
Planete Causse-Tarn, 311
Pointue-Roche, 253
Pont de Montvert, 303
Pont-Fromentières, 262
Porte des Fées, 232
Potala, Rocher, 16
Pourtalas, 299
Pradel, 248

Prés Marty, 225
Puy de la Tourte, 223
Rancune-Dent, 213
Remigny, 156
Restant-Long Rocher, 17
Retournac, 247
Reverend-Jonte, 314
Rivalet, 204
Roc Armand, 179
Roc d'Hozières, 222
Roche-Coche, 173
Rochettes, 202
Rompon, 266
Rory, 236
Sabots, Roche, 16
Saffres, 78
Saint Germain Est, 14
Saint-Denis-Vaux, 159
Sainte-Catherine, 64
Saint-Floret, 202
Saint-Genest, 179
Saint-Julien-Tournel, 302
Saint-Just, 230
Saint-Sauves, 208
Saint-Vincent, 189
Salers, 216
Salette, 187
Saurier, 206
Saussois, 26
Sauviat, 198
Semur-en-Auxois, 71
Solutre, 164
St-Julien-Chaz, 248
St-Symp-Coise, 238
St-Symp-Lay, 238
Suin, 175
Surgy, 40
Tarn-Gorges, 304
Tennessee-Tarn, 309
Teu, 158
Thorrenc, 258
Top Secret, 267
Tortue, 253
Tour, 265
Tournay, 261
Tras les Baumes, 272
Trésor-Zébra-Tarn, 310
Trois Pignons, 16
Tuilière-Roche, 209
Urlande, 221
Valcivières, 198
Vergisson, 168
Viel Audon, 278
Vieux-Château, 64
Volpie, 199
Yzeron, 239
Zébra-Tarn, 310